COMPLETE COURSE Fifth Edition

CENTURY 21®

KEYBOARDING, FORMATTING, AND DOCUMENT PROCESSING

JERRY W. ROBINSON, Ed.D.
Senior Editor
South-Western Publishing Co.

JACK P. HOGGATT, Ed.D.
Professor of Business Education
and Administrative Management
University of Wisconsin,
Eau Claire

JON A. SHANK, Ed.D.
Professor of Administrative Management
and Business Education
Robert Morris College,
Coraopolis (PA)

ARNOLA C. OWNBY, Ed.D.
Professor of Office Administration
and Business Education
Southwest Missouri State University

LEE R. BEAUMONT, Ed.D.
Professor of Business, Emeritus
Indiana University of Pennsylvania

T. JAMES CRAWFORD, Ph.D.
Professor of Business/Education, Emeritus
Indiana University

LAWRENCE W. ERICKSON, Ed.D.
Professor of Education, Emeritus
University of California (LA)

TA20EA
PUBLISHED BY
SOUTH-WESTERN PUBLISHING CO.
CINCINNATI, OH DALLAS, TX LIVERMORE, CA

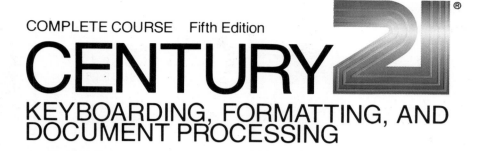

ACKNOWLEDGMENTS

Contributing Authors

Several teachers prepared selected materials for this textbook and correlating laboratory materials and tests. Their names are listed here as evidence of our appreciation of their helpful participation.

Connie M. Forde, Ph.D.
Mississippi State University

John E. Gump, Ph.D.
Eastern Kentucky University

Donna M. N. Newhart, Ph.D.
Western Carolina University

Marilyn K. Popyk
Henry Ford Community College
Dearborn, Michigan

Other Contributors

In addition to the authorship team and editorial staff who prepare and process the manuscript that becomes a textbook, thousands of others contribute in vital ways to the quality of the final product. Among these are teachers and students too numerous to thank individually. We mention these groups here as an expression of appreciation and thanks.

Senior Acquisitions Editor: Karen Schmohe
Production Editor: Deborah M. Luebbe
Associate Editors/Production: Denise A. Blust, Diane M. Bowdler, M. Elizabeth Druhan, Susan Richardson
Designer: J. E. Lagenaur
Production Artist: Richard Moore
Photo Researcher: Fred M. Middendorf
Photographer: Diana W. Fleming
Marketing Manager: Al S. Roane

Photo Credits

COVER PHOTO:	© Geoff Gove/The IMAGE BANK © Steven Hunt/The IMAGE BANK
PHOTO, p. vi, top:	International Business Machines Corporation*
PHOTO, p. vi, bottom:	Brother
PHOTO, p. vii:	International Business Machines Corporation*
GLOSSARY PHOTOS, pp. xiii-xvi:	
"Disk"	Courtesy BASF Corporation Information Systems
"Facsimile"	Courtesy of AT&T
"Sheet feeder"	Photo Courtesy Xerox Corporation
PHOTO, p. ix:	Apple Computer, Inc.**
PHOTO, p. 128:	© Jose Carrillo, Ventura, CA
PHOTO, p. 167:	© Walter Hodges/West Light
PHOTO, p. 293:	Bob Daemmrich
PHOTO, p. 325:	Unisys Corp.
PHOTO, p. 337:	Hilton Hotels Corporation
PHOTO, p. 364:	© Wayne Michael Lottinville
PHOTO, p. 389:	Courtesy of ACCO World Corporation
PHOTO, p. 428:	© Michael Philip Manheim/The Stock Solution
PHOTO, p. 434:	© The Stock Solution
PHOTO, p. 443:	© 1989, Comstock
PHOTO, p. 449:	© Wayne Michael Lottinville
PHOTO, p. 464:	© 1987, Comstock
PHOTO, p. 471:	Courtesy of International Business Machines Corporation
PHOTO, p. 488:	© Royce Bair/The Stock Solution
PHOTO, p. RG13: "Offset printer"	Courtesy of A.B.Dick Company

* IBM is a registered trademark of International Business Machines Corporation.

** Apple and the Apple logo are registered trademarks of Apple Computer, Inc.

Any reference made to or use of any of these names or logos in this textbook refers to the foregoing credits.

ISBN: 0-538-60073-X

Library of Congress Catalog Card Number: 90-61015

1 2 3 4 5 6 7 8 9 10 11 12 13 14 H 9 8 7 6 5 4 3 2 1

Printed in the United States of America

PREFACE

Keyboarding instruction is in a period of transition. Some schools still use predominantly electric typewriters for teaching/learning. Other schools have a mix of electric and electronic typewriters along with a few computers. Increasing numbers are moving almost exclusively to computers and word processors. The highest percentage of schools, however, have a mix of all these kinds of teaching/learning equipment.

Thus, this new Fifth Edition of *Century 21 Keyboarding, Formatting, and Document Processing* is designed and written to accommodate these differing configurations of learning conditions.

But whatever the equipment used for learning, instruction must center around the three historical thrusts of emphasis: *keyboarding* (the manipulative skills), *formatting* (the arrangement, placement, and spacing) of commonly used documents, and *document processing* (the production in quantity of documents of quality). This *Century 21* series of learning materials focuses heavily on these three fundamental components.

In addition to keyboarding, formatting, and document processing, two other components deserve and receive frequent emphasis: *language skills* (without which keyboard learning is of little consequence) and *familiarity with electronic word processing equipment* (without which keyboarding skill cannot be widely applied in the modern workplace).

Century 21 Keyboarding, Formatting, and Document Processing gives appropriate attention to each of these aspects of instruction at strategic times in its four cycles. Emphasis moves from the simplest and most basic to the more complex and less often used. The amount of time and emphasis given to each facet of learning is carefully geared to the difficulty of the learning task and the level of skill required for effective job performance.

Basic Keyboarding Skills

Basic keyboarding skill consists of the fluent manipulation of the letter keys, the figure/symbol keys, and the basic service keys by "touch" (without looking).

Mastery of keyboard operation is assured by presenting just two keys in each practice session and by providing both intensive and extensive repetition of those keys.

The first phase of 25 lessons is devoted almost exclusively to alphabetic keyboarding skill development. Thereafter, emphasis on alphabetic keyboarding skill is provided mainly in periodic units of intensive practice.

Keyboarding skill on the top row is delayed until correct technique has been developed on the alphabetic keys and an essential level of keyboarding skill has been demonstrated.

Scientifically designed drills that are computer controlled are used to develop maximum skill in minimum time on the letter and figure/symbol keys. For computer users, Appendix A (on pp. A-2 to A-7) teaches the operation of the numeric keypad. These lessons should be used in addition to, not instead of, the figure-learning lessons of Unit 3.

During keyboard learning, this new edition places first emphasis on technique of keyboard operation (*without* time pressure) and second emphasis on speed of manipulative performance (*with* strategic timed writings). Then, when appropriate, it emphasizes accuracy of copy produced (with *restricted-speed* paced practice). This plan of emphasis is in harmony with generally accepted principles of skill learning and with a large body of keyboarding research findings.

Formatting Skills

Formatting includes arranging, placing, and spacing copy according to accepted conventions for specific documents (letters, memos, reports, tables, forms, and so on). It involves learning and following efficient, orderly steps for making machine adjustments, for making within-document decisions, and for evaluating final format acceptability.

Whether one learns to format on a typewriter, computer, or word processor, the concepts and principles are the same. What does differ are the machine-specific procedural steps for accomplishing the task.

This Fifth Edition emphasizes streamlined formats that may be completed with speed and ease, regardless of the equipment used. This new edition also includes many documents that permit the use of the time-saving features of word processing software. In Appendix B (pp. A-8 to A-24), students have an opportunity to practice automatic features and word processing functions of electronic equipment *before* attempting to use them in completing textbook documents.

Century 21 begins format learning with the simplest formats in the first cycle (block style letters, unbound reports, and simple tables with blocked columnar headings). Later cycles present the other letter and report formats and introduce the more complex formats for tables and other documents.

What is learned in one cycle is reviewed and reinforced in the next cycle before new formats or variants of familiar ones are presented.

Document Processing Skills

Document processing is the production of a series of usable documents over an extended period of time. It involves the combining of keyboarding and formatting skills with job-task planning, application of language skills, proofreading/correcting, materials handling, and efficient disposition of work produced.

Century 21 provides this integrative training through a four-step plan of production skill-building and a series of realistic office job simulations. The methods used have been classroom tested and found effective.

Basic Language Skills

Language skills are vital to the successful production of usable documents. *Century 21* begins language skills learning/review early and continues it frequently in manageable segments throughout the course. Beginning with rule-guided activities for capitalization, number expression, and word division, the activities expand to include punctuation, grammar, spelling, and word choice (commonly confused words). Using a study/learn/apply tactic, students get a thorough review of basic language skills. Periodic composing activities give students an opportunity to apply these learnings. In addition, many documents have embedded errors that students are expected to detect and correct.

Basic Computer Orientation

Word processing equipment and software have changed the language of keyboarding applications. *Century 21* uses the vocabulary of word processing and a simple set of abbreviations like computer operating commands in giving directions for practice activities. Further, many of its timed writings and documents are about computer and word processing applications and systems.

In these and other ways, this Fifth Edition of *Century 21 Keyboarding, Formatting, and Document Processing* provides the best materials of the right amounts for this period of transition. Students who successfully complete the *Century 21* activities will be well-prepared for entering and succeeding in the modern workplace.

CONTENTS

Cycle 3 *Lessons 151-225*
Formatting/Processing Business Documents

Cycle 4 *Lessons 226-300*
Modern Office Simulations

ELECTRIC (IBM Selectric II)

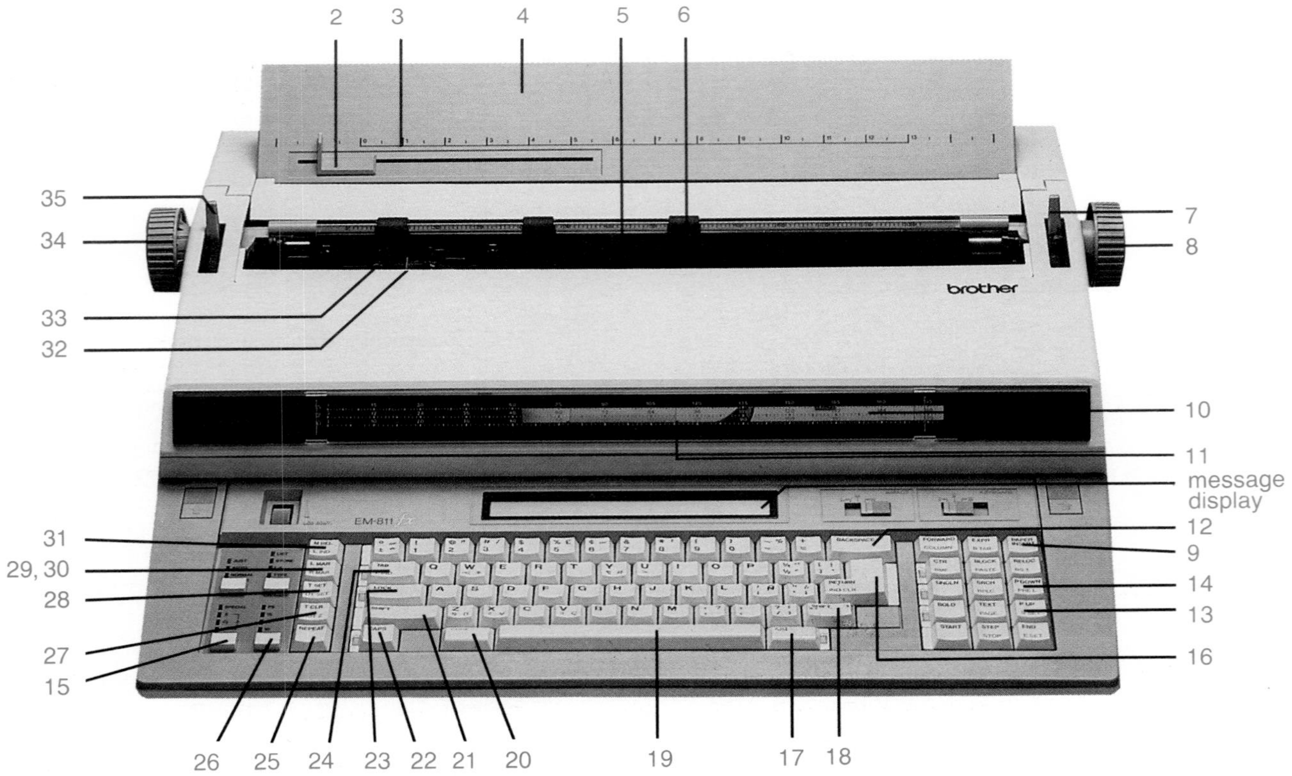

ELECTRONIC (Brother EM-811fx)

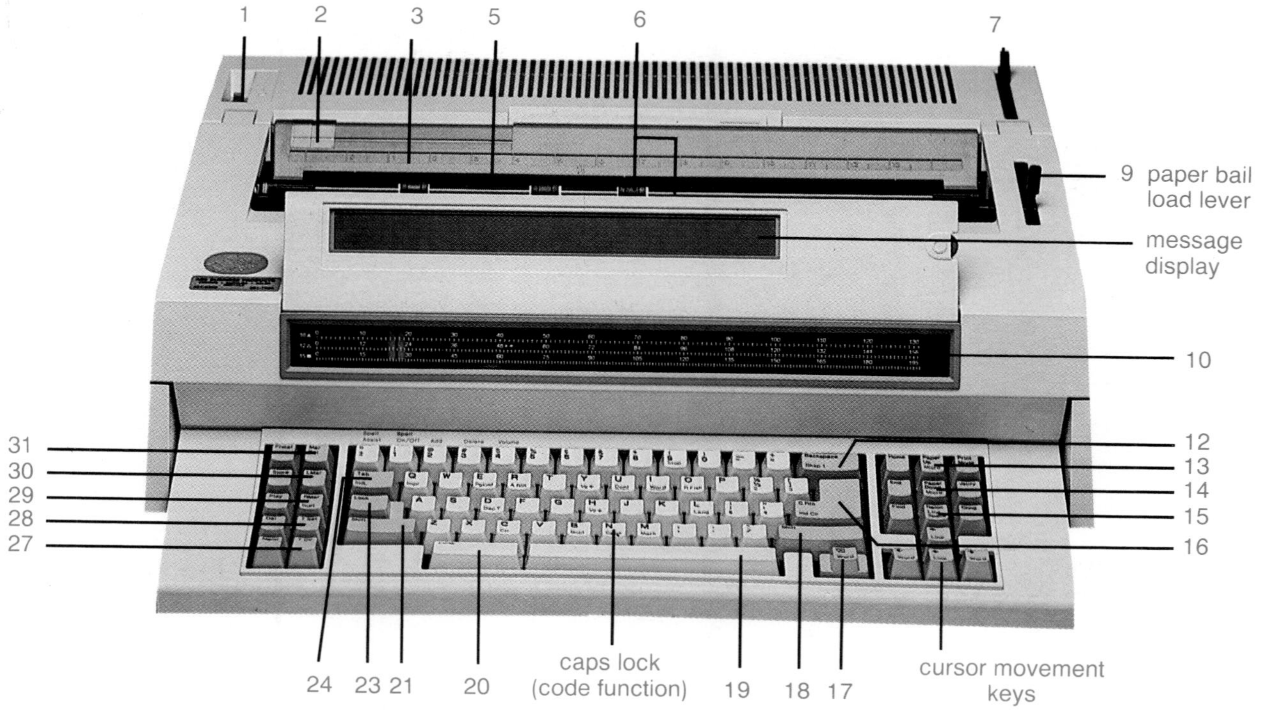

ELECTRONIC (IBM Wheelwriter 30 Series II)

The diagrams above show the parts of an electric and two electronic typewriters. Illustrated on pp. viii-ix is an array of microcomputers to which your keyboarding skills will transfer.

Since all typewriters have similar parts, you will probably be able to locate the parts on your machine using one of these diagrams. However, if you have the User's Manual that comes with your machine, use it to identify the exact location of each machine part, including special parts that may be on one machine but not on another.

1 **ON/OFF control**--used to turn machine on or off (not shown on Brother EM-811--under left platen knob)

2 **paper guide**--used to position paper for insertion

3 **paper guide scale**--used to set paper guide at desired position

4 **paper support**--used to support paper in machine (not on IBM Wheelwriter or Selectric)

5 **platen**--used to feed paper into machine and to provide a hard surface for daisy wheel or element to strike

6 **paper bail** and **paper bail rolls**--used to hold paper against platen

7 **paper release lever**--used to adjust position of paper after insertion

8 **right platen knob**--used to turn platen manually (not on IBM Wheelwriter)

9 **paper insert key**--used to feed paper into machine and advance paper to proper position for keying (not on Selectric); some machines also have an eject key

10 **line-of-writing** or **format scales**--used to plan margin settings and tab stops

11 **print point indicator**--used to position print carrier at desired point (on Selectric--red piece behind left margin set lever; not visible on IBM Wheelwriter)

12 **backspace key**--used to move print point to the left one space at a time

13 **paper up key**--used to advance paper one-half line at a time; can be used for paper insertion and ejection; also called **page up key** and **index key**

14 **paper down key**--used to retract paper one-half line at a time (not on Selectric); also called **page down key**

15 **line space selector**--used to select line spacing, such as single spacing or double spacing

16 **return key**--used to return print carrier to left margin and to advance paper up to next line of writing

17 **correction key**--used to erase ("lift off") characters

18 **right shift key**--used to key capital letters and symbols controlled by left hand

19 **space bar**--used to move print carrier to the right one space at a time

20 **code key**--used with selected character or service keys to key special characters or to perform certain operations (not on Selectric)

21 **left shift key**--used to key capital letters and symbols controlled by the right hand

22 **caps lock key**--used to lock shift mechanism for *alphabet characters only* (not on Selectric)

23 **shift lock key**--used to lock shift mechanism for *all* keyboard characters

24 **tab key**--used to move print carrier to tab stops

25 **repeat key**--used to repeat the previous keystroke (IBM Wheelwriter and Selectric have a feature that causes certain keys to repeat when held down)

26 **pitch selector**--used to select pitch (type size); some machines (like the IBM Wheelwriter) adjust pitch automatically depending upon the daisy wheel inserted

27 **tab clear key**--used to erase tab stops

28 **tab set key**--used to set tab stops

29 **right margin key**--used to set right margin

30 **left margin key**--used to set left margin

31 **margin release key**--used to move print carrier beyond margin settings

32 **print carrier**--used to carry ribbon cassette, daisy wheel or element, correction tape, and print mechanism to print point (not visible on IBM Wheelwriter or Selectric)

33 **aligning scale**--used to align copy that has been reinserted (not visible on IBM Wheelwriter)

34 **left platen knob**--used to feed paper manually; also **variable line spacer** on machines with platen knobs (not on IBM Wheelwriter)

35 **paper bail lever**--used to move paper bail forward when inserting paper manually (Selectric has one at each end of the paper bail)

IBM Personal System/2
Model 30

Tandy 1000
Personal Computer SX

Apple IIe

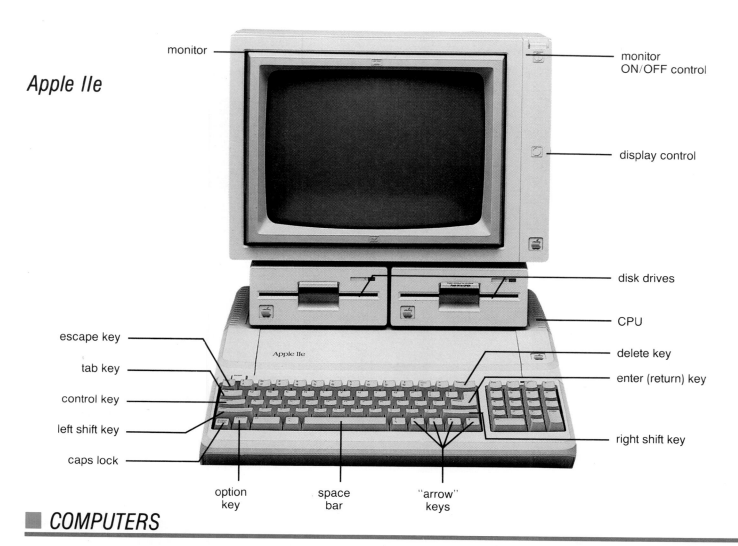

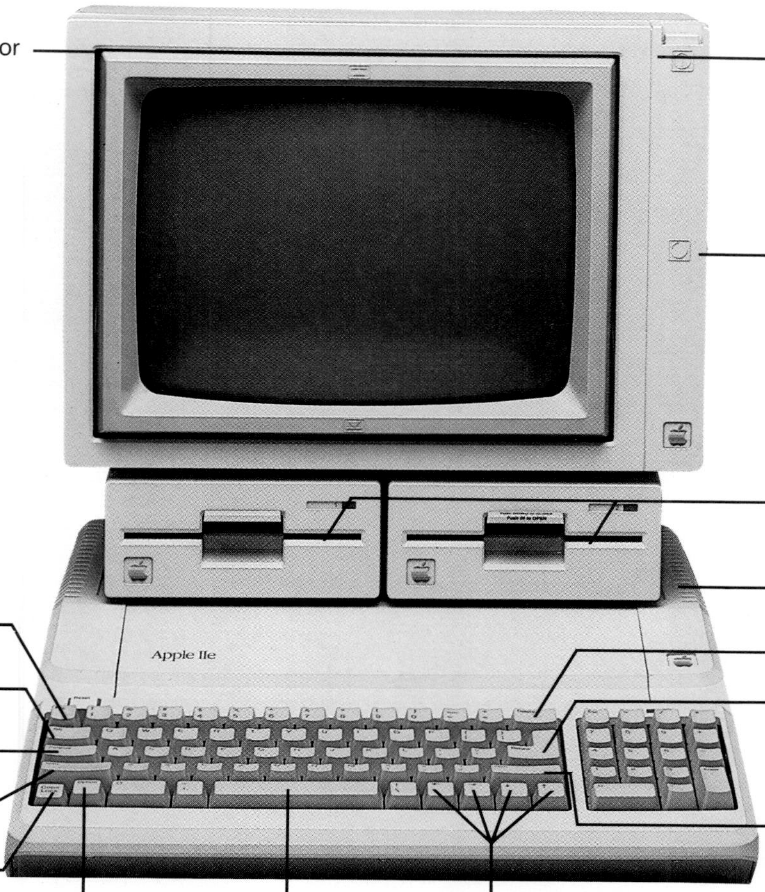

COMPUTERS

The diagram above shows the parts of various microcomputers/word processors with some examples of different types of machines.

Microcomputers/word processors have similar parts, though the names of these parts and their arrangement may differ. With the help of the User's Manual for your equipment, you should be able to identify each item labeled in the illustration above.

The particular word processing software that you use will determine the specific uses of so-called "function keys." Therefore, you must familiarize yourself with the User's Manual for your software as well as the one for your equipment.

The number in parentheses with some items in the alphabetized list at right refers to a comparable machine part on an electric or electronic typewriter (pp. vi-vii).

alternate (ALT) key--used with selected function keys to perform certain operations (called **option key** on Apple IIe)

"arrow" keys--used to move cursor in the direction of the arrow

caps lock key--used to lock shift mechanism for alphabet characters only (22)

control (CTRL) key--used with selected function keys to perform certain operations

CPU (Central Processing Unit)--the piece of equipment that holds the hardware or "brain" of the computer

delete key--used to remove characters from the screen one by one

display control(s)--used to adjust contrast and brightness in display

disk drive--a device into which a disk is inserted so information can be either retrieved or recorded

enter (return) key--used to return cursor to left margin and down to the next line; also, to enter system commands (16)

escape (ESC) key--used to cancel a function or exit a program section

left shift key--used to key capital letters and symbols controlled by the right hand (21)

monitor--the piece of equipment used to display text, data, and graphic images on screen

ON/OFF control--used to "power up" or "power down" the system (1) (Apple IIe CPU control not shown--back of CPU, your left side)

right shift key--used to key capital letters and symbols controlled by the left hand (18)

space bar--used to move cursor to right one space at a time or to add space between characters (19)

tab key--used to move cursor to tab stops (24)

1 Insert Paper

Electronic Typewriters

1. Align **paper guide** (2) with *0* (zero) on the **paper guide scale** (3). Turn typewriter on using **ON/OFF control** (1).

2. With your left hand, place paper on **paper support** (4), left edge against **paper guide.**

3. With your right index finger, strike the **paper insert key** (9). Paper will feed to a preset point on the sheet.

4. If paper is not straight, pull **paper release lever** (7) toward you (or upward on some machines).

5. Straighten paper; then push **paper release lever** back.

6. Slide **paper bail rolls** (6) to divide paper into thirds (or fourths if there are three rolls).

Electric Typewriters

1. Align **paper guide** (2) with *0* (zero) on the **paper guide scale** (3) or **line-of-writing** or **format scale** (10).

2. Pull **paper bail lever** (35) toward you (or upward on some machines).

3. With your left hand, place paper on **paper support** (4), left edge against the **paper guide.**

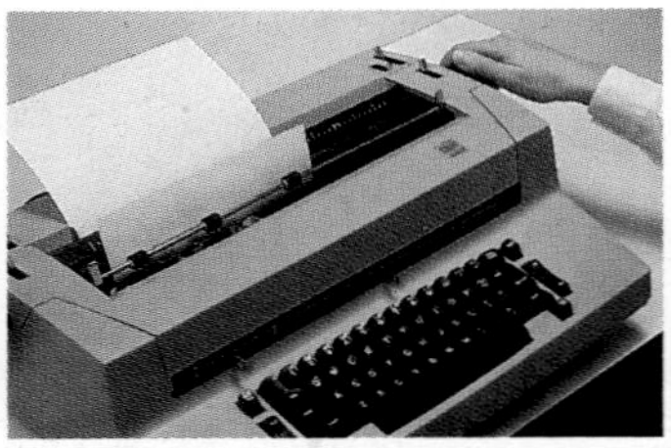

4. With your right hand, turn the right **platen knob** (8) or strike the **index key** (13) until paper is about 1½" above the **aligning scale** (33).

5. If paper is not straight, pull **paper release lever** (7) toward you or upward, straighten paper, and push lever back.

6. Slide **paper bail rolls** (6) to divide paper into thirds (or fourths if there are three rolls).

2 Set Line Space Selector

Many machines offer 3 choices for line spacing--1, 1½, and 2--indicated by bars or numbers on the **line space selector** (15).

Set the **line space selector** as directed for lines to be keyed in Phase 1:

- on (–) or 1 to single-space (SS)
- on (=) or 2 to double-space (DS)

To quadruple space (QS), set the **line space selector** on (–) or 1 to SS and strike the **return key** 4 times; alternatively, set the **line space selector** on (=) or 2 to DS and strike the **return key** twice.

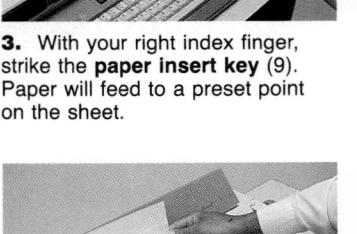

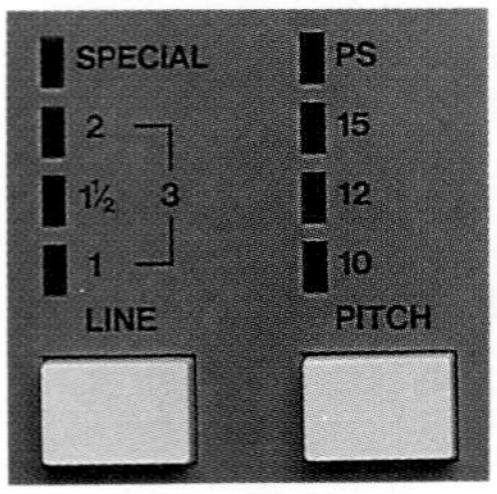

1 Lines 1 and 2 are single-spaced (SS).
2 Lines 2 and 4 are double-spaced (DS).
3 1 blank line space
4 Lines 4 and 8 are quadruple-spaced (QS).
5
6 3 blank line spaces (2 DS)
7
8 Set the selector on "1" or "–" to SS.

3 *Plan Margin Settings*

A machine may have pica type (10-pitch type--10 spaces to a horizontal inch) or may have elite type (12-pitch type--12 spaces to a horizontal inch).

Machines have at least one **line-of-writing** or **format scale** (10) that reads as follows: from *0* to at least 90 for machines with *pica* type; from *0* to at least 110 for machines with *elite* type.

When 8½" × 11" paper is inserted into the machine (short side at top) with left edge of paper at *0* on the **line-of-writing** or **format scale,** the exact center point is 42½ for pica machines and 51 for elite machines. Use 42 for pica center and 51 for elite center.

To center lines of copy, set left and right margins the same number of spaces left and right from center point. Diagrams at right show margin settings for 50-, 60-, and 70-space lines. When you begin to use the warning bell, 5 or 6 spaces may be added to the right margin.

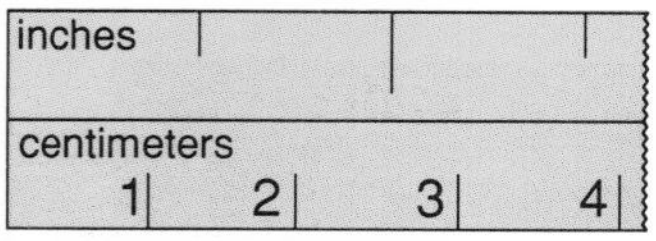

Pica, 10 keystrokes per inch
Elite, 12 keystrokes per inch

Pica center

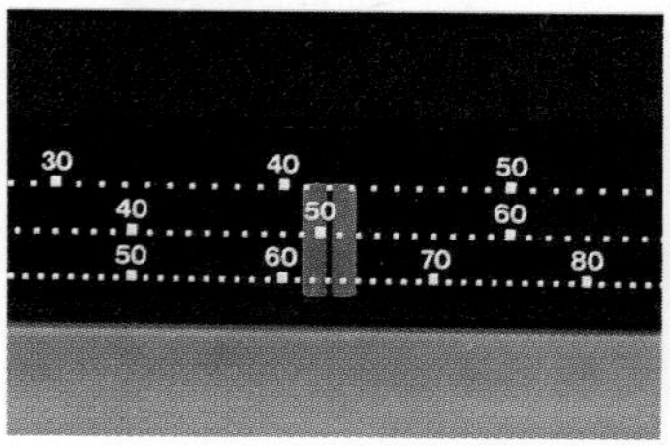

Elite center

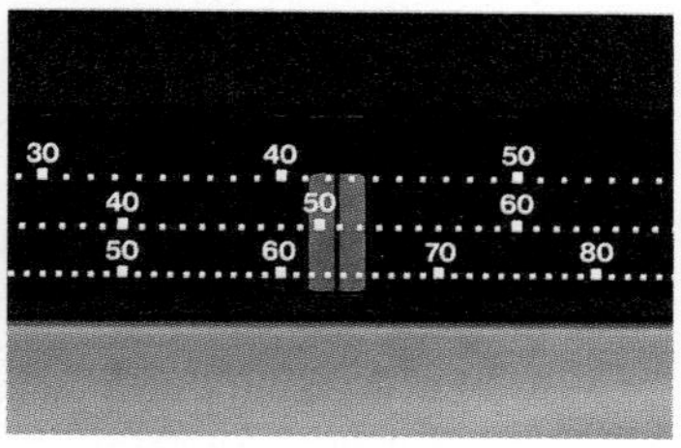

Elite (12-pitch)

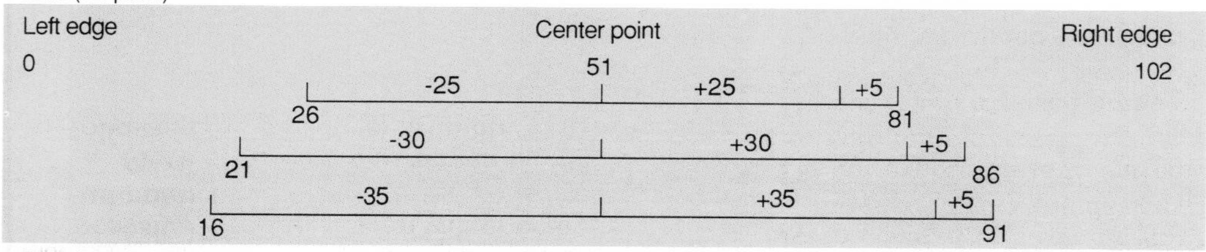

Pica (10-pitch)

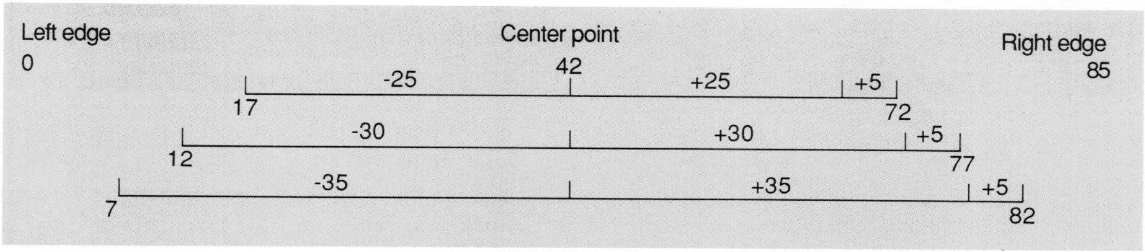

4 *Set Margins*

General information for setting margins on a typewriter is given here. The procedure for your particular model may be slightly different; therefore, consult the User's Manual or Operator's Guide for your machine.

Set left margin for a 50-space line for each lesson in Phase 1; set right margin position at right end of **line-of-writing** or **format scale** (10).

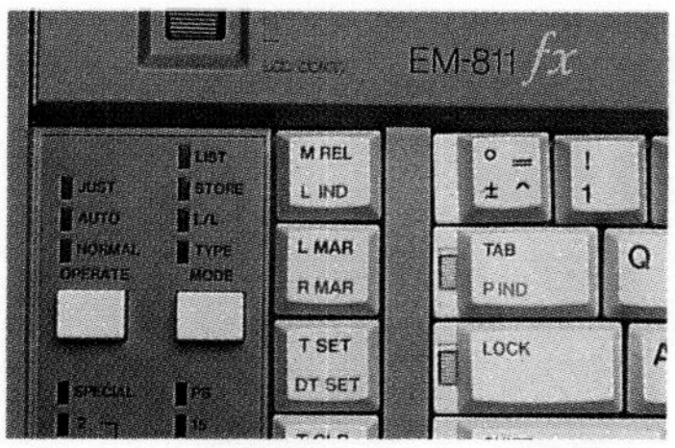

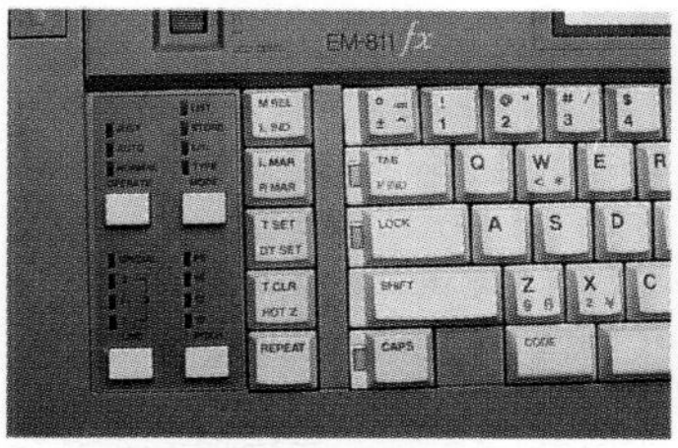

Electronic margin settings

1. Use the **space bar** (19) to move the **print carrier** (32) to the desired left margin position on the **line-of-writing** or **format scale;** strike the left **margin key** (30); on some models, depress the **code key** (20) at the same time.

2. Space to the desired right margin position and strike the **right margin key** (29) and the **code key,** if necessary.

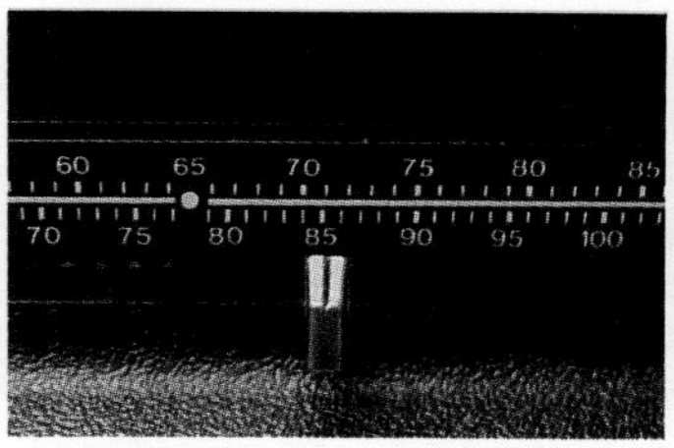

Push-lever margin settings

1. Use the **space bar** (19) to move the **element** (32) to about the middle of the **line-of-writing** or **format scale.**

2. Push in on the **left margin set lever** (see diagram); slide it to the desired left margin position on the **line-of-writing** or **format scale.**

3. Repeat, using the **right margin set lever** (see diagram).

Key set margin settings

1. At current left margin position, depress the **margin set key** and simultaneously move the **carriage** to the desired left margin position; release the **margin set key.**

2. Using the **space bar** (19) or **tab key** (24), move the **carriage** to the current right margin position.

3. Depress the **margin set key** and simultaneously move the **carriage** to the desired right margin position; release the **margin set key.**

5 *Set Other Electronic Typewriter Options*

Mode select

Set the **mode select key** for ordinary keystroking. Later, you may choose to use other typewriter modes.

Operation/Auto select

Set the **operation select key** on "normal"; later, set it on "auto" when directed by your teacher to use automatic return.

Keyboard select

Set the **keyboard select switch** to correspond to the daisy wheel used (position 1 = standard).

Impact select

Set the **impact select switch** on "light" unless heavy, hard-surfaced paper is used.

GET READY TO KEYBOARD: Computers

Computer work area

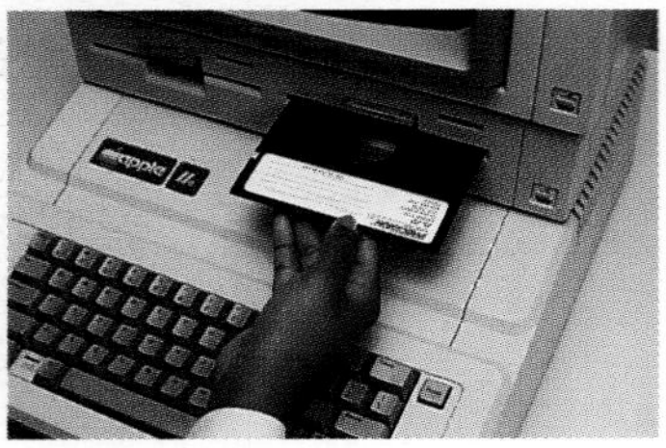

Diskette insertion

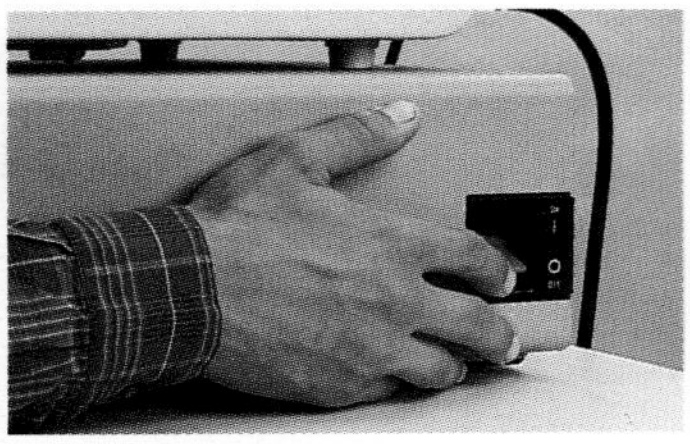

Power switch

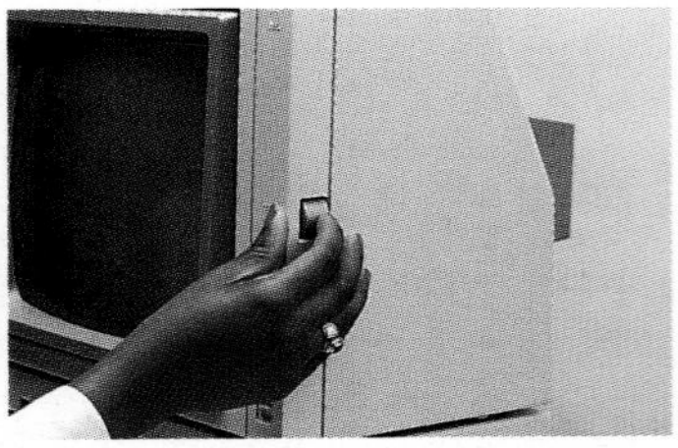

Display control

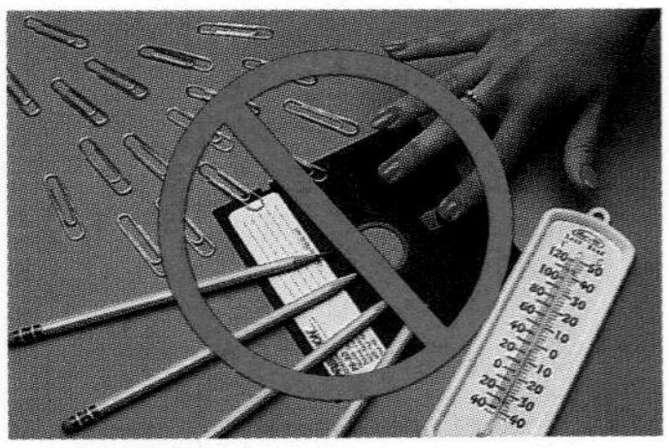

Diskette care

GET READY TO KEY

1. Position the keyboard so that the center of the alphabetic keyboard (the space between the *G* and *H*) is lined up with the center of your body. Position the front edge of the keyboard even with the front edge of the desk. If the keyboard is adjustable, adjust the angle so that the keyboard tilts slightly upward for ease of operation.

2. Turn the disk(s) you will use label-side *up*. Note the oval window at one edge. When directed to insert the disk, you will insert this edge into the slot of the disk drive.

3. Note whether you are using a single- or a dual-drive system. If there are two disk drives, you will use Drive 1. (Ask your teacher to identify the correct drive if drives are not numbered or are color-coded.)

4. Check that the power cords are plugged into a power source outlet.

5. Check that the monitor and keyboard are connected to the computer.

6. Locate the display controls (contrast and brightness) so that you may adjust them if nothing appears on the screen in Step 7.

7. Use one of the following "Power up" (turn on) procedures depending on the brand of equipment you are using.

For the Apple IIe, Apple IIc, and Apple IIGS computers, "Power up" as follows:

a. Turn on the monitor.

b. Open the door of the disk drive; insert the program disk; and close the door.

c. Turn on the computer by operating the ON/OFF control. *(If the computer is already on, hold down the Control, "open apple," and Reset keys simultaneously.)* The title screen will appear automatically.

d. Move from screen to screen by following the on-screen prompts.

For the IBM and Tandy 1000 computers, "Power up" as follows:

a. Insert the DOS disk into the disk drive and close the door.

b. Turn on the computer by operating the ON/OFF control. Make sure that the monitor (if separate) and printer (if one is connected to your computer) are also on. *If the computer is already on, hold down the control (CTRL) and alternate (ALT) keys and strike the delete (DEL) key at the same time.*

c. When the computer prompts you to enter the date, either do so *or* strike the enter key. When the computer prompts you to enter the time, either do so *or* strike the enter key.

d. The computer will display the message A⟩. *(If DOS has been installed on the program disk, go to Step 7f.)*

e. Remove the DOS disk from Drive A and insert the appropriate program disk in the drive; then close the door.

f. Key the specific command for the software in use (see User's Manual).

g. Move from screen to screen by following the on-screen prompts.

CARE OF DISKETTES

1. Do not bend or fold a disk or attach a paper clip to it.

2. Keep disks away from direct sunlight, magnets, and x-ray devices.

3. Do not expose disks to extremely hot or cold temperatures.

4. Do not touch exposed areas of disks.

5. Use only felt-tipped pen when writing on disk labels.

6. Use care when inserting disks into and removing them from disk drives. Do so only when the disk drive light is *off*. If the door of the disk drive doesn't close easily, remove the disk and reinsert it. *Never force the door to close.*

7. Store each disk in its envelope when not in use.

Control key (CTRL)

Cursor

Disk (diskette)

Disk drive

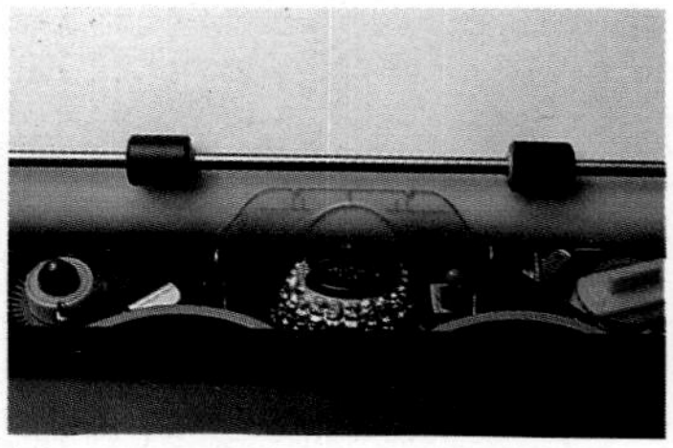
Element

ACCURACY degree of freedom from errors measured from zero--usually expressed as 1 error, 2 errors, etc.; sometimes as errors a minute (eam) or percent of error.

AUTOMATIC CENTERING a formatting feature of automated equipment that places text at an equal distance from the right and left margin settings (equal copy on either side of the center point).

AUTOMATIC UNDERLINE a formatting feature that automatically underscores text.

BACKSPACE to move the print carrier or print point (element, daisy wheel, or cursor) to the left one space at a time by striking the backspace ("back arrow") key once for each character or space.

BACKUP COPY a copy of an original storage medium such as a diskette.

BLOCK a word processing feature that defines a specific portion of text; used with the copy, move, and delete features.

BOILERPLATE stored text that can be merged with previously stored or new text to create new documents.

BOLD a formatting feature that prints the designated text darker than the rest of the copy to add emphasis.

CAPS LOCK a key that causes *all letters* to be CAPITALIZED without having to depress a shift key for each stroke; differs from the **SHIFT LOCK**, which causes *all shifted characters (letters and symbols)* to print.

CENTERING the placing of text so that half the copy is on each side of the center point.

CONTROL the power to cause the hands and fingers to make correct motions; also the ability to hold keystroking speed down so that errors (mistakes) are kept to an expected or acceptable number.

CONTROL KEY (CTRL) a special key that is pressed at the same time another key is struck, causing that key to perform a specific operation.

COPY a word processing feature that allows the operator to define text at one location and duplicate it in another location; also, material that has been or is to be keyed.

CPU (Central Processing Unit) the internal operating unit or "brains" of an electronic computer system.

CURSOR a lighted point on a display screen where the next character or space can be entered.

DEFAULT STANDARDS preset specifications in word processing software that control line length, tabs, etc.

DELETE to remove from text a segment of copy such as a character, a word, a line, a sentence, etc.; also, a word processing feature that allows the operator to eliminate a defined block of text.

DESKTOP PUBLISHING using microcomputers, laser printers, and special software to create near typeset-quality documents.

DIRECTORY a listing of documents filed on computer software.

DISK (DISKETTE) a magnetic, Mylar-coated record-like disk (encased in a protective cover) used for recording, reading, and writing by a central processing unit (CPU). Common sizes are 5¼″ and 3½″.

DISK DRIVE the unit into which a disk is inserted to be read or written on by the central processing unit (CPU).

DOCUMENT formatted information such as a letter, memo, report, table, or form.

DOS (Disk Operating System) a program recorded on a disk that causes a computer to operate or function.

DOUBLE-SPACE (DS) to use vertical line spacing that leaves one blank line space between printed lines of copy; equals 2 single-spaced lines.

EDIT to arrange, change, and correct existing text; editing includes proofreading but is not limited to it.

ELECTRONIC FILES information stored in machine-readable form.

ELECTRONIC MAIL information transmitted electronically from one computer to another without transmitting hard copy.

ELEMENT a ball-shaped printing device on the print carrier of many electric and electronic typewriters.

ELITE a type size that prints 12 characters per inch; see **CHARACTER PITCH.**

ENTER to input keystrokes; see **KEY.**

ERROR any misstroke of a key; also any variation between source copy and displayed or printed copy; departure from acceptable format (arrangement, placement, and spacing).

ESCAPE KEY (ESC) a key that lets the user cancel a function or exit one segment of a program and go to another.

Facsimile

Function keys

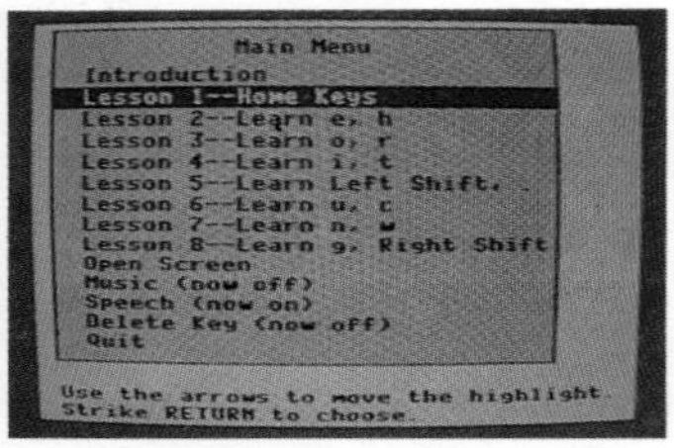

Menu

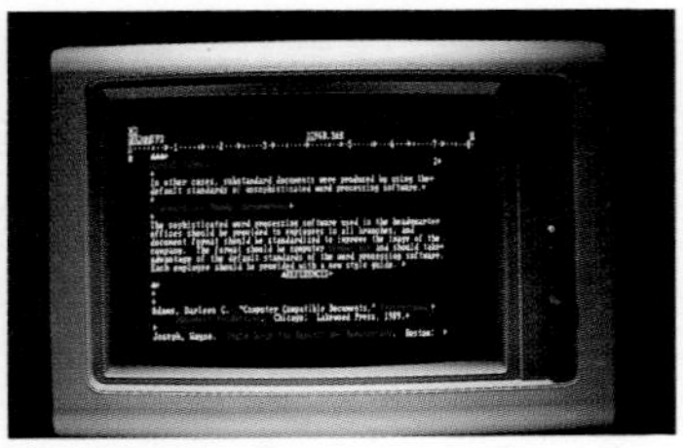

Monitor

Numeric keypad

FACSIMILE the use of scanning devices and telephone lines to transfer text and images; a copy of such text/images; commonly abbreviated "FAX."

FINAL COPY copy that is free of error and ready for use or distribution.

FONT a set of characters of a named type style.

FORMAT the style (arrangement, placement, and spacing) of a document; also to arrange a document in proper form or style.

FORMATTING the process of arranging a document in proper form or style.

FUNCTION KEYS special keys on computers and word processors that are used alone or in combination with other keys to perform special operations such as setting margins, centering copy, etc.

GWAM (Gross Words a Minute) a measure of the rate of keyboarding speed; GWAM = total standard 5-stroke words keyed divided by the time required to key those words.

HANGING INDENT a word processing feature that positions the first line of a segment of text at the left margin or other point and indents the remaining lines a specific number of spaces to the right; frequently used with enumerations.

HARD COPY typewritten or printed copy.

HARDWARE the physical equipment that makes up a computer or word processing system.

HIGHLIGHTING identifying on-screen text by changing the color or light intensity.

INDENT to set copy farther to the right than the left margin; for example, the first line of a paragraph.

INFORMATION PROCESSING the task of putting text and data into usable form, as in letters, tables, and memos.

INPUT text and data that enter an information system; also the process of entering text and data.

INSERT (INSERTION) to add new text to existing text without rekeying the entire document; also the text that is added.

KEY to strike keys to print or display text and data; also called enter, key in, keyboard, input, and type.

KEYBOARD an arrangement of keys on a "board" that is attached to a typewriter, computer, or word processor; also the act of keying or typing.

MARGINS specification of the number of spaces (or inches) at the left and right of printed lines; also the number of characters (inches) per line; also the number of line spaces above the page beginning (first line of type) or below the last line of type.

MEMORY data storage location in a computer, word processor, or electronic typewriter.

MENU a listing of available software options that appears on a display screen.

MERGE to assemble new documents from stored text such as form paragraphs; to combine stored text such as form letters with stored or newly keyed text (variables such as names and addresses).

MICROCOMPUTER a small-sized computer with a keyboard, screen, and auxiliary storage; its central processor is usually a single CPU chip.

MONITOR a TV-like screen used to display text, data, and graphic images; also called CRT, display screen, and video display terminal (VDT).

MOVE a word processing feature that allows the operator to define text at one location and shift it to another location.

NUMERIC KEYPAD an arrangement of figure keys and special keys, such as +, −, and =, to the right of most microcomputer keyboards; used for keying all-number copy and for calculations.

OPERATOR'S GUIDE (USER'S MANUAL) a set of instructions accompanying equipment or software that tells/shows how the hardware/software features are made to work.

OUTPUT data or documents that leave an information system, usually presented to the user as a screen display or a printout.

OVERSTRIKE a word processing feature that replaces existing text with newly keyed text; also, to key new text in place of existing text.

PAGINATION dividing text into segments that will print on a page; can be automatic or operator specified.

PICA a type size that prints 10 characters per inch; see **CHARACTER PITCH.**

PRINT to produce (using a printing device) a paper copy of information displayed on a screen or stored in computer, word processor, or typewriter memory.

PRINT COMMANDS software options for specifying the character pitch, margins, line spacing, justification, number of copies, page numbering, etc., of a document to be printed.

PRINTER a device attached to a computer or word processor that produces a paper (hard) copy of electronically stored text.

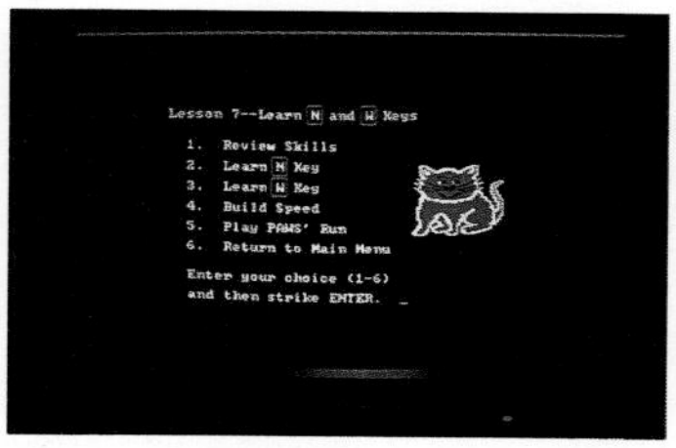

Prompt

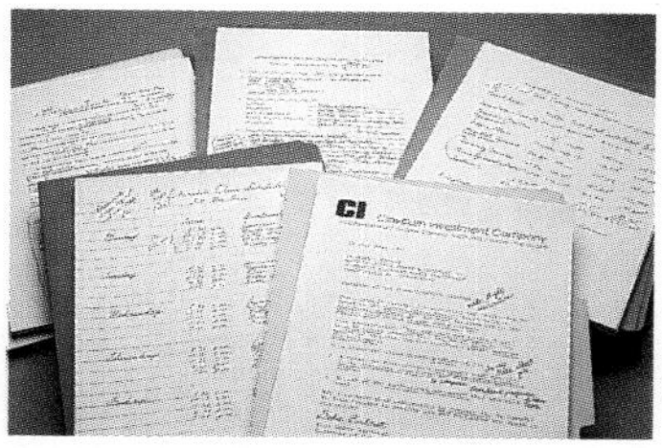

Source documents

Text (data) entry
from a voice record

User's Manual

PROMPT a message displayed in the window of an electronic typewriter or on the screen of a computer or word processor telling the user that the machine is awaiting a specific response.

PROOFREAD to compare copy on a display screen or printout to the original or source copy and to correct errors (or mark them for correction); one of the steps in editing text.

PROOFREADER'S MARKS notations used to indicate changes and corrections needed to convert draft copy to final copy.

QUADRUPLE-SPACE (QS) to use vertical line spacing that leaves 3 blank line spaces between printed lines of copy; equals 4 single-spaced lines or 2 double-spaced lines.

RATE the speed of doing a task; keying or typing rate is usually expressed in gross words a minute (GWAM) or lines per hour.

RETRIEVE a software function that recovers information that has been stored (saved).

RETURN to strike the return or enter key to cause the print carrier or cursor to move to left margin and down to next line.

SAVE (STORE) a software function that records keystrokes on a magnetic medium (disk) so that the data may be retrieved later; on some software, STORE records text and removes it from the screen while SAVE records and leaves it on the screen.

SEARCH a word processing feature that locates a specified series of characters or words in a document for editing purposes.

SHIFT KEY a key that is depressed as another key is struck to make capital letters and certain symbols.

SHIFT LOCK see **CAPS LOCK.**

SINGLE-SPACE (SS) to use vertical line spacing that leaves no blank space between printed lines of copy.

SOFTWARE instructions, or programs, that tell a computer or word processor what to do; may be contained on a disk or on computer hardware.

SOURCE DOCUMENTS original papers (documents) from which information (data and/or text) is keyed.

SPACE BAR a long bar at the bottom of a keyboard used to move the print carrier or cursor to the right one space at a time; also used to add space between on-screen characters.

SPACING the number of blank line spaces between printed lines--usually indicated as SS (0), DS (1), or QS (3).

SPELLING VERIFICATION SOFTWARE a program that identifies misspelled words in a document generated on a computer, word processor, or electronic typewriter.

TAB KEY a key that when struck causes the print carrier or cursor to skip to a preset position; used to indent paragraphs or other document parts.

TECHNIQUE a keyboard operator's form or keying style.

TEXT (DATA) ENTRY the process of transferring text (data) from the writer's mind or from a written or voice record into a word processing system.

USER'S MANUAL see **OPERATOR'S GUIDE.**

VARIABLES information (such as names, addresses, or financial data) in prestored files that is inserted in standard documents to personalize messages; see **MERGE.**

WIDOW/ORPHAN a word processing feature that prevents the occurrence of widows and orphans (see definitions above) during automatic paging.

WORD PROCESSING the act of writing and storing letters, reports, and other documents on a computer, electronic typewriter, or word processor; may also include printing of the final document.

WORD WRAP a word processing feature that permits information to be keyed on successive lines without having to strike the return key at the end of each line.

ABBREVIATIONS YOU SHOULD KNOW

BM bottom margin
CH center horizontally
CS columnar spacing; space between columns
CV center vertically
DS double-space; double spacing
GWAM gross words a minute
LL line length
LM left margin
LP LabPac (workbook)
LS line spacing
N-PRAM net production rate a minute
PB page beginning
PI paragraph indent
QS quadruple-space; quadruple spacing
RM right margin
SM side margins
SS single-space; single spacing

LESSONS 1 – 25

PHASE 1

LEARN ALPHABETIC KEYBOARDING TECHNIQUE

All professional and business offices in the modern workplace use a typewriter-like keyboard to enter data, retrieve information, and communicate facts and ideas. To achieve success in most careers today, you must be able to operate a keyboard with skill -- on a typewriter, computer, or word processor.

Fortunately, the alphabetic keyboards on these kinds of equipment have standard key locations. As a result, if you learn to key on one kind of machine, you can readily adapt to other keyboarding machines.

Your goal during the next few weeks is to learn to operate a letter keyboard with proper technique (good form) and at a reasonable level of keyboarding speed.

Phase 1 (Lessons 1-25) will help you learn:

1. To adjust (format) equipment for correct margins and vertical line spacing.

2. To operate the letter keyboard by touch (without looking at the keyboard).

3. To use basic service keys with skill: space bar, return/enter key, shift keys, caps lock, and tabulator.

4. To key words, sentences, and paragraphs with proper technique and without time-wasting pauses between letters and words.

5. To review/improve language skills.

300b (continued)

words

Document 2
Table with Horizontal Rulings

Format and key the table on a full sheet. Center the table horizontally and vertically. Center column headings; CS: 10.

THE ORIGINAL 13 STATES 5

19

State	Order of Statehood	Date of Statehood	words
			30
			44
Connecticutt	~~6~~ 5th	January 9, 1~~8~~788	50
Del~~e~~aware	1st	December 7, 1787	56
Georgia	4th	January 2, 1788	62
Maryland	7th	April 28, 1788	68
Massachusetts	~~5~~ 6th	February 6, 1788	75
New Hampshire	9th	June 21, 1788	81
New Jersey	3rd	December 18, 178~~0~~7	88
New York	11th	July 26, 1788	93
North Carolina	12th	November 21, 1789	101
Pennsylvania	2nd	December 12, 1787	108
Rhode Island	13th	May 29, 1790	115
South Carolian	8th	May 23, 1788	121
virginia	10th	June 25, 1788	127

141

Source: Fabulous Facts About the 50 States. 151

Document 3
Purchase Order

LP p. 193

Format and key the purchase order shown at the right with the changes that have been indicated.

Document 4
Table with Horizontal Rulings

Rekey Document 2 with the following changes:

DS the table; CS: 8; list the items in order of statehood (1-13).

Arlington Local School District
605 Baychester Avenue
Bronx, NY 10475-2294
(212) 638-7391

PURCHASE ORDER

Purchase Order No.: FM-3892-A 2

LEARNING ESSENTIALS
1388 MONTGOMERY STREET
SAN FRANCISCO CA 94133-4611

Date: March 25, 19-- 12
16
Terms: n/30 24
Shipped Via: Arrow Express 27

Quantity	Description/Stock Number	Price		Per	Total		words
25	Essential Word Skills (6803-WS)	6	95	ea	173	75	37
25	Learn to Capitalize (2475-LC)	5	87	ea	146	75	47
~~10~~ 5	Picture Punctuation (3820-PP)	6	25	ea	~~62~~ 31	~~50~~ 25	56
~~10~~ 5	Reader Review (5970-RR)	5	10	ea	~~51~~ 25	~~00~~ 50	66
					~~434~~ 377	~~00~~ 25	68
	Less 10% discount				~~43~~ 37	~~40~~ 73	74
					~~390~~ 339	~~60~~ 52	75

By ____________________

UNIT 1 *LESSONS 1 – 20*

Learn Letter Keyboarding Technique

Learning Goals

1. To learn to operate letter keys and punctuation keys with correct technique.

2. To learn to operate service keys (SHIFT and RETURN/ENTER keys, SPACE BAR, CAPS LOCK, and TABULATOR) with correct technique.

3. To learn to operate letter, punctuation, and service keys by touch (without looking).

4. To learn to key sentences and paragraphs with correct technique and speed.

Format Guides

1. PAPER GUIDE at *0* (for typewriters).

2. Line length (LL): 50 spaces; see *Get Ready to Keyboard: Typewriters* (p. x) or *Computers* (p. xii).

3. Line spacing (LS): single-space (SS) drills; double-space (DS) paragraphs (¶s).

4. Page beginning (PB): line 6 or line 10, according to teacher directions.

Lesson 1 — *Home Keys (ASDF JKL;)*

Line length (LL): 50 spaces
Line spacing (LS): single (SS)

1a ▶ *Get Ready to Keyboard*

1. Arrange work area as shown at right.

Typewriter

- front frame of machine even with front edge of desk
- book at right of machine, top raised for easy reading
- paper at left of machine
- unneeded books and supplies placed out of the way

Computer

- keyboard directly in front of chair, front edge even with edge of table or desk
- monitor placed for easy viewing; disk drives placed for easy access
- diskette package within easy reach
- book at right of computer, top raised for easy reading
- unneeded books and supplies placed out of the way

2. Turn on equipment (ON/OFF control of typewriter or computer/monitor).

3. Make needed machine (format) adjustments (see pages x-xi, typewriter; page xii, computer).

4. Insert paper into typewriter (see page x). If using a computer printer, turn printer on and check paper supply and paper feed.

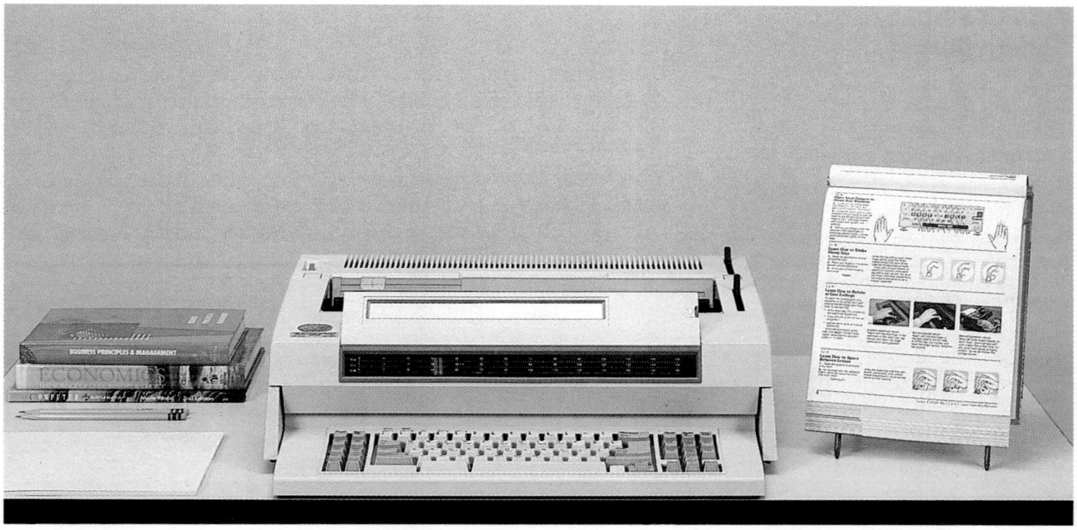

Properly arranged work area: typewriter

Properly arranged work area: computer

300a ► 5 Conditioning Practice

Key each line twice. Then take two 30″ writings for speed on line 4 followed by two 30″ writings for control on line 1.

alphabet 1 Jack or Megan will buy the exquisite bracelet made of topaz in Denver.

figures 2 Their office buildings are at 2581 State, 7349 Dorbe, and 608 Sherman.

fig/sym 3 Kent & Sons donated $3,500 (Check #478) to the United Way on 12/16/91.

speed 4 They may both make the goals if they keep busy in their own cornfield.

| 1 | 2 | 3 | 4 | 5 | 6 | 7 | 8 | 9 | 10 | 11 | 12 | 13 | 14 |

300b ► 45 Evaluate Document Processing Skills: Tables/Forms

Time Schedule

Plan and prepare .... 5′
Timed production .... 30′
Proofread, compute *n-pram*... 10′

1. Arrange materials for ease of handling (LP p. 193 and 199).

2. Format and key Documents 1-4 for 30′. Proofread and correct errors before removing each document from machine or screen.

3. After time is called, proofread again and circle any uncorrected errors. Compute *n-pram.*

Document 1
Letter with Table

LP p. 199

Format and key the letter at the right in block format with mixed punctuation. Address the letter to

Mrs. Dorothy A. Romine
Arlington Grade School
605 Baychester Avenue
Bronx, NY 10475-2294

Date the letter **March 10, 19--** and supply any missing letter parts.

words

opening lines 24

Despite the fact that you are bringing another ^school year to a 37
close, it is time to start planning for next year. Learning 49
Essentials is eager to assist again ni that planning. 62

You may be interested in the new products that we will have 74
available in time for the start of the next school year. 86
Our pilot-test schools have been very enthusiastic about the 98
following ~~five~~ six products. 103

Product	Order No.	Unit Price	words
			116
Essential Word Skills	6803-WS	$6.95	124
Fun with Contractions	8319-FC	4.75	131
Learn to Capitalize	2475-LC	5.87	138
Picture Punctuation	3820-PP	6.25	144
Enhance Your Vocabulary	1024-EV	7.35	152
Reader Review	5970-RR	5.10	158

SS

Brochures ~~about~~ describing the products are enclosed. If you would 170
like examination copies of any of these products, mail the 182
card attached to each brochure. 188

Sincerely, 190

Jamison R. Cleworth 194
Sales Representative 201

A 10 percent discount will be given on orders 210
totaling $100 or more that are received before 220
June 15.

221/**239**

1b ▶ *Take Keyboarding Position*

Proper position is the same for typewriters and computers. The essential features of proper position are illustrated at right and listed below:

- fingers curved and upright over home keys
- wrists low, but not touching frame of machine or keyboard
- forearms parallel to slant of keyboard
- body erect, sitting back in chair
- feet on floor for balance

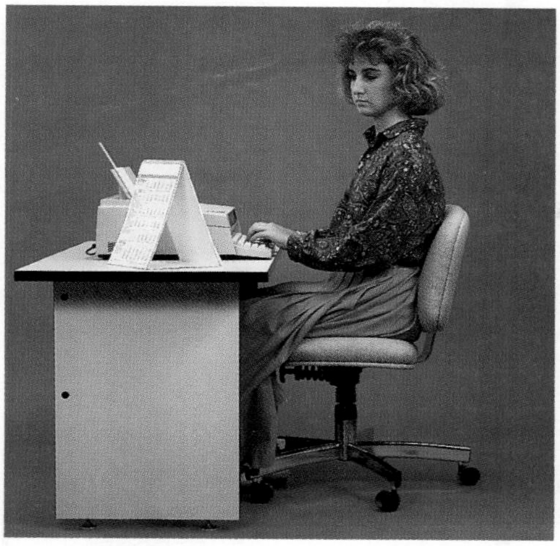

Proper position at typewriter

Proper position at computer

1c ▶ *Place Your Fingers in Home-Key Position*

1. Locate the home keys on the chart: **a s d f** for left hand and **j k l ;** for right hand.

2. Locate the home keys on your keyboard. Place left-hand fingers on **a s d f** and right-hand fingers on **j k l ;** *with your fingers well-curved and upright (not slanting).*

3. Remove your fingers from the keyboard; then place them in home-key position again, curving and holding them *lightly* on the keys.

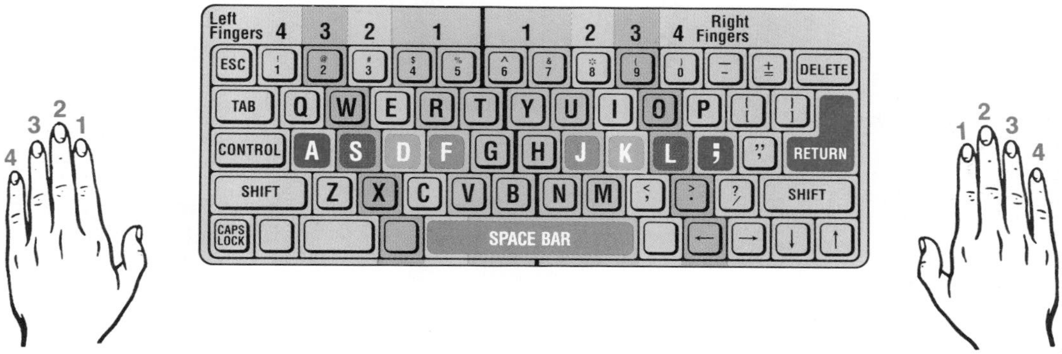

1d ▶ *Learn How to Strike Home Keys and Space Bar*

1. Read the keystroking technique statement and study the illustrations at right.

2. Read the spacing technique statement and study the illustrations at right.

3. Place your fingers in home-key position as directed in 1c, above.

4. Strike each letter key for the first group of letters in the line of type below the technique illustrations.

5. After striking **;** (semicolon), strike the SPACE BAR once.

6. Continue to key the line; strike the SPACE BAR once at the point of each color arrow.

Keystroking technique

Strike each key with a light tap with the tip of the finger, snapping the fingertip toward the palm of the hand.

Spacing technique

Strike the SPACE BAR with the right thumb; use a quick down-and-in motion (toward the palm). Avoid pauses before or after spacing.

Space once

```
fdsajkl; f d s a j k l ; ff jj dd kk ss ll aa ;;
```

299b (continued)

Use the information given below to prepare the reference page.

Yukl, Gary A. Leadership in Organizations. 2d ed. Englewood Cliffs, NJ: Prentice-Hall, Inc., 1989.

Lundy, James L. Lead, Follow, or Get Out of the Way. San Diego: Slawson Communications, Inc., 1986.

References: 56 words.

Document 3
Unbound Report

plain full sheets

Rekey Document 2 as an unbound report.

words

Leadership styles 141

A leadership style is the approach a person (leader) 152
uses to get others to accomplish goals and objectives. 163
Leader ship styles can eb classified as either authoritarian 175
or participative. Styles are also classified as autocratic 187
~~or~~ and democratic. 190

Authoritarian style. The authoritarian style of 204
leadership allows for ~~very~~ little or no imput from group 214
members in the decision-making process. This style is also 226
referred to as "autocratic." 232

Participative style. The participative style of 246
leadership ~~believes that~~ allows for group members to ~~should~~ be actively 256
involved in the decision-making process and encourages input 268
from the members of the group. "Democratic" is another name 281
for this style. 284

In reality, ~~it is not uncommon for~~ a person's individual style ~~to~~ 292
~~be~~ is often a combination of ~~these~~ two styles rather than strictly ~~totally~~ authori- 305
tarian or strictly ~~totally~~ participative. 312

Characteristics of Respected Leaders 327

Debate over which style of leadership is most effective 338
has taken place formany years. Advantages and disadvantages 350
of each are often discussed. However, most responses given 362
in a survey htat requested participants to list character- 374
istics that contribute to their respect for ~~of~~ leaders can be 385
found in the participative style of leadership (Lundy 1986, 388
13-16) These characteristics include ~~such items as~~ the following: 409

1. Communicates, allows input, is willing to listen. 419

2. Is objective, open-minded, tolerant, rational, rea- 430
sonable, impartial, fair. 435
3. Delegates, trusts subordinates, allows room to 446
achieve. 447
4. Motivates, challenges, inspires, is team-oriented. 458
5. Is available, approachable; provides feedback; 469
trains, guides, coaches. 473

1e ▶ Learn How to Return at Line Endings

Return the *printing point indicator* of a typewriter or the *cursor* of a computer to the left margin and move down to the next line as follows:

- Strike the RETURN key on electric and electronic typewriters.
- Strike the RETURN/ENTER key on computers.

Study the illustrations at right and return 4 times (quadruple-space) below the line you completed in 1d, page 3.

Typewriter return

Reach with the little finger of the right hand to the RETURN key, tap the key, and return the finger quickly to home-key position.

Computer return

Reach with the little finger of the right hand to the RETURN/ENTER key, tap the key, and return the finger quickly to home-key position.

1f ▶ Practice Home-Key Letters and Spacing

1. Place your hands in home-key position (left-hand fingers on **a s d f** and right-hand fingers on **j k l ;**).

2. Key the lines once as shown: single-spaced (SS) with a double-space (DS) between 2-line groups.

Do not key the line numbers.

Fingers curved and upright

Down-and-in spacing motion

Spacing hint

With the LINE SPACE SELECTOR set for single spacing, return twice at the end of the line to double-space (DS).

Strike SPACE BAR once to space

```
1 j jj f ff k kk d dd l ll s ss ; ;; a aa jkl; fdsa
2 j jj f ff k kk d dd l ll s ss ; ;; a aa jkl; fdsa
```
Strike the RETURN/ENTER key twice to double-space (DS)

```
3 a aa ; ;; s ss l ll d dd k kk f ff j jj fdsa jkl;
4 a aa ; ;; s ss l ll d dd k kk f ff j jj fdsa jkl;
```
DS

```
5 jf jf kd kd ls ls ;a ;a fj fj dk dk sl sl a; a; f
6 jf jf kd kd ls ls ;a ;a fj fj dk dk sl sl a; a; f
```
DS

```
7 a;fj a;sldkfj a;sldkfj a;sldkfj a;sldkfj a;sldkfj
8 a;fj a;sldkfj a;sldkfj a;sldkfj a;sldkfj a;sldkfj
```
Strike the RETURN/ENTER key 4 times to quadruple-space (QS)

1g ▶ Practice Return Technique

each line twice single-spaced (SS); double-space (DS) between 2-line groups

Reach out with little finger; tap RETURN/ENTER key quickly; return finger to home key.

```
1 a;sldkfj a;sldkfj
```
DS

```
2 ff jj dd kk ss ll aa ;;
```
DS

```
3 fj fj dk dk sl sl a; a; asdf ;lkj
```
DS

```
4 fj dk sl a; jf kd ls ;a fdsa jkl; a;sldkfj
```
QS

299a ▶ 5 Conditioning Practice

Each line twice. Then take two 30″ writings for speed on line 4 followed by two 30″ writings for control on line 1.

alphabet 1 He was extremely helpful in moving the jazz band quickly to the stage.

figures 2 For more information on our rates, phone 615-889-2743, Extension 5077.

fig/sym 3 He bought 50 shares of BB&Q at $36.95 ($1,847.50) with 12% commission.

speed 4 If the firms do the tax audit, we may make the signs for their social.

| 1 | 2 | 3 | 4 | 5 | 6 | 7 | 8 | 9 | 10 | 11 | 12 | 13 | 14 |

299b ▶ 45 Evaluate Document Processing Skills: Reports/News Release

Time Schedule

Plan and prepare .... 5′
Timed production .... 30′
Proofread; compute *n-pram* .... 10′

1. Arrange materials for ease of handling (LP p. 197).

2. Format and key Documents 1-3 for 30′. Proofread and correct errors before removing each document from machine or screen.

3. After time is called, proofread again and circle any uncorrected errors. Compute *n-pram.*

Document 1
News Release

LP p. 197

Format and key the material to the upper right as a news release for release immediately with **Marsha G. Chen, 612-392-4219,** as the contact.

words

opening lines 8

(¶1) Minneapolis, MN, March 26, 19--. Gerald M. Richardson, Mall 20
Manager, announced today that construction of the new Oak Ridge Mall in 35
downtown Minneapolis is nearing completion and that stores will be opening 50
for business on May 1. The grand opening of the mall is scheduled for the 65
week of May 7. 68

(¶2) Richardson reported that 85% of the mall's 1.25 million square feet 82
of store space had been leased. "With the normal occupancy rate of a new 96
mall being 80% on opening day, we are confident that the mall is going to be 112
a huge success." The mall includes approximately 150 shops anchored by 126
three major department store chains. The fourth anchor is the Oak Ridge 141
Hotel which features a Supper Club & Dinner Theatre. 152

(¶3) Richardson stated that developers have focused on making the mall a 165
place that provides family entertainment as well as shopping. At the center 181
of the mall is a small amusement park for the children, featuring miniature 196
golf, a skating rink, and various food establishments. 207

Document 2
Leftbound Report

plain full sheets

Format and key the material at the right as a leftbound report. Prepare a reference page on a separate sheet.

LEADERSHIP 2

The term leadership is very difficult to define. {Even} those 14
who ~~do~~ {have done} extensive research in the area {have found} ~~find~~ an abundance of 29
definitions. ~~with most~~ {Many} of these definitions reflect ~~ing~~ the 39
individual perspectives of the person defining the term. 51
One researcher, after doing a comprehensive review of the 62
leadership literature, concluded that there are almost as 74
many definitions of leadership as there are persons who have 86
attempted to define the concept (Yukl, 1989, 2). Even 97
though one definition is difficult to {agree on} ~~attain~~, a greater un- 109
derstanding of leadership can be gained by looking at dif- 121
ferent leadership styles and characteristics of respected 132
leaders. 134

(continued, p. 500)

1h ▶ Key Letters, Words, and Phrases

1. Key the lines once as shown; strike the RETURN/ENTER key twice to double-space (DS) between lines.

2. If time permits, rekey the drill at a faster pace.

Fingers curved and upright

Spacing hint
Space once after **;** used as punctuation.

Technique hint
Keep fingers curved and upright over home keys with right thumb just barely touching the SPACE BAR.

1 aa ;; ss ll dd kk ff jj a; sl dk fj jf kd ls ;a jf

DS

2 a a as as ad ad ask ask lad lad fad fad jak jak la

DS

3 all all fad fad jak jak add add ask ask ads ads as

DS

4 a lad; a jak; a lass; all ads; add all; ask a lass

DS

5 as a lad; a fall fad; ask all dads; as a fall fad;

1i ▶ End of Lesson

Standard typewriter

1. Raise PAPER BAIL or pull it toward you.

2. Pull PAPER RELEASE LEVER toward you.

3. Remove paper with your left hand. Push PAPER RELEASE LEVER back to its normal position.

4. Turn machine off.

Electronic typewriter

1. Press the PAPER UP (or EJECT) key to remove paper.

2. Turn machine off.

Computer

1. Remove diskette from disk drive and store it.

2. If directed to do so, turn equipment off.

Review Lesson 1 — Home Keys (ASDF JKL;)

Line length (LL): 50 spaces
Line spacing (LS): single (SS)

R1a ▶ Get Ready to Keyboard

Typewriters

1. Arrange your work area (see page 2).

2. Get to know your equipment (see pages vi-vii).

3. Make machine adjustments and insert paper into machine (see pages x-xi).

4. Take keyboarding position (see illustration at right and features of proper position on page 3).

Computer

1. Arrange your work area (see page 2).

2. Get to know your equipment (see pages viii-ix).

3. Make format adjustments unless you are using the built-in default margins and spacing (see page xii).

4. Take keyboarding position (see illustration at right and features of proper position on page 3).

298b (continued)

words

Document 2
Formal Memorandum

LP p. 193

Format and key the material at the right as a formal memorandum to **Margaret Comstock, Personnel Manager** from **Thomas Salazar, Assistant Personnel Manager.** Date the memo **March 6, 19--.** Use **EMPLOYEE MORALE** for the subject line.

opening lines 22

After our meeting last week, I called Research 32
Dynamics to discuss the possibility of their conduct- 42
ing the study for us on employee morale. I met 52
with three of their research specialists to outline 62
what we want from the research. 69
They are interested in working with us on 77
the project, and I feel that they will be able to 87
provide us with the information we need. They 97
will present a proposal to us during the week 106
of May 13. Let me know which day and time 114
would best fit your schedule, and I will 123
arrange for the meeting. 127/**139**

Document 3
Business Letter

LP p. 195

Format the material at the right as a modified block letter with mixed punctuation and blocked paragraphs. Use the **current date,** and address the letter to

Ms. Rosetta N. Johnson
2682 Gingham Court
Orlando, FL 32828-8461

Include an appropriate salutation and complimentary close.

The letter is from **Marcia G. Ogden, Studio Manager**

Special features:

Company name in closing lines:

SANDBERG PHOTOGRAPHY STUDIO

Supply any missing parts.

Document 4
Simplified Memorandum

plain full sheet

Rekey Document 2 as a simplified memorandum.

opening lines 20

the primary Sandberg Photography
Customer satisfaction is ~~a major~~ goal of ~~ours.~~ ~~In order~~ 33
Studio.
to determine how we can imporve our photography service we 47
rely on customer feed back. 53
recent
since you were a customer of our studio, we would like to 66
solicit input from you regarding your perception of the ser- 77
vice you received ~~when you did business with us the last~~ 81
n c
~~time.~~ The enclosed questionaire is divided into sebtions. 92
The first section is the second, the third,
to evaluate the receptionist; the photographer; thesales 113
the last, your # e
representative; and the quality of ~~the~~ photos. Pleas take a 127
few n providing
~~couple of~~ minutes to complete the questionaire, ~~to give~~ us 138
with better
~~the~~ information to ~~better~~ serev you in the future. 149
Certificate
The enclosed ~~coupon~~ for a 25 percent discount on your next 162
p
sitting is a token of our apreciation for helping us to con- 174
primary
tinue focusing on our ~~major~~ goal--customer satisfaction. 185

closing lines 208/**221**

R1b ▶ Review Home-Key Position

1. Locate the home keys on the chart: **a s d f** for left hand and **j k l ;** for right hand.

2. Locate the home keys on your keyboard. Place left-hand fingers on **a s d f** and right-hand fingers on **j k l ;** *with fingers well-curved and upright (not slanting).*

3. Remove fingers from the keyboard; then place them in home-key position again, curving and holding them *lightly* on the keys.

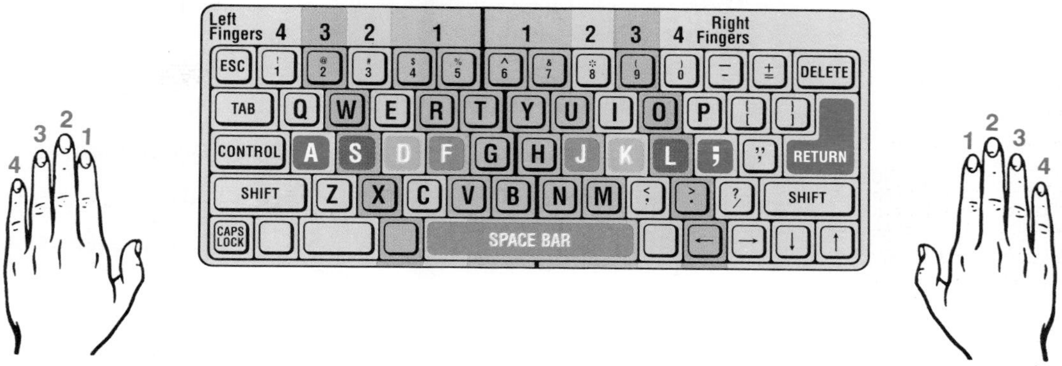

R1c ▶ Review Keystroking, Spacing, and Return Technique

Keystroke

Curve left-hand fingers and place them over **a s d f** keys. Curve right-hand fingers and place them over **j k l ;** keys. Strike each key with a quick-snap stroke; release key quickly.

Space

To space after letters, words, and punctuation marks, strike the SPACE BAR with a quick down-and-in motion of the right thumb. Do not pause before or after spacing stroke.

Typewriter return

Reach the little finger of the right hand to the RETURN key, strike the key, and release it quickly.

Computer return

Reach the little finger of the right hand to the RETURN/ENTER key, strike the key, and release it quickly.

Key the lines once as shown: single-spaced (SS) with a double space (DS) between 2-line groups.

Do not key the line numbers.

Spacing hint
To DS when in SS mode, strike the RETURN/ENTER key twice at the end of the line.

Strike SPACE BAR once to space

```
1 f ff j jj d dd k kk s ss l ll a aa ; ;; fdsa jkl;
2 f ff j jj d dd k kk s ss l ll a aa ; ;; fdsa jkl;
```
Strike the RETURN key twice to double-space (DS)

```
3 j jj f ff k kk d dd l ll s ss ; ;; a aa asdf ;lkj
4 j jj f ff k kk d dd l ll s ss ; ;; a aa asdf ;lkj
```
DS

```
5 a;a sls dkd fjf ;a; lsl kdk jfj a;sldkfj a;sldkfj
6 a;a sls dkd fjf ;a; lsl kdk jfj a;sldkfj a;sldkfj
```
Strike the RETURN key 4 times to quadruple-space (QS)

R1d ▶ Improve Home-Key Stroking

1. Review the technique illustrations in R1c, above.

2. Key the lines once as shown: single-spaced (SS) with a double space (DS) between 2-line groups.

Goal: To improve keystroking, spacing, and return technique.

```
1 f f ff j j jj d d dd k k kk s s ss l l ll a a aa;
2 f f ff j j jj d d dd k k kk s s ss l l ll a a aa;
```
DS

```
3 fj dk sl a; jf kd ls ;a ds kl df kj sd lk sa ;l j
4 fj dk sl a; jf kd ls ;a ds kl df kj sd lk sa ;l j
```
DS

```
5 sa as ld dl af fa ls sl fl lf al la ja aj sk ks j
6 sa as ld dl af fa ls sl fl lf al la ja aj sk ks j
```
QS

298a ▶ 5 Conditioning Practice

Key each line twice. Then take two 30″ writings for speed on line 4 followed by two 30″ writings for control on line 1.

alphabet 1 Wayne Mazzilli very quickly expressed his own feelings on the subject.

figures 2 The call numbers for the last two books are HD52.7.L86 and SG40.9.L13.

fig/sym 3 Invoice #694 was billed to credit card #C17305 for $805.23 on 8/02/92.

speed 4 If they are too busy with work, the visitor may be a problem for them.

| 1 | 2 | 3 | 4 | 5 | 6 | 7 | 8 | 9 | 10 | 11 | 12 | 13 | 14 |

298b ▶ 45 Evaluate Document Processing Skills: Letters/Memos

Time Schedule

Plan and prepare .... 5′
Timed production .... 30′
Proofread; compute *n-pram* .... 10′

1. Arrange materials for ease of handling (LP pp. 191-195).

2. Format and key Documents 1-4 for 30′. Proofread and correct errors before removing each document from machine or screen.

3. After time is called, proofread again and circle any uncorrected errors. Compute *n-pram*.

Note: To find *n-pram* (net production rate per minute), deduct 10 words for each uncorrected error; divide remainder by 30 (time).

Document 1
Business Letter
LP p. 191

Format in block style with open punctuation the letter shown at the right. Address the letter to

Mr. Robert T. Cline
Nagle College of Business
310 McDowell Avenue, S
Chicago, IL 60609-7395

Use **March 4, 19--** as the date and prepare the letter to be sent **REGISTERED.**

Include the following postscript:

If you decide not to purchase the materials, please return them by June 4.

Supply any missing letter parts.

words

opening lines 27

Subject: Laura McKinzie Presentation Materials 36

Here is the McKinzie material developed for im- 46
proving presentation skills for your review. As I in- 56
dicated to you during our conversation, the materials 67
are comprehensive and include three videos, a text, 78
transparencies, and a workbook. 84

Once you have had the opportunity to review the 94
materials, you will see how extremely helpful they 104
are for instructing future businesspeople on the art of 115
making an effective presentation. Several colleges in 126
your area currently use this material. Also, many 136
business organizations throughout the United States 147
have purchased the materials and are using them 156
for in-house training for their employees. 165

If you have any questions after reviewing the 174
materials, please call me at 1-800-639-6700. 184

Sincerely 187

EDUCATIONAL SPECIALISTS, INC. 192

Marshall G. Pearson 196
Sales Representative 200

closing lines 218/**236**

R1e ▶ *Improve Return Technique*

each line twice single-spaced (SS); double-space (DS) between 2-line groups

Goals

- curved, upright fingers
- quick-snap keystrokes
- down-and-in spacing
- quick return without spacing at line ending

Return without moving your eyes from the copy.

Technique hint
Reach out with the little finger, not the hand; tap RETURN/ENTER key quickly; return finger to home key.

1 a;sldkfj a;sldkfj
DS
2 a ad ad a as as ask ask
DS
3 as as jak jak ads ads all all
DS
4 a jak; a lass; all fall; ask all dads
DS
5 as a fad; add a jak; all fall ads; a sad lass
QS

R1f ▶ *Key Home-Key Words and Phrases*

each line twice single-spaced (SS); double-space (DS) between 2-line groups

Goals

- curved, upright fingers
- eyes on copy in book or on screen
- quick-snap keystrokes
- steady pace

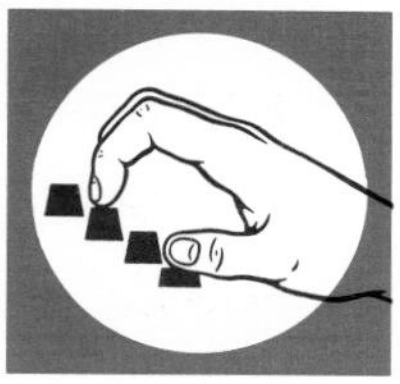
Correct finger curvature

Correct finger alignment

Down-and-in spacing motion

1 a jak; a jak; ask dad; ask dad; as all; as all ads
Return twice to DS
2 a fad; a fad; as a lad; as a lad; all ads; all ads
DS
3 as a fad; as a fad; a sad lass; a sad lass; a fall
DS
4 ask a lad; ask a lad; all jaks fall; all jaks fall
DS
5 a sad fall; a sad fall; all fall ads; all fall ads
DS
6 add a jak; a lad asks a lass; as a jak ad all fall

R1g ▶ *End of Lesson*

Standard typewriter

1. Raise PAPER BAIL or pull it toward you.

2. Pull PAPER RELEASE LEVER toward you.

3. Remove paper with your left hand. Push PAPER RELEASE LEVER back to its normal position.

4. Turn machine off.

Electronic typewriter

1. Press the PAPER UP (or EJECT) key to remove paper.

2. Turn machine off.

Computer

1. Remove diskette from disk drive and store it.

2. If directed to do so, turn equipment off.

297c ▶ 30
Evaluate Language Skills

LL: 70 spaces
LS: DS

1. The sentences at the right contain errors in capitalization, number expression, punctuation, grammar, and word choice.

2. As you key each sentence (with number and period), make all necessary corrections, including any keyboarding errors you may make.

3. After you key all sentences, proofread each one and mark each keyboarding error that was not corrected.

Capitalization/Number Expression

1. 9 fbla members from Utah may attend the Meeting in Washington, d.c.
2. they will arrive on flight 62 at ten thirty a.m. with president Chi.
3. She was invited to lunch at the Hotel lombardozzi on 5th avenue.
4. The singing statesmen will perform on friday, january 25, at 7 p.m.
5. Does the Mississippi river divide minneapolis and st. paul?
6. The united parcel service will still deliver on christmas eve.
7. The Roberts live at nine pacific view drive in San diego, california.

Punctuation

8. If we leave a week early we will go to Houston Dallas and Austin.
9. The man said "If you are staying for lunch please raise your hand."
10. The new president Jason Masters will take office in May.
11. I believe Dr. James you will be able to meet with him after lunch.
12. During the summer of 1991 10975 students attended the university.
13. The senator Sandra Myers is a charming intelligent person.
14. Tom my cousin was born on Friday July 2, 1976 in Oxford Maine.

Subject/Verb/Pronoun Agreement

15. Either Mr. Dixon or Ms. Jay were invited to be our guest of honor.
16. The executive committee have made arrangements for the next meeting.
17. Some of the report are finished. All of the boys are working on it.
18. The new desks that you ordered has arrived; the chairs have not.
19. Dr. Jones and Dr. Blassingame is in charge of the project.
20. Most of the administrators was pleased with his decision.

Word Choice

21. The two of them decided the report was too long too be acceptable.
22. They gave her a complement on the weigh she threw the baseball.
23. If they are write about the date, it does not make cents to weight.
24. The heir to the throne seams to be adapt at flying an airplane.
25. I am confidant that he will learn a good lessen from her advise.
26. The cereal number is written right at the bottom of the envelop.
27. They will let us know within the our if the site is acceptable.
28. He seems to recent the weigh they choose to cite his work.
29. She was told to be very implicit with her plans for paying the lone.
30. There mite be a big deference in the two types of stationery.

Read Before Beginning Lesson 2

Standard Procedures for Getting Ready to Keyboard

DO at the beginning of each practice session:

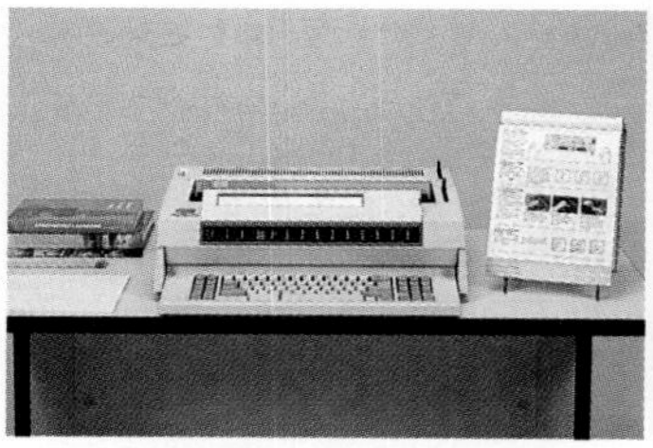

Work area properly arranged

Typewriter

1. Arrange work area as shown at left.
2. Adjust PAPER GUIDE to line up with *0* (zero) on the LINE-OF-WRITING or FORMAT SCALE. See page x.
3. Insert paper (long edge against the PAPER GUIDE). See page x.
4. Set the LINE SPACE SELECTOR to single-space (SS) your practice lines. See page x.
5. Set line length (LL) for a 50-space line: left margin (LM) at center −25; right margin (RM) at center +25 or at right end of LINE-OF-WRITING or FORMAT SCALE. See page xi.

Computer

1. Arrange work area as shown on page 2.
2. Check to see that the computer, display screen, and printer (if any) are properly plugged in.
3. Choose the appropriate diskette for your computer and for the lesson you are to complete.
4. "Power up" the computer, following the steps given in the User's Guide or the Operator's Manual for your computer.
5. Align the front of the keyboard with the front edge of the desk (table).

Standard Plan for Learning New Keys

All keys except the home keys (ASDF JKL;) require the fingers to reach in order to strike them. Follow these steps in learning the reach stroke for each new key:

1. ***Find*** the new key on the keyboard chart given with the new key introduction.
2. ***Look*** at your own keyboard and find the new key on it.
3. ***Study*** the reach-technique drawing at the left of the practice lines for the new key. (See page 9 for illustrations.) Read the printed instructions.
4. ***Identify*** the finger to be used to strike the new key.
5. ***Curve*** your fingers; place them in home-key position (over ASDF JKL;).
6. ***Watch*** your finger as you reach it to the new key and back to home position a few times (keep it curved).
7. ***Refer*** to the set of 3 drill lines at the right of the reach-technique drawing. Key each line twice single-spaced (SS):

- once *slowly*, to learn the new reach;
- once *faster*, to get a quick-snap stroke.

Double-space (DS) between 2-line groups.

Technique Emphasis During Practice

Of all the factors of proper position at the keyboard, the position of the hands and fingers is most important because they do the work.

Position the body in front of the keyboard so that you can place the fingers in a vertical (upright) position over the home keys with the fingertips just touching the faces of the keys. Move your chair forward or backward or your elbows in or out a bit to place your fingers in this upright position. Do not let your fingers lean over onto one another toward the little fingers.

Curve the fingers so that there is about a 90-degree angle at the second joint of the index fingers. In this position, the fingers can make quick, direct reaches to the keys and snap toward the palm as reaches are completed. A quick-snap stroke is essential for proper keystroking.

Place the thumbs *lightly* on the SPACE BAR with the tip of the right thumb pointing toward the *n* key; tuck the tip of the left thumb slightly into the palm to keep it out of the way. Strike the SPACE BAR with a quick down-and-in motion of the right thumb.

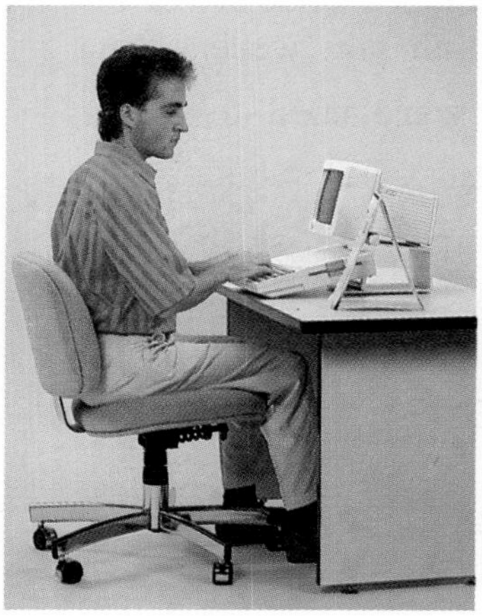

Body properly positioned

Fingers properly upright

Fingers properly curved

Thumb properly positioned

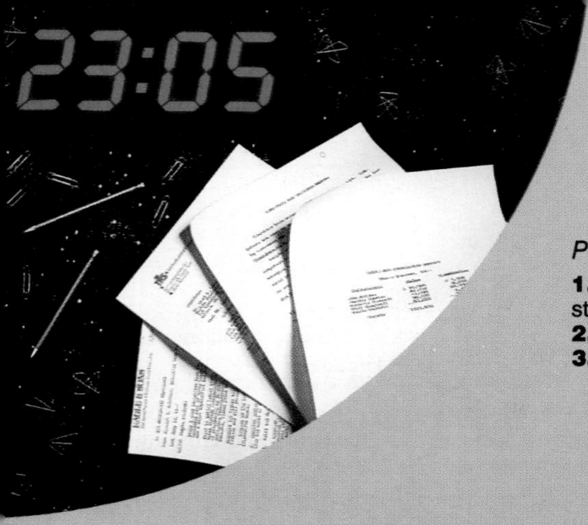

UNIT 71 LESSONS 297 – 300

Evaluate Keyboarding/Language/Document Processing Skills

Performance Goals

1. To measure your skill in keyboarding straight-copy material.
2. To evaluate your language skills.
3. To measure your document processing skill.

Format Guides

1. Paper guide at *0* (for typewriters).
2. LL: 70 spaces for drills and ¶s; as appropriate for documents.
3. LS: SS drills; DS ¶s; as required by document formats.
4. PI: 5 spaces for ¶s; as appropriate for document formats.

Lesson 297 *Evaluate Keyboarding/Language Skills*

297a ▶ 5 Conditioning Practice

Key each line twice. Then take two 30″ writings for speed on line 4 followed by two 30″ writings for control on line 1.

alphabet 1 Suzann gave the four new job descriptions to me to re-examine quickly.
figures 2 If you use F5-6091 rather than F25-7384, you can access the data file.
fig/sym 3 Kennedy & Nelson's last order (#2987), dated July 15, was for $31,640.
speed 4 Their problems with the forms may end when they go to see the auditor.

| 1 | 2 | 3 | 4 | 5 | 6 | 7 | 8 | 9 | 10 | 11 | 12 | 13 | 14 |

297b ▶ 15 Evaluate Straight Copy

Take two 5′ writings on the ¶s at the right. Record *gwam* and errors on better writing.

all letters used | A | 1.5 si | 5.7 awl | 80% hfw |

Text	*gwam* 1′	5′	
You are nearing the end of your keyboarding classes. The skill	13	3	53
level you have attained is much better than that with which you started	27	5	55
when you were given keyboarding instruction for the very first time.	41	8	58
During the early phase of your training, you were taught to key the let-	55	11	61
ters of the alphabet and the figures by touch. During the initial period	69	14	64
of learning, the primary emphasis was placed on your keying technique.	83	17	67
After learning to key the alphabet and figures, your next job was	13	19	69
to learn to format documents. The various types of documents formatted	27	22	72
included letters, tables, and manuscripts. During this time of training,	42	25	75
an emphasis also was placed on increasing the rate at which you were	55	28	78
able to key. Parts of the lessons keyed at this time also were used to	70	31	81
help you recognize the value of and to improve language skills.	82	33	83
The final phase of your training dealt with increasing your skill	13	36	86
at producing documents of high quality at a rapid rate. Directions were	28	39	89
provided for keying special documents; drills were given to build skill;	42	42	92
and problems were provided to assess your progress. You also were given	57	44	94
a number of simulations to allow you to apply what you had learned. Now	72	47	97
you have a skill that you will be able to use throughout your life.	85	50	100

gwam 1′ | 1 | 2 | 3 | 4 | 5 | 6 | 7 | 8 | 9 | 10 | 11 | 12 | 13 | 14 |
5′ | 1 | 2 | 3 |

Line length (LL): 50 spaces
Line spacing (LS): single (SS)

2a ▶ Get Ready to Keyboard

1. Arrange work area (see p. 2).
2. Adjust machine for 50-space line, single spacing (SS). (For typewriters, see pp. x-xi; for computer, see p. xii.)
3. Insert paper if necessary (see p. x) or check paper supply in printer.

Your teacher may guide you through the steps appropriate for your machine.

2b ▶ Review Home Keys

each line twice single-spaced (SS): once slowly; again, at a faster pace; double-space (DS) between 2-line groups

all keystrokes learned

```
1 a;sldkfj a; sl dk fj ff jj dd kk ss ll aa ;; fj a;
2 as as ad ad all all jak jak fad fad fall fall lass
3 a jak; a fad; as a lad; ask dad; a lass; a fall ad
```

Return 4 times to quadruple-space (QS) between lesson parts

2c ▶ Learn H and E

Use the *Standard Plan for Learning New Keys* (see p. 8) for each key to be learned. Study the plan now.

Relate each step of the plan to the drawings and copy at right and below. Then key each line twice SS; leave a DS between 2-line groups.

Reach technique for **h**

Learn **h**

```
1 j j hj hj ah ah ha ha had had has has ash ash hash
2 hj hj ha ha ah ah hah hah had had ash ash has hash
3 ah ha; had ash; has had; a hall; has a hall; ah ha
```

Return twice to double-space (DS) after you complete the set of lines

Reach technique for **e**

Learn **e**

```
4 d d ed ed el el led led eel eel eke eke ed fed fed
5 ed ed el el lee lee fed fed eke eke led led ale ed
6 a lake; a leek; a jade; a desk; a jade eel; a deed
```

Do not attempt to key the color verticals separating word groups in Line 7.

Combine **h** and **e**

```
7 he he he|she she she|shed shed|heed heed|held held
8 a lash; a shed; he held; she has jade; held a sash
9 has fled; he has ash; she had jade; she had a sale
```

Return 4 times to quadruple-space (QS) between lesson parts

292b-296b (continued)

Document 10
Memorandum
plain sheet
This memo should go to **John C. Richardson;** I'll initial it.
Date: **February 8, 19--**

Your excellent promotion of the Rose Bowl Tour has resulted in a record accomplishment for GGTA. The table below compares last year's Football Pasadena tour with this year's Rose Bowl tour--and shows why I'm commending you.

	Football Pasadena	Rose Bowl Tour	Percent of Change
Students	90	126	40.0
Faculty and Staff	121	160	32.2
Berkeley Residents	42	46	9.5
Alumni Members	128	192	50.0
Other	26	16	(38.5)
Total	407	540	

A comparison of the two totals for the tours shows an increase of 133 participants (32.7 percent.) An increase is seen in all groups except the "Other" category. You increased the football tour number by one-third in just a one year's time. Good work, John!

Documents 11-13
Form Letters
LP pp. 185-189
Will you prepare these letters; I'll sign them. You'll find the addresses for Carlos, Kelley, and Vice in the February 3 telephone log. The variable information is shown on this note.

Document 11
V1 **$1,450**
V2 **Miss Carlos**
Document 12
V1 **$1,300**
V2 **Mr. Kelley**
Document 13
V1 **$1,350**
V2 **Mr. and Mrs. Vice**

Date: **February 9, 19--**

A detailed itinerary of your travel arrangements for April 1 - 8 is enclosed for your close review. Brochures describing our scheduled tours and optional tours plus tips on apropriate clothes clothing for this climate are also enclosed. In addition, I have included several leaflets recounting describing historical events in the development of sites we will visit in New Zealand as it is today.

Your preregistration frdm for the New Zealand tour and check for (V1) was received today. You will be traveling to exciting New Zealand with a group of 75 other people. I am delighted that I will to be accompanying this tour group as its guide.

(V2), thank you for choosing GGTA; I look foreward to serving you on you tour.

2d ▶ Improve Keyboarding Technique

1. Key the lines once as shown: SS with a DS between 2-line groups.

2. Key the lines again at a faster pace.

Do not attempt to key the line identifications, line numbers, or color verticals separating word groups.

Space once after ; used as punctuation.

Fingers curved

Fingers upright

home row
1 ask ask|has has|lad lad|all all|jak jak|fall falls
2 a jak; a lad; a sash; had all; has a jak; all fall
DS

h/e
3 he he|she she|led led|held held|jell jell|she shed
4 he led; she had; she fell; a jade ad; a desk shelf
DS

all keys learned
5 elf elf|all all|ask ask|led led|jak jak|hall halls
6 ask dad; he has jell; she has jade; he sells leeks
DS

all keys learned
7 he led; she has; a jak ad; a jade eel; a sled fell
8 she asked a lad; he led all fall; she has a jak ad

Lesson 3 — I and R

Line length (LL): 50 spaces
Line spacing (LS): single (SS)

Time schedule

A time schedule for the parts of this lesson and lessons that follow is given as a guide for pacing your practice. The numeral following the triangle in the lesson part heading indicates the number of minutes suggested for the activity. If time permits, rekey selected lines from the various drills.

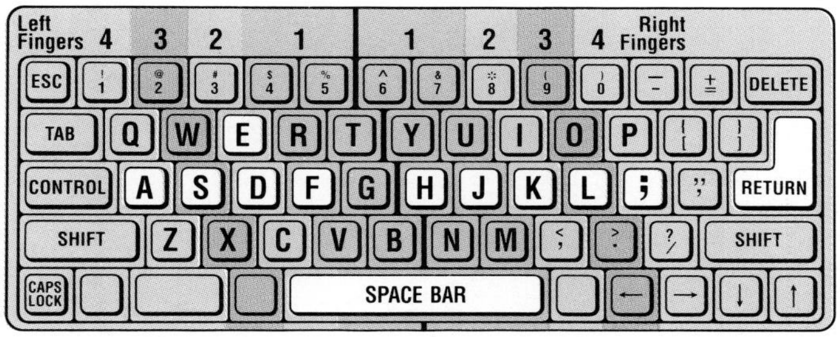

3a ▶ 5 Get Ready to Keyboard

Follow the steps on page 8.

3b ▶ 7 Conditioning Practice

each line twice SS; DS between 2-line groups

Goals

First time: Slow, easy pace, but strike and release each key quickly.

Second time: Faster pace, move from key to key quickly; keep element or cursor moving steadily.

Technique hints

1. Keep fingers upright and well-curved.

2. Try to make each reach without moving hand or other fingers forward or downward.

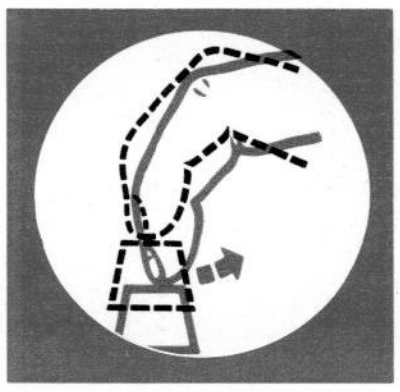

home keys
1 a;sldkfj a;sldkfj as jak ask fad all dad lads fall
Return twice to DS

h/e
2 hj hah has had sash hash ed led fed fled sled fell
DS

all keys learned
3 as he fled; ask a lass; she had jade; sell all jak
Return 4 times to quadruple-space (QS) between lesson parts

292b-296b (continued)

Document 8
Itinerary
plain sheet

Will you prepare this itinerary for a client, **CARL E. FILBECK**. Just refer to the itinerary for the dates of the trip and the destinations. Here's a model to follow.

ITINERARY FOR CARL E. FILBECK

February 24-26, 19--

Trip to Washington, D.C., and New York City

THURSDAY, FEBRUARY 24 (SAN FRANCISCO TO WASHINGTON, D.C.)

7:35 a.m. Leave San Francisco International Airport on Nationwide Flight 2533 (nonstop). Park automobile in long-term parking.

2:50 p.m. Arrive Washington D.C. Take airport shuttle to Washington City Inn, 299 North Circle Drive, Telephone: 555-2111.

7:00 p.m. Tickets to Washington Symphony. Take taxi to Washington Concert Hall, 2991 H Avenue.

FRIDAY, FEBRUARY 25 (WASHINGTON, D.C. TO NEW YORK CITY)

8:00 a.m. Washington City Tour with stops at Arlington National Cemetery, Washington Monument, and Lincoln, Jefferson, and Vietnam memorials.

2:25 p.m. Leave Washington, D.C., on Eastrack--Train #788 for New York City.

5:05 p.m. Arrive New York City. Take taxi to Grand Hotel, 232 South Liberty Street. Telephone: 555-6961.

8:30 p.m. Ticket to New York City Opera for the production of La Boheme.

SATURDAY, FEBRUARY 26 (NEW YORK CITY TO SAN FRANCISCO)

9:00 a.m. Vintage Tour of Manhattan.

6:05 p.m. Leave LaGuardia International Airport on Nationwide Flight 3222 (nonstop) to San Francisco.

7:20 p.m. Arrive San Francisco International Airport.

THURSDAY, FEBRUARY 23 (SAN FRANCISCO TO WASHINGTON, D.C.)

7:25 a.m.	Leave San Francisco International Airport Nationwide Flight 2533 (nonstop). Park automobile in long term parking.
2:50 a.m.	Arrive Washington D.C. Take airport shuttle to Washington City Inn, 299 North Circle Dr., Telephone: 555-2111.
7:00 p.m.	Tickets to Symphony. Take taxi to Washington Concert Hall, 2991 H Avenue.

FRIDAY, FEBRUARY 25 (WASHINGTON, D.C. TO NEW YORK)

8:00 a.m.	Washington City Tour with stops at Arlington National Cemetery, Washington Monument, Lincoln and Jefferson ~~Memorials~~, and Vietnam Memorial.
2:25 p.m.	Leave Washington, D.C. on Eastrack--Train #788 for New York City.
5:05 p.m.	Arrive New York City. Take taxi to Grand Hotel, 232 South Liberty St.
~~8:00~~ p.m.	Ticket to New York City Opera for the production of "La Boheme."

SATURDAY, FEBRUARY 26 (NEW YORK CITY TO SAN FRANCICSO)

9:00 a.m.	~~Liberty~~ Tour of ~~New York City~~.
6:05 p.m.	Leave LaGuardia Airport on Nationwide flight 3222 (nonstop) to San Francisco.
7:20 p.m.	Arrive San Francisco International Airport.

Document 9
Letter Composition
plain sheet

Use these notes to draft a letter to
Coastal Airlines
2999 Southwood Drive
San Francisco, CA 94112-0933
I'd like to review your rough draft.

Date: **February 8, 19--**

1. Ask on behalf of our client, Ms. Alice B. Fulton, to have the price ($632.38) of her unused airline ticket (round-trip to Charleston, West Virginia) refunded to us.
2. Explain that the client's physician admitted her to a hospital on February 7, the day of her planned departure.
3. State that the airline ticket and a letter from the client's physician about her condition are enclosed.

3c ▶ 18
Learn I and R

1. Key each line twice SS (slowly, then faster); DS between 2-line groups.

2. If time permits, key each line once more.

Goals

- curved, upright fingers
- finger-action keystrokes
- quick return, eyes on textbook copy

Follow the *Standard Plan for Learning New Keys* outlined on page 8.

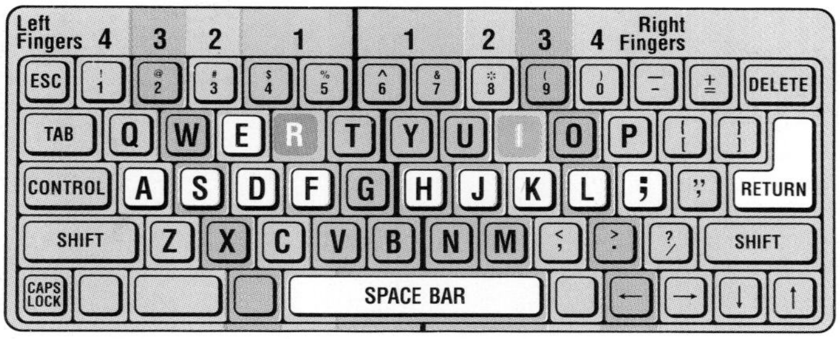

Reach technique for **i**

Reach technique for **r**

Learn **i**

```
1 k k ik ik is is if if did did aid aid kid kid hail
2 ik ik if if is is kid kid his his lie lie aid aide
3 a kid; a lie; if he; he did; his aide; if a kid is
```
DS

Learn **r**

```
4 f f rf rf jar jar her her are are ark ark jar jars
5 rf rf re re fr fr jar jar red red her her far fare
6 a jar; a rake; a lark; red jar; hear her; are dark
```
DS

Combine **i** and **r**

```
7 fir fir|rid rid|sir sir|ire ire|fire fire|air airs
8 a fir; if her; a fire; is fair; his ire; if she is
9 he is; if her; is far; red jar; his heir; her aide
```
Quadruple-space (QS) between lesson parts

3d ▶ 20 Improve Keyboarding Technique

1. Key the lines once as shown: SS with a DS between 2-line groups.

2. Key the lines again at a faster pace.

Goals

- curved, upright fingers
- finger-action keystrokes
- down-and-in spacing
- quick return, eyes on textbook copy

reach review
```
1 hj ed ik rf hj de ik fr hj ed ik rf jh de ki fr hj
2 he he if if all all fir fir jar jar rid rid as ask
```
DS

h/e
```
3 she she|elf elf|her her|hah hah|eel eel|shed|shelf
4 he has; had jak; her jar; had a shed; she has fled
```
DS

i/r
```
5 fir fir|rid rid|sir sir|kid kid|ire ire|fire fired
6 a fir; is rid; is red; his ire; her kid; has a fir
```
DS

all keys learned
```
7 if if|is is|he he|did did|fir fir|jak jak|all fall
8 a jak; he did; ask her; red jar; she fell; he fled
```
DS

all keys learned
```
9 if she is; he did ask; he led her; he is her aide;
10 she has had a jak sale; she said he had a red fir;
```

292b-296b (continued)

Polynesian Cultural Center Dinner and Show

~~This tour includes~~ the play "Polynesia: Our Way of Life," a visit to four Polynesian villages, bountiful buffets, and island music by live musicians. ~~Authentic~~ island handicrafts can be purchased at the numerous gift shops.

await the tourists on this truly memorable side trip.

Pearl Harbor and U. S. S. Arizona Memorial

This historical ~~tour~~ excursion includes a guided tour of Pearl Harbor. Tourists will be able to board the U.S.S Arizona Memorial and pay tribute to the service men who were aboard ~~the U.S.S Arizona~~ during the bombing of Pearl Harbor.

and the U.S.S. Arizona Memorial

Document 7
Table
plain sheet

I've developed this price list of optional side trips for the Baseball Hawaii Tour. I need the table for my meeting at 2 with the SHC Alumni Association officers. Oh, alphabetize the list please, and title it **OPTIONAL EXCURSIONS FOR BASEBALL HAWAII TOUR.**

Excursion	Price per Person
Sea Life Tour	$ 20.00
~~Big Island Luau~~	~~40.00~~
Oahu Cultural Dinner and Show	85.50
Catamaran dinner Sail	35.00
~~Polynesian Show + Dinner~~	~~75.00~~
Snorkeling/Beach Picnic	42.00
Diamond/head Crater Tour	30.00
~~Roundtop Park Tour~~	~~25.00~~
Nuuanu Valley Tour	30.00 ~~25.00~~
National Memorial Cemetery Tour	15.00
Honolulu Whaling Museum	20.00 ~~15.00~~
Pearl of the Pacific Tour	100.00
Waikiki Museum	12.50
Honolulu City Tour	20.00

4a ▶ 3 Review Get-Ready Procedures

1. Review the steps for arranging your work area (see p. 2).

2. Review the steps required to ready your machine for keyboarding (see pp. x-xi for typewriters; see p. vii for computers).

3. Review the steps for inserting paper into a typewriter (see p. x) or checking the paper supply in a printer (see p. xii).

4. Take good keyboarding position:

- fingers curved and upright
- wrists low, but not touching frame of machine
- forearms parallel to slant of keyboard
- body erect, sitting back in chair
- feet on floor for balance

4b ▶ 5 Conditioning Practice

each line twice SS; DS between 2-line groups; if time permits, rekey selected lines

all keystrokes learned

1 a;sldkfj fj dk sl a; jh de ki fr hj ed ik rf fj a;
2 a if is el he la as re led fir did she has jak jar
3 he has fir; she had a jak; a jade jar; a leek sale
QS

4c ▶ 10 Improve Space-Bar Technique

1. Key each line twice SS; DS between 2-line groups. Space *immediately* after keying a word; make the space a part of the word it follows.

2. If time permits, rekey lines 1-3.

Use down-and-in motion

Short, easy words

1 if is ha la ah el as re id did sir fir die rid lie
2 ad lad lei rah jak had ask lid her led his kid has
3 hah all ire add iris hall fire keel sell jeer fall
DS

Short-word phrases

4 if he|he is|if he is|if she|she is|if she is|as is
5 as he is|if he led|if she has|if she did|had a jak
6 as if|a jar lid|all her ads|as he said|a jade fish
QS

4d ▶ 10 Improve Return Technique

1. Key each line twice SS; DS between 2-line groups. Keep up your pace at the end of the line, return quickly, and begin the new line immediately.

2. If time permits, rekey the drill.

Reach out and tap return

1 if he is;
2 as if she is;
3 he had a fir desk;
4 she has a red jell jar;
5 he has had a lead all fall;
6 she asked if he reads fall ads;
7 she said she reads all ads she sees;
8 his dad has had a sales lead as he said;
QS

Document 6
Report
plain sheet
This report describes the Baseball Hawaii Tour and is to be enclosed with the form letters you just completed.

BASEBALL HAWAII TOUR

College Baseball, exciting travel, beautiful islands, and delicious food are all attractions of the Baseball Hawaii tour, the first tour of this type made available by Golden Gate Travel Agency. This tour is scheduled for May 12-16 in conjunction with the invitational baseball tour of the Sidney Hillman College baseball team in Hawaii. Baseball Hawaii includes round-trip airfare, hotel acommodations, a guided tours of Pearl Harbor/U.S.S. Arizona Memorial, and a dinner-show at the Polynesian Cultural Center. of course an added attractive on is 5 ~~college~~ baseball tickets to the SHC invitational games. Rates per person are $1,450~~.00~~ for single, $1,350~~.00~~ for double, and $1300~~.00~~ for triple.

Hotel Acommodations

The tour will begin in Honolulu on the island of Oahu. You will have delux e accommodations at the fabulous Hotel Waikiki for two nights. On the Big Island of Hawaii, you will be entertained at the Aloha Resort for two nights. The Kona Palace is the lodging place for the final night of this five-day tour.

Baseball Games

The top-ranked SHC Warriors will play the third-ranked Pacifica University Whales for two exciting action-packed games. ~~To~~ The highlight of the ~~baseball~~ activties in Honolulu will be a luau for the Baseball Hawaii Tour group.

The next two games will be played in Hilo, located on the Big Island of Hawaii. The grand final e ~~game~~ will be played on the spectacular Kona coast.

(continued, p. 492)

4e ▶ 10
Build Keying Speed by Repeating Words

Each word in each line is shown twice. Practice a word the first time at an easy speed; repeat it at a faster speed.

1. Key each line once SS; DS after the third line. Use the plan suggested above.

2. Key each line again. Try to keep the printing point or cursor moving at a steady speed. QS at the end of the drill.

Technique hint
Think and say the word; key it with quick-snap strokes using the fingertips.

Goal: to speed up the combining of letters

1 is is|if if|ah ah|he he|el el|irk irk|aid aid|aide
2 as as|ask ask|ad ad|had had|re re|ire ire|are hare
3 if if|fir fir|id id|did did|el el|eel eel|jak jaks

QS

4f ▶ 12
Build Keying Speed by Repeating Phrases

1. Key each line once SS. Speed up the second keying of each phrase.

2. Key the lines once more to improve your speed.

Space with right thumb

Use down-and-in motion

Goal: to speed up spacing between words

1 ah ha|ah ha|if he|if he|as if|as if|as he|as he is
2 if a|if a|a fir|a fir|a jar|a jar|irk her|irks her
3 he did|he did|if all|if all|if she led|if she fled
4 a lad|a lad|if her|if her|as his aide|as his aides

Lesson 5 — O and T

Line length (LL): 50 spaces
Line spacing (LS): single (SS)

5a ▶ 8
Conditioning Practice

each line twice SS (slowly, then faster); DS between 2-line groups

In this lesson and the remaining lessons in this unit, the time for the *Conditioning Practice* is changed to 8 minutes. During this time you are to arrange your work area, ready your machine for keyboarding, and practice the lines of the *Conditioning Practice.*

Fingers curved

Fingers upright

home row 1 a sad fall; had a hall; a jak falls; as a fall ad;
3d row 2 if her aid; all he sees; he irks her; a jade fish;
all keys learned 3 as he fell; he sells fir desks; she had half a jar

QS

Documents 2-5
Form. Letters
LP pp. 177-183

I need to have this form letter processed for my signature. Send the form letter to the four clients who called about the Baseball Hawaii Tour. Their names and addresses are listed on the Telephone Log for February 3.

Date: **February 5, 19--**

The Golden Gate Travel Agency is proud to announce the Baseball Hawaii Tour for the Sidney Hillman College baseball team, students, facutly, and alumni. This unique tour is scheduled for May 12-16. It features five exciting SHC baseball games to be played on two beautiful islands.

The five-day tour will start in Honolulu at the magnificent Hotel Waikiki. For 2 days you can enjoy Waikiki beach, sight-seeing, shopping, and 2 baseball games at Pacifica University. After the last ballgame, you will then fly to Hilo, located on the big island of Hawaii. There you will be staying at the beauti-ful Aloha Resort, known for its gracious hospitality and delicious food. Two baseball games and a delectable luau are planned just for the Baseball Hawaii tour are special highlights.

No ¶ The final stop of the tour is Kona Coast and the Kona Pal-ace. Waterfalls, grand architecture, famous Hawaiian restau-rants and the last baseball game awaits you. ¶ Join the baseball team, faculty, students, and alumni for a spring break never too be forgotten. Please read it carefully, share it with friends and family, and then sign up today. Simply call (916) 555-1238 and begin your plans planning for a spring break filled with relaxation, enchanting scenery, and SHC baseball.

A detailed description of the Baseball Hawaii Tour is enclosed.

5b ▶ 20
Learn O and T

each line twice SS (slowly, then faster); DS between 2-line groups; if time permits, key lines 7-9 again

Follow the *Standard Plan for Learning New Keys* outlined on page 8.

Reach technique for **o**

Reach technique for **t**

Learn **o**

1 l l ol ol do do of of so so lo lo old old for fore
2 ol ol of of or or for for oak oak off off sol sole
3 do so; a doe; of old; of oak; old foe; of old oak;
DS

Learn **t**

4 f f tf tf it it at at tie tie the the fit fit lift
5 tf tf ft ft it it sit sit fit fit hit hit kit kite
6 if it; a fit; it fit; tie it; the fit; at the site
DS

Combine **o** and **t**

7 to to|too too|toe toe|dot dot|lot lot|hot hot|tort
8 a lot; to jot; too hot; odd lot; a fort; for a lot
9 of the; to rot; dot it; the lot; for the; for this
QS

5c ▶ 22 Improve Keyboarding Technique

1. Key the lines once as shown: SS with a DS between 2-line groups.

2. Key the lines again at a faster pace.

Goals

- curved, upright fingers
- quick-snap keystrokes
- down-and-in spacing
- quick return, eyes on textbook copy

Goal: quick-snap keystrokes; quiet hands

reach review
1 hj ed ik rf ol tf jh de ki fr lo ft hj ed ol rf tf
2 is led fro hit old fit let kit rod kid dot jak sit
DS

h/e
3 he he|she she|led led|had had|see see|has has|seek
4 he led|ask her|she held|has fled|had jade|he leads
DS

i/t
5 it it|fit fit|tie tie|sit sit|kit kit|its its|fits
6 a kit|a fit|a tie|lit it|it fits|it sits|it is fit
DS

o/r
7 or or|for for|ore ore|fro fro|oar oar|roe roe|rode
8 a rod|a door|a rose|or for|her or|he rode|or a rod
DS

space bar
9 of he or it is to if do el odd off too for she the
10 it is|if it|do so|if he|to do|or the|she is|of all
DS

all keys learned
11 if she is; ask a lad; to the lake; off the old jet
12 he or she; for a fit; if she left the; a jak salad

292a-296a ▶ 5 (daily)

Equipment Check

each line twice SS; DS between 2-line groups

alphabet 1 Tim quarreled with the angry zookeeper about the five jackal exhibits.

figures 2 On May 27, 1991, she reported 3,468 professional and 150 life members.

fig/sym 3 Wails & Simms offered 37,850 shares of common stock at $14.62 (up 9%).

speed 4 Jane is to pay a neighbor at the lake to fix their auto and a bicycle.

| 1 | 2 | 3 | 4 | 5 | 6 | 7 | 8 | 9 | 10 | 11 | 12 | 13 | 14 |

292b-296b ▶ 45 (daily)

Document Processing

Key as many of the following documents as you can during each daily session. Watch for unmarked errors in source documents. Proofread and correct each document before you remove it from the machine or print a copy.

Document 1
Table
plain sheet

Use my telephone log to compile an alphabetical list of clients interested in the New Zealand tour. Use the information on this sheet.

Main heading: **PROSPECTS FOR NEW ZEALAND TOUR**
Secondary heading: Date of the telephone log
Column heads: **Name Address Telephone**

TELEPHONE LOG FOR February 3, 19--

NAME	ADDRESS	TELEPHONE	INQUIRY
Miss Maria R. Carlos	200 Jackson St.	361-9661	New Zealand
	Oakland, CA 94607-0101		
Dr. Miriam J. Harrison	2604 College Ave.	236-9830	Baseball Hawaii
	Berkeley, CA 94704-1374		
Mr. & Mrs. Joseph F. Vice	5 Panoramic Way	236-1100	New Zealand
	Berkeley, CA 94704-6016		
Ms. J. Tracy Kavanagh	106 Eton Ave.	231-7661	New Zealand
	Berkeley, CA 94705-1696		
Mr. & Mrs. Lance D. Abbott	1907 Bonita Ave.	235-2698	Baseball Hawaii
	Berkeley, CA 94704-1562		
Miss Amber C. Kent	P. O. Box 615	469-0168	New Zealand
	Berkeley, CA 94701-0615		
Mr. Iyabode O. Adamou	605 Peralta Ave.	235-3361	Baseball Hawaii
	Berkeley, CA 94707-2277		
Dr. & Mrs. W. S. Duff	3165 Telegraph Ave.	246-9987	Baseball Hawaii
	Berkeley, CA 94705-3626		
Mr. Tom C. Kelly	P. O. Box 1096	259-8163	New Zealand
	University, CA 94707-1096		

Line length (LL): 50 spaces
Line spacing (LS): single (SS)

6a ▶ 8 Conditioning Practice

each line twice SS (slowly, then faster); DS between 2-line groups

all letters learned

home row 1 has a jak; ask a lad; a fall fad; had a jak salad;
o/t 2 to do it; as a tot; do a lot; it is hot; to dot it
e/i/r 3 is a kid; it is far; a red jar; her skis; her aide
QS

6b ▶ 20 Learn N and G

each line twice SS (slowly, then faster); DS between 2-line groups; if time permits, key lines 7-9 again

Follow the *Standard Plan for Learning New Keys* outlined on page 8.

Reach technique for **n**

Reach technique for **g**

Learn **n**

1 j j nj nj an an and and end end ant ant land lands
2 nj nj an an en en in in on on end end and and hand
3 an en; an end; an ant; no end; on land; a fine end
DS

Learn **g**

4 f f gf gf go go fog fog got got fig figs jogs jogs
5 gf gf go go got got dig dig jog jog logs logs golf
6 to go; he got; to jog; to jig; the fog; is to golf
DS

Combine **n** and **g**

7 go go|no no|nag nag|ago ago|gin gin|gone gone|long
8 go on; a nag; sign in; no gain; long ago; into fog
9 a fine gig; log in soon; a good sign; lend a hand;
QS

6c ▶ 5 Improve Return Technique

1. Key each line twice SS; DS between 2-line groups. Keep up your pace at the end of the line, return quickly, and begin new line promptly.

2. If time permits, rekey the drill.

1 she is gone;
2 he got an old dog;
3 she jogs in a dense fog;
4 she and he go to golf at nine;
5 he is a hand on a rig in the north;
QS

Reach out and tap return

UNIT 70 LESSONS 292 – 296

Golden Gate Travel, Inc.

Production Goals

1. To process a variety of documents from various kinds of source copy.

2. To compose a business letter.

3. To use information from several sources in processing documents.

4. To reinforce proofreading and language skills.

Documents Processed

1. Tables
2. Form letters
3. Report
4. Itinerary
5. Letter
6. Memorandum

GOLDEN GATE TRAVEL, INC.

Before you begin the work of this simulation, read the material and study the format guides at the right.

Work Assignment

You have notified Cal-Temp that you will assume a full-time position in two weeks. Your final temporary assignment is at Golden Gate Travel, Inc., a travel agency that caters to college students, professors, and other campus personnel. The agency is located in Berkeley at 2144 Shattuck Avenue.

Mrs. Linda T. Mitchell manages the agency, and she will originate most of the documents you process. Mr. John C. Richardson, one of the seven travel agents, will also ask you to prepare a document. Usually Mrs. Mitchell and Mr. Richardson will talk with you rather than write directions for you to follow. (Linda Mitchell's words are printed in blue; John Richardson's, in red.)

Mrs. Mitchell has developed communication guidelines that include rules for composing letters and for formatting various documents. Use your previously acquired knowledge when you're not given specific instructions. Review these communication guidelines now and refer to them as needed during your time at Golden Gate Travel.

Rules for Composing Letters

1. Make letters short, uncomplicated. If two or three sentences are enough to make your point, don't write more.

2. Plan each letter--no matter how short--before you draft it. Decide the steps (inform, explain, ask, apologize, etc.) to be taken in the letter and the order of the steps.

3. Include the C qualities: Make the letter courteous (express goodwill), considerate (show respect for reader), clear (state exact meaning), concise (omit unnecessary words), concrete (refer to specific things and actions), complete (say whatever is needed to fulfill purpose of the letter), and correct (accurate in content, language, and format).

4. Edit and revise. Add, delete, or move sentences and paragraphs in a draft as needed. Proofread for errors in grammar, punctuation, capitalization, number expression, spelling, and keystroking; and check for errors in format. Use standard proofreader's marks.

Format Guides

Letters. Block format, open punctuation; agency letterhead; standard complimentary closing--**Sincerely.** Sender's name and title on one or two lines depending upon length:

```
Sincerely



Linda T. Mitchell, Manager
```

```
Sincerely



John C. Richardson
Travel Agent
```

Memos. Simplified format; titles omitted following recipient's and sender's names; plain full-size sheets.

Tables. Center vertically (DS) and horizontally (CS: 6-10) on plain full-size sheets. Column headings are centered over columns. Two-line entries are keyed SS, with a DS between entries. Within letters, memos, or reports, DS above/below table and SS the items; center between side margins of the document.

Reports and Other Documents. Unbound format; page number at upper-right margin, except on page 1 (not numbered); plain full-size sheets.

6d ▶ 17 Improve Keyboarding Technique

1. Key the lines once as shown: SS with a DS between 2-line groups.

2. Key the lines again at a faster pace.

Goals

- curved, upright fingers
- quick-snap keystrokes
- down-and-in spacing
- quick return, eyes on textbook copy

reach review
1 a;sldkfj ed ol rf hj tf nj gf lo de jh ft nj fr a;
2 he jogs; an old ski; do a log for; she left a jar;
DS

n/g
3 an an|go go|in in|dig dig|and and|got got|end ends
4 go to; is an; log on; sign it; and golf; fine figs
DS

space bar
5 if if|an an|go go|of of|or or|he he|it it|is is|do
6 if it is|is to go|he or she|to do this|of the sign
DS

all keys learned
7 she had an old oak desk; a jell jar is at the side
8 he has left for the lake; she goes there at eight;
DS

all keys learned
9 she said he did it for her; he is to take the oars
10 sign the list on the desk; go right to the old jet

Lesson 7 Left Shift and . (Period)

Line length (LL): 50 spaces
Line spacing (LS): single (SS)

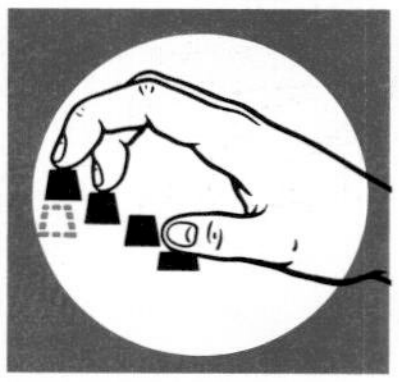
Finger-action keystrokes

Down-and-in spacing

Quick out-and-tap return

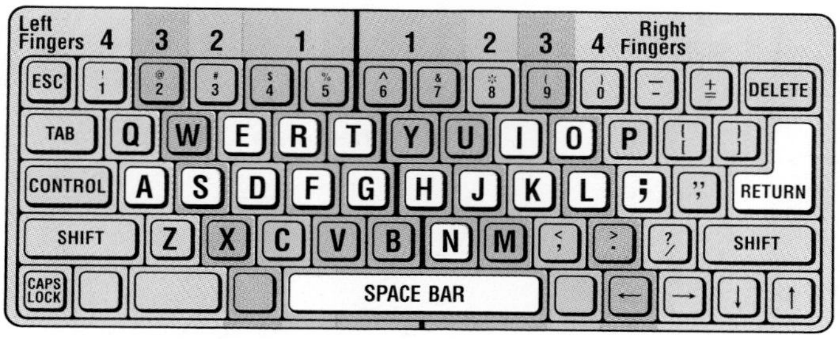

7a ▶ 8 Conditioning Practice

each line twice SS (slowly, then faster); DS between 2-line groups

reach review
1 ed ik rf ol gf hj tf nj de ki fr lo fg jh ft jn a;

space bar
2 or is to if an of el so it go id he do as in at on

all keys learned
3 he is; if an; or do; to go; a jak; an oak; of all;
QS

7b ▶ 5 Improve Space-Bar/Return Technique

1. Key each line once SS; return and start each new line quickly.

2. If time permits, rekey the drill at a faster pace.

1 the jet is hers;
2 she has gone to ski;
3 he asked her for one disk;
4 all the girls left for the lake;
5 she is to take this list to his desk;
6 he is at the lake to ski if the fog lifts;
7 he is to see her soon if the jet lands at nine;
QS

287b-291b (continued)

Document 13
Statement of Change in Financial Condition

plain sheet

This statement of change in financial condition is for **OLYMPIC MUSEUM** and covers the fiscal year ended December 31, 19-- (*previous year*).

Sources of working capital:		
Excess of support and revenue before capital additions	$ 12,500	
Capital additions	67,200	
Excess of support and revenue after capital additions		$ 79,700
Depreciation and		45,800
Deferred revenue & restricted gifts received in excess of expenses incurred		220,600
Investments sold		835,900
		$1,182,000
Uses of working capital:		
Fixed assets purchased	$ 98,700	
Investments purchased	901,400	
		1,000,100
Increase in working capital		$ 181,900
Changes in working capital:		
Cash	($ (2,750)	
Receivables	10,300	
Investments	480	
Inventories	139,700	
Prepayments	10,600	
Accts. Pay. & Accrued Expenses	(3,500)	
Deferred revenue and restricted gifts, current portion	27,070	
		$ 181,900

Document 14
Collection Form Letter

plain sheet

Prepare this collection letter to be added to the series in the office procedures manual. Identification: **Stage 4 Ultimatum.**

¶ A copy of your account is enclosed. Your cooperation is required to settle the long-overdue balance. Please notify me within 10 days of the date of this letter, telling me of your plan for payment. ¶ If we do not receive payment or a ~~word~~ response from you within 10 days, we will have to assume that you do not intend to settle the account voluntarily. In that case, we will be forced to use other means of collecting the amount due.

7c ► 20 Learn Left Shift Key and . (Period)

each line twice SS (slowly, then faster); DS between 2-line groups; if time permits, rekey each line

Spacing hints

Space *once* after . used at end of abbreviations and following letters in initials. *Do not* space after . *within* abbreviations.

Space *twice* after . at the end of a sentence except at line endings. There, return without spacing.

Control of LEFT SHIFT key

Reach technique for . (period)

Reach *down* with *right third* finger; space twice after . at end of sentence.

Learn **Left Shift Key** (Shift; strike key; release both quickly.)

1 a a Ja Ja Ka Ka La La Hal Hal Kal Kal Jae Jae Lana
2 Kal rode; Kae did it; Hans has jade; Jan ate a fig
3 I see that Jake is to aid Kae at the Oak Lake sale

DS

Learn . (period)

4 l l .l .l fl. fl. ed. ed. ft. ft. rd. rd. hr. hrs.
5 .l .l fl. fl. hr. hr. e.g. e.g. i.e. i.e. in. ins.
6 fl. ft. hr. ed. rd. rt. off. fed. ord. alt. asstd.

DS

Combine **Left Shift** and .

7 I do. Ian is. Ola did. Jan does. Kent is gone.
8 Hal did it. I shall do it. Kate left on a train.
9 J. L. Han skis on Oak Lake; Lt. Haig also does so.

QS

7d ► 17 Improve Keyboarding Technique

1. Key the lines once as shown: SS with a DS between 2-line groups.

2. Key the lines again at a faster pace.

Goals

- curved, upright fingers
- finger-action keystrokes
- quiet hands and arms
- down-and-in spacing
- out-and-down shifting
- quick out-and-tap return

Technique hint: Eyes on copy except when you lose your place.

abbrev./initials
1 He said ft. for feet; rd. for road; fl. for floor.
2 Lt. Hahn let L. K. take the old gong to Lake Neil.

DS

3d row emphasis
3 Lars is to ask at the old store for a kite for Jo.
4 Ike said he is to take the old road to Lake Heidi.

DS

key words
5 a an or he to if do it of so is go for got old led
6 go the off aid dot end jar she fit oak and had rod

DS

key phrases
7 if so|it is|to do|if it|do so|to go|he is|to do it
8 to the|and do|is the|got it|if the|for the|ask for

DS

all letters learned
9 Ned asked her to send the log to an old ski lodge.
10 O. J. lost one of the sleds he took off the train.

287b-291b (continued)

Document 10
Memorandum
plain sheet
Date this memo **January 20, 19--** and send it to **Randall Collins, Chair; Roberta Osborne;** and **Eugenia Rodriguez. Karl Coppersmith** will initial it. Use **Mission Statement of Our Firm** as the subject.

We are
~~Our firm is~~ in the process of preparing an Employees' Handbook. You have been assigned to the committee responsible for ~~devel-oping~~ writing the philosophy or mission statement of our firm. I have asked Randall to chair this ~~section~~ committee, and he will ~~inform you of~~ call the first meeting.

believe
Listed below are some topics that I ~~feel~~ should be ~~included~~ addressed in our philosophy. Please do not feel that you must confine your thinking to this list. 1. Concern for the general public interest 2. Concern for the financial well-being of ~~all~~ our clients 3. Reinvestment of profits in the training and advancement of partners and ~~other~~ staff 4. Growth plans 5. Development of specialties such as auditing governmental units or concentration in ~~particular~~ certain fields 6. Extent of autonomy for partners

date
As the publication for the handbook is early April, may I please have your report by March 1. xx

---

Document 11
Proposal Resume
plain sheet
When accounting firms submit bids for jobs, resumes of the key staff members who may be involved are included with each bid. Prepare the proposal resume at the right.

EUGENIA RODRIGUEZ, CPA

QS

Certification — Certified Public Accountant, licensed, state of California. Member: CA (sp) Society of CPAs. (SS)

Experience — Bouchard & Roberson, Oakland, California.

1990-1991 -- Senior accountant

1987-1989 -- Staff accountant

SS: Prepared ~~annual tax~~ financial statements and federal and state tax returns for individuals and small businesses. planned, coordinated, and ~~conducted~~ (stet) certified audits.

EDUCATION — B.S. in Business Administartion, SanMateo University, 1987. (SS, #)

M.B.A., with high honors, Oakland University, 1989.

COMMUNITY (SS)
SERVICE — Pres. (sp), ~~The~~ Business and Professional Woman's (e) Club, 1990-1991, Oakland. (SS)

Document 12
Engagement Letter
LP p. 175
Prepare an engagement letter (refer to Document 6) for **Mr. Coppersmith** to sign. Here is the information you will need.

V1 **January 21, 19--**
V2 **Mr. Umeki Yoshino**
183 Stoneyford Drive
Daly City, CA 94015-2264
V3 **Mr. Yoshino**
V4 **January 17, 19--**
V5 (*Insert previous year*)
V7 **Umeki Yoshino**

Line length (LL): 50 spaces
Line spacing (LS): single (SS)

8a ▶ 8 Conditioning Practice

each line twice SS (slowly, then faster); DS between 2-line groups; if time permits, practice each line again

Space once

reach review 1 ik rf ol ed nj gf hj tf .l ft. i.e. e.g. rt. O. J.

spacing 2 a an go is or to if he and got the for led kit lot

left shift 3 I got it. Hal has it. Jan led Nan. Kae is gone.

QS

8b ▶ 10 Improve Return Technique

1. Key each pair of lines once as shown: SS with a DS between 2-line groups.

2. Repeat the drill at a faster pace.

Return hint

Keep up your pace to the end of the line; return immediately; start the new line without pausing.

Eyes on copy as you return

1 Nan has gone to ski;
2 she took a train at nine.

DS

3 Janet asked for the disk;
4 she is to take it to the lake.

DS

5 Karl said he left at the lake
6 a file that has the data she needs.

DS

7 Nadia said she felt ill as the ski
8 lift left to take the girls to the hill.

QS

8c ▶ 10 Build Keyboarding Skill: Space Bar/Left Shift

each line twice SS; DS between 2-line groups

Goals

- to reduce the pause between words
- to reduce the time taken to shift/strike key/release when making capital letters

Down-and-in spacing

Out-and-down shifting

Space bar (Space *immediately* after each word.)

1 if is an he go is or ah to of so it do el id la ti

2 an el | go to | if he | of it | is to | do the | for it | and so

3 if she is | it is the | all of it | go to the | for an oak

DS

Left shift key (Shift; strike key; release both quickly.)

4 Lt. Ho said he left the skiff at Ord Lake for her.

5 Jane or Hal is to go to Lake Head to see Kate Orr.

6 O. J. Halak is to ask for her at Jahn Hall at one.

QS

287b-291b (continued)

Document 8
News Release

plain sheet

Prepare the news item at the right for immediate release. Suggest this title: **RODRIGUEZ JOINS REGENCY AGENCY.** Give **Mr. Coppersmith**'s name and telephone number (**213-555-6879**) as the contact.

Daly City, January 19, 19--. Regency (Acctg.) sp Services, Inc., is pleased to announce that Ms. Eugenia Rodriguez, CPA, has recently joined the agency. Ms. Rodriguez received her bachelor's degree in business administration from San Mateo (Univ.) sp and her master's degree from Oakland (Univ.) sp She passed the CPA exam in May. For the past (3) sp years Ms. Rodriguez has been associated with Bouchard & Roberson in Oakland where she specialized in tax services for small businesses and for individuals.

Regency (Acctg.) sp Services, Inc., currently has a staff of 12 employees, including 2 CPAs. The agency's offices are located at 400 Serramonte (Blvd.) sp in Daly City. (# # #) center

---

Document 9
Balance Sheet

plain sheet

Key the balance sheet for **Robert and Kathy Pearson** for the period ending **December 31, 19--.** Add leaders.

Assets DS		
Cash	$ 3,500	
Bonus Receivable	10,000	
Stock Options	4,6(46)	
Cash Value of life insurance	~~5~~ 5,500	
Residence	83,000	
Personal Effects	45,000	
Total Assets		$151,~~554~~ 664
Liabilities DS		
Income Taxes--Current (Yr.) (Bal.) sp	$ 4,400	
Mortgage Payable	44,000	
Total liabilities		$ ~~48,400~~ 52,136
Net Worth DS		
(Robt.) sp ~~&~~ and Kathy Pearson, Net Worth		~~103,264~~ 99,528
Total Liabilities And Net Worth		$151,664
Car Loan ~~Outstanding~~ Payable	2,910	
Credit Card (Bal.) sp	826	

8d ▶ 22 Improve Keyboarding Skill

each line twice SS (slowly, then faster); DS between 2-line groups

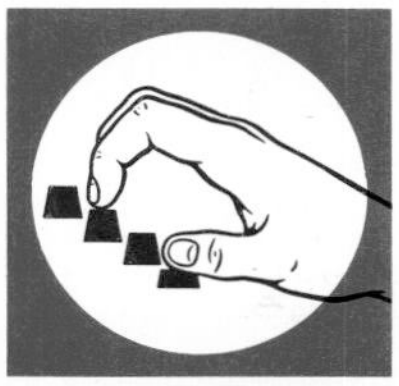

Correct finger curvature

Correct finger alignment

Key words (*Think, say,* and *key* the words.)

1 an the did oak she for off tie got and led jar all
2 go end air her dog his aid rid sit and fir ask jet
3 talk side jell gold fled sign stir fork high shall

DS

Key phrases (*Think, say,* and *key* the phrases.)

4 to do|it is|of an|if he|is to|or do|to it|if he is
5 to aid|if she|he did|of the|to all|is for|is a tie
6 is to ask|is to aid|he or she|to rig it|if she did

DS

Easy sentences (Strike keys at a brisk, steady pace.)

7 Joan is to go to the lake to get her old red skis.
8 Les asked for a list of all the old gold she sold.
9 Laska said she left the old disk list on his desk.

Lesson 9 U and C

Line length (LL): 50 spaces
Line spacing (LS): single (SS)

9a ▶ 8 Conditioning Practice

each line twice SS (slowly, then faster); DS between 2-line groups

1 nj gf ol rf ik ed .l tf hj fr ki ft jn de lo fg l.
2 lo fir old rig lot fit gin fog left sign lend dike
3 Olga has the first slot; Jena is to skate for her.

QS

9b ▶ 5 Build Keyboarding Skill: Space Bar/Left Shift

Key the lines once as shown: SS with a DS between 3-line groups. Keep hand movement to a minimum.

space bar

1 Ken said he is to sign the list and take the disk.
2 It is right for her to take the lei if it is hers.
3 Jae has gone to see an old oaken desk at the sale.

DS

left shift

4 He said to enter Oh. for Ohio and Kan. for Kansas.
5 It is said that Lt. Li has an old jet at Lake Ida.
6 L. N. is at the King Hotel; Harl is at the Leland.

QS

287b-291b (continued)

Document 5
Balance Sheet

plain sheet

Key this balance sheet; add leaders. Use these headings:

MARY'S COUNTRY CRAFTS
Balance Sheet
December 31, 19--

Assets
DS

Cash		$16,735
Accts. [sp] Receivable		753
Mdse. [sp] on hand		3,243
DS Total Assets		$20,731

Liabilities
DS

Accts. [sp] Payable	$417	
Utilities	190	
Wages Payable	625	
DS Total Liabilities		$ 1,232

Owner's Equity
DS

Mary Castleton, Capital		19,499
DS Total Liabilities and Owner's Equity		$20,731

Document 6
Engagement Letter

plain sheet

Key the engagement letter at right for inclusion in the Office Procedures Manual. The identification of this form letter is **Engagement Letter for Representing Client Before the IRS.**

Key **V1, V2,** etc., to show where variable information will be inserted.

Format the closing lines, including an "approval" line and date line according to the document format guides in the Manual. (You will use Document 6 to prepare Documents 7 and 12.)

Document 7
Engagement Letter

LP p. 173

Prepare an engagement letter (Document 6) for **Mr. Coppersmith**'s signature. Use the following information.

V1 **January 17, 19--**
V2 **Mr. and Mrs. Robert Pearson**
One Park Manor Drive
Daly City, CA 94015-2265
V3 **Mr. and Mrs. Pearson**
V4 **January 16, 19--**
V5 (*Insert previous year*)
V7 **Robert Pearson**
Kathy Pearson

Include two approval lines and two date lines; DS between the two sets of lines.

```
This letter summarizes our discussion of (V4), concerning the
terms of our engagement.  If the letter does not accurately
reflect your understanding of ~~them~~ these terms, call us for
clarification[.] ~~of the terms~~

We will represent you before the Internal Revenue Service and
exert our best efforts to obtain a ~~settlement~~ satisfactory
settlement of any issues that may arise in the examination of
your (V5) income tax return.  We will not audit or otherwise
~~verify~~ attempt to verify the information you have submitted,
although we may ask ~~you~~ for clarification or further details
on some matters.

Our fee, charged at standard billing rates for tax work plus
out-of-pocket expenses, will be based upon the amount of time
required for our services.  A copy of our current fees ~~is and~~
and billing policies ~~are~~ is enclosed.

If this ~~agreement~~ letter accurately sets forth your [and date] under-
standing of the engagement, ~~sign below~~ please sign below in
the space[s] provided and return ~~it~~ the letter to us.  Retain a
copy for your files.
```

9c ▶ 20
Learn U and C

each line twice SS (slowly, then faster); DS between 2-line groups; if time permits, repeat selected lines

Follow the *Standard Plan for Learning New Keys* outlined on page 8.

Reach technique for **u**

Reach technique for **c**

Learn **u**

```
1 j j uj uj us us us jug jug jut jut due due fur fur
2 uj uj jug jug sue sue lug lug use use lug lug dues
3 a jug; due us; the fur; use it; a fur rug; is just
```
DS

Learn **c**

```
4 d d cd cd cod cod cog cog tic tic cot cot can cans
5 cd cd cod cod ice ice can can code code dock docks
6 a cod; a cog; the ice; she can; the dock; the code
```
DS

Combine **u** and **c**

```
7 cud cud cut cuts cur curs cue cues duck ducks clue
8 a cud; a cur; to cut; the cue; the cure; for luck;
9 use a clue; a fur coat; take the cue; cut the cake
```
QS

9d ▶ 17 Improve Keyboarding Technique

1. Key the lines once as shown: SS with a DS between 2-line groups.

2. Key the lines again at a faster pace.

Technique goals

- reach *up* without moving hands away from you
- reach *down* without moving hands toward your body
- use quick-snap keystrokes

3d/1st rows
```
1 in cut nut ran cue can cot fun hen car urn den cog
2 Nan is cute; he is curt; turn a cog; he can use it
```
DS

l. shift and .
```
3 Kae had taken a lead.  Jack then cut ahead of her.
4 I said to use Kan. for Kansas and Ore. for Oregon.
```
DS

key words
```
5 and cue for jut end kit led old fit just golf coed
6 an due cut such fuss rich lack turn dock turf curl
```
DS

key phrases
```
7 an urn|is due|to cut|for us|to use|cut off|such as
8 just in|code it|turn on|cure it|as such|is in luck
```
DS

all keys learned
```
9 Nida is to get the ice; Jacki is to call for cola.
10 Ira is sure that he can go there in an hour or so.
```

287b-291b (continued)

Document 2
Memorandum

plain sheet

Prepare this memo for **Karl Coppersmith** to initial. Leave the TO: line blank; names will be keyed in later.

Date the memo **January 16, 19--,** and use **UNITED WAY FUND DRIVE** as the subject.

¶ Yesterday marked the beginning of the ^current fund drive for the United Way of San Mateo County. ~~It~~ ^The United Way is an organization that addresses the needs of people ^in our area through financial support and volunteer work. ¶ The attached literature lists the ~~groups~~ ^organizations receiving financial aid and includes an (Inv.)[sp] for your contribution. If you wish to give ^to the United Way through a payroll deduction, simply see Marie Getz. You may ~~indicate~~ ^request that your gift go to a specific ~~group~~ ^organization. xx Attachment

Document 3
Income Statement

plain sheet

Format this income statement. The heading is

MARY'S COUNTRY CRAFTS/Income Statement/For the Year Ended December 31, 19-- (*previous year*).

Note: To key the double underline on a typewriter, first underline the total in the usual way. Then roll the paper up ½ line space and key the second underline. If your equipment will not permit you to key a double underline, use a ruler and pen or pencil to draw the second underline.

(Add remaining leaders)

Income:		
Sales	$46,764	
Craft Classes	2,503	
Total Income		$49,267
Operating expenses:		
Rent Expense	$12,000	
Wages Expense	8,320	
Advertising Expense	295	
Depreciation Expense	1,440	
Utilities expense	2,368	
(Mdse.)[sp] Expense	3,815	
Supplies Expense	~~280~~ 380	
Total ^Operating expenses		28,618
Net Income For The (Yr.)[sp]		$20,649

Document 4
Statement of Owner's Equity

plain sheet

Key the Statement of Owner's Equity at the right.

MARY'S COUNTRY CRAFTS
Statement of Owner's Equity
For the Year Ended December 31, 19--
} DS

QS

Mary Castleton, Capital January 1, 19-- (*previous year*)	$18,350
Add:	
Net Income for (Yr.)[sp]	20,649
	$38,999
Less:	
Capital Withdrawn during (Yr.)[sp]	19,500
Mary Castleton, Capital December 31, 19--	$19,499

Line length (LL): 50 spaces
Line spacing (LS): single (SS)

10a ▶ 8 *Conditioning Practice*

each line twice SS (slowly, then faster); DS between 2-line groups

all letters learned

1 a;sldkfj a;sldkfj uj cd ik rf nj ed hj tf ol gf .l
2 is cod and cut for did end off got the all oak jug
3 Hugh has just taken a lead in a race for a record.

QS

10b ▶ 20 *Learn W and Right Shift Key*

each line twice SS (slowly, then faster); DS between 2-line groups; if time permits, repeat each line

Follow the *Standard Plan for Learning New Keys* outlined on page 8.

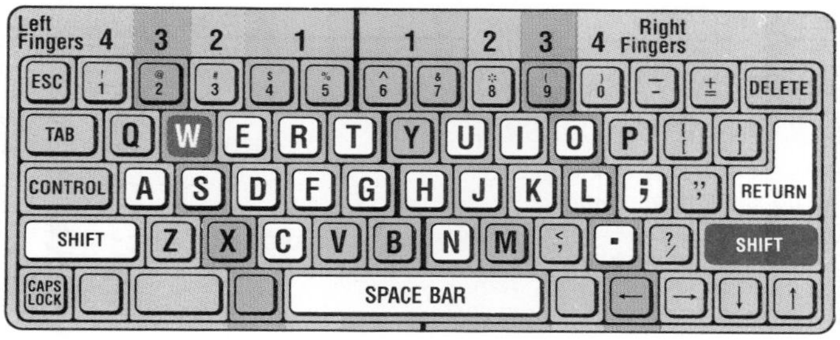

Reach technique for **w**

Learn **W**

1 s s ws ws sow sow wow wow low low how how cow cows
2 sw sw ws ws ow ow now now row row own own tow tows
3 to sow; is how; so low; to own; too low; is to row

DS

Control of RIGHT SHIFT key

Reach *down* with *right little* finger; shift, strike, release.

Technique hint
Shift, strike key, and release both in a quick 1-2-3 count.

Learn **Right Shift Key**

4 A; A; Al Al; Cal Cal; Ali or Flo; Di and Sol left.
5 Ali lost to Ron; Cal lost to Elsa; Di lost to Del.
6 Tina has left for Tucson; Dori can find her there.

DS

Combine **W** and **Right Shift**

7 Dodi will ask if Willa went to Town Center at two.
8 Wilf left the show for which he won a Gower Award.
9 Walt will go to Rio on a golf tour with Newt Lowe.

QS

10c ▶ 5 *Review Spacing with Punctuation*

each line once DS

Spacing hint
Do not space after an internal period in an abbreviation.

No space — Space once

1 Use i.e. for that is; cs. for case; ck. for check.
2 Dr. Wong said to use wt. for weight; in. for inch.
3 R. D. Roth has used ed. for editor; Rt. for Route.
4 Wes said Ed Rowan got an Ed.D. degree last winter.

QS

287a-291a ▶ 5 (daily)

Equipment Check

each line twice SS; DS between 2-line groups

alphabet 1 Lack of oxygen caused dizziness for Jeb who quickly moved up the hill.

figures 2 Please verify the $3,679 total on Invoice No. 4802 dated September 15.

fig/sym 3 K & S (6948 Loretta Street) is having a 50% sale from September 17-23.

speed 4 Iris did key in the surname and title of the auditor on the amendment.

| 1 | 2 | 3 | 4 | 5 | 6 | 7 | 8 | 9 | 10 | 11 | 12 | 13 | 14 |

287b-291b ▶ 45 (daily)

Document Processing

Process as many of the following documents as you can during each work period. Proofread and correct each document before you remove it from the typewriter or print a copy.

Document 1
Partial Audit Report

plain sheet

Key this rough draft as page 12 of a report (leftbound).

Organization and Facilities

Sufficiency of Working Capital

As a result of our audit for the year ended December 31, 19--, we offer these suggestions concerning the status of your capital. Our audit reveals that the corporation has been operating with insufficient capital. Long-range plans must be made to insure that the corporation has a sufficient ~~amount of~~ working capital in the future. The best from of working capital is still cash in the bank.

Providing for adequate record storage

A ~~few~~ record-storing inadequacies were discovered during our examination.

1. In our tests of the inventory records, we could not locate the records from Sept. 19--.

2. General ledgers, journal books, and other records are not clearly marked.

3. Record-storage area is cluttered; records are stacked on top or in front of other records.

Since we found it time-consuming and frustrating to locate the necessary records, we ~~suggest~~ that the records area be cleaned, organized, and efficiently maintained. All records must be clear ~~and~~ marked and should be ~~readily~~ accessable.

10d ▶ 17 Improve Keyboarding Technique

1. Key the lines once as shown: SS with a DS between 2-line groups.

2. Key the lines again at a faster pace.

Goal: finger-action reaches; quiet hands and arms

w and r. shift
1 Dr. Rowe is in Tulsa now; Dr. Cowan will see Rolf.
2 Gwinn took the gown to Golda Swit on Downs Circle.
DS

n/g
3 to go|go on|no go|an urn|dug in|and got|and a sign
4 He is to sign for the urn to go on the high chest.
DS

key words
5 if ow us or go he an it of own did oak the cut jug
6 do all and for cog odd ant fig rug low cue row end
DS

key phrases
7 we did|for a jar|she is due|cut the oak|he owns it
8 all of us|to own the|she is to go|when he has gone
DS

all keys learned
9 Jan and Chris are gone; Di and Nick get here soon.
10 Doug will work for her at the new store in Newton.

Lesson 11 B and Y

Line length (LL): 50 spaces
Line spacing (LS): single (SS)

Fingers curved

Fingers upright

11a ▶ 8 Conditioning Practice

each line twice SS (slowly, then faster); DS between 2-line groups

reach review
1 uj ws ik rf ol cd nj ed hj tf .l gf sw ju de lo fr

c/n
2 an can and cut end cue hen cog torn dock then sick

all letters learned
3 A kid had a jag of fruit on his cart in New Delhi.
QS

11b ▶ 5 Improve Space-Bar/Return Technique

1. Key each line once SS; return and start each new line quickly.

2. On line 4, see how many words you can key in 30 seconds (30″).

1 Dot is to go at two.
2 He saw that it was a good law.
3 Rilla is to take the auto into the town.
4 Wilt has an old gold jug he can enter in the show.
QS

gwam 1′ | 1 | 2 | 3 | 4 | 5 | 6 | 7 | 8 | 9 | 10 |

A standard word in keyboarding is 5 characters or any combination of 5 characters and spaces, as indicated by the number scale under line 4.

***gwam* = gross words a minute**

To find 1-minute (1′) *gwam*:

1. Note on the scale the figure beneath the last word you keyed. That is your 1′ *gwam* if you key the line partially or only once.

2. If you completed the line once and started over, add the figure determined in Step 1 to the figure 10. The resulting figure is your 1′ *gwam*.

To find 30-second (30″) *gwam*:

1. Find 1′ *gwam* (total words keyed).

2. Multiply 1′ *gwam* by 2. The resulting figure is your 30″ *gwam*.

UNIT 69 LESSONS 287 – 291

Regency Accounting Services, Inc. (An Accounting Office Simulation)

Production Goals

1. To format formal memos on plain paper.
2. To process letters commonly written by accountants.
3. To format financial statements and other specialized documents.

Documents Processed

1. Partial audit report
2. Memorandums
3. Financial statements
4. Engagement letters
5. News release
6. Proposal resume
7. Collection letter

REGENCY ACCOUNTING SERVICES, INC.

Before you begin the work of this simulation, read the introductory material and study the format guide summary at the right.

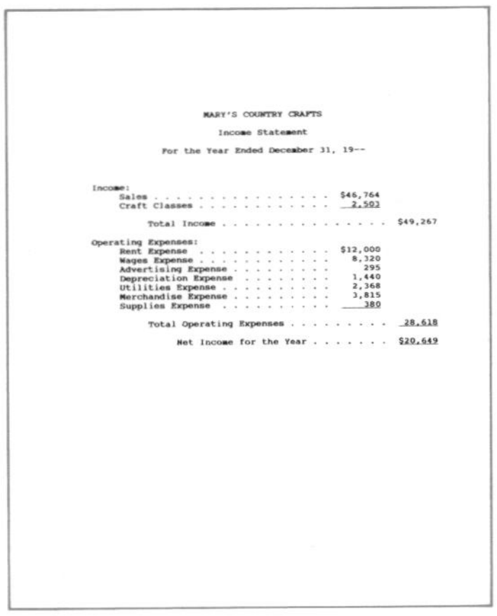

MARY'S COUNTRY CRAFTS
Income Statement
For the Year Ended December 31, 19--

Income:		
Sales	$46,764	
Craft Classes	2,503	
Total Income		$49,267
Operating Expenses:		
Rent Expense	$12,000	
Wages Expense	8,320	
Advertising Expense	295	
Depreciation Expense	1,440	
Utilities Expense	2,368	
Merchandise Expense	3,815	
Supplies Expense	380	
Total Operating Expenses		28,618
Net Income for the Year		$20,649

Income Statement

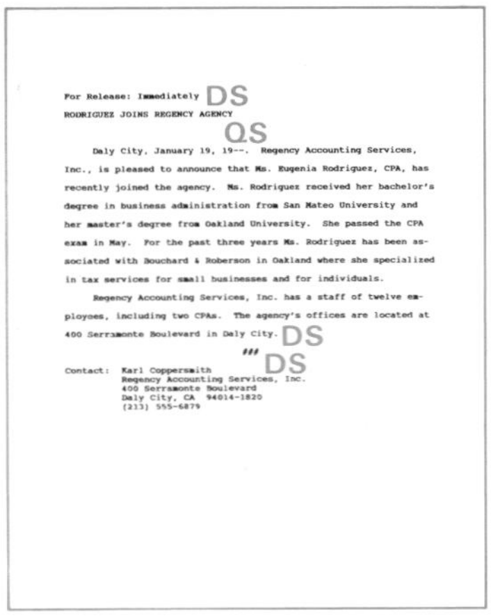

For Release: Immediately DS
RODRIGUEZ JOINS REGENCY AGENCY
QS

Daly City, January 19, 19--. Regency Accounting Services, Inc., is pleased to announce that Ms. Eugenia Rodriguez, CPA, has recently joined the agency. Ms. Rodriguez received her bachelor's degree in business administration from San Mateo University and her master's degree from Oakland University. She passed the CPA exam in May. For the past three years Ms. Rodriguez has been associated with Bouchard & Roberson in Oakland where she specialized in tax services for small businesses and for individuals.

Regency Accounting Services, Inc. has a staff of twelve employees, including two CPAs. The agency's offices are located at 400 Serramonte Boulevard in Daly City. DS

###
DS

Contact: Karl Coppersmith
Regency Accounting Services, Inc.
400 Serramonte Boulevard
Daly City, CA 94014-1820
(213) 555-6879

News Release

You are assigned to work as a temporary replacement for one of the office assistants at Regency Accounting Services, Inc., 400 Serramonte Boulevard, Daly City, CA 94014-1820. Regency consists of two Certified Public Accountants (CPAs), four assisting accountants, and an office support staff.

Most of your work will be for Karl Coppersmith, CPA, whose job title is senior accountant; but you report directly to Roberta Osborne, office supervisor. Miss Osborne has given you an office procedures manual to review. More form letters are to be added to the manual in the near future.

While reviewing the office procedures manual, you note the following:

1. Letters are formatted attractively on letterhead in the modified block format (blocked paragraphs) with mixed punctuation. Name of the firm is keyed in ALL CAPS in the closing lines. The preferred complimentary closing is **Very truly yours**.

2. Memos, prepared on plain paper, have the guide words TO, FROM, DATE, and SUBJECT keyed and blocked 1″ from the left edge. Enumerated items are listed in "hang indent" format. SS 2-line entries; DS between enumerated items.

3. Financial statements, such as balance sheets, statements of financial condition, and income statements, are compiled in leftbound report style (1½″ left margin and 1″ right margin). The page beginning ranges from line 6 to line 12 depending upon the length of the statement. One-page statements are preferred. Leaders are used in all financial statements.

4. Reports of 5 pages or more typically include headers at the top of each page. To create a header, place the title at the left margin on line 6 (same line as the page number).

5. Abbreviations, often used in handwritten drafts, are not used in final documents. Common abbreviations include

accts.	accounts	mdse.	merchandise
bal.	balance	mo.	month(s)
cr.	credit	qtr.	quarter(ly)
dr.	debit	stmt.	statement
ins.	insurance	yr.	year(s)

6. Accuracy is essential on all documents; financial statements MUST be error-free.

Document Format Guides

Form Letters. The form or standard part of a form letter is arranged on plain paper. Each form letter has a title or identification keyed on line 12. Variables are indicated by V1 (date), V2 (letter address), V3 (salutation), etc. The closing lines are formatted normally, except that the sender's name is variable information.

The engagement letter, used to clarify the accounting tasks to be performed for clients, includes an "approval" line (3″) for the client's signature and a line (1½″) for the date. These lines are arranged below the closing lines of the letter as shown here:

Very truly yours, DS
REGENCY ACCOUNTING SERVICES, INC.
QS

Karl Coppersmith, CPA
Senior Accountant
DS
xx DS
Enclosures
DS
Approved:
DS
Umeki Yoshino Date

Financial Statements. All financial documents have a 3-line heading, DS, containing the client's name, title of the statement, and the date or period the statement covers. Recommended: CS--4 spaces between amount columns. Long items should be keyed on two lines--not extended into the intercolumn space. Leaders are used to make statements more readable. Periods and spaces must align vertically. A leader must end at least two spaces to the left of the figures.

News Releases. PB: line 10; SM: 1″; DS. **For Release:** is keyed at the left margin followed by the release date. The suggested title of the article is keyed at the left margin in ALL CAPS. **Contact:** followed by a name, address, and telephone number is keyed at the left margin below the symbols ###.

11c ▶ 20
Learn B and Y

each line twice SS (slowly, then faster); DS between 2-line groups; if time permits, practice selected lines again

Follow the *Standard Plan for Learning New Keys* outlined on page 8.

Reach technique for **b**

Learn **b**

1 f f bf bf fib fib rob rob but but big big fib fibs
2 bf bf rob rob lob lob orb orb bid bid bud bud ribs
3 a rib; to fib; rub it; an orb; or rob; but she bid
DS

Reach technique for **y**

Learn **y**

4 j j yj yj jay jay lay lay hay hay day day say says
5 yj yj jay jay eye eye dye dye yes yes yet yet jays
6 a jay; to say; an eye; he says; dye it; has an eye
DS

Combine **b** and **y**

7 by by buy buy boy boy bye bye byte byte buoy buoys
8 by it; to buy; by you; a byte; the buoy; by and by
9 Jaye went by bus to the store to buy the big buoy.
QS

11d ▶ 17 Improve Keyboarding Technique

1. Key the lines once as shown: SS with a DS between 2-line groups.

2. Key the lines again at a faster pace.

Goals

- reach *up* without moving hands away from you
- reach *down* without moving hands toward your body
- use quick-snap keystrokes

reach review
1 a;sldkfj bf ol ed yj ws ik rf hj cd nj tf .l gf uj
2 a kit low for jut led sow fob ask sun cud jet grow
DS

3d/1st rows
3 no in bow any tub yen cut sub coy ran bin cow deck
4 Cody wants to buy this baby cub for the young boy.
DS

key words
5 by and for the got all did but cut now say jut ask
6 work just such hand this goal boys held furl eight
DS

key phrases
7 to do|can go|to bow|for all|did jet|ask her|to buy
8 if she|to work|and such|the goal|for this|held the
DS

all letters learned
9 Kitty had auburn hair with big eyes of clear jade.
10 Juan left Bobby at the dog show near our ice rink.

gwam 1' | 1 | 2 | 3 | 4 | 5 | 6 | 7 | 8 | 9 | 10 |

286a ▶ 5 Conditioning Practice

each line twice SS (slowly, then faster); then a 1′ writing on line 4

alphabet 1 Gladyce bought two dozen quarts of jam and five extra jars of pickles.

figures 2 The team batting average went from .389 on June 16 to .405 on June 27.

bottom row 3 Dr. Betz gave him an extensive physical examination on Monday morning.

speed 4 When they fix the chair by the door, they may also work on the mantle.

| 1 | 2 | 3 | 4 | 5 | 6 | 7 | 8 | 9 | 10 | 11 | 12 | 13 | 14 |

286b ▶ 15 Improve Language Skills

LL: 70 spaces
LS: DS

1. The sentences at the right contain errors in spelling, punctuation, capitalization, and grammar.

2. As you key each sentence (with number and period), make all necessary corrections, including any keystroking errors you may make.

3. After you key all sentences, proofread each one and mark each error that was not corrected.

1. The Jay cooperation has a divers product line.
2. It seams to me that they should be farther than lesson 5.
3. The jefferson memorial was Dedicated on April 13 1943.
4. The implemintation of the Knew policy were succesful.
5. The mississippi and colorodo is two rivers in the us.
6. The recent events wayed heavily n his conscious.
7. Toms' resent promotion was the bases of jack's resentment.
8. It is importent too decrease expenditers on Foreign Oil.
9. Did dr. Sanchez enjoy her trip to south america in july?
10. His recomendation was to by the Knewer vehicle.
11. The Mark Twain museum are located in Hannibal Missour.
12. Will president Chi deliver the Keynote Address on Friday may 23.
13. Ten of the sixteen computers was damaged during shipment.
14. The new desks are three ft. wide and five ft. long.
15. King louis XVI was executed in paris on january 21 1793.

286c ▶ 10 Improve Keyboarding Technique

Key each sentence twice; once for speed, then slower for accuracy; key difficult sentences again as time permits.

Balanced-hand 1 Diana may make the girls keep the lamb and fowl down by the city dock.

Double letters 2 Warren better have the three drill books when Annette arrives at noon.

Combination 3 Their box with the forms in it was left in my room by the old dresser.

3d row 4 Terri requested Peter to report your errors to the proper authorities.

Adjacent-key 5 News of a lower oil and crop production created very serious problems.

Shift key 6 Jana lived in New York City before moving to Salt Lake City in August.

Figures 7 I showed homes at 1856 Hatch, 297 Wren, and 403 Elm Street on July 30.

286d ▶ 20 Improve Basic Keyboarding Skills

1. Take a 1′ writing on each paragraph of 285d; determine *gwam* and errors on each writing.

2. Take two 5′ writings on 285d. Record *gwam* and errors of the better writing.

Before you begin each practice session:

- Position your body directly in front of the keyboard; sit erect, with feet on the floor for balance.
- Curve your fingers deeply and place them in an upright position over the home keys.
- Position the textbook or screen for easy reading (at about a 90° angle to the eyes).

Body properly positioned

Fingers properly curved

Fingers properly upright

12a ► 8 Conditioning Practice

each line twice SS (slowly, then faster); DS between 2-line groups; if time permits, practice each line again

all keystrokes learned

```
1 we ok as in be on by re no us if la do ah go C. J.
2 for us; in a jet; by the bid; cut his leg; to work
3 Fran knew it was her job to guide your gold truck.
```
QS

12b ► 12 Improve Space-Bar/Shift-Key Technique

1. Key the lines once as shown: SS with a DS between 2-line groups.

2. Key the lines again at a faster pace.

Down-and-in spacing

Out-and-down shifting

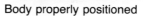

Space bar (Space *immediately* after each word)

```
1 an by win buy den sly won they than flay when clay
2 in a way|on a day|buy a hen|a fine day|if they win
```
DS

```
3 Jay can bid on the old clay urn he saw at the inn.
4 I know she is to be here soon to talk to the club.
```
DS

Shift keys (Shift; strike key; release both quickly)

```
5 Lt. Su; Nan and Dodi; Karl and Sol; Dr. O. C. Goya
6 Kara and Rod are in Italy; Jane and Bo go in June.
```
DS

```
7 Sig and Bodie went to the lake with Cory and Lana.
8 Aida Rios and Jana Hardy work for us in Los Gatos.
```
QS

285c ▶ 10
Improve Keyboarding Technique

1. Key lines 1-10 once as shown.

2. Take a 1′ writing on lines 2, 4, 6, 8, and 10. Try to maintain your line 2 rate on the other writings.

3. Compute *gwam* and compare rates on each writing.

Balanced-hand	1	and fix elf hair jams sick pays quay ruby fuzz vigor works towns sight
	2	Lana may make the proficient girls handle the problems with the forms.
Double letters	3	add book tree offer dinner accept bottle pepper yellow message command
	4	Debbie usually corrects all the keying errors in her business letters.
Combination	5	sir see man kept were them kind key very best social audit within have
	6	If she is able to leave the downtown area by noon, she may be on time.
3d row	7	up put top pop two your yoyo were tire quite quote quiet teeter terror
	8	They were quite polite to the witty reporter who requested your story.
Adjacent-key	9	as we buy open milk over save newer power union ponder return reporter
	10	Broken sewer pipes created havoc prior to the popular fashion exhibit.

| 1 | 2 | 3 | 4 | 5 | 6 | 7 | 8 | 9 | 10 | 11 | 12 | 13 | 14 |

285d ▶ 20
Improve Basic Keyboarding Skills

1. A 1′ writing on each paragraph; determine *gwam* and errors on each writing.

2. Two 5′ writings on the ¶s. Record *gwam* and errors of the better writing.

all letters used | A | 1.5 si | 5.7 awl | 80% hfw |

	gwam 1′	5′	
All students should ponder the advantages of continuing their edu-	13	3	58
cation after finishing high school. A greater number of jobs than ever	28	6	61
before require post high school training in order to meet the minimum	42	8	63
standards of entry level. Many jobs that were previously open to indi-	56	11	66
viduals who had a high school diploma no longer exist, or technology has	71	14	69
changed the duties of the job to such an extent that some type of train-	85	17	72
ing after high school is now required in order to be qualified.	98	20	75
The secretarial position is an example of a job that has changed a	13	22	77
great deal by improved technology. Years ago, one of the major duties for	28	25	81
this type of work was to be able to use a manual typewriter with a	42	28	83
great deal of skill. Today the position has changed into one that re-	56	31	86
quires competence in operating word processing equipment and the ability	71	34	89
to utilize the computer as well as deal with customers and clients in	85	36	92
a skillful manner.	88	37	92
These changes are examples of how the current job market has made	13	40	95
it important for people to contemplate attending college in order to be	28	43	98
considered for some of the higher paying jobs. Advocates of more school-	42	46	101
ing also mention having a richer and more rewarding life as a reason	56	48	104
for continuing school. These factors are just a few of the reasons why,	71	51	106
over the years, young people, as well as old, have enrolled in some form	85	54	109
of advanced schooling.	90	55	110

gwam 1′ | 1 | 2 | 3 | 4 | 5 | 6 | 7 | 8 | 9 | 10 | 11 | 12 | 13 | 14 |
gwam 5′ | 1 | 2 | 3 |

12c ▶ 15 Improve Keyboarding Skill

1. Key the lines once as shown: SS with a DS between 2-line groups.

2. Key the lines again at a faster pace.

Goals

- curved, upright fingers
- quiet hands and arms
- quick spacing -- no pause between words
- finger-reach action to shift keys

Finger-action keystrokes

Down-and-in thumb motion

Key words and phrases (*Think, say,* and *key* words and phrases.)

1 by dig row off but and jet oak the cub all got rid
2 ah she own dug irk buy cog jak for yet ask led urn
DS

3 of us|if the|all of|and do|cut it|he got|to do the
4 is to be|as it is|if we do|in all the|if we own it
DS

All letters learned (Strike keys at a brisk, steady pace.)

5 Judy had gone for that big ice show at Lake Tahoe.
6 Jack said that all of you will find the right job.
DS

7 Cindy has just left for work at the big ski lodge.
8 Rudy can take a good job at the lake if he wishes.
QS

gwam 1′ | 1 | 2 | 3 | 4 | 5 | 6 | 7 | 8 | 9 | 10 |

12d ▶ 15 Check Keyboarding Skill

1. Key each line once DS. To DS when in SS mode, return twice at the end of the line.

2. Take a 20-second (20″) timed writing on each line. Your rate in gross words a minute (*gwam*) is shown word-for-word above the lines.

3. Take another 20″ writing on each line. Try to increase keystroking speed.

Goal: At least 15 *gwam*.

20″ gwam

3 | 6 | 9 | 12 | 15 | 18 | 21 | 24 | 27 | 30

1 Al is to do it.

2 Di has gone to work.

3 Jan is to go to the sale.

4 Rog is to row us to your dock.

5 Harl has an old kayak and two oars.

6 She told us to set a goal and go for it.

7 It is our job to see just how high we can go.

8 Jake will go to the city to work on the big signs.
QS

ENRICHMENT ACTIVITY: Reach Review

1. Key each line twice SS (slowly, then faster); DS between 2-line groups.

2. Rekey the drill for better control of reaches.

1 June had left for the club just as the news ended.
2 Bro led a task force whose goal was to lower cost.
3 Lyn knew the surf was too rough for kids to enjoy.
4 Ceil hikes each day on the side roads near school.

gwam 1′ | 1 | 2 | 3 | 4 | 5 | 6 | 7 | 8 | 9 | 10 |

UNIT 68 LESSONS 285 – 286

Improve Keyboarding and Language Skills

Learning Goals

1. To improve/refine technique and response patterns.
2. To increase keystroking speed and to improve accuracy on straight copy.
3. To improve language skills.

Format Guides

1. Paper guide at *0* (for typewriters).
2. LL: 70 spaces.
3. LS: SS drills; DS ¶s.
4. PI: 5 spaces.

Lesson 285 *Keyboarding/Language Skills*

285a ▶ 5 *Conditioning Practice*

Key each line twice. Then take two 30″ writings for speed on line 4 followed by two 30″ writings for control on line 1.

alphabet 1 James very quickly placed the two extra megaphones behind the freezer.

figures 2 The 120 computers were purchased in 1987; the 34 typewriters, in 1965.

shift keys 3 Terra McKinney and Margo Norton are new initiates of Delta Pi Epsilon.

speed 4 When we do the work for him, we may also fix their neighbor's bicycle.

| 1 | 2 | 3 | 4 | 5 | 6 | 7 | 8 | 9 | 10 | 11 | 12 | 13 | 14 |

285b ▶ 15 *Improve Language Skills*

LL: 70 spaces
LS: DS

1. The sentences at the right contain errors in spelling, punctuation, capitalization, and grammar.

2. As you key each sentence (with number and period), make all necessary corrections, including any keystroking errors you may make.

3. After you key all sentences, proofread each one and mark each error that was not corrected.

1. The united states tennis open will begin in new york next week.
2. There baby was born on the fifteenth of november at three thirty p.m.
3. When the alarm went off at the christmas party the crowd disbursed.
4. Tom and nancy Selby's vacationed in Denmark switzerland and Holland.
5. Mary has received her exceptance letter; Tom and Bob has not.
6. All of the homes on Vine street was damaged by the terrible whether.
7. The business professionals of America will meet on tuesday, May 15.
8. Some of the lone payments was received before the do date of may 1.
9. The federal reserve bank of minneapolis is on Marquette avenue.
10. They will spend independence day at their cottage in south Dakota.
11. The advise she recieved encouraged her to move foreward with the job.
12. The lincoln center is between amsterdam and columbus avenues.
13. They should apreciate the principle for the job she has dun.
14. please duplicate twelve copies of Page 4 and 15 copies of Page 5.
15. The office is located on the corner of 3rd Avenue and Maple lane.
16. You will find the answer to you question in section 9 on page 406.
17. Only 1 of the teachers are planning to attend the Senior play.
18. your Biology test will cover chapter 12 which starts on Page 256.
19. Gehrig ruth and mantle are just a few new york, yankee idles.
20. Pedro c. Ramirez immerged as the leading Presidential candidate.

13a ▶ 8 Conditioning Practice

each line twice SS (slowly, then faster); DS between 2-line groups

reach review 1 bf ol rf yj ed nj ws ik tf hj cd uj gf by us if ow

b/y 2 by bye boy buy yes fib dye bit yet but try bet you

all letters learned 3 Robby can win the gold if he just keys a new high.

QS

13b ▶ 20 Learn M and X

each line twice SS (slowly, then faster); DS between 2-line groups; if time permits, practice selected lines again

Follow the *Standard Plan for Learning New Keys* outlined on page 8.

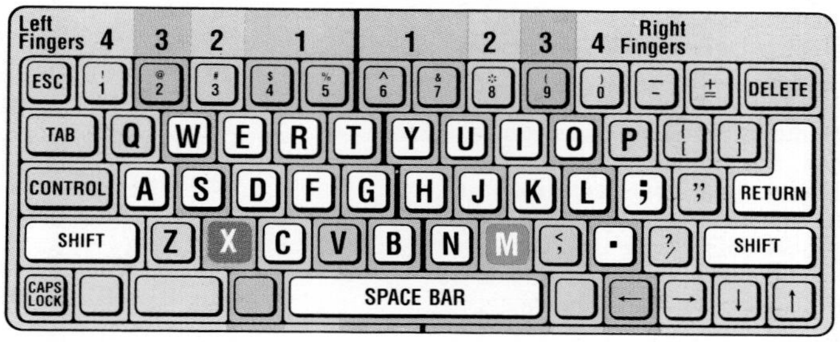

Reach technique for **m**

Reach technique for **x**

Learn **m**

1 j j mj mj am am am me me ma ma jam jam ham ham yam

2 mj mj me me me may may yam yam dam dam men men jam

3 am to; if me; a man; a yam; a ham; he may; the hem

DS

Learn **x**

4 s s xs xs ox ox ax ax six six fix fix fox fox axis

5 xs xs sx sx ox ox six six nix nix fix fix lax flax

6 a fox; an ox; fix it; by six; is lax; to fix an ax

DS

Combine **m** and **x**

7 me ox am ax ma jam six ham mix fox men lax hem lox

8 to fix; am lax; mix it; may fix; six men; hex them

9 Mala can mix a ham salad for six; Max can fix tea.

QS

13c ▶ 5 Review Spacing with Punctuation

each line once DS

▽ Do not space after an internal period in an abbreviation.

1 Mrs. Dixon may take her Ed.D. exam early in March.

2 Lex may send a box c.o.d. to Ms. Fox in St. Croix.

3 J. D. and Max will go by boat to St. Louis in May.

4 Owen keyed ect. for etc. and lost the match to me.

QS

280b-284b (continued)

Documents 10-11
Job Descriptions

2 plain sheets

Until now, Gateway has had one job description for all medical assistants, who performed both administrative (office) and clinical (medical) tasks. An increase in our patient load indicates a need to divide job duties between two types of medical assistants. From the job description at the right, prepare two separate job descriptions in report format.

Prepare a job description for **Medical Assistant--Administrative.** For the **Job Summary** key **The medical assistant--administrative performs typical office procedures.** Under **Job Duties** list items 1, 2, 9, 11, 12, and 15-18 (renumber the items, beginning with 1).

Prepare a job description for **Medical Assistant--Clinical.** For the **Job Summary** key **The medical assistant--clinical helps patients** *(copy remainder of sentence from original).* Under **Job Duties** list items 3-8, 10, 13, and 14 (renumber the items, beginning with 1).

L. Sanchez

JOB DESCRIPTION

Job Title: Medical Assistant

Job Summary: The medical assistant performs typical office procedures, helps patients prepare for examinations, assists physicians as requested, and performs basic clinical procedures.

Job Duties:

1. Greet patients.
2. Inspect patients' records for accuracy and completeness.
3. Gather essential patient information, prepare/drape patients, measure temperature, height, weight, blood pressure, etc.
4. Administer all injections and maintain accurate record of each.
5. Sterilize instruments and maintain quality of instruments.
6. Maintain examination rooms, workstations, and equipment.
7. Obtain and process specimens and attach Holter monitor and electrocardiograph.
8. Complete lab request forms.
9. Perform patient education activities.
10. Assist physician upon request.
11. Screen patients' telephone calls to determine need for/urgency of appointments.
12. Order medical supplies and prescription medications.
13. Obtain samples from pharmaceutical suppliers.
14. Organize and control pharmaceutical samples on sample shelves.
15. Maintain detailed records of all prescriptions filled in the office.
16. Maintain the supply closets.
17. Keep the patient information booklets and other handouts up to date.
18. Set up examination rooms each afternoon, including patients' charts, for the next day.

Documents 12-13
Continuation Sheets

2 plain sheets

Dr. Lloyd made the notes at the right as he examined two of his young patients. Copy the notes to separate sheets, one for each patient's file. Center the words **CONTINUATION SHEET** on line 6; DS. Key the examination date in the six-digit format at the left margin; reset the margin 4 spaces to the right to key the notes single-spaced.

On Alexa Beerman's sheet, add the following note you recorded when Alexa's mother called in this morning (key your initials at end of note).

12/17-- TC axillary temp. 97.6 F w/i 6 hrs. after last dose. Stopped Tylenol. xx

L. Sanchez

12/16--

CARL D. JOHNSON. Age--6 mos. Hgt. 26" Wt. 16 lbs., 10 oz. Head circum. 44 2/3 cm. Immunizations--DTP, OPV. Denver Developmental passed.

12/16-- ALEXA K. BEERMAN. Age--10 weeks. Hgt. 17½" Wt. 10 lbs., 2 oz. Head circum. 35½ cm. Axillary temp. 99.3 F. Rx for fever, 0.4 ml. Tylenol, q.i.d. /24 hrs. only.

13d ► 17 Improve Keyboarding Technique

1. Key the lines once as shown: SS with a DS between 2-line groups.

2. Key the lines again at a faster pace.

Technique goals

- reach *up* without moving hands away from you
- reach *down* without moving hands toward your body
- use quick-snap keystrokes

Goal: finger-action keystrokes; quiet hands and arms

3d/1st rows
1 by am end fix men box hem but six now cut gem ribs
2 me ox buy den cub ran own form went oxen fine club
DS

space bar
3 an of me do am if us or is by go ma so ah ox it ow
4 by man buy fan jam can any tan may rob ham fun guy
DS

key words
5 if us me do an sow the cut big jam rub oak lax boy
6 curl work form born name flex just done many right
DS

key phrases
7 or jam|if she|for me|is big|an end|or buy|is to be
8 to fix|and cut|for work|and such|big firm|the call
DS

all keys learned
9 Jacki is now at the gym; Lex is due there by four.
10 Joni saw that she could fix my old bike for Gilda.

Lesson 14 P and V

LL: 50
LS: SS

14a ► 8 Conditioning Practice

each line twice SS (slowly, then faster); DS between 2-line groups; if time permits, practice each line again

all letters learned

one-hand words
1 in we no ax my be on ad on re hi at ho cad him bet

phrases
2 is just|of work|to sign|of lace|to flex|got a form

all letters learned
3 Jo Buck won a gold medal for her sixth show entry.
QS

14b ► 6 Improve Shift-Key/Return Technique

Key each 2-line sentence once SS as "Return" is called every 30 seconds (30"). Leave a DS between sentences.

Goal: To reach the end of each line just as the 30" guide ("Return") is called.

> The 30" *gwam* scale shows your gross words a minute if you reach the end of each line as the 30" guide is called.

Eyes on copy as you shift and as you return

	gwam 30"	20"
1 Marj is to choose a high goal	12	18
2 and to do her best to make it.	12	18
DS		
3 Gig said he had to key from a book	14	21
4 for a test he took for his new job.	14	21
DS		
5 Alex knows it is good to hold your goal	16	24
6 in mind as you key each line of a drill.	16	24
DS		
7 Nan can do well many of the tasks she tries;	18	27
8 she sets new goals and makes them one by one.	18	27
QS		

No family history of cardiac disease exists. Her mother died of breast cancer at 87.

Pyhsical examination revealed that pateints' neck is supple without jvd. Breathe is even with few scattered rhonchi. Heart had regular rhythm without murmur, gallop, or click. PMI was not palpable; S 1 and S 2 were normal. Pulse was 2 + and regular in carotids and radials, and carotid up strokes were normal. Blood pressure 110/60 in her right arm, seated and standing. Juguler venus pulse pressure was 5 centimeters of water and normal in contuor. The lungs were clear. The left ventricle impulse was within the midclavicular line. All heart sounds were normal. Review of her electrocardiagram of March 17, 19-- revealed a normal sinus rhythm and a normal PR interval of 0.18.

In summary, Mrs. Johnson is a pleasant woman, in relatively good health, who is satisfied with her presented life style. Her history of occassional chest discomfort and prier occurrence of subendocardial myocardial infraction do not indicate cardiac diseases. I advice no further cardiac evaluation for 1 year unless the patient should expereince an increase in frequency or a change in character of the chest discomfort.Under either circumstance farther evaluation, including in-hospital rest and exercise first pass study, is advised. No cardiac treatment is recommended now other than prn sublingual nitroglycerin.

I would like to evaluate the patient again in 10-12 months. Thank you for refering Mrs. Johnson to me.

14c ▶ 20 Learn P and V

each line twice SS (slowly, then faster); DS between 2-line groups; if time permits, practice selected lines again

Follow the *Standard Plan for Learning New Keys* outlined on page 8.

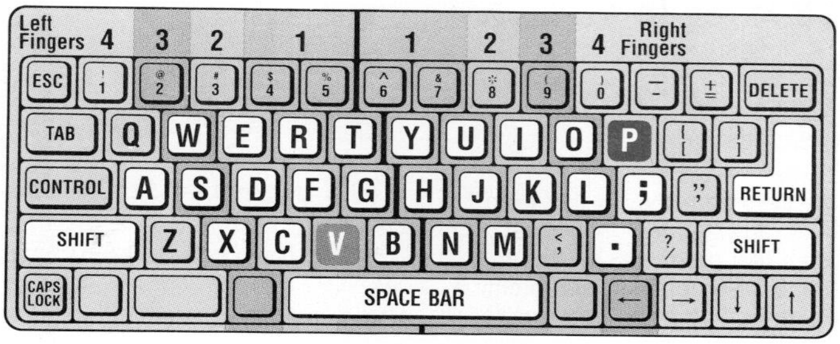

Reach technique for **p**

Reach *up* with *right little* finger.

Learn **p**

1 ; ; p; p; pa pa up up apt apt pen pen lap lap kept
2 p; p; pa pa pa pan pan nap nap paw paw gap gap rap
3 a pen; a cap; apt to pay; pick it up; plan to keep
DS

Learn **v**

4 f f vf vf via via vie vie have have five five live
5 vf vf vie vie vie van van view view dive dive jive
6 go via; vie for; has vim; a view; to live; or have
DS

Reach technique for **v**

Reach *down* with *left first* finger.

Combine **p** and **v**

7 up cup vie pen van cap vim rap have keep live plan
8 to vie; give up; pave it; very apt; vie for a cup;
9 Vic has a plan to have the van pick us up at five.
QS

14d ▶ 16 Improve Keyboarding Technique

1. Key the lines once as shown: SS with a DS between 2-line groups.

2. Key the lines again at a faster pace.

Technique goals

- reach *up* without moving hands away from you
- reach *down* without moving hands toward your body
- use quick-snap keystrokes

Goal: finger-action keystrokes; quiet hands and arms

reach review
1 vf p; xs mj ed yj ws nj rf ik tf ol cd hj gf uj bf
2 if lap jag own may she for but van cub sod six oak
DS

3d/1st rows
3 by vie pen vim cup six but now man nor ton may pan
4 by six but now may cut sent me fine gems five reps
DS

key words
5 with kept turn corn duty curl just have worn plans
6 name burn form when jury glad vote exit came eight
DS

key phrases
7 if they|he kept|with us|of land|burn it|to name it
8 to plan|so sure|is glad|an exit|so much|to view it
DS

all letters learned
9 Kevin does a top job on your flax farm with Craig.
10 Dixon flew blue jets eight times over a city park.

280b-284b (continued)

Documents 6-8
Form Letters
plain paper and
LP pp. 167-169

Dr. Liebman revised this form letter advising his patients about a lab test (urinalysis). First, format the letter on plain paper, omitting the date, letter address, salutation, and complimentary close, and keying **V1** and **V2** as shown. Then prepare a letter to the two patients named on these cards. Variable information (date, time) is shown on the cards. Date the letters **December 16.**

L. Sanchez

Ellison, Suzy B. (Miss)

4292 El Camino, Apt. 16
Palo Alto, CA 94306-8372

V1 December 22
V2 9:00 a.m.

Luebber, Richard M. (Mr.)

16 Thunderbird Ct.
Oakland, CA 94605-7127

V1 December 23
V2 9:30 a.m.

~~In order~~ to obtain accurate results from urinanalysis, you should (1) maintnain a normal in take of liquids during the 24-hour specimen collection period & (2) take the total ~~entire~~ specimen to the lab the morning the collection is complete ~~taken~~. In adition, these following substances should be avoided four at least 24 hours prier to beginning the collection: (Alphabetize each list below.)

coffee/tea	aspirin
chocolate	chlorpomazine
citrus fruits	~~serotonin~~
vanilla/~~chocolate~~	resperine
	pentobarbital

Remember, your lab apointment is on V1 at V2. The lab is in the Gateway Medical Center building on the ground floor.

Document 9
Letter to Referring Physician
LP p. 171
1 plain sheet

Dr. Myers dictated the letter at the right following her evaluation of a patient referred to her by Dr. Lopez. One of your coworkers transcribed the dictation, producing this rough draft. Prepare the letter for Dr. Myers' signature, using this address:

Dr. Barbara M. Lopez
Bayside Professional Building
2000 Bay Street
San Francisco, CA 94213-6008

Date the letter **December 16, 19--.**

L. Sanchez

The Evaluation of Carol Jo Johnson has been completed. As you know she is a 69 year old white female who states that she had a heart attack 15 years ago. A review ofher clinic chart shows a history of sub-endocardial myocardial infraction. The pateint experiences episodes of chest discomfort that she describes as a "sharp to aching" sensation over the upper left quadrant. The sensation occurs suddenly and seems ~~to be~~ unrelated to activities. She reported that releif typicaly is gained by taking sub-lingual nitroglycerin. The patient reported no significant limitations in her usual activity. No orthopnea, PND, or petal edema was reported. Ms. Johnson reported that 2 years ago she discontinued smoking cigaretes after smoking a pack daily for over 25 years.

(continued, p. 476)

15a ▶ 8 Conditioning Practice

each line twice SS (slowly, then faster); DS between 2-line groups; if time permits, practice selected lines again

all letters learned 1 do fix all cut via own buy for the jam cop ask dig

p/v 2 a map; a van; apt to; vie for; her plan; have five

all letters learned 3 Beth will pack sixty pints of guava jam for David.

QS

15b ▶ 20 Learn Q and , (Comma)

each line twice SS (slowly, then faster); DS between 2-line groups; if time permits, practice each line again

Follow the *Standard Plan for Learning New Keys* outlined on page 8.

Reach technique for **q**

Learn **q**

1 a qa qa aq aq quo quo qt. qt. quad quad quit quits

2 qa quo quo qt. qt. quay quay aqua aqua quite quite

3 a qt.; pro quo; a quad; to quit; the quay; a squad

DS

Learn **,** (comma)

4 k k ,k ,k kit, kit; Rick, Ike, or I will go, also.

5 a ski, a ski; a kit, a kit; a kite, a kite; a bike

6 Ike, I see, is here; Pam, I am told, will be late.

DS

Reach technique for **,** (comma)

Reach *down* with *right second* finger; space once after , used as punctuation.

Combine **q** and **,**

7 Enter the words quo, quote, quit, quite, and aqua.

8 I have quit the squad, Quen; Raquel has quit, too.

9 Marquis, Quent, and Quig were quite quick to quit.

QS

15c ▶ 5 Review Spacing with Punctuation

each line once DS

▽ Space once after comma used as punctuation.

1 Aqua means water, ▽ Quen; also, ▽ it is a unique blue.

2 Quince, enter qt. for quart; also, sq. for square.

3 Ship the desk c.o.d. to Dr. Quig at La Quinta Inn.

4 Q. J. took squid and squash; Monique, roast quail.

QS

280b-284b (continued)

Documents 3 and 4
Statements of Account
LP pp. 163-165

Will you prepare statements of account from these patients' Accounts Receivable Ledger sheets. Wherever a zero balance appears, key only the lines *below* the zero balance.

Add the current year to the six-digit date; for example, 12/13/92. Key **.00** following all amounts.

Key the codes in the Service column as shown. For your information, a list of Gateway's codes is attached.

L. Sanchez

Service Codes

HC--Hospital Care
OC--Office Care
PRO--Procedures
INJ--Injections
OS--Lab, X-Ray, or Other Service
INS--Insurance Payment
ROA--Received on Account

ACCOUNTS RECEIVABLE LEDGER

Mr. Angelo Patti, 3740 San Bruno Ave., San Francisco, 94134-1833

DATE	PROFESSIONAL SERVICE	CHARGES	PAYMENTS	CURRENT BALANCE
11/22	OC	125	0	125
11/29	INJ	10	0	135
11/30	INS		25	110

ACCOUNTS RECEIVABLE LEDGER

Miss Lena M. Moss, 67 Eddy St., San Francisco, 94102-3331

DATE	PROFESSIONAL SERVICE	CHARGES	PAYMENTS	CURRENT BALANCE
10/01	OC, PRO	120	0	120
10/18	INJ	8	0	128
10/30	ROA		128	0
12/02	OC	40	0	40
12/09	INJ	8	0	48

Document 5
Partnership Contract
plain paper

This document, revised by Mr. Beard, is page **8** of Gateway's partnership contract, prepared as a leftbound report. Prepare a final draft for Mr. Beard.

On the same line as the page number key this *header* at the left margin: **Articles of Partnership--Gateway Medical Center.** The main heading (line 10 or line 12) is **ARTICLE XIX--COVENANT AGAINST COMPETITION,** followed by a QS. (In all articles of the contract, paragraphs are numbered as shown.)

L. Sanchez

<u>P19.01</u>. Each shareholder in Gateway Medical Center covenants and agrees that ~~if he chooses to withdraw~~ in the event of his or her withdrawal, voluntary or involuntary, he or she will not engage in the practice of medicine in ~~any county in the State of~~ San Francisco County, California, for a period of ~~one~~ two (~~1~~ 2) years from the time of such withdrawal.

<u>P19.02</u>. The former shareholder will not practice medicine either directly or indirectly, for his or her own account or for others, during the ~~one~~ two-year period. Furthermore, during said period of ~~one~~ two years from the date that he or she leaves the employment of Gateway Medical Center, he or she will not engage in any business in ~~any county in the State of~~ San Francisco County, California, that competes in any manner with the business of the Corporation.

15d ▶ 17 Improve Keyboarding Technique

1. Key the lines once as shown: SS with a DS between 2-line groups.

2. Key the lines again at a faster pace.

Technique goals

- reach *up* without moving hands away from you
- reach *down* without moving hands toward your body
- use quick-snap keystrokes

Goal: finger-action keystrokes; quiet hands and arms

reach review
1 qa .l ws ,k ed nj rf mj tf p; xs ol cd ik vf hj bf
2 yj gf hj quo vie pay cut now buy got mix vow forms
DS

3d/1st rows
3 six may sun coy cue mud jar win via pick turn bike
4 to go|to win|for me|a peck|a quay|by then|the vote
DS

key words
5 pa rub sit man for own fix jam via cod oak the got
6 by quo sub lay apt mix irk pay when rope give just
DS

key phrases
7 an ox|of all|is to go|if he is|it is due|to pay us
8 if we pay|is of age|up to you|so we own|she saw me
DS

all letters learned
9 Jevon will fix my pool deck if the big rain quits.
10 Verna did fly quick jets to map the six big towns.

Lesson 16 Review

LL: 50
LS: SS

Fingers properly curved

Fingers properly aligned

16a ▶ 8 Conditioning Practice

each line twice SS (slowly, then faster); DS between 2-line groups; if time permits, practice each line again

all letters learned

review
1 Virgil plans to find that mosque by six with Jack.

shift keys
2 Pam, Van, and Quin have to be in New Hope by five.

easy sentence
3 Vi is to aid the girl with the sign work at eight.
QS

gwam 1′ | 1 | 2 | 3 | 4 | 5 | 6 | 7 | 8 | 9 | 10 |

16b ▶ 10 Key Block Paragraphs

each paragraph (¶) once SS as shown; DS between ¶s; then key the ¶s again at a faster pace

To find 1-minute (1′) *gwam*:

1. Note the figure at the end of your last complete line.

2. Note from the scale under the ¶s the figure below where you stopped in a partial line.

3. Add the two figures; the resulting number is your *gwam*.

Paragraph 1 *gwam* 1′

Do not stop at the end of the line before you make 10
a return. Keep up your pace at the end of a line, 20
and return quickly after you strike the final key. 30
DS

Paragraph 2

Make the return with a quick motion, and begin the 10
next line with almost no pause. Keep your eyes on 20
the copy as you return to save time between lines. 30
QS

gwam 1′ | 1 | 2 | 3 | 4 | 5 | 6 | 7 | 8 | 9 | 10 |

280b-284b (continued)

TIME SAVED BY AUTOMATION

Task	Time Required Current Method	Time Required Medic 1000
Appointment scheduling	1 hour	15 minutes
Monthly billing	2 days	30 minutes
Proving a daysheet	15 minutes	2-5 minutes
Processing claim forms	4-5 hours	10 minutes
Patient checkout	5 minutes	10 seconds

Document 2
Software Options Table

plain paper

Use these MEDIC 1000 menus, printed from my computer screen, to create a four-column table. Use these main and secondary headings:

MEDIC 1000 SOFTWARE

Basic Options Available*

Use the first four Main Menu options as column headings; block the submenu options under the column heads as shown by arrows. Don't key the option numbers. Key a divider line; then, this note: ***Custom options available in six upgrade modules.**

L. Sanchez

MAIN MENU

{1} Scheduling

{2} Accounting

{3} Bill/Collect/Insure

{4} Practice Management

{E} Exit to Operating System

SCHEDULING MENU

{1} Appointments
{2} Follow-up
{3} Recalls
{4} Reminders
{5} Daily list

ACCOUNTING MENU

{1} Gen. ledger
{2} Daysheet
{3} Payroll
{4} Profit/Loss
{5} A/Payable

BILL/COLLECT/INSURE MENU

{1} A/Receivable
{2} Claim forms
{3} Batch posting
{4} Statements
{5} Form letters

PRACTICE MANAGEMENT MENU

{1} Inventories
{2} Patient files
{3} Diag. codes
{4} Proced. codes
{5} Referrals

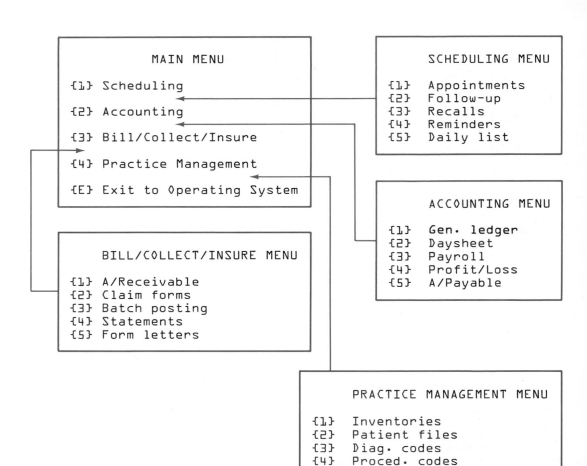

16c ▶ 12 Build Keyboarding Skill: Space Bar/Shift Keys

each line twice SS; DS between 4-line groups

Goals
- to reduce the pause between words
- to reduce the time taken to shift/strike key/release when making capital letters

Down-and-in spacing

Out-and-down shifting

Space bar (Space *immediately* after each word.)

```
1 so an if us am by or ox he own jay pen yam own may
2 she is in|am to pay|if he may|by the man|in a firm
                                                   DS
3 I am to keep the pens in a cup by a tan mail tray.
4 Fran may try to fix an old toy for the little boy.
                                                   DS
```

Shift keys (Shift; strike key; release both quickly.)

```
5 J. V., Dr. or Mrs., Ph.D. or Ed.D., Fourth of July
6 Mrs. Maria Fuente; Dr. Mark V. Quin; Mr. T. C. Ott
                                                   DS
7 B. J. Marx will go to St. Croix in March with Lex.
8 Mae has a Ph.D. from Miami; Dex will get his Ed.D.
                                                   QS
```

16d ▶ 10 Improve Keyboarding Skill

each line twice SS (slowly, then faster); DS between 4-line groups

Technique goals
- quick-snap keystrokes
- quick joining of letters to form words
- quick joining of words to form phrases

Key words and phrases (*Think, say,* and *key* words and phrases.)

```
1 ox jam for oak for pay got own the lap via sob cut
2 make than with them such they when both then their
                                                   DS
3 to sit|an elf|by six|an oak|did go|for air|the jam
4 to vie|he owns|pay them|cut both|the quay|for they
                                                   DS
```

Key sentences (Strike keys at a brisk, steady pace.)

```
all letters learned
5 I may have six quick jobs to get done for low pay.
6 Vicky packed the box with quail and jam for Signe.
                                                   DS
all letters learned
7 Max can plan to bike for just five days with Quig.
8 Jim was quick to get the next top value for Debby.
                                                   QS
```

16e ▶ 10 Check Keyboarding Skill

1. Take a 30-second (30″) timed writing on each line. Your rate in gross words a minute (*gwam*) is shown word-for-word above the lines.

2. If time permits, take another 30″ writing on each line. Try to increase your keyboarding speed.

Goal: At least 18 *gwam*.

30″ gwam

```
        2|   4|   6|   8|  10|  12|   14|   16|   18|   20|
1 I am to fix the sign for them.
2 Jaye held the key to the blue auto.
3 Todd is to go to the city dock for fish.
4 Vi paid the girl to make a big bowl of salad.
5 Kal may keep the urn he just won at the quay show.
|       2|   4|   6|   8|  10|  12|   14|   16|   18|   20|
```

If you finish a line before time is called and start over, your *gwam* is the figure at the end of the line PLUS the figure above or below the point at which you stopped.

280a-284a ▶ 5 (daily)

Equipment Check

each line twice SS; DS between 2-line groups

alphabet	1	This quiet but perky jazz dancer will give fox-trot lessons on Monday.
figures	2	A total of 2,574 people attended the ball games on September 30, 1986.
fig/sym	3	Inventory list No. 182 included these stock numbers: #3597 and #6463.
speed	4	Both of the neurotic men did sue for the right to air the title fight.

| 1 | 2 | 3 | 4 | 5 | 6 | 7 | 8 | 9 | 10 | 11 | 12 | 13 | 14 |

280b-284b ▶ 45 (daily)

Document Processing

Key as many of the following documents as you can during each daily session. Watch for unmarked errors in these original documents. Proofread and correct each document before you remove it from the machine or print a copy.

Document 1
Software Selection Memo

2 plain sheets

December 12, 19--

Prepare this memo to **All Staff Members;** I'll initial it. For the subject line use **MEDIC 1000 WINS HANDS DOWN.** The table to be inserted is on page 473.

L. Sanchez

The soft ware selection commitee completed it's feasibility study with input from you, and the results indicate that Medic 1000 is best suited to Gateways' needs. All members agreed that of the three medical software package studied, Medic 1000 represents the best combination of funtion & price.

Members of the commitee spent 3 working days at the vendors location using the software to determine the time required to complete their jobs. The table below "tells the story."

Medic 1000 is to be installed on our computer net work, for a three-month trial, within three weeks. Inhouse training will be offered by the vendor next month (dates to be announced). In the meantime, stop by Brook Sloan's office any Tuesday or Thursday and see the presentation of Medic 1000 to and skim the user manuals. The attachment shows the wide vareity of menu options available.

The initial training will involve a two-hour hands-on workshop in the training room, plus 4 hours of vendor assistance at each workstation. The first group of trainees will also be able to assist the individuals trained later.

During the trial, all of you will be asked to provide feedback. Then if the Medic 1000 installation is not to be permanant the other two options, Caduceus II and Hippocrates will be studied farther.

Lesson 17 Z and : (Colon)

LL: 50
LS: SS

17a ▶ 8 Conditioning Practice

each line twice SS; then a 1′ writing on line 3; find *gwam:* total words keyed

all letters learned 1 Jim won the globe for six quick sky dives in Napa.
spacing 2 to own|is busy|if they|to town|by them|to the city
easy sentence 3 She is to go to the city with us to sign the form.
gwam 1′ | 1 | 2 | 3 | 4 | 5 | 6 | 7 | 8 | 9 | 10 |

17b ▶ 20 Learn Z and : (Colon)

each line twice SS (slowly, then faster); DS between 2-line groups; if time permits, practice selected lines again

Follow the *Standard Plan for Learning New Keys* outlined on page 8.

Reach technique for **z**

Reach technique for **:** (colon)

Left shift and strike ; key; space twice after : used as punctuation.

Language skills notes

- Space twice after **:** used as punctuation.
- Capitalize the first word of a complete sentence following a colon.

Learn **z**

1 a a za za zap zap zap zoo zoo zip zip zag zag zany
2 za za zap zap zed zed oz. oz. zoo zoo zip zip maze
3 zap it, zip it, an adz, to zap, the zoo, eight oz.

Learn **:** (colon)

4 ; ; :; :; Date: Time: Name: Room: From: File:
5 :; :; To: File: Reply to: Dear Al: Shift for :
6 Two spaces follow a colon, thus: Try these steps:

Combine **z** and **:**

7 Zelda has an old micro with : where ; ought to be.
8 Zoe, use as headings: To: Zone: Date: Subject:
9 Liza, please key these words: zap, maze, and zoo.
10 Zane read: Shift to enter : and then space twice.

17c ▶ 5 Spacing Checkup

Key each line once SS. In place of the blank line at the end of each sentence, key the word "once" or "twice" to indicate the proper spacing.

1 After a . at the end of a sentence, space ______.
2 After a ; used as punctuation, space ______.
3 After a . following an initial, space ______.
4 After a : used as punctuation, space ______.
5 After a , within a sentence, space ______.
6 After a . following an abbreviation, space ______.

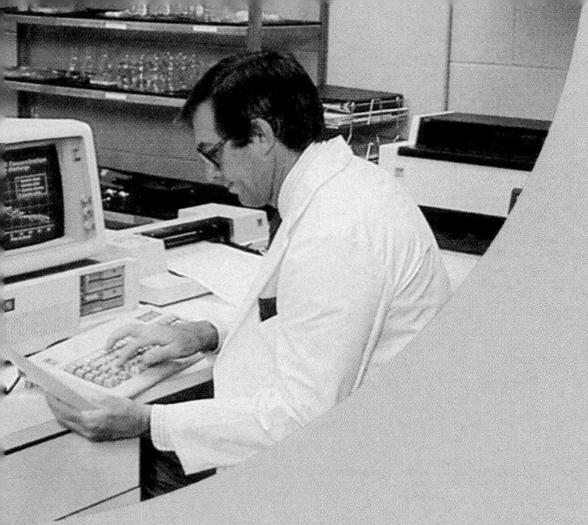

UNIT 67 LESSONS 280 – 284
Gateway Medical Center (A Health Services Simulation)

Production Goals

1. To adapt previously acquired formatting and language skills to documents processed in medical offices.

2. To improve your ability to use judgment in the absence of specific directions.

3. To improve your ability to organize work and materials.

Documents Processed

1. Simplified memorandum with table
2. Four-column table
3. Statements of account
4. Partnership contract
5. Form letters
6. Block format letter
7. Job descriptions
8. Continuation sheets

GATEWAY MEDICAL CENTER

Read the "Work Assignment" before beginning the documents on pages 472-477. When processing documents in this simulation, refer to the format guides and other information provided here.

Work Assignment

Gateway Medical Center welcomes a new "temp"--you. As a temporary medical assistant at Gateway, you'll apply many of the document production skills you acquired at Bayview Legal Services and in school.

Gateway Medical Center is a corporation of 15 physicians, who offer primary care specialties including family practice, internal medicine, and cardiology. Office support is provided by three small support teams, each with a supervisor. An office manager, Mr. Charles W. Beard, oversees all office support personnel.

Your supervisor is Ms. Louise M. Sanchez. The physicians supported by your team--Dr. Janice Myers, cardiologist; Dr. Matthew W. Lloyd, family practitioner, and Dr. Kyle A. Liebman, internist--request document processing services from Ms. Sanchez, who then assigns the documents to someone in your support team.

During your initial meeting Ms. Sanchez emphasizes the importance of complete accuracy in a medical office, noting that patients' health--even their lives--are at stake when errors occur in medical documents. In particular, Ms. Sanchez cautions you always to transcribe a doctor's handwritten notes or dictation *verbatim;* that is, word for word and with the exact punctuation. In addition, of course, she stresses that careful proofreading is a *must* in this office.

Your supervisor says she usually will give you directions in writing, because she realizes that temporary medical assistants may need to "go over" the directions more than once. Until you become familiar with the office procedures and materials, she'll provide additional information you'll need, such as patients' address cards, with her written directions.

Ms. Sanchez then provides you with a copy of "Procedures Manual for Medical Assistants" and suggests that you take time to read carefully the document format guides that she has highlighted.

Procedures Manual for Medical Assistants

The following is a description of the standard document formats used at Gateway Medical Center.

Memorandums--Simplified Format

Stationery: plain sheets.
PB: line 10.
SM: 1″. All memo parts begin at LM.
LS: QS below date and last line of body; DS below other parts; SS paragraphs.

Letters--Block Format/Open Punctuation

Stationery: Gateway letterhead.
PB: line 12.
SM: 1″. All letter parts begin at LM.
LS: Same as memorandums.
Signature Line: Key the doctor's medical title (M.D.) on the same line following his/her name.

Tables

Stationery: plain sheet, unless in body of letter or memorandum.
CV: center vertically.
CH: center horizontally.
Column Headings: blocked.
CS: determined by operator.
LS: DS below main, secondary, and column headings, and between items; in body of letter or memorandum, DS above and below table.

Reports--Medical and Nonmedical

Stationery: plain sheets.
PB: line 10 or line 12 (page 1); line 6 (other pages).
SM: 1″ unless "leftbound" is specified; then, 1½″ LM, 1″ RM.
LS: QS below main heading; DS elsewhere.
Enumerations: SS; DS between items; hang indent.
PE: at about line 60.

17d ▶ 17 Improve Keyboarding Technique

1. Key the lines once as shown: SS with a DS between 2-line groups.

2. Key the lines again at a faster pace.

Technique goals

- curved, upright fingers
- quiet hands and arms
- steady keystroking pace

q/z
1 zoo qt. zap quo zeal quay zone quit maze quad hazy
2 Zeno amazed us all on the quiz but quit the squad.

p/x
3 apt six rip fix pens flex open flax drop next harp
4 Lex is apt to fix apple pie for the next six days.

v/m
5 vim mam van dim have move vamp more dive time five
6 Riva drove them to the mall in my vivid lemon van.

easy sentences
7 Glen is to aid me with the work at the dog kennel.
8 Dodi is to go with the men to audit the six firms.

alphabet
9 Nigel saw a quick red fox jump over the lazy cubs.
10 Jacky can now give six big tips from the old quiz.

Lesson 18 CAPS LOCK and ? (Question Mark)

LL: 50
LS: SS

18a ▶ 8 Conditioning Practice

each line twice SS; then a 1′ writing on line 3; find *gwam:* total words keyed

alphabet 1 Lovak won the squad prize cup for sixty big jumps.
z/: 2 To: Ms. Mazie Pelzer; From: Dr. Eliza J. Piazzo.
easy sentence 3 He is to go with me to the dock to do work for us.

gwam 1′ | 1 | 2 | 3 | 4 | 5 | 6 | 7 | 8 | 9 | 10 |

18b ▶ 7 Key Block Paragraphs

Key each paragraph (¶) once as shown; DS between ¶s; then key the ¶s again at a faster pace.

If your teacher directs, take a 1′ writing on each ¶; find your rate in *gwam* (see page 30).

Paragraph 1 *gwam* 1′

The space bar is a vital tool, for every fifth or 10
sixth stroke is a space when you key. If you use 20
it with good form, it will aid you to build speed. 30

Paragraph 2

Just keep the thumb low over the space bar. Move 10
the thumb down and in quickly toward your palm to 20
get the prized stroke you need to build top skill. 30

gwam 1′ | 1 | 2 | 3 | 4 | 5 | 6 | 7 | 8 | 9 | 10 |

276b-279b (continued)

Document 7
List of Pending Cases

plain full sheet

Miss Lee has requested an updated list of cases that are pending. She will need this list tomorrow for the meeting of staff attorneys.

She has revised last week's list of pending cases (shown at the right). She has numbered the cases, putting them in alphabetical order for you. To save time, use blocked column headings.

Add a two-line main heading:

LIST OF PENDING CASES
JUNG JIN LEE

For the secondary heading, use **November 11, 19--.**

Arrange names in alphabetical order

	Client Name	~~Client Number~~ Case No.	Matter
6	Thomas P. Smothers	14,865	Divorce
	~~Watson & Watson, Inc.~~	~~16,521~~	~~Tax Planning~~
3	Bor-Rung Ousmane	15,313	Loan Closing
2	Follin, Follin & Guest, Inc.	15,989	Estate and Tax Planning
4	E. Jon and ~~Connie~~ Constance M. Qualles	15,231	House Closing
7	Jose F. Vinicki	13,775	Bankruptcy
1	Helga A. Fitz	15,128	Personal Injury
5	Simo Company, Inc.	15,001	Proof of Claim

Document 8
Acknowledgment of Signature by Notary Public

LP p. 161

Process the acknowledgment for Case No. 14,865. In the first paragraph, replace the blanks; insert client's name (from Document 7); insert the appropriate pronoun (her or his).

In the other paragraphs, key 1½" lines where indicated; the day and month will be written in by the notary public.

STATE OF CALIFORNIA

COUNTY OF ALAMEDA

Personally appeared before me, the undersigned authority in and for the jurisdiction aforesaid, the within named _______________, who being by me first duly sworn, states on _______________ oath that all facts and matters contained in the above complaint are true and correct as therein stated and that the complaint is not filed by collusion with the defendant.

Witness my signature this the _______________ day of _______________, 19--,

____
(INSERT NAME OF CLIENT)

SWORN TO and subscribed before me on this the _______________ day of _______________, 19--.

____
NOTARY PUBLIC

MY COMMISSION EXPIRES:

____

(SEAL)

18c ▶ 15 Learn CAPS LOCK and ? (Question Mark)

each line twice SS (slowly, then faster); DS between 2-line groups; if time permits, practice each line again

Depress the CAPS LOCK to key a series of capital letters.
To release the LOCK to key lowercase letters, strike LEFT or RIGHT SHIFT key on most typewriters; strike the LOCK again on most computers. Learn now how this is done on the equipment you are using.

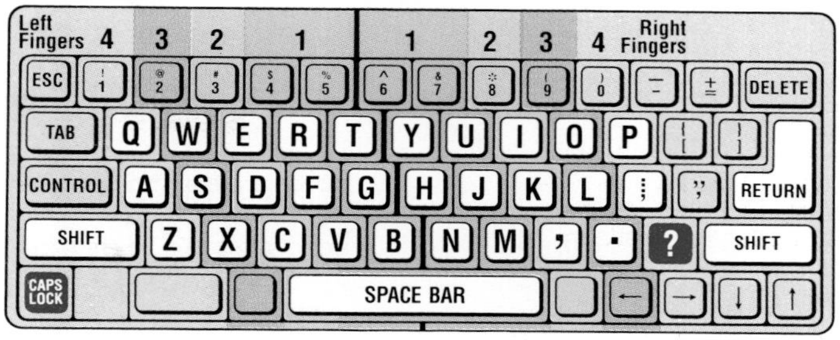

Reach technique for CAPS LOCK

Reach technique for **?** (question mark)

Left shift; reach *down* with *right little* finger; space twice after **?** at end of sentence.

Learn **CAPS LOCK**

```
1 Hal read PENTAGON and ADVISE AND CONSENT by Drury.
2 Oki joined FBLA when her sister joined PBL at OSU.
3 Zoe now belongs to AMS and DPE as well as to NBEA.
```

Learn **?** (question mark) — Space twice

```
4 ; ; ?; ?; Who?  What?  When?  Where?  Why?  Is it?
5 Who is it?  Is it she?  Did he go?  Was she there?
6 Is it up to me?  When is it?  Did he key the line?
```

18d ▶ 20 Improve Keyboarding Technique

1. Key the lines once as shown: SS with a DS between 2-line groups.

2. Key the lines again at a faster pace.

3. If time permits, take a 1′ writing on line 11 and then on line 12; find *gwam*.

Technique goals

- reach *up* without moving hands away from you
- reach *down* without moving hands toward your body
- use CAPS LOCK to make ALL CAPS

Goal: finger-action keystrokes; quiet hands and arms

```
CAPS LOCK/?     1 Did she join OEA?  Did she also join PSI and DECA?
                2 Do you know the ARMA rules?  Are they used by TVA?

z/v             3 Zahn, key these words:  vim, zip, via, zoom, vote.
                4 Veloz gave a zany party for Van and Roz in La Paz.

q/p             5 Paul put a quick quiz on top of the quaint podium.
                6 Jacqi may pick a pink pique suit of a unique silk.

key words       7 they quiz pick code next just more bone wove flags
                8 name jack flax plug quit zinc wore busy vine third

key phrases     9 to fix it|is to pay|to aid us|or to cut|apt to own
               10 is on the|if we did|to be fit|to my pay|due at six

alphabet       11 Lock may join the squad if we have six big prizes.
easy sentence  12 I am apt to go to the lake dock to sign the forms.

gwam 1′  | 1 | 2 | 3 | 4 | 5 | 6 | 7 | 8 | 9 | 10 |
```

To find 1′ *gwam*: Add 10 for each line you completed to the scale figure beneath the point at which you stopped in a partial line. The total is your 1′ *gwam*.

5. The said ingestion of Kwell lotion by the ward and resulting injuries to the ward were ~~was~~ a direct and proximate result of the gross negligence of the Tseng Pharmacy, Inc., its agents and employees, in the following particulars:

A. By failing to ~~properly~~ dispense medication ~~pursuant~~ according to a prescription therefor;

C ~~B~~. By ~~negligently~~ substituting a toxic substance for the prescribed medicine with total disregard for the consequences of its use by a ~~small~~ child.

B ~~C~~. By failing to properly label medication;

6. As a direct and proximate result of the negligence of defendant, its agents and employees aforedescribed, plaintiff's ward was painfully and seriously injured. Injuries sustained by plaintiff's ward include, but are not limited to, burns and blisters of the face, lips, mouth, and tongue. Likewise, as a result, plaintiff's ward was severely nauseated for an extended period of time and required treatment not only for nausea and the burns and blisters but also for the internal effects of ingestion of Kwell lotion. All of said injuries are the direct and proximate result of the negligence of the said defendant.

WHEREFORE, PREMISES CONSIDERED, plaintiff demands judgment of and against said defendant in such amount sufficient to compensate plaintiff's ward for all losses and damages sustained by ward, which amount is in excess of the minimum jurisdiction limitations of the Circuit Courts of the State of California, together with costs of court.

~~Respectfully~~ Submitted by,

Begin the closing lines at the center of the line of writing. Below Submitted by, QS and key a blank line for the signature; SS and key the following:

Kelly Q. Janqusek
Attorney for Plaintiff

Lesson 19 Tabulator

LL: 50
LS: SS

19a ▶ 8 Conditioning Practice

each line twice SS; then a 1′ writing on line 3; find *gwam:* total words keyed

On most typewriters: Comma and **period** as well as **colon** and **question mark** can be keyed when the CAPS LOCK is on.

On most computers: CAPS LOCK affects only the letter keys; shifted punctuation marks require the use of one of the SHIFT keys.

alphabet 1 Zosha was quick to dive into my big pool for Jinx.

CAPS LOCK 2 Type these ZIP Codes: OR, MD, RI, NV, AL, and PA.

easy sentence 3 Ian kept a pen and work forms handy for all of us.

gwam 1′ | 1 | 2 | 3 | 4 | 5 | 6 | 7 | 8 | 9 | 10 |

19b ▶ 12 Learn Tabulator

TYPEWRITERS

To clear electric tabs:

1. Move print element to *extreme* right using SPACE BAR or TAB key.

2. Hold CLEAR key down as you return print element to *extreme* left to remove all tab stops.

To clear electronic tabs:

1. Strike TAB key to move print element to the tab stop you want to clear.

2. Depress the TAB CLEAR key to remove the stop.

3. To remove all stops, depress TAB CLEAR key, then REPEAT key.

To set tab stops (all machines):

1. Move print element to desired tab position by striking SPACE BAR or BACKSPACE key.

2. Depress TAB SET key. Repeat procedure for each stop needed.

Tabulating procedure:

Strike the TAB key with the closest little finger; release it quickly and return the finger to home-key position.

COMPUTERS

Most computer programs have preset (default) tabs as shown in the following tab line:

----T ----T---- T---- T ----T---- T
5 10 15 20 25 30

Procedures for removing default tabs and setting tab stops vary. Use the Operator's Manual for your equipment/software to learn proper procedures.

Drill procedure:

1. Clear all tab stops, as directed above.

2. Set a tab stop 5 spaces to the right of left margin stop.

3. Set the LINE-SPACE SELECTOR on "2" for DS.

4. Key the paragraphs (¶s) once DS as shown, indenting the first line of each ¶.

Tab ⟶ The tab key is used to indent blocks of copy such as these.

Tab ⟶ It should also be used for tables to arrange data quickly and neatly into columns.

Tab ⟶ Learn now to use the tab key by touch; doing so will add to your keying skill.

276b-279b (continued)

Document 6
Complaint--Personal Injury

plain full sheets

Kelly Q. Janqusek spoke recently with a new client, Helga A. Fitz, who is the guardian of James P. Cox. Ms. Janqusek will file a complaint against Tseng Pharmacy (defendant) in **Alameda** County circuit court for Mrs. Fitz on behalf of her ward, James P. Cox.

Although the complaint cannot be finalized until additional information is received from the attending physician at Alameda County Hospital, Ms. Janqusek requests that you prepare a first draft on plain paper for her review.

The case (No. **15,219**) is styled as follows: **HELGA A. FITZ** (PLAINTIFF) V. **TSENG PHARMACY, INC.** (DEFENDANT). Do not key the underlines; simply insert the appropriate information in the blanks.

IN THE CIRCUIT COURT OF ________________ COUNTY

STATE OF CALIFORNIA

________________, GUARDIAN OF THE ESTATE PLAINTIFF

V. NO. ________________

________________ DEFENDANT

COMPLAINT

Comes now ________________, guardian of the estate of ________________, unmarried minor, plaintiff in the above styled and numbered cause, by and through her attorneys of record, and files this complaint against ________________, defendant and for cause of action would show unto the Court the following facts, to-wit:

1. Plaintiff is an adult resident citizen of ________________ County, California, and is the duly appointed and acting guardian of the estate of ________________, an unmarried minor and present citizen of ________________ County, California. Plaintiff was duly appointed guardian of the estate of her ward by a decree of the Chancery Court of ________________ County, California.

2. ________________ is a corporation, organized and existing under the laws of the State of California, and whose registered agent for service of process is Victoria P. Lane, 1305 Franklin Street, Oakland, CA 94612-2033.

3. On or about January 13, 19-- plaintiff's ward had a cold and was treated by his personal physician, Dr. Emily Long. Dr. Long prescribed medication that was filled by Tseng Pharmacy, Inc. The plaintiff administered the prescription to the ward. Immediately the ward began to vomit and heave.

4. Approximately 30 minutes thereafter, an agent or employee of Tseng Pharmacy, Inc., appeared at plaintiff's residence and took afore said prescription, presented another bottle of medicine, and told her to take the ward to the emergency room. The ward had ingested Kwell Lotion, a toxin not intended for internal use. Plaintiff immediately took her ward to the emergency room of Alameda Hospital where he was treated.

(continued, p. 469)

19c ▶ 10 Improve Keyboarding Technique

each pair of lines twice SS; DS between 4-line groups

Lines 1-2

1. Clear tab stops; then, beginning at left margin, set a tab stop every 9 spaces until you have set 5 tab stops.

2. Key the first word in Column 1; tab to Column 2 and key the first word in that column, and so on. There will be 5 blank spaces between the columns.

tabulator

1 coal Tab turn Tab they Tab paid Tab worn Tab right
2 them kept fuel corn dual their

shift-key sentences

3 The best dancers are: Ana and Jose; Mag and Boyd.
4 Did Ms. Paxon send us the letter from Dr. LaRonde?

CAPS LOCK

5 Masami saw the game on ESPN; Krista saw it on NBC.
6 The AMS meeting is on Tuesday; the DPE, on Friday.

19d ▶ 14 Build Keyboarding Speed

1. Key each pair of lines once as shown: SS with a DS between pairs.

2. Take a 1′ writing on each of lines 5-8; find *gwam* on each writing. (1′ *gwam* = total 5-stroke words keyed.)

3. If time permits, take another 1′ writing on line 7 and line 8 to improve speed.

Goal: At least 21 *gwam*.

Key words and phrases (*Think, say,* and *key* words and phrases.)

1 ad my we in be on at up as no are him was you gets
2 girl quay turn rush duty down maps rich laid spend

3 an ad|to fix|an oak|to get|the zoo|via jet|in turn
4 if they|to risk|by them|the duty|and paid|she kept

Key easy sentences (Key the words at a brisk, steady pace.)

5 He is to aid the girls with the work if they wish.
6 Jan may go to the city for the bid forms for them.

7 He may go to the lake by dusk to do the dock work.
8 I did all the work for the firm for the usual pay.

gwam 1′ | 1 | 2 | 3 | 4 | 5 | 6 | 7 | 8 | 9 | 10 |

19e ▶ 6 Check Keyboarding Skill

1. Clear tab stops and set a new stop 5 spaces to the right of the left margin.

2. Set your equipment to DS the lines of the paragraphs (¶s).

3. Key each ¶ once DS as shown.

4. Take a 1′ writing on each ¶; find *gwam* on each writing. (1′ *gwam* = figure above the last word keyed.)

Key easy paragraphs containing all letters

. 2 . 4 . 6 . 8 .
¶ 1 Good form means to move with speed and quiet
10 . 12 . 14 . 16 . 18 .
control. My next step will be to size up the job
20 . 22 . 24 . 26 . 28
and to do the work in the right way each day.

. 2 . 4 . 6 . 8 .
¶ 2 To reach my goal of top speed, I have to try
10 . 12 . 14 . 16 . 18 .
to build good form. I will try for the right key
20 . 22 . 24 . 26 . 28
each time, but I must do so in the right way.

276b-279b (continued)

Document 4
Labor and Materials Statement

plain full sheet

Mr. Gonzales' client, Mr. Sims, gave him this copy of Exhibit A, which will be attached to the Proof of Claim (Document 3). This table provides supporting evidence in the Sims case.

1. Verify the accuracy of amounts in the last column (for example, for the first item, multiply 20 × 40.00) and make needed corrections.
2. Verify the accuracy of the total.
3. Process the table DS.

Labor and Materials Statement
For Overton Inn, Ltd.
September 1, 19--

Description	Unit Cost	Total
Labor, 20 hours	$ 40.00	$ 800.00
Carpet, 450 sq. yd.	18.99	8,545.50
Padding, 450 sq. yd.	1.00	45.00
3/4" molding, 500 ft.	.75	375.00
Paneling, 5 sheets	18.00	90.00
Nails, 2 lbs.	1.73	34.60
Paint, 15 gallons	19.59	293.85
Total		$10,557.81

Document 5
Form Letters

LP pp. 157-159

I need to have this form letter processed for my signature, **Jose B. Arias, Office Manager.** I drafted the message hurriedly, so you may need to correct errors in spelling and grammar. Use the date, addresses, and variables (V) listed below.

November 10, 19--

Mr. J. K. Randall
Randall Cablevision, Inc.
One Westwood Court
Oakland, CA 94611-2788
V1: **two years**
V2: **Subchapter S Corporation**
V3: **Mr. Randall**
V4: **Randall Cablevision, Inc.**

Mrs. Carmen G. Anglin
Cottage Crafters, Ltd.
1624 Jackson Street
Oakland, CA 94612-3205
V1: **year**
V2: **partnership**
V3: **Mrs. Anglin**
V4: **Cottage Crafters, Ltd.**

The professional staff at Bayview Legal Services, Inc., feels priviledged to have ~~had the opportunity to~~ provide[d] legal services to your organization [for the past (V1)] ~~this year~~. Our top priority have been to provide up-to-date, ~~timely~~ information as a basis for accurate advise about your [(V2)] ~~(type of organization)~~.

In anticipation of our continuing this business relationship, I have enclosed a proposal for next years retainer of legal services. Bayview would like to serve your legal needs in the ~~coming year~~ [~~future~~ stet]. To better serve you we have implemented a sophisticated telecommunication system, which will be in place ~~January 1~~ [stet] [~~by the first of next month~~]. Also, each member of our staff is committed to serving you in the most professional and competent manner.

[(V3)] ~~(Title and last name)~~, please consider our proposal carefully and call me at 555-3129 to discuss continuing our legal service to [(V4)] ~~(name of company)~~.

20a ▶ 8 Conditioning Practice

each line twice SS; then a 1′ writing on line 3; find *gwam*

alphabet 1 Quig just fixed prize vases he won at my key club.

spacing 2 Marcia works for HMS, Inc.; Juanita, for XYZ Corp.

easy sentence 3 Su did vow to rid the town of the giant male duck.

gwam 1′ | 1 | 2 | 3 | 4 | 5 | 6 | 7 | 8 | 9 | 10 |

20b ▶ 20 Check/Improve Keyboarding Technique

each line once SS; if time permits, key each line again at a faster pace

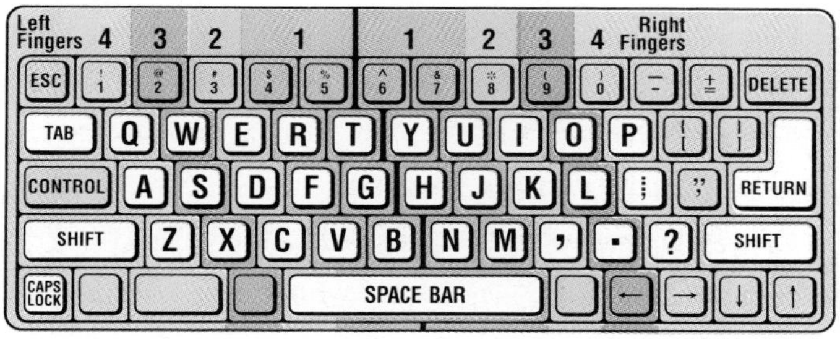

Ask your teacher to check your keyboarding technique as you key the following lines.

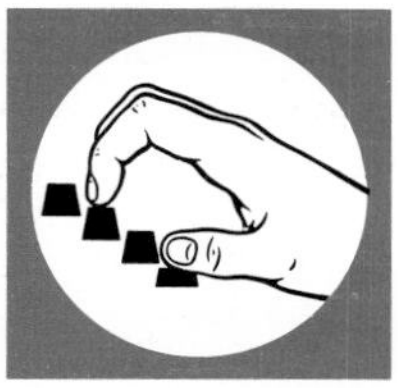

Fingers curved

Reach review (Keep on home row the fingers not used for reaching.)

1 old led kit six jay oft zap cod big laws five ribs

2 pro quo | is just | my firm | was then | may grow | must try

3 Olga sews aqua and red silk to make six big kites.

Fingers upright

Space-bar emphasis (*Think, say,* and *key* the words.)

4 en am an by ham fan buy jam pay may form span corn

5 I am | a man | an elm | by any | buy ham | can plan | try them

6 I am to form a plan to buy a firm in the old town.

Finger-action keystroking

Shift-key emphasis (Reach *up* and reach *down* without moving the hands.)

7 Jan and I are to see Ms. Han. May Lana come, too?

8 Bob Epps lives in Rome; Vic Copa is in Rome, also.

9 Oates and Co. has a branch office in Boise, Idaho.

Down-and-in spacing

Easy sentences (*Think, say,* and *key* the words at a steady pace.)

10 Eight of the girls may go to the social with them.

11 Corla is to work with us to fix the big dock sign.

12 Keith is to pay the six men for the work they did.

gwam 1′ | 1 | 2 | 3 | 4 | 5 | 6 | 7 | 8 | 9 | 10 |

20c ▶ 6 Think as You Key

Key each line once SS. In place of the blank line at the end of each sentence, key the word that correctly completes the adage.

1 All that glitters is not ______.

2 Do not cry over spilt ______.

3 A friend in need is a friend ______.

4 A new broom always sweeps ______.

5 A penny saved is a penny ______.

Document 3
Proo, of Claim

LP pp. 153-155

Using the information provided below by Joseph W. Gonzalez, the attorney handling the case, process a Proof of Claim for the Sims case. Format and key the Proof of Claim given at the right, replacing the details with Mr. Gonzelez' information.

RE: OVERTON INN, LTD.
A PARTNERSHIP COMPOSED OF
STEPHEN P. GODDARD
GENERAL MANAGER
NO. 15,001

Changes in ¶s:

¶1: **Matthew K. Sims, who resides at 901 Fairhaven Way, Oakland, CA 94947-3366, is President of Sims Company, Inc.**

¶2: **sum of ten thousand five hundred fifty-seven and 81/100 dollars ($10,557.81).**

¶3: **labor performed and materials furnished to the Overton Inn, Ltd., renovation project.**

Special Notes:
Place the dateline a QS below the last line of the document. The dateline should be 1½" long. Use the Sims company name and replace the name under the By line. Key the "penalty" ¶ as shown.

IN THE UNITED STATES BANKRUPTCY COURT

NORTHERN DISTRICT OF CALIFORNIA

IN RE: RESEARCH TECHNOLOGY, INC.
A LIMITED PARTNERSHIP COMPOSED OF
SANDRA F. GIACHELLI
GENERAL PARTNER NO. ~~88-0013702 BKS-EEL~~

PROOF OF CLAIM

DS the #s

1. The undersigned, ~~Howard D. Delk, who resides at 5302 Estates Drive, Oakland, CA 94618-4172,~~ is President of ~~Innovative Software, Inc.~~, a corporation organized under the laws of the State of California, with its principal place of business in Oakland, California, and is duly authorized to make this Proof of Claim on behalf of said corporation.

2. The debtor was at the time of the filing of the petition initiating this case, and is still indebted to this claimant in the ~~sum of ($12,331.99)~~.

3. The consideration for this debt is as follows: ~~licensed software and 40 hours of support supplied to Research Technology, Inc.~~

4. A true and correct copy of the statement of account upon which this claim is founded is attached hereto as Exhibit A.

5. No judgment has been rendered on the claim of ~~Innovative Software, Inc.~~

6. The amount of all payments on this claim has been credited and deducted for the purpose of making this proof of claim.

7. This claim is not subject to any set off or counterclaim.

8. This claim is a general unsecured claim except to the extent that a lien, if any, described herein is sufficient to satisfy the claim.

Dated: ________________

INNOVATIVE SOFTWARE, INC.

BY: ______________________________
HOWARD ~~D.~~ DELK, PRESIDENT

PENALTY FOR PRESENTING FRAUDULENT CLAIM: FINE OF NOT MORE THAN $5,000.00 OR IMPRISONMENT FOR NOT MORE THAN FIVE YEARS, OR BOTH. TITLE 18 USC. SECTION 152.

20d ▶ 7 Check/Improve Keyboarding Speed

1. Take a 30-second (30″) timed writing on each line. Your rate in *gwam* is shown word-for-word above the lines.

2. If time permits, take another 30″ writing on each line. Try to increase your keyboarding speed.

Goal: At least 22 *gwam*.

30″ gwam

```
    2    4    6    8    10    12    14    16    18    20    22
1 He bid for the rich lake land.
2 Suzy may fish off the dock with us.
3 Pay the girls for all the work they did.
4 Quen is due by six and may then fix the sign.
5 Janie is to vie with six girls for the city title.
6 Duane is to go to the lake to fix the auto for the man.
    2    4    6    8    10    12    14    16    18    20    22
```

If you finish a line before time is called and start over, your *gwam* is the figure at the end of the line PLUS the figure above or below the point at which you stopped.

20e ▶ 9 Check/Improve Keyboarding Speed

1. Take a 1′ writing on each paragraph (¶); find *gwam* on each writing.

2. Using your better *gwam* as a base rate, select a *goal rate* and take two 1′ guided writings on each ¶ as directed at the bottom of the page.

Copy used to measure skill is triple-controlled for difficulty:
E = easy HA = high average
LA = low average D = difficult
A = average

Difficulty index (shown above copy)

E	1.2 si	5.1 awl	90% hfw
	1 Syllable intensity	2 Average word length	3 High-frequency words

Difficulty index

all letters used | E | 1.2 si | 5.1 awl | 90% hfw |

```
              .    2    .    4    .    6    .    8    .
Tab     How you key is just as vital as the copy you
   10   .   12   .   14   .   16   .   18   .
work from or produce.  What you put on paper is a
   20   .   22   .   24   .   26   .   28   .
direct result of the way in which you do the job.
              .    2    .    4    .    6    .    8    .
Tab     If you expect to grow quickly in speed, take
   10   .   12   .   14   .   16   .   18   .
charge of your mind.  It will then tell your eyes
   20   .   22   .   24   .   26   .   28   .
and hands how to work through the maze of letters.
```

Guided (Paced) Writing Procedure

Select a practice goal

1. Take a 1′ writing on ¶ 1 of a set of ¶s that contain superior figures for guided writings, as in 20e above.

2. Using the *gwam* as a base, add 4 *gwam* to determine your goal rate.

3. Choose from Column 1 of the table at the right the speed nearest your goal rate. At the right of that speed, note the 1/4′ points in the copy you must reach to maintain your goal rate.

Quarter-minute checkpoints

gwam	1/4′	1/2′	3/4′	Time
16	4	8	12	16
20	5	10	15	20
24	6	12	18	24
28	7	14	21	28
32	8	16	24	32
36	9	18	27	36
40	10	20	30	40

4. Note from the word-count dots and figures above the lines in ¶ 1 the checkpoint for each quarter minute. (Example: Checkpoints for 24 *gwam* are 6, 12, 18, and 24.)

Practice procedure

1. Take two 1′ writings on ¶ 1 at your goal rate guided by the quarter-minute calls (1/4, 1/2, 3/4, time).

Goal: To reach each of your checkpoints just as the guide is called.

2. Take two 1′ writings on ¶ 2 of a set of ¶s in the same way.

3. If time permits, take a 2′ writing on the set of ¶s combined, without the guides.

Speed level of practice

When the purpose of practice is to reach out into new speed areas, use the *speed* level. Take the brakes off your fingers and experiment with new stroking patterns and new speeds. Do this by:

1. Reading 2 or 3 letters ahead of your keying to foresee stroking patterns.

2. Getting the fingers ready for the combinations of letters to be keyed.

3. Keeping your eyes on the copy in the book.

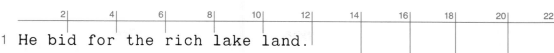

276a-279a ▶ 5 (daily)

Equipment Check

each line twice SS; DS between 2-line groups

alphabet 1 Dez will have to get a jet flight back to Rio to my unique exposition.

figures 2 At 6:30 p.m. on June 27, 1991, 458 guests attended the garden wedding.

fig/sym 3 A May 5, 1992, sales increase of $7,068 (43%) was praised by everyone.

speed 4 The girl paid a visit to the downtown auto firm to sign the work form.

| 1 | 2 | 3 | 4 | 5 | 6 | 7 | 8 | 9 | 10 | 11 | 12 | 13 | 14 |

276b-279b ▶ 45 (daily)

Document Processing

Mr. Jose B. Arias, the office manager, hands you a series of eight documents to be formatted and keyed. Using the notes given with each document, process as many documents as you can in each work session. Proofread and correct each document before removing it from your machine or printing a copy. Be alert for any unmarked errors that need to be corrected.

Document 1
Letter

LP. 151

Process, for **Miss Jung Jin Lee's** signature, the letter at the right. Miss Lee's title is **Attorney-at-Law.**

Date: **November 8, 19--**

Letter address:
The Honorable S. Troy Adams
Judge of the Chancery Court
Oakland Courthouse
1225 Fallon Street
Oakland, CA 94612-1038

Reference line:
RE: Chancery Court #169008

Salutation:
Dear Judge Adams

Subject line:
Jordan v. Jordan

The case ~~shown~~ above is ready for trail. I have discussed court dates with the attorney of the other party, and we have agreed that both parties can be available for a court appearance on November 28 or 30 or December 5, 8, or 15.

If you are ~~un~~avilable on anyone of these dates, let us know. Then we can make final plans to appear in your court on that date.

Judge Adams, you should be aware of an important problem. The parties have been unable to agree on child custody arangements. Mr. Jordan is considering relocating in Pittsburgh; therefor, weekend visitation rights would not be possible. We hope to reach an agreement before appearing in court.

We look forsward to recieving confirmation of one of these suggested dates.

Document 2
Memo

plain full sheet

I want the memo addressed to **All Attorneys and Paralegal Staff.** Use **November 8, 19--** as the date. Supply a subject line. Use my name, **Jose B. Arias,** as the writer of the memo.

A staff meeting for attorneys and para legal staff will be held on Friday, november 12, at 10 a.m. in Conference Room C.

Withe the implimentation of the new telecomunication system in our office we must develop procedures that will continue to safeguard confidential information. In preparation for this meeting on Friday, please review the enclosed draft of new procedures concerning record protection. These new procedures will supersede procedures currently printed in the <u>Office Procedures Manual</u>.

During the past years Bayview has ~~earned~~ an outstanding reputation for confidential handling of legal services. Our clients continue to depend upon us to keep their private matters in confidence. If we are to maintain our reputation problems of confidentiality must be a major concern. I look forward to your contributions at this meeting ~~on Friday~~.

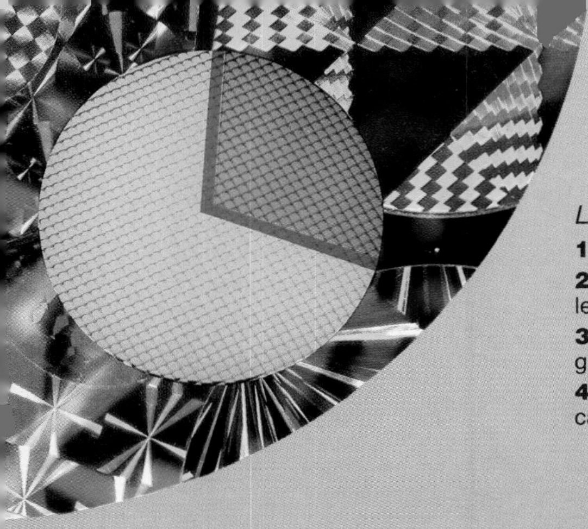

UNIT 2 LESSONS 21 – 25

Improve Keyboarding/Language Skills

Learning Goals

1. To improve keyboarding technique.

2. To improve control of letter reaches and letter combinations.

3. To improve speed on sentence and paragraph copy.

4. To review and improve language skills: capitalization.

Format Guides

1. ***Paper Guide*** at *0* (for typewriters)

2. Line length (LL): 50 spaces; see *Get Ready to Keyboard: Typewriters* (p. x) or *Computers* (p. xii).

3. Line spacing (LS): Single-space (SS) drills; double-space (DS) paragraphs (¶s).

4. Paragraph indention (PI): 5 spaces when appropriate.

Lesson 21 *Keyboarding/Language Skills*

LL: 50
LS: SS

21a ▶ 6 Conditioning Practice

each line twice SS; then a 1′ writing on line 3; find *gwam*

alphabet	1	Nat will vex the judge if she bucks my quiz group.
punctuation	2	Al, did you use these words: vie, zeal, and aqua?
easy sentence	3	She owns the big dock, but they own the lake land.

gwam 1′ | 1 | 2 | 3 | 4 | 5 | 6 | 7 | 8 | 9 | 10 |

21b ▶ 22 Improve Keyboarding Technique

1. Key the lines once as shown: SS with a DS between 2-line groups.

2. If time permits, key the lines again to improve keying ease and speed.

Technique goals

- fingers deeply curved and upright
- eyes on copy
- finger-action keystrokes
- hands and arms quiet, almost motionless

Reach review

ed/de	1	ed de led ode need made used side vied slide guide
	2	Ned said the guide used a video film for her talk.
ju/ft	3	ju ft jug oft jet aft jug lift just soft jury loft
	4	Judy left fifty jugs of juice on a raft as a gift.
ol/lo	5	ol lo old lot lob lox log sold loan fold long told
	6	Lou told me that her local school loans old books.
ws/sw	7	ws sw was saw laws rows cows vows swam sways swing
	8	Swin swims at my swim club and shows no big flaws.
ik/ki	9	ik ki kit ski kin kid kip bike kick like kiwi hike
	10	The kid can hike or ride his bike to the ski lake.
za/az	11	za az zap adz haze zany lazy jazz hazy maze pizzas
	12	A zany jazz band played with pizzazz at the plaza.
alphabet	13	Olive Fenz packed my bag with six quarts of juice.
	14	Jud aims next to play a quick game with Bev Fritz.

gwam 1′ | 1 | 2 | 3 | 4 | 5 | 6 | 7 | 8 | 9 | 10 |

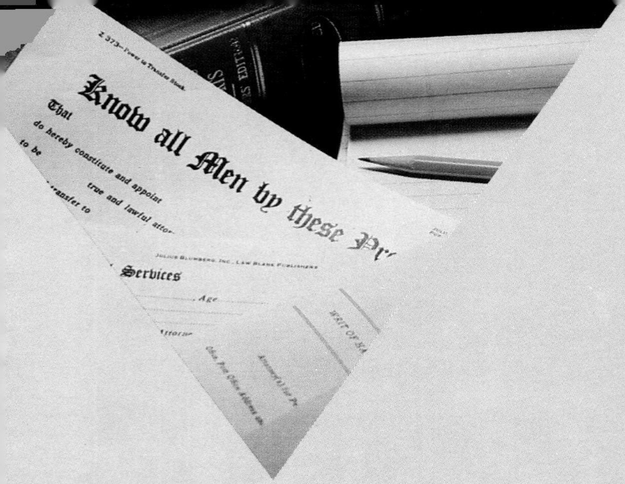

UNIT 66 *LESSONS 276 – 279*

Bayview Legal Services, Inc. (A Legal Office Simulation)

Production Goals

1. To prepare, in an acceptable form with all errors corrected, documents processed in a legal office.
2. To improve your document processing skills by keying from rough-draft and script source documents.
3. To improve proofreading skills by detecting and correcting errors.

Documents Processed

1. Block format letter
2. Simplified memo
3. Proof of Claim
4. Tables
5. Form letter with variables
6. Complaint
7. Acknowledgment of Signature

BAYVIEW LEGAL SERVICES, INC. (A Legal Office Simulation)

Before you begin the work of this simulation, read the introductory material and study the Format Guides for Legal Documents, Letters, Memos, and Tables at the right.

Your first temporary work assignment is in the office of Bayview Legal Services, Inc., 1540 San Pablo Avenue, Oakland, CA 94612-9475. Bayview consists of a group of five attorneys and a paralegal staff who share an on-site information processing center (IPC). Your position is in Bayview's IPC, preparing a variety of documents for the office manager, Jose B. Arias, and three attorneys: Miss Lee, Mr. Gonzalez, and Ms. Janqusek.

This legal firm is committed to following standard operating procedures. Its personnel have found that the organization is more effective when everyone follows these procedures. Therefore, review carefully the following guidelines taken from the Office Procedures Manual of Bayview Legal Services, Inc. If a formatting guide is not given, use your previously acquired knowledge to decide the format features for a document.

Accuracy

To serve the intended purpose, a legal document must be free of errors. In particular, the names of people and places and all figures must appear without error or obvious correction. Correct any errors made by the originator of a document; check spelling, punctuation, and grammar (a court case may rest on a misplaced comma).

Stationery

Legal documents and interoffice memos should be prepared on 8½″ × 11″ paper. (If ruled paper is to be used, it will be specified.) Letters are processed on the firm's letterhead.

Format Guides for Legal Documents

Margins. Each page should have a left margin of 1½″ and a right margin of ½″. On ruled paper, set the left margin 2 spaces to the right of the double rule; set the right margin 3-5 spaces to the left of the single rule. The standard page beginning (PB) is line 12; the bottom margin (BM) may be 1″ to 2″. (At least two lines of the body of a document must appear on the same page as the signatures.)

Titles. The title of a legal document (example, PROOF OF CLAIM) is keyed in all capital letters. A single line that extends from margin to margin is keyed above and below the title of the document. (See model below.)

```
                 IN THE UNITED STATES BANKRUPTCY COURT
                   NORTHERN DISTRICT OF CALIFORNIA
IN RE:  OVERTON, INN, LTD.
        A PARTNERSHIP COMPOSED OF
        STEPHEN P. GODDARD
        GENERAL MANAGER                        NO.  88-0026500-EEL  SS
__________________________________________________________________  DS
                          PROOF OF CLAIM                            SS
__________________________________________________________________  DS
          1.  The undersigned, Matthew K. Sims, who resides at
```

Paragraph indention and spacing. Paragraphs should be indented 10 spaces. The body of a legal document, including numbered paragraphs, generally should be double-spaced.

Page numbers. A page number should be centered at the bottom of each page, including the first, a DS below the last line of text and preceded and followed by a hyphen (example, -2-).

Signature lines. Lines for signatures should be about 3″ long. When more than one signature is needed, DS between the lines.

Format Guides for Letters, Memos, and Tables

Letters. Prepare letters in block format with open punctuation. Use 1½″ side margins and begin approximately a DS below the letterhead. If a letter is about a client's case, key a reference line a DS above the salutation and a subject line a DS below the salutation. For the reference line, key RE: followed by the court case number. For the subject line, key the case "style"; that is, the name of the case (example, Humphrey v. Gow). For the complimentary close, use Sincerely yours.

Memos. Prepare interoffice memos in simplified format. Omit all titles with recipients' and senders' names.

Tables. DS tables on plain full sheets, centered vertically and horizontally with 6-10 spaces between columns.

21c ▶ 12
Check/Improve Keyboarding Speed

1. Take one 1' timed writing and two 1' *guided* writings on ¶ 1 as directed on page 38.

2. Take one 1' timed writing and two 1' *guided* writings on ¶ 2 in the same way.

3. As time permits, take one or two 2' timed writings on ¶s 1 and 2 combined *without* the call of the guide; find *gwam*.

1' gwam goals

▽ 17 = acceptable
⊡ 21 = average
⊙ 25 = good
◇ 29 = excellent

all letters used | E | 1.2 si | 5.1 awl | 90% hfw

gwam 2'

| . 2 . 4 . 6 . 8
Keep in home position all of the fingers not 5
| 10 . 12 . 14 . 16 ▽ 18 .
being used to strike a key. Do not let them move 10
| 20 ⊡ 22 . 24 ⊙ 26 . 28 ◇
out of position for the next letters in your copy. 15
| . 2 . 4 . 6 . 8
Prize the control you have over the fingers. 19
| 10 . 12 . 14 . 16 ▽ 18 .
See how quickly speed goes up when you learn that 24
| 20 ⊡ 22 . 24 ⊙ 26 . 28 ◇
you can make them do just what you expect of them. 29

gwam 2' | 1 | 2 | 3 | 4 | 5 |

21d ▶ 10 Improve Language Skills: Capitalization

1. Read the first rule highlighted in color at the right.

2. Key the **Learn** sentence below it, noting how the rule has been applied.

3. Key the **Apply** sentence, supplying the needed capital letters.

4. Read and practice the other rules in the same way.

5. If time permits, key the three **Apply** sentences again to increase decision-making speed.

Capitalize the first word in a sentence.

Learn 1 Mindy left her coat here. Can she stop by for it?
Apply 2 do you plan to go today? the game begins at four.

Capitalize personal titles and names of people.

Learn 3 I wrote to Mr. Katz, but Miss Dixon sent the form.
Apply 4 do you know if luci and lex bauer are with dr. tu?

Capitalize names of clubs, schools, organizations, and companies.

Learn 5 The Beau Monde Singers will perform at Music Hall.
Apply 6 lennox corp. now owns the hyde park athletic club.

| Lesson 22 | Keyboarding/Language Skills | LL: 50 LS: SS |

22a ▶ 6
Conditioning Practice

each line twice SS; then a 1' writing on line 3; find *gwam*

alphabet 1 Wusov amazed them by jumping quickly from the box.
spacing 2 am to|is an|by it|of us|an oak|is to pay|it is due
easy 3 It is right for the man to aid them with the sign.

gwam 1' | 1 | 2 | 3 | 4 | 5 | 6 | 7 | 8 | 9 | 10 |

22b ▶ 12
Check/Improve Keyboarding Speed

1. Take one 1' timed writing and two 1' *guided* writings on ¶ 1 of 21c, above, as directed at the bottom of page 38.

2. Key ¶ 2 of 21c, above, in the same way.
Goal: To increase speed.

3. As time permits, take one or two 2' timed writings on ¶s 1 and 2 combined; find *gwam*.

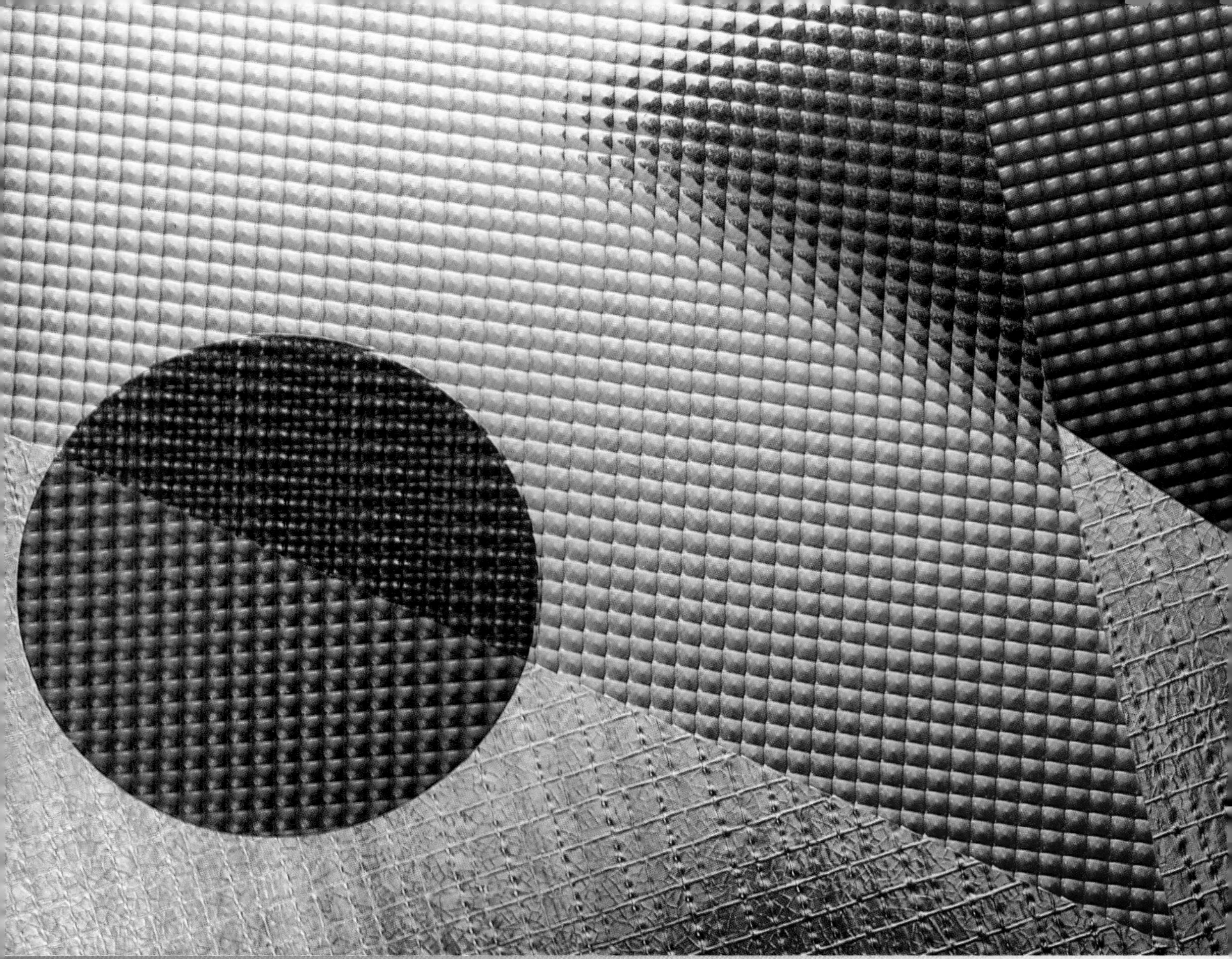

LESSONS 276 – 300

PHASE 12

CAL-TEMP OFFICE AIDS, INC., PROFESSIONAL OFFICE SITUATIONS

You have opted for employment with Cal-Temp Office Aids, Inc., a temporary service agency in Oakland, California. As a Cal-Temp employee, you will be assigned to several professional offices in the San Francisco Bay area, including Bayview Legal Services, Inc., in Oakland; Gateway Medical Center in San Francisco; Regency Accounting Services, Inc., in Daly City; and Golden Gate Travel, Inc., in Berkeley.

As you move from one office to another, your position title will change; but in each office your primary duty will be to process the documents. Mostly, you will process the types of documents that are familiar to you--letters, reports, memos, tables, forms, etc. You also will prepare documents peculiar to the professions represented; at first, these types of documents may be unfamiliar to you.

Naturally, you will need to apply the language skills you have learned in school and on previous jobs; plus you will continue to polish and assess these skills by using special drills at home between your job assignments. The specialized vocabulary of each profession adds a new area of language-skill development.

No two offices anywhere are exactly alike. As a Cal-Temp employee, you will be challenged to become more self-reliant in adapting to differences and changes--a valuable trait not only in simulated work settings, but, especially, in *real* ones.

22c ▶ 20 *Improve Keyboarding Technique: Response Patterns*

1. Key each pair of lines twice SS; DS between 4-line groups.

2. Take a 1′ writing on line 10 and then on line 12; find *gwam* (total words keyed) on each writing.

3. Take another 1′ writing on the slower line to increase your speed on more difficult copy.

PRACTICE HINTS

Balanced-hand lines: *Think, say,* and *key* the words by word response at a fast pace.

One-hand lines: *Think, say,* and *key* the words by letter response at a steady but unhurried pace.

Letter response
Many one-hand words (as in lines 3-4) are not easy to key. Such words may be keyed letter-by-letter and with continuity (steadily, without pauses).

Word response
Short, balanced-hand words (as in lines 1-2) are so easy to key that they can be keyed as words, not letter-by-letter. Think and key them at your top speed.

balanced-hand words	1	ah do so go he us if is of or to it an am me by ox
	2	ha for did own the for and due pay but men may box
one-hand words	3	as up we in at on be oh ax no ex my ad was you are
	4	ad ink get ilk far him few pop set pin far imp car
balanced-hand phrases	5	of it|he is|to us|or do|am to|an ox|or by|is to do
	6	do the|and for|she did|all six|the map|for the pay
one-hand phrases	7	as on|be in|at no|as my|be up|as in|at him|saw you
	8	you are|oil tax|pop art|you get|red ink|we saw him
balanced-hand sentences	9	The man is to go to the city and do the auto work.
	10	The girl is to go by bus to the lake for the fish.
one-hand sentences	11	Jimmy saw you feed a deer on a hill up at my mill.
	12	Molly sat on a junk in oily waters at a bare reef.

gwam 1′ | 1 | 2 | 3 | 4 | 5 | 6 | 7 | 8 | 9 | 10 |

22d ▶ 12 *Improve Language Skills: Capitalization*

1. Read each rule and key the **Learn** and **Apply** sentences beneath it.

2. If time permits, practice the **Apply** lines again to increase decision-making speed.

Capitalize the days of the week.

Learn 1 Did you ask if the OEA contest is to be on Friday?
Apply 2 does FBLA meet on wednesday, thursday, and friday?

Capitalize the months of the year.

Learn 3 August was very hot, but September is rather cool.
Apply 4 they are to spend july and august at myrtle beach.

Capitalize names of holidays.

Learn 5 Kacy and Zoe may visit their parents on Labor Day.
Apply 6 gus asked if memorial day comes at the end of may.

Capitalize the names of historic periods and events and special events.

Learn 7 The Fourth of July honors the American Revolution.
Apply 8 bastille day is in honor of the french revolution.

275b (continued)

words

Document 3
Job Description

LP p. 131

Key a job description in the proper format from the rough draft shown at the right.

JOB TITLE: Director, Public Relations; UNIT: Public Re- 8
lations Office; REPORTS TO: Exexecutive Vice President; SUB- 16
ORDINATE STAFF: Six Section Chiefs; DATE: May 2, 19--; 22
D.O.T: 165.067-010 24

GENERAL STATEMENT OF THE JOB

Under the supervision of the Executive Vice President, 35
plans, organizes, and ~~supervises~~ directs a public relations 45
program ~~intended~~ designed to promote goodwill, ~~inspire~~ de- 53
velop confidence, and create a favorable public image for 65
the company. 67

SPECIFIC DUTIES OF THE JOB

1. Plans and directs development and comunication of ~~data~~ 78
information designed to keep the public informed of the com- 90
pany's ~~deeds~~ accomplishments and point of view. 3~~2~~. Estab- 101
lishes policies and procedures for all official contact with 113
the public by any employee. 2~~3~~. Supervises the development 125
and conduct of promotional activities such as exhibits, 136
films and tours. 5~~4~~. Represents the company at public, so- 148
cial, and business events. 6~~5~~. Conducts periodic surveys to 160
determine the public's ~~concept~~ perception and opinoin of the 170
company. 4~~6~~. Coordinates the participation of company 181
~~agents~~ representatives in community improvement, welfare, 190
and social-beterment ~~activities~~ programs. 198

Document 4
Table

Center the table vertically and horizontally; DS the items.

BOUTIQUES INTERNATIONAL, LTD. 6

Pension Benefits by Years of Service 13

Average Salary*	20 Years	25 Years	30 years**	words
$25,000	$ 9,175	$11,450	$13,750	28
35,000	12,854	16,300	19,250	36
45,000	16,[5]~~1~~15	20,610	24,750	41
55,000	20,185	25,[1]~~2~~90	30,250	47
65,000	23,85[5]~~4~~	29,77[0]~~9~~	35,750	53
75,000	27,525	34,[3]~~4~~50	41,250	59
85,000	31,[1]~~2~~95	38,930	46,750	64
95,000	[34]~~43~~,865	43,510	52,250	70

75

*Highest 3 consecutive years out of final 10. 88

**Benefits increase 2.5% per year for every year 98
after 30 years. 101

23a ▶ 6 Conditioning Practice

each line twice SS; then a 1′ timed writing on line 3; find *gwam*

alphabet 1 Marjax made five quick plays to win the big prize.
CAPS LOCK 2 Did you say to send the cartons by UPS or by USPS?
easy 3 I am to pay the six men if they do the work right.

gwam 1′ | 1 | 2 | 3 | 4 | 5 | 6 | 7 | 8 | 9 | 10 |

23b ▶ 20 Improve Keyboarding Technique: Response Patterns

1. Key each set of lines twice SS (slowly, then faster); DS between 6-line groups.

2. Take a 1′ writing on line 10, on line 11, and on line 12; find *gwam* on each; compare rates.

3. If time permits, rekey the slowest line.

Combination response

Normal copy (as in lines 7-9) includes both word- and letter-response sequences.

Use *top* speed for easy words, *lower* speed for words that are harder to key.

letter response
1 be in as no we kin far you few pin age him get oil
2 see him|was nil|vex you|red ink|wet mop|as you saw
3 Milo saved a dazed polo pony as we sat on a knoll.

word response
4 ox if am to is may end big did own but and yam wit
5 do it|to cut|he got|for me|jam it|an owl|go by air
6 He is to go to the city and to do the work for me.

combination response
7 am at of my if on so as to be or we go up of no by
8 am in|so as|if no|is my|is up|to be|is at|is up to
9 Di was busy at the loom as you slept in the chair.

letter 10 Jon gazed at a phony scarab we gave him in a case.
combination 11 Pam was born in a small hill town at the big lake.
word 12 Keith is off to the lake to fish off the big dock.

gwam 1′ | 1 | 2 | 3 | 4 | 5 | 6 | 7 | 8 | 9 | 10 |

23c ▶ 12 Improve Language Skills: Capitalization

1. Read each rule and key the **Learn** and **Apply** sentences beneath it.

2. If time permits, practice the **Apply** lines again to increase decision-making speed.

Capitalize names of cities, states, and other important places.

Learn 1 When you were in Nevada, did you visit Hoover Dam?
Apply 2 did he see paris from the top of the eiffel tower?

Capitalize geographic names, regions, and locations.

Learn 3 Val drove through the Black Hills in South Dakota.
Apply 4 we canoed down the missouri river near sioux city.

Capitalize names of streets, roads, avenues, and buildings.

Learn 5 Jemel lives at Bay Towers near Golden Gate Bridge.
Apply 6 our store is now in midtown plaza on kenwood road.

275b ▶ 45 *Evaluate Document Processing Skills: Form and Tables*

Time Schedule
Plan and prepare .... 5′
Timed production ....30′
Proofread; compute *n-pram* .....10′

1. Arrange materials for ease of handling. Use LP pp. 129-131.
2. Key Documents 1-4 for 30′. Proofread and correct errors before removing documents from machine.
3. After time is called, proofread again and circle any uncorrected errors. Compute *n-pram.*

Document 1
Grievance Statement
LP p. 129
Key the formal grievance statement with 1″ side margins. Use **your name** as that of the steward.

FORMAL STATEMENT OF GRIEVANCE words

EMPLOYEE Joan T. Clark I.D. NO. 43725 CLOCK NO. 891 5
JOB TITLE Data Entry Operator DEPARTMENT Administrative 12
STATEMENT OF GRIEVANCE
Before my previous supervisor, James Friel, retired, he 23
promised me that I would receive a merit raise on October 35
16, after two years of service. Even though I received a 46
performance rating of excellent, my new supervisor, Mrs. 58
Mary Robb, refuses to recommend me for a merit raise because 70
she says she is not familiar with my work. I feel that this 82
is unfair treatment and that I should receive my raise 93
immediately. 96

Employee Signature ________ Steward Signature ________ 11/30/19-- Date 98

Document 2
Table
Center the table vertically and horizontally. DS the items.

Documents 3 and 4 are on p. 462.

BOUTIQUES INTERNATIONAL, LTD. 6

Bonus for Employees Program 12

Job No.	Title	Bonus*	
			18
169.167-014	Administrative assistant	$ 500	28
247.387-010	Advertising ~~Clerk~~ Specialist	200	36
162.117-018	Contract Specailist	4 ~~3~~00	43
186.117-014	~~Financial manager~~ Controller	1,000	49
249.131-014	Customer Services Supervisor	500	58
166.167-033	Employment Manager	8 ~~5~~00	65
166.267-018	Job Analyst	300	71
189.167-022	Management Trainee	300	78
161.116-014	Records Management Director	1,000	88
201.362-030	Secretary I, II	300	95
189 ~~18~~.117-010	Research Director tr	1,000	103
922.687-058	Wharehouse Worker	100	109
203.362-022	Word Processer Operator	300	117

______________ 121

*Fifty percent payable when hired; 50% payable ~~six~~ three 132
months after satisfactory job performance. 140

23d ▶ 12 Check/Improve Keyboarding Speed

1. Take one 1′ timed writing and two 1′ *guided* writings on ¶ 1 as directed on page 38.

2. Take one 1′ timed writing and two 1′ *guided* writings on ¶ 2 in the same way.

3. As time permits, take one or two 2′ timed writings on ¶s 1 and 2 combined *without* the call of the guide; find *gwam.*

1′ *gwam* goals

▽ 19 = acceptable
⊡ 23 = average
⊙ 27 = good
◇ 31 = excellent

all letters used | E | 1.2 si | 5.1 awl | 90% hfw |

gwam 2′

```
      .    2    .    4    .    6    .    8    .
    The level of your skill is a major item when      5
 10    .   12    .   14    .   16    .   18    ▽
you try to get a job.  Just as vital, though, may    10
 20    .   22    ⊡   24    .   26    ⊙   28    .
be how well you can express ideas in written form.   15
      .    2    .    4    .    6    .    8    .
    It might amaze you to learn what it is worth     19
 10    .   12    .   14    .   16    .   18    ▽
to a company to find those who can write a letter    24
 20    .   22    ⊡   24    .   26    ⊙   28    .
of quality as they key.  Learn to do so in school.   29
```

gwam 2′ | 1 | 2 | 3 | 4 | 5 |

Lesson 24 Keyboarding/Language Skills

LL: 50
LS: SS

24a ▶ 6 Conditioning Practice

each line twice SS; then a 1′ writing on line 3; find *gwam*

alphabet 1 Jack viewed unique forms by the puzzled tax agent.
? 2 Where is Elena? Did she call? Is she to go, too?
easy 3 Title to all of the lake land is held by the city.

gwam 1′ | 1 | 2 | 3 | 4 | 5 | 6 | 7 | 8 | 9 | 10 |

24b ▶ 12 Improve Language Skills: Capitalization

1. Read each rule and key the **Learn** and **Apply** sentences beneath it.

2. If time permits, practice the **Apply** lines again to increase decision-making speed.

Capitalize an official title when it precedes a name and elsewhere if it is a title of high distinction.

Learn 1 In what year did Juan Carlos become King of Spain?
Learn 2 Masami Chou, our class president, made the awards.
Apply 3 will the president speak to us in the Rose Garden?
Apply 4 mr. koch, our company president, chairs the group.

Capitalize initials; also capitalize letters in abbreviations if the letters would be capitalized when the words are spelled out.

Learn 5 Does Dr. R. J. Anderson have an Ed.D., or a Ph.D.?
Learn 6 He said that UPS stands for United Parcel Service.
Apply 7 we have a letter from ms. anna m. bucks of boston.
Apply 8 m.d. means Doctor of Medicine, not medical doctor.

24c ▶ 12 Check/Improve Keyboarding Speed

Practice again the 2 ¶s above, using the directions in 23d.

Goal: To improve your speed by at least 2 *gwam.*

274b (continued)

Document 2
Unbound Report

Key this report in the unbound format. Correct all marked and unmarked errors. Heading: **REPORT OF OPEN HOUSE**

words

heading 4

The annual Open House of Boutiques International in the 15
New Orleans [complex] ~~office~~ was held on July 15, 19--. During the 27
hours of 9 a.m. and noon, 126 people toured our [facilities] ~~company~~; dur- 40
ing the hours of 1 p.m. and 4 p.m., 237 [additional] ~~more~~ people took the 53
tour. Note should be [taken] ~~made~~ of the [big] increase [during] ~~in~~ the afternoon 67
hours. At the 2 p.m. and 2:30 p.m. tours, the meeting room 79
was unable to accomodate the number of people present [; and] we 91
[were forced to] ~~asked~~ some people to wait for the [next] ~~following~~ tour. 103

The tour of the mail room went smoothly; and the expla- 114
nation of our order processing system was a highlight of the 126
tour [;] thanks in great measure to the interesting presentation 139
given by Maria Rodriques [, one of our machine operators.] 150

The tour through warehouse B [en route to the shipping department] was not a success. The 168
noise of the equipment prevented any explaination of the op- 179
erations. Further, the [continuous] stream of people through the 192
warehouse tended to disrupt [operations] ~~work~~. 200

The refreshments served in the employee's dining room 211
were welcomed by all visitors. The group [immediately] ~~just~~ before and 224
after the noon hour, however, disrupted operations [of the kitchen personnel]. 240

The following recomendations are made [to improve future tours of this nature]. 256

DS

1. Backup accomodations should be provided for the over- 267
flow during the afternoon hours. 273

SS

[3] ~~2~~. The refreshments at the close of the tour should be 285
served in a location other than the employee's dining room. 297

[2. The tour through Warehouse B should be eliminated.] 309

24d ▶ 20 Master Difficult Reaches

1. Key each set of lines twice SS (slowly, then faster); DS between 8-line groups.

2. Note the lines that caused you difficulty; practice them again to develop a steady pace (no pauses between letters).

Adjacent (side-by-side) keys (as in lines 1-4) can be the source of many errors unless the fingers are kept in an upright position and precise motions are used.

Long direct reaches (as in lines 5-8) reduce speed unless they are made without moving the hands forward and downward.

Reaches with the outside fingers (as in lines 9-12) are troublesome unless made without twisting the hands in and out at the wrist.

Adjacent-key letter combinations

1 Rena saw her buy a red suit at a new shop in town.
2 Opal will try to stop a fast break down the court.
3 Jeremy knew that we had to pool our points to win.
4 Her posh party on their new patio was a real bash.

Long direct reaches with same finger

5 Herb is under the gun to excel in the second race.
6 My fervor for gym events was once my unique trait.
7 Music as a unique force is no myth in any country.
8 Lynda has since found many facts we must now face.

Reaches with 3d and 4th fingers

9 The poet will opt for a top spot in our port town.
10 Sam said the cash price for gas went up last week.
11 Zane played a zany tune that amazed the jazz band.
12 My squad set a quarter quota to equal our request.

Lesson 25 Keyboarding/Language Skills

LL: 50
LS: SS

25a ▶ 6 Conditioning Practice

each line twice SS; then a 1′ writing on line 3; find *gwam*

alphabet 1 Kevin can fix the unique jade owl as my big prize.
capitalization 2 Rule: When : precedes a sentence, cap first word.
easy 3 Dodi is to make a visit to the eight island towns.

gwam 1′ | 1 | 2 | 3 | 4 | 5 | 6 | 7 | 8 | 9 | 10 |

25b ▶ 20 Improve Keyboarding Technique: Response Patterns

1. Key each set of lines twice SS; DS between 6-line groups.

2. Take a 1′ writing on line 10, on line 11, and on line 12 to increase speed; find *gwam* on each.

Goal: At least 24 *gwam* on line 12.

letter response
1 kilo beef yams were only date upon gave milk rates
2 my car|oil tax|you are|was him|raw milk|as you see
3 We ate plump plum tarts in a pink cafe on a barge.

word response
4 also form town risk fuel auto goal pens iris visit
5 apt to|go for|is also|the goal|fix them|go for the
6 Roxie is also apt to go for the goal of good form.

combination response
7 an in of at is fix pop for him ham are pen far men
8 in the|at the|and tar|for him|due you|she saw them
9 An odor of wax and tar was in the air at the mill.

letter 10 Zac gave only a few facts in a case on wage taxes.
combination 11 He set off for the sea by dusk to see a rare loon.
word 12 It is right for them to audit the work of the men.

gwam 1′ | 1 | 2 | 3 | 4 | 5 | 6 | 7 | 8 | 9 | 10 |

274b ▶ 45 *Evaluate Document Processing Skills: Reports*

Time Schedule

Plan and prepare .... 5′
Timed production .... 30′
Proofread; compute *n-pram* ... 10′

1. Arrange materials for ease of handling.

2. Key Documents 1-2 for 30′. Proofread and correct errors before removing each page from the machine. If you complete both documents before time is called, rekey the report in Document 1 in the topbound format.

3. After time is called, proofread again and circle any uncorrected errors. Compute *n-pram.*

Document 1
Leftbound Report with Textual Citations

1. Key this unedited manuscript in the form of a leftbound report. Correct all errors, including unmarked ones.

2. The complete reference information has been included in the text of the report. As you prepare the report, insert the proper textual citation.

3. Place an alphabetized reference list on the final page (at the end of the report).

Document 2 is on p. 460.

words

ANNUAL REPORT OF THE HUMAN RESOURCES DEPARTMENT 10

Employment 14

The company employed an average of 4,657 people during 25
the ~~last~~ past fiscl year. A total of 389 employees were ~~found~~ 35
hired during the year. Of this number, 174 were replacements 48
for ~~those~~ employees who had left the company ~~and~~ while 215 58
were hired as additional personel. One of the major problem 70
areas has been the shortage of managerail and administrative 82
personnel. Despite ~~continued~~ increased recruiting efforts, we 93
have had difficulty finding qualified ~~individuals~~ people. As 103
forcast by the Bureau of Labor Statistics [Kutscher, Robert E., 114
"An Overview of the Year 2000," Occupational Outlook Quarter- 114
ly, Spring 1988, p. 9], these occupations are among the fastest 124
growing and, therefore, will continue to be a recruitment 135
problem. An analysis of the individuals employed ~~by~~ 145
under our BONUS FOR EMPLOYEES PROGRAM ~~verifies~~ proves the 155
well-established belief that "(employee) referrals can be a 167
very good source of job applicants." [Cunningham, William H., 177
Aldag, Ramon J., and Swift, Christopher M., Introduction to 180
Business, Cincinnati: South-Western Publishing Co., 1984, p. 182
158.] 183

Employee Benefits 190

Without cost to employees, the company ~~offers~~ provides 200
health insurance, life insurance, retirement ~~pay~~ benefits, 211
liberal vacations, ~~five~~ six holidays, sick ~~leave~~ and jury duty 221
leave, and a profit sharing plan. A national survey [Bates, 233
Judith K., "A Survey of Desired Employee Benefits," Glick As- 233
sociates, February 1989, p. 19] indicates that the desire for a 242
child care center (or compensation for child care) is growing, 254
~~indicating~~ reflecting an increase in the number of house 263
holds in which both parents work. We anticipate that child 275
care will be a major issue when we ~~discuss~~ negotiate our next 286
labor contract. In preparation for this ~~probability~~ 295
eventuality, we have initiated a study to ~~find~~ determine the 306
feasibility and cost of providing this care benefit. 317

Human Relations 323

The company had a good human relations record this year. 335
We had ~~but~~ only six complaints filed under Title VII of the 346
Civil Rights act of 1964, as amended. All but two of these 358
have been resolved. A total of 32 greivances were filed under 370
the terms of our labor contract. Of these, 18 were resolved 383
at the supervisory level, 10 were resolved by the appeals com- 395
mitte, and 4 were referred to an arbitrator. Through mutual 407
agreement with our unions, ~~discussions~~ negotiations for the 417
next master contract will ~~start~~ begin at an earlier date than 428
previously ~~set~~ scheduled. It is hoped that the longer period 440
allowed for considering the issues by both sides ~~may~~ will help 452
prevent any work stop pages. 457

references 536

25c ▶ 14 Check/Improve Keyboarding Speed

1. Take a 1′ writing on each ¶; find *gwam* on each; record the better *gwam*.

2. Take a 2′ writing on ¶s 1 and 2 combined; find *gwam*.

3. Using your better *gwam* in Step 1 as a base rate, take two 1′ *guided* writings on ¶ 1 as directed on page 38.

4. Using the same goal rate, take two 1′ writings on ¶ 2 in the same way.

5. Take another 2′ writing on ¶s 1 and 2 combined; find *gwam*.

6. Record your best 1′ *gwam* and your better 2′ *gwam*.

Goals

1′: At least 22 *gwam*.
2′: At least 20 *gwam*.

all letters used | E | 1.2 si | 5.1 awl | 90% hfw

	gwam 2′
You must realize by now that learning to key	5
requires work. However, you will soon be able to	10
key at a higher speed than you can write just now.	15
You will also learn to do neater work on the	19
machine than you can do by hand. Quality work at	24
higher speeds is a good goal for you to have next.	29

gwam 2′ | 1 | 2 | 3 | 4 | 5 |

25d ▶ 10 Check Language Skills: Capitalization

1. Key each sentence once SS, capitalizing words according to the rules you have learned in this unit.

2. Check with your instructor the accuracy of your application of the rules.

3. If time permits, rekey the lines in which you made errors in capitalization.

The references refer to previous lesson parts containing capitalization rules.

page references		
21d	1	this stapler is defective. please send a new one.
21d	2	ask if alma and suzan took the trip with ms. diaz.
23c	3	texas and mexico share the rio grande as a border.
21d, 23c, 24b	4	miss jackson is an auditor for irs in los angeles.
21d, 22d	5	alice said thanksgiving day is always on thursday.
21d, 23c	6	marcus saw the play at lincoln center in new york.
21d, 22d	7	our school year begins in august and ends in june.
23c	8	is the dubois tower on fifth avenue or oak street?
21d, 24b	9	send the dental supplies to byron c. tubbs, d.d.s.
21b, 24b	10	when did senator metcalf ask to see the president?

ENRICHMENT ACTIVITY: Think as You Key

Key each line once SS. At the end of each line, supply the information (noted in parentheses) needed to complete the sentence. In Items 3 and 6, also choose the correct article (*a* or *an*) to precede the information you supply.

1 My full name is *(first/middle/last).*
2 I attend *(name of school).*
3 I am learning to key on a/an *(brand of typewriter/computer).*
4 My main goal has been to develop *(technique/speed/accuracy).*
5 My favorite class in school is *(name of subject).*
6 My career goal is to be a/an *(name of job).*
7 My main hobby is *(name of hobby).*
8 I spend most of my free time *(name of activity).*

273b (continued)

Document 3
News Release

LP p. 127

Key the news release for immediate release with **Michelle T. Worthington, 504-565-6459,** as the contact.

Document 4
Simplified Memorandum

If time permits, rekey Document 1, p. 456, as a simplified memo.

Total words: 237

words

heading 10

NEW ORLEANS, LA, September 1, 19--. Mark E. 19
La Grande, chairperson of Boutiques International, Ltd., 30
announced today that the ~~officers~~ management of the com- 39
pany will recommend that the (lc) Board of (lc) Directors in- 49
crease the quarterly cash dividend on its common stock 60
from 54 cents to 60 cents ~~per~~ a share. The recommenda- 70
tion will be ~~set forth~~ made at the next regular meeting 79
of the board, ~~which is~~ scheduled for September 15. 87

The increased dividend, if approved by the board, 97
will be effective with the regularly scheduled third-quarter 109
dividend payment, Annualized, the cash dividend will be 125
$2.40 a share, an 11.1 % ~~percent~~ increase over the present 135
$2.16 a share. 138

Mr. La Grande ~~said~~ stated that the increased dividend 148
was the ~~direct~~ result of the company's policy of sharing 158
the profits with its stock holders. He ~~reported~~ noted 167
that the net income of the company had ~~risen~~ increased 177
22.9% over the previous fiscal year. 184

Boutiques International, Ltd., sells fine wares from 195
all over the world by ~~post~~ direct mail and in shops lo- 205
cated throughout the (sp) U.S. The company has branch 217
offices in London, Paris, Rome, and Hong Kong. 226

227

payable September 30.

LESSONS 26 – 50

PHASE 2

LEARN ALPHANUMERIC KEYBOARDING TECHNIQUE AND CORRESPONDENCE FORMATTING

In the 25 lessons of this phase, you will:

1. Learn to key figures and basic symbols by touch and with good technique.

2. Improve speed/control on straight copy, handwritten (script) copy, rough-draft (corrected) copy, and statistical copy (copy containing figures and some symbols).

3. Review/improve language skills.

4. Apply your keyboarding skill in preparing simple personal and business documents.

The copy from which you have keyed up to now has been shown in pica (10-pitch) typewriter type. In Phase 2 much of the copy is shown in large, easy-to-read printer's type.

All drill lines are written to an exact 60-space line to simplify checking. Some paragraphs and problem activities, however, contain lines of variable length. Continue to key them line-for-line as shown until you are directed to do otherwise.

273b (continued)

words

We will [intensify] ~~escalate~~ our recruiting efforts thru [sp] our normal 103
channels. In addition, I [recommend] ~~suggest~~ that we begin recruiting 115
qualified persons through our [present] ~~current~~ employees by [initiating] a bonus 129
program. Under this program, employees will be encouraged to 142
"earn money and [do] ~~to~~ a freind a favor" by [recommending] ~~suggesting~~ individuals 155
for specific jobs. For thier efforts, employees will be paid 167
a bonus as [shown] ~~indicated~~ on the enclosed BONUS FOR EMPLOYEES PRO- 178
GRAM. Experience [has shown] ~~indicates~~ that present employees can be 190
[highly] ~~greatly~~ effective in recruting [i] people and that employee [referrals] ~~sug-~~ 203
~~gestions~~ are often of a [higher] ~~better~~ quality than those obtained 213
through other sources. 218

DS

If you approve, we will [announce] ~~put~~ this program in the next edi- 230
tion of our Employee [lc] Newsletter [lc]. 237/**253**

Document 2
Form Letter
LP p. 125

Key the letter dated **August 14** for the signature of **Harold J. Peterson, Director, Customer Service Center,** to the address below. Use block format with open punctuation.

Mrs. Vicki T. Goldblum
1638 Park Avenue
New York, NY 10035-4442

opening lines 20

Because you are one of our most valued customers and a col- 31
lector of fine crystal, we are pleased to offer you a preview 44
of some special items that will be included in our next catalog. 57
You are among a select few to receive this opportunity to ob- 69
tain unusual items at reduced prices. 77

You will find many new and exciting items in the enclosed leaf- 89
let. Please note these extraordinary crystal items: 100

**Galway Irish Crystal in a Fleur-de-lis Pattern 110
**Cavan Irish Crystal Flower Bowls 117
**Waterford Crystal's new "Essex Suite" 125
**Austrian Crystal Lamps 130
**Swarovsky's Crystal Circus Animal Collection 139

Many of these items are "special editions" and are available 151
in limited quantities. Our next catalog will be mailed to the 164
general public on September 15. Prior to that date, you will 176
have the opportunity to order the items you desire; and, to 188
show our appreciation for your continued patronage, we offer 200
you a discount of 10% on your order. 208

Be sure to send your order on or before September 15 to take 220
advantage of this singular offer. 227

closing lines 244/**256**

Document 3 is on p. 458.

UNIT 3 LESSONS 26 – 30

Learn the Figure Keyboard

Learning Goals

1. To learn the location of each figure key.
2. To learn how to strike each figure key properly and with the correct finger.
3. To build keyboarding speed and technique on copy containing figures.
4. To improve keyboarding speed and technique on alphabetic copy.
5. To learn to center lines horizontally (side-to-side).

Format Guides

1. ***Paper guide*** at *0* (for typewriters).
2. Line length (LL): 60 spaces; see *Get Ready to Keyboard: Typewriters* (p. x) or *Computers* (p. xii).
3. Line spacing (LS): single-space (SS) drills; double-space (DS) paragraphs (¶s).
4. Paragraph indention (PI): 5 spaces when appropriate.

Lesson 26 — 8 and 1

Line length (LL): 60 spaces
Line spacing (LS): single (SS)

26a ▶ 6 Conditioning Practice

each line twice SS; then a 1′ writing on line 3; find *gwam*

alphabet 1 Max was quick to fly a big jet plane over the frozen desert.
spacing 2 Any of them can aim for a top goal and reach it if they try.
easy 3 Nan is to go to the city hall to sign the land forms for us.

gwam 1′ | 1 | 2 | 3 | 4 | 5 | 6 | 7 | 8 | 9 | 10 | 11 | 12 |

26b ▶ 18 Learn 8 and 1

each line twice SS (slowly, then faster); DS between 2-line groups; if time permits, practice each line again

Follow the *Standard Plan for Learning New Keys* outlined on page 8.

Reach technique for **8**

Reach technique for **1**

Learn **8**

1 k k 8k 8k kk 88 k8k k8k 88k 88k Reach up for 8, 88, and 888.
2 Key the figures 8, 88, and 888. Please open Room 88 or 888.

Learn **Figure 1**

3 a a 1a 1a aa 11 a1a a1a 11a 11a Reach up for 1, 11, and 111.
4 Add the figures 1, 11, and 111. Has just 1 of 111 finished?

Combine **8** and **1**

5 Key 11, 18, 81, and 88. Just 11 of the 18 skiers have left.
6 Reach with the fingers to key 18 and 188 as well as 1 and 8.
7 The stock person counted 11 coats, 18 slacks, and 88 shirts.

272c ▶ 15 Evaluate Keyboarding Skills

Take two 5′ writings on the ¶s at the right. Record *gwam* and errors on the better writing.

all letters used | A | 1.5 si | 5.7 awl | 80% hfw

gwam 1′ | 5′

The system for processing documents in an office varies depending 13 3 62
upon the size of the office, the number of employees, the types of equip- 29 6 64
ment, and other factors. There are some major steps, though, which are 42 8 67
found in most offices. In the first step, the author of a document sub- 57 11 70
mits it in some manner. The words are then keyboarded, usually in rough- 71 14 73
draft form, and sent back to the author. The author edits the document, 86 17 76
makes any changes he or she wants, and returns it for final copy. 99 20 79

Many executives believe that they can best organize their ideas by 112 22 81
putting them on paper with pen or pencil. This may explain why many 126 25 84
documents are written by hand initially. Since no equipment is required, 141 28 87
this might be considered as a cost-effective way of producing documents. 156 31 90
On the other hand, the time involved by a highly paid person adds consid- 170 34 93
erably to the cost. Furthermore, much that is written by hand is dif- 184 37 96
ficult to read, which adds to the time and cost of keying the document. 198 40 99

Some executives who know how to key may provide rough drafts of 211 42 101
their material. A more effective means of preparing documents, however, 226 45 104
is machine dictation. The author can dictate at any time and at any con- 240 48 107
venient place, and the operator can key the material quickly in a timely 255 51 110
manner. The cost of the equipment, though, may be a drawback. Further, 269 54 113
the time required in training both the authors and the operators in the 284 57 116
proper use of the equipment may be a negative factor. 294 59 118

gwam 1′ | 1 | 2 | 3 | 4 | 5 | 6 | 7 | 8 | 9 | 10 | 11 | 12 | 13 | 14
gwam 5′ | 1 | 2 | 3

273b ▶ 45 Evaluate Document Processing Skills: Correspondence

Time Schedule

Plan and prepare .... 5′
Timed production .... 30′
Proofread; compute *n-pram* .... 10′

1. Arrange materials for ease of handling. Use LP pp. 123-131.

2. Key Documents 1-3 for 30′. Proofread and correct errors before removing documents from machine. If you complete the documents before time is called, key Document 1 in the simplified memo format.

3. After time is called, proofread again; circle any uncorrected errors; compute *n-pram.*

Document 1
Formal Memorandum LP p. 123

words

TO: Lucille K. Phillips, Vice President of Administration 11

FROM: Henry K. O'Brian, Director of Human Resources 20

DATE: August ~~5~~ [7], 19-- SUBJECT: Bonus for Employees [Program] 29

We are [presently] ~~currently~~ faced with a shortage of manager~~ia~~[ai]l, 39
administrative[,] and office personnel. Through our [usual] ~~normal~~ 51
source[s] ~~of~~ recruitment--advertising, private [and public] employment agen- 64
cies, educational institutions, and ~~P~~[p]rofessional organi- 75
zations--we have not been able to fill a number of vacancies 88
in [key] ~~some~~ areas. 91

(continued, p. 457)

26c ▶ 14 Improve Keyboarding Technique

1. Each pair of lines (1-6) twice SS (slowly, then faster); DS between 4-line groups.

2. A 1′ writing on line 7 and on line 8; find *gwam* on each writing.

Technique goals

- reach *up* without moving the hand forward
- reach *down* without twisting the wrists or moving the elbows in and out

Row emphasis

home/3d
1 she quit | with just | that play | fair goal | will help | they did go
2 Dru said you should try for the goal of top speed this week.

home/1st
3 hand axe | lava gas | can mask | jazz band | lack cash | a small flask
4 Ms. Hamm can call a cab, and Max can flag a small black van.

figures
5 The quiz on the 18th will be on pages 11 to 18 and 81 to 88.
6 Just 11 of the 118 boys got 81 of the 88 quiz answers right.

easy
7 Ty is to pay for the eight pens she laid by the audit forms.
8 Keith is to row with us to the lake to fix six of the signs.

gwam 1′ | 1 | 2 | 3 | 4 | 5 | 6 | 7 | 8 | 9 | 10 | 11 | 12 |

26d ▶ 12 Improve Keyboarding Speed: Guided Writing

1. A 1′ writing on each ¶; find *gwam* on each writing.

2. Using your better *gwam* as a base rate, select a *goal rate* 2-4 *gwam* higher than your base rate.

3. Take three 1′ writings on each ¶ with the call of the quarter-minute guide (see page 38 for directions).

Quarter-minute checkpoints

gwam	1/4′	1/2′	3/4′	Time
16	4	8	12	16
20	5	10	15	20
24	6	12	18	24
28	7	14	21	28
32	8	16	24	32
36	9	18	27	36
40	10	20	30	40

all letters used | E | 1.2 si | 5.1 awl | 90% hfw |

gwam 2′

How much time does it take you to return at the end of 6
the line? Do you return with a lazy or a quick reach? Try 12
not to stop at the end of the line; instead, return quickly 18
and move down to the next line of copy. 21

How much time does it take you to strike the shift key 27
and the letter to make a capital? Just a bit more practice 33
will help you cut by half the time you are now using. When 39
you cut the time, you increase your speed. 43

gwam 2′ | 1 | 2 | 3 | 4 | 5 | 6 |

Lesson 27 — 9 and 4

LL: 60
LS: SS

27a ▶ 6 Conditioning Practice

each line twice SS; then a 1′ writing on line 3; find *gwam*

alphabet 1 Joby quickly fixed a glass vase and amazed the proud owners.
figures 2 She told us to add the figures 11, 88, 18, 81, 118, and 881.
easy 3 Ciel may make a bid on the ivory forks they got in the city.

gwam 1′ | 1 | 2 | 3 | 4 | 5 | 6 | 7 | 8 | 9 | 10 | 11 | 12 |

27b ▶ 12 Improve Keyboarding Speed: Guided Writing

Practice again the 2 ¶s above, using the directions in 26d.

Goal: To improve your speed by at least 2-4 *gwam*.

UNIT 65 LESSONS 272 – 275

Evaluate Keyboarding/Language/Document Processing Skills

Performance Evaluated

1. To measure straight-copy speed and accuracy.

2. To evaluate language skills.

3. To measure production skills on correspondence, reports, and tables and forms.

Format Guides

1. Paper guide at *0* (for typewriters).

2. LL: 70 spaces for drills, paragraphs, and Language Skills activity; as required for documents.

3. LS: DS for Language Skills activity and paragraphs; as required for documents.

272a-275a ▶ 5 (daily) Conditioning Practice

each line twice SS (slowly, then faster); if time permits take 1′ writings on line 4

alphabet 1 Wilbur realized expert judges may check the value of the unique books.

figures 2 Published in 1987, this text has 546 pages, 130 pictures, and 27 maps.

fig/sym 3 I earned a commission of $3,149 (6%) on the sale of Lot #758 on May 2.

speed 4 If we wish them to do so, both of them may go with us to the sorority.

| 1 | 2 | 3 | 4 | 5 | 6 | 7 | 8 | 9 | 10 | 11 | 12 | 13 | 14 |

272b ▶ 30 Evaluate Language Skills

1. In each sentence at the right, items have been underlined. The underlines indicate that there *may* be an error in spelling, punctuation, capitalization, grammar, or in the use of words or figures.

2. Study each sentence carefully. Key each line with the number and period. If an underlined item is incorrect, correct it as you key the sentence. In addition, correct any typographical errors you may make as you work.

3. When you have completed the sentences, and *before* you remove the copy, study each sentence carefully and correct any errors you may have missed.

1. She said: “they must insure complience with the electrical code.”
2. Keep in mind: installation of the permanant wiring must be done now.
3. Do you beleive that ten 5-gallon cans will be suficient?
4. We must have acess to Conference Room Six for our meeting.
5. The profesional mens’ banquet was held at Gibbs’ country estate.
6. More than twenty-six foriegn managers will receive benifits.
7. Mary went to the librery, Ralph visited the planning comission.
8. According to “The New York Times,” the firm’s President will resign.
9. Approximately 10% of the participents voted “yes.”
10. He questioned the expendeture on Line 27 in Report 206-A.
11. Ed Boyle the company Treasurer will implement the fiscle plan.
12. My question is this--What was the maximum morgage rate last year?
13. The custumer shipped the material in a large, wooden crate.
14. Each of the comittee members are expected to initial the report.
15. Its almost certain the committee will issue their report imediately.
16. Whose facilaties were used in monitoring the quality of the items?
17. Lopez’s frequent absences was the subject of the correspondence.
18. The climate here is similer to that in southern California.
19. Don’t she work on the avenue of the Americas in New York city?
20. The analyss was included on Page 39 of Fiscal study #14.

27c ▶ 18 *Learn 9 and 4*

each line twice SS (slowly, then faster); DS between 2-line groups; if time permits, practice each line again

Follow the *Standard Plan for Learning New Keys* outlined on page 8.

Reach technique for **9**

Reach technique for **4**

Learn **9**

use the letter "l"
1 l l 9l 9l ll 99 l9l l9l 99l 99l Reach up for 9, 99, and 999.
2 Key the figures 9, 99, and 999. Have only 9 of 99 finished?

Learn **4**

3 f f 4f 4f ff 44 f4f f4f 44f 44f Reach up for 4, 44, and 444.
4 Add the figures 4, 44, and 444. Please study pages 4 to 44.

Combine **9** and **4**

5 Key 44, 49, 94, and 99. Only 49 of the 94 joggers are here.
6 Reach with the fingers to key 49 and 499 as well as 4 and 9.
7 My goal is to sell 44 pizzas, 99 tacos, and 9 cases of cola.

27d ▶ 5 *Improve Keyboarding Skill: Figures*

1. Key each of lines 1-3 twice SS (slowly, then faster); DS between 2-line groups.

2. If time permits, key each line again to improve speed.

Figure sentences

use the figure "1"

1 Keep the fingers low as you key 11, 18, 19, 48, 94, and 849.
2 On March 8, 1991, 44 people took the 4 tests for the 8 jobs.
3 He based his May 1 report on pages 449 to 488 of Chapter 19.

27e ▶ 9 *Learn to Center Lines Horizontally*

plain full sheet

Get ready to center

1. Set LM and paper guide at *0;* set RM at 85 (10-pitch) or 102 (12-pitch).

2a. *If machine has an automatic centering feature,* learn to use it and follow the *Drill procedure* given in Column 2.

2b. *If machine does not have an automatic centering feature:*
(1) clear all tab stops.
(2) set a tab stop at center point: 42, 10-pitch; 51, 12-pitch.
(3) Study *How to center on a typewriter* in the color block at the right.
(4) Follow the *Drill Procedure* below.

Drill procedure

1. Beginning on line 10, center each line of Drill 1 horizontally (side to side), SS.

2. Space down 4 times and center each line of Drill 2 horizontally, SS.

3. Center Drill 3 in the same manner.

How to center on a typewriter

1. Tabulate to center point.

2. From center, backspace *once* for each 2 letters, spaces, figures, or punctuation marks in the line.

3. Do not backspace for an odd or leftover stroke at the end of the line.

4. Begin keying where backspacing ends.

Example:

● center point

backspace ▶ 1 | 1 | 1 | 1 | 1 | 1 | 1 | 1 | 1

LE|AR|NI|NG|space T|O space|CE|NT|ER

1
to
wish
profit
problems
amendments

2
a
the
their
foreign
committee

3
I
work
handle
quantity
patient

~~dollars~~ in retail sales, direct mail ~~gets~~ almost 20 percent of the total--a considerable increase over the 14 percent ~~gained~~ in the 1970's. The increase in sales through direct mail ~~have~~ led ~~more and more~~ of the Fortune 500 companies to begin direct mail sales, ~~as well as~~ such famous department stores as Neiman-Marcus and Tiffany & Co.

There are many advantages ~~of~~ using direct mail advertising. One of the major advantages is that, thanks to the computerized mailing list, mail can be sent directly to individuals who ~~may be~~ interested in ~~a specific company's~~ product or produces. A new sceience, "individual demographics," can pinpoint with amazing accuracy the buying preferences of individuals through a computerized analysis of ZIP Codes, automobile registration, birth and marriage certificates, ~~credit ratings,~~ and other personal information frequently gained through questionnaires.

~~It is currently posible for any~~ company ~~to~~ rent a mailing tailored to meet its specific needs. Recently, Boutiques International, Ltd. conducted a sample survey in ~~two~~ large, Metropolitan Areas to determine the type of people interested in a new product line we ~~are~~ planning to ~~put on the~~ market. From an analysis of that survey, we can ~~now~~ order a ~~a~~ mailing list of people with specific characteristics--people who are most apt to buy our new product.

28a ▶ 6 Conditioning Practice

each line twice SS; then a 1′ writing on line 3; find *gwam*

alphabet 1 Roz may put a vivid sign next to the low aqua boat for Jack.

figures 2 Please review Figure 8 on page 94 and Figure 14 on page 189.

easy 3 Tien may fix the bus panel for the city if the pay is right.

gwam 1′ | 1 | 2 | 3 | 4 | 5 | 6 | 7 | 8 | 9 | 10 | 11 | 12 |

28b ▶ 18 Learn 0 and 5

each line twice SS (slowly, then faster); DS between 2-line groups; if time permits, practice each line again

Follow the *Standard Plan for Learning New Keys* outlined on page 8.

Reach technique for **0**

Learn **0** (zero)

1 ; ; 0; 0; ;; 00 ;0; ;0; 00; 00; Reach up for 0, 00, and 000.

2 Snap the finger off the 0. I used 0, 00, and 000 sandpaper.

Learn **5**

3 f f 5f 5f ff 55 f5f f5f 55f 55f Reach up for 5, 55, and 555.

4 Reach up to 5 and back to f. Did he say to order 55 or 555?

Reach technique for **5**

Combine **0** and **5**

5 Reach with the fingers to key 50 and 500 as well as 5 and 0.

6 We asked for prices on these models: 50, 55, 500, and 5500.

7 On May 5, I got 5 boxes each of 0 and 00 steel wool for her.

28c ▶ 12 Improve Keyboarding Technique: Figures

each line twice SS; DS between 2-line groups

Language skills notes

1. No space is left before or after : when used with figures to express time.

2. Most nouns before numbers are capitalized; exceptions include *page* and *line*.

No space

1 Flight 1049 is on time; it should be at Gate 48 at 5:50 p.m.

2 The club meeting on April 5 will be in Room 549 at 8:10 a.m.

3 Of our 105 workers in 1989, 14 had gone to new jobs by 1991.

4 I used Chapter 19, pages 449 to 458, for my March 10 report.

5 Can you meet us at 1954 Maple Avenue at 8:05 a.m. August 10?

6 Of the 59 students, 18 keyed at least 40 w.a.m. by April 18.

Document 12
Partial Text of Speech

Mrs. Scott: Please key in the form of a leftbound report this partial text of a speech Ms. Perez plans to present at the national meeting of FBLA.

Document 13
Partial Text of Speech

Mrs. Scott: Please key the partial text of speech on 5″ × 8″ cards with top and side margins of ½″ and bottom margins of ¼″ to ½″. Omit the title, and number each card at the left margin on the second line from the top edge. DS the text.

MILLIONS OF DOLLARS WORTH OF JUNK

"Junk" is a ~~term that~~ *word* we apply to something worthless, such as trash *or garbage*. Many ~~individuals~~ *people* call advertisements they recieve through the postal service "junk mail." And yet, this *so-called* "junk" generates millions and millions of dollars in sales ~~each year~~ *annually*. In marketing ~~parlance~~ *STET*, "junk mail" is *known as* direct mail--and important and ~~rewarding~~ *valuable* means of advertising.

The most popular media for advertising on a national and local basis are news papers and magazines; television ranks second; and direct mail, third. An interesting trend in the ~~amount~~ *percentage* of funds ~~spent~~ *expended* for advertising was first ~~noticed~~ *noted* in the 1970's. The per cent of expenditures on newspapers and magazine advertising began to ~~go down~~ *decreases* whereas the percent for direct mail began to increase. At first, *this trend* ~~it~~ was believed, ~~that~~ *to be* ~~it was~~ only a temporary aberration, but the trend has ~~been~~ continued. In the 1980's, money spent on newspaper and magazine advertising dropped more than 4% [sp]; the percent for direct mail increased by just about 3 percent. This *amount* may not seem to be ~~such~~ a ~~big number~~ *significant figure*, but it assumes some importance when *we* ~~you~~ remember that, nationwide, more than $100 billion is spent each year on advertising. Some experts have foerecast [r] that advertising expenditures for direct mail will double in the 1990's.

Despite ~~In spite of~~ the grumbling about "junk mail," sales generated through this media [um] have continued to ~~grow~~ *increase*. The most recent figures reveal that of the more than $1.5 trillion

28d ▶ 14 Improve Keyboarding Technique: Response Patterns

1. Each pair of lines twice SS (slowly, then faster); DS between 4-line groups.

2. A 1′ writing on line 2 and on line 4; find *gwam* on each writing.

3. If time permits, rekey the slower line.

letter response
1 face pump ever milk area jump vast only save upon safe union
2 As we were in a junk, we saw a rare loon feast on a crawdad.

word response
3 quay hand also body lend hang mane down envy risk corn whale
4 Tisha is to go to the lake with us if she is to do the work.

combination response
5 with only | they join | half safe | born free | firm look | goal rates
6 I sat on the airy lanai with my gaze on the sea to the east.

gwam 1′ | 1 | 2 | 3 | 4 | 5 | 6 | 7 | 8 | 9 | 10 | 11 | 12 |

Lesson 29 — *7 and 3*

LL: 60
LS: SS

29a ▶ 6 Conditioning Practice

each line twice SS; then a 1′ writing on line 3; find *gwam*

alphabet 1 Gavin made a quick fall trip by jet to Zurich six weeks ago.
figures 2 Key 1 and 4 and 5 and 8 and 9 and 0 and 190 and 504 and 958.
easy 3 The man is to fix the big sign by the field for a city firm.

gwam 1′ | 1 | 2 | 3 | 4 | 5 | 6 | 7 | 8 | 9 | 10 | 11 | 12 |

29b ▶ 18 Learn 7 and 3

each line twice SS (slowly, then faster); DS between 2-line groups; if time permits, practice each line again

Follow the *Standard Plan for Learning New Keys* outlined on page 8.

Reach technique for **7**

Reach technique for **3**

Learn **7**

1 j j 7j 7j jj 77 j7j j7j 77j 77j Reach up for 7, 77, and 777.
2 Key the figures 7, 77, and 777. She checked Rooms 7 and 77.

Learn **3**

3 d d 3d 3d dd 33 d3d d3d 33d 33d Reach up for 3, 33, and 333.
4 Add the figures 3, 33, and 333. Read pages 3 to 33 tonight.

Combine **7** and **3**

5 Key 33, 37, 73, and 77. Just 37 of the 77 skiers have come.
6 Please order 7 Model 337 computers and 3 Model 737 printers.
7 On August 7, the 33 bikers left on a long trip of 377 miles.

267b-271b (continued)

Document 7
Advertising Budget

Mrs. Scott: Key this budget beginning on line 12. Center the material horizontally. Compute the new total for each location.

BOUTIQUES INTERNATIONAL, LTD.

DS

Advertising Budget for Fiscal Year Beginning September 1, 19--

Eastern Division

Media	New York	Washington D.C.	Atlanta	Miami
Newspapers	$ 480,000 ~~432,000~~	$ 400,000 ~~360,000~~	320,000 ~~$288,000~~	$ 400,000 ~~360,000~~
Magazines	150,000 ~~135,000~~	125,000 ~~112,500~~	100,000 ~~90,000~~	125,000 ~~112,500~~
Television	270,000 ~~243,000~~	225,000 ~~202,500~~	180,000 ~~162,000~~	225,000 ~~202,500~~
Radio	210,000 ~~189,000~~	175,000 ~~157,500~~	140,000 ~~126,000~~	175,000 ~~157,500~~
Direct Mail	390,000 ~~351,000~~	325,000 ~~292,500~~	260,000 ~~234,000~~	325,000 ~~292,500~~
Total	$1,350,000	$1,125,000	$900,000	$1,125,000

DS

Documents 8-11
Simplified Memorandums with Table

Mrs. Scott: Prepare memorandums for Miss Perez dated **June 12** to each of the boutique managers on the list below. Also, prepare mailing envelopes for the memorandums.

Using the information from the advertising budget table you already keyed, center the budget figures in table form with two headings in ALL CAPS: **MEDIA** and **AMOUNT**. DS above and below the headings, but SS the entries.

New York manager:
Mr. Byron T. St. George
Boutiques International, Ltd.
769 Fifth Avenue
New York, NY 10022-3969

Washington, D.C. manager:
Ms. Leona M. Jones
Boutiques International, Ltd.
2652 Virginia Avenue, NW
Washington, DC 20037-5697

Atlanta manager:
Mrs. Margaret J. Fulton
Boutiques International, Ltd.
260 Peachtree Street, NW
Atlanta, GA 30303-6568

Miami manager:
Ms. Juanita R. Sanchez
Boutiques International, Ltd.
2927 Florida Avenue
Miami, FL 33133-5281

The figures below represent the projected advertising ~~funds~~ budget for your office for the fiscal year beginning September 1, 19--. The figures have been increased 10% over this year's budget to compensate for anticipated increase^s in ~~prices~~ costs caused by inflation~~ary pressures~~.

(Insert figures for specific office)

This budget ~~allocates~~ allots funds for local advertising only. As in the past, all national advertising ~~campaigns~~ will be conducted by this office in ~~cooperation~~ coordination with you and the managers of ~~all of the~~ our other boutiques.

Please let me have your ~~ideas~~ comments on this projected budget and any ~~other~~ recommended changes by June ~~19~~ 26. Keep in mind that once the budget has been ~~set~~ approved, no changes may be made without the ~~advanced~~ prior approval of this office.

29c ▶ 12 Improve Keyboarding Technique: Figures

each line twice SS (slowly, then faster); DS between 2-line groups; if time permits, practice each line again

3/7	1	Flights 337 and 377 will be replaced by Flights 733 and 737.
5/0	2	You had 500 books and 505 workbooks but returned 50 of each.
4/9	3	For the answer to Problem 94, see Unit 9, page 494, line 49.
1/8	4	Irv will be 18 on Tuesday, October 18; he weighs 181 pounds.
all figures learned	5	Key these figures as units: 18, 37, 49, 50, 73, 81, and 94.
	6	We sold 18 spruce, 37 elms, 49 maples, and 50 choice shrubs.

29d ▶ 14 Practice Centering Lines

1. Review *Get ready to center* and *How to center on a typewriter* in 27e, page 49, and adjust your equipment as directed there.

2. Beginning on line 8 of a half sheet (long edge at top), center each line of Problem 1. DS the lines.

3. Beginning on line 10, center the lines of Problem 2 in the same way.

1

IMPORTANT TERMS
income tax
gross national product
balance of trade
consumer price index
national debt
social security

2

FBLA ANNOUNCES
NEW OFFICERS
Christopher Linden, President
Mary Ann Stokes, Vice President
ElVon Gibbs, Secretary
Carla Johnson, Treasurer

Lesson 30 — 6 and 2

LL: 60
LS: SS

30a ▶ 6 Conditioning Practice

each line twice SS; then a 1′ writing on line 3; find *gwam*

alphabet	1	Jared helped Mazy quickly fix the big wood stove in the den.
figures	2	Bella lives at 1847 Oak Street; Jessi, at 5039 Duard Circle.
easy	3	They may make their goals if they work with the usual vigor.

gwam 1′ | 1 | 2 | 3 | 4 | 5 | 6 | 7 | 8 | 9 | 10 | 11 | 12 |

30b ▶ 14 Check Keyboarding Technique

1. Key each of lines 1-10 twice SS as your teacher checks your keyboarding technique; DS between 4-line groups.

2. If time permits, take a 1′ writing on line 11 and on line 12; find *gwam* on each writing.

finger reaches to top row	1	if 85 | am 17 | or 94 | me 73; | dot 395 | lap 910 | kept 8305 | corn 3947
	2	In 1987, we had 305 workers; in 1991, we had a total of 403.
quiet hands and arms	3	Celia doubts if she can exceed her past record by very much.
	4	Brian excels at softball, but many say he is best at soccer.
quick-snap keystrokes	5	Ella may go to the soap firm for title to all the lake land.
	6	Did the bugle corps toot with the usual vigor for the queen?
down-and-in spacing	7	Coy is in the city to buy an oak chair he wants for his den.
	8	Jan may go to town by bus to sign a work form for a new job.
out-and-down shifting	9	Robb and Ty are in Madrid to spend a week with Jae and Aldo.
	10	Are you going in May, or in June? Elena is leaving in July.
easy sentences	11	Rick paid for both the visual aid and the sign for the firm.
	12	Glena kept all the work forms on the shelf by the big chair.

gwam 1′ | 1 | 2 | 3 | 4 | 5 | 6 | 7 | 8 | 9 | 10 | 11 | 12 |

267b-271b (continued)

Document 6
Questionnaire

Mrs. Scott: Key the questionnaire using these format guides.

- side margins, 1″
- column width, 3″
- space between columns, ½″

Key the questions so that the columns are *approximately* the same length.

Line 6 {QUESTIONNAIRE FOR SPECIAL PEOPLE

QS

GETTING TO KNOW YOU . . . . so that we may ~~treat~~ serve you as a person and not just as another customer, will you please complete the following short questionnaire and return it in the enclosed envelope. For your cooperation, you may deduct 10% on your next purchase of $50 or less. Just use the certificate enclosed.

1. Are you married?
___Yes ___No

2. What is your 6 age group?
___18-24 5 ___35-45 ___65+ 56-
___25-34 ___50-64 ___ 66+
6 5 46-55

5 3. How many children under the age of 18 do you have?
___None __1 __2 __3 or more

6 4. Which magazines do you read on a regular basis?
___Reader's Digest
___People
___Time
___Better Homes and gardens
___Fortune
___Sports Illustrated
___National Geographic
___Cosmopolitan

~~5. Do you have a~~
~~___Microwave oven~~
~~___VCR~~
~~___CD player~~
~~___Stereo~~

7 6. What is your annual income?
___$15,000 to $29,999
___$30,000 to $44,999
___$45,000 to $59,999
___$60,000 to $74,999
___$75,000 to $89,999
___$90,000+

4 8. What is your educational level?
___High school
___Junior college
___Four-year college
___Master's degree
___Advanced degree

8. Which three of the ~~following~~ se activities do you enjoy most?
___Watching TV
___Reading
___Traveling
___Playing sports
___Attending concerts
___Gardening
___Fishing or hunting
___Attending the theater
___~~Playing cards~~ Handicrafts

9. Recently, you purchased an item by Molyneaux. Was this item for yourself or a gift?
~~9.~~ ___Myself ___Gift

11 STET ~~10.~~ If this item was for yourself, how would you rate it?
___Excellent
___Good
___Satisfactory
___Disappointing

12 STET ~~11.~~ What attracted you to this product?
___Attractive package
___Pleasing scent
___Handsome container

13 STET ~~12.~~ Would you purchase this item again?
___Yes
___No
___Undecided

14 STET ~~13.~~ In your opinion, is the price of this item
___About right ___Too high

3. What is your ZIP Code?

___ ___ ___ ___ ___

30c ▶ 12 Check Keyboarding Speed

1. A 1′ writing on ¶ 1 and then on ¶ 2; find *gwam* on each ¶.

2. Two 2′ writings on ¶s 1 and 2 combined; find *gwam* on each writing.

3. A 3′ writing on ¶s 1 and 2 combined (or if your teacher prefers, an additional 1′ writing on each ¶).

1′ gwam goals

- ▽ 21 = acceptable
- ⊡ 25 = average
- ⊙ 29 = good
- ◇ 33 = excellent

all letters used | E | 1.2 si | 5.1 awl | 90% hfw |

	gwam 2′	3′
Time and motion are major items in building our keying	6	4
power. As we make each move through space to a letter or a	12	8
figure, we use time. So we want to be sure that every move	18	12
is quick and direct. We cut time and aid speed in this way.	24	16
A good way to reduce motion and thus save time is just	29	19
to keep the hands in home position as you make the reach to	35	23
a letter or figure. Fix your gaze on the copy; then, reach	41	27
to each key with a direct, low move at your very best speed.	47	31

gwam 2′ | 1 | 2 | 3 | 4 | 5 | 6

3′ | 1 | 2 | 3 | 4

30d ▶ 18 Learn 6 and 2

each line twice SS (slowly, then faster); DS between 2-line groups; if time permits, practice each line again

Follow the *Standard Plan for Learning New Keys* outlined on page 8.

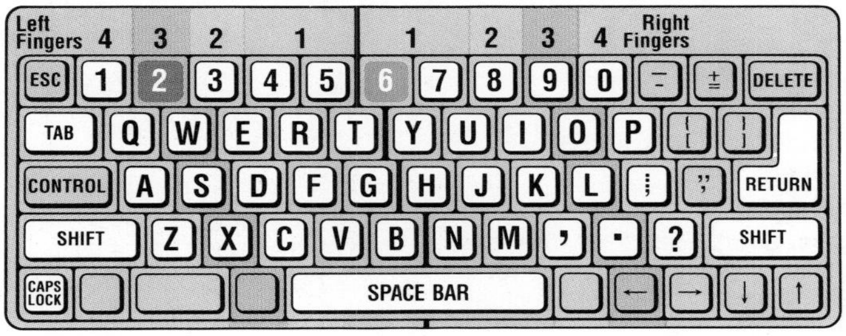

Reach technique for **6**

Reach technique for **2**

Learn **6**

1 j j 6j 6j jj 66 j6j j6j 66j 66j Reach up for 6, 66, and 666.

2 Key the figures 6, 66, and 666. Have only 6 of 66 finished?

Learn **2**

3 s s 2s 2s ss 22 s2s s2s 22s 22s Reach up for 2, 22, and 222.

4 Add the figures 2, 22, and 222. Review pages 2 to 22 today.

Combine **6, 2,** and other figures

5 Key 22, 26, 62, and 66. Just 22 of the 66 scouts were here.

6 Reach with the fingers to key 26 and 262 as well as 2 and 6.

7 Key figures as units: 18, 26, 37, 49, 50, 62, 162, and 268.

8 The proxy dated April 26, 1990, was vital in Case No. 37584.

267b-271b (continued)

Document 2
Table

Mrs. Scott: Center the table vertically and horizontally.

Common Metric Measures
(With Approximate U.S. Equivalents)

Unit	Symbol	Equivalent
kilometer	km	0.62 mile
meter	m	37.37 inches
centimeter	cm	0.39 inch
millimeter	mm	0.039 inch
liter	l* or L*	1.057 quarts
milliliter	ml	0.27 fluidram
kilogram	kg	2.2046 pounds
gram	g	0.035 ounce

*May also be spelled in full (liter).

Documents 3, 4, and 5
Letters

LP p. 117-121

Mrs. Scott: Please key this letter for Mr. Novak, dated **June 10,** in the block format, open punctuation, to the addressees below. Place appropriate columnar headings over the tabular items.

Mr. Byron T. St. George, Manager
Boutiques International, Ltd.
769 Fifth Avenue
New York, NY 10022-3969

Ms. Marcy L. LaCruz, Manager
Boutiques International, Ltd.
102 Rodeo Drive
Los Angeles, CA 90035-4729

Mr. Thomas C. Harding, Manager
Boutiques International, Ltd.
2600 January Avenue
St. Louis, MO 63139-2233

Boutiques International Ltd. has entered into an exclusive agreement with Molyneaux Parfums, Ltd., of Paris, to market a new line of perfumes and toiletries.

~~[struck out]~~ Before marketing these items nationally, we have decided to market test a sample of the items in three Metropolitan Areas: New York, ~~and~~ Los Angelos, and St. Louis. The test will determine (1) the relative effectiveness of two copy ads and (2) the ~~kinds~~ types of people interested in these ~~items~~ products. Via Airfreight, you will recieve 500 each of the following items to be ~~sold~~ retailed at the prices ~~shown~~ indicated.

Molyneaux Parfum No. 12, 7.5 m l	$62.95
Nouveau Eau De Toilette, 100 ml	72.99
LeOrleans Skin Creanm, 75 ml	29.00
Bule De Bain 2 L	48.50

A complete record of the name and address of each purchaser will be ~~made~~ kept. Two weeks after purchase, a copy of the inclosed questionnaire will be ~~sent~~ mailed to the purchaser. Completed questionnaires will be ~~mailed~~ returned to ~~us~~ this office.

~~Two~~ Three ad cmapiagns will be conducted. One will begin July 1 and continue for two weeks; one will begin August 1 and continue for two weeks; one will begin September 1 and continue for two weeks. Print copy for the ads will be faxed on June 15.

Please call me if you have any questions about this market test.

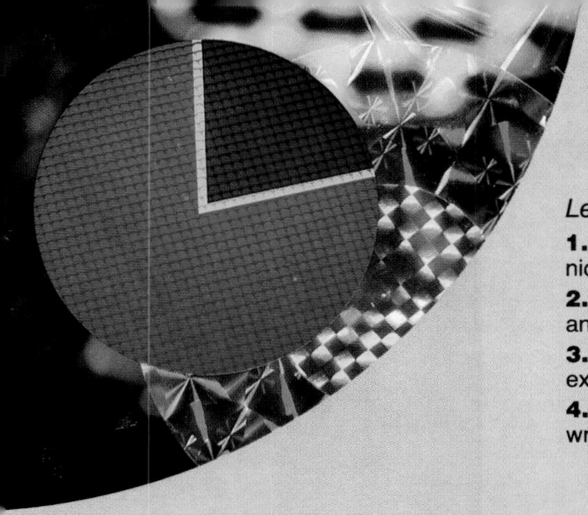

UNIT 4 LESSONS 31 – 32
Improve Keyboarding/Language Skills

Learning Goals

1. To improve alphabetic keyboarding technique and speed.
2. To improve numeric keyboarding technique and control (accuracy).
3. To review/improve language skills in number expression.
4. To acquire skill in keying longer paragraph writings.

Format Guides

1. ***Paper guide*** at *0* (for typewriters).
2. LL: 60 spaces; see *Get Ready to Keyboard: Typewriters* (p. x) or *Computers* (p. xii).
3. LS: SS drills; DS ¶s.
4. PI: 5 spaces when appropriate.

Lesson 31 *Keyboarding/Language Skills*

LL: 60
LS: SS

31a ▶ 6 Conditioning Practice

each line twice SS; then a 1′ writing on line 3; find *gwam*

alphabet 1 Linda may have Jack rekey parts two and six of the big quiz.
6/2 2 Our house at 622 Gold Circle will be paid for June 26, 2006.
easy 3 Jena is to go to the lake towns to do the map work for them.

| 1 | 2 | 3 | 4 | 5 | 6 | 7 | 8 | 9 | 10 | 11 | 12 |

31b ▶ 10 Improve Language Skills: Number Expression

1. Read the first rule highlighted in color at the right.
2. Key the **Learn** sentence below it, noting how the rule has been applied. Use the 60-space line for which your machine is set.
3. Key the **Apply** sentence, supplying the appropriate number expression.
4. Practice the other rules in the same way.
5. If time permits, key the three **Apply** sentences again to improve number control.

Spell a number that begins a sentence even when other numbers in the sentence are shown in figures.

Learn 1 Twelve of the new shrubs have died; 38 are doing quite well.
Apply 2 40 members have paid their dues, but 15 have not done so.

Use figures for numbers above ten, and for numbers one to ten when they are used with numbers above ten.

Learn 3 She ordered 2 word processors, 15 computers, and 3 printers.
Apply 4 Did he say they need ten or 12 sets of Z11 and Z13 diskettes?

Use figures to express dates and times.

Learn 5 He will arrive on Paygo Flight 62 at 10:28 a.m. on March 21.
Apply 6 Candidates must be in Ivy Hall at eight ten a.m. on May one.

31c ▶ 18 Improve Keyboarding Technique: Service Keys

1. Each pair of lines twice SS (slowly, then faster); DS between 4-line groups.
Note: For lines 5-6, clear all tabs and set 7 new ones 8 spaces apart, beginning at the left margin.
2. Two 1′ writings on line 7 and on line 8; find *gwam* on each writing.

space bar 1 to my | is in | of the | to buy | for the | may sign | the form | pay them
2 Kenton may sign the form at my farm for the corn and barley.

shift keys & CAPS LOCK 3 Aida or Coyt; Hafner and Co.; Have you read OF MICE AND MEN?
4 Frankie read LINCOLN by Vidal; Kate read ALASKA by Michener.

tabulator 5 ape tab 103 tab six tab 282 tab she tab 263 tab cut tab 375
6 for tab 495 tab nap tab 610 tab own tab 926 tab and tab 163

alphabet 7 Roz fixed the crisp okra while Jan made a unique beef gravy.
easy 8 Alfie is to go to work for the city to fix bus sign emblems.

gwam 1′ | 1 | 2 | 3 | 4 | 5 | 6 | 7 | 8 | 9 | 10 | 11 | 12 |

UNIT 64 LESSONS 267 – 271
Advertising Department

Learning Goals

1. To increase your skills in planning and organizing a variety of production jobs.
2. To produce a variety of business documents of high quality within a reasonable time and with a minimum of assistance.
3. To become familiar with the functions performed and the documents produced in an Advertising Department.

Documents Processed

1. Formal Memorandum
2. Tables
3. Letters
4. Simplified Memorandums
5. Questionnaire
6. Manuscript of Speech
7. Speech Cards

267a-271a ▶ 5 (daily) Conditioning Practice

each line twice SS (slowly, then faster); if time permits, take 1′ writings on line 1

alphabet 1 After key tax cuts, we bought major equipment that vitalized our work.
figures 2 Change line item 25 on page 109 from 3,876 to 3,576 units we produced.
fig/sym 3 Does Model #37215-A printer (Serial #40689) sell for $1,647 or $2,398?
speed 4 Is the sign to the ancient chapel in the big field visible to the eye?

| 1 | 2 | 3 | 4 | 5 | 6 | 7 | 8 | 9 | 10 | 11 | 12 | 13 | 14 |

267b-271b ▶ 45 (daily) Document Processing

1. You have been assigned to work as a word processing operator in the Advertising Department under the direction of Mrs. Joanna P. Scott, the office manager. Miss Rita L. Perez is the director of advertising; Mr. Robert T. Novak is the assistant director.

2. In this job, you will be required to prepare a variety of documents. Follow the directions given for each document. If no directions are given, use your best judgment.

3. Unless otherwise directed, complete each document in final form. Correct all marked and unmarked errors and those you may make.

4. Before beginning, review the material about the Advertising Department on page 427 as well as the major duties and special instructions.

Document 1
Formal Memorandum
LP p. 115

Mrs. Scott: Please key this memo to **All Copywriters** for Mr. Novak. Date it **June 9.** Use the subject **Metric Copy.**

business

A 1988 act of Congress provides that agencies of the government XXXX must use the metric system of measurement in XXX
activities. Since that time, a number of industreis with
whom we deal have begun converting to metric XXXXXX. XX XX
XXXXXXXXXXXXXXX therefore, XXXX all copywriters should be
familier with the metric system.

Attached is a table of the most commonly used metric XXXXX
measures. In preparing copy using metric measures, follow
these guide lines. DS

1. Key metric units as abbreviations: 23 g (23 grams). Do
not pluralize abbreviationss and do not use a period after an
abbreviation except at the end of a sentence.
2. Key metric unit letter abbreviations in lower case unless the unit name was derived from a propr name, such as
"C" for Celsius. An uppercase L may be used as an abbreviation
for liter to avoid confusing the lowercase l with the figure 1.
3. Space between a figure and the unit abbreviation that follows: 3 g (3 grams).

4. Express temprature in this manner: 24 C.
5. When the measure is a decimal, place a zero XX XXXXX XX
before the decimal: 0.54 cm (0.54 centimeter).
6. Groups of three digits should be separated by a space
rather than by comas: 0.142 035 g (0.142 035 gram).

DS between enumerated items.

31d ▶ 16 Improve Keyboarding Skill: Guided Writing

1. Take one 1′ timed writing and two 1′ *guided* writings on ¶ 1 as directed on page 38.
2. Take one 1′ timed writing and two 1′ *guided* writings on ¶ 2 in the same way.
3. Take two 2′ timed writings on ¶s 1 and 2 combined; find *gwam* on each.
4. Take one 3′ timed writing on ¶s 1 and 2 combined; find *gwam*.

1′ gwam goals
▽ 23 = acceptable
⊡ 27 = average
⊙ 31 = good
◈ 35 = excellent

all letters used | E | 1.2 si | 5.1 awl | 90% hfw |

	gwam 2′	3′
Although copy lines in your book are even at the right	6	4
margin, they may not be when you key them. The reason for	11	8
this is that type used by a printer is not uniform in width	17	12
as is that on your equipment. Be sure to recognize this.	23	15
Do not think that just because your copy is even at the	29	19
right, it contains no errors. To be sure that your work is	35	23
correct, you must check it to see that each character and	41	27
space is an exact match with the copy from which you work.	46	31

gwam 2′ | 1 | 2 | 3 | 4 | 5 | 6 |
3′ | 1 | 2 | 3 | 4 |

Lesson 32 Keyboarding/Language Skills

LL: 60
LS: SS

32a ▶ 6 Conditioning Practice

each line twice SS; then a 1′ writing on line 3; find *gwam*

alphabet 1 Jung quickly baked extra pizzas for the film festival crowd.
figures 2 I moved from 3748 Oak Street to 1059 Jaymar Drive on May 26.
easy 3 She paid the big man for the field work he did for the city.

gwam 1′ | 1 | 2 | 3 | 4 | 5 | 6 | 7 | 8 | 9 | 10 | 11 | 12 |

32b ▶ 10 Improve Language Skills: Number Expression

1. Read the first rule highlighted in color at the right.
2. Key the **Learn** sentence below it, noting how the rule has been applied. Use the 60-space line for which your machine is set.
3. Key the **Apply** sentence, supplying the appropriate number expression.
4. Practice the other rules in the same way.
5. If time permits, key the three **Apply** sentences again to improve number control.

Use figures for house numbers except house number *One*.

Learn 1 My home is at 9 Vernon Drive; my office, at One Weber Plaza.
Apply 2 The Nelsons moved from 4037 Pyle Avenue to 1 Maple Circle.

Use figures to express measures and weights.

Learn 3 Gladys Randoph is 5 ft. 6 in. tall and weighs 119 lbs. 6 oz.
Apply 4 This carton measures one ft. by six in. and weighs five lbs.

Use figures for numbers following nouns.

Learn 5 Review Rules 1 to 22 in Chapter 6, pages 126 and 127, today.
Apply 6 Case 2659 is reviewed in Volume five, pages eight and nine.

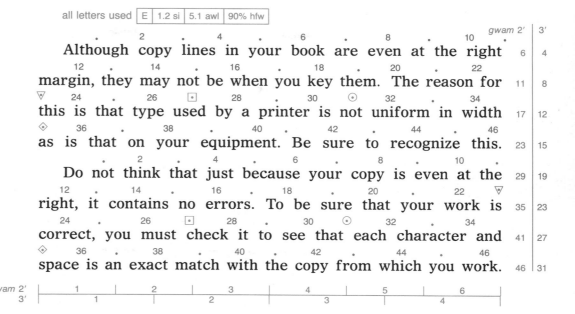

Document 12
Grievance Procedures

plain paper

Mrs. Schwartz: Key the grievance procedures as an unbound manuscript. Correct all marked and unmarked errors.

Document 13
Grievance Procedures

plain paper

Mrs. Schwartz: Key the grievance procedures as a leftbound manuscript for inclusion in the company's Standard Operating Procedures. After the first paragraph, single-space the steps that follow, but double-space between them.

BOUTIQUES INTERNATIONAL, LTD.

Grievance Procedures for Unionized Employees*

All actions taken by the company that effect employees will be based on the principals of fairness and individual merit. All employees have the right to fair and equitable treatment. If ~~at any time~~ an employee believes that this basic right has been violated, she or he may take the following steps.

Step 1. The employee will discuss the problem with his ~~superior~~ supervisor. The ~~superior~~ supervisor will determine the exact nature of the problem and ~~provide~~ offer a solution.

Step 2. In the event the employee is not satisfied with the solution offered by ~~his~~ the supervisor, the employee will then ~~state his~~ submit the problem in writing using Form 201, "Grievance Statement," ~~which will be sent to the superior of the employees' supervisor.~~ to the supervisor's superior. The superior will study the problem, talk with both parties, if necessary, ~~and provide~~ and render a written decision.

Step 3. If the employee is not satisfied with the written decision, she or he will ~~send~~ refer the problem to the union representative, who will ~~discuss~~ take up the matter with the union committee and, if necessary, the appeals committee.

Step 4. If the problem is not ~~solved~~ resolved during any of the ~~other~~ previous steps, the matter will ~~given~~ be referred to an arbitrator, who will determine an equitable settlement, which will be binding on all parties.

*Source: Master Labor Agreement, Provision 692.1.

32c ▶ 12
Check/Improve Keyboarding Speed

1. Two 1′ writings on each ¶; find *gwam* on each writing.

2. A 2′ writing on ¶s 1 and 2 combined; find *gwam.*

3. A 3′ writing on ¶s 1 and 2 combined; find *gwam.*

Goals

1′: At least 24 *gwam.*
2′: At least 23 *gwam.*
3′: At least 22 *gwam.*

all letters used | E | 1.2 si | 5.1 awl | 90% hfw

Text	gwam 2′	3′
Success does not mean the same thing to everyone. For	6	4
some, it means to get to the top at all costs: in power, in	12	8
fame, and in income. For others, it means just to fulfill	18	12
their basic needs or wants with as little effort as required.	24	16
Most people fall within the two extremes. They work quite	30	20
hard to better their lives at home, at work, and in the social	36	24
world. They realize that success for them is not in being at	42	28
the top but rather in trying to improve their quality of life.	48	32

gwam 2′ | 1 | 2 | 3 | 4 | 5 | 6
3′ | 1 | 2 | 3 | 4

32d ▶ 12
Learn to Proofread Your Copy

1. Note the kinds of errors marked in the ¶ at right.

2. Note how the proofreader's marks above the copy are used to make corrections in the ¶.

3. Proofread the copy you keyed in the 3′ writing above and mark for correction each error you made.

Goal: To learn the first step in finding and correcting your errors.

= space ∧ = insert ⁀ = close up ⌐ = delete ∿ = transpose (tr)

Sucess does not mean thesame thing to every one. For
some, it means to get the top att all costs:in power, in
fame, and in incone. For others it means juts to fulfill
thier basic needs or or wants with as little effort required.

Line 1	Line 2	Line 3	Line 4
1 Omitted letter	1 Omitted word	1 Misstroke	1 Transposition
2 Failure to space	2 Added letter	2 Omitted comma	2 Added word
3 Faulty spacing	3 Faulty spacing	3 Transposition	3 Omitted word

32e ▶ 10
Think as You Key

Key each line once SS. In place of the blank line at the end of each sentence, key the word or word group that correctly completes the sentence.

1 A small mass of land surrounded by water is a/an ______.
2 A large mass of land surrounded by water is a/an ______.
3 The earth rotates on what is called its ______.
4 When the sun comes up over the horizon, we say it ______.
5 When the sun goes down over the horizon, we say it ______.
6 A device used to display temperature is a/an ______.
7 A device used to display atmospheric pressure is a/an ______.
8 A device used to display time is a/an ______.

262b-266b (continued)

Document 10
Statement of Policy

plain paper

Mrs. Schwartz: Please key this statement of policy as an unbound manuscript. DS the enumerated items. Correct the marked errors and any unmarked errors.

STATEMENT OF POLICY

Fair and Equitable Treatment of Employees

QS

The basic policy of Boutiques International, Ltd., is to select the ~~person~~ individual best qualified to fill each position regardless of race, color, creed, sex, ~~or~~ age, or national origin. All ~~employees~~ individuals in positions of autherity have the responsibility to ensure that all employees are treated fairly and equitably in all personel actions.

To insure (e) that this policy is known and understood by all concerned, the following ~~steps~~ actions will be taken.

1. A ~~state~~ statement of the policy will be ~~given~~ sent to all of those who are in positions of authority including, but not restricted to, supervisors, administrators, and the heads of all organizational elements.

2. Seminars will be held on a ~~recurring~~ periodic basis for supervisory personel to review and up date this policy.

3. All advertisements for personnel will include the statement ~~that~~ "We are an "equal opportunity employer."

4. During their oreintation ~~period~~ program, new employees will be given a statement of the ~~firm's~~ company's fair and ~~equal~~ equitable treatment policy, together with a copy of the ~~steps~~ procedures to be followed in the event ~~an~~ any employee feels that he or she has been the subject of discrimination.

Document 11
Simplified Memorandum

plain paper

Mrs. Schwartz: Please compose and key a simplified memorandum, dated **April 16,** for **Mr. O'Brian** to **Lucille K. Phillips, Vice President for Administration,** submitting the revised statement of policy on "Fair and Equitable Treatment of Employees" for her approval.

Tell Ms. Phillips that the policy has been revised to reflect the latest U.S. Supreme Court rulings on the implementation of the Equal Opportunity Act of 1972 as reflected in the amendments to the "Uniform Guidelines on Employee Selection Procedures," published by the Equal Employment Opportunity Commission.

Ask Ms. Phillips to expedite her approval, since the next seminar for supervisors on fair and equitable treatment of employees is scheduled for **April 25.**

ENRICHMENT ACTIVITY: Response Pattern Drills

Practice Procedure

1. Key each line of a group (words, phrases, and sentences) 3 times: first, to improve keyboarding technique; next, to improve keyboarding speed; then, to build precise control of finger motions.

2. Take several 1′ writings on the 2 sentences at the end of each set of lines to measure your skill on each kind of copy.

3. As time permits, repeat the drills, keeping a record of your speed scores to see how your skill grows.

Each of the 120 *different* words used in the drills is among the 600 most-used words in the English language. In a study of over 2 million words in personal and business communications, these 120 words accounted for over 40 percent of all word occurrences. Thus, they are important to you in perfecting your keyboarding skill. Practice them frequently for both speed and accuracy.

Balanced-hand words of 2-5 letters (Use word response.)

words

1 of is it he to by or us an so if do am go me the six and but

2 a box may did pay end man air own due big for they with when

3 make them also then such than form work both city down their

4 end they when wish hand paid name held down sign field world

phrases

5 to me | of us | and may | pay for | big box | the six | but due | own them

6 am to work | is to make | a big city | by the name | to do such work

sentences

7 He may wish to go to the city to hand the work form to them.

8 The city is to pay for the field work both men did for them.

gwam 1′ | 1 | 2 | 3 | 4 | 5 | 6 | 7 | 8 | 9 | 10 | 11 | 12 |

One-hand words of 2-5 letters (Use letter response.)

words

9 a in be on we up as my at no was you are him get few see set

10 far act war tax only were best date case fact area rate free

11 you act few ever only fact card upon after state great water

phrases

12 at no | as my | on you | we are | at best | get set | you were | only date

13 get you in | act on my case | you set a date | get a rate on water

sentences

14 Get him my extra tax card only after you set up a case date.

15 As you see, you are free only after you get a case date set.

gwam 1′ | 1 | 2 | 3 | 4 | 5 | 6 | 7 | 8 | 9 | 10 | 11 | 12 |

Double-letter words of 2-5 letters (Speed up double letters.)

words

16 all see too off will been well good miss feel look less call

17 too free soon week room fill keep book bill tell still small

18 off call been less free look need week soon will offer needs

phrases

19 a room | all week | too soon | see less | call off | need all | will see

20 see a need | fill a book | miss a bill | all will see | a good offer

sentences

21 It is too soon to tell if we will need that small book room.

22 They still feel a need to offer a good book to all who call.

gwam 1′ | 1 | 2 | 3 | 4 | 5 | 6 | 7 | 8 | 9 | 10 | 11 | 12 |

Balanced-hand, one-hand, and double-letter words of 2-5 letters

words

23 of we to in or on is be it as by no if at us up an my he was

24 and all war six see you men too are may get off pay him well

25 such will work best then keep were good been only city needs

26 make soon ever wish tell area name bill upon paid tell great

phrases

27 is too great | they will be | box was small | their offer was good

28 if at all | may get all | off the case | to tell him | to keep after

sentences

29 If you wish to get to the rate you set, keep the hand still.

30 All of us do the work well, for only good form will pay off.

gwam 1′ | 1 | 2 | 3 | 4 | 5 | 6 | 7 | 8 | 9 | 10 | 11 | 12 |

262b-266b (continued)

Documents 6-9
Form Letters

LP pp. 107-113

Mrs. Schwartz: Please key these letters dated **April 9** to the following applicants, using the form letters indicated. The letters will be signed by Mr. O'Brian.

Applicant 1
Mrs. Velma T. Monroe
Rural Route 5
Baton Rouge, LA 70807-2323
Position: **job analyst**
Letter 26

Applicant 2
Mr. Jun Hori
2030 North Magnolia Street
Hammond, LA 70401-9824
Position: **legal advisor**
Letter 27

Applicant 3
Miss Jennifer P. Jackson
1228 Broadway Street
New Orleans, LA 70118-7127
Position: **executive secretary**
Letter 28

Applicant 4
Mr. Mark C. Johnson
2309 Florida Street
Kenner, LA 70062-7216
Position: **records manager**
Letter 27

Form Letter 26

Thank you for your recent letter in which you applied for a position as a/an (insert title of position). We appreciate your interest in Boutiques International, Ltd.

Will you please complete the enclosed application form and return it to us promptly. After we have had an opportunity to review your background, we shall be able to determine if you have the necessary qualifications to fill the position.

Within two weeks after we receive your application form, we shall let you know if we have a vacant position for which you are qualified.

Form Letter 27

We acknowledge, with thanks, your application for a position as a/an (insert title of position). We may have a position for which you are qualified.

Will you please call our office at 504-3000, Ext. 280, and arrange for a personal interview so that we can discuss the position with you.

We are looking forward to meeting you as a prospective employee of Boutiques International, Ltd.

Form Letter 28

Recently, you were interviewed by a member of our staff for the position of (insert title of position) in the office of Boutiques International, Ltd. The competition for this job was very keen, and it was quite difficult to select the person to fill the position.

We regret that you were not selected for the position. We shall keep your application on file for six months and will call you if another vacancy occurs for which you may be qualified.

Again, we thank you for your interest in becoming an employee in our company.

UNIT 5 LESSONS 33 – 38
Learn Symbol-Key Operation

Learning Goals

1. To learn locations of basic symbol keys.
2. To learn how to strike symbol keys properly, with the correct fingers.
3. To improve keyboarding speed/technique on alphabetic and statistical copy.
4. To review/improve language skills.
5. To improve horizontal centering skill.

Format Guides

1. ***Paper guide*** at *0* (for typewriters).
2. LL: 60 spaces; see *Get Ready to Keyboard: Typewriters* (p. x) or *Computers* (p. xii).
3. LS: SS drills; DS ¶s.
4. PI: 5 spaces when appropriate.

Lesson 33 — */ and $*

LL: 60
LS: SS

33a ▶ 6 *Conditioning Practice*

each line twice SS; then a 1′ writing on line 3; find *gwam*

alphabet 1 Di will buy from me as prizes the six unique diving jackets.
figures 2 The January 17 quiz of 25 points will test pages 389 to 460.
easy 3 Both of us may do the audit of the work of a big title firm.

| 1 | 2 | 3 | 4 | 5 | 6 | 7 | 8 | 9 | 10 | 11 | 12 |

33b ▶ 18 *Learn / and $*

each line twice SS (slowly, then faster); DS between 4-line groups; if time permits, practice the lines again

/ = diagonal
$ = dollar sign

Do not space between a figure and the / or the **$** sign.

Reach technique for /

Reach *down* to / with *right little* finger.

Reach technique for **$**

Shift; then reach *up* to **$** with *left first* finger.

Learn / (diagonal)

1 ; ; /; /; ;; // ;/; ;/; 2/3 4/5 and/or We keyed 1/2 and 3/4.
2 Space between a whole number and a fraction: 7 2/3, 18 3/4.

Learn **$** (dollar sign)

3 f f $f $f ff $$ f$f f$f $4 $4 for $4 Shift for $ and key $4.
4 A period separates dollars and cents: $4.50, $6.25, $19.50.

Combine / and **$**

5 I must shift for $ but not for /: Order 10 gal. at $16/gal.
6 Do not space on either side of /: 1/6, 3/10, 9 5/8, 4 7/12.
7 We sent 5 boxes of No. 6 3/4 envelopes at $11/box on June 2.
8 They can get 2 sets of disks at $49.85/set; 10 sets, $39.85.

262b-266b (continued)

Document 3
Formal Memorandum

LP p. 105

Mrs. Schwartz: Since the Records Section is very busy, Ms. Morris has asked us to help her. Please key this memorandum for her to **Mr. O'Brian,** dated **April 7,** with the subject **Transfer of Documents.**

As requested in your memo (sp) of March ~~26~~ 28, we have begun transferring the paper files in our office to electronic media. I do not anticipate any difficulty in meeting the target dates.

Attatched is a ~~new~~ revised job description for the Director of Human Resources. The revision ~~represents~~ includes a few minor ~~major~~ editorial changes and two major changes.

1. Since training is now a responsibility of the Education and Training Department, which was ~~set up~~ established on February 1, this duty has been eliminated from the job description.

3. The responsibility for planning for human resources in the future has been added to the ~~revised~~ job description.

Document 4
Table

plain paper

Mrs. Schwartz: Key this table; center it vertically and horizontally.

Document 5
Table

plain paper

Mrs. Schwartz: Key the table on employee benefits again, making these changes:

1. Change the secondary heading to read **(Not Including Administrative Personnel).**

2. Key the benefits in alphabetical order.

3. Add this source note preceding the footnote. **Source: In-House Survey Conducted March, 19--.**

BENEFITS DESIRED BY A MAJORITY OF EMPLOYEES*

(In-House Survey Conducted March, 19--)

Benefit	Percent
Paid Vacations	100%
Paid Holidays	99
Life Insurance	95
Health Insurance	~~94~~ 96
Parking Facilities	92
Jury Duty Leave	90
Funeral Leave	90
Rest Time	82
Pension Plan	74
Paid Sick Leave	70
Educational Assistance	68
Employee Discounts	56

*Not including benefits required by law such as Social Security and workers' compensation.

33c ▶ 10 Check Language Skills: Number Expression

1. Read each handwritten (script) line, noting mentally where changes are needed in spacing and number expression.
2. Key each line once SS, making needed changes; then check accuracy of work against rules on pages listed at left of sentences.
3. If time permits, key each line again at a faster speed.

page references

54 1 *15 voted for the amendment, but 12 voted against it.*

54 2 *Of the twenty divers, only three advanced to the state finals.*

54 3 *The curtain rises at eight thirty p.m. on Saturday, October ten.*

55 4 *My office is at ten Park Place; my home, at 1 Key Largo.*

55 5 *Buy one doz. eggs, two lbs. of butter, and 8 oz. of cream.*

55 6 *Check your answers on pages ten and eleven of Chapter One.*

33d ▶ 16 Improve Keyboarding Skill

plain full sheet; begin on line 10

1. Clear tabs; set a tab at the center point.
2. Center each of lines 1-5; DS.
3. QS and key each of lines 6-11 once SS; DS between 2-line groups.
4. If time permits, rekey the drill.

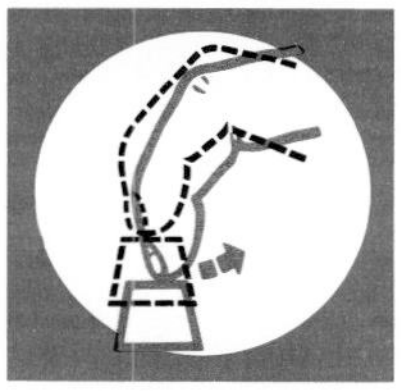

Quick-snap keystroke

center lines

1 WORD PROCESSING TERMS

2 automatic centering

3 delete and insert

4 store and retrieve

5 global search and replace

space bar
6 by us of an am to go by an urn of elm to pay she may and jam
7 Karen is to pay the man for any of the elm you buy from him.

CAPS LOCK
8 They are to see the musical play INTO THE WOODS on Saturday.
9 HBO will show THE KING AND I on Monday, May 13, at 8:30 a.m.

alphabet 10 Sprague is amazed at just how quickly he fixed the blue van.
figures 11 Invoice No. 2749 totals $163.85 plus $4.20 shipping charges.

| 1 | 2 | 3 | 4 | 5 | 6 | 7 | 8 | 9 | 10 | 11 | 12 |

Lesson 34 % and -

LL: 60
LS: SS

34a ▶ 6 Conditioning Practice

each line twice SS; then a 1′ writing on line 3; find *gwam*

alphabet 1 Lopez knew our squad could just slip by the next five games.
figures 2 Check Numbers 267, 298, 304, and 315 were still outstanding.
easy 3 Dixie works with vigor to make the theory work for a profit.

| 1 | 2 | 3 | 4 | 5 | 6 | 7 | 8 | 9 | 10 | 11 | 12 |

34b ▶ 16 Improve Keyboarding Technique

1. Key lines 1-11 of 33d, above, once each as shown.
2. Take a 1′ writing on line 7 and on line 10 of 33d.

Goals:
- to refine technique
- to increase speed

262b-266b (continued)

Document 2
Job Description

LP p. 103

Mrs. Schwartz: Please key this corrected job description making the changes that are marked.

JOB DESCRIPTION

JOB TITLE Director of Human Resources UNIT Human Resources Dept.

REPORTS TO Vice President for Administration

SUBORDINATE STAFF ~~Eleven~~ Ten Section Chiefs

DATE ~~July 9,~~ April 6 19-- D.O.T. 166.117-018

GENERAL STATEMENT OF THE JOB

Under the general direction of the Vice President for Administration, establishes the objectives, policies, and procedures for the efficient and effective use of human resources so that the overall objectives of the company will be achieved successfully.

SPECIFIC DUTIES OF THE JOB

1\. Analyzes and evaluates jobs to determine the tasks performed and the qualifications required to complete the tasks, as a basis for recruiting, placing, and compensating employees.

7 ~~2~~. Provides employees with a variety of benefits that best suit~~s~~ their needs.

2 ~~3~~. Provides human resources required by all organizational elements by recruiting and selecting qualified employees.

~~4. Improves the value of human resources through training and, at the same time, aids employees to reach their full potential.~~

3 ~~5~~. Improves relations with employees through collective bargaining with unions and by implementing effective procedures for redressing grievances.

4 ~~6~~. E~~I~~nsures that employees enjoy a safe working environment through safety campaigns, inspections, and education; investigates and corrects causes of all accidents.

6 ~~7~~. Maintains and safeguards all employee records.

8\. Assures, through equal opportunity programs, that all employees are treated equitably, regardless of race, color, ~~religion,~~ creed, age, and sex.

9\. Establishes affirmative action programs to e~~i~~nsure and improve the recruitment and hiring of minorities.

5 ~~10~~. Provides for the physical ~~medical~~ well-being of employees through in-house medical facilities and a comprehensive health insurance plan.

10\. Forecasts, through careful planning, the scope and conduct of an effective human resources program in the future.

34c ▶ 18 Learn % and -

each line twice SS (slowly, then faster); DS between 4-line groups; if time permits, practice the lines again

% = percent sign
- = hyphen

Do not space between a figure and the %, nor before or after - or -- (dash) used as punctuation.

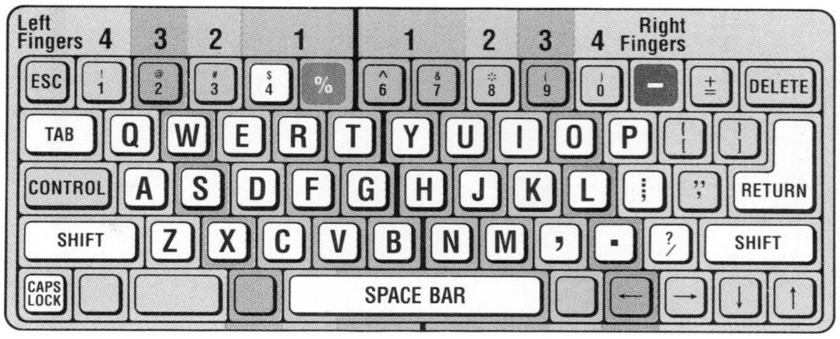

Reach technique for %

Shift; then reach *up* to % with *left first* finger.

Reach technique for -

Reach *up* to – with *right little* finger.

Learn % (percent sign)

1 f f %f %f ff %% f%f f%f 5% 5% Shift for the % in 5% and 15%.
2 Do not space between a number and %: 5%, 75%, 85%, and 95%.

Learn - (hyphen)

3 ; ; -; -; ;; -- ;-; ;-; 4-ply I use a 2-ply tire on my bike.
4 I gave each film a 1-star, 2-star, 3-star, or 4-star rating.

Combine % and -

5 He can send the parcel by fourth-class mail at a 50% saving.
6 A dash is two unspaced hyphens--no space before or after it.
7 The new prime rate is 12%--but you have no interest in that.
8 You need 60 signatures--51% of the members--on the petition.

34d ▶ 10 Build Keyboarding Skill Transfer

1. Take a 1′ writing on ¶ 1; find *gwam*.

2. Take a 1′ writing on ¶ 2 and on ¶3; find *gwam* on each writing.

3. Compare rates. On which ¶ did you have the highest *gwam?*

4. Take two 1′ writings on each of the slower ¶s, trying to equal your highest *gwam* of the first 3 writings.

Note: Most students key straight copy at the highest *gwam;* handwritten (script) copy at the next highest; and statistical copy at the lowest *gwam.*

To find *gwam,* use the 1′ *gwam* for partial lines in ¶s 1 and 2, but *count* the words in a partial line in ¶ 3.

all letters/figures used | LA | 1.4 si | 5.4 awl | 85% hfw

gwam 1′

You should try now to transfer to other types of copy 11
as much of your straight-copy speed as you can. Handwritten 23
copy and copy in which figures appear tend to slow you down. 35
You can increase speed on these, however, with extra effort. 48

An immediate goal for handwritten copy is at least 90% 11
of the straight-copy rate; for copy with figures, at least 23
75%. Try to speed up balanced-hand figures such as 26, 84, 35
and 163. Key harder ones such as 452 and 890 more slowly. 47

Copy that is written by hand is often not legible, and 11
the spelling of words may be puzzling. So give major atten- 23
tion to unclear words. Question and correct the spacing used 35
with a comma or period. You can do this even as you key. 47

gwam 1′ | 1 | 2 | 3 | 4 | 5 | 6 | 7 | 8 | 9 | 10 | 11 | 12 |

UNIT 63 LESSONS 262 – 266

Human Resources Department

Learning Goals

1. To become familiar with some of the major functions performed in a Human Resources Department.
2. To increase your knowledge of typical documents processed and tasks performed in a Human Resources Department.
3. To improve your skill in formatting special documents.

Documents Processed

1. Formal Memorandum
2. Job Description
3. Table
4. Form Letters
5. Statement of Policy
6. Simplified Memorandum
7. Grievance Procedures

262a-266a ▶ 5 (daily) *Conditioning Practice*

each line twice SS (slowly, then faster); if time permits, take 1′ writings on line 4

alphabet	1	Suzi quickly indexed jokes for the performance she will give publicly.
figures	2	Based on 5,349,700 shares sold, the new stock rose 6 points to 83 1/2.
fig/sym	3	The balance ($829.35) was paid by Bell & Erby on May 6 by Check #7410.
speed	4	It may be a big problem if both of the men bid for the city dock work.

| 1 | 2 | 3 | 4 | 5 | 6 | 7 | 8 | 9 | 10 | 11 | 12 | 13 | 14 |

262b-266b ▶ 45 (daily) *Document Processing*

1. You will now work as a keyboard technician in the Human Resources Department under the direction of Mrs. Rachel Schwartz, who is the administrative assistant to Henry K. O'Brian, Director of Human Resources.
2. In this job, you will be required to prepare a number of documents for members of the Human Resources Department. Before beginning, review the material about the department on page 427 as well as the major duties and special instructions.
3. Follow directions given for each document. If no format is specified, use your best judgment.
4. Unless directed to prepare a draft copy, key all documents in final form. Correct all marked and unmarked errors.

Document 1
Formal Memorandum
LP p. 101

Please key this memorandum for Mr. O'Brian, dated March 28, to Diane T. Morris, Chief of Records. Use the subject "Transfer of Documents."

SS Lucille K. Phillips, vice president for administration, has notified me that *to the extent possible,* all documents will be transfered from paper files to electronic files by means of an optical ~~scanner~~ *character* recognition (OCR) *scanner*. Listed below is the schedule for converting records in your files.

DS

Access Code	Documents	Target Date
8 18 3010	Individual Personel Records	April 30
8 18 3020	Correspondence	May 15
8 18 3030	Job Descriptions	June 1

SS Prior to converting the job descriptions, you should review and revise *where necessary,* all job description that are ~~two~~ *three* or more years old. When you do so please send me a copy of the job descriptoin for ~~this~~ *my* position.

35a ▶ 6 Conditioning Practice

each line twice SS; then a 1′ writing on line 3; find *gwam*

alphabet 1 Racquel just put back five azure gems next to my gold watch.
figures 2 Joel used a comma in 1,203 and 2,946 but not in 583 and 750.
easy 3 The auto firm owns the big signs by the downtown civic hall.

| 1 | 2 | 3 | 4 | 5 | 6 | 7 | 8 | 9 | 10 | 11 | 12 |

35b ▶ 10 Check Language Skills: Capitalization

1. Read and key each line once SS, making needed changes in capitalization.
2. Check accuracy of work against rules on pages listed; rekey any line that contains errors in capitalization.

page references
40, 41 1 did mr. reid assign Unit 8 for monday? beth read it sunday.
40 2 did miss perez excuse john and anita xica from history class?
40 3 gloria said that juan will attend midway college next year.
40, 42 4 the golden gate bridge connects san francisco and sausalito.
40, 41 5 our labor day holiday is the first monday in september.
40, 42 6 concordia bank is located at mason street and laurel avenue.
40, 43 7 muriel getz, the club secretary, wrote to president marquis.
40, 43 8 dr. p. c. vickers has an m.d. and a ph.d. from johns hopkins.

35c ▶ 18 Learn # and &

each set of lines twice SS (slowly, then faster); DS between groups; if time permits, practice the lines again

= number/pounds
& = ampersand (and)

Do not space between # and a figure; space once before and after **&** used to join names.

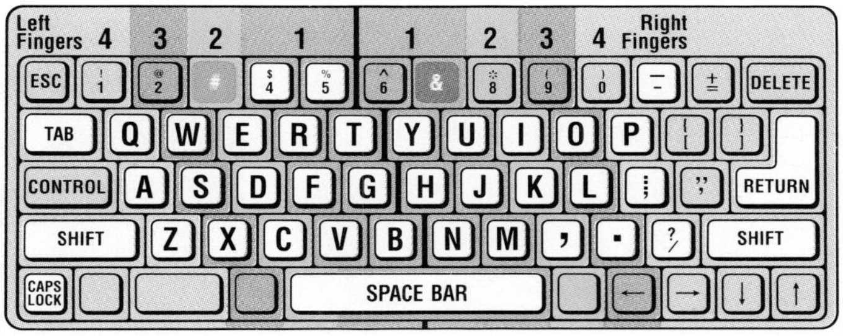

Reach technique for #

Shift; then reach *up* to # with *left second* finger.

Reach technique for **&**

Shift; then reach *up* to **&** with *right first* finger.

Learn # (number/pounds)

1 d d #d #d dd ## d#d d#d 3# 3# Shift for # as you enter #33d.
2 Do not space between a number and #: 3# of #633 at $9.35/#.

Learn & (ampersand)

3 j j &j &j jj && j&j j&j 7& 7& Have you written to Poe & Son?
4 Do not space before or after & in initials; i.e., CG&E, B&O.

Combine # and &

5 Shift for # and &. Recall: # stands for number and pounds.
6 Names joined by & require spaces; a # sign alone does, also.
7 Letters joined by & are keyed solid: List Stock #3 as C&NW.
8 I bought 20# of #830 grass seed from Locke & Uhl on March 4.

261c ▶ 20 *Improve Language Skills: Proofread/Correct*

1. The paragraphs at the right include errors in spelling, punctuation, capitalization, and keystroking.

2. Key the paragraphs as an unbound report, correcting errors as you work. Title: **MATHEMATICS AND YOUR FUTURE.**

3. When you have completed the report, proofread it carefully and correct any errors you may have missed.

words

heading 6

When asked to name there favorite sujbect in school, very few peopel list 20
mathematics. This is probably true because solving problems with numbers 35
require thought concentration and extra effort. When we study math; how- 50
ever; we develope skills in solving problems; we learn to think thru a prob- 66
lem logicaly, and we increase our ability to make good decisions. Farther--we 82
enhance our ability to analyse situations and come to valid conclusoins. in 97
many instances, their are no substitutes for applying mathematics in solving 112
are problems. 115

In to day's complex world, it is allmost impossible to exist without useing 130
math. We use math everytime we buy an item, keep a cheking acount, verify 146
the deductions made from our pay checks, and prepare our Income Taxes. 160
In a sense math governs our personel lives since we must plan our spending 175
and savnigs to avoid going to deeply into debt. A budget can help us to use 191
our money wisely so that we can injoy life with out magor money problems. 205

Mathematics is becoming more and more important in the busness world. 220
Those with good back grounds in math qualify for a wider variety of jobs. 235
One who can do only simpel arithmetic for example cannot hope to be pro- 249
moted to a job wich require the worker to analyse and interpret financiel 264
statements. Workers often find that they lose job oportunities to others who 280
has higher levels of math skills. Math is a skill of such importence that it is 297
worth puting extra effort in to it. 304

261d ▶ 10 *Improve Keystroking Skills: Figures and Symbols*

1. Key each sentence. Do not correct errors.

2. Proofread the sentences carefully and correct errors in pencil.

3. Rekey the sentences from your corrected copy. Correct all errors.

1 The vote on Amendment 901-A was 518 "ayes" (58%) and 376 "nays" (42%).

2 The interest on Note #512846 is $356.25 ($7,500 for 6 months at 9.5%).

3 On May 9, I ordered 50 reams of 20# 8 1/2″ × 11″ paper (Stock #36472).

4 The Ajax Copier (Model #43895-B) lists for $2,687 less a 10% discount.

5 My statement of 1/8/90 (Account #93462) showed a balance of $4,593.76.

6 Sales (as of June 30) were $21,540,871--an increase of 29.6% over May.

7 The report stated, "Taxes for 1990 were $378,640--an increase of 25%."

8 The desks (Catalog #502648-P) ordered from C&L will cost $371.90 each.

35d ▶ 16 Improve Keyboarding Skill Transfer

1. Take a 1′ writing on ¶ 1; find *gwam*.

2. Take a 1′ writing on ¶ 2; find *gwam*.

3. Take two more 1′ writings on the slower ¶.

4. Take a 2′ writing on ¶ 1 and on ¶ 2; find *gwam* on each writing (2′ *gwam* = 1′ *gwam* ÷ 2).

5. Take 2 more 2′ writings on the slower ¶.

Goal: To transfer at least 75% of your straight-copy speed to statistical copy.

To determine % of transfer:
¶ 2 *gwam* ÷ ¶ 1 *gwam*

all letters/figures used | LA | 1.4 si | 5.4 awl | 85% hfw

Figures appear often in personal and business documents. It is vital, therefore, that you learn to key them rapidly. If you will just keep your hands in position and reach with your fingers, you will soon be amazed at your ability to key all figures with ease.

Learn to read and key figures in distinct groups. For example, read 165 as one sixty-five and key it that way. Tackle the longer sequences in like manner. Read 1078 as ten seventy-eight and handle it as 2 units. Try this trick for 2493, also.

Lesson 36

(and)

LL: 60
LS: SS

36a ▶ 6 Conditioning Practice

each line twice SS; then a 1′ writing on line 3; find *gwam*

alphabet 1 Jacques could win a prize for eight more dives by next week.
figures 2 In 1987, we had only 135 computers; as of 1990 we owned 264.
easy 3 The girls paid for the eight antique urns with their profit.

| 1 | 2 | 3 | 4 | 5 | 6 | 7 | 8 | 9 | 10 | 11 | 12 |

36b ▶ 12 Recall/Improve Language Skills: Capitalization and Number Expression

1. Read the first rule highlighted in color.

2. Key the **Learn** sentence below it, noting how the rule has been applied.

3. Key the **Apply** sentence, supplying the appropriate capitalization and/or number expression.

4. Practice the other rules in the same way.

5. If time permits, key the four **Apply** lines again to improve decision-making speed.

Capitalize nouns preceding numbers (except *page* and *line*).

Learn 1 Please see Rule 10 in Unit 3, page 45, lines 27 and 28.
Apply 2 See volume 12, section 38, page 564, lines 78-90.

Spell (capitalized) names of small-numbered streets and avenues (ten and under).

Learn 3 I walked several blocks along Third Avenue to 65th Street.
Apply 4 At 6th Street she took a taxi to his home on 43d Avenue.

Use figures for a series of fractions, but spell isolated fractions and indefinite numbers.

Learn 5 Carl has a 1/4 interest in Parcel A, 1/2 in B, and 2/3 in C.
Learn 6 Nearly forty-five members voted; that is almost two thirds.

Apply 7 Guide calls: one fourth, 1/2, 3/4, and 1--each 15 seconds.
Apply 8 Over 50 students passed the test; that is about 1/2.

260c ▶ 15 Improve Straight-Copy Skill

Take two 5′ writings on the ¶s at the right. Record *gwam* and errors on the better writing.

all letters used | A | 1.5 si | 5.7 awl | 80% hfw

	gwam 1′	5′	
Today we live in an age of information brought about by the amazing	14	3	61
growth in data and word processing by the computer. Success in business	28	6	64
demands information upon which vital decisions can be made. A computer	43	9	67
can produce volumes of data in the form of words and figures in a very	57	11	70
short time. Data, however, is simply the raw facts which must be re-	71	14	73
fined into useful information. Though a number of techniques may be	84	17	75
used to submit pertinent information, a formal report is often used.	98	20	78
As an employee in an office, you may be asked to assist in the	13	22	81
preparation of reports--to collect the essential data, outline the im-	27	25	84
portant concepts to be emphasized, and perhaps to prepare a first draft.	41	28	86
When the originator of the report has completed it, your job will be to	56	31	89
prepare it in an appropriate format. When doing so, it might also be	70	34	92
your responsibility to recheck the report for clarity and conciseness	84	36	95
and to verify that all facts and figures used are correct.	95	39	97
The operator who keys a report can do a great deal to assure that	13	41	100
the report is favorably received by arranging it so that it is attrac-	27	44	103
tive and neat. An untidy, poorly prepared report is certain to give a	41	47	106
bad impression. Extra attention must be given to the format of a re-	55	50	108
port; especially the margins and spacing. The report should be free	69	52	111
of errors in spelling, grammar, punctuation, and in the use of words	83	55	114
or figures. Each page should be proofread carefully to recheck all of	97	58	117
these points.	100	59	117

gwam 1′ | 1 | 2 | 3 | 4 | 5 | 6 | 7 | 8 | 9 | 10 | 11 | 12 | 13 | 14 |
gwam 5′ | 1 | 2 | 3 |

Lesson 261 Improve Basic Skills

261a ▶ 5 Conditioning Practice

each line twice SS (slowly, then faster); if time permits, take 1′ writings on lines 1 and 4

alphabet 1 Pete found gold jewelry and necklaces in the excavation in Mozambique.

figures 2 Make a copy of the material on pages 12, 39, 56, 74, 83, 106, and 109.

fig/sym 3 They paid a local tax of 2% ($327.76) and a sales tax of 5% ($819.40).

speed 4 If the men work with proficiency, the big coalfield may make a profit.

| 1 | 2 | 3 | 4 | 5 | 6 | 7 | 8 | 9 | 10 | 11 | 12 | 13 | 14 |

261b ▶ 15 Improve Straight-Copy Skill

1. Take two 5′ writings on the ¶s in 260c.

2. Strive to increase speed by 2 *gwam* with fewer errors.

3. Record *gwam* and errors on the better writing.

36c ▶ 18 *Learn (and)*

each set of lines twice SS (slowly, then faster); DS between groups; if time permits, practice the lines again

(= left parenthesis
) = right parenthesis

Do not space between **(** **)** and the copy they enclose.

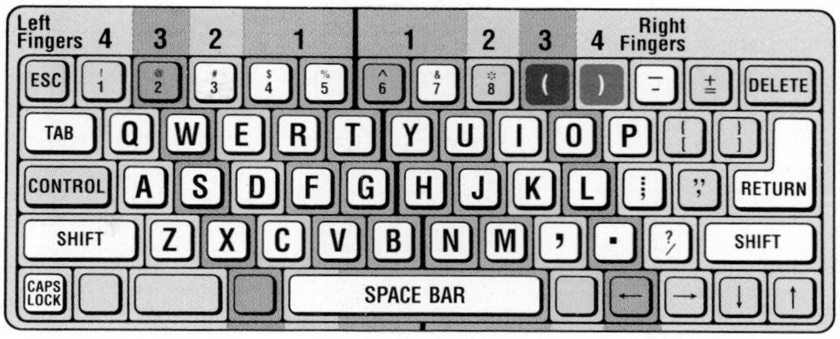

Reach technique for **(**

Shift; then reach *up* to **(** with *right third* finger.

Reach technique for **)**

Shift; then reach *up* to **)** with *right little* finger.

Learn **(** (left parenthesis)

use the letter "l"

1 l l (l (l ll ((l(l l(l 9(9(Shift for the (as you key (9.
2 As (is the shift of 9, use the l finger to key 9, (, or (9.

Learn **)** (right parenthesis)

3 ; ;);); ;;)) ;); ;); 0) 0) Shift for the) as you key 0).
4 As) is the shift of 0, use the ; finger to key 0,), or 0).

Combine **(** and **)**

5 Hints: (1) depress shift; (2) strike key; (3) release both.
6 Tab steps: (1) clear tabs, (2) set stops, and (3) tabulate.
7 Her new account (#495-3078) draws annual interest at 6 1/2%.

36d ▶ 14 Improve Keyboarding Skill

full sheet; line 10

1. Clear tabs; set a tab at center point.
2. Center each of lines 1-5; DS.
3. QS and key each of lines 6-13 once SS; DS between 2-line groups.
4. If time permits, rekey the drill.

center lines

1 DENTAL SERVICES, INC.
2 Announces New Dental Center
3 in
4 Eastwood Circle Mall
5 Opening the First of March

letter response

6 upon ever join save only best ploy gave pink edge pump facts
7 You acted on a phony tax case only after a union gave facts.

word response

8 visit risks their world field chair proxy throw right eighty
9 Lana may sign the form to pay for the giant map of the city.

combination response

10 also fast sign card maps only hand were pair link paid plump
11 To get to be a pro, react with zest and care as the pros do.

alphabet
12 Shep quickly coaxed eight avid fans away from the jazz band.

fig/sym
13 Of 370 students, only 35 (9.46%) failed to type 18-20 w.a.m.

UNIT 62 LESSONS 260 – 261
Improve Basic Skills

Learning Goals

1. To improve your basic keyboarding skills with emphasis on figures and symbols.
2. To increase your keystroking speed and to improve your accuracy on straight copy.
3. To improve your communications skills.

Format Guides

1. Paper guide at *0* (for typewriters).
2. LL: 70 spaces for drills, timed writings and language skills.
3. LS: SS sentence drills with a DS between groups; DS paragraph writings and language skill sentences.
4. PI: 5 spaces.

Lesson 260 *Improve Basic Skills*

260a ▶ 5 Conditioning Practice

each line twice SS (slowly, then faster); if time permits, take 1′ writings on lines 2 and 3

alphabet 1 Equalizing my daily work load was the objective of the office experts.

figures 2 On July 15, my telephone number was changed from 634-5817 to 932-8026.

fig/sym 3 The sales tax on Invoice #14397-610 will be $329.62 (4% of $8,240.50).

speed 4 When he is at the dock, my neighbor may fix the rotor of the big auto.

| 1 | 2 | 3 | 4 | 5 | 6 | 7 | 8 | 9 | 10 | 11 | 12 | 13 | 14 |

260b ▶ 30 Improve Language Skills: Proofread/Correct

1. In each sentence at the right, items have been underlined. The underlines indicate that there *may* be an error in spelling, punctuation, capitalization, grammar, or in the use of words or figures.

2. Study each sentence carefully. Key the line number. If an underlined item is incorrect, correct it as you key the sentence. In addition, correct any keyboarding errors you may make as you work.

3. When you have completed the sentences and *before* you remove the copy, study each sentence carefully and correct any errors you may have missed.

1. In doctor Millers' opinion, the patiant can be released.
2. Did the custumer order 6 or 8 banners for the festival?
3. She said its a posibility we will meet in the world trade center.
4. Mary_ our President_ will preside at the instalation of officers.
5. Ron's and Betty's joint report was about our foriegn policy.
6. This is the point, will they receive their benifits?
7. If she don't apply now, she can not obtain a masximum morgage.
8. The firm of Martin & Hayes have been hired to raise the wharehouse.
9. Wanda choose a large, red book to record her expendatures.
10. According to table 3789_ 42% of the funds have all ready been spent.
11. The facultie will meet in room 1,082 at 3:00 PM.
12. In edition we flue to these cities, Oslo, Cairo, Paris, and Rome.
13. Each man drove their own car to the sight of the Shopping Center.
14. Jill said, 'the theater was pact for the commissions' report.'
15. Did he autherize us to buy 12 copies of the book "Fiscul Planning"?
16. In the passed, 6 absences was grounds for disciplinary action.
17. Whose responsible for implementing the plan; Don or Leslie?
18. This year_ Ross's comissions rose from the $60s to the mid $80s.
19. The superviser, who just arrived, will establish new scedules.
20. In my judgement_ only 1/4 of the man were at the confrence.

37a ▶ 6 Conditioning Practice

each line twice SS; then a 1′ writing on line 3; find *gwam*

alphabet 1 Bowman fixed prized clocks that seven judges say are unique.
figures 2 Only 1,473 of the 6,285 members were at the 1990 convention.
easy 3 She lent the field auditor a hand with the work of the firm.

| 1 | 2 | 3 | 4 | 5 | 6 | 7 | 8 | 9 | 10 | 11 | 12 |

37b ▶ 20 Learn ' (Apostrophe) and " (Quotation Mark)

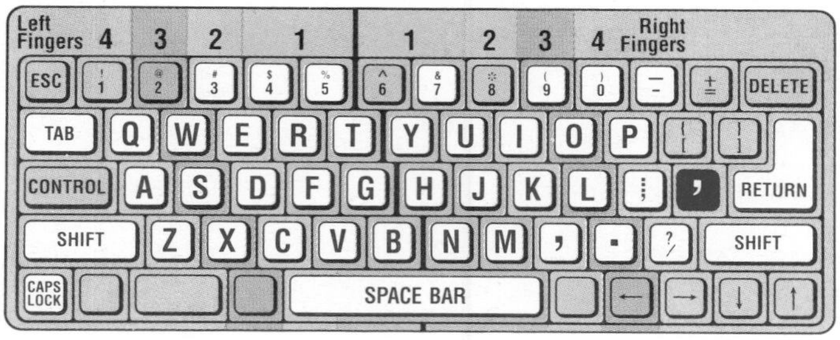

Apostrophe: The **'** is to the right of **;** and is controlled by the *right little finger.*

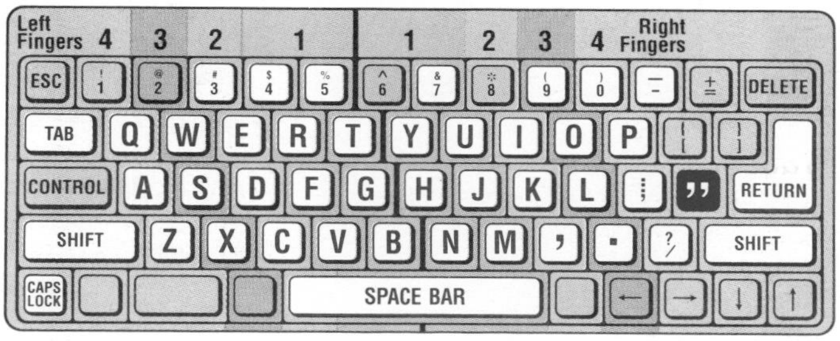

Quotation mark: Key **"** (the shift of **'**) with the *right little finger.* Remember to depress the left shift before striking **"**.

Learning procedure

1. Locate new symbol on appropriate chart above. Read the reach technique given below the chart.

2. Key twice SS the appropriate pair of lines given at right; DS between pairs.

3. Repeat Steps 1 and 2 for the other new symbol.

4. Key twice SS lines 5-8.

5. If time permits, rekey the lines with which you had difficulty.

Language skills note

Capitalize the first and all important words in titles of publications.

Learn ' (apostrophe)

1 ; ; '; '; ;; '' ;'; ;'; it's he's I'm I've It's hers, I see.
2 I'm not sure if it's Hal's; but if it's his, I'll return it.

Learn " (quotation mark)

3 ; ; "; "; ;; """ ;"; ;"; "Keep on," she said, but I had quit.
4 I read "Ode on a Grecian Urn," "The Last Leaf," and "Trees."

Combine ' and "

5 "If it's Jan's or Al's," she said, "I'll bring it to class."
6 "Its" is an adjective; "it's" is the contraction of "it is."
7 Miss Uhl said, "To make numbers plural, add 's: 8's, 10's."
8 O'Shea said, "Use ' (apostrophe) to shorten phrases: I'll."

Alternative practice

On some keyboards, ' is the shift of **8** and " is the shift of **2**. If these are the locations of ' and " on your keyboard, key each set of lines at right twice SS; then key each of lines 5-8 in 37b, above, twice SS.

apostrophe 1 k k 'k 'k kk '' k'k k'k Is this tie Ike's? No, it's Dick's.
2 On Vic's keyboard the ' is on 8; on Lei's, it's in home row.

quotation mark 3 s s "s "s ss """ s"s s"s 2" 2" "Go for a high goal," he said.
4 Did Mrs. Negron use "there" for "their" and "two" for "too"?

255b-259b (continued)

Document 14
Table
plain full sheet

Mr. Devereau: Please key this updated report of the company's participation in the United Community Fund Campaign.

BOUTIQUES INTERNATIONAL, LTD.

United Community Fund Campaign

Report of Progress as of October ~~1~~ 15, 19--

Organizational Unit	Percent of Participation	Amount
Administration Division	~~42%~~ 64%	$ ~~882~~ 1,344
Advertising Department	~~51~~ 72	~~1,020~~ 1,440
Customer Service Center	~~58~~ 81	~~1,160~~ 1,620
Finance Division	~~48~~ 67	~~709~~ 989
General Services Department	~~60~~ 84	~~902~~ 1,263
Human Resources Department	~~55~~ 74	~~1,154~~ 1,553
Information Processing Center	~~67~~ 86	~~737~~ 946
Industrial Relations Department	~~45~~ 68	~~682~~ 1,031
Legal Department	~~70~~ 84	~~1,750~~ 2,100
Maintenance Department	~~40~~ 52	~~255~~ 332
Marketing Division	~~63~~ 85	~~756~~ 1,020
Planning and Research Department	~~72~~ 89	~~1,083~~ 1,339
Public Relations Office	~~80~~ 92	~~1,679~~ 1,931
Purchasing Division	~~53~~ 71	~~799~~ 1,071

Document 15
Formal Memorandum
LP p. 99

Mr. Devereau: Key this memorandum from **Miss Jackson** to **Henry K. O'Brian, Director of Human Resources.** Date the memo **May 20.** Use as a subject line: **TOYS-FOR-TOTS CAMPAIGN.**

¶ Will you please include the following notice in the next edition of the "Employees' Newsletter":

¶ Again this year we will participate in the annual "Toys-for-Tots" campaign conducted by the local Army Reserve Units.

¶ Please help us by volunteering to participate ~~in this worthwhile campaign~~ as a coordinator in your area. Call Dan Devereau (Extension 592) who will act as the overall coordinator for the campaign.

We are getting an early start this year in gathering volunteers for this worthwhile campaign.

37c ▶ 10 Improve Language Skills: Capitalization

1. Read the first rule highlighted in color.
2. Key the **Learn** sentences below it, noting how the rule has been applied.
3. Key the **Apply** sentences, supplying the appropriate capitalization.
4. Practice the other rule in the same way.
5. If time permits, key the **Apply** lines again at a faster speed.

> Capitalize the first word of a direct quotation unless the quote is built into the structure of the sentence.

Learn 1 Yu-lan quoted the rule: "Spell the hour used with o'clock."
Learn 2 I didn't say that "making more errors makes us more human."

Apply 3 Kathleen quoted Pope: "to err is human, to forgive divine."
Apply 4 Ms. Ohms said to "Keep your eyes on the copy as you key."

> Capitalize the first word of the first part of an interrupted quotation, but not the first word of the second part.

Learn 5 "To reduce errors," he said, "drop back slightly in speed."
Apply 6 "curve your fingers," she urged, "and keep them upright."

37d ▶ 14 Improve Keyboarding Technique

1. Key each pair of lines once as shown: SS with a DS between pairs.
2. Take two 1′ writings on line 11 and on line 12; find *gwam* on each writing.
3. If time permits, rekey the slower line.

Technique goals
- curved, upright fingers
- quick-snap keystrokes
- quiet hands and arms

shift-key sentences
1 He and Vi crossed the English Channel from Hove to Le Havre.
2 J. W. Posner has left Madrid for Turin for some Alps skiing.

fig/sym sentences
3 I signed a 20-year note--$67,495 (at 13.8%)--with Coe & Han.
4 Order #29105 reads: "16 sets of Cat. #4718A at $36.25/set."

adjacent-key sentences
5 We spent a quiet week at the shore prior to the open season.
6 If we buy her coffee shop, should we buy the gift shop, too?

long-reach sentences
7 My niece has a chance to bring the bronze trophy back to us.
8 We once had many mussels, but not since the recent harvests.

alphabetic sentences
9 Pam was quickly given the bronze trophy by six fussy judges.
10 Quent got six big jigsaw puzzles from the very dapper clerk.

easy sentences
11 Did he rush the rotor of the giant robot to the island firm?
12 The busy girl works with a fury to fix the signals by eight.

| 1 | 2 | 3 | 4 | 5 | 6 | 7 | 8 | 9 | 10 | 11 | 12 |

Lesson 38 — _ and *

LL: 60
LS: SS

38a ▶ 6 Conditioning Practice

each line twice SS; then a 1′ writing on line 3; find *gwam*

alphabet 1 Quig was just amazed by the next five blocks of his players.
figures 2 On October 30, 1991, the 287 members met from 5 to 6:45 p.m.
easy 3 Keith may hang the sign by the antique door of the big hall.

| 1 | 2 | 3 | 4 | 5 | 6 | 7 | 8 | 9 | 10 | 11 | 12 |

38b ▶ 14 Improve Keyboarding Technique

1. Key lines 1-12 of 37d, above, once SS as shown; DS between pairs.

2. Take two 1′ writings on line 11 and one on line 12; find *gwam* on each writing.

Goals:
- to refine technique
- to increase speed.

255b-259b (continued)

Document 12
Simplified Memorandum
plain full sheet

Mr. Devereau: Key this message as a simplified memorandum from **Ms. Quan** in reply to **Miss Jackson**'s memo of May 3. Date the memo **May 16.** Subject line: **SCHEDULE FOR OPEN HOUSE.**

As you requested in your memo (sp) of May 3, attached is a copy of the proposed schedule for the open house to be ~~conducted~~ held on July 15.

The tours will begin at 30-minute intervals ~~beginning~~ from 9 a.m. until 4 p.m. with a 1-hour (sp) break for lunch ~~beginning~~ at noon. Upon arrival, the guests will be directed to the Meeting room, which will accomodate 30 people. There ~~guests~~ they will receive a breif greeting and then view the company film which was recently updated.

Inasmuch as Warehouse B is on the route from the Shipping Complex to the Shipping Dept. (sp), I have added a "walk-through" tour of the Warehouse (lc).

A schedule of the ~~individuals~~ people who will be responsible for each ~~part~~ segment of the tour will be ~~prepared within a very short time.~~ published no later than June 1.

Document 13
Schedule
plain full sheet

Mr. Devereau: Key the open house schedule which will be attached to the memo to Miss Jackson. Quadruple-space after the heading information and between the activities.

BOUTIQUES INTERNATIONAL, LTD.

Open House

July ~~12~~ 15, 19--

Time	Activity	Location
9:00 a.m.	Greetings Film: "Boutiques International--at Home and Abroad"	Meeting Room
9:20 a.m.	Tour of Mail Room	Mail Room
9:30 a.m.	Explanation of Order Processing	Computer Room
9:45 a.m.	Tour of Shipping Department (Through Warehouse B en route)	Shipping ~~Room~~ Complex
10:00 a.m.	Refreshments	~~Executive Conference Room~~ Employees' Lounge

38c ▶ 18 Learn __ (Underline) and * (Asterisk)

Underline: Key __ (the shift of -) with the *right little finger.* Remember to depress the left shift before striking __.

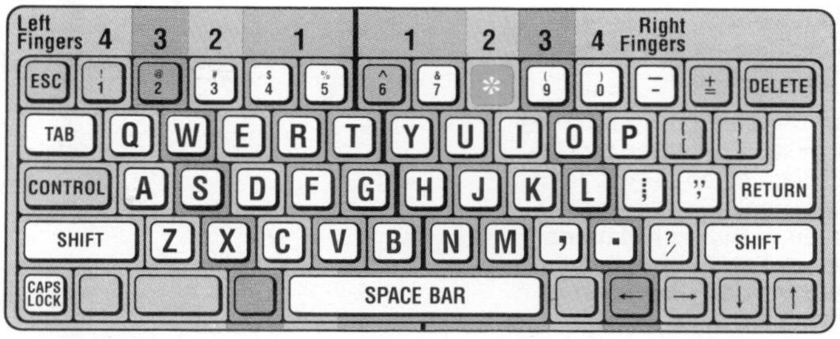

Asterisk: Key * (the shift of **8**) with the *right second finger.* Remember to depress the left shift before striking *.

Learning procedure

1. Locate new key on appropriate chart above. Read the reach technique given below the chart.

2. Key twice SS the appropriate pair of lines given at right; DS between pairs.

3. Repeat Steps 1 and 2 for the other new key.

4. Key twice SS lines 5-6.

5. If time permits, rekey the lines with which you had difficulty.

> **Note:** If you are using a computer, insert the proper codes for underlining.

Key the word; backspace to beginning to underline it.

Learn __ (underline)

1 ; ; _; _; ;; _ _ ;_; ;_; We are to underline ready and begin.
2 To succeed, you should plan the work and then work the plan.

Learn * (asterisk)

3 k k *k *k kk ** k*k k*k She used * for a single source note.
4 All discounted items show an *, thus: 48K*, 588*, and 618*.

Combine __ and *

5 Use an * to mark often-confused words such as then and than.
6 *Note: Book titles (like Lorna Doone) are often underlined.

38d ▶ 12 Check/Improve Keyboarding Skill

1. A 1′ writing on each ¶; find *gwam* on each.

2. A 2′ writing on ¶s 1-2 combined; find *gwam.*

3. An additional 1′ writing on each ¶; find *gwam*.

4. An additional 2′ writing on ¶s 1-2 combined; find *gwam.*

5. If time permits, take a 3′ writing on ¶s 1-2 combined; find *gwam.*

***1′ gwam* goals**

- ▽ 25 = acceptable
- ⊡ 29 = average
- ⊙ 33 = good
- ◈ 37 = excellent

all letters used | LA | 1.4 si | 5.4 awl | 85% hfw

	gwam 2′	3′
One reason we learn to key is to be able to apply that	6	4
skill as we format personal and business documents--letters,	12	8
reports, and tables, for example. Your next major goal will	18	12
be to learn the rules that govern how we arrange, place, and	24	16
space the most commonly used documents.	28	18
In one way or another, we must memorize the features	33	22
that distinguish one style of letter or report from another.	39	26
Our ability to retain in our minds the vital details will	45	30
help us place and space documents quickly and avoid having	51	34
to look up such facts as we key letters or reports.	56	37

gwam 2′ | 1 | 2 | 3 | 4 | 5 | 6
3′ | 1 | 2 | 3 | 4

255b-259b (continued)

Document 9
Simplified Memorandum
plain full sheet

Mr. Devereau: Key this message as a simplified memorandum, dated **May 3,** from **Miss Jackson** to **Nancy P. Quan,** a **Public Relations Specialist.** Subject line: **ANNUAL BOUTIQUES INTERNATIONAL OPEN HOUSE.**

¶ Will you please assume responsibility for planning and ~~organizing~~ supervising the annual Boutiques International open house for the public, which has been scheduled for July 15.

¶ Last year's open house proved ~~quite~~ very successful and can be used as a basis for planning this year's event. You will find copies of last year's schedule in the files. This year, however, I would like to eliminate the visit to the executive conference room and substitute in its place a ~~trip~~ visit to the employees' lounge where refreshments ~~may~~ can be served.

¶ Please let me have your ~~suggestions~~ recommendations for a schedule of events for the open house by May ~~15~~ 18.

Document 10
Letter
LP p. 97

Mr. Devereau: Key this letter in block format for **Miss Jackson**'s signature to **Dr. Helen N. Tanner, President of the Allied Service Clubs, 926 Canal Street, New Orleans, LA 70112-4579.** Date the letter **May 5** and send a copy to **Christine C. Mays.**

Thank you for inviting Boutiques International ~~us~~ to participate in the annual banquet of the Allied Service Clubs of New Orleans to be held at the Park plaza hotel on June 20 at 7 p.m. [caps: Plaza, Hotel]

Ms. Christine C. Mays, our director of sales, will represent us at this important meeting. Ms. Mays has been a member of the New Orleans Chamber of Commerce for the past nine ~~a number of~~ years and was recently elected Vice President of that group. [lc: vice president]

As you requested, Ms. Mays will be prepared to speek for a period of not more than (10) [sp] minutes at the conclusion of the banquet. She will send you a transcript of her remarks within the next ~~a~~ few weeks.

Boutiques International appreciates and welcomes the opportunity to participate in this major public affair.

Document 11
Simplified Memorandum
plain full sheet

1. Compose and key a simplified memorandum to **Ms. Mays** from **Miss Jackson** dated **May 5** to which you will attach a copy of the letter to Dr. Tanner (Document 10). Supply an appropriate subject line.

2. Call Ms. Mays' attention to the fact that Miss Jackson has promised that she will send a transcript of her remarks within the next few weeks.

3. Request Ms. Mays to send a copy of her remarks to the Public Relations Office before she sends them to Dr. Tanner.

ENRICHMENT ACTIVITY: Timed Writing

The ¶s are counted internally for 1′ guided and unguided writings and at the side and bottom for 2′ and 3′ measurement writings. The ¶s may be used whenever additional timed writing practice is desired.

1. Take a 1′ writing on ¶ 1; determine *gwam.*

2. Add 4 *gwam* to set a new goal rate.

3. Take two 1′ writings on ¶ 1, trying to maintain your goal rate each 1/4 minute.

4. Key ¶ 2 in the same way.

5. Take a 2′ unguided writing on each ¶. If you complete a ¶ before time is called, begin that ¶ again.

6. Take a 3′ writing on ¶s 1-2 combined; determine *gwam.*

gwam	¼′	½′	¾′	Time
16	4	8	12	16
20	5	10	15	20
24	6	12	18	24
28	7	14	21	28
32	8	16	24	32
36	9	18	27	36
40	10	20	30	40
44	11	22	33	44
48	12	24	36	48

all letters used | LA | 1.4 si | 5.4 awl | 85% hfw |

	gwam 2′	3′
When you need to adjust to a new situation in which new	6	4
people are involved, be quick to recognize that at first it	12	8
is you who must adapt. This is especially true in an office	18	12
where the roles of workers have already been established. It	24	16
is your job to fit into the team structure with harmony.	30	20
Learn the rules of the game and who the key players are;	6	23
then play according to those rules at first. Do not expect	12	27
to have the rules modified to fit your concept of what the	18	31
team structure and your role in it should be. Only after you	24	36
become a valuable member should you suggest major changes.	30	39

gwam 2′ | 1 | 2 | 3 | 4 | 5 | 6
gwam 3′ | 1 | 2 | 3 | 4

ENRICHMENT ACTIVITY: Centering Horizontally

plain full sheets; begin on line 24

1. Clear tabs; set a tab at center point.

2. Set line spacing to DS.

3. Center each line of the first announcement.

4. Center each line of the second announcement, correcting errors as marked.

= delete and close up
= capitalize
= transpose (tr)
= insert a space

Announcement 1

SUPER SAVER SALE

Up to 35% Off

Rings, Necklaces, Bracelets

at

THE GEM SHOP

December 1 through 15

10 a.m.-6 p.m.

Towne Shopping Center

Announcement 2

SCHOOL OF PERFORMMING ARTS

presents

"The Mouse that Roared"

on

January 21 and 22

2:30 and 8:00 p.m.

Marx Theatre

Matinee:$4.50; Evening: $5.50

255b-259b (continued)

Document 4
Letter
LP p. 87

Mr. Devereau: Key this letter to **Mr. Christopher P. Chase, President of the New Orleans United Community Fund, 920 Common Street, New Orleans, LA 70112-4786** for **Miss Jackson**'s signature. Date the letter **April 26** and prepare it in modified block format with indented ¶s. Be sure to correct all marked and unmarked errors.

It is with pleasure and pride that I accept your invitation to ~~conduct~~ chair the annual campaign of the New Orleans United Community Fund which will ~~kick off~~ begin in Sept. of this year.

As you ~~recommended,~~ suggested, I am inviting four ~~individuals~~ leaders in the community to join me, as a steering comittee, to plan, organize, and direct the campaign. These people are

Mrs. Lorraine T. Feliciana, Special Assistant
Office of the Mayor

The Reverend Father John P. Delacroix, Vice ~~Chairman~~ Chancellor
Xavier Theological Seminary

Ms. Alica B. Currant, Director
Citizens Action Group

Mr. Ralph C. Baronne, Vice President
New Orleans Business Association

Through regular reports, I will keep you informed of the activities and progress of ~~the~~ steering comittee.

Documents 5-8
Letters on Executive-Size Stationery
LP pp. 89-95

Mr. Devereau: Key this letter to the individuals listed in Document 4 for **Miss Jackson**'s signature. Date the letter **April 28** and prepare it in modified block format. Be sure to correct all marked and unmarked errors. The address for each individual is given below.

Mrs. Feliciana:
1300 Perdido Street
New Orleans, LA 70112-4001

Father Delacroix:
7300 Palmetto Street
New Orleans, LA 70125-4321

Ms. Currant:
202 Loyola Avenue
New Orleans, LA 70112-5094

Mr. Baronne:
820 Gravier Street
New Orleans, LA 70112-5183

Mr. Christopher T. Chase, president of the New Orleans United Community Fund, has ~~asked~~ invited me to ~~conduct~~ chair the annual campaign of the Community fund which will ~~start~~ begin in September of this year.

I am ~~quite~~ very pleased that you agreed in our tele phone conversation today to join ~~me~~ in this worth while effort by becoming a member of the steering committee. The first meeting of the committee will be held in the conferance room of Boutiques International on May ~~14~~ 15 at ~~9~~ 10 a.m.

This campaing should ~~prove to~~ be an interesting and exciting ~~one,~~ challenge and I am looking forward to working ~~together~~ with you to acheive our campaign ~~objectives~~ goals.

UNIT 6 *LESSONS 39 – 42*

Learn to Format Personal-Business Correspondence

Learning Goals

1. To learn how to format personal-business letters in block style.
2. To learn how to format simplified memos in block style.
3. To learn how to divide words correctly at line endings.
4. To improve basic keyboarding skills.

Format Guides

1. ***Paper guide*** at *0* (for typewriters).
2. LL: 60 spaces or as directed for documents; see *Get Ready to Keyboard: Typewriters* (p. x) or *Computers* (p. xii).
3. LS: SS except when formatting special parts of letters and memos which require DS and QS.

FORMATTING GUIDES: LETTERS AND MEMORANDUMS IN BLOCK STYLE

11300 Lower Azusa Road
El Monte, CA 91732-4725
October 24, 19--

Ms. Laura J. Marsh
2274 Cogswell Road
El Monte, CA 91732-3846

Dear Ms. Marsh

How fortunate you are to have Dr. Mark C. Gibson as a speaker for the November 18 meeting of the El Monte PTA. If he speaks as well as he writes, your meeting will be a success.

Because I strongly support the effort El Monte schools are making to assure computer literacy for all students, I would like to bring three guests, not two, to the meeting. All three names are listed on the enclosed card. If the limit is two guests per member, please let me know.

We need parental support for the computer literacy program to be the success it should be. You are to be commended for arranging this informative program for us.

Cordially yours

Alice M. Wiggins

Mrs. Alice M. Wiggins

Enclosure

Personal-Business Letter

October 28, 19--

Leon Deitz

FOREIGN EXCHANGE STUDY

On Thursday, November 15, Mr. Earl Bosma of Rotary, International will be here to discuss the foreign study program with prospective exchange students.

The meeting will be at 11:15 a.m. in Conference Room A of Tredwell Library. After the general session, Mr. Bosma will visit with each applicant separately. Your appointment is at 2:30 p.m.

Please be prompt for these meetings and bring all your application materials with you.

Eileen P. Roth

Eileen P. Roth, Assistant Principal

xx

Simplified Memorandum

Block Format

When *all* lines of a letter or memorandum begin at the left margin (LM) as shown in the illustrated models, the document is arranged in *block format* (style). Block format is easy to learn and easy to arrange. It is widely used for both personal and business correspondence.

Parts of a Personal-Business Letter

The basic parts of personal-business letters (those written by individuals to conduct business) are described below in order of their occurrence. (See model letter on p. 70.)

Return address. The return address consists of a line for the street address and one for the city, state, and ZIP Code. Key the street address (or post office box or route number) on line 14 from the top edge of the sheet; key the city, state name abbreviation, and ZIP Code on line 15.

Date. Key the date (month, day, and year) a single space (SS) below the last line of the return address.

Letter address. Begin the letter address on the fourth line space (QS) below the date. If the letter is addressed to a company, the address *may* include an attention line (the first line of the address) to call the letter to the attention of a specific person, department, or job title.

Salutation. Key the salutation (greeting) a double space (DS) below the letter address.

Body. Begin the letter body (message) a DS below the salutation. Block the paragraphs (¶s) of the body and SS them with a DS between ¶s.

Complimentary close. Key the complimentary close (farewell) a DS below the last line of the body.

Name of writer. Key the name of the writer (the originator of the message) a QS below the complimentary close. The name may be preceded by a personal title such as ***Miss***, ***Mrs.***, or ***Ms.*** to indicate how a female prefers to be addressed in a response.

Enclosure notation. An enclosure notation indicates that something other than the letter is included in the envelope. When appropriate, key the word *Enclosure* or *Enclosures* a DS below the name of the writer.

Parts of a Simplified Memorandum

Simplified memorandums are often used by a quick and easy means of written communication between members of clubs, by schools for making announcements and summarizing information, and by people who frequently exchange information. (See model memorandum on p. 74.)

The parts of simplified memorandums are described below in order of their occurrence. By eliminating the address of the addressee, the salutation, and the complimentary close, the simplified memo format saves time and reduces opportunity for error.

Date. Key the date (month, day, and year) on line 10 from the top edge of a full sheet or on line 6 of a half sheet.

Name of addressee. Key the name(s) of the person(s) to receive the memo a QS below the date. No personal title(s) should be used before the name(s), but an official title (such as *Principal* or *President*) may follow a name, preceded by a comma.

Subject. The subject line specifies the topic discussed in the memo. Key the subject line in ALL CAPS a DS below the name of the addressee.

Body. Block the ¶s in the body (message) a DS below the subject line. SS the ¶s with a DS between them.

Name of writer. Key the name of the writer a QS below the last line of the body. A personal title does not precede the name, but an official title may follow it, preceded by a comma.

Reference initials. If the keyboard operator is not the writer of the message, key the operator's initials (lowercased) a DS below the name of the writer.

Attachment/enclosure notation. If a supporting document is attached to the memo, key an attachment notation a DS below the name of the writer (or below the reference initials, if any). If the enclosure is not attached to the memo, use the word *Enclosure* rather than *Attachment.*

255b-259b (continued)

Document 2
Leftbound Report
plain full sheets

Mr. Devereau: Prepare the information contained in Document 1 as a leftbound report which will be included in the company's organizational manual.

Use as a heading: **OFFICE OF PUBLIC RELATIONS.**

5~~4~~. Arrange for and conduct public contact programs to promote goodwill for the company.

7~~5~~. Provide corporate ~~and~~ leadership in community improvements and participate in welfare and social-betterment programs.

4~~6~~. Prepare fact sheets, audio news releases, scripts, photographs, motion pictures, tapes, or vidio recordings to distribute to media representatives and others who may be interested in publicizing company activities.

6~~7~~. Prepare, edit, or clear all speeches to be given by company executives at public ~~affairs.~~ functions.

Document 3
News Release
LP p. 85

Mr. Devereau: Key this news release for immediate release with **Miles T. Nicolas 504-565-6452** as the contact.

¶ NEW ORLEANS, LA, April 16, 19--. Ground-breaking ceremonies for the Prentiss ~~Memorial~~ Recreation Center will be held May 3 at 10 a.m., according to an announcement by Ramon C. Delachaise, president of Boutiques International, Ltd. The recreation center will be located along the Mississippi River adjacent to Bridge City. "The Prentiss Recreation Center will serve as an enduring ~~a living~~ memorial to Gregory T. Prentiss, the founder of Boutiques International," said Mr. Delachaise. "It has been designed to serve the citizens of New Orleans, all of whom have contributed to our success."

¶ The new recreation center will include a gymnasium with complete locker facilities, an arts and crafts center, and an auditorium for meetings, theatrical productions, and concerts. Future plans call for the addition of an indoor swimming pool.

¶ The entire cost of the center will be funded by the Prentiss Foundation. When completed, the center will be operated by the New Orleans Department of Parks and Recreation with funds augmented by the Prentiss Foundation.

# # #

Lesson 39 Personal-Business Letters

LL: 60
LS: SS

39a ▶ 6 Conditioning Practice

each line twice SS; then a 1′ writing on line 3; find *gwam*

alphabet 1 Jake led a big blitz which saved the next play for my squad.
fig/sym 2 Beth has ordered 26 5/8 yards of #304 linen at $7.19 a yard.
speed 3 Good form is the key if all of us wish to make the big goal.

| 1 | 2 | 3 | 4 | 5 | 6 | 7 | 8 | 9 | 10 | 11 | 12 |

39b ▶ 9 Improve Language Skills: Word Division

1. Read each rule and key the **Learn** and **Apply** lines beneath it.

Note: As you key the **Apply** lines, insert a hyphen in each word at the point (if any) where the word can best be divided.

2. Check with your teacher the accuracy of your **Apply** lines; if time permits, rekey the **Apply** lines in which you made word-division errors.

Divide a word only between syllables; words of one syllable, therefore, should not be divided.

Learn 1 per-sons, through, in-come, straight, pur-pose, con-tracts
Apply 2 expects, brought, control, methods, thoughts, practice

Do not separate a one-letter syllable at the beginning of a word or a one- or two-letter syllable at the end of a word.

Learn 3 ideal, prior, ready, ahead, around, event, lengthy, ef-fort
Apply 4 again, early, party, ideal, quickly, about, adhere, enough

Divide a word between double consonants except when adding a syllable to a word that ends in double letters.

Learn 5 mat-ters, writ-ten, sud-denly, add-ing, will-ing, run-ning
Apply 6 summer, college, carried, current, telling, stopping

39c-40c ▶ 35 (daily) Format Personal-Business Letters in Block Style

plain full sheets
LL: 60 spaces
LS: single
PB: line 14

1. Study the formatting guides for personal-business letters on p. 68 and the model letter illustrating block format on p. 70. Note the vertical and horizontal placement of letter parts and the spacing between them.

2. On a plain full sheet, format and key line-for-line a copy of the letter on p. 70. Do not correct your errors as you key.

3. Proofread your copy of the letter and mark it for correction. (See list of proofreader's marks on Reference Guide p. RG10 at back of book.)

4. Format and key the letter again from your own copy, errors corrected.

5. If time permits, begin processing the letters on p. 71. Save any partially completed letter to finish during the next class period. Correct your errors as you key.

Lesson 40 Personal-Business Letters

LL: 60
LS: SS

40a ▶ 6 Conditioning Practice

each line twice SS; then a 1′ writing on line 3; find *gwam*

alphabet 1 Jacki had won first place by solving my tax quiz in an hour.
fig/sym 2 Our 1990 profit was $58,764 (up 23% from the previous year).
speed 3 Roddy may sign the six forms and work with the city auditor.

| 1 | 2 | 3 | 4 | 5 | 6 | 7 | 8 | 9 | 10 | 11 | 12 |

UNIT 61 LESSONS 255 – 259
Public Relations Office

Learning Goals

1. To acquaint you with some of the major functions of a public relations office.
2. To increase your proficiency in producing typical documents processed in public relations operations.
3. To improve your ability to process special documents using your best judgment.

Documents Processed

1. Formal Memorandums
2. Leftbound Report
3. News Release
4. Letters
5. Simplified Memorandums
6. Schedule
7. Table

255a-259a ▶ 5 (daily)
Conditioning Practice

each line twice SS (slowly, then faster); DS between 2-line groups; if time permits, take 1′ writings on line 4

alphabet 1 Black may join in requesting to have six of the township lots rezoned.

figures 2 The company hired 357 employees in 1989, 401 in 1990, and 624 in 1992.

fig/sym 3 Panel 74296A will measure exactly 50.80 cm by 68.58 cm (1′8″ by 2′3″).

speed 4 If the firm's audit is right, half of the men did sign a formal proxy.

| 1 | 2 | 3 | 4 | 5 | 6 | 7 | 8 | 9 | 10 | 11 | 12 | 13 | 14 |

255b-259b ▶ 45 (daily)
Document Production

1. Your next job as a keyboard technician will be in the Office of Public Relations. You will work under the direction of F. Daniel Devereau, who is the administrative assistant to Michelle C. Jackson, Director of Public Relations.

2. In this job you will be required to prepare a variety of documents originated by members of the Public Relations staff.

3. Follow directions given for each document. If no format is specified, use your best judgment.

4. Unless directed to prepare a draft copy, key all documents in final form. Correct all marked and unmarked errors.

Document 1
Formal Memorandum
LP p. 83

Mr. Devereau: Prepare a formal memorandum from **Miss Jackson** to **ALL EXECUTIVES, ADMINISTRATORS, AND SUPERVISORS,** dated **April 15,** with the subject: **Public Relations Office.**

We at Boutiques International have always sought to be exemplary corporate citizens and have reconized our responsibility to contribute to and improve the communitys in which we operate. In reality, it is the task job of every member of Boutiques International to be an "embassador of goodwill" by mantaining friendly and cooperative relations with the citizens of our communitys.

To insure that we "put our best food forward," the Public Relations section of the Marketing Divisoin has been active for many years. Public relations has become increasingly important and, in recognition of that fact, the Executive Board has established the Office of Public Relations, effective April 12 15. which will become a member of the special staff reporting directly to the executive vice president, Seymore T. Brown.

The duties of the Public Relations Office will be to

1. Establish and conduct a public relations program designed to create and maintain a favorable corporate image with the public.

3 2. Inform the public of those ways in which the firm serves the interests of society.

2 3. Communicate to the public information regading the companys' programs, activities, achievements, and point of view.

(continued, p. 435)

		words in parts	total words
Return address	2274 Cogswell Road ▼ Line 14	4	4
	El Monte, CA 91732-3846	9	9
Date	October 15, 19--	12	12
	Quadruple-space (QS): strike return key 4 times		
Letter address	Mrs. Alice M. Wiggins	17	17
	11300 Lower Azusa Road	21	21
	El Monte, CA 91732-4725 Double-space (DS): strike return key twice	26	26
Salutation	Dear Mrs. Wiggins DS	30	30
Body	The El Monte PTA is devoting its next meeting to the important	13	42
	topic "Computer Literacy." The meeting is on November 18 and	25	55
	begins at 7 p.m. DS	29	59
	Our speaker will be Dr. Mark C. Gibson. For the past several	41	71
	years, he has written the "Personal Computer" column in the	53	83
	Los Angeles Post. His talk will combine wisdom and wit. DS	68	98
	To assure Dr. Gibson a large audience, we are asking selected	80	110
	members to bring as guests two parents who are not active mem-	93	123
	bers of our group. Please use the enclosed return card to	105	134
	give me the names of your guests by November 1. DS	114	144
	I shall appreciate your assistance. DS	121	152
Complimentary close	Cordially yours QS	3	155
	Laura J. Marsh		
Writer	Ms. Laura J. Marsh DS	7	159
Enclosure notation	Enclosure	9	160

Shown in pica (10-pitch) type on a 60-space line, photo-reduced

Personal-Business Letter in Block Format

251b-254b (continued)

Document 16
Announcement

full sheet

Miss Morales: Please prepare the announcement attractively on the page.

BOUTIQUES INTERNATIONAL, LTD.

Chinaware Replacement Service

Did some one break a plate of your ~~best~~ favorite chinaware service? Are some of your ~~plates~~ cups chipped? We are ~~happy~~ pleased to announce another personal service to ~~assist~~ help you ~~in replacing~~ replace ~~any~~ certain peice s of chinaware which may be chipped, cracked, or broken. This special service applies to all sets of china included in our current catalog.

The ~~price~~ cost for replacement service is quiet nominal. An example for our best selling chinaware is ~~given~~ shown below.

DS

Royal Worcester, Mayfair Pattern

STOCK NUMBER	PIECE	~~PRICE~~ COST *
FC473021	Bread and Butter Plate (B, P → lowercase)	$ ~~8~~9.75
FC473022	Cereal bowl	~~19~~18.00
FC473023	Coffee pot	51.00
FC473024	Cup (tea)	17.50
FC473025	~~Large~~ Dinner plate	18.25
FC473026	Pepper shaker	16.00
FC473027	Salad plate	1~~4~~5.90
FC473028	Salt shaker	16.00
FC473029	Saucer	1~~0~~9.00
FC473030	Souffle	31.00

For ~~further~~ information, regarding your pattern, please call 1-800-504-3022.

* Shipping not included.

40b ▶ 9 *Improve Language Skills: Word Division*

1. Read each rule and key the **Learn** and **Apply** lines beneath it.

Note: As you key the **Apply** lines, insert a hyphen in each word at the point (if any) where the word can best be divided.

2. Check with your teacher the accuracy of your **Apply** lines; if time permits, rekey the **Apply** lines in which you made word-division errors.

> Divide a word after a single-letter vowel syllable that is not a part of a word ending.

Learn 1 ori-ent, usu-ally, vari-ous, sepa-rate, genu-ine, situ-ated
Apply 2 editor, educate, holiday, evaluate, celebrate, maximum

> Divide a word before the word endings *-able, -ible, -acle, -ical,* and *-ily* when the vowel **a** or **i** is a separate syllable.

Learn 3 mir-acle, heart-ily, prob-able, convert-ible, opti-cal
Apply 4 edible, handily, lyrical, tropical, variable, musical

> Do not divide a word that contains a contraction (a word in which one or more omitted letters have been replaced by an apostrophe).

Learn 5 we've, didn't, hadn't, you're, haven't, they'll, couldn't
Apply 6 we'll, hasn't, you'll, you've, aren't, doesn't, shouldn't

39c-40c ▶ 35 (continued)

1. Continue processing the series of personal-business letters given below and on p. 72. See 39c-40c, p. 69, for formatting guides. Color verticals indicate line endings.

2. Before removing a letter from the machine, proofread it and correct any errors.

Letter 1 (words)

5802 Lehman Drive 4
Colorado Springs, CO 80918-1123 10
October 20, 19-- 14
QS
Ms. Lorna K. Ryan, Director 19
Placement Services, Inc. 24
350 E. Colfax Avenue 28
Denver, CO 80203-6285 33
DS
Dear Ms. Ryan 36
DS
Today's <u>Times Star</u> quotes you as saying in a 47
recent talk that "more workers fail as a result 56
of personal traits than because of weak techni- 66
cal skills." 67
DS
I want to quote this statement in a paper I am 78
writing titled "Why Beginning Workers Fail," 87
and I would like to know the research studies 96
to which you referred so that I can include them 106
in my reference list. 111
DS
If you will send me the research references you 120
used to sup- port your statement, I shall be most 130
grateful. I am sure the references will be of 139
great help to me in preparing my paper. 147
DS
Sincerely yours 151
QS
Edward R. Shields 154

Letter 2 (words)

2405 Siesta Avenue 4
Las Vegas, NV 89121-2683 9
October 22, 19-- 12

Learning Tutor, Inc. 17
752 S. Bascom Avenue 21
San Jose, CA 95128-3605 26

Ladies and Gentlemen 30

On October 8 I ordered from your fall catalog a 40
copy of MATH TUTOR IX (Catalog #A2937) de- 48
signed for use on the Eureka GS. I have had the 57
diskette a week. 61

I follow the booting instructions step-by-step 70
but am unable to boot the program on my 78
Eureka GS. I took the diskette to the store 87
where I bought my computer, but the manager 96
could not boot the program on the same model 105
computer. 107

Will you please check the booting instructions 117
in the User's Guide to see if they are correct. 127
If they are, please send a replacement diskette 136
and I will return the faulty one to you. 145

Sincerely yours 148

Miss Ellen M. Marcos 152

Letters 3, 4, and 5 are on p. 72.

251b-254b (continued)

Documents 12-15
Letters

LP pp. 75-81

Miss Morales:

Prepare the letter to the managers of our branches in London, Paris, Rome, and Hong Kong. You will find their names and addresses and the names of the customer service managers in the files.

Key the letter, dated **October 16,** in modified block format with indented ¶s and open punctuation.

Provide an appropriate salutation and subject line. The letter will be signed by **Mr. Peterson.**

INFORMATION FROM THE FILES:

London Branch:

Mr. Anthony P. Middleton, Manager, Boutiques International, Ltd., 10 Berkeley Street, London, England W1X 6NE
Mr. Thomas Browne

Paris Branch:

Ms. Lilli S. Carpentier, Manager, Boutiques International, Ltd., 8 Place de la Republique, Paris, France 75011
Mr. Francois P. Casini

Rome Branch:

Mrs. Maria DiAngelo, Manager, Boutiques International, Ltd., Via Aurelia Antica 411, Rome, Italy 00165
Mrs. Concetta P. Firpo

Hong Kong Branch:

Mr. Kunio T. Lee, Manager, Boutiques International, Ltd., 48 Nathan Road, Kowloon City Centre, Hong Kong
Ms. Tiem Kim

~~There will be~~ a meeting of all customer service managers (will be held) on November 15 at the Pierre Hotel in New Orleans. A tentative list of ~~items~~ topics to be discussed follows.

1. Implementing ~~plans~~ (procedures) for ~~establishing~~ providing wedding consultants for customers.
2. ~~Planning~~ (Developing) new personalized services.
3. Revising current policies ~~about~~ regarding return of merchandise.
4. Analyzing major ~~customer~~ complaints (received from customers.)
5. ~~Beginning~~ Implementing the SELL USA Campaign.
6. ~~Discussing~~ (Reviewing) special problems in customer relations encountered by each branch office.

Will you please arrange for your customer service manager, (name), to ~~come~~ fly to New Orleans arriving on November 14. A reservation ~~was~~ has been made for (him, her) at the Pierre Hotel.

If you have any ~~more~~ additional topics you would like to add to the agenda for this ~~conference~~ meeting, please send them to my assistant, Miss Carla J. Morales, ~~as soon as you possibly can.~~ (before November 1.)

39c-40c (continued)

Letter 3 words

5209 W. Grand Avenue 4
Chicago, IL 60639-3372 9
October 23, 19-- 12

Dr. Dallas T. Johnson 17
Drug Rehabilitation Center 22
4056 W. Melrose Street 27
Chicago, IL 60641-2940 32

Dear Dr. Johnson 35

With the approval of the principal of Columbus 44
High School, | the Student Leadership Club is 53
sponsoring a series of assembly | programs this 62
year dealing with student problems in learn- 71
ing | and life. One of these student assemblies 81
will address the | serious problem of teenage drug 90
abuse. 92

As chair of the program committee, I would es- 101
pecially like | you, or a member of your staff, to 111
talk to us on this timely | topic. A presentation 121
similar to the one you made last year | on local 130
TV would be ideal. 134

Can you give us 45 minutes of your time on 143
Friday, March 10, | at 10:15 a.m. We need your 152
help, and we will appreciate it. | If you prefer 162
to call, my telephone number (after 4 p.m.) is | 171
277-2048. 173

Sincerely yours 176

Juan F. Ramirez 179

Letter 4 words

11300 Lower Azusa Road 5
El Monte, CA 91732-4725 10
October 24, 19-- 13

Ms. Laura J. Marsh 17
2274 Cogswell Road 21
El Monte, CA 91732-3846 26

Dear Ms. Marsh 29

How fortunate you are to have Dr. Mark C. 37
Gibson as a speaker | for the November 18 meet- 46
ing of the El Monte PTA. If he speaks | as well 55
as he writes, your meeting will be a success. 65

Because I strongly support the effort El Monte 74
schools are mak- | ing to assure computer liter- 83
acy for all students, I would like | to bring three 93
guests, not two, to the meeting. All three | names 103
are listed on the enclosed card. If the limit is 113
two | guests per member, please let me know. 122

We need parental support for the computer lit- 131
eracy program to | be the success it should be. 140
You are to be commended for ar- | ranging this 149
informative program for us. 155

Cordially yours 158

Mrs. Alice M. Wiggins 162

Enclosure 164

Letter 5

1. Format and key the handwritten copy as a personal-business letter in block style. Key it on a plain full sheet, line-for-line as shown.

2. Use your own **return address;** date the letter **October 25** of the **current year.**

3. Address the letter to:

Shutterbug Shops, Inc.
812 Olive Street
St. Louis, MO 63101-4460

4. Use your **full name** (first name, middle initial, and surname) in the closing lines. Females should include a personal title (Miss, Ms., or Mrs.).

words
opening lines 25

Ladies and Gentlemen 29

The enclosed copy of my credit card statement shows that you 42
have not yet issued a credit for the Lycon Camera (Catalog 53
#C288) that I returned to you more than three weeks ago. 65

Will you please check to see whether a credit of $137.95 has 77
now been issued; and, if not, see that it is issued promptly. 90
I wish to pay the invoice less the appropriate credit. 101

Sincerely yours/Enclosure 106

251b-254b (continued)

Document 9
Table
full sheet

Miss Morales: Center this table vertically and horizontally.

FINE CHINA DEPARTMENT

Best-Selling Dinnerware Sets During the Month of ~~August~~ September

Stock Number	Dinnerware	Sets Sold
FC47302	Royal Worcester, Mayfair Pattern	~~672~~ 685
FC58491	Wedgwood, Eaton Pattern	~~613~~ 593
FC47802	Aynsley, Spring Flower Pattern	~~589~~ 591
FC69524	Noritake, Fugi Pattern	~~542~~ 563
FC70635	Royal Doulton, Floral Pattern	~~497~~ 508
FC89524	Coalport, Golden Wheat Pattern	~~403~~ 423
FC34000	Golden Tara, Irish Summer Pattern	~~371~~ 385
FC56222	Spode, Rose Garden Pattern	~~295~~ 271
FC67404	Wedgwood, Avon Pattern	~~228~~ 253
~~FC43090~~ FC47305	~~Delft, Blue Onion Pattern~~ Royal Doulton, Gold Leaf Pattern	~~196~~ 246

Document 10
Formal Memorandum
LP p. 73

Miss Morales: Please key this memo, dated **October 9,** from **Mr. Peterson** to **Richard C. Murray** who is the **Director of Marketing.** Subject: **THE PERSONAL TOUCH.**

Document 11
Table
full sheet

Miss Morales: Please rekey the table in Document 9 to show the figures for both months. Make all necessary changes.

The heading for Column 3 will be **August** and the heading for Column 4 will be **September**.

To farther (u) customize our ~~contacts~~ relations with our customers, I ~~suggest~~ recommend that we have ~~each~~ the packer place the following message in each order.

Dear ~~Boutiques International~~ Customer

Thank you for patronizing Boutiques International.

My name is ______________________________. I hope you will be pleased by the care I have taken to package your order. If you have any questions about your order, please call 1-800-504-3220.

Have a good day.

I beleive that this message will add another "personal touch" to our contacts with our customers and, at the same time, give packers a greater feeling of satisfaction and pride. To save time in packing, a rubber stamp with his or her name on it can be provided each packer.

41a ▶ 6 Conditioning Practice

each line twice SS; then a 1′ writing on line 3; find *gwam*

alphabet 1 Five kids quickly mixed the prizes, baffling one wise judge.

fig/sym 2 Joe asked, "Is the ZIP Code 45209-2748 or is it 45208-3614?"

speed 3 The firms may make a profit if they handle their work right.

| 1 | 2 | 3 | 4 | 5 | 6 | 7 | 8 | 9 | 10 | 11 | 12 |

41b ▶ 9 Improve Language Skills: Word Division

1. Read each rule and key the **Learn** and **Apply** lines beneath it.

Note: As you key the **Apply** lines, insert a hyphen in each word at the point (if any) where the word can best be divided.

2. Check with your teacher the accuracy of your **Apply** lines; if time permits, rekey the **Apply** lines in which you made word-division errors.

When two words are hyphenated to make up a compound word, divide only after the designated hyphen.

Learn 1 ill-advised, self-satisfied, well-groomed, self-concerned

Apply 2 illmannered, self con-tained, well-mean-ing, self centered

When two single-letter syllables occur together in a word, divide between them.

Learn 3 gradu-ate, gradu-ation, evalu-ate, evalu-ation, initi-ation

Apply 4 devaluation, insinuation, variation, anxiety, attenuation

Avoid dividing proper names, dates, and figures.

Learn 5 Edna J. Jackson; May 15, 1997; $300,000; Atlanta or Savannah

Apply 6 Sep-tember 28, 1996; Portland, Cali-fornia; Edward S. Ebe-ling

41c-42c ▶ 35 (daily) Format Memorandums in Simplified Style

plain full sheets
LL: 1-inch side margins
Pica (10-pitch) = 10-75
Elite (12-pitch) = 12-90
LS: single
PB: line 10

1. Study the formatting guides for simplified memos on p. 68 and the model memo illustrating the simplified format on p. 74. Note the vertical and horizontal placement of memo parts and the spacing between them.

2. On a plain full sheet, format and key a copy of the memo on p. 74; do not correct your errors as you key. Center the assembly topic as shown.

3. Proofread your copy of the memo, marking any errors that need to be corrected.

4. Format and key the memo again from your own copy, errors corrected.

5. If time permits, begin processing the memos on p. 75. Save any partially completed memo to finish during the next class period. Correct your errors as you key.

MANAGING LINE ENDINGS

The format for memos requires 1-inch side margins (10 pica spaces; 12 elite). Thus, the line length for pica or 10-pitch machines is 65 spaces; for elite or 12-pitch machines, 78 spaces. As a result, line endings for pica and elite equipment will differ.

Users of standard typewriters should add about 5 spaces to the right margin stop setting and be guided by the warning bell to return, add a short word, or divide a word at the end of the line. Doing so will cause the right margin to be more nearly 1 inch and will result in a less-ragged right margin.

Users of computers or word processors should study their software to learn how to manage line endings. Procedures vary from program to program and depend upon whether hard returns or the word wrap feature is used.

251b-254b (continued)

Document 7
Announcement

full sheet

Miss Morales: Use your best judgment in centering this announcement attractively on the page. Use as a heading: **EXCLUSIVELY FOR BOUTIQUES INTERNATIONAL CUSTOMERS.** Change the ALL-CAPS paragraph headings to ALL-CAPS side headings.

Document 8
Announcement

full sheet

Miss Morales: Marketing has decided to delay the special wedding arrangements for approximately six months. Rekey Document 7, omitting the paragraph on wedding arrangements. Also, move paragraph 1 to the end of the document and move the final paragraph to the beginning of the document.

SPECIAL TOLL-FREE NUMBERS FOR OUR CUSTOMERS~~,~~ ¶ For Orders. Call 1-800-504-3210 24 hours a day, 7 days a week to order items on approved accounts or credit cards. ¶ For Information. Call 1-800-504-3220 for any questions on orders previously placed. ¶ For Account Information. Call 1-800-504-3230 for any questions regarding your account. Be sure to have your account number available.

GIFT SERVICE~~.~~ What shall I give Uncle Dwight for his birthday? Is there ~~anything~~ something special I can give my wife (or husband) on our anniversary? For help with gift ~~in~~ shopping ~~for a gift,~~ simply call a member of our staff at 1-800-504-3240. Our trained experts can help you ~~to~~ select a gift for any occasoin. Your gift will be ~~packaged~~ placed in a handsome gift box with an appropriate card.

NEED QUICK DELIVERY? All orders are filled the day following reciept. Please allow more time for items marked with asterisks {**}. If you need an item ~~earlier,~~ quickly we can offer one- or two-day service by either PRIORITY MAIL or FEDERAL EXPRESS. ~~SERVICE.~~

WEDDING ARRANGEMENTS~~.~~ Is there a wedding in your future? Our special consultants can aid you in all ~~aspects~~ phases of planning the wedding, including etiquette, attire of wedding party, and selection of trousseau. ~~We~~ They can also provide advise (advice) on the selection of silver ware style and patterns for china and glassware. ~~We~~ They will even tape the wedding ceremony and reception for your enjoyment in years to come. ~~through the years.~~ Call ~~TOLL FREE~~ 1-800-504-3250 for complete details.

COMPLETE CUSTOMER SATISFACTION IS OUR GOAL~~.~~ Our ~~aim~~ policy is to provide you superior products ~~excellent items~~ at ~~good~~ reasonable prices. If you are not completely satisfied with your purchase, simply return the item within 30 days for a full refund. The only exception to this policy is personalized items which may be returned only if we have made an error.

		words in parts	total words
Date	October 29, 19-- Line 10 (line 6 of a half sheet)	3	3
	QS		
Addressee	Student Leadership Program Committee	11	11
	DS		
Subject	DALLAS JOHNSON TO ADDRESS ASSEMBLY	18	18
	DS		
Body	Dr. Dallas T. Johnson telephoned to say that he will be pleased	13	31
	to address the special student assembly on March 10 on the topic	26	44
	DS		
	TEENAGE DRUG ABUSE	30	47
	DS		
	Dr. Johnson will use slides to present data on the incidence of	42	60
	drug use among teenagers. He will use a short film to highlight	55	73
	differences in attitudes and behavior before and after drug use.	69	86
	Finally, a young adult who has undergone treatment at the Drug Re-	82	100
	habilitation Center will tell us about her experiences with drugs.	95	113
	DS		
	This assembly should be very interesting, but sobering.	106	125
	QS		
	Juan F. Ramirez		
Writer	Juan F. Ramirez	3	128

Shown in pica (10-pitch) type with 1-inch side margins, photo-reduced

Simplified Memorandum in Block Format

Lesson 42 — *Simplified Memorandums*

LL: 60
LS: SS

42a ▶ 6
Conditioning Practice

each line twice SS; then a 1′ writing on line 3; find *gwam*

alphabet 1 Quincy worked six jigsaw puzzles given him for his birthday.

fig/sym 2 I deposited Hahn & Ober's $937.48 check (#1956) on March 20.

speed 3 Vivian may lend them a hand with the audit of the soap firm.

| 1 | 2 | 3 | 4 | 5 | 6 | 7 | 8 | 9 | 10 | 11 | 12 |

251b-254b (continued)

Documents 2-6
Form Letters from Boilerplate

LP pp. 63-71

Miss Morales: We use boilerplate files to create many documents used in responding to customer orders. A boilerplate file, such as this one, contains standardized paragraphs which can be combined to create documents.

Prepare letters dated **October 6, 19--,** to the addressees below for **Mr. Peterson's** signature using the paragraphs indicated and inserting the appropriate information. Use block format, open punctuation, with these letters of average length.

Document 2

Mr. Jeremy R. Polk
16301 Thomas Street
Biloxi, MS 39532-6785

1-1 **a lead crystal bud vase**
2-3 **Ireland; three weeks**
3-2

Document 3

Mr. Kevin T. Miles
4210 Ash Lane
Dallas, TX 75223-9569

1-2 **a solid brass desk clock**
2-1 **$78.75**
3-4

Document 4

Mrs. Rose L. Moss
250 Florida Boulevard
Baton Rouge, LA 70801-4042

1-4 **a Limoges jewelry box**
2-3 **France; two weeks**
3-2

Document 5

Ms. Alyse C. Brown
9601 Kanis Road
Little Rock, AR 72205-6930

1-3 **October 1; lead crystal swan**
2-4 **September 27**
3-4

Document 6

Dr. C. Elinor Crane
1410 Coleman Avenue
Macon, GA 31207-5286

1-1 **a silver vanity set**
2-2 **ten days**
3-1

Paragraphs for Form Letters

Paragraph 1 Options

1-1 Thank you, (name of customer), for your recent order for (name of item).

1-2 Thank you, (name of customer), for your inquiry regarding your order for (name of item).

1-3 Your letter of (date of letter) indicates that you have not yet received the (item) you ordered.

1-4 This letter will confirm our telephone conversation today regarding your order for (item).

Paragraph 2 Options

2-1 Unfortunately, our stock of this item has been completely depleted and we are unable to obtain additional quantities. By separate mail, we are sending a refund check in the amount of $(amount).

2-2 This item is not currently in stock; however, we expect a shipment within the next (number of days) and will ship it at that time. We regret the delay.

2-3 As you know, this item is a special order from a firm in (location); and we have not received the item from them. We do expect, however, to ship the item to you within the next (time period).

2-4 Your order was shipped on (date) and should have arrived by now. If you have not received it, please let me know immediately so that I can check it for you.

Paragraph 3 Options

3-1 Thank you for shopping with Boutiques International. We look forward to serving you in the future.

3-2 Please call me (800-504-3200) between 9 a.m. and 5 p.m. Central Time if you have any additional questions.

3-3 For your special shopping needs, keep in mind that Boutiques International is eager to serve you.

3-4 Enclosed is a copy of our latest catalog. Be sure to look for the many new, unique items now available.

42b ▶ 9
Language Skills: Composing Sentences

Compose a 1- or 2-sentence answer to each question.

1 Why are you learning to operate a typewriter or computer?

2 By the end of the course, in what ways do you want to be able to use your skill?

3 In what ways could this course be made more helpful to you?

4 In what ways do you think you could improve your performance?

41c-42c ▶ 35 (continued)

See 41c-42c, p. 73, for formatting guides. Correct your errors as you key.

Memo 1 — words

October 24, 19-- 3
QS
All Seniors 6
DS
CHOOSING A COLLEGE OR UNIVERSITY 12
DS
A voluntary assembly for seniors is planned for 22
3 p.m. next Friday, November 5, in the cafete- 31
ria. The purpose is to give you information and 41
answer your questions about choosing and get- 50
ting into the college or university of your choice 60
upon graduation. 64
DS
Each guest speaker will summarize entrance 72
requirements and opportunities at his or her 81
college or university. A question/answer period 91
will follow. You may direct your questions to 101
the person of your choice: Miss Micaela Stokes 110
of Central Community College, Dr. Louise 118
Bolan of Midland State University, or Mr. John 128
Hawkes of Metropolitan College of Business. 137
DS
If you plan to attend, sign your name below. 146
QS
Melissa Briggs, Senior Class President 154

Memo 2 — words

October 28, 19-- 3
Leon Deitz 6
FOREIGN EXCHANGE STUDY 10

On Thursday, November 15, Mr. Earl Bosma 18
of Rotary, International will be here to discuss 28
the foreign study program with prospective 37
exchange students. 41

The meeting will be at 11:15 a.m. in Conference 50
Room A of Tredwell Library. After the general 60
session, Mr. Bosma will visit with each applicant 70
separately. Your appointment is at 2:30 p.m. 79

Please be prompt for these meetings and bring 88
all your application materials with you. 97

Eileen P. Roth, Assistant Principal 104

xx (Use your own initials for reference) 104

Memo 3

Format and key Memo 2 again but address it to **Cora Jordan.** Change the appointment time to **1:15 p.m.**

Memo 4

1. Read the rough-draft memo, noting the changes to be made. (See key to proofreader's marks below.)

2. Format and key the copy as a simplified memo. Use the **current date** and use **Keyboarding Students** as the addressee. Correct marked errors and any errors you make as you key. **Note:** Try to maintain an acceptable right margin of 1 inch, fairly even.

∧	= insert
#	= add space
∾	= transpose
℘	= delete
⁀	= close up
≡	= capitalize

words

AL — opening lines 7

AUTOMATICLY CONTROLLED RIGHT MARGINS 15

Some machines have built in software that control right mar- 28
gin; others, such as computers, depend upona separate software 41
disk too control how the lines end. 48

However the rihgt margin is controll though, you can override 61
the defaults to change a line ending. adding or dividing a 74
wrod may make the right margin ragged. You must fol low the 87
proceedure in your user's guide to make line ending changes. 99

Liang Chih, Keyboarding Teacher 106

xx 106

UNIT 60 *LESSONS 251 – 254*
Customer Service Center

Learning Goals

1. To increase your skill in planning, organizing, and formatting a variety of documents.
2. To key in acceptable formats a series of typical documents processed in a Customer Service Center.
3. To increase your production skill.

Documents Processed

1. Unbound Report
2. Letters
3. Sales Announcement
4. Table
5. Simplified Memorandum

Lessons 251-254

251a-254a ▶ 5 (daily)
Conditioning Practice

each line twice SS (slowly, then faster); if time permits, take 1′ writings on line 4

alphabet	1	Jan Zweibel quickly solved the problem by using very complex formulas.
figures	2	They purchased four calculators: Nos. 40741, 51902, 63254, and 68037.
fig/sym	3	Kern & Werner offered a discount of $437 (10% and 2%) on Order 864591.
speed	4	She may sue the panel of men if they entitle the six girls to the pay.

| 1 | 2 | 3 | 4 | 5 | 6 | 7 | 8 | 9 | 10 | 11 | 12 | 13 | 14 |

251b-254b ▶ 45 (daily)
Document Processing

Your first experience as a keyboard technician will be in the Customer Service Center under the supervision of Miss Carla T. Morales, administrative assistant to Harold J. Peterson, who is the director of the center. Before you begin work, Miss Morales asks you to review the functions of the Customer Service Center on p. 427 as well as your major duties and the special instructions.

Document 1
Statement of Policy

full sheet

Miss Morales: Prepare this Statement of Policy in final form as an unbound report. Watch for and correct any unmarked errors. Use **CUSTOMER RELATIONS** as a main heading; use **Statement of Policy** as a secondary heading.

The success and continued growth of Boutiques International depends upon satisfied customers. To ensure continued progress, we must strive to increase and retain the number of customers who de sire the goods and servides we provide ~~our customers.~~

Satisfing our customers demands that we determine there specefic requirements, desires, and preferances. Each customer must be made to feel that we are totaly comitted to serving him or her in an affective manner.

Courtesy and attention are key concepts in customer relations. All customer contacts, specificaly complaints, must be treated in a manner that will convince the customer that we have his or her best interests at heart. All questions and compleints will be resolved ~~quickly~~ in a prompt and curteous manner.

To provide ~~add~~ the "personal touch," all contacts with customers who have major problems or questions will be made in person whenever possible. In matters of vital importance, a representative from the nearest local branch will visit the customers; in other cases, the customer will be contacted by telephone. Each personal contact will be followed by a letter of confirmation. Minor or routine questions and problems will be resolved by correspondence.

Boutiques International has earned a reputation for providing goods of the highest qualety at reasonabel prices. We are also noted for the personal specialised services we provide all customers. We must continually strive to up hold our reputation so that we will merit customer confidance and satisfaction.

UNIT 7 *LESSONS 43 – 46*

Learn to Format Business Correspondence

Learning Guides

1. To learn how to format business letters in block style.

2. To improve skill in formatting/keying simplified memos and personal-business letters.

3. To improve basic keyboarding skills.

4. To review/improve language skills.

Format Guides

1. ***Paper guide*** at *0* (for typewriters).

2. LL: 60 spaces for drills, ¶s, and personal-business letters; see *Get Ready to Keyboard: Typewriters* (p. x) or *Computers* (p. xii); 1″ SM for memos; as directed by *Letter Placement Guide* for business letters.

3. LS: SS (except for letter/memo parts).

4. PI: 5 spaces when appropriate.

FORMATTING GUIDES: BUSINESS LETTERS IN BLOCK STYLE

Visual Systems Inc.
2201 Sixth Avenue • Seattle, WA • 98121-3645 • Tel. 206-651-7388

November 14, 19--

Business Management Systems
Attention Sales Manager
748 S. Market Street
Tacoma, WA 98402-1365

Ladies and Gentlemen

IMPROVE SALES BY 10 PERCENT

If you could close 10 percent more sales a year, would you spend a day of your time to learn how? If so, we want to welcome you to "Success by Visual Persuasion."

This special seminar is designed for high-level managers like you who want quick, easy ways to prepare visual presentations that are a cut above the chalkboard and flipchart. Using a lecture/electronic technique, a seminar leader will show you how to use built-in outlining, drawing, and charting tools. You will even learn how to get full-color effects in overheads and slides.

To improve your sales by 10 percent a year, read the enclosed brochure about the seminar; then complete and return the registration card. You will be glad you did.

Sincerely yours

Robert L. Marsh

Robert L. Marsh, Director

xx

Enclosure

Block Style, Pica

Visual Systems Inc.
2201 Sixth Avenue • Seattle, WA • 98121-3645 • Tel. 206-651-7388

November 14, 19--

Business Management Systems
Attention Sales Manager
748 S. Market Street
Tacoma, WA 98402-1365

Ladies and Gentlemen

IMPROVE SALES BY 10 PERCENT

If you could close 10 percent more sales a year, would you spend a day of your time to learn how? If so, we want to welcome you to "Success by Visual Persuasion."

This special seminar is designed for high-level managers like you who want quick, easy ways to prepare visual presentations that are a cut above the chalkboard and flipchart. Using a lecture/electronic technique, a seminar leader will show you how to use built-in outlining, drawing, and charting tools. You will even learn how to get full-color effects in overheads and slides.

To improve your sales by 10 percent a year, read the enclosed brochure about the seminar; then complete and return the registration card. You will be glad you did.

Sincerely yours

Robert L. Marsh

Robert L. Marsh, Director

xx

Enclosure

Block Style, Elite

2″ = 20 pica spaces
24 elite spaces

1½″ = 15 pica spaces
18 elite spaces

1″ = 10 pica spaces
12 elite spaces

Block Letter Style

In block letter style (format), all lines begin at the left margin (LM). Open punctuation is used, which means that no punctuation follows the salutation or complimentary close.

Letter Stationery

Most business letters are processed on standard-size letterheads (8½″ × 11″) with the company name, address, and telephone number printed at the top.

Simplified memorandums may be processed on letterheads, too. If the letterhead is too deep to key the date on line 10, place it a DS below the letterhead.

Letter Placement/Spacing

A placement guide such as the one shown below will help you place letters.

Dateline placement. Vertical placement of the dateline varies according to letter length (the longer the letter, the higher the date placement). If a deep letterhead prevents placing the date on the line suggested in the *Letter Placement Guide,* place it a DS below the letterhead.

Letter address. The letter address is always started a QS below the dateline. If the letter is addressed to a company, the address may include an attention line (the first line of the address) to call the letter to the attention of a specific person, department, or job title.

Salutation. The salutation is placed a DS below the letter address. If the first line of the address is a company name, the salutation *Ladies and Gentlemen* is used. If the first line of the letter address is a person's name, the salutation includes the name: *Dear Mr. Wells; Dear Ms. Sanchez.*

Subject line. A subject line identifies the topic of the letter. It is placed a DS below the salutation in ALL CAPS.

Body. The body or letter message begins a DS below the salutation (or below the subject line, if any). Body paragraphs (¶s) are SS with a DS between ¶s.

Complimentary close. The complimentary close is placed a DS below the last line of the body.

Writer's name and title. The writer's name is placed a QS below the complimentary close. The writer's business title may follow the name on the same line, preceded by a comma, or may be placed on the next line.

Reference initials. If the keyboard operator is not the writer of the message, the operator's initials (lowercased) are keyed a DS below the writer's name or title.

Enclosure notation. If anything other than the letter is to be included in the envelope, the word *Enclosure* (or *Enclosures*) is keyed a DS below the initials.

Copy notation. If a copy of the letter is to be sent to someone other than the addressee, the letter *c,* followed by a space and the recipient's name, is placed a DS below the enclosure notation. If two people are to receive copies, both names are placed on the same line with a comma and space between them.

Note: Not all letters require subject lines, reference initials, enclosure notations, and copy notations. Regardless of which special elements are needed, key them in the order given with a DS between them.

LETTER PLACEMENT GUIDE

Letter Classification	5-Stroke Words in Letter Body	Side Margins	Margin Settings		Dateline Position (from Top Edge of Paper)
			Elite	Pica	
Short	Up to 100	2″	24-78*	20-65*	18
Average	101-200	1½″	18-84*	15-70*	16
Long	201-300	1″	12-90*	10-75*	14
Two-Page	More than 300	1″	12-90*	10-75*	14
6″ Line	All letters	1¼″	15-87*	12-72*	As above

*Plus 3-7 spaces for the typewriter bell cue — usually add 5.

BOUTIQUES INTERNATIONAL, LTD.

As part of your orientation program, Miss Angela E. Benson, a personnel administrator in the Human Resources Department, asks you to study these excerpts from the COMPANY INFORMATIONAL HANDBOOK.

Excerpts from COMPANY INFORMATIONAL HANDBOOK

Functions of Special Offices

Customer Service Center

1. Promotes customer satisfaction.
2. Studies customer needs and preferences.
3. Solves customer problems in an expeditious manner.
4. Resolves any customer complaints promptly and equitably.
5. Provides personal, specialized customer services.

Public Relations Office

1. Strives to create and maintain public goodwill.
2. Prepares informational materials, including booklets and speeches.
3. Cooperates with public and private organizations in community projects.
4. Serves as a clearinghouse for all official contacts with the public.
5. Plans and conducts special activities to enhance public goodwill.

Human Resources Department

1. Provides required human resources.
2. Develops programs to help employees reach their maximum potential under safe and healthful working conditions.
3. Establishes a fair and equitable schedule of compensation, including desirable employee benefits.
4. Evaluates performance of employees.
5. Monitors equal opportunity policies.

Advertising Department

1. Stimulates and promotes the sale of goods.
2. Selects appropriate media for promoting sales.
3. Prepares sales promotional material.
4. Plans and conducts special advertising campaigns.
5. Upholds ethical standards in sales promotion.

Formatting Documents

Each major office of the company is free to adopt any document format it chooses. Follow directions given by the document originator. If no format is specified, use your best judgment in placing the material neatly on the page.

Job Competencies

To be successful as a keyboard technician you must possess these qualifications.

1. Excellent keyboarding skills.
2. A thorough knowledge of grammar, punctuation, spelling, and formatting.
3. The ability to use reference materials such as dictionaries, directories, and manuals.
4. Good proofreading skills.
5. The ability to listen, understand, and follow directions.
6. The ability to plan, organize, and complete your work with a minimum of assistance.
7. The ability to get along well with others.

Major Duties

Under the direction of a specified supervisor, you will do the following:

1. Compile information as the basis for preparing business documents.
2. Key documents such as correspondence, reports, forms, and tables.
3. Prepare business documents from handwritten or rough-draft copy and from source materials.
4. Compose short documents based on data and instructions provided.
5. Compute amounts in pencil or by using a calculator.

Special Instructions

As a keyboard technician, you will be expected to

1. Use the proper format for a document.
2. Provide date for correspondence (use the current date if a date is not given).
3. Provide an appropriate salutation, complimentary close, keyed signature and title of the originator of correspondence, and your initials.
4. Include the proper notation if the content of the document indicates there are enclosures or attachments.
5. Correct errors you make as you prepare a document in final form.
6. Correct any unmarked errors made by the originator of the document in spelling, punctuation, grammar, and word usage.
7. Proofread all documents and correct any errors you may have missed *before* you remove a document from the machine.
8. Produce neat, error-free, usable business documents.

43a ▶ 6 Conditioning Practice

each line twice SS; then a 1′ writing on line 3; find *gwam*

alphabet 1 Rex just left my quiz show and gave back a prize he had won.

fig/sym 2 Review reaches: $40, $84, 95%, #30, 5-point, 1/6, B&O 27's.

speed 3 Di may profit by good form and a firm wish to make the goal.

| 1 | 2 | 3 | 4 | 5 | 6 | 7 | 8 | 9 | 10 | 11 | 12 |

43b ▶ 14 Learn to Format Letter Parts

2 plain full sheets

Drill 1

1. Begin return address on line 14 so that the date is placed on line 16.

2. After keying the salutation, space down 14 lines to begin closing lines.

SM: 1½″
pica: 15-70 + 5
elite: 18-84 + 5
PB: line 16

Drill 2

1. Study the business-letter formatting guides on p. 76; check each placement point with the model letter on p. 78 and with the copy in Drill 2 at right.

2. Key the drill according to the spacing annotations in color within the drill.

Drill 1: **Personal-Business Letter**

3204 Mount Holly Road
Charlotte, NC 28216-3746
November 10, 19-- ←Line 16
QS (Return 4 times)

Mrs. Juanita L. Ruiz
1859 Boston Road
Springfield, MA 01129-3467 DS

Dear Mrs. Ruiz DS

Space down 14 times (using ***index*** or ***return/enter*** key) to allow for body of letter.

Cordially yours QS (Return 4 times)

Ms. Gloria C. Ainsley DS

Enclosure

Drill 2: **Business Letter**

Line 16→ November 10, 19-- QS (Return 4 times)

Attention Mr. Kevin J. Marx
Kendall Computers, Inc.
733 Marquette Avenue
Minneapolis, MN 55402-1736 DS

Ladies and Gentlemen DS

Space down 14 times (using ***index*** or ***return/enter*** key) to allow for body of letter.

Sincerely yours QS (Return 4 times)

Evan L. Ritchey, Director
Word Processing Center DS

tbh DS

Enclosure DS

c Miss Mary E. Durbin

43c ▶ 30 Learn to Format Business Letters

3 plain full sheets; SM: 1½″; PB: line 16

1. Study the model letter on p. 78 which illustrates *block style* with *open punctuation.* Note the vertical and horizontal placement of letter parts.

2. On a plain full sheet, key the letter shown on p. 78. Use the typewriter bell cue or word wrap feature to return at line endings.

3. Proofread/correct your copy.

4. If time permits, take a 2′ writing on the opening lines (date through subject line); then a 2′ writing on the closing lines (complimentary close to the end). Use plain full sheets.

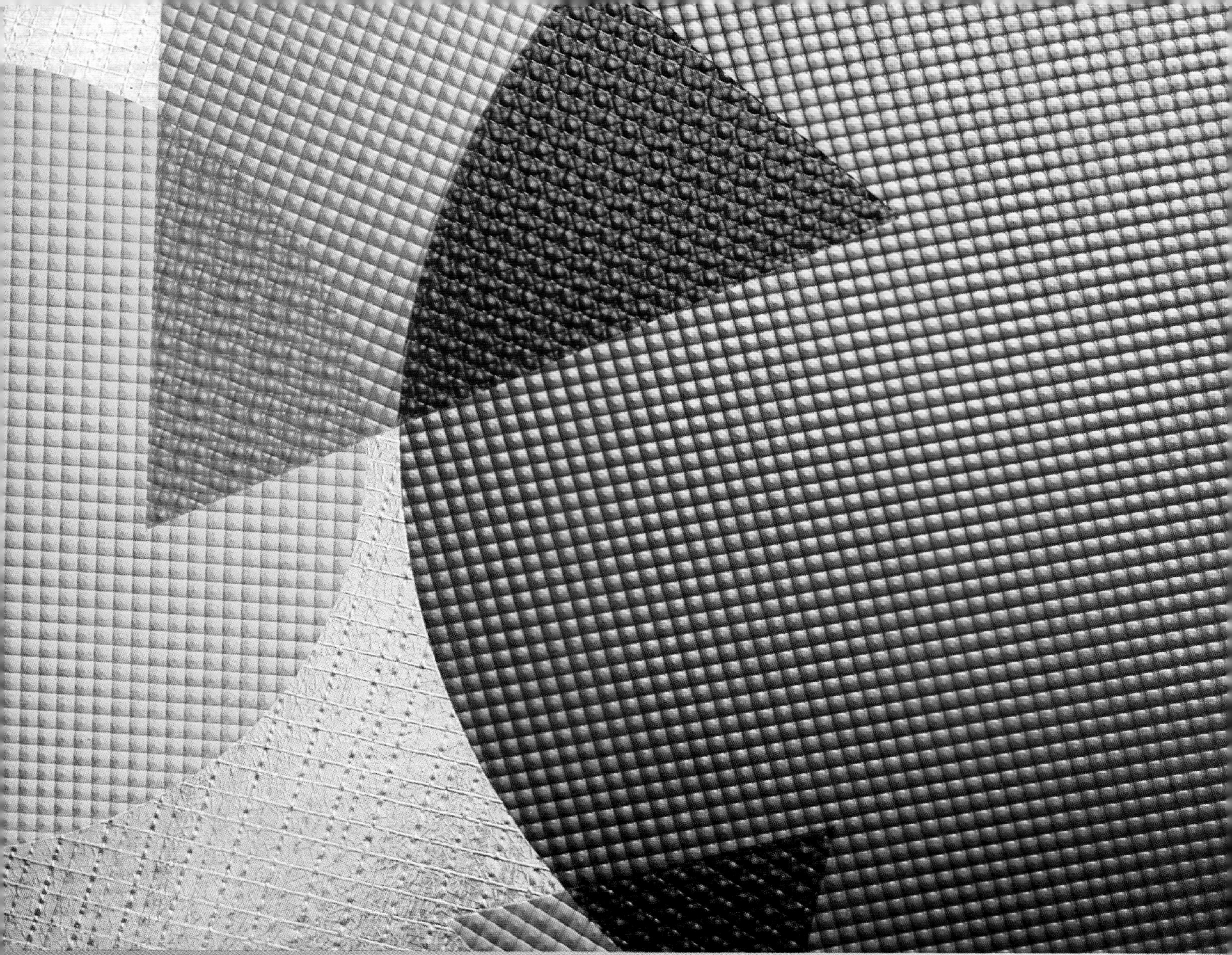

LESSONS 251 – 275

PHASE 11

BOUTIQUES INTERNATIONAL, LTD. SPECIAL OFFICE SIMULATIONS

You have been hired as a keyboard technician by **Boutiques International, Ltd.**, a mail order firm that sells fine wares from all over the world. The company's headquarters are located at **801 Canal Street, New Orleans, LA 70112-3500.** The company has branch offices in London, Paris, Rome, and Hong Kong, and shops in major cities throughout the United States.

Initially, you will work at the company's headquarters as a replacement for employees who are ill or on vacation. This will give you an opportunity to work in some of the special offices of the company.

Your goals at Boutiques International are to

1. Increase your knowledge of typical office procedures.

2. Learn how to plan and organize your work.

3. Produce acceptable documents quickly and efficiently.

4. Improve your basic keyboarding and communications skills.

5. Become familiar with the functions of some of the special offices of a large corporation--Customer Service Center, Public Relations Office, Human Resources Department, and Advertising Department.

MERKEL-EVANS, Inc.

1321 Commerce Street • Dallas, TX 75202-1648 • Tel. (214) 871-4400

		words in parts	total words
Date	November 10, 19-- Line 16	4	4
	Quadruple-space (QS): strike return key 4 times		
Letter address	Mrs. Evelyn M. McNeil	8	8
	4582 Campus Drive	12	12
	Fort Worth, TX 76119-1835 Double-space (DS): strike return key twice	17	17
Salutation	Dear Mrs. McNeil DS	20	20
Body	The new holiday season is just around the corner, and	11	31
	we invite you to beat the rush and visit our exciting	22	42
	Gallery of Gifts. Gift-giving can be a snap this year	33	53
	because of our vast array of gifts "for kids from one	43	64
	to ninety-two." DS	47	67
	What's more, many of our gifts are prewrapped for pre-	57	78
	sentation. All can be packaged and shipped right here	68	89
	at the store. DS	71	92
	A catalog of our hottest gift items and a schedule of	82	103
	holiday hours for special charge-card customers are en-	93	113
	closed. Please stop in and let us help you select that	104	125
	special gift, or call us if you wish to shop by phone. DS	115	136
	We wish you happy holidays and hope to see you soon. DS	126	147
Complimentary close	Cordially yours QS	3	150
	Carol J. Suess		
Writer's name and title	Ms. Carol J. Suess, Manager DS	9	155
Reference initials	rj DS	9	156
Enclosure notation	Enclosures	11	158

Shown in pica (10-pitch) type with 1½-inch side margins, photo-reduced

Business Letter in Block Format, Open Punctuation

248b-250b (continued)

DIANNA E. WARRENS
3559 Longfellow Drive
Portland, ME 04107-7486
(207) 256-8673

EDUCATION

High School: Memorial High School (received diploma in May, 1990)

Business Courses: Keyboarding for Information Processing
Document Processing Applications
Office Procedures/Machine Transcription
Business Computer Applications

Current Skill Level: Keyboarding straight-copy rate: 70 words a minute.
Machine transcription rate: 35 words a minute.

SCHOOL ACTIVITIES

Business Professionals of America, Community Service Chairperson during junior and senior years (responsible for organizing and conducting various community service projects for organizations in the Portland area.)

Member of National Honor Society, junior and senior years.

Senior Class Secretary (responsible for preparing agenda and recording minutes of meetings.)

WORK EXPERIENCE

Administrative Assistant, Karsten Insurance Company, Portland, ME, January 1990 to present. Work 20 hours a week performing tasks assigned by the office manager; key correspondence, process insurance applications and claims, answer telephone, greet clients, and file correspondence.

Camp Counselor, Parks and Recreation Department, Portland, ME, summers 1988 and 1989. Organized, directed, and supervised activities for camp participants.

REFERENCES

Ms. Audra Westbrook, Office Manager, Karsten Insurance Company, 3619 Quebec Street, Portland, ME 04101-7475, (207) 249-8324.

Mr. Jason Thrasher, Director, Parks and Recreation Department, 2990 Ridgeway Road, Portland, ME 04104-1830 (207) 836-2990.

Ms. Mary St. James, Business Instructor, Memorial High School, 688 Cleveland Street, Portland, ME 04103-2701 (207) 836-3800.

Resume

APPLICATION FOR EMPLOYMENT

PLEASE PRINT WITH BLACK INK OR USE TYPEWRITER *AN EQUAL OPPORTUNITY EMPLOYER*

NAME (LAST, FIRST, MIDDLE INITIAL)	SOCIAL SECURITY NUMBER	CURRENT DATE
Warrens, Dianna E.	701-325-4899	June 4, 19--

ADDRESS (NUMBER, STREET, CITY, STATE, ZIP CODE): 3559 Longfellow Drive, Portland, ME 04107-7486
HOME PHONE NO.: (207) 256-8673

REACH PHONE NO.:
U.S. CITIZEN? YES x NO
DATE YOU CAN START: June 15, 19--

ARE YOU EMPLOYED NOW? Yes
IF SO, MAY WE INQUIRE OF YOUR PRESENT EMPLOYER? Yes

TYPE OF WORK DESIRED: Office
REFERRED BY: Jasper Employment Agency
SALARY DESIRED: $ Open

IF RELATED TO ANYONE IN OUR EMPLOY, STATE AND NAME AND POSITION: No

DO YOU HAVE ANY PHYSICAL CONDITION THAT MAY PREVENT YOU FROM PERFORMING CERTAIN KINDS OF WORK? YES NO x IF YES, EXPLAIN

HAVE YOU EVER BEEN CONVICTED OF A FELONY? YES NO x IF YES, EXPLAIN

EDUCATION

	EDUCATIONAL INSTITUTION	LOCATION (CITY, STATE)	DATES ATTENDED FROM MO.	FROM YR.	TO MO.	TO YR.	DIPLOMA, DEGREE, OR CREDITS EARNED	CLASS STANDING (CHK QUARTER) 1	2	3	4	MAJOR SUBJECTS STUDIED
COLLEGE												
HIGH SCHOOL	Memorial High School	Portland, Maine	8	86	5	90	Diploma	x				Business
GRADE SCHOOL												
OTHER												

LIST BELOW THE POSITIONS THAT YOU HAVE HELD (LAST POSITION FIRST)

1. NAME AND ADDRESS OF FIRM: Karsten Insurance Company, 3619 Quebec Street, Portland, ME 04101-7475
DESCRIBE POSITION RESPONSIBILITIES: Keyed correspondence, processed routine insurance claims, answered telephone, greeted clients, and filed documents.
NAME OF SUPERVISOR: Ms. Audra Westbrook
EMPLOYED (MO-YR) FROM: 1/90 TO: present
REASON FOR LEAVING:

2. NAME AND ADDRESS OF FIRM: Parks and Recreation Department, 2990 Ridgeway Road, Portland, ME 04104-1830
DESCRIBE POSITION RESPONSIBILITIES: Organized, directed, and supervised activities for six-year-old camp participants.
NAME OF SUPERVISOR: Mr. Jason Thrasher
EMPLOYED (MO-YR) FROM: Summers TO: 1988 and 1989
REASON FOR LEAVING: It was a summer job only.

3. NAME AND ADDRESS OF FIRM:
DESCRIBE POSITION RESPONSIBILITIES:
NAME OF SUPERVISOR:
EMPLOYED (MO-YR) FROM: TO:
REASON FOR LEAVING:

I UNDERSTAND THAT I SHALL NOT BECOME AN EMPLOYEE UNTIL I HAVE SIGNED AN EMPLOYMENT AGREEMENT WITH THE FINAL APPROVAL OF THE EMPLOYER AND THAT SUCH EMPLOYMENT WILL BE SUBJECT TO VERIFICATION OF PREVIOUS EMPLOYMENT, DATA PROVIDED IN THIS APPLICATION, ANY RELATED DOCUMENTS, OR RESUME. I KNOW THAT A REPORT MAY BE MADE THAT WILL INCLUDE INFORMATION CONCERNING ANY FACTOR THE EMPLOYER MIGHT FIND RELEVANT TO THE POSITION FOR WHICH I AM APPLYING, AND THAT I CAN MAKE A WRITTEN REQUEST FOR ADDITIONAL INFORMATION AS TO THE NATURE AND SCOPE OF THE REPORT IF ONE IS MADE.

Dianna E. Warrens
SIGNATURE OF APPLICANT

Application Form

3559 Longfellow Drive
Portland, ME 04107-7486
June 1, 19--

Ms. Lydia Kent
Personnel Director
Norton Industries
333 Highland Street
Portland, ME 04103-8488

Dear Ms. Kent:

Mr. Keith Riles, director of the Jasper Employment Agency, informed me of the employment opportunity in your document processing department with Norton Industries. Mr. Riles shared the job description and outlined the requirements for the position. I believe I possess the necessary qualifications and would like to be considered for the position.

Last week I graduated from Memorial High School. While attending Memorial, all of my elective credits were used to take courses from the business department. From these courses I acquired skills in the areas of document processing, office procedures, computer applications, and transcription techniques.

My part-time job with Karsten Insurance Company allowed me to apply and refine the skills I gained from the course work. The job also required me to deal with the public, work under pressure to meet deadlines, work as part of a team, and learn how to operate new office equipment.

A career in today's technology-oriented office is very exciting to me. Since I am eager to begin that career on a full-time basis, I shall call your office next week after you have had an opportunity to review the resume which is enclosed. I look forward to discussing the document processing position with you.

Sincerely,

Dianna E. Warrens

Enclosure

Letter of Application

3559 Longfellow Drive
Portland, ME 04107-7486
June 8, 19--

Ms. Lydia Kent
Personnel Director
Norton Industries
333 Highland Street
Portland, ME 04103-8488

Dear Ms. Kent:

Thank you for allowing me to meet with you to discuss the position in your document processing department. Being able to observe the department in action and meet with Mr. Conrad as well as several other employees gave me a much better understanding of the requirements of the job as well as the opportunities available with Norton Industries.

The company tuition reimbursement program is particularly appealing to me. It was a very difficult decision for me to forego further schooling in order to start a career immediately. Your program would allow me to do both.

If there is additional information that I can provide to assist you in making your decision, I would be happy to do so. I am looking forward to hearing from you.

Sincerely,

Dianna E. Warrens

Follow-Up Letter

44a ▶ 6 Conditioning Practice

each line twice SS; then a 1′ writing on line 3; find *gwam*

alphabet 1 Zoe just may have to plan a big, unique dance for next week.
fig/sym 2 Tami asked, "Can't you touch-key 65, 73, $840, and 19 1/2%?"
speed 3 Six of the big firms may bid for the right to the lake land.

| 1 | 2 | 3 | 4 | 5 | 6 | 7 | 8 | 9 | 10 | 11 | 12 |

44b ▶ 8 Language Skills: Simple Sentences

1. Study the guides in the color blocks at right and the sentences that illustrate the guides.
2. Key the **Learn** sentences as shown, noting the words that comprise the subject and predicate of each sentence.
3. On a separate sheet of paper, key vertically the numbers 1 through 8, DS.
4. Key the subject and predicate of each **Learn** sentence opposite the appropriate number.
5. Check work with teacher.

A *simple* sentence consists of a single independent clause which contains a subject (noun or pronoun) and a predicate (verb).

Learn 1 Pam is president of her class. *(single subject/single predicate)*
Learn 2 Kevin walks to and from school. *(single subject/single predicate)*
Learn 3 Reading mystery novels is my favorite pastime.
Learn 4 The captain of the team is out with a badly sprained ankle.

A simple sentence may have as its subject more than one noun or pronoun and as its predicate more than one verb.

Learn 5 She bought a new bicycle. *(single subject/single predicate)*
Learn 6 Marv and I received new bicycles. *(compound subject/single predicate)*
Learn 7 Alice washed and waxed her car. *(single subject/compound predicate)*
Learn 8 He and I cleaned and cooked the fish. *(compound subject and predicate)*

44c ▶ 6 Improve Keyboarding Skill: Rough-Draft Copy

1. Using a 60-space line, key a 2′ writing on the ¶, making the marked changes as you key.
2. Proofread your copy and find *gwam.*
3. Key another 2′ writing; try to increase your speed.

∧	= insert
ℓ	= delete
#	= add space
∽	= transpose
⁀	= close up

all letters used | LA | 1.4 si | 5.4 awl | 85% hfw |

gwam 2′

~~When~~ As you key from corrected ~~marked~~ copy, read just a lit(t)le ahead 6
of where ~~your~~ you are keying. Doing ~~this~~ so will keep you from missing 12
changes that need to ~~must~~ be made. Learn to reco(g)nize quickly the~~e~~ 18
correction s(y)mbols so that you don't have to ~~reduce~~ lower your speed 24
or stop to(#)read. Exp~~ce~~(ec)t to copy rough~~-~~draft at about eighty-(∧) 30
five per cent of your straight(∧)copy speed. 35

44d-45d ▶ 30 (daily) Improve Formatting Skill: Letters and Memos

5 letterheads (LP pp. 29-38) or plain full sheets

Note: Correct your errors as you key unless otherwise directed.

1. Begin formatting/processing the average-length letters and the memo on pp. 81-82 (use the *Letter Placement Guide* on p.76). Try to finish the documents in two class periods.

2. Proofread/correct each document before removing it from your typewriter or the screen of your computer.

3. If a document cannot be completed within a class period, complete the line on which you are working and save the document for later completion.

Application Form

Many companies require that their standard application form be completed even though a resume and application letter have been sent. In some cases the applicant must complete the form in longhand at the company location. In other cases the applicant may take the form and return it later, in which case it should be keyed. In either case, particular attention should be given to neatness and accuracy. In addition, directions should be followed carefully.

One way to help ensure neatness is to make a photocopy of the form to complete as a rough-draft copy. Then the final form can be completed more easily.

Follow-Up Letter

The follow-up letter is an important part of the job search. It is a thank you for the time given and courtesies extended to you during the interview. If you can honestly do so, discuss the positive impressions you have of the company and indicate your continued interest in the job.

Lessons 248-250 Apply for Employment

248a-250a ▶ 5 (daily) *Conditioning Practice*

Each day check to see that equipment is in good working order by keying the lines at the right at least twice.

alphabet 1 Mr. Gomez was quite favorably pleased with the six market projections.

figures 2 Only 1,985 of the 12,476 voting delegates had registered by 10:30 p.m.

fig/sym 3 I sent Check #714 for $4,368.90 to C. L. Walker & Sons on November 25.

speed 4 If they pay me to do so, I may make their formal gowns for the social.

| 1 | 2 | 3 | 4 | 5 | 6 | 7 | 8 | 9 | 10 | 11 | 12 | 13 | 14 |

248b-250b ▶ 45 (daily) *Prepare Employment Documents*

Documents 1-4
LP p. 47 and
7 plain full sheets

Your teacher encourages you to apply for the job with **Boutiques International, Ltd.**, which is described in the job announcement shown at the right. Using the illustrations on page 425 as guides, prepare the following employment documents.

1. Resume. Using your personal data, compose at the keyboard a resume. Revise and key a final copy.

2. Letter of Application. Compose at the keyboard your application letter to **Mr. Henry K. O'Brian.** Revise and key a final copy.

3. Application Form (LP p. 47). On a plain sheet, key the information that you will include on the application form used by Boutiques International, Ltd. for all potential employees. Key the application form, using the personal data that you keyed on the plain sheet.

4. Follow-Up Letter. Compose at the keyboard a follow-up letter similar to the one on the next page. Revise and key a final copy.

KEYBOARDING TECHNICIAN

Large international mail order firm hiring keyboarding technicians. Firm looking for applicants who have

- excellent keyboarding skills.
- a good knowledge of formatting, grammar, spelling, and punctuation.
- the ability to listen to, understand, and follow directions.
- the ability to plan, organize, and complete work with a minimum of assistance.
- the ability to work well with others.

Send letter of application and resume to

Mr. Henry K. O'Brian
Director of Human Resources
Boutiques International, Ltd.
801 Canal Street
New Orleans, LA 70112-3500

An Equal Opportunity Employer

45a ▶ 6 Conditioning Practice

each line twice SS; then a 1′ writing on line 3; find *gwam*

alphabet 1 Wayne froze the ball, having just made the six quick points.
fig/sym 2 Flo moved from 583 Iris Lane to 836 - 42d Avenue on 10/7/91.
speed 3 Suella may row to the small island to dig for the big clams.

| 1 | 2 | 3 | 4 | 5 | 6 | 7 | 8 | 9 | 10 | 11 | 12 |

45b ▶ 8 Improve Language Skills: Compound Sentences

1. Study the guides in the color blocks at right and the sentences that illustrate the guides.

2. Key the **Learn** sentences as shown, noting the words that comprise the subjects and predicates of each sentence.

3. On a separate sheet of paper, key vertically the numbers 1 through 8, DS.

4. Key the subject-predicate of both clauses in each **Learn** sentence opposite the appropriate number. Use a diagonal (/) to separate the subject-predicate of one clause from that of the other.

5. Check work with teacher.

A *compound* sentence contains two or more independent clauses connected by a coordinating conjunction (*and, but, for, or, nor, yet, so*).

Learn 1 Jay Sparks likes to hike, and Roy Tubbs likes to swim.
Learn 2 The computer is operative, but the printer does not work.
Learn 3 You may eat in the hotel, or you may choose a cafe nearby.
Learn 4 The sky is clear, the moon is out, and the sea is very calm.

Each clause of a compound sentence may have as its subject more than one noun/pronoun and as its predicate more than one verb.

Learn 5 Ben and I saw the game, and Bob and Marla went to a movie.
Learn 6 Nick dived and swam, but the others fished off the boat.
Learn 7 You may play solitaire, or you and Joe may play checkers.
Learn 8 Jan huffed and puffed up the hill, but Eloise scampered up.

45c ▶ 6 Improve Keyboarding Skill: Script Copy

1. Using a 60-space line, key a 2′ writing on the ¶.

2. Proofread your copy and find *gwam.*

3. Key another 2′ writing; try to increase speed.

all letters used | LA | 1.4 si | 5.4 awl | 85% hfw |

gwam 2′

Whether you key documents for personal or for business 5
use, much of the copy will be in handwritten or rough-draft 11
form. So adjust your speed in order to do work of quality. 18
Seize the next opportunity to prove that you can handle both 24
kinds of copy without too great a loss in speed and control. 30
With practice, you can process such copy with speed and ease. 36

44d-45d ▶ 30 (continued)

letterheads and plain full sheets as listed in 44d-45d, p. 79

Use *Letter Placement Guide* on p. 76 for business letters.

1. Continue formatting/processing the average-length documents given on pp. 81-82.

2. Proofread/correct each document before removing it from the typewriter or the screen of your computer.

3. If you finish all documents before time is called, start over with Document 1; *OR* rekey one of the documents that contains errors. Use plain paper.

4. Assemble your work in document number order and turn it in.

Your teacher may evaluate your work in terms of number of lines or documents satisfactorily processed.

UNIT 59 LESSONS 248 – 250

Apply for Employment

Learning Goals

1. To learn the appropriate content and format for employment documents.
2. To prepare your personal employment documents for a specified job.

Documents Prepared

1. Resume
2. Application Letter
3. Application Form
4. Follow-Up Letter

APPLY FOR EMPLOYMENT

Now that you have completed your cooperative work experience, you are ready to apply for a job. Guidelines for preparing employment documents are provided at the right; examples are illustrated on page 425. Review these guidelines and examples carefully.

Employment Document Guidelines

Employment documents provide applicants an opportunity to present their best qualities to prospective employers. These qualities are represented by the specific content of the documents as well as by the format, neatness, and accuracy of the documents. The care with which these documents are prepared is a strong indication to a company of the highest level of performance they can expect of the applicant; therefore, special attention should be given to their preparation.

The most common types of employment documents are the resume (or personal data sheet), application letter, application form, and the follow-up letter.

Resume

The resume should be a factual presentation of your skills, abilities and traits that would be of value to the prospective employer. It is usually one page and contains the following major categories of information: personal, education, school activities, work experience, and references. The order in which the major categories are listed may vary, with the most significant qualifications for the particular job listed first. However, personal information is usually listed first and references are usually listed last.

Personal information typically includes name, address, and telephone number. Other personal information should only be included if it relates directly to the job qualifications.

The education section is a listing of the high schools you have attended. If you have attended more than one high school, you should list the schools attended in reverse chronological order (most recent school listed first). In this section you may also list courses completed that are specifically related to the job, skill levels achieved if appropriate (such as keyboarding speed), and grades earned. Grade point average, if B or above, may be listed.

In the school activities section, list organization memberships, offices held, scholarships, awards, and honors. In particular, list activities that will demonstrate leadership abilities.

List work experience in reverse chronological order with a brief description of duties. If experience is limited, jobs not related to the business office, such as babysitting or lawn mowing, should be listed because such jobs demonstrate responsibility and initiative.

Include a variety of references, such as teachers and former employers. Always request permission from the people you plan to list as references before using their names.

Application Letter

The letter of application should include three sections. The first section (paragraph) may state something positive about the company, how the applicant learned of the opening, and the specific position the applicant is seeking.

The second section may contain two or three paragraphs which provide evidence that the applicant is qualified for the position. Avoid merely repeating the information on the resume. This is the time to interpret that information and to show how those qualifications can be beneficial to the company. The applicant should focus on what he/she can do for the company--not what the job will do for him/her.

The last section (paragraph) should request an interview. Some authorities suggest that the applicant should be proactive rather than reactive, meaning that the applicant should suggest a time to call the company to request an interview rather than ask the company to call or write to set up the interview. The logic of this recommendation is that company representatives may become so busy that they neglect to respond to the letter; whereas, they may respond positively to a telephone request for the interview. This action is appropriate only after allowing adequate time for the company representative to inspect the application letter and resume.

44d-45d (continued)

Document 1: Business Letter in Block Format, Open Punctuation

words

November 12, 19-- 4

Miss Carmen J. Blanco, Chair 9
Business Education Department 15
Dolphin Vocational High School 22
104 N. Andrews Avenue 26
Fort Lauderdale, FL 33301-2859 32

Dear Miss Blanco 36

Your order for six Genesis GS computers and 45
two printers is being processed. We are pleased 54
to include you in the growing number of users 64
of this quality equipment. 69

We plan to deliver and install these machines at 79
three o'clock on November 18 to avoid disrupt- 88
ing classroom activities. Please let me know if 98
this date and time are convenient for you. 107

Only a few minutes are required to install the 116
equipment, but we want to test two or three 125
programs to be certain that everything is work- 134
ing properly. 137

Please telephone me at the number shown above 147
to confirm or change the appointment. 154
(words in body: 121)

Sincerely yours 158

Kermit L. Dahms, Sales Manager 164

xx (Use your own initials for reference) 164

c DeRon S. Jackson 168

Document 2: Business Letter in Block Format, Open Punctuation

words

November 12, 19-- 4

Mr. Duane R. Burk, Office Manager 10
Huesman & Schmidt, Inc. 15
662 Woodward Avenue 19
Detroit, MI 48226-1947 24

Dear Mr. Burk 27

Thank you for letting our representative, Miss 36
Tina Chun, discuss with you and your staff our 46
new line of landscaped office modules. 54

Using in-scale templates, Miss Chun has rede- 63
signed the general work area of your word 71
processing center. Her mock-up offers you 80
important features: ideal use of space in indi- 89
vidual workstations, stationary panels to create 99
private work areas without a feeling of cloister, 109
and traffic patterns that are least disruptive 118
to others. 121

May we show you this portable display and dis- 130
cuss the low cost of improving the productivity 140
and harmony of your office staff. A color photo- 149
graph of the mock-up is enclosed. Please call 159
me to set a convenient date and time for us to 168
spend about an hour with you. 174
(words in body: 149)

Sincerely yours 178

Virgil P. Thompson 181
Assistant Sales Manager 186

xx (Use your initials) 187

Enclosure 189

Document 3
Simplified Memo in Block Format

letterhead (LP p. 33) or plain full sheet; SM: 1"; PB: line 10

Date: **November 13, 19--**
Addressees: **Ana Wells**
DeRon Jackson
Subject: **APPOINTMENT FOR GENESIS INSTALLATION**
Writer's name: **Kermit L. Dahms**
Reference: **your initials**

Documents 4, 5, and 6 are on p. 82.

Two-Addressee Memo

```
October 28, 19--

Leon Deitz, Cora Jordan

FOREIGN EXCHANGE STUDY

On Thursday, November 15, Mr. Earl
will be here to discuss the foreign
```

words

opening lines 16

Miss Blanco of Dolphin Vocational High School called to con- 28
firm the appointment for DeRon Jackson to install the six 39
Genesis GS computers and two printers in her word processing 52
lab. The appointment is at 3 p.m. on Friday, November 18. 64

Be sure to take the three _User's Manuals_ for the basic soft- 78
ware programs we are providing. Miss Blanco wants three 90
of her teachers to have a brief hands-on demonstration of 101
the basic operating procedures. 108

closing lines 111

Document 2
Reference Page

Using the information given below, prepare a reference page for the report.

Kleinschrod, Walter A. "A Multisensory Approach to PC Training." Today's Office. May 1989, 66.

Tedesco, Eleanor Hollis, and Robert B. Mitchell. Administrative Office Systems Management. New York: John Wiley & Sons, 1987.

Document 3
Unbound Report with Footnotes

Rekey Document 1 as an unbound report with footnotes. Use the information below when keying footnotes.

---

[1]Walter A. Kleinschrod, "A Multisensory Approach to PC Training," Today's Office, May 1989, p. 66.

[2]Eleanor Hollis Tedesco and Robert B. Mitchell, Administrative Office Systems Management (New York: John Wiley & Sons, 1987), p. 183.

words

Formalized classes taught by company employees 380
(trainers) are also offered by many larger organizations. 392
In addition to teaching classes, the trainers are available 404
DS readily to assist employees with questions about ^specific software 417
features. 420

The User's Manual 427

another resource is the user's manual
~~Users' manuals are also~~ used for training purposes. 440
The users manual provides descriptions, examples, and in- 451
structions regarding the use of the particular software prod- 463
DS uct. For the real computer novice, the user's manual is 475
usually the least effective training resource. However, after 487
developing some skill with the ~~the~~ software, employees can ex- 499
pand their expertise with the software by referring to the 511
user's manual as a base source. 517

No single method for computer training ~~employees~~ can be 526
recommended. Most organizations use a combination of ~~the~~ 537
DS methods ~~listed above~~ to keep human resources functioning at a 547
competitive level. 551

references 609

ENRICHMENT ACTIVITY: Timed Writings

IMPROVE KEYBOARDING: SPEED AND CONTROL

Use the paragraphs to increase your skills. Follow the procedure below.

1. Take two 1′ speed writings on each of the three paragraphs; find *gwam* and determine errors on each writing.

2. Take two 1′ control writings on each of the three paragraphs. Strive for no more than 2 errors on each 1′ writing.

3. Take a 5′ writing on the three paragraphs combined; find *gwam;* determine errors.

all letters used | D | 1.8 si | 6.3 awl | 70% hfw

	gwam 1′	5′	
With today's automated equipment, more documents are created in	13	3	61
the office than ever before. Most office managers are concerned about	27	5	64
managing the enormous number of documents that flow in and out of their	41	8	67
firms. Many of these documents are essential for a firm's daily opera-	56	11	70
tions. Executives use these important documents to arrive at decisions	70	14	73
that affect the direction of their firm. These decisions are more often	85	17	76
the right ones when they are based on documented information rather than	99	20	79
on intuition.	102	20	79
Because of the usefulness of the documents to executives, many	13	23	82
firms now control documents via a records management program. A few of	27	26	84
the functions of such a program include document retrieval, retention,	41	29	87
protection, and disposition. Each of these functions is essential for	55	31	90
the efficient handling of a firm's documents. How adequately the docu-	70	34	93
ments are managed in a firm is directly related to the quality of the	84	37	96
staff employed in the records management program.	93	39	98
Larger firms will utilize a records management department or cen-	13	42	100
ter to operate the records program. A variety of jobs are available in	27	45	103
such centers for individuals interested in working with records. The	41	47	106
required qualifications will vary by the type of position. A high school	56	50	109
graduate with some training in filing and office procedures may qualify	71	53	112
for a job as a records manager. Duties such as sorting, indexing, fil-	85	56	115
ing, and retrieving documents are performed by the records manager.	98	59	117

gwam 1′ | 1 | 2 | 3 | 4 | 5 | 6 | 7 | 8 | 9 | 10 | 11 | 12 | 13 | 14 |
gwam 5′ | 1 | 2 | 3 |

44d-45d (continued)

Document 4
Business Letter with Attention and Subject Lines
Use *Letter Placement Guide*, page 76.

words

November 14, 19-- | Attention Sales Manager | Business Management 12
Systems | 748 S. Market Street | Tacoma, WA 98402-1365 | Ladies and 25
Gentlemen | IMPROVE SALES BY 10 PERCENT 33

If you could close 10 percent more sales a year, would you spend a day of 48
your time to learn how? If so, we want to welcome you to 59

SUCCESS BY VISUAL PERSUASION 65

This special seminar is designed for high-level managers like you who want 80
quick, easy ways to prepare visual presentations that are a cut above the 95
chalkboard and flipchart. Using a lecture/electronic technique, a seminar 110
leader will show you how to use built-in outlining, drawing, and charting tools. 127
You will even learn how to get full-color effects in overheads and slides. 142

To improve your sales by 10 percent a year, read the enclosed brochure 156
about the seminar; then complete and return the registration card. You will 171
be glad you did. (143) 175

Sincerely yours | Robert L. Marsh, Director | xx | Enclosure 186

Document 5
Personal-Business Letter from Rough Draft
Recall
LL: 60 spaces; PB: line 14

words

22149 West chester Road 5
Cleveland, OH 44122-3756 10
November 15, 19-- 13

QS

Mr. Trevor L. DeLong 18
5202 Regency Drive 21
Cleveland, OH 44129-2756 27

Dear Trevor 29

never
A news item inthe Shaker Hieghts <u>Gazette</u> says that you are 42
to be graduated from Case Western Reserve at midyear. 53
With honors no less. Congratulations. 61
When you were a student at Woodmere High I worried that you 73
might not put your potential to work in a serious way. But 86
evidently you have been able to continue your athletic 97
goals and at the same time pursue an academic major suc- 108
cessfully. I am glad you have done credit to us at Wood- 119
mere. We are quiet proud of you. 126

What are your plans after graduation? Whatever they are 138
your former teachers at Woodmere wish you well. I would 149
enjoy a note from you which I would share with the others. 161

Cordially yours 165

QS

Willis R. Lowenstein 169

Document 6
Business Letter with Changes

1. Rekey Document 4 with changes; use **November 18, 19--** as the date.
2. Address the letter to:
Mrs. Lou Ann Rich, Manager
Management Services Corp.
10778 Main Street
Bellevue, WA 98004-1946
3. Supply an appropriate salutation.
4. Use the same closing lines.

247a ▶ 5 Conditioning Practice

Key each line twice. Then take two 30″ writings for speed on line 4 and two 30″ writings for control on line 1.

alphabet 1 Many of the duck plaques were just the right size for David's exhibit.
figures 2 Checks 63, 79, 85, 104, and 122 were not included with this statement.
fig/sym 3 They paid $5,896 in taxes ($2,740) and interest ($3,156) on the house.
speed 4 It may be the duty of the island officials to handle the tax problems.

| 1 | 2 | 3 | 4 | 5 | 6 | 7 | 8 | 9 | 10 | 11 | 12 | 13 | 14 |

247b ▶ 45 Evaluate Formatting Skills: Reports

Time Schedule
Plan and prepare .... 5′
Timed production .... 30′
Proofread; compute *n-pram* .. 10′

1. Format and key Documents 1, 2, and 3 for 30 minutes. Proofread and correct errors before removing documents from the machine.

2. After time is called (30′), proofread again and circle any uncorrected errors. Compute *n-pram.*

Document 1
Leftbound Report with Internal Citations

Prepare the report given at the right as a leftbound report.

INSERT A

1. Employees work at their own pace.

2. Instruction is individualized. Training can be scheduled when trainees need it rather than when class enrollment is large enough.

3. Employees receive instruction at their desk terminals, making the instruction cost-effective. There is no need to send either employees or instructors to training sites. Travel costs and employee/instructor travel time are eliminated (Tedesco and Mitchell, 1987, 183).

words

TRAINING RESOURCES 4

According to a 1989 projection, American firms will buy 15
more than 29 million copies of software and purchase 5 million 28
additional personal computers togo along with the 40 million 40
that are used in American business offices. Instruction of 60
some type is essential for training office personnel to oper- 72
ate this hardware and software that is being purchased. 86
The instruction is bieng provided in a variety of ways. 99
Tutorials (computer-based training) instructor-directed 111
training, and users' manuals are frequently being used to 123
train office personnel to become proficient users of the 136
technology that is a vital part of today's offices. 147
Tutorials 150
Many software packages come with tutorials. The 160
tutorials provide instruction that allows the learner to 172
master the basics of the software package. Tutorials use 183
prompts that ask questions or give instructions to guide the 195
learner through the material. Some of the advantages of this 208
type of training are listed below. 215

INSERT A 317

Instructor-Directed Training
Many companies use a variety of instructor-directed ap- 324
proaches to training personnel on hardware and software. 341
These include classroom instruction offered by educational 356
institions and classroom instruction offered by vendors. 371

(continued, p. 422)

46a ▶ 6 Conditioning Practice

each line twice SS; then a 1′ writing on line 3; find *gwam*

alphabet 1 Vicky landed quite a major star for her next big plaza show.
fig/sym 2 Items marked * are out of stock: #139*, #476A*, and #2058*.
speed 3 Dodi is to handle all the pay forms for the small lake town.

| 1 | 2 | 3 | 4 | 5 | 6 | 7 | 8 | 9 | 10 | 11 | 12 |

46b ▶ 14 Learn to Address Envelopes

1. Study the guides at right and the illustrations below.

2. Format a small (No. 6¾) and a large (No. 10) envelope for each of the addresses given below the illustration (LP pp. 39-46). Use your own return address on the small envelopes.

3. If time permits, practice folding standard-sized sheets of paper for both large and small envelopes. (See Reference Guide page RG7.)

Envelope address

Set a tab stop 10 spaces left of center of a small envelope, and 5 spaces left of center for a large envelope.

Space down 12 lines from top edge of a small envelope, and 14 spaces for a large envelope. Begin the address at the tab stop position.

Style

Use *block style,* SS. Use ALL CAPS; omit punctuation. Place city name, 2-letter state name abbreviation, and ZIP Code on last address line. Two spaces precede the ZIP Code.

Return address

Use *block style,* SS, and caps and lowercase or ALL CAPS. Begin on line 2 from top of envelope, 3 spaces from left edge.

Special notations

Place *mailing notations* such as REGISTERED and SPECIAL DELIVERY below the stamp position on line 8 or 9.

Place *addressee notations* such as PERSONAL and HOLD FOR ARRIVAL a DS below the return address and 3 spaces from left edge of envelope.

Formatting Personal and Business Envelopes as Recommended by the U.S. Postal Service

small, number 6¾ (6½″ × 3⅝″)

large, number 10 (9½″ × 4⅛″)

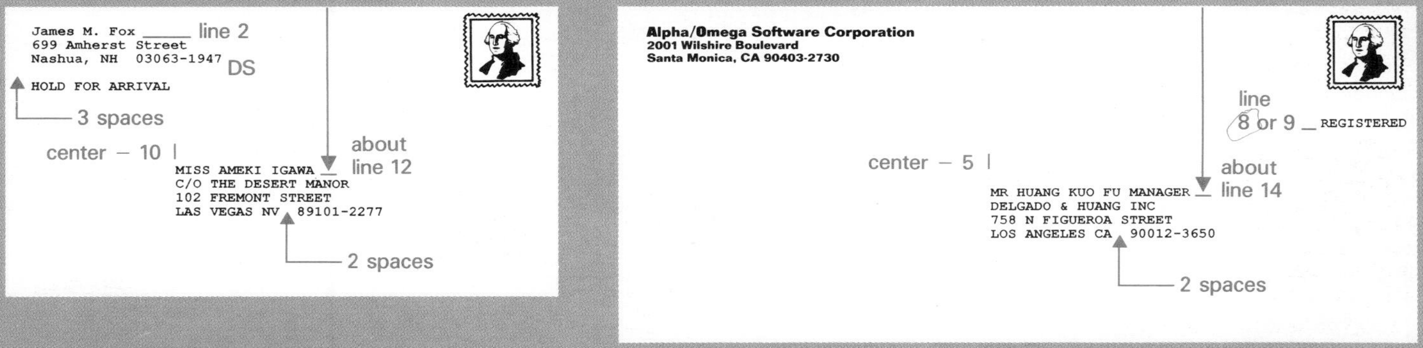

Note: The ALL CAPS unpunctuated address format may also be used for the letter address when window envelopes or automated addressing equipment (computers) is used.

MRS SONIA J CARDONA ASST VP
GENESIS ELECTRONICS INC
700 E DURANGO BLVD
SAN ANTONIO TX 78205-2649

MS HAN CHING YU
GOLDEN GATE REALTY CO
785 MARKET STREET
SAN FRANCISCO CA 94103-2277

DR NIGEL P OATMAN
407 UNIVERSITY AVENUE
SYRACUSE NY 13210-1246

MR GEORGE V WHITNEY
ROUTE 1 BOX 457
DALTON GA 30720-1457

246b (continued)

Document 2
Table

Format and key the table at the right on a full sheet. Center column headings; CS: 8.

words

SPECIAL RESORT ACTIVITIES 5

May-September 8

Activity	Date(s)	Coordinator	words
			19
Festival of the Stars	May 15-17	J. Dennis Phelps	29
Mesa Ski Exhibit	May 29	Scott Snell	36
Hot Air Balloon Day	June 15	Marsha Schneider	45
American Jazz Festival	June 28	Carlos Santiago	55
Wildlife Art Exhibit	July 15	Rhea Bosworth	63
Mesa Bicycle Classic	July 29	Sydna Mincher	72
Little Big-Top Circus	August 8	Cha Xang	80
Hang Gliding Contest	August 20	Scott Snell	89
Mesa Golf Classic	September 3-4	Carmen Pascual	98

Document 3
Purchase Order

LP p. 43

Key the purchase order shown at the right with the changes that have been marked.

Document 4
Purchase Order

LP p. 43

Key the purchase order again, making the following changes:

Order only **1 1" Changeable Letter Set.** Include **1 2" Changeable Letter Set (B5915)** with the order. The 2" set sells for **$37.50 each.**

MESA MOUNTAIN RESORT
727 Apache Road
Boulder, CO 80537-5565
(303) 234-5989

PURCHASE ORDER

MONTOYA OFFICE SUPPLY
5889 WILLOUGHBY AVENUE
LOS ANGELES CA 90038-6222

Purchase Order No.: B3617 1

Date: March 18, 19-- 9

Terms: 2/10, n/30 13 21

Shipped Via: Bel Aire Freight 24

Quantity	Description/Stock Number	Price		Per	Total		words
1	Diskette Tray Cabinet ~~(Q2813)~~ (Q3604)	~~279~~ 239	~~98~~ 46	ea	~~279~~ 239	~~98~~ 46	34
1	Desktop Organizer (P3709)	86	95	ea	86	95	43
2	Changeable Letter Board (B5613)	79	49	ea	158	98	53
2	1" Changeable Letter Set (B4321)	18	50	ea	37	00	64
					~~562~~ 522	~~91~~ 39	65

By ____________________

46c ▶ 22 Check Business Letter Formatting Skill

2 letterheads (LP pp. 47-50) or plain full sheets

Document 1
Business Letter with USPS Address

1. Format and key the average-length letter.
2. Use the USPS address format as shown; assume a window envelope will be used.
3. Proofread and correct your copy before removing it from your typewriter or computer.

Document 2
Business Letter with Variations

Format the letter again from your corrected copy, making these changes:
Date: **November 17, 19--**
Address, traditional format:
Mr. Edwin C. Phipps
Elmwood Vocational School
1262 Asylum Avenue
Hartford, CT 06105-2828
Salutation: supply one
Subject: **WORLD CHAMPIONS**
Copy notation: **c Ms. Eloise M. Rozic**

	words
November 16, 19--	4
MISS JANELLE A QUIN	8
CENTRAL HIGH SCHOOL — Use USPS format.	12
1000 LINCOLN AVENUE	16
EVANSVILLE IN 47714-2330	21
Dear Miss Quinn	24
Thanks for conveying the intrest of your students inthe	36
keying speeds achieved by those who have won international	48
typewriting contests.	52
Margaret Hama won hte last inter national contest, held	64
in 1941. She keyed for an hour on an electric typewriter	75
at a speed of 149 net words a minute (errors penalized).	87
The next highest speed was attained by Albert Tangore who	99
won the 1923 contest on a manual typewriter atthe rate of	110
147 words a minute.	115
~~Even though~~ later claims have been ~~made~~ to the title World	126
Champion Typist," the international contests were discon-	137
tinued during World War II and to our knowledge have not	149
been ~~started again.~~	152
Good luck to you and you students as you seek champion	163
ship speed. (141)	166
Sincerely Yours	169
Mrs. Allison K. Boyles	173
Educational director — cap	178
xx (Use your initials)	178/195

46d ▶ 8 Language Skills: Complex Sentences

1. Study the guides in the color blocks at right and the sentences that illustrate the guides.
2. Key the **Learn** sentences as shown, noting the clauses that are independent (can stand alone as a sentence) and dependent (cannot stand alone as a sentence).
3. On a separate sheet of paper, key vertically the numbers 1 through 8, DS.
4. Key the subject and predicate of the independent clause and then of the dependent clause of each sentence opposite the appropriate number. Use a diagonal (/) to separate the subject-predicate of one clause from that of the other clause.
5. Check work with teacher.

A complex sentence contains only one independent clause but one or more dependent clauses.

Learn 1 The book that you gave Juan for his birthday is lost.
Learn 2 If I were you, I would speak to Paula before I left.
Learn 3 Miss Gomez, who chairs the department, is currently on leave.
Learn 4 Students who use their time wisely usually succeed.

The subject of a complex sentence may consist of more than one noun or pronoun; the predicate may consist of more than one verb.

Learn 5 All who were invited to the party also attended the game.
Learn 6 If you are to join, you should sign up and pay your dues.
Learn 7 After she and I left, Cliff and Pam sang and danced.
Learn 8 Although they don't know it yet, Fran and Bret were elected.

245b (continued)

Document 3
Simplified Memorandum
plain paper
Key the memorandum shown at the right in simplified format. Date the memo **March 16, 19--,** and send it to **Conrad G. Nelson, Manager.** Use **EQUIP-MENT PURCHASE UPDATE** as the subject line. The memo is from **K. Renae Stevens, Purchasing Director.**

Document 4
Simplified Memorandum
plain paper
Rekey Document 3. Add the following as the final paragraph of the memo.

If you are hesitant about postponing a final decision or would like to discuss the situation further, please let me know.

Last week I met with Ms. Karla Sather, Fenton Office Ma- 24
and Mr. Jerome Reynolds, JB Office Products,
chines, to discuss our equipment needs. I also spent part of 46
 equipment
last week in Los Angeles visiting several vendors to make sure 60
 is
that I havent overlooked anything that currently available. 73
 l
The capabilities of some of the equipment are realy un- 84

believable. However, I truly beleive that we should postpone 95

making any final decisions for a few months. Several of the 108
 s
vendor mentioned that they are expecting major break throughs 120
 Ms. Sather
to be announced very shortly. Karla also mentioned that she 133
 e
expects a signficant descreased in the cost of the equipment 145

that I am currently considering. 152

Lesson 246 Evaluate Forms and Table Skills

246a ▶ 5
Conditioning Practice

Key each line twice. Then take two 30" writings for speed on line 4 and two 30" writings for control on line 1.

alphabet 1 Quin may reject my idea of leaving two dozen oak trees by the complex.

figures 2 As of July 30, 12,465 copies of the 1987 edition were still available.

fig/sym 3 We received their order (#152-67) amounting to $3,498 on September 20.

speed 4 The eight city officials may sign the forms when they see the auditor.

| 1 | 2 | 3 | 4 | 5 | 6 | 7 | 8 | 9 | 10 | 11 | 12 | 13 | 14 |

246b ▶ 45 Evaluate
Formatting Skills:
Forms and Tables

Time Schedule
Plan and prepare 5'
Timed production 30'
Proofread; compute *n-pram* .. 10'

1. Arrange materials for ease of handling (LP p. 43).

2. Format and key Documents 1-4 for 30'. Proofread and correct errors before removing documents from machine.

3. After time is called (30'), proofread again and circle any uncorrected errors. Compute *n-pram.*

Document 1
Table
Format and key the table at the right on a full sheet. Center column headings; leave 6 spaces between columns 1 and 2; leave 4 spaces between columns 2 and 3.

LODGING RATES

April 1, 19-- through March 31, 19--

Dates	Traditional	Garden Terrace
April 1 - May 20	$60.75	$75.75
May 21 - September 10	75.75	90.75
September 11 - December 10	55.00	70.00
December 11 - January 5	68.00	83.00
January 6 - February 1	53.50	68.50
February 2 - March 31	68.50	83.00

3
10
23
29
42
49
55
63
70
77
84
96

Documents 2-4 are on p. 420.

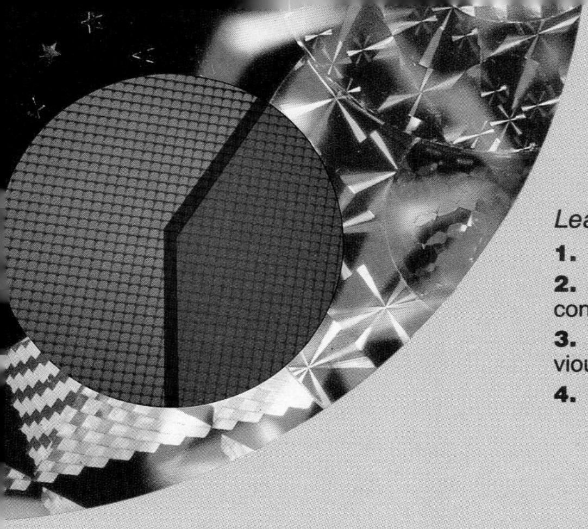

Improve Keyboarding/Language Skills

Learning Goals

1. To improve keyboarding technique.
2. To check/improve keyboarding speed and control (accuracy).
3. To check application of language skills previously learned.
4. To extend compose-as-you-key skills.

Format Guides

1. ***Paper guide*** at *0* (for typewriters).
2. LL: 60 spaces; see *Get Ready to Keyboard: Typewriters* (p. x) or *Computers* (p. xii).
3. LS: SS drills; DS ¶s, language skills, and composing activities.
4. PI: 5 spaces when appropriate.

Lesson 47 *Keyboarding/Language Skills*

LL: 60
LS: SS

47a ▶ 6 Conditioning Practice

each line twice SS; then a 1′ writing on line 3; find *gwam*

alphabet 1 Jarvis will take the next big prize for my old racquet club.
fig/sym 2 My income tax for 1990 was $5,274.62--up 3% over 1989's tax.
speed 3 A neighbor paid the girl to fix the turn signal of the auto.

| 1 | 2 | 3 | 4 | 5 | 6 | 7 | 8 | 9 | 10 | 11 | 12 |

47b ▶ 9 Check/Improve Language Skills

LL: 60 spaces; LS: DS

1. Key each line, supplying capitalization as needed.
2. Check accuracy of work with teacher.
3. If time permits, rekey each line in which you made capitalization errors.

1 elana cruz agreed to serve as president of delta pi epsilon.
2 was it pope who said, "to err is human, to forgive divine"?
3 the address by dr. morales will be given in assembly hall.
4 fujio kimura began work for miramir, inc., on september 15.
5 the giant christmas tree in rockefeller plaza was stunning.
6 "be very quiet," she said, "and listen to the stillness."
7 she said to check the data in volume 4, section 2, page 29.
8 a labor day buffet dinner will be held at 201 fifth street.

47c ▶ 15 Improve Keyboarding Technique

LL: 60 spaces; LS: SS
Tabs: Set 2, 24 spaces apart, starting at LM

1. Each line twice SS; DS between 4-line groups.
2. A 1′ writing on each of lines 8, 10, and 12; find *gwam* on each.
3. If time permits, rekey the two lines on which you had the lowest *gwam.*

tabulator
1 if they work *tab* as they fear *tab* he may serve
2 he paid them my land case she may save

shift keys
3 Jane and Robb go to a New Year's party with Donna and Spiro.
4 R. J. Appel was paid by the Apollo Insurance Co. of Jackson.

space bar
5 It is up to me to do my best in each try to make a new goal.
6 Andy may use his pen to sign the form for a job in the city.

letter response
7 A tax rate was set in my area only after we set a case date.
8 We are free only after we get him set up on a tax rate case.

combination response
9 I shall bid on the antique vase only if I regard it as rare.
10 You are to sign all of the artwork you turn in to be graded.

word response
11 He is to do the work for both of us, and she is to pay half.
12 The girl with the titian hair owns the title to the autobus.

| 1 | 2 | 3 | 4 | 5 | 6 | 7 | 8 | 9 | 10 | 11 | 12 |

245a ▶ 5 Conditioning Practice

Key each line twice. Then take two 30″ writings for speed on line 4 and two 30″ writings for control on line 1.

alphabet 1 Greg fixed the four new pairs of jumper cables very quickly for Shizu.

figures 2 There were 28 computer graphs and 17 tables between pages 309 and 456.

fig/sym 3 The next two flights (#308 & #796) leave Chicago at 1:45 and 2:00 p.m.

speed 4 The city may pay Eva and me to work on the problem of the title forms.

| 1 | 2 | 3 | 4 | 5 | 6 | 7 | 8 | 9 | 10 | 11 | 12 | 13 | 14 |

245b ▶ 45 Evaluate Formatting Skills: Letters and Memorandums

Time Schedule

Plan and prepare .... 5′
Timed production .... 30′
Proofread; compute *n-pram* .. 10′

1. Arrange materials for ease of handling (LP pp. 39-41).

2. Format and key Documents 1-4 for 30′. Proofread and correct errors before removing documents from machine.

3. After time is called (30′), proofread again and circle any uncorrected errors. Compute *n-pram.*

Note: To find *n-pram* (net production rate per minute), deduct 15 words for each uncorrected error; divide remainder by 30 (time).

Document 1
Letter
LP p. 39
Format in block style with mixed punctuation the letter shown at the right.

words

March 15, 19-- Mr. Ross A. Medina 5410 Peppermint Drive San Jose, CA 14
95148-3167 Dear Mr. Medina: 19

We are pleased to provide you with more information about Mesa Mountain Resort. Mesa Mountain is a great place to spend time relaxing and enjoying the great outdoors at affordable prices. 57

Guests at our resort can choose from a variety of activities. Sailing, hiking, fishing, golfing, and rafting are just a few of the many activities that are available for guest participation on a daily basis. The mountain water slide, hot air balloon rides, nature trails, and an abundance of outdoor beauty bring our guests back year after year. 127

Two special resort activities are planned for each month of the summer. These activities range from the jazz festival to the hang gliding contest. A complete listing along with the dates of the activities is enclosed. 171

We are confident that if you come to Mesa Mountain Resort, you will make it a part of your yearly vacation plans. To make reservations, call 1-800-234-6891. 203

Sincerely, Ms. Michelle C. Slattery Director of Sales and Marketing xx 217
Enclosures 219/232

Document 2
Letter
LP p. 41
Format in block style with open punctuation the letter shown at the right.

Address letter to
Ms. Kathleen C. Travis
729 Manhattan Drive
Huntington Beach, CA 92647-4248
Date the letter **March 16, 19--**

Closing lines:
Sincerely

Jonathan W. Sutter
Customer Relations

opening lines 21

Thank you for bringing to our attention the problems you 33
when checking out on March 5 — been
encountered. The situation has reveiwed with the desk clerk 52
confident — in dealing with our guests
and we are sure that he will use more tact in the future. 70

r — r
The eror with your bill was ours. You reservation was 81
" " accomodated — with " "
for our Traditional room; we gave you our Garden Terrace room. 98
" " room
Unfortunately we also charged you for the Garden Terrace. A 111
between the two rooms
check is enclosed that reflects the difference in cost. 127

p
We apreciate your providing us with this information. 138
quality of
Only through customer feed back that we can improve the ser- 151
#
vice we offer ourguests. 157

closing lines 169/183

Documents 3 and 4 are on p. 419.

47d ▶ 20 Check/Improve Keyboarding Skill

1. A 1′ writing on ¶ 1; find *gwam*. Add 2-4 words to set a new goal.

2. Two 1′ writings on ¶ 1 at your new goal rate, guided by ¼′ guide call.

3. Key ¶ 2 in the same way.

4. A 2′ writing on ¶ 1 and then on ¶ 2. If you finish a ¶ before time is called, start over.

5. A 3′ writing on ¶s 1-2 combined; find *gwam*.

gwam	¼′	½′	¾′	1′
20	5	10	15	20
24	6	12	18	24
28	7	14	21	28
32	8	16	24	32
36	9	18	27	36
40	10	20	30	40
44	11	22	33	44
48	12	24	36	48
52	13	26	39	52
56	14	28	42	56

all letters used | LA | 1.4 si | 5.4 awl | 85% hfw |

gwam 2′ | 3′

What is it that makes one person succeed and another 5 | 4
fail when the two seem to have about equal ability? Some 11 | 7
have said that the difference is in the degree of motivation 17 | 11
and effort each brings to the job. Others have said that an 23 | 16
intent to become excellent is the main difference. 28 | 19

At least four items are likely to have a major effect 5 | 22
on our success: basic ability, a desire to excel, an aim 11 | 26
to succeed, and zestful effort. If any one of these is ab- 17 | 30
sent or at a low point, our chances for success are lessened. 23 | 34
These features, however, can be developed if we wish. 29 | 38

gwam 2′ | 1 | 2 | 3 | 4 | 5 | 6
gwam 3′ | 1 | 2 | 3 | 4

Lesson 48 Keyboarding/Language Skills

LL: 60
LS: SS

48a ▶ 6 Conditioning Practice

each line twice SS; then a 1′ writing on line 3; find *gwam*

alphabet 1 Bevis had quickly won top seed for the next games in Juarez.

fig/sym 2 The Diamond Caper (Parker & Sons, #274638) sells for $19.50.

speed 3 Shana may make a bid for the antique bottle for the auditor.

| 1 | 2 | 3 | 4 | 5 | 6 | 7 | 8 | 9 | 10 | 11 | 12 |

48b ▶ 9 Check/Improve Language Skills

LL: 60 spaces; LS: SS groups, DS between groups

1. Lines 1-2: Insert hyphens where words can be divided.

2. Lines 3-5: Correct the errors in capitalization.

3. Lines 6-8: Key numbers as words/figures when appropriate.

4. Check work with teacher; rekey incorrect sentences.

Word division

1 into yearly ideals annual indeed little smaller sessions
2 suggest sizable service taxicab variation self-analysis

Capitalization

3 the junior achievement meeting will be at 3 p.m. in room 44.
4 rick reviewed the article "ethics in business" on wednesday.
5 mrs. thomas assigned lines 10-20 of beowulf for november 16.

Number expression

6 The package measures thirty-two by twenty-four by eight cm.
7 When you get to 5th Street, turn west toward 10th Avenue.
8 We are to study Units one and two of Chapter 10 this week.

243c ▶ 30 Prepare For Evaluation: Letters, Memos, and Tables

Prepare a list of the problems at the right.

Prepare for the production measurement of letters, memos, and tables by keying the problems from your list. Use plain sheets for all documents.

Letter: p. 302, 172c, Document 1
Memo: p. 302, 172c, Document 3
Table: p. 352, 204c, Table 1
Table: p. 350, 203d, Table 1

Lesson 244 Prepare for Evaluation: Forms and Reports

244a ▶ 5 Conditioning Practice

Key each line twice; then take two 30" writings for *speed* on line 4 and two 30" writings for *control* on line 1.

alphabet 1 Maria Jackson will have the best grade for the six philosophy quizzes.

figures 2 Is the Little Rock, AR, ZIP Code I requested 72205-3674 or 72205-1698?

fig/sym 3 The loan (#270-38) was made on 12/14/89 for $68,000 at a rate of 9.5%.

speed 4 Both of them may go with me to the lake to do the work on the chapels.

| 1 | 2 | 3 | 4 | 5 | 6 | 7 | 8 | 9 | 10 | 11 | 12 | 13 | 14 |

244b ▶ 15 Evaluate Language Skills Application

1. Key each sentence, with the number and period, making the needed corrections. DS between sentences.

2. After keying all sentences, proofread each one. Mark any correction that still needs to be made.

1. Their home that is located at Ten Silver Lake Road are for sail.
2. The number of applicants recieving financial aid have increased.
3. The finance committee members is working on that recomendation
4. Everyone in the class are making arrangments to attend the play.
5. The balence do on their account is three hundred dollars.
6. Christina was born on January ten 1970 in brooklyn New York.
7. Do you no if she has scheduled a concert for anaheim california?
8. Is Dr. Van Burens' ph.d in chemistry from harvard or columbia?
9. Mr. and mrs. j. b. West live at 1 devney drive near 5th Avenue.
10. The center on our team is six ft. two in. tall and weighs 200 lbs.
11. They took the cold wet dog to the washington humane association.
12. Can you accomodate sixteen people for dinner on Thursday, May 22nd?
13. The plain from Los Angeles will arrive at approximately eleven p.m.
14. There corperate loan with First national bank of Miami was approved.
15. The Friday activitys were arranged too celebrate independence day.
16. Its our commitment to establish a Monument at 23 Lexington Avenue.
17. If you right to senator Swindell be sure to include your resume.
18. Each year at regestration the coach said "This mite be the year."
19. Rebecca has all ready past the exam on chapter 8, pages 316-359.
20. The mens' supervisers will meet inside if the whether is still bad.

244c ▶ 30 Prepare for Evaluation: Forms and Reports

Prepare a list of the problems at the right.

Prepare for the production measurement of forms and reports by keying the problems from your list.

Forms: p. 358, 208c, Document 1, LP p. 37
Report: p. 283, 159c, Document 3, plain paper
Report: p. 284, 160b, Document 1, plain paper

48c ▶ 15 Improve Keyboarding Speed: Skill Comparison

1. A 1′ writing on each line; find *gwam* on each writing.

2. Compare rates and identify the 4 slowest lines.

3. A 1′ writing on each of the 4 slowest lines.

4. As time permits in later lessons, do this drill again to improve speed and control.

fig/sym	1	Ed asked, "How much is due by May 28 on Account #4039-1657?"
figures	2	By May 25 in 1990 we had planted 375 trees and 1,648 shrubs.
one-hand	3	My war on waste at a union mill was based upon minimum data.
long-reach	4	Myra said I must curb at once my urge to glance at my hands.
adjacent-key	5	Coila hoped for a new opal ring to wear to her next concert.
double-letter	6	Bobby will sell the cookbook for a little less than it cost.
combination	7	He may join us for tea at the pool if he wishes to see them.
balanced-hand	8	Did they make the right title forms for the eight big firms?

| 1 | 2 | 3 | 4 | 5 | 6 | 7 | 8 | 9 | 10 | 11 | 12 |

48d ▶ 20 Check/Improve Keyboarding Skill

1. A 3′ writing on ¶s 1-2 combined; find *gwam*, circle errors.

2. A 2′ writing on ¶s 1-2 combined; find *gwam*, circle errors.

3. A 1′ writing on each ¶; find *gwam* on each writing.

4. Another 3′ writing on ¶s 1-2 combined; find *gwam*, circle errors.

5. As time permits, take 1′ guided writings on each ¶ to improve:

- **speed** (increase goal rate).
- **accuracy** (reduce goal rate).

all letters used | LA | 1.4 si | 5.4 awl | 85% hfw |

Text	*gwam* 2′	3′
Planning is the first step in composing a message. The	6	4
plan should include a goal, what you want to accomplish. It	12	8
also should include a list of the points you will use to con-	18	12
vince the reader of your point of view or of the action you	24	16
want taken. The list should be arranged in logical sequence.	30	20
Your goal is the major idea behind the topic sentence.	36	24
The topic sentence is often stated first, followed next by	41	28
facts and ideas that support it. You may instead decide to	47	32
work up to the main idea at the end. In either case, you	53	35
itemize the information and tie it to the main thought.	59	39

gwam 2′ | 1 | 2 | 3 | 4 | 5 | 6 |
gwam 3′ | 1 | 2 | 3 | 4 |

ENRICHMENT ACTIVITY: Composing

LL: 60 spaces; LS: DS; PB: line 12

1. Select a topic from those given at right.

2. Compose two or three ¶s giving your plans (or point of view) regarding the topic.

3. Edit and proofread your copy; then process a final draft with errors corrected.

1 My future education plans
2 The harmful effects of steroid use
3 The job I want and why
4 Why I want to excel
5 Why I do not care to be No. 1
6 How to reduce teenage drinking
7 My plans for a future career
8 Is winning the most important goal
9 Why cheating is wrong
10 How to reduce teenage drug abuse
11 My plans for next summer
12 How I do my homework

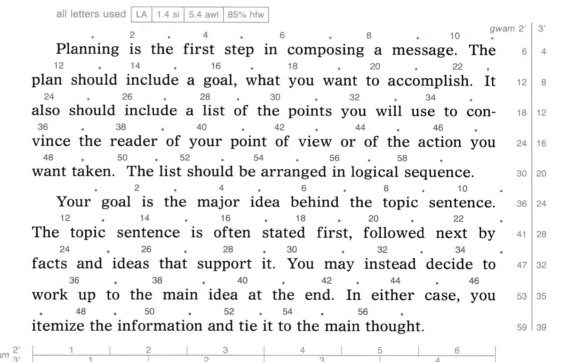

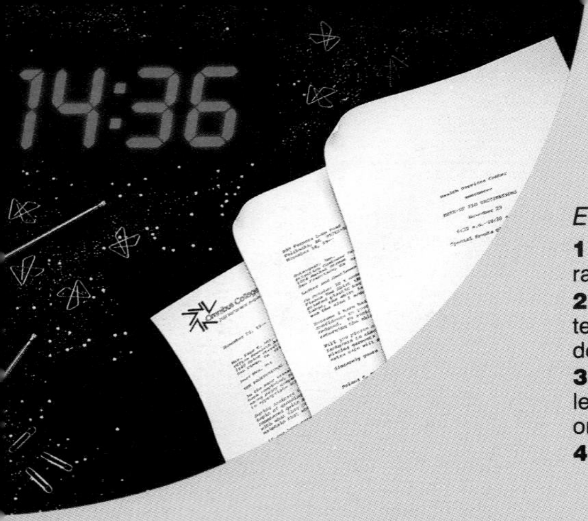

UNIT 58 LESSONS 243 – 247
Evaluation

Evaluation Goals

1. To evaluate straight-copy speed and accuracy.
2. To improve skill in formatting and keying letters, memos, tables, reports, and purchase orders.
3. To evaluate skill in formatting and keying letters, memos, tables, reports, and purchase orders.
4. To evaluate language skills.

Format Guides

1. Paper guide at *0* (for typewriters).
2. LL: 70 spaces for drills and language skills activities; as required by document formats.
3. LS: SS for drills and language skills activities unless otherwise instructed; as required by document formats.
4. PI: 5 spaces, when appropriate.

Lesson 243 *Prepare for Evaluation: Letters, Memorandums, and Tables*

243a ▶ 5 Conditioning Practice

Key each line twice. Then take two 30″ writings for speed on line 4 and two 30″ writings for control on line 1.

alphabet 1 Maxine was amazed frequently by the project check arriving so quickly.
figures 2 The combined population of the same 23 towns in 1989 was only 146,750.
double letters 3 The litter of kittens with the funny feet put the boys in a good mood.
speed 4 With their profit they may pay for an emblem of the shantytown chapel.

| 1 | 2 | 3 | 4 | 5 | 6 | 7 | 8 | 9 | 10 | 11 | 12 | 13 | 14 |

243b ▶ 15 Evaluate Straight-Copy Skill

Take two 5′ writings; record *gwam* and errors on the better writing.

all letters used | A | 1.5 si | 5.7 awl | 80% hfw |

gwam 3′ | 5′

Information shown in a graphic form has always been a vital part of 5 3 60
the communication process--whether or not the message presented is in an 9 6 62
oral or written form. Most of the graphics used in the past were created 14 9 65
by a media or art center. Today, because of the computer, however, more 19 12 68
data than ever is being shown with the use of graphics. Computers using 24 14 71
various software programs make it quite easy to prepare graphic data to 29 17 74
enhance the process of communicating. 31 19 76
Graphics are used for a variety of reasons. One of the major rea- 36 21 78
sons is that graphics can help the writer or speaker send a clear and a 41 24 81
complete message using as few words as possible. Some have said that 45 27 84
a picture is worth a thousand words. Graphics also allow the sender to 50 30 87
emphasize specific parts of the message as well as to add more interest 55 33 90
to the message. Recent progress in computer technology has greatly en- 59 36 93
hanced the graphic-producing abilities of many business firms. 64 38 95
Many different types of graphics can be used to help present data. 68 41 98
A few common types of graphics that computers are now able to generate 73 44 101
include maps, bar graphs, and pie charts. The capabilities of desktop 78 47 103
publishing further enhance the visuals that can be used to present all 82 49 106
kinds of information. In the future, as graphics become an expected 87 52 109
part of information, they will be sure to play an even greater role in 92 55 112
the exchange of ideas in the business world. 95 57 114

gwam 3′ | 1 | 2 | 3 | 4 | 5 |
5′ | 1 | 2 | 3 |

UNIT 9 LESSONS 49 – 50

Measure Keyboarding/Formatting Skills

Measurement Goals

1. To demonstrate that you can key straight-copy ¶s for 3 minutes at the speed and control level specified by your teacher.

2. To demonstrate that you can format and key personal-business and business letters in block style.

3. To demonstrate that you can format and key simplified memos in block style.

4. To demonstrate that you can center lines horizontally.

Format Guides

1. ***Paper guide*** at *0* (for typewriters).

2. LL: 60 spaces for drills, ¶s, and personal-business letters; as format requires on business letters and memos. See *Get Ready to Keyboard: Typewriters* (p. x) or *Computers* (p. xii).

3. LS: SS drills and documents; DS ¶s.

4. PI: 5 spaces when appropriate.

Lesson 49 *Keyboarding/Formatting Skills*

49a ▶ 6 Conditioning Practice

each line twice SS; then a 1′ writing on line 3; find *gwam*

alphabet 1 Jocko will place a high bid for my next prized antique vase.

fig/sym 2 Ora asked, “Wasn’t R&N’s check #285367 deposited on 1/4/90?”

speed 3 When did the field auditor sign the audit form for the city?

| 1 | 2 | 3 | 4 | 5 | 6 | 7 | 8 | 9 | 10 | 11 | 12 |

49b ▶ 14 Check Keyboarding Skill

1. A 1′ writing on ¶ 1; find *gwam;* circle errors.

2. A 1′ writing on ¶ 2; find *gwam;* circle errors.

3. A 2′ writing on ¶s 1 and 2 combined; find *gwam;* circle errors.

4. A 3′ writing on ¶s 1 and 2 combined; find *gwam;* circle errors.

all letters used | LA | 1.4 si | 5.4 awl | 85% hfw |

	gwam 2′	3′
As you work for higher skill, remember that how well you	8	4
key fast is just as important as how fast you key. How well	12	8
you key at any speed depends in major ways upon the technique	18	12
or form you use. Bouncing hands and flying fingers lower the	24	16
speed, while quiet hands and low finger reaches increase speed.	31	20
Few of us ever reach what the experts believe is perfect	36	24
technique, but all of us should try to approach it. We must	42	28
realize that good form is the secret to higher speed with	48	32
fewer errors. We can then focus our practice on the improve-	54	36
ment of the features of good form that will bring success.	60	40

gwam 2′ | 1 | 2 | 3 | 4 | 5 | 6 |
gwam 3′ | 1 | 2 | 3 | 4 |

49c-50c ▶ 30 (daily) Measure Formatting Skills

3 letterheads (LP pp. 61-66)
3 plain full sheets
error correction supplies

1. Begin processing the documents on pp. 89-90 (use the *Letter Placement Guide* on p. 76). You have two class periods to complete the documents.

Note: Complete the line on which you are working when the class ends so that if necessary you can reinsert the paper and continue the document in the next class period.

2. Correct any errors you make as you key.

3. Before you remove a document from the machine or screen, proofread and correct your copy.

4. If you complete all documents before time is called, start over.

239b-242b (continued)

Documents 13-14
Ruled Forms
LP p. 35

SANDRA MORENO
Administrative
Assistant

I have written in the information on photocopies of the registration forms for the symposium Ms. Jones will be attending. Please key this information on the original forms. *Sm*

Symposium Registration Form
(July 24-26)

Jones	Ann
Last Name	First Name
Midwestern Office Products	
Firm/Affiliation	
3871 Bridge Avenue	
Address	
Davenport IA	52807-7002
City State	Zip
(319)887-2424	(319)887-5767
Office Telephone	Home Telephone

Payment Method:

X Credit Card ____ Check

Secure Card 6815 0716 10106 1/95
Card Name and Number — Expiration Date

Signature

Mail to: International Technology Symposium
510 Gettysburg Court
Washington, DC 20335-2111

Hotel Reservation Form

Jones	Ann
Last Name	First Name
Midwestern Office Products	
Firm/Affiliation	
3871 Bridge Avenue	(319)887-2424
Address	Phone
Davenport IA	52807-7002
City State	Zip
July 23	July 26
Arrival Date	Departure Date

Payment Method:
(First night's deposit required to confirm reservation.)

X Credit Card ____ Check (to McKinley Inn for $105)

Secure Card 6815 0716 10106 1/95
Card Name and Number — Expiration Date

Signature

Mail to: McKinley Inn
5568 Georgia Avenue
Washington, DC 20335-2464

Document 15
Income Statement

SANDRA MORENO
Administrative
Assistant

Ms. Koontz needs an income statement for the first quarter for a meeting tomorrow. I called the Accounting Department to get the figures that are marked on the copy of the First-Quarter Budgeted Income Statement. Some formatting guides are marked on the copy to assist you as you key the document. *Sm*

1½"

MIDWESTERN OFFICE PRODUCTS
~~Budgeted~~ Income Statement
For Quarter Ending March 31, 19--

QS

1" LM — 2 sp — 1" RM

~~Expected~~ Sales revenue		~~$1,125,000~~	1,234,680
Deduct ~~expected~~ cost of goods sold		~~675,000~~	740,808
~~Estimated~~ Gross margin		$ ~~450,000~~	493,872
Deduct ~~estimated~~ expenses controllable by department managers:			
Sales	~~$205,000~~ 224,790		
Information Processing	~~58,000~~ 56,500		
Accounting	~~47,000~~ 48,550		
Personnel	~~29,000~~ 28,350	~~339,000~~	358,190
Margin for non controllable expenses . .		$ ~~111,000~~	135,682
Deduct expenses noncontrollable by departments:			
Administration	$ 45,000		
Occupancy	25,000	70,000	
~~Estimated~~ net income before taxes . . .		$ ~~41,000~~	65,682

(Indent 2 — Sales through Personnel)

50a ▶ 6 Conditioning Practice

each line twice SS; then a 1′ writing on line 3; find *gwam*

alphabet 1 Fitz may have a jinx on our squad, but we kept the gold cup.
fig/sym 2 Pay invoice #6382 for $4,279 (less discounts of 10% and 5%).
speed 3 Sign the work form for the six men to do the city dock work.

| 1 | 2 | 3 | 4 | 5 | 6 | 7 | 8 | 9 | 10 | 11 | 12 |

50b ▶ 14 Check Keyboarding Skill

1. Repeat the timed writings called for in the directions for 49b, p. 88.

Goals: To improve your 1-, 2-, and 3-minute *gwam* or to reduce excessive errors.

2. As time permits, do additional writings to improve speed or reduce errors.

49c-50c ▶ 30 (continued)

1. Continue formatting the documents below and on p. 90 which you began in Lesson 49c.

2. Proofread and correct your work before removing it from the machine or screen.

3. If you complete all documents before time is called, start over.

Document 1: Personal-Business Letter words
plain full sheet; LL: 60 spaces; PB: line 14

899 Farmers Loop Road 4
Fairbanks, AK 99712-3647 9
November 18, 19-- 12

Attention Customer Service 18
Outergear, Inc. 21
1354 Market Street 25
San Francisco, CA 94103-2746 31

Ladies and Gentlemen 35

On October 30 I ordered from your winter cata- 44
log a Heavyweight Fleece Tee Shirt (#M628). 53
Although the packing slip and the printed plastic 63
bag label clearly state that the shirt is a Large, 73
the shirt label shows that the size is Medium. 83
Large was the size I ordered. 89

Because I have had a similar experience twice 98
in the past, my confidence in your ability to fill 108
my orders accurately is reduced. To avoid the 118
nuisance and expense of packaging and return- 126
ing the shirt, I will keep it to use as a gift. 136

Will you please caution your packers or the 145
appropriate manufacturers to check sizes and 154
colors more carefully before placing garments 163
in prelabeled bags. I'm certain that the extra 173
care will make your other customers happier, 182
too. 183

Sincerely yours 186

Roland C. Marshall 190

Documents 3, 4, and 5 are on p. 90.

Document 2: Business Letter words
LP p. 61

November 18, 19-- 4

Mr. Leslie D. Banks 8
George Washington High School 14
2165 E. 2700 South Street 19
Salt Lake City, UT 84109-3720 25

Dear Mr. Banks 28

Your question about the effect of word process- 37
ing equipment on the need for keying accuracy 46
is a good one. 50

Accuracy of documents processed is just as 58
vital now as ever before. The ease with which 68
keying errors can now be corrected, however, 77
has shifted the emphasis from number of input 86
errors made to skill in finding and correcting 95
these errors. 98

A major weakness of those who take employ- 106
ment tests is their inability to detect and correct 117
the errors they make. Therefore, we suggest 126
that employee training should emphasize proof- 135
reading and error correction rather than error- 144
free initial input. 148

A grading system rewarding efficient proofread- 158
ing and correction skills instead of penalizing 167
errors of initial input is worthy of your serious 177
consideration. (words in body: 152) 180

Sincerely yours 184

Ms. Audrey M. Lindsay 188
Employment Office Manager 193

xx 194/**214**

239b-242b (continued)

Document 12 Report

> SANDRA MORENO
> Administrative Assistant
>
> Here is a rough-draft document with the highlights of the speech Ms. Koontz has prepared for the July 15 annual meeting of the sales representatives. She would like it keyed as a topbound manuscript with footnotes for distribution after the presentation. Use **REMARKS BY PRESIDENT SARA KOONTZ** for the main heading and **19-- Annual Sales Representatives Meeting** for the secondary heading.
>
> SM

Insert A

1. In every sale, even at the individual consumer level, more decision makers are involved.
2. The time needed to close a sale has increased dramatically.
3. Where before customers used to accept "generic" solutions and products, now they are demanding specific, "custom-made" solutions.
4. Customers are now looking for a different, higher-level, longer-term relationship with the salespeople and the companies with which they deal.[1]

Insert B

1. Recruiting top salespeople.
2. Ability to keep top salespeople.
3. Quality of training.
4. Opening accounts.
5. Holding new accounts.
6. Product/technical knowledge.
7. Reputation among customers.[2]

Footnote Information

[1]Larry Wilson, Changing the Game: The New Way to Sell (New York: Simon and Schuster, Inc., 1987), pp. 21-22.

[2]"America's Best Sales Forces," Sales & Marketing Management, June 1989, p. 34.

[3]Ibid., pp. 39-45.

I have two objectives ~~that I have~~ for this years ~~annual~~ sales meeting. First I would like to recieve recommendations from you on changes that need to be made to increase sales and how management can assist with the proposed changes. Second, I would like your assistance in develpping a sales philosophy for Midwestern Office Products.

Major Changes in Selling

There are major shifts taking place in the field of sales. According to Wilson, these changes included the following.

Insert A

During your afternoon meetings consider these changes and the implications they have for ~~our~~ Midwestern Office Products sales strategies. If your discussion brings out areas where changes are needed make recommendations along with ~~reasons~~ justification for the changes. Management ~~We~~ will consider these reccommendations as plans are made to enhance the sales efforts.

Sales Philosophy

Sales & Marketing Management recently conducted a survey with participants from various industries. The participants were to asked rate the top 10 companies within their own industries according to the companies efectiveness in these 7 sales ~~areas.~~ functions

Insert B

Each of the companies that ranked number one in its area of specialization had a strong sales Philosophy as the basis for its success. Slogans that capsulize the sales philosophies of a few of these succesful companes are lsited below to help generate discus sion on an appropriate sales philosophy for Midwestern ~~Office products~~.

DS

Caterpillar. "Give the customer something that he will be able to make money with."

International Business Machines. "Providing information systems technology--hardware, software, and services--to enable our customers to be successful in whatever business they are in."

Xerox Corporation. "To develop a sales force that uses quality tools, understands customer requirements, and can provide total solutions to all customer requirements."[3]

49c-50c (continued)

Document 3
Simplified Memo

LP p. 63 or plain full sheet; SM: 1″; PB: line 10

DATE: **November 19, 19--**
Addressee: **Maya Lee Agular**
Subject: **MAKE-UP FLU VACCINATIONS**
Writer's name: **William D. Jent**
Reference: **your initials**
Enclosure notation: supply

words

opening lines 12

Maya, please prepare in final form and post on all bulletin 24
boards the enclosed rough-draft announcement of the 34
make-up flu vaccinations on November 23. 43

Dr. Preston and his assistant will be available only from 54
8:30 a.m. to 10:30 a.m. Will you please set up a schedule in- 66
dicating at what time the members of each department are 78
to arrive at the Special Events Dining Room. A copy of the 90
schedule should be sent to each affected employee a day 101
or two before November 23. 107

closing lines 112

Document 4
Announcement

plain full sheet

Beginning on line 26, center each line of the announcement, DS.

Health Service^s Center 5
announces 7
MAKE-UP FLU VAC^c INATIONS 12
November ~~24~~ 23 14
8:30^a.m.-10:30 a.m. 18
Spec~~ai~~ial Events^Dining Room 24

Document 5
Business Letter

LP p. 65

Date: **November 20, 19--**
Address the letter to:
Mrs. Kaye E. Ott, Manager
Office Research Associates
1140 Union Street
San Diego, CA 92101-4488
Salutation: supply
Subject: **THE PROFESSIONAL IMAGE**
Complimentary close: supply
Writer's name and title:
Miss Alexis L. Morse
Professor of Business
Reference: **your initials**
Copy notation: **J. Ellen Hicks**

opening lines 30

In the ^research many projects you and your as^s ociates have ^completed ~~done,~~ you 45
must have discovered soem patterns ^among ~~in~~ major companies in 57
terms of dress#codes or guides to appr^o priate ^attire ~~dress~~ and groom- 70
ing for#the office. 74

During seminars I have ^conducted ~~completed~~ this ^past year on the topic of 87
grooming and dressing for succes^s, I have ^encountered ~~found~~ quiet a few 100
working ^students ~~people~~ who take issue with what they call my "conser- 112
vative attitude." They maintain that where they work, "any- 124
thing goes." 127

If you have surveyed business practice^s in this fac^e it of 138
employe^e conduct, i shall appreciate you^r sharing your findings 151
with me. Perhap^s with your help, I can ^convince ~~tell~~ students that "any- 165
thing goes" is ^not a viable optoin in most offices. (144) 175

closing lines 190/**208**

239b-242b (continued)

Document 6
Agenda

SANDRA MORENO
Administrative Assistant

Prepare the attached agenda for the August Board of Directors meeting. *Sm*

DS

AGENDA
Board of Directors Meeting
August 1, 19--

1. Opening Remarks . . . . Sara C. Koontz, President
2. Facilities Expansion . . . . . Ann M. Jones, VicePresident
3. Compensation Program . . . . . Ann M. Jones
4. Report on Sales Rep Meeting . . Sydna T. Espinoza, Sales
5. Second Quarter Earnings . . . . Sara C. Koontz
6. Adjournment

3. Learning Center Justification . . T. M. Chaney, Sales Manager

Documents 7-8
Address Cards LP p. 35

SANDRA MORENO
Administrative Assistant

Ms. Koontz would like address cards prepared from the attached business cards. *Sm*

FIRST NATIONAL BANK
Miss Jennifer S. Alexander
Executive Vice President
3526 East 15th Street
Davenport, IA 52803-5522
(319) 632-4477

Fenton & Collinsworth Architects
200 Iowa Street
Davenport, IA 52801-7317
Mr. Richard A. Collinsworth, AIA
(319) 721-7710

Documents 9-11
Simplified Memorandums

SANDRA MORENO
Administrative Assistant

Three members of the sales staff exceeded last year's first-quarter hardware sales by more than five percent. **Ms. Koontz** would like the attached memorandum sent to

- **Eva Lewis** (17.4%)
- **Kerry Munson** (7.5%)
- **Dave Bromberg** (7.3%)

Date the memo **June 12;** use **FIRST-QUARTER SALES** for the subject line; use the figures in parentheses to complete the memorandum; correct any unmarked errors you may find and any keying errors you may make. *Sm*

Congratulations (first name)! I just recieved the first-quarter sales repot Thomas Channey. Your 19-- sales for that quarter have increased by (percentage) over salesa for the same quarter fo last year.

Your efforts have helped us surpass the goal we set for company sales for last quarter. Overall, there was 5.5% increase during that period. When the sales made by the new sale representative are included with the figures, the company hsows a 13.5% increase. If sales continue at this rate we will easily accede the 11% projected growth rate for the year.

LESSONS 51 – 75

PHASE 3 LEARN TO FORMAT REPORTS AND TABLES

In the 25 lessons of Phase 3, you will:

1. Learn to format and process reports, reference lists, title or cover pages, and topic outlines.
2. Learn to format and process data in columnar or table form.
3. Improve basic keyboarding and language skills.
4. Apply your formatting skills to process a series of documents typical of those prepared in the office of a recreation center.
5. Measure and evaluate your basic document processing skills.

Drills and timed writings in this phase are to be keyed on a 70-space line. Line length for problems varies according to the format required.

You will work at various times from model typescript, from print, and from handwritten (script) and rough-draft (corrected) copy. Keyboarding for personal and business purposes is often done from script and rough draft.

239b-242b (continued)

Letter 4:
Mrs. Janet A. Garrison
1701 Kruse Avenue
Davenport, IA 52804-3553

Paragraphs: B2, M, E2
Years: **15**
Department: **Information Processing Center**
SM

Letter File for Employees Quitting or Retiring

B1 I am sorry to hear that you will be leaving Midwestern Office Products. We sincerely appreciate your efforts on behalf of the company during the past (number) years.

B2 It seems impossible that you are retiring. The years do have a way of quickly passing. If one considers the status of Midwestern Office Products (number) years ago and where it is today, it is easy to recognize that time has passed swiftly.

M You have made significant contributions to the (name of department) and to the overall success of Midwestern. Because of talented people like you, our firm has become one of the leaders in serving the technology needs of organizations in this area. Your effort in helping us attain this leadership status is genuinely appreciated.

E1 Best wishes in your future professional endeavors.

E2 Best wishes in your future personal endeavors.

Document 5
Itinerary

SANDRA MORENO
Administrative Assistant

Prepare the itinerary in final form for Ms. Jones.
SM

ITINERARY

Ann M. Jones

International Technology Symposium

QS

July 23

3:15 p.m.	Depart Davenport on Atlantic Airlines--Flight #618 for Washington D.C.
6:05 p.m.	Arrive Washington D. C. Accomodations at McKinley Inn, 4568 Georgia Avenue (m; 5; .)

July 24

7:00 a.m.	Breakfast with Martin Johnson at hotel.
8:00 a.m.	International technology symposium, meetings until 4:00 p.m.
5:30 p.m.	Dinner with Chi Xang at Capitol Hilton.

July 25

8:00 a.m.	International Technology Symposium, meetings until 2:00 p.m.
3:00 p.m.	Meeting with Marshall Sneed.
7:30 p.m.	John F. Kennedy Center for the Performing Arts performance of the Washington Opera.

July 26

8:30 a.m.	Depart Washington D.C. on Atlantic Air Lines-- (lc) SS Flight #482 for Davenport.
10:25 a.m.	Arrive Davenport.

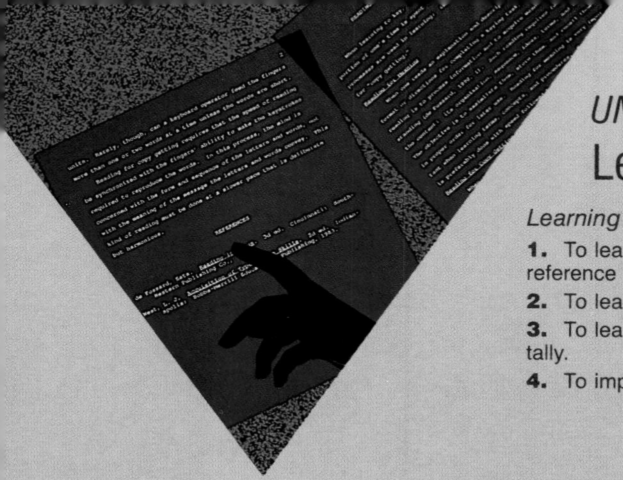

UNIT 10 *LESSONS 51 – 57*

Learn to Format Reports and Outlines

Learning Goals

1. To learn to format and key unbound reports, reference lists, and title pages.
2. To learn to format and key topic outlines.
3. To learn to align copy vertically and horizontally.
4. To improve basic keyboarding skills.

Format Guides

1. ***Paper guide*** at *0* (for typewriters).
2. LL: 70 spaces for drills and ¶s; as required for document formats.
3. LS: SS drills; DS ¶s; as required for document formats.
4. PI: 5 spaces for ¶s and reports.

FORMATTING GUIDES: UNBOUND REPORTS

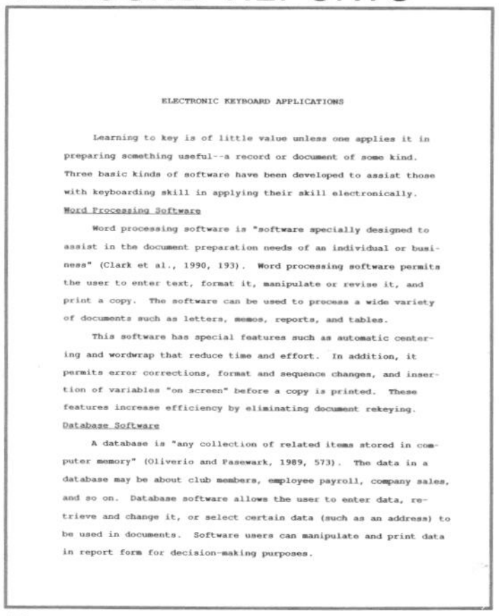

ELECTRONIC KEYBOARD APPLICATIONS

Learning to key is of little value unless one applies it in preparing something useful--a record or document of some kind. Three basic kinds of software have been developed to assist those with keyboarding skill in applying their skill electronically.

Word Processing Software

Word processing software is "software specially designed to assist in the document preparation needs of an individual or business" (Clark et al., 1990, 193). Word processing software permits the user to enter text, format it, manipulate or revise it, and print a copy. The software can be used to process a wide variety of documents such as letters, memos, reports, and tables.

This software has special features such as automatic centering and wordwrap that reduce time and effort. In addition, it permits error corrections, format and sequence changes, and insertion of variables "on screen" before a copy is printed. These features increase efficiency by eliminating document rekeying.

Database Software

A database is "any collection of related items stored in computer memory" (Oliverio and Pasewark, 1989, 573). The data in a database may be about club members, employee payroll, company sales, and so on. Database software allows the user to enter data, retrieve and change it, or select certain data (such as an address) to be used in documents. Software users can manipulate and print data in report form for decision-making purposes.

Page 1

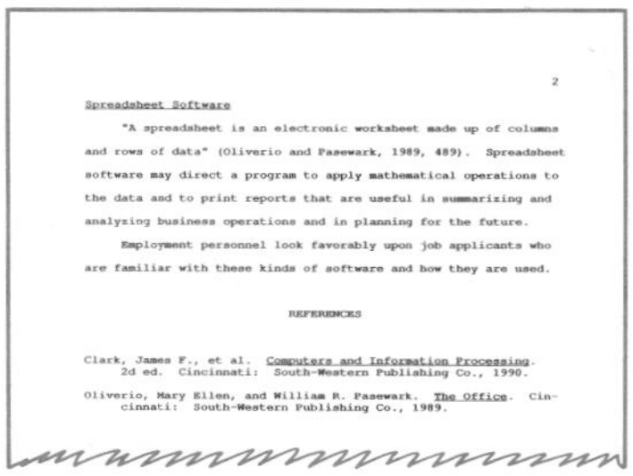

2

Spreadsheet Software

"A spreadsheet is an electronic worksheet made up of columns and rows of data" (Oliverio and Pasewark, 1989, 489). Spreadsheet software may direct a program to apply mathematical operations to the data and to print reports that are useful in summarizing and analyzing business operations and in planning for the future.

Employment personnel look favorably upon job applicants who are familiar with these kinds of software and how they are used.

REFERENCES

Clark, James F., et al. Computers and Information Processing. 2d ed. Cincinnati: South-Western Publishing Co., 1990.

Oliverio, Mary Ellen, and William R. Pasewark. The Office. Cincinnati: South-Western Publishing Co., 1989.

Page 2

Automatic centering of report headings

Some machines can automatically center lines horizontally. If you are using such a typewriter or computer, refer to the Operator's Manual or User's Guide to learn how to center automatically. You may then center report headings and title page lines without using the manual backspace-from-center method.

UNBOUND REPORT FORMAT

Many short reports are prepared without covers or binders. Such reports are called *unbound reports*. If they consist of more than one page, the pages are fastened together in the upper left corner by a staple or paper clip.

Standard Margins

Unbound reports are formatted with standard 1-inch (1″) *side margins* (SM): 10 pica (10-pitch) spaces; 12 elite (12-pitch) spaces. With the *paper guide* set at *0* on the *line-of-writing* or *format scale*, this means that the left margin (LM) is set at 10 on 10-pitch machines or at 12 on 12-pitch machines. If computer margins are preset, the margins may have to be reset to leave the right number of spaces in each SM.

A *top margin* of about 2″ is customarily used on the first page of unbound reports, so the title is placed on line 12. In school settings where the same report is done by users of both 10- and 12-pitch machines, a 1½″ top margin (PB: line 10) may be used for 10-pitch machines so that all students have similar end-of-page decisions to make.

A 1″ *bottom margin* is recommended. Because the internal spacing of report parts varies, a bottom margin of exactly 1″ is often not possible. For that reason, a bottom margin of *at least* 1″ is acceptable. An exact 1″ bottom margin would place the last line of copy on line 60 from the top edge of the paper.

Report Margin Summary

	10-pitch	12-pitch
Line Length (LL)	10-75	12-90
Page Beginning (PB)		
Page 1	line 10/12	line 12
Page 2 (page #)	line 6	line 6
Page Ending (PE)	line 60 or less	line 60 or less

Page Numbering

The first page of an unbound report is usually not numbered. On the second and subsequent pages, the page number is placed on line 6 at the right margin (RM). A DS is left below the page number so that the first line of the report body appears on line 8.

Internal Spacing of Reports

A QS is left between the report title and the first line of the body. Multiple-line titles are DS. A DS is left above and below side headings and between paragraphs, which are usually DS but may be SS when specified.

Internal (textual) Citations

References used to give credit for quoted or paraphrased material are cited in parentheses in the report body. This internal (textual) citation method of documentation is rapidly replacing the footnote method because it is easier and quicker. Internal citations should include the name(s) of the author(s), the year of publication, and the page number(s) of the material cited.

Quotation marks are used for direct quotes, but not for paraphrased material. An ellipsis (. . .) is used to indicate any material omitted from a quotation.

> "Many changes are occurring today in office organization . . . and technology" (VanHuss and Daggett, 1990, 1).

Reference Lists

All references cited in a report are listed alphabetically by author surnames at the end of a report (usually on a separate page) under the heading REFERENCES. A QS appears between the heading and the first reference. The reference page uses the same top margin and side margins as the first page of the report except that a page number appears on line 6 at the RM.

Each reference is SS with a DS between references. The first line of each reference begins at the LM; other lines are indented 5 spaces. If the reference list appears on the last page of the report body, a QS is left between the last line of copy and the heading REFERENCES.

239a-242a ▶ 5 (daily)
Conditioning Practice

Each day check to see that the equipment is in good working order by keying the lines at the right at least twice.

alphabet 1 Joaquin and Kay were puzzled over the exact amount of my storage bill.

figures 2 Nevada sent 187 of the 936 entries, Idaho sent 450, and Utah sent 299.

fig/sym 3 Invoice #687 for $2,958.40 was sent to J&K Supply Company on March 13.

speed 4 If I go to the city to see the man with the maps, I may visit the spa.

| 1 | 2 | 3 | 4 | 5 | 6 | 7 | 8 | 9 | 10 | 11 | 12 | 13 | 14 |

239b-242b ▶ 45 (daily)
Document Production: Executive Office

Documents 1-4
Modified Block Letters
LP pp. 27-33

SANDRA MORENO
Administrative Assistant

Ms. Koontz would like letters dated **June 10, 19--**, prepared from the attached boilerplate for the following individuals who have accepted positions or who have terminated employment.

Letter 1:
Mr. Joshua T. Heintz
424 Bluff Drive
Davenport, IA 52802-6112

Paragraphs: B, M2, E1
Department: **Information Processing Center**

Letter 2:
Ms. Lea S. Fong
725 East Street
Davenport, IA 52803-2141

Paragraphs: B, M3, E3
Department: **Accounting Department**

Letter 3:
Mr. Dennis M. Dupree
858 Glen Place
Davenport, IA 52804-7834

Paragraphs: B, M1, E1
Department: **Sales Department**

Letter File for New Employees

B Welcome to Midwestern Office Products! We are pleased that you have chosen to become part of our organization, and we are looking forward to your assistance in helping us achieve our goals and objectives in the years ahead.

M1 You will enjoy working with Thomas Chaney. He has been with the company for 12 years and is highly regarded by his colleagues. Since he was promoted to sales manager five years ago, company sales have grown tremendously. The new sales strategies that he implemented have been very successful.

M2 If you enjoy working with the latest technology, I am certain that you will enjoy being part of Olivia Reinhold's staff. Our Information Processing Center was recently featured in a national office technology magazine and is the envy of many organizations, due to the efforts of Ms. Reinhold and her talented staff.

M3 You will enjoy working with Rhonda Little; she is outstanding. She is one of those rare individuals who possesses people skills as well as technical expertise. She has completely computerized the Accounting Department since being appointed accounting supervisor.

E1 I am confident that your association with us will be rewarding. I am looking forward to visiting with you in person at the next meeting of the (name of the department).

E2 Your association with us will be rewarding. I am looking forward to meeting you the next time I visit the (name of the department).

E3 I am confident that your work in the (name of the department) will be rewarding. I am looking forward to meeting you soon.

Document 4 is on p. 412.

51a ▶ 6 Conditioning Practice

each line twice SS (slowly, then faster); DS between 2-line groups; if time permits, rekey selected lines

alphabet 1 The six boys quickly removed juicy chunks from a sizzling pot of stew.

figures 2 They washed 59 cars, 28 vans, 47 campers, and 30 bikes on November 16.

fig/sym 3 The 164 copies (priced at $8.75 each) may be shipped on June 29 or 30.

speed 4 Dodi may make fuchsia gown for the civic social to be held downtown.

| 1 | 2 | 3 | 4 | 5 | 6 | 7 | 8 | 9 | 10 | 11 | 12 | 13 | 14 |

51b ▶ 6 Improve Language Skills: Word Choice

1. Study the spelling/definitions of the words in the color block at right.

2. Key line 1 (the **Learn** line), noting the proper choice of words.

3. Key lines 2-3 (the **Apply** lines), choosing the right words to complete the lines correctly.

4. Key the remaining lines in the same way.

5. Check your accuracy; rekey lines containing word-choice errors.

its (adj) of or relating to itself as the possessor

it's (contr) it is; it has

than (conj/prep) used in comparisons to show difference between items

then (n/adv) that time; at that time

Learn 1 It's time for the dog to have its food.
Apply 2 Before (its, it's) time to bid, check (its, it's) number.
Apply 3 If (its, it's) not yours, return it to (its, it's) shelf.

Learn 4 If she is older than you, then I am older than you.
Apply 5 We (than, then) decided that two hours were more (than, then) enough.
Apply 6 Fewer (than, then) half the workers were (than, then) put on overtime.

51c ▶ 8 Review How to Center Lines Horizontally

Begin on line 28 of a plain full sheet. Center each line horizontally, DS.

Automatic procedure
If your equipment has automatic centering, see your User's Guide to review centering procedure.

Manual procedure

1. Move *cursor* or *printing point indicator* to center of paper.

2. From this point, backspace once for each 2 characters and spaces in the line to be centered. (Disregard any leftover letter.)

HORIZONTAL CENTERING

Equal Left and Right Margins

Half of Copy to Left of Center

Half of Copy to Right of Center

Variance of One or Two Spaces Acceptable

51d ▶ 30 Learn to Format an Unbound Report and Reference List

1. Study the report formatting information on p. 92.

2. On 2 plain full sheets, format the model report shown on pp. 94-95. Do not correct your errors as you key.

3. When you have finished, proofread your copy, mark it for correction, and prepare a final copy with all errors corrected.

Note: Line endings of elite/pica solutions differ.

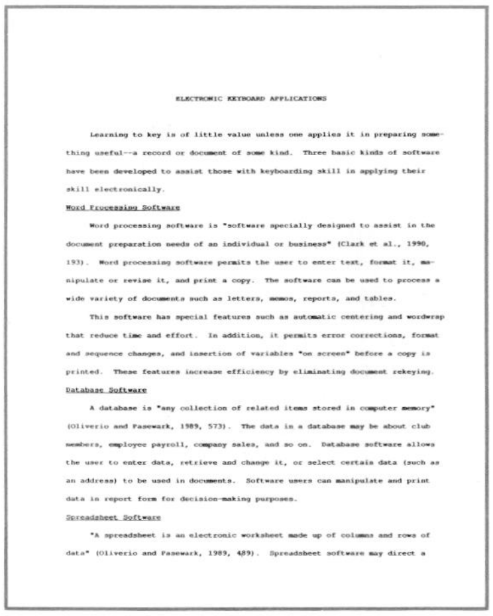
ELECTRONIC KEYBOARD APPLICATIONS

Learning to key is of little value unless one applies it in preparing something useful--a record or document of some kind. Three basic kinds of software have been developed to assist those with keyboarding skill in applying their skill electronically.

Word Processing Software

Word processing software is "software specially designed to assist in the document preparation needs of an individual or business" (Clark et al., 1990, 193). Word processing software permits the user to enter text, format it, manipulate or revise it, and print a copy. The software can be used to process a wide variety of documents such as letters, memos, reports, and tables.

This software has special features such as automatic centering and wordwrap that reduce time and effort. In addition, it permits error corrections, format and sequence changes, and insertion of variables "on screen" before a copy is printed. These features increase efficiency by eliminating document rekeying.

Database Software

A database is "any collection of related items stored in computer memory" (Oliverio and Pasewark, 1989, 573). The data in a database may be about club members, employee payroll, company sales, and so on. Database software allows the user to enter data, retrieve and change it, or select certain data (such as an address) to be used in documents. Software users can manipulate and print data in report form for decision-making purposes.

Spreadsheet Software

"A spreadsheet is an electronic worksheet made up of columns and rows of data" (Oliverio and Pasewark, 1989, 489). Spreadsheet software may direct a

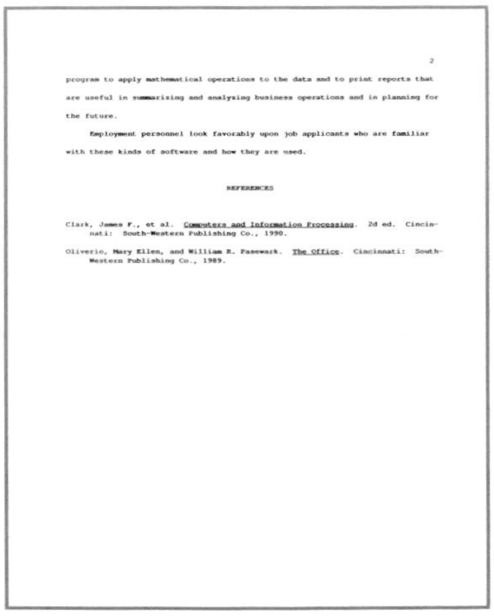
2

program to apply mathematical operations to the data and to print reports that are useful in summarizing and analyzing business operations and in planning for the future.

Employment personnel look favorably upon job applicants who are familiar with these kinds of software and how they are used.

REFERENCES

Clark, James F., et al. Computers and Information Processing. 2d ed. Cincinnati: South-Western Publishing Co., 1990.

Oliverio, Mary Ellen, and William R. Pasewark. The Office. Cincinnati: South-Western Publishing Co., 1989.

Elite (12-pitch) Layout

UNIT 57 *LESSONS 239 – 242*

Executive Office

Production Goals

1. To improve your ability to plan and organize work.
2. To improve your ability to make decisions or acceptable judgments.
3. To apply your language skills.
4. To assess the quality of work processed.
5. To integrate knowledge and skills previously acquired.

Documents Processed

1. Letters
2. Itinerary
3. Agenda
4. Address Cards
5. Simplified Memorandums
6. Topbound Report with Footnotes
7. Ruled Forms
8. Income Statement (Table)

MIDWESTERN OFFICE PRODUCTS: EXECUTIVE OFFICE

Before beginning the documents on pages 411-415, read the copy at the right. When planning the assigned documents, refer to the formatting guides given here to refresh your memory about proper formatting and spacing of documents.

Work Assignment

Because a full-time employee has been hired in the Sales Department, you have been reassigned to work in the Executive Office of Midwestern Office Products. Your work will be assigned by Ms. Sandra Moreno, who is the administrative assistant in the Executive Office.

The documents you process during this assignment will be for Ms. Sara C. Koontz, the company president, or for Ms. Ann M. Jones, the administrative vice president. Ms. Moreno will attach written instructions for each of the documents you are to process.

Excerpts from Midwestern's "Guide to Document Formats" that are applicable to the Executive Office are included here. Refer to the Guide as needed when processing the various documents. Use your textbook as a reference when Ms. Moreno's directions and the Guide are not sufficiently detailed.

When necessary, supply missing parts for documents. Use your judgment when specific formatting directions are not given. Correct errors in punctuation, spelling, capitalization, etc. Proofread each document carefully (even if your equipment includes a spell-check program) to produce correctly formatted, error-free documents.

Boilerplate Document

A boilerplate document is a letter or memo created by combining selected paragraphs that previously have been composed and filed (stored). Midwestern uses boilerplate paragraphs for documents created on a recurring basis. Paragraphs are labeled as beginning (B), middle (M), and ending (E) to ensure that the boilerplate documents will "flow" smoothly. Each boilerplate letter consists of a beginning and ending paragraph and, of course, one or more middle paragraphs. The different software packages utilized by the departments have various names for the function used to merge the files of the stored paragraphs. If you are keying on this kind of electronic equipment, consult your user's manual for the software package your department uses to determine the name and operation of this function.

Guide to Document Formats

Use the following guides as a quick reference to document formats.

Memorandums--Simplified

Stationery: plain sheets.
SM: 1″.
Memo parts: all begin at LM.
LS: QS below date and last line of body; DS below other parts; SS paragraphs.
PB: line 10.

Letters--Modified Block, Mixed Punctuation

Stationery: letterheads (executive size).
SM: 1″.
LS: SS with DS between paragraphs.
PB: line 12.

Reports--Topbound

Stationery: plain sheets.
References: footnotes.
SM: 1″.
PB (first page): line 12, 10-pitch;
line 14, 12-pitch.
PB (second and succeeding pages):
line 10.
BM: at least 1″.
LS: DS text.
Enumerations: SS with SS between items; key in hang-indent format.

Address Card

NAME Alexander, Jennifer S. (Miss)
TITLE Executive Vice President
ADDRESS First National Bank
3526 East 15th Street
Davenport, IA 52803-5522
TELEPHONE NO. (319) 632-4477

Line 10, pica (10-pitch)
Line 12, elite (12-pitch)

words

Title ELECTRONIC KEYBOARD APPLICATIONS 7

QS (space down 2 DS)

Report body Learning to key is of little value unless one applies it in 19
preparing something useful--a record or document of some kind. 31
Three basic kinds of software have been developed to assist those 45
with keyboarding skill in applying their skill electronically. 57

DS

Side heading <u>Word Processing Software</u> 67

DS

Word processing software is "software specially designed to 79
assist in the document preparation needs of an individual or busi- 92
Internal citation ness" (Clark et al., 1990, 193). Word processing software permits 106
the user to enter text, format it, manipulate or revise it, and 118
print a copy. The software can be used to process a wide variety 132
of documents such as letters, memos, reports, and tables. 143

DS

This software has special features such as automatic center- 155
1" ing and word wrap that reduce time and effort. In addition, it 1" 168
permits error corrections, format and sequence changes, and inser- 181
tion of variables "on screen" before a copy is printed. These 193
features increase efficiency by eliminating document rekeying. 206

DS

Side heading <u>Database Software</u> 213

DS

A database is "any collection of related items stored in com- 225
Internal citation puter memory" (Oliverio and Pasewark, 1989, 573). The data in a 238
database may be about club members, employee payroll, company sales, 252
and so on. Database software allows the user to enter data, re- 265
trieve and change it, or select certain data (such as an address) to 278
be used in documents. Software users can manipulate and print data 292
in report form for decision-making purposes. 301

At least 1"

Shown in pica (10-pitch) type, photo-reduced

Unbound Report

(continued, p. 95)

238a ▶ 5 Conditioning Practice

each line twice SS (slowly, then faster); if time permits rekey selected lines

alphabet 1 Quin, zip your fox jacket and get your gloves to brave the March wind.

fig/sym 2 Fred Jones & Company's telephone number was changed to (381) 509-2647.

left shift 3 Lisa appointed Jack, Paul, Ingrid, Helen, and Mae to make decorations.

speed 4 Turn down the lane by the foggy lake to see the hay and the cornfield.

| 1 | 2 | 3 | 4 | 5 | 6 | 7 | 8 | 9 | 10 | 11 | 12 | 13 | 14 |

238b ▶ 18 Improve Straight-Copy Speed and Accuracy

1. Three 1′ writings on ¶ 1 for speed. **Goal:** Increase speed by 2-4 *wam.*
2. Follow Step 1 for ¶ 2.
3. Three 1′ writings on ¶ 1 for accuracy. **Goal:** No more than 1 error a minute.
4. Follow Step 3 for ¶ 2.
5. A 3′ writing on all ¶s.
6. Determine *gwam*/errors.

all letters used | A | 1.5 si | 5.7 awl | 80% hfw |

	gwam 3′	
To realize maximum benefit from the many time-management techniques	5	62
that can be used, one should make a major effort at self-management.	9	66
One step in this process involves making a list of the less enjoyable	14	71
tasks performed. Then a scheme to associate some pleasure with these	19	76
tasks, such as doing them with a friend or following them with a reward,	23	81
should be implemented to help reduce the drudgery of the tasks.	28	85
Another self-management exercise is to analyze a task that never	32	89
gets done by questioning why one doesn't really want to complete that	37	94
unfinished job. Psychologists tell us that actions reflect our desired	41	99
behavior and that sometimes when we say that we would like to do some-	46	103
thing but do not have the time, we probably just do not want to do it.	51	108
Understanding this point can help one to learn to apply the pleasure	55	113
technique to tedious tasks.	57	115

gwam 3′ | 1 | 2 | 3 | 4 | 5 |

238c ▶ 12 Check Language Skills

Key the paragraph at the right correcting errors in subject/verb agreement and pronoun/antecedent agreement. Correct keyboarding errors.

Since neither of the other committee members were prepared for the meeting, each of them were asked to submit a written report by next week. After that time, the committee can meet again to compile their final recommendation to the president. Before making the decision, however, all members will cast its votes concerning the recommendation. The president hopes that the chairperson as well as committee members are happy with the final recommendation.

238d ▶ 15 Improve Keyboarding Skill

Repeat 237d, p. 408, as directed.

Page number — Line 6 2

DS

Side heading — <u>Spreadsheet Software</u> 310

DS

"A spreadsheet is an electronic worksheet made up of columns 322

Internal citation — and rows of data" (Oliverio and Pasewark, 1989, 489). Spreadsheet 335

software may direct a program to apply mathematical operations to 349

1" → the data and to print reports that are useful in summarizing and ← 1" 362

analyzing business operations and in planning for the future. 374

DS

Employment personnel look favorably upon job applicants who 386

are familiar with these kinds of software and how they are used. 399

QS (space down 2 DS)

REFERENCES 402

QS, then change to SS

List of references — Clark, James F., et al. <u>Computers and Information Processing</u>. 422
2d ed. Cincinnati: South-Western Publishing Co., 1990. 433

DS

Oliverio, Mary Ellen, and William R. Pasewark. <u>The Office</u>. Cin- 448
cinnati: South-Western Publishing Co., 1989. 457

Unbound Report, Page 2

Lesson 52 *Unbound Reports*

LL: 70
LS: SS

52a ▶ 6 Conditioning Practice

each line twice SS (slowly, then faster); DS between 2-line groups; if time permits, rekey selected lines

alphabet 1 Four giddy children were amazed by the quick, lively jumps of the fox.

figures 2 This new edition boasts 1,380 photographs, 926 charts, and 475 graphs.

fig/sym 3 Check #1657 for $48.90, dated May 23, is made out to McNeil & O'Leary.

speed 4 He may hand me the clay and then go to the shelf for the die and form.

| 1 | 2 | 3 | 4 | 5 | 6 | 7 | 8 | 9 | 10 | 11 | 12 | 13 | 14 |

52b ▶ 6 Improve Language Skills: Word Choice

1. Study the spelling/definitions of the words in the color block at right.

2. Key line 1 (the **Learn** line), noting the proper choice of words.

3. Key lines 2-3 (the **Apply** lines), choosing the right words to complete the lines correctly.

4. Key the remaining lines in the same way.

5. Check your accuracy; rekey lines containing word-choice errors.

do (vb) to bring about; to carry out

due (adj) owed or owing as a debt; having reached the date for payment

hear (vb) to gain knowledge of by the ear

here (adv) in or at this place; at this point; in this case; on this point

Learn 1 If you pay when it is due, the cost will be less.
Apply 2 (Do, Due) you expect the plane to arrive when it is (do, due)?
Apply 3 (Do, Due) you want me to indicate the (do, due) date of the invoice?

Learn 4 Did you hear the sirens while you were here in the cellar?
Apply 5 (Hear, Here) is the new CD you said you want to (hear, here).
Apply 6 To (hear, here) well, we should see if we can get seats (hear, here).

237c ▶ 12
Check Language Skills

Key the paragraph at the right correcting errors in spelling and word usage (commonly confused words). Correct keyboarding errors.

The comittee decided to except the advice of the consultant concerning the installation of electrical outlets. The principal reason for doing so was their knowledge of the consultant's prior succesful projects. The comittee members knew that they had to have acess to more outlets if they were to move foreword with plans to expand, and they were confidant that the consultant had studied their needs and their facilaties carefully. They believed that such a profesional person would weigh the alternatives and make a reccomendation that would be in their best intrest.

237d ▶ 15
Improve Keyboarding Skill

1. A 1′ writing on ¶ 1; find *gwam*.
2. Add 4-8 *gwam* to the rate attained in Step 1, and note quarter-minute checkpoints from table below.
3. Take two 1′ guided writings on ¶ 1 to increase speed.
4. Practice ¶s 2 and 3 in the same way.
5. A 5′ writing on ¶s 1-3 combined; find *gwam* and determine errors.

Quarter-Minute Checkpoints

gwam	1/4′	1/2′	3/4′	1′
40	10	20	30	40
44	11	22	33	44
48	12	24	36	48
52	13	26	39	52
56	14	28	42	56
60	15	30	45	60
64	16	32	48	64
68	17	34	51	68
72	18	36	54	72

all letters used | A | 1.5 si | 5.7 awl | 80% hfw

	gwam 1′	5′	
Speaking before a group of people can cause a great deal of anxiety	14	3	61
for an individual. This anxiety is so extensive that it was ranked as	28	6	64
the greatest fear among adults in a recent survey. Such fear suggests	42	8	67
that many people would rather perish than go before the public to give	56	11	69
a talk. Much of this fear actually comes from a lack of experience and	71	14	72
training in giving public speeches. People who excel in the area of	84	17	75
public speaking have developed this unique skill through hard work.	98	20	78
Planning is a key part to giving a good talk. The talk should be	13	22	80
organized into three basic parts. These parts are the introduction, the	28	25	83
body, and the conclusion. The introduction is used to get the attention	42	28	86
of the audience, to introduce the topic of the talk, and to establish	56	31	89
the credibility of the speaker. The body of the speech is an organized	71	34	92
presentation of the material the speaker is conveying. The conclusion	85	37	95
is used to summarize the main points of the talk.	95	39	97
Several things can be done to lower the level of anxiety during a	13	41	99
talk. Learning as much as possible about the audience prior to the	27	44	102
talk can reduce uncertainty. Advanced planning and preparing are essen-	41	48	105
tial; the lack of either is a major cause of anxiety. Having the main	56	50	108
points written on note cards to refer to when needed is also helpful.	70	52	111
Using visual aids can also lessen the exposure a person feels. These	84	55	113
are but a few ideas that may be used to develop better speaking skills.	98	58	116

gwam 1′ | 1 | 2 | 3 | 4 | 5 | 6 | 7 | 8 | 9 | 10 | 11 | 12 | 13 | 14 |
5′ | 1 | 2 | 3 |

52c ▶ 8 Learn to Format a Report Title Page

A title or cover page is prepared for many reports. Using the following guides, format a title page for the report you prepared in Lesson 51.

1. Center the title in ALL CAPS on line 16 of a plain full sheet (from top edge down 8 DS).

2. Center your name in capital and lowercase letters on the 16th line below the title.

3. Center the school name a DS below your name.

4. Center the current date on the 16th line below the school name.

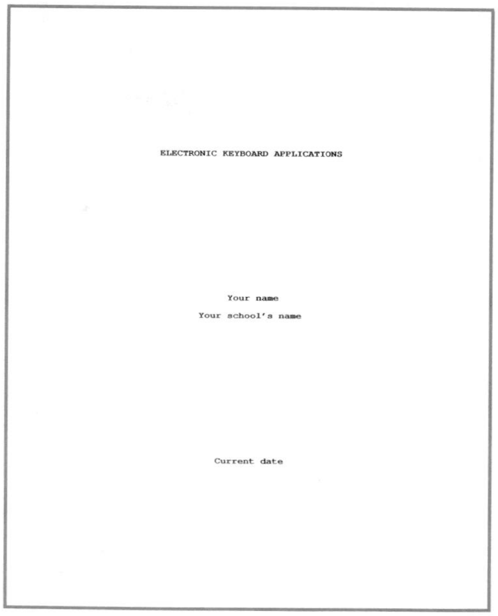
ELECTRONIC KEYBOARD APPLICATIONS

Your name

Your school's name

Current date

52d ▶ 30 Format a Book Report in Unbound Report Style

1. Review the formatting guides on p. 92.

2. Format the following material as a 2-page unbound report on 2 plain full sheets.

3. Place the reference below the last line of copy on the second page of the report.

4. Correct any errors you make as you key.

5. Staple the pages together across the upper left corner or fasten them with a paper clip.

words

BOOK REPORT 2

by 3

George Timberwolf 6

Ordinary People is a heartrending, and 17
at times heartwarming, family novel in which 26
"ordinary people" under pressure become spe- 35
cial after all. 38

Calvin Jarrett is a determined, successful 47
provider. Beth is his organized and efficient, 56
but proud and self-centered, wife. They had 65
two sons, Buck and Conrad. Now they have 74
just one. Buck, the older and the leader, was 83
drowned in a storm while sailing with Conrad, 92
the younger and the follower. Conrad held on; 102
Buck let go. 105

Devastated by the death of his brother, 113
Conrad comes to blame himself and attempts 121
suicide. After months in a hospital for phys- 130
ical and psychological care, he returns, still 140
guilt-ridden, to a home environment that is less 149
than warm and understanding. His mother does 159
nothing to help relieve his feelings of guilt; 168
rather, she is concerned with what her friends 177
and neighbors will think of his behavior. 186
Empathy and affection appear alien to her 194
nature, and Buck was her favorite son. Thus 203
it is left to the father, who is well-intentioned 213
but often ineffective, to maintain parental ties 223
to the boy. 226

Conrad withdraws further into himself and 234
away from his parents and friends. Only as a 243
result of psychiatric care with Dr. Berger and 253
his father's growing understanding and accep- 262
tance is he able to rebuild his self-image and 271
self-esteem and to absolve himself of guilt. 280
Conrad manages to reaccept his former friends 289
and even to forgive his mother for her inability 299
to show him affection and understanding--to 308
say nothing of forgiveness. 314

The characters are so finely drawn they 322
seem real. The story is so carefully woven 331
that the reader is pulled along by an unwind- 339
ing string from beginning to end, as in a mys- 348
tery thriller. Principles of human strength 357
born of suffering are laced throughout the 366
story. One is left with the conviction that 375
even for "ordinary people" under stress, there 384
is a way out of the darkness. 391

REFERENCE 393

Guest, Judith. Ordinary People. New York: 405
Ballantine Books, 1979. 409

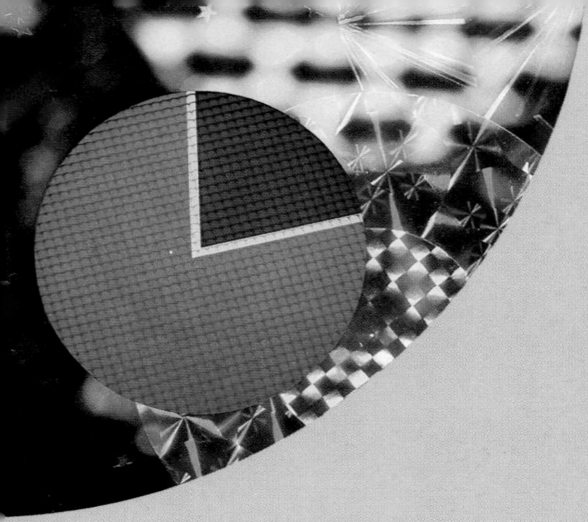

UNIT 56 LESSONS 237 – 238

Improve Keyboarding/Language Skills

Learning Goals

1. To improve keyboarding speed and accuracy on straight copy.
2. To assess straight-copy speed and accuracy.
3. To check language skills.

Format Guides

1. Paper guide at *0* (for typewriters).
2. LL: 70 spaces.
3. LS: SS sentence drills with DS between groups; DS paragraph writings.
4. PI: 5 spaces.

Lesson 237 *Improve Keyboarding/Language Skills*

237a ▶ 5 Conditioning Practice

each line twice SS (slowly, then faster); if time permits, rekey selected lines

alphabet	1	I drove the jazz quartet up to the front walk in my big luxurious car.
figures	2	Mid-State's office ordered Models #30271 and #46958 at $1,269.41 each.
right shift	3	Did Eric, Betty, and Todd make the debate team along with Ann and Wes?
speed	4	Both of the haughty men risk a big penalty if they dismantle the auto.

| 1 | 2 | 3 | 4 | 5 | 6 | 7 | 8 | 9 | 10 | 11 | 12 | 13 | 14 |

237b ▶ 18 Improve Straight-Copy Speed and Accuracy

1. Three 1′ writings on ¶ 1 for speed. **Goal:** Increase speed by 2-4 *wam* on each writing.
2. Follow Step 1 for ¶ 2.
3. Three 1′ writings on ¶ 1 for accuracy. **Goal:** No more than 1 error a minute.
4. Follow Step 3 for ¶ 2.
5. A 3′ writing on ¶s 1 and 2 combined.
6. Determine *gwam*/errors.

all letters used | A | 1.5 si | 5.7 awl | 80% hfw

	gwam 3′	
All people have exactly the same number of hours a day for the	4	61
tasks that are required, for the tasks that are elective, and for ac-	9	66
tivities that are just for pleasure. Some people, though, organize	13	71
their schedules in such a way as to accomplish noticeably more of the	18	75
tasks and activities than do others. Do such individuals have a deep	23	80
secret, or do they just have superior time-management skills?	27	84
If the answer is that these are people who excel in applying good	31	88
time-management techniques, then they are apt to recognize the necessity	36	93
of establishing priorities. To establish priorities means that they	41	98
must judge which tasks or activities are the most essential and place	45	103
those items high on their priority list. Then they must schedule their	50	107
day to work steadily to complete with few deviations the items in the	55	112
order in which they appear on the list.	57	115

gwam 3′ | 1 | 2 | 3 | 4 | 5 |

53a ▶ 6 Conditioning Practice

each line twice SS (slowly, then faster); DS between 2-line groups; if time permits, rekey selected lines

alphabet	1	Joey paid the exotic woman a quarter each for three black gauze veils.
figures	2	Jan sold 14 rings, 293 clips, 50 watches, 168 clocks, and 70 tie pins.
fig/sym	3	After May 5, Al's new address will be 478 Pax Avenue (ZIP 92106-1593).
speed	4	Ivor may make the goal if he works with vigor and with the right form.

| 1 | 2 | 3 | 4 | 5 | 6 | 7 | 8 | 9 | 10 | 11 | 12 | 13 | 14 |

53b ▶ 6 Improve Language Skills: Word Choice

1. Study the spelling/definitions of the words in the color block at right.

2. Key line 1 (the **Learn** line), noting the proper choice of words.

3. Key lines 2-3 (the **Apply** lines), choosing the right words to complete the lines correctly.

4. Key the remaining lines in the same way.

5. Check your accuracy; rekey lines containing word-choice errors.

hour (n) the 24th part of a day; a particular time

our (adj) of or relating to ourselves as possessors

know (vb) to be aware of the truth of; to have understanding of

no (adv/adj/n) in no respect or degree; not so; indicates denial or refusal

Learn	1	It is our intention to complete the work in an hour or two.
Apply	2	If I drive steadily, we should reach (hour, our) house in an (hour, our).
Apply	3	We should earn one credit (hour, our) for (hour, our) computer class.
Learn	4	Did you know that there are to be no quizzes this week?
Apply	5	If you (know, no) the chapter, you should have (know, no) fear of a quiz.
Apply	6	Did you (know, no) that they scored (know, no) touchdowns in the game?

53c ▶ 38 Format an Unbound Report with Long Quotation

Document 1
Report

On two plain full sheets, format the report given at right and on the next page as a 2-page unbound report, DS. Correct any errors you make as you key.

Long quotations
When keying quotations of more than 3 typed lines, SS and indent them 5 spaces from the LM. Leave a DS above and below them.

words

TYPEWRITERS: AN ENDANGERED SPECIES? 7

For well over a decade, experts in office automation 18
have predicted the demise of the typewriter. In their view 30
the computer is destined to take over the word processing 42
role enjoyed by the typewriter for over a century. Yet, a 53
recent report (Fernberg, 1989, 49-50) indicates that elec- 65
tronic typewriter shipments over the last three years aver- 76
aged about a billion dollars a year. Further, the Computer 88
and Business Equipment Manufacturers' Association projects 100
that the annual growth rate will remain constant at 1.5 per- 112
cent over the next five years. With sales holding steady at 124
over a million units a year, the electronic typewriter does 136
not appear endangered. It is likely here to stay--and for 148
good reasons. 151

<u>Typewriter Familiarity</u> 160

Virtually anyone who has learned to key can sit down at 171
the electronic typewriter and within a few minutes operate it 184
with amazing ease and speed. According to Paez (1985, 55): 196

SS

> A familiar keyboard, which requires fewer keystrokes and 207
> has a simpler, less code-intensive user interface, makes 219
> the transition to a high-end typewriter much easier than 230
> the transition to a personal computer with the same func- 241
> tions. 243

(continued, p. 98)

232b-236b (continued)

Document 12
Modified Block Letter
LP p. 25

> **LINDA HENRY**
> **Office Supervisor**
>
> Perry A. McDaniel, one of our Sales Representatives, would like the attached form letter sent to
>
> **Mrs. Julia C. Ward**
> **Word Processing Supervisor**
> **James and Associates**
> **2100 Claude Road**
> **Hunstville, AL 35806-8000**
>
> Variable 1:
> **electronic typewriters**
>
> Variable 2:
> **(319) 887-4404**
>
> Date letter May 11
> LH

Here is the information you requested regarding guarantee, service, and training programs for our <variable 1>.

Equipment Guarantee. All equipment is guaranteed for three months from the date of delivery. During the warranty period, equipment will be repaired or replaced at no charge. After the warranty has expired, you can continue to have us service the equipment at an hourly rate charge plus parts.

Service. A response time of eight hours or less is guaranteed for all service calls. If the equipment requires longer than eight hours to service, a loaner will be provided free of charge until the equipment is repaired. Our service, we have been told, is among the best customer service provided in the industry.

Training Programs. Our Educational Division provides seminars to assure that our customers are utilizing the many capabilities of the equipment. The seminars are provided free of charge during the first six months after the purchase of the equipment. Technicians are available during every workday to respond to any questions a customer has about the equipment.

I enjoyed meeting with you and demonstrating our <variable 1>. If you have additional questions about our products or customer service policies, just call me at <variable 2>.

Sincerely

Document 13
Sales Figures

> **LINDA HENRY**
> **Office Supervisor**
>
> Prepare a table comparing the January-March Hardware and Software sales figures for last year with this year's. Use the sales figures in Document 4 for this year's figures.
>
> LH

JANUARY-MARCH SALES COMPARISON

Past Two Years

Sales Representative	Hardware Last Year	Hardware This Year	Software Last Year	Software This Year
Sam Johnson	$144,846	$ xxx,xxx	$ 2,617	$ x,xxx
Bob Black	--		--	
Eva Lewis	138,558		5,032	
Kerry Munson	113,654		3,624	
Mary Ramirez	149,695		3,780	
Lydia Mendez	131,860		3,159	
Perry McDaniel	151,985		6,870	
Dave Bromberg	162,598		5,254	
Totals	$993,196	$x,xxx,xxx	$30,336	$xx,xxx

53c (continued)

words

Typewriter Flexibility 252

An electronic typewriter can preform some function com- 263
puters cannot, but a personal computer (PC) cannot be used as 275
a mere typewriter (nor should it be). Perhaps that is why 287
one large survey found that 85 percent of secretaries who use 299
PCs also use typewriters. Using microchip technology, sophis- 312
ticated electronic typewriters can perform many of the auto- 324
matic functions and editing functions of which computers are 336
capable. 338

Automatic Functions. Among the features of ~~electric~~ 353
typewriters are autematic centering, returning, right margin 365
justifing and hang-indenting. These features are ~~avi~~able on 378
computers as well, but some users of both kinds of equipment 390
say that the typewriter is more "user freindly." 400

Editing Functions. ~~Many~~ electronic typewriters permit 415
operators to backspace/delete, insert copy, move copy from 426
one plce to another, and search and replace specific words or 439
terms in an document. Some are equiped with templates that 451
make form fill-in easy; others permits the merging of in- 462
formation from diferent sources. All these functions are 474
performed without ~~needing to~~ rekey documents. 482

Typewriter Sophistication 492

Electronic typewriters range from low-end machines with 503
limited features and without editing windows to high-end 514
machaines with full page displsys, diskete storage, and com- 526
plete text-editing capabilities. The price range varies with 539
the ~~amount~~ of advanced features included. Some machines are 551
upgradable so that the aproppriate level of sophistocation 563
can be obtained without replacing machines. 572

Document 2
Reference Page
Format the references on a separate plain full sheet.

REFERENCES 574

Audion, Mark. "~~Using~~ Electronic Typewriters: The Basics, 584
Plus. . . ." Today's Office, July 1986, 55-64. 597

Fernberg, Patricia M. "Electric Typewriters: Understanding 610
the Product." Modern Office Technology, March 1989, 625
48-50. 627

Paze, Patricia. "Typewriters: Technology with an Easy 638
Touch." Today's Office, September 1985, 55-72. 650

Document 3
Title Page
Format a title page for the report on a plain full sheet. Use your own name and school name and the current date.

232b-236b (continued)

Document 9
Simplified Block Letter
LP p. 21

> **LINDA HENRY**
> **Office Supervisor**
>
> Format the attached information as a simplified block letter for **Thomas M. Chaney** to use in the exhibit area of the Regional Office Automation Convention. Use the following for the letter address.
>
> **Convention Participants**
> **Hotel Tuscany**
> **3400 Fillmore Street**
> **Davenport, IA 52806-4721**
>
> Date letter May 25 LH

Welcome to the [19--] Regional [Office] Automation Convention. I'm sure you are enjoying learning about the lastest develop ments in the fast paced world of [office] thechnology.

One piece of equipment ~~that is~~ being demonstrated is the Elec II 40-character display, electronic typewriter. The typewriter has 32 K of basic memory, text merging in memory capability, and a [print] speed of 17 [#] characters per second. The list price for the typewriter is $1,285. A word processor upgrade and a sheet feeder are additional features that can be added to enhance the ~~electronic~~ typewriteer capabilities.

If you have any questions regarding the ~~equipment,~~ [Elec II] please ask the person demonstrating the equipment or one of our sales representatives [at the exhibit area].

Documents 10-11
Formal Memorandums
LP p. 23

> **LINDA HENRY**
> **Office Supervisor**
>
> Key two copies of the attached information as formal memorandums on half sheets for Mr. Chaney. One copy goes to **Lori Chin** and other copy to **Malcolm Deters.** (Both work in the Information Processing Center.) Date the memos **May 10** and supply a subject line.
>
> LH

Thank you for agreeing to assist our sales representatives at the 19-- Regional Office Automation Convention on May 25. ~~An informational~~ meeting [to] ~~will~~ be held on May 15 [will] ~~to give you the opportunity to to~~ help you prepare for the convention. ~~At this time~~ [Then] you can meet our convention sales force and discuss with them the types of ~~documents~~ [information processing applications] you will demonstrate. ~~during the convention.~~

Any questions you have [about] ~~regarding~~ this assignment will be answered during this meeting. I am looking forward to working with you.

54a ▶ 6 Conditioning Practice

each line twice SS (slowly, then faster); DS between 2-line groups; if time permits, rekey selected lines

alphabet 1 After a wild jump ball, the guards very quickly executed a zone press.
figures 2 The invoice covered 115 sofas, 270 desks, 476 chairs, and 1,398 lamps.
fig/sym 3 Order the #284, #365, and #1790 cartons (untaped) from O'Brien & Sons.
speed 4 A big firm kept half of the men busy with their work down by the lake.

| 1 | 2 | 3 | 4 | 5 | 6 | 7 | 8 | 9 | 10 | 11 | 12 | 13 | 14 |

54b ▶ 6 Improve Language Skills: Word Choice

1. Study the spelling/definitions of the words in the color block at right.

2. Key line 1 (the **Learn** line), noting the proper choice of words.

3. Key lines 2-3 (the **Apply** lines), choosing the right words to complete the lines correctly.

4. Key the remaining lines in the same way.

5. Check your accuracy; rekey lines containing word-choice errors.

lead (vb) to guide or direct; to be first
led (vb) the past tense of lead

choose (vb) to select; to decide on
chose (vb) the past tense of choose

Learn 1 Max is to lead the parade; Pam led it last year.
Apply 2 The Falcons (lead, led) now; the Friars (lead, led) at the half.
Apply 3 Marj (lead, led) at the ninth hole, but she does not (lead, led) now.

Learn 4 Jose chose a Eureka computer; I may choose a Futura.
Apply 5 After he (choose, chose) a red cap, I told him to (choose, chose) blue.
Apply 6 Mae (choose, chose) me as a partner; Janice may (choose, chose) me.

54c ▶ 38 Format an Unbound Report with Enumerated Items

Document 1
Report
On 2 plain full sheets, format and key the copy given at right and on page 100 as an unbound report. Place the reference list below the last line of copy on page 2 of the report. Correct any errors you make as you key.

words

BASIC STRATEGIES FOR EFFECTIVE STUDY 7

Effective learning depends upon good study habits. Efficient study skills 22
do not simply occur; they must first be learned and then applied consis- 37
tently. Good study strategies include a preset time for study, a desirable 52
place to study, and a well-designed study plan. 62

<u>A Time for Study</u> 68

All of us think we have more things to do than we have time to do, and 82
studying gets shortchanged. It is important to prepare a schedule of daily ac- 98
tivities that includes time slots for doing the studying we have to do. Within 114
each study slot, write in the specific study activity; for example, "Read Unit 6 130
of accounting; do Problems 1-5." Keep the schedule flexible so that it can be 146
modified after you assess your success in meeting your study goals within 161
each time slot. 164

<u>A Place to Study</u> 171

Choose the best place to study and use the same one every day. Doing so 185
will help to put you in a study mood when you enter that place. According to 201
Usova (1989, 37), "The library is not always a desirable place to study." Choose 217
a place that has the fewest distractions such as people traffic, conversation, 233
telephone, TV, and outside noises. Study is usually best done alone and in the 249
absence of sights and sounds that distract the eye and ear. In your chosen 264
quiet place, force the mind to concentrate on the task at hand. 277

<u>A Plan for Study</u> 284

Research on the effects of specific study skills on student performance 298
(Dansereau, 1985, 39) suggests that the following study tactics help to im- 313
prove academic performance. 319

(continued, p. 100)

232b-236b (continued)

Document 8
Price List

LINDA HENRY
Office Supervisor

Attached is a price list that has been marked with price increases and new products. Prepare a new price list for distribution to sales representatives reflecting those changes. These changes will be effective as of June 1. A few formatting marks have been included to assist you in preparing the copy. *LH*

List the groups of equipment in alphabetical order.

PRICE LIST

DS

Effective May 1, 19--

Blocked Headings *QS*

Printers	Price	Order Number
Star I	$ 249	100-PSI
Star II	329	200-PSII
Super Star	*489*	*300-PSS*
Quality I	~~399~~ *419*	150-PQI
Quality II	~~459~~ *479*	250-PQII

DS *QS*

Typewriters	Price	Order Number
Star 6000	$ ~~799~~ *829*	6000-ETS
Star 6086	~~899~~ *939*	6086-ETS
Elec I	1,085	349-ETEI
Elec II	1,285	350-ETEII
EIT 521	849	521-ETEIT
EIT 621	1,089	621-ETEIT

Copiers	Price	Order Number
Quality Copier I	$6,939	305-CQCI
Quality Copier II	9,729	310-CQCII
Pro Copier 380	4,349	380-CPC
Pro Copier 690	6,799	690-CPC

Computers	Price	Order Number
McGregger 600	$1,299	600-COM-MG
McGregger 6000	1,999	6000-COM-MG
Werner I	~~1,549~~ *1,599*	300-COM-WI
Werner II	*2,349*	*400-COM-WII*
PC-50 Dixon	2,459	50-COM-DIX
PC-95 Dixon	2,949	95-COM-DIX

54c (continued)

words

Enumerated items

1. Block a series of numbered items 5 spaces from the LM (at ¶ indent point).

2. SS each item, but DS between items and above and below the series.

3. For a long series, reset the LM (or use automatic indent if your equipment has this feature).

1. Skim a unit or a chapter, noting headings, topic sentences, key words, 334
and definitions. This overview will clue you to what you are about to 348
study. 350

2. As you read a unit or chapter, convert the headings into questions; then 365
seek answers to those questions as you read. 374

3. If you own the book, use color marking pens to highlight important 389
ideas: headings, topic sentences, special terms, definitions, and support- 403
ing facts. If you don't own the book, make notes of these important ideas 418
and facts. 421

4. After you have completed a unit or chapter, review the highlighted 435
items (or your notes which contain them). 444

5. Using the headings stated as questions, see if you can answer those 458
questions based on your reading. 465

6. Test yourself to see if you can recall definitions of important terms and 480
lists of supporting facts or ideas. 488

A high correlation exists between good study habits and good grades for 502
the courses taken in school. 508

Document 2
Title Page
Format a suitable title page for the report, using your name and school name and the current date.

REFERENCES 510

Dansereau, D. F. "Learning Strategy Research." Thinking and Learning 529
Skills. Vol. 1. Hillsdale, NJ: Lawrence Erlbaum, 1985, 21-40. 543
Usova, George M. Efficient Study Strategies. Pacific Grove, CA: Brooks/ 563
Cole Publishing Company, 1989. 569

Lesson 55 Unbound Reports

LL: 70
LS: SS

55a ▶ 6 Conditioning Practice

each line twice SS (slowly, then faster); DS between 2-line groups; if time permits, rekey selected lines

alphabet 1 Liquid oxygen fuel was used to give this big jet rocket amazing speed.

figures 2 We proofread 275 letters, 18 reports, 369 invoices, and 40 statements.

fig/sym 3 This rug (12′ × 13′6″) was $814.95, but it is now on sale for $710.50.

speed 4 Pay them for their work and then go with us to the city for the forms.

| 1 | 2 | 3 | 4 | 5 | 6 | 7 | 8 | 9 | 10 | 11 | 12 | 13 | 14 |

55b ▶ 6 Improve Language Skills: Word Choice

1. Study the spelling/definitions of the words in the color block at right.

2. Key line 1 (the **Learn** line), noting the proper choice of words.

3. Key lines 2-3 (the **Apply** lines), choosing the right words to complete the lines correctly.

4. Key the remaining lines in the same way.

5. Check your accuracy; rekey lines containing word-choice errors.

your (adj) of or relating to you or yourself as possessor

you're (contr) you are

for (prep/conj) used to indicate purpose; on behalf of; because; because of

four (n) the fourth in a set or series

Learn 1 As soon as you receive your blue book, you're to write your name on it.
Apply 2 (Your, You're) to write the letter using (your, you're) best English.
Apply 3 When (your, you're) computer is warmed up, (your, you're) to begin work.

Learn 4 All four workers asked for an appointment with the manager.
Apply 5 At (for, four) o'clock the lights went off (for, four) an hour.
Apply 6 The (for, four) boys turned back, (for, four) they feared the lightning.

232b-236b (continued)

Document 6
Purchase Order
LP p. 17

LINDA HENRY
Office Supervisor

Prepare a purchase order for the computer accessories that Mr. Mundy has requisitioned. I have written the stock numbers and price information on the requisition. Order the items from this company.

Ellis Computer Products
425 East Ivy Avenue
St. Paul, MN 55101-2444

Use the following information to complete the purchase order.

Purchase Order No.: **QZ 1039**
Date: **May 8, 19—**
Terms: **2/10, n/30**
Shipped Via: **Watson Freight**

LH

MIDWESTERN OFFICE PRODUCTS PURCHASE REQUISITION

3871 BRIDGE AVENUE, DAVENPORT, IA 52807-7002 (319) 887-1462

Deliver to: Marvin Mundy Requisition No. 38569
Location: 400E Date May 6, 19--
Job No. 698-Drake Date Required May 20, 19--

Quantity	Description	Price	Total
20	Computer Locks (9461-C)	27.95 ea	559.00
10	Surge Protectors (7648-C)	36.15 ea	361.50
5	Five-way Switchboxes (5230-G)	109.00 ea	545.00
10	Keyboard Extension Cables (7609-B)	16.45 ea	164.50
1	Standby Power System (1568-G)	279.95 ea	279.95
			1,909.95

Requisitioned by: Marvin Mundy

Document 7
Formal Memorandum
LP p. 19

LINDA HENRY
Office Supervisor

Mr. Chaney would like the attached information formatted as a formal memo and sent to **Ms. Olivia Reinhold, IPC Supervisor**. Date the memo **May 8, 19--** and supply an appropriate subject line.

LH

The 19-- Regional Office Automation Convention will be held at the Hotel Tuscany here in Davenport on May 25. We are planning to give demonstrations of the Elec II electronic typewriter, the Pro Copier 690, and the McGregger 6000 computer. President Koontz suggested that personnel from the Information Processing Center give the demonstrations. Would it be possible for you to assist us by providing IPC personnel?

If so, we would like the individuals you select to be specialists with the equipment who can present the professional image that is critical to advance our sales efforts. I'll phone you within a few days to give you specific details about the convention.

55c ▶ 38 *Format an Unbound Report*

Process report with references on page 2; prepare title page; correct errors.

words

READING FOR KEYBOARDING AND FORMATTING 8

When learning to key, format, and process 16
documents, a major portion of one's time is 25
spent reading. Two different reading processes 35
are used in learning: reading for meaning and 44
reading for "copy getting." 50

<u>Reading for Meaning</u> 58

When one reads an explanation and descrip- 66
tion of a document format or directions for com- 75
pleting a keying task, the purpose of reading is 85
to process information and to acquire meaning 94
or understanding (de Fossard, 1990, 1). Such 103
reading requires focusing on the content: its 113
organization, sequence, ideas, terms, and facts. 123
The objective is to assimilate them, store them, 133
and recall them in proper order for later use. 142
Reading for meaning is very important when 151
learning terms, concepts, and procedures. Such 160
reading is preferably done with speed followed 170
by review. 172

<u>Reading for Copy Getting</u> 182

When one reads a drill or document for the 191
purpose of copying it by means of a keyboard, 200
one reads to "get the copy" to feed through the 210
brain at the speed the fingers are able to re- 219
cord it by striking the keys (West, 1983, 227
130). The purpose is not to understand the 236
message or to get meaning from it; rather, the 245
purpose is to reproduce the message character 254
for character. In initial learning, this process 264
is done on a letter-by-letter basis. As skill 274
grows, however, the process begins to include 283
"chains" of letters and short words that are 292
perceived and responded to as units. Rarely, 301
though, can a keyboard operator feed the fin- 310
gers more than one or two words at a time un- 319
less the words are short. 324

Reading for copy getting requires that the 333
speed of reading be synchronized with the fin- 342
gers' ability to make the keystrokes required to 352
reproduce the words. In this process, the mind 361
is concerned with the form and sequence of the 371
letters and words, not with the meaning of the 380
message the letters and words convey. This 389
kind of reading must be done at a slower pace 398
that is deliberate but harmonious. 405

REFERENCES 407

de Fossard, Esta. <u>Reading in Focus</u>. 3d ed. 420
Cincinnati: South-Western Publishing Co., 428
1990. 430

West, L. J. <u>Acquisition of Typewriting Skills</u>. 446
2d ed. Indianapolis: Bobbs-Merrill Educa- 455
tional Publishing, 1983. 459

Lesson 56 Outlines

LL: 70
LS: SS

56a ▶ 6 *Conditioning Practice*

each line twice SS (slowly, then faster); DS between 2-line groups; if time permits, rekey selected lines

alphabet 1 Suzi can equal a track record by jumping twelve feet at the next meet.

figures 2 The data are given in Figures 26 and 27 of Part 14, Unit 39, page 508.

fig/sym 3 Rizzo & Lewis wrote Check #728 for $301.95 and Check #745 for $648.50.

speed 4 Eighty of the men may work for the island firms if they make a profit.

| 1 | 2 | 3 | 4 | 5 | 6 | 7 | 8 | 9 | 10 | 11 | 12 | 13 | 14 |

56b ▶ 9 *Learn to Align Roman Numerals*

Use drill sheet from 56a; center heading a QS below your warm-up lines; LL: 40 spaces; LS: DS.

Automatic procedure
If your equipment has an automatic aligning feature, see the User's Guide for information on how to set tabs and align numerals.

Manual procedure
1. Clear all tab stops; from LM, space forward to set new tab stops as indicated by the KEY below and the guides above the columns at right.

2. Center the heading.

3. As you key Roman numerals, tabbing from column to column, align them at the right. To do this, space forward or backward from the tab stop as needed.

Margin release
To begin the numeral III in Column 1, depress the *margin release key* with the nearer little finger and backspace once into the LM.

ROMAN NUMERALS

margin ↓	tab ↓	tab ↓
I	IV	VII
II	V	VIII
III	VI	IX

KEY | 3 | 16 | 2 | 16 | 4 |

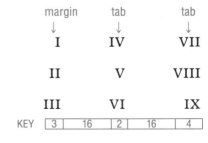

232b-236b (continued)

Document 4
Sales Report

> **LINDA HENRY**
> **Office Supervisor**
>
> Prepare the attached Quarterly Sales Report in final form for Mr. Chaney. *LH*

Note: Be sure to keep a copy of this document since you will need information from this table to complete Document 13.

QUARTERLY SALES REPORT

January-March 19--

alphabetize

Representative	Hardware	Software	*Printware*
Mary Ramirez	$ 153,132	*$* 5,520	*$ 1,183*
Sam Johnson	144,690	2,579	*1,567*
Lydia Mendez	133,409	4,407	*249*
Bob Black	*79,234*	*2,135*	*498*
Perry McDaniel	157,095	8,195	*489*
Kerry Munson	122,167	3,397 *8*	*918*
Dave Bromburg *e*	174,459	3,096	*2,821*
Eva Lewis	162,598	7,240	*2,040*
Totals	*$ 1,126,703*	*$ 36,570*	*$ 9,765*

Document 5
Invoice
LP p. 17

> **LINDA HENRY**
> **Office Supervisor**
>
> Grovesdale Business College requested us to delay their order until they met with department members. They have now decided to purchase the PC-95 Dixon rather than the PC-50.
> Key an invoice with the information and changes marked on their purchase order. Our Order No. is **C63-896**; use **May 8** for the date. *LH*

GROVESDALE BUSINESS COLLEGE
4225 WILSON AVENUE, DES MOINES, IA 50317-6700
515-245-7171

PURCHASE ORDER

MIDWESTERN OFFICE PRODUCTS
3871 BRIDGE AVENUE
DAVENPORT IA 52807-7002

Purchase Order No.: 108-493Z
Date: May 4, 19--
Terms: 3/10, n/30
Shipped Via: Dalton Transit

Quantity	Description/Stock Number	Price	Per	Total
2	Elec II Typewriters (350-ETEII)	1,285 00	ea	2,570 00
2	Quality II Printers (250-PQII)	479 00	ea	958 00
2	PC-~~50~~ *95* Dixon Computers (~~50~~ *95*-COM-DIX)	~~2,459 00~~ *2,949 00*	ea	~~4,918 00~~ *5,898.00*
				~~8,446 00~~ *9,426 00*
	Sales Tax			~~422 30~~ *471 30*
				~~8,868 30~~ *9,897 30*

By ____________________

56c ▶ 35 Learn to Format Topic Outlines

Outline 1
Format the outline on a plain full sheet.

SM: 1″ (pica, 10 spaces; elite, 12 spaces)
PB: line 10 (pica) or line 12 (elite)

Automatic procedure
If your equipment has the land-indent feature, see the User's Guide for the appropriate tab procedure.

Manual procedure
Set margins and tabs as indicated by the color notes on the outlines.

Note: Major headings are preceded by I., II., etc.; first-order headings by A., B., etc.; and second-order headings by 1., 2., etc.

Language skills notes

1. Outline title is in ALL CAPS and may be underlined.

2. Major headings are in ALL CAPS and are not underlined.

3. Important words of first-order subheadings are capitalized.

4. First word only of second-order subheadings is capitalized.

```
                    SPACING TOPIC OUTLINES
                                          Leave 3 blank line spaces—
              2 spaces                    QS (quadruple space)
Space forward once from margin
 I.  VERTICAL SPACING          Leave 1 blank line space—
                               DS (double space)
Reset margin → A.  Title of Outline
1st tab →          1.  Line 12, elite (12-pitch); line 10, pica (10-pitch)
(Set 2 tab stops   2.  Followed by 3 blank line spaces (QS)
4 spaces apart)  B.  Major Headings
                   1.  First major heading preceded by a QS; all others
2d tab →               preceded by 1 blank line space (DS)
                   2.  All followed by a DS
                   3.  All subheadings single-spaced (SS)
                                                          DS
Use margin release; backspace 5 times
II.  HORIZONTAL SPACING
                  DS
     A.  Title of Outline Centered over the Line of Writing
     B.  Major Headings and Subheadings
         1.  Identifying Roman numerals at left margin (periods
             aligned) followed by 2 spaces
         2.  Identifying letters and numbers for each subsequent
             level of subheading aligned below the first word of
             the preceding heading, followed by 2 spaces
```

Outline 2
Format the outline on a plain full sheet.

SM: 1″; PB: line 10 (pica) or line 12 (elite); correct errors

```
                    EMPLOYMENT COMMUNICATIONS
                                              QS
 I.  PERSONAL DATA SHEET

     A.  Personal Information     lc
         1.  Name, address, and Telephone number
         2.  Social Security number (work permit number) if needed
         3.  Personal interests:  hobbies/recreational interests
     B.  Educational Information
         1.  Schools attended and dates of attendance
         2.  Special areas of study; activities; awards received
     C.  Work Experience
         1.  Jobs held; what you experienced; commendations
         2.  Volunteer work
 DS  D.  References (Teachers, Work Supervisors)
II.  LETTER OF APPLICATION

     A.  Source of Information about Job Opening
     B.  Expression of Interest in Being Interviewed for the Job
     C.  Brief Summary of Work Skills and How They Fit the Job
         1.  Special courses that are applicable to the job
         2.  Work experiences that make you qualified for the job
     D.  Request for Interview

III. THANK-YOU LETTER FOLLOWING INTERVIEW
 DS  A.  Appreciation for Courtesies Shown Dur(z→r)ing Company Visit
     B.  Positive Impressions of Company and Employees
     C.  Expression of Continued Interest in the Job
```

232b-236b (continued)

the workplace, the current problem of educating/training company personal with today's hardware and software is going to grow. In a recent study, one out of every there businesses surveyed reported trouble with getting the proper training (Stoltenberg, 1988, 63). Midwestern customers are not ~~one of the three having~~ among those reporting trouble because of the training available through the LC.

Benefits of Support Services

DS Customer surveys have shown that the level of customer satisfaction has increased since the implementation of training programs through the LC. The indirect advertising done by satisfied customers has resulted in increased revenues. **This fact is not surprising since positive word-of-mouth advertising** is one of the most powerful information sources for attracting potential customers; while negative word-of-mouth advertising can be one of the most destructive sources (Berkowitz, Kerin, and Rudelius, 1989, 104).

This word-of-mouth advertising is working for Midwestern. During the last 12 months, Sales Representatives has reported a much higher referral rate as well as in increased number of new contacts initiated through the customer. A large number of these contacts mention training as being an important factor in their decisions regarding equipment purchases. The LC is essential to making these sales.

Document 3
Agenda

LINDA HENRY
Office Supervisor

Format the attached agenda for the sales representatives meeting in July.

LH

Leaders: Key leaders by alternating periods and spaces, noting whether the first period is on an odd or even space. End leaders 2 or 3 spaces to the left of the beginning of the second column.

AGENDA

Business Meeting for Sales Representatives

8:30 a.m., July 15

DS

1. Greetings . . . . Sara C. Koontz, President
2. Proposed District Realignment . . Ann M. Jones, Vice President
3. New Product Presentations . . . .

   SuperStar Printer . . . . Lori A. Chin
   Werner II Computer . . . . . . Malcolm J. Deters

4. Computerized Expense Reporting . . Rhonda C. Little
5. Convention assignments . . . . . . Thomas M. Chaney
7. Adjournment
6. Incentive Program Changes . . . . Ann M. Jones

Lesson 57 Measurement

LL: 70
LS: SS

57a ▶ 6 Conditioning Practice

each line twice SS (slowly, then faster); DS between 2-line groups; if time permits, rekey selected lines

alphabet 1 Marvin, the tax clerk, was puzzled by the quaint antics of the judges.

figures 2 The shop is 278.4 meters long, 90.6 meters wide, and 13.5 meters high.

fig/sym 3 Guy Moss's order (#30-967) is for 42 almanacs, 15 atlases, and 8 maps.

speed 4 Vivian may go to the ancient island city by the lake to work for them.

| 1 | 2 | 3 | 4 | 5 | 6 | 7 | 8 | 9 | 10 | 11 | 12 | 13 | 14 |

57b ▶ 35 Check Formatting Skill: Unbound Reports

4 plain full sheets; correction supplies

1. Format and key the report in unbound style.

2. Format the reference list on a separate sheet.

REFERENCES

Hamel, Ruth. "Making Summer Earnings Work for You." <u>USA Weekend</u>, 2-4 June 1989, 10-11.

Kushner, John. <u>How to Find and Apply for a Job</u>. Cincinnati: South-Western Publishing Co., 1989.

3. If time permits, prepare a title page using your name and school name and the current date.

words

THE IMPORTANCE OF WORK EXPERIENCE 7

A part-time or summer job pays more than money. Although the money 20
earned is important, the work experience gained has a greater long-term 35
value when one applies for a full-time job after graduation from school. Job 50
application forms (the application blank and the personal data sheet) ask you 66
to list jobs you have held and to list as references the names of individuals 82
who supervised your work. As one young person was heard to remark, "You 96
can't get a job without experience and you can't get experience without a 111
job." That dilemma can be overcome, however, by starting to work early in 126
life and by accepting simpler jobs that have no minimum age limit and do not 141
require experience. 146

<u>Jobs Teens Can Do</u> 153

Start early at jobs that may not pay especially well but help to establish a 168
working track record: baby-sitting, delivering newspapers, mowing lawns, 183
assisting with gardening, and the like. Use these work experiences as spring- 198
boards for such later jobs as sales clerk, gas station attendant, fast food 213
worker, lifeguard, playground supervisor assistant, and office staff assistant 229
(after you have developed basic office skills). As you progress through these 245
work exploration experiences, try increasingly to get jobs that have some re- 260
lationship to your career plans. If, for example, you want a career involving 276
frequent contact with people--as in sales--seek part-time and summer work 291
that gives you experience in dealing with people (Hamel, 1989, 10). 305

<u>How to Handle Yourself on the Job</u> 318

Whatever the job you are able to get, the following pointers will help you 333
succeed in getting a good recommendation for the next job you seek. 347

1. Be punctual. Get to work on time and return from lunch and other 361
breaks promptly. 364

2. Get along well with others. Do your job well and offer to assist others 380
who may need help. Take direction with a smile instead of a frown. 394

3. Speak proper English. Teenage jargon is often lost on the adults who 408
are likely to be your supervisors. 416

4. Dress the part. Observe the unwritten dress code; dress as others on 430
the job do. Always be neat and clean. 438

references 487

Document 2
Report

<table>
<tr><td>

LINDA HENRY
Office Supervisor

Mr. Chaney would like the attached material prepared as a leftbound report. Correct any un-marked errors that you find as you key the docu-ment. The table insert and information for the reference page are shown below. *L H*

</td></tr>
</table>

Table Insert

<table>
<tr><td colspan="2">

LINDA HENRY
Office Supervisor

</td></tr>
<tr><td>Year</td><td>% Increase</td></tr>
<tr><td>1</td><td>2%</td></tr>
<tr><td>2</td><td>6%</td></tr>
<tr><td>3</td><td>12%</td></tr>
<tr><td>4</td><td>22%</td></tr>
<tr><td>5</td><td>33%</td></tr>
<tr><td colspan="2" align="center">*L H*</td></tr>
</table>

References

<table>
<tr><td>

LINDA HENRY
Office Supervisor

Berkowitz, Eric N., Roger A. Kerin, and William Rudelius. Marketing. 2d ed. Boston: Richard D. Irwin, Inc., 1989.

Romei, Lura K. "Pick a key—any key...." Modern Office Technology, March 1989, 12.

Stoltenberg, John."Turn-ing Problems Into Profits." Working Woman, May 1988, 63. *L H*

</td></tr>
</table>

LEARNING CENTER JUSTIFICATION

Justifying the existence of the company Learning Center is a rela-tively simple task. The growth rate of revenues for the 5-year period prior to the existence of the LC was 10% (2% per year). Since the LC was implemented 5 years ago, company revenues have increased significantly, as illustrated below.

(Insert Table)

Without the LC, this growth would not have been possible. More important, however, is the fact that the LC has been utilized ex-tensively during the past year and is an integral part of the projected growth. Without the support provided by the LC, the projected growth will not happen. Several recent articles docu-ment the need for providing quality training for personnel working with today's technology.

Need for Support Services

For most business organizations to be successful in the information age, it is critical that sophisticated technol-ogy (hardware and software) be operated by personnel who have been educated/trained to utilize the capabilities of the technology. Romei (1989, 12) believes that cor-porations need to recognize that putting computers on desks is only part of solving the technology puzzle. The other part is investing money to train personnel so they may be-come productive users of the investment in hardware and software. Through user training, the LC assures our clients a high return on their technology investments.

More businesses than ever are eager to tap into the productivity-boosting and cost-saving potential of new software and hardware. As more technology is introduced into

57c ▶ 9 Check Keyboarding Skill: Straight Copy

LL: 70 spaces; LS: DS
PI: 5 spaces

1. Take two 3′ writings on ¶s 1-2 combined; find *gwam;* circle errors.

2. If time permits, take a 1′ writing on each ¶ to build skill.

all letters used | A | 1.5 si | 5.7 awl | 80% hfw |

	gwam 3′	5′
In excess of a hundred different makes and models of personal com-	4	3
puters are now on the market. An amazing number of software packages	9	5
are available to use in them. Each software package has its own com-	14	8
mands to make an operating system work. Commands that are given in one	18	11
package often do not work for another program.	22	13
An operation guide usually is prepared for each disk package. The	26	16
guide shows you how to power up and power down the system, how to format	31	19
a disk, how to copy a disk if permissible, and how to perform various	36	21
other major functions of which the program is capable. It is necessary	40	24
to learn the commands required to make your program function.	44	27

gwam 3′ | 1 | 2 | 3 | 4 | 5
gwam 5′ | 1 | 2 | 3

ENRICHMENT ACTIVITY: Keyboarding Skill

Skill Comparison: Straight Copy

1. Take two 1′ writings on ¶ 1; find *gwam.*

2. Take two 1′ writings on ¶ 2; find *gwam.*

3. Compare the better *gwam* figures of the two ¶s.

4. Take two additional 1′ writings on the slower ¶; try to equal or exceed the best *gwam* achieved in Steps 1 and 2.

5. Take two 3′ writings on ¶s 1-2 of 57c above; find *gwam* and circle errors on each writing.

all letters used in the two paragraphs

| E | 1.2 si | 5.1 awl | 90% hfw |

¶ 1 Do you think it is all right to cheat as long as you do not get caught? Some people do. They think that what they get away with does not concern anyone except themselves. If you cheat to move ahead, you deny someone else the right to the prize, and that is wrong.

| A | 1.5 si | 5.7 awl | 80% hfw |

¶ 2 Some of the major rules by which we live have been devised to protect us from one another; that is, to prevent one person or group from taking unfair advantage of another person or group. Equally important tenets are intended to keep us from being unfair to ourselves.

232a-236a ▶ 5 (daily)
Conditioning Practice

Check each day to see that the equipment is in good working order by keying the lines at the right at least twice.

alphabet 1 To what extent was Kazumori involved with my projects before quitting?
figures 2 Please ship Order 1750 for 36 word processors, 49 desks, and 28 lamps.
fig/sym 3 Sales discounts (5%) in 1990 amount to $14,682, an increase of $1,735.
speed 4 If they go to the social with us, they may also visit their six girls.

| 1 | 2 | 3 | 4 | 5 | 6 | 7 | 8 | 9 | 10 | 11 | 12 | 13 | 14 |

232b-236b ▶ 45 (daily)
Document Production: Sales Department

Document 1
Simplified Block Letter
LP p. 15

LINDA HENRY
Office Supervisor

Here is a rough draft of a letter Mr. Chaney would like keyed in simplified block letter format. Since the letter will be sent to all sales representatives, we will do a mail merge using our sales rep address file. Key the letter address exactly as it appears on the rough draft. Mr. Chaney would like the following postscript included with the letter. "**Please notify me immediately if there are other items you would like included on the agenda for the business meeting.**" LH

Note: Key the letter address as shown with the variables keyed inside the <   >'s. If your machine does not have the <   > keys, use the (   )'s.

May 6, 19--

<Sales Representative>
<Address>
<City, State, and ZIP>

ANNUAL MEETING FOR SALES REPRESENTATIVES

The annual meeting for company sales representatives is scheduled for July 15. Please arrange your schedules so that you will be able to spend the ~~day~~ entire with us at corporate headquarters.

The business meeting for sales reps is scheduled for 8:30 a.m. in the conference room. District realignment, new expense reporting procedures, and incentive program changes will be discussed. Since these items have a major impact on all sales reps, you will want to be present. The afternoon ~~will~~ sessions are still being planned. You will receive a complete program within the next (2) Sp weeks.

I am looking forward to seeing you again on the 15th.

~~Sincerely your,~~

Thomas M. Chaney, SALES MANAGER

xx

Enclosure

c Ann M. Jones

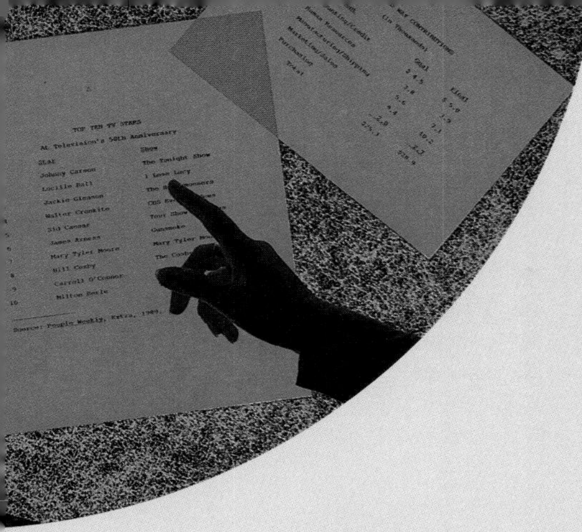

UNIT 11 LESSONS 58 – 64

Learn to Format Simple Tables

Learning Goals

1. To learn to center (format) 2- and 3-column tables.

2. To learn to align figures at the right (or at the decimal point).

3. To improve keyboarding skill on copy containing figures and symbols.

4. To improve language skills.

Format Guides

1. ***Paper guide*** at *0* (for typewriters).

2. LL: 70 spaces for drills and ¶s; as required for table formats.

3. LS: SS drills; DS ¶s; as required for table formats.

4. PI: 5 spaces for ¶s.

FORMATTING GUIDES: TABLES

Parts of a Simple Table

A table is a systematic arrangement of data, usually in rows and columns. Tables range in complexity from those with only two columns and a main heading to those with several columns and special features. The tables in this unit are limited to those with the following parts:

1. Main Heading (title) in ALL CAPS
2. Secondary Heading in capital and lowercase letters
3. Column Headings (blocked)
4. Body (column entries)
5. Source Note
6. Total line

The first tables to be formatted consist of only a main heading and two columns of data. The tables progress gradually in complexity so that, finally, they include three columns and several of the listed parts.

Spacing Table Parts

Short, simple tables are usually double-spaced (DS) throughout, but single-spaced (SS) column entries are acceptable. Keying all lines DS makes table processing easier, especially on computers which may require special commands to change line spacing within a document.

Horizontal/Vertical Placement of Tables

Tables are placed on the page so that the left and right margins (LM, RM) are approximately equal and the column spacing (CS), or number of spaces between columns, is exactly equal. This means that about half the characters and spaces in each line are at the left of horizontal center; about half are at the right. (Horizontal center is 42 for pica machines; 51 for elite.)

When prepared on separate sheets, tables are placed so that the top and bottom margins are approximately equal. This means that about half the lines are above vertical center; about half are below. (Vertical center of a full sheet is at line 33.) Tables that are placed slightly above vertical center (sometimes called the "reading position") are considered to look more appealing than those that are placed at or below exact vertical center.

BASIC UNITS OF METRIC MEASURE

Units and Names

Unit of length	meter (m)
Unit of mass (weight)	kilogram (kg)
Unit of temperature	kelvin (K)
Unit of time	second (s)
Unit of electrical current	ampere (A)
Unit of luminous intensity	candela (cd)
Unit of substance	mole (mol)

TOP TEN TV STARS

At Television's 50th Anniversary

No.	Star	Show
1	Johnny Carson	The Tonight Show
2	Lucille Ball	I Love Lucy
3	Jackie Gleason	The Honeymooners
4	Walter Cronkite	CBS Evening News
5	Sid Caesar	Your Show of Shows
6	James Arness	Gunsmoke
7	Mary Tyler Moore	Mary Tyler Moore Show
8	Bill Cosby	The Cosby Show
9	Carroll O'Connor	All in the Family
10	Milton Berle	Texaco Star Theater

Source: People Weekly, Extra, 1989.

Aligning Data in Columns

Words in columns are aligned at the left. Figures, however, are usually aligned at the right or at the decimal point. On typewriters, alignment is done by spacing forward or backward from the tab stops. With some computer software, aligning is done automatically; for other software, it is necessary to set tabs at the leftmost figure of the columns and space forward for the shorter entries. (See User's Guide for appropriate procedure.)

Note to computer users
If your printer has only full-sheet continuous-feed paper, center half-sheet tables vertically on the upper half of a full sheet (the top 33 lines). Alternatively, center all tables on full sheets (66 lines).

UNIT 55 LESSONS 232 – 236
Sales Department

Production Goals

1. To integrate knowledge and skills previously learned.
2. To improve the efficiency (speed and accuracy) with which you complete documents.
3. To improve ability to follow standard formatting guides.
4. To manage time wisely in the production process.

Documents Processed

1. Letters
2. Formal Memorandums
3. Tables
4. Leftbound Report with Internal Citations
5. Agenda
6. Invoice
7. Purchase Order

MIDWESTERN OFFICE PRODUCTS: SALES DEPARTMENT

Before beginning the documents on pages 399-406, read the copy at the right. When planning the assigned documents, refer to the formatting guides given here to refresh your memory about proper formatting and spacing of documents.

Work Assignment

One of the secretaries in the Sales Department quit yesterday without giving notice. Ms. Linda Henry, the office supervisor for the Sales Department, has requested the Information Processing Center (IPC) supervisor to provide a temporary replacement until a permanent replacement can be hired. Since your work in the IPC has been of such high quality, Ms. Reinhold has asked you to assist Ms. Henry.

The majority of the documents you process during this assignment will be for the sales manager, Mr. Thomas M. Chaney. Ms. Henry will attach written instructions for each of the documents you are to process.

You will be given the Sales Department's "Guide to Document Formats," which summarizes the formats used by Midwestern Office Products. Refer to this Guide as needed when processing the various documents. Personnel in the Sales Department use either the modified block letter style or the simplified block letter style. Ms. Henry will indicate the originator's preference with her written instructions. Since Midwestern Office Products has based its word processing manual on your textbook, you may also use the text as a reference when Ms. Henry's directions and the "Guide to Document Formats" are not sufficiently detailed.

When necessary, supply missing parts for documents. For some documents you will be required to use your judgment since specific formatting directions will not be given. Correct errors in punctuation, spelling, capitalization, etc. Proofread each document carefully (even if your equipment includes a spell-check program) to produce correctly formatted, error-free documents.

Guide to Document Formats

Use the following guides as a quick reference to document formats.

Memorandums--Formal
Stationery: forms with preprinted headings.
SM: 1″.
LS: DS between major parts of memo and between paragraphs. SS paragraphs.

Letters--Simplified Block
Stationery: letterheads.
SM: Set for 6″ line.
LS: SS with a DS between paragraphs.
PB: line 12.

Letters--Modified Block
Stationery: letterheads.
SM: short, 2″; average, 1½″; long, 1″.
LS: SS with a DS between paragraphs.
PB: short, line 18; average, line 16; long, line 14.

Reports--Leftbound
Stationery: plain sheets.
References: internal citations.
SM: left, 1½″; right, 1″.
PB (first page): line 10, 10-pitch;
line 12, 12-pitch.
PB (second page): line 6, page number;
line 8, text.
BM: at least 1″.
LS: DS text; SS tables.

Agendas
Stationery: plain sheets.
SM: 1″.
LS: DS, unless otherwise indicated.
PB: line 10.

Tabulated Documents
Stationery: plain full sheets.
LS: DS or SS, as indicated.
CV (center vertically).
CH (center horizontally).
CS: Even number of intercolumn spaces. Use more space between 2-column groups (when 2 columns are grouped under one common heading) than between individual columns.
Column Headings: Centered over column unless otherwise indicated. If 2 columns are grouped together below one heading, center heading over both columns.

58a ▶ 6 Conditioning Practice

each line twice SS (slowly, then faster); if time permits, rekey lines 2 and 4

alphabet 1 Tex just received quite a sizable rebate check from the wagon company.

figures 2 On June 23 she served 461 hamburgers, 597 sodas, and 80 bags of chips.

fig/sym 3 Invoice #14729 was paid by Byron & Gibb's check (#6058) on January 13.

speed 4 Did the chair signal the man to name the auditor of the downtown firm?

| 1 | 2 | 3 | 4 | 5 | 6 | 7 | 8 | 9 | 10 | 11 | 12 | 13 | 14 |

58b ▶ 9 Review Horizontal Centering

1. Set a tab stop at the horizontal center point of the paper.

2. Beginning a QS below your warm-up lines, center each line of Drill 1 horizontally, DS.

3. Center Drill 2 in the same way, a QS below Drill 1.

Drill 1

SCHOLASTIC AWARD WINNERS

David Crum

Flora Fuentes

Suzi Kwan

Christopher Leis

Drill 2

CENTERING CONCEPTS

Horizontal: side to side

Vertical: top to bottom

Horizontal center: half left; half right

Vertical center: half top; half bottom

58c ▶ 35 Learn to Format a Two-Column Table

half sheet (long edge at top); DS all lines

Automatic formatting
If your equipment has automatic centering and table formatting features, refer to your User's Guide to learn to format tables. Otherwise, follow steps at right.

1. Study the guides for vertical and horizontal centering given at right.

2. Using the model table on page 107, set LM to begin Column 1; set a tab stop for Column 2 with 10 spaces between columns (CS: 10).

3. Determine the line on which to place the heading of the DS table.

4. Format/key the model.

5. Proofread and check the formatting of your completed table; mark corrections; prepare a final copy with all errors corrected.

Vertical Centering (VC) of Tables

1. Count the lines to be keyed and the blank line spaces to be left between lines (1 blank line space between DS lines).

2. Subtract *lines needed* from *total lines available* (33 for half sheet; 66 for full sheet).

3. Divide the remainder by 2 to determine top margin. If the number that results ends in a fraction, *drop the fraction.* If an odd number results, *use the next lower even number.*

Example: lines available = 33
total lines needed = 13
20 ÷ 2 = 10

place heading on line 10

Horizontal Centering (HC) of Columns

1. Move margin stops to ends of scale.

2. Clear all tabulator stops.

3. Move printing point to horizontal center of paper, which is 42 for pica (10-pitch) machines and 51 for elite (12-pitch) machines.

4. If column spacing (CS) is not specified, decide how many spaces to leave between columns (preferably an even number).

5. Set left margin stop:
a. From horizontal center point, backspace once for each 2 characters and spaces in longest line of each column and once for each 2 spaces to be left between columns. If longest line in one column has an odd number of strokes, combine extra stroke with first stroke in next column, as in **check####proofread.**

◀ 1 1 1 1 1 1 1 1 1
ch|ec|kp|ro|of|re|ad|##|##

If you have 1 stroke left over after backspacing for all columnar items, disregard the extra stroke.
b. Set LM at point where all backspacing ends.

6. Set tabulator stop(s):
a. From LM, space forward once for each character and space in longest line of first column and once for each space to be left between first and second columns.
b. Set tab stop at this point for second column.
c. When there is a third column, continue spacing forward in the same way to set a tab stop for it.

231a ▶ 5 Conditioning Practice

each line twice SS (slowly, then faster); if time permits, rekey selected lines

alphabet 1 Avoid such fizzling fireworks because they just might explode quickly.
figures 2 Ava's three trips earned air mileage of 1,086, 1,923, and 1,475 miles.
fig/sym 3 The #5346 item will cost McNeil & Company $921.78 (less 10% for cash).
speed 4 Pamela may sign the form for the men to do the dock work for the city.

| 1 | 2 | 3 | 4 | 5 | 6 | 7 | 8 | 9 | 10 | 11 | 12 | 13 | 14 |

231b ▶ 18 Improve Straight-Copy Speed and Accuracy

1. Three 1′ writings on ¶ 1 for speed. **Goal:** Increase speed by 2-4 *wam.*
2. Follow Step 1 for ¶ 2.
3. Three 1′ writings on ¶ 1 for accuracy. **Goal:** No more than 1 error a minute.
4. Follow Step 3 for ¶ 2.
5. A 3′ writing on all ¶s.
6. Find *gwam;* circle errors.

all letters used | A | 1.5 si | 5.7 awl | 80% hfw |

gwam 3′

In today's automated office, integrated software can help not only 5 60
to save time but also to expand capabilities and improve the quality 9 64
of the final product. It enables an office worker to develop a spread- 14 69
sheet quickly, change that data into graph form, and then move the graph 19 74
into a report. In the report, text can then be used to analyze and give 24 79
additional meaning to the data shown in the graph. 27 82

This kind of integration can be realized in one of three ways: 31 86
with a single package, with a software series, or with an integrator 36 91
program. The single package is better than the other two because it 40 95
requires just a few steps to move data from one program to another. 45 100
The software series has separate programs, but they use common com- 49 105
mands for ease in moving the data. The integrator moves data between 54 109
unlike programs. 55 110

gwam 3′ | 1 | 2 | 3 | 4 | 5 |

231c ▶ 12 Check Language Skills

Most of the sentences at the right contain errors in number usage, spelling, or word choice, as labeled. Key each sentence, with the number and period, correcting errors in the copy and any keyboarding errors you may make.

Number usage

1. 22 seniors, 12 juniors, and 8 sophomores left on May tenth.
2. My address was 428 East Sixtieth Street; now it is 1 Park Place.
3. We purchased 12 computers, 6 printers, and 18 tables.

Spelling

4. My recomendation is that you select your categories soon.
5. Arrangments have allready been made to purchase the stationary.
6. Base your decision on experiance and careful analasis of the data.

Word choice

7. Did you hear that your required to choose your class ring today?
8. Want you speak to the heir of the property about cleaning the flue?
9. The bases of the recent duel was a disagreement about a loan.

231d ▶ 15 Assess Keyboarding Skill

Repeat 230d, p. 396, as directed.

Center

Main heading **YEARBOOK STAFF** DS

Body

Editor-in-Chief	Susan Druhan DS
Assistant Editor	Elizabeth Poole
Business Manager	Robert Banks
Photography/Layout	Denise Richardson
Advertising/Sales	Diane Blust
Advisor	Anthony Diaz

| 18 | 10 | 17 |

Two-Column Table Centered Vertically and Horizontally

Lesson 59 Simple Two-Column Tables

LL: 70
LS: SS

59a ▶ 6 Conditioning Practice

each line twice SS (slowly, then faster); if time permits, rekey lines 2 and 4

alphabet 1 Fine cooks brought piquant flavor to exotic foods with zesty marjoram.

figures 2 I reviewed 50 magazines, 127 books, 189 pamphlets, and 364 newspapers.

fig/sym 3 Items marked * (as PC-478* and WP-360*) were reduced 15% May 26, 1991.

speed 4 The panel may then work with the problems of the eight downtown firms.

| 1 | 2 | 3 | 4 | 5 | 6 | 7 | 8 | 9 | 10 | 11 | 12 | 13 | 14 |

59b ▶ 9 Review Procedures for Vertical/Horizontal Centering

half sheet (long edge at top); DS all lines

Using the model table above, see how quickly you can format and key the copy.

1. Review vertical/horizontal centering steps on page 106, if necessary.

2. Leave 12 spaces between columns (CS: 12).

3. Check work for proper placement. Is the heading on line 10? Are the LM and RM about the same width? Are there 12 spaces between columns?

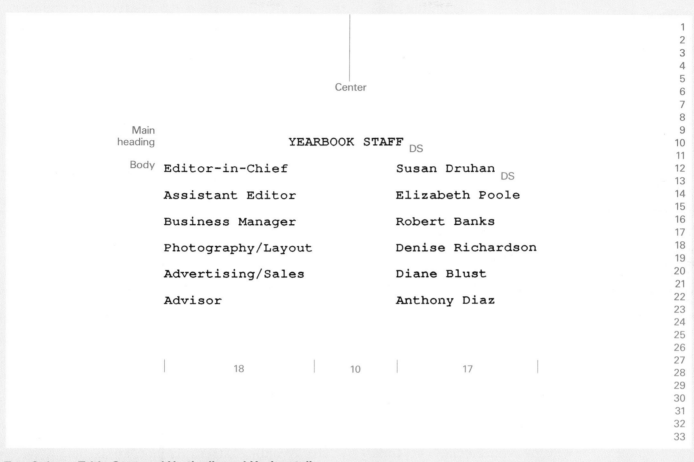

230c ▶ 12
Check Language Skills

The sentences at the right contain errors in punctuation, capitalization, and spelling, as labeled. Key each sentence, with the number and period, correcting errors in the copy as well as any keyboarding errors you may make.

Punctuation

1. Although Terry ran well he was beaten by Franklin, Julio and James.
2. Di, the chair of the committee collected reports from the members.
3. Efficient loyal employees are valued by most companies.

Capitalization

4. The President of the Latin Club called the meeting to order on time.
5. Will school be dismissed on president's day?
6. Here is my advice: exercise slowly at first and speed up gradually.

Spelling

7. The hotel was able to accommodate all of the corperate employes.
8. The bank was expecially pleased that the morgage was released.
9. The supervisor offerred technicle assistance on the project.

230d ▶ 15
Assess Keyboarding Skill

Two 5′ writings. Record *gwam*/errors for the better of the two writings on LP p. 1.

all letters used | A | 1.5 si | 5.7 awl | 80% hfw

Text	gwam 1′	5′	
Stress qualifies as either good or bad depending on the circum-	13	3	59
stances and ability of people to cope. It is good when it has resulted	27	5	62
from a pleasant event, such as a promotion. In addition, it may in-	41	8	65
crease job performance if the pressure is not too great. On the other	55	11	67
hand, stress is bad when caused by an unpleasant event, such as being	69	14	70
passed over for a prized promotion. Furthermore, it may interfere with	83	17	73
the performance of a task when the pressure is excessive.	95	19	75
The major point to recognize is that stress is quite normal and	107	21	78
will be experienced at times by all. Avoiding stress is not an issue,	122	24	81
but learning to handle day-to-day stress in a proper manner is. A few	136	27	84
methods that work are taking the time for regular exercise, getting	149	30	86
enough sleep, and eating well-balanced meals. These specific methods	163	33	89
relate to personal habits. In addition, using some stress reducers	177	35	92
that more directly relate to the job will also be helpful.	189	38	94
A good way to reduce stress in the office is to use techniques	201	40	97
known to improve time management. These include analyzing the tasks	215	43	99
performed to see if all are necessary, judging which ones are most im-	229	46	102
portant so that priorities can be set, and using most of the time to	243	49	105
do the jobs that are most important. Office workers who do not use	256	51	108
these procedures may expend considerable energy in less valuable tasks	271	54	110
and feel stressed when more important ones go unfinished.	282	56	113

gwam 1′ | 1 | 2 | 3 | 4 | 5 | 6 | 7 | 8 | 9 | 10 | 11 | 12 | 13 | 14

gwam 5′ | 1 | 2 | 3

59c ▶ 35 Format Two-Column Tables with Main Headings

2 half sheets (long edge at top), 1 full sheet; DS all headings and column entries

Table 1
Center table vertically on a half sheet; center horizontally with 10 spaces between columns (CS: 10).

PERSONNEL RECORD		words
		3
Employee Name	Jorge L. Ortega	9
Street Address	1624 Melody Drive	16
City	Midwest City	20
State	OK	21
ZIP Code	73110-2856	25
Telephone	733-1958	29

Table 2
Center table vertically on a half sheet; center horizontally with 12 spaces between columns (CS: 12).

Table 3
Reformat Table 2 on a full sheet with 14 spaces between columns (CS: 14). Correct all errors you make as you key. Keep the list and master the spelling of the words.

COMMONLY MISSPELLED WORDS		
		5
accommodate	corporate	10
adequate	customer	13
appropriate	electrical	18
categories	eligible	22
committee	employees	26
compliance	immediately	30
compliment	implemented	35
correspondence	international	41

Lesson 60 Simple Two-Column Tables

LL: 70
LS: SS

60a ▶ 6 Conditioning Practice

each line twice SS (slowly, then faster); if time permits, two 1′ writings on line 4

alphabet 1 A judge will quiz expert witnesses before he makes any vital decision.
figures 2 Please order 1,520 pencils, 894 pens, 350 file boxes, and 76 dividers.
fig/sym 3 Order #5-207 (May 24) from Kline & Co. totals $98.56, less 2/10, n/30.
speed 4 It is a civic duty to handle their problem with proficiency and vigor.

| 1 | 2 | 3 | 4 | 5 | 6 | 7 | 8 | 9 | 10 | 11 | 12 | 13 | 14 |

60b ▶ 10 Learn to Align Figures

QS below your drill lines in 60a; then key the drill at right twice SS, with 12 spaces between columns (CS: 12).

Computer users
Set a tab stop for the longest item in each column (after Column 1). To align the figures, space forward as necessary. (See your User's Guide for alternative procedures).

Typewriter users
Set a tab stop for the digit in each column (after Column 1) that requires the least forward and backward spacing to align the figures at the right. To align the figures, space forward ▶ or backward ◀ as necessary.

margin

492	—tab→	1640	—tab→	2288
63		930		826
110		4610		1049
374		475		638
85		928		1177
211		2017		405
KEY 3	12	4	12	4

UNIT 54 LESSONS 230 – 231
Improve Keyboarding/Language Skills

Learning Goals

1. To improve keyboarding speed and accuracy on straight copy.
2. To assess straight-copy speed and accuracy.
3. To check language-skills competency.

Format Guides

1. Paper guide at *0* (for typewriters).
2. LL: 70 spaces for drills and paragraphs.
3. LS: SS drill lines; DS paragraphs.
4. PI: 5 spaces for paragraphs.

Lesson 230 Improve Keyboarding/Language Skills

230a ▶ 5 Conditioning Practice

each line twice SS (slowly, then faster); if time permits, rekey selected lines

alphabet	1	Open your gift quickly, but avoid scuffing the floor Zelma just waxed.
figures	2	Flights leave for Denver at 6:48, 9:36, 10:27, and 11:56 each morning.
fig/sym	3	The coat costs $358.14 (with a 20% discount), and I have only $297.60.
speed	4	Did six or eight firms bid on the authentic map of the ancient island?

| 1 | 2 | 3 | 4 | 5 | 6 | 7 | 8 | 9 | 10 | 11 | 12 | 13 | 14 |

230b ▶ 18 Improve Straight-Copy Speed and Accuracy

1. Three 1′ writings on ¶ 1 for speed. **Goal:** Increase speed by 2-4 *wam.*
2. Follow Step 1 for ¶ 2.
3. Three 1′ writings on ¶ 1 for accuracy. **Goal:** No more than 1 error a minute.
4. Follow Step 3 for ¶ 2.
5. One 3′ writing on both ¶s.
6. Find *gwam;* circle errors.

all letters used | A | 1.5 si | 5.7 awl | 80% hfw

	gwam 3′	5′	
Some people seem to have a greater level of job stress than others,	5	3	35
and the reason for the differences may not be revealed by just a quick	9	6	38
observation. Without taking time to analyze a situation, one may assume	14	8	41
that the jobs of highly stressed people are much more demanding; but a	19	11	43
close examination may point out that the real discrepancy is in the way	24	14	46
people react to a potentially stressful situation.	27	16	48
For example, some job-related problems, such as the quality of	31	19	51
work performed by co-workers, cannot be resolved by the office worker.	36	22	54
The reaction of one person may be to recognize and accept the situation	41	25	57
whereas the reaction of another may be to worry about the dilemma. The	46	27	59
person whose attitude is to make the best of such a plight will likely	50	30	62
become less stressed than the one who worries.	53	32	64

gwam 3′ | 1 | 2 | 3 | 4 | 5
gwam 5′ | 1 | 2 | 3

60c ▶ 34 Format Two-Column Tables with Secondary Headings

2 half sheets (long edge at top), 1 full sheet

Table 1
Center table vertically on a half sheet; center horizontally with 8 spaces between columns (CS: 8). DS all headings and column entries.

		words
BASIC UNITS OF METRIC MEASURE		6
Units and Names		9
Unit of length	meter (m)	14
Unit of mass (weight)	kilogram (kg)	21
Unit of temperature	kelvin (K)	28
Unit of time	second (s)	32
Unit of electrical current	ampere (A)	40
Unit of luminous intensity	candela (cd)	48
Unit of substance	mole (mol)	54

Table 2
1. Center table vertically on a half sheet; center horizontally with 8 spaces between columns (CS: 8).
2. Set line spacing to SS the column entries; strike ***return/ enter*** key twice to DS below the headings and between classes of information.
3. Align figures at decimals.

> **Note**
> Because the figure "1" and the letter "l" are so similar, "L" is often used as the abbreviation for "liter."

Table 3
Reformat Table 2 on a full sheet with 10 spaces between columns (CS: 10). Correct all errors you make as you key.

		words
COMMON U.S./METRIC EQUIVALENTS		6
Approximate Values		10
1 inch	25.4 millimeters (mm)	16
1 inch	2.54 centimeters (cm)	22
1 foot	0.305 meter (m)	26
1 yard	0.91 meter (m)	31
1 mile	1.61 kilometers (km)	36
1 pint	0.47 liter (l or L)	42
1 quart	0.95 liter (l or L)	47
1 gallon	3.785 liters (l or L)	54
1 ounce	28.35 grams (g)	59
1 pound	0.45 kilogram (kg)	64

Lesson 61 Three-Column Tables

LL: 70
LS: SS

61a ▶ 6 Conditioning Practice

each line twice SS (slowly, then faster); if time permits, rekey lines 2 and 4

alphabet 1 Peter may quit cutting flax when jet black clouds cover the azure sky.
figures 2 I ordered 36 desks, 49 chairs, 15 tables, 80 lamps, and 72 file trays.
fig/sym 3 Su paid a $72.48 premium on a $5,000 insurance policy (dated 6/13/91).
speed 4 Eighty of the city firms may form a panel to handle the fuel problems.

| 1 | 2 | 3 | 4 | 5 | 6 | 7 | 8 | 9 | 10 | 11 | 12 | 13 | 14 |

61b ▶ 9 Build Skill in Formatting Tables

full sheet; CS: 10; DS all lines

Using Table 1 above, see how quickly you can format and key the copy.

1. Review vertical/horizontal centering steps on page 106 if necessary.

2. Check work for proper placement. Is the heading on line 24? Are the LM and RM about the same width? Are there 10 spaces between columns?

226b-229b (continued)
Documents 11 and 12
Tables

OLIVIA REINHOLD
IPC Supervisor

From the information attached, please process two double-spaced tables, one comparing the Star 6087 and EIT 621 (columns 1, 2, and 3) and one comparing the Star 6087 and the Elec II (columns 1, 2, and 4). OR

ELECTRONIC TYPEWRITER FEATURES

Features	Star 6087	EIT 621	Elec II
Basic Memory	31K	32K	32K
Upgradeable Memory	no	to 6~~5~~4K	no
Display	24 characters	40 characters	40 characters
Print Speed	16 cps	17 cps	17 cps
Maximum Writing Line	13.2"	14"	13.5"
Characters on Printwheel	92	100	92
Search Capability	yes	yes	no
Automatic Bold	no	yes	yes
Sheet Feeder	no	no	optional
Text Merging in Memory	no	~~no~~ yes	yes
Word Processor Upgrade	optinoal	no	optional
Suggested List Price	$899	$1,089	$1,285

Source: Electronic Typewriter Guide, 1992.

Document 13
Simplified Memo
plain paper

OLIVIA REINHOLD
IPC Supervisor

Please process this memo from **Carlos J. Menez, Director of Human Resources,** to **All Department Managers.** Date 1/20 OR

"Greater Graphics" is a half day seminar promoting the increased use of graphics with a desktop publishing system. This program is sponsored by Brooks Information Systems. It will be held on February 15, 19--, from 9:00am to 11:30am, at the Brooks Building, 450 Cedar Street, Room 618.

The fee for this seminar is $50 and will be paid from the HRD budget for the first twelve people making a reservation through my ofice.

Please disbribute this information to the people in your department who you think should consider attending.

61c ▶ 35 Format Three-Column Tables

2 half sheets, 1 full sheet
DS all lines; block column headings

Table 1
Three-Column Table with Total Line
half sheet; CS: 6

Note: Do not count $ as part of a column.

Keying *Total* Lines

1. Underline the last figures in the columns so that the underlines extend over the *Total* figures.
2. DS below the underlined figures.
3. Indent the word "Total" 5 spaces; key the totals; align figures at decimals.

UNITED WAY CONTRIBUTIONS

(In Thousands)

Department	Goal	Final	words
			5
			8
Department	Goal	Final	16
Accounting/Credit	$ 4.5	$ 5.0	23
Human Resources	3.8	3.9	28
Manufacturing/Shipping	5.6	7.1	34
Marketing/Sales	9.4	10.2	39
Purchasing	2.0	2.7	45
Total	$25.3	$28.9	49

Table 2
Three-Column Table with Source Note
half sheet; CS: 8

DS above and below the 1½" rule above the source note (15 underline spaces, pica; 18 underline spaces, elite).

HEISMAN TROPHY WINNERS

(Best College Football Player of the Year)

Year	Player	College	words
			5
			13
Year	Player	College	21
1984	Doug Flutie	Boston College	27
1985	Bo Jackson	Auburn	32
1986	Vinny Testaverde	Miami (Fla.)	39
1987	Tim Brown	Notre Dame	44
1988	Barry Sanders	Oklahoma State	51
1989	Andre Ware	Univ. of Houston	57

______________ 61

Source: The World Almanac, 1990. 71

Table 3
Reformat Table 1 on a full sheet with CS: 10. Correct all errors you make as you key.

Lesson 62 Two- and Three-Column Tables

LL: 70
LS: SS

62a ▶ 6 Conditioning Practice

each line twice SS (slowly, then faster); if time permits, two 1′ writings on line 4

alphabet 1 Zoya picked a bouquet of vivid flowers growing next to the jungle gym.
figures 2 Order 196 was for 38 vests, 72 jackets, 40 skirts, and 25 plaid suits.
fig/sym 3 I said, "The quiz covering pages 35-149 and 168-270 will be on May 5."
speed 4 She is to pay the six firms for all the bodywork they do on the autos.

| 1 | 2 | 3 | 4 | 5 | 6 | 7 | 8 | 9 | 10 | 11 | 12 | 13 | 14 |

62b ▶ 9 Build Skill in Formatting Tables

full sheet; CS: 10
DS all lines

Using Table 2 above, see how quickly you can format and key the copy.

1. Review vertical/horizontal centering steps on page 106 if necessary.

2. Check work for proper placement. Is the heading on line 22? Are the LM and RM about the same width? Are there 10 spaces between columns?

226b-229b (continued)

Documents 9 and 10
Letters LP p. 11-13

OLIVIA REINHOLD
IPC Supervisor

Please process the attached letter for **Miss Patricia S. Wilmer, Manager of Exhibits.** Send it to the addressee shown on the attached business card. Fill in the blanks as follows:

Paragraph 1, **Madison, Wisconsin**

Paragraph 2, **Tonya Swartz**

Date 1/20 OR

Thomas M. Imuta, President
Imuta and Barone Industries
414 Corydon Road
Eau Claire, WI 54701-6600

~~Integrated program.~~ Integrated ~~packages~~ software permit the creation, editing, and ~~integration~~ consolidation of text, graphics, spreadsheets, and data bases with much less effort than would otherwise be required. In particular, the editing of text should be ~~fin~~ completed at this stage ~~here~~ where it can be done much more efficiently than in the DTP program. Then the document is moved to the DTP program for farther manipulation.

DTP program.

Page layout and design are perfected in the DPT program. ~~Metzner (1988, 34) elaborates:~~ Text can be flowed around the various graphic presentations, such as charts, tables, and drawings. Headings and head lines can be sized and styled. Borders can be added and cover pages can be designed to generate professional-quality output (Metzner, 1988, 34).

OLIVIA REINHOLD
IPC Supervisor

Miss Wilmer would like another copy of the letter you just processed. She cannot remember the name of the office manager to whom you should send the letter, so use the salutation **"Ladies and Gentlemen"** and address the letter as follows:

Attention Office Manager
Wetherby and Associates
726 Alliance Road
Rockford, IL 61103-3799

Fill in the blanks as follows:

Paragraph 1, **Kansas City, Missouri**

Paragraph 3, **Al Davidson**

Date 1/20 OR

Thank you for stopping by our exhibit during the recent Office Systems Conference in ____________. We appreciate your interest in all of our new products.

Since you expressed interest in desktop publishing we are enclosing a ~~desktop publishing~~ report that may be helpful as you plan to ~~add~~ implement desktop publishing in your company. In addition we would like to give you and your company's most likely users an on-site demonstration of our DTP 8000 system.

____________ our Office Systems Consultant for your area, will call you next week to arrange a convenent time.

(Send a copy to consultant--Tonya or Al.)

62c ▶ 35 Build Skill in Formatting Tables

2 half sheets, 1 full sheet

Table 1
Two-Column Table with Source Note
half sheet, DS; CS: 14

Remember to DS above and below the 1½″ rule above the source note.

		words
PLAYS MOST OFTEN STAGED BY HIGH SCHOOLS		8
(Times Produced by Schools Surveyed)		15
You Can't Take It with You	42	21
Bye Bye Birdie	35	25
Arsenic and Old Lace	31	30
Guys and Dolls	27	33
The Music Man	24	37
____________		41
Source: International Thespian Society.		49

Table 2
Three-Column Table with Column Headings and Source Note

1. Center table on a half sheet with CS: 8.

2. Set line spacing to SS the column entries; strike ***return/enter*** key twice to DS above and below the headings and divider rule.

Table 3
Reformat Table 2 on a full sheet, but DS the entries and use CS: 10. Correct all errors you make as you key.

			words
JOHN R. WOODEN AWARD WINNERS			6
(Best College Basketball Player of the Year)			15
Year	Player	College	22
1984	Michael Jordan	North Carolina	30
1985	Chris Mullin	St. John's	37
1986	Walter Berry	St. John's	43
1987	David Robinson	Navy	49
1988	Danny Manning	Kansas	55
1989	Sean Elliott	Arizona	61
____________			65
Source: The World Almanac, 1990.			75

Lesson 63 Prepare for Measurement

LL: 70
LS: SS

63a ▶ 6 Conditioning Practice

each line twice SS (slowly, then faster); if time permits, rekey lines 2 and 4

alphabet 1 Chan just dropped a queer pink vase we got on sale for my next bazaar.

figures 2 What is the sum of 16 3/8 and 27 4/5 and 49 1/2 and 10 2/3 and 17 1/6?

fig/sym 3 There is a credit (on 3/9) of $481.23 and a debit (on 3/25) of $70.62.

speed 4 He may go with us to a small town by the lake to do the work for them.

| 1 | 2 | 3 | 4 | 5 | 6 | 7 | 8 | 9 | 10 | 11 | 12 | 13 | 14 |

63b ▶ 44 Prepare for Measurement

2 half sheets, 1 full sheet; correction supplies

correct errors

To prepare for measurement in Lesson 64, format and key each of the tables on p. 112 according to the directions given with the problems.

Refer to the centering guides on p. 106 as needed.

If you finish all the tables before time is called, start over with Table 1. Use a full sheet and DS all the lines.

226b-229b (continued)

Document 7
Purchase Order LP p. 9

> OLIVIA REINHOLD
> IPC Supervisor
>
> Please process this purchase order. I suggest that you verify the $ amounts by calculating extensions and the total.
>
> OR

MIDWESTERN OFFICE PRODUCTS
3871 BRIDGE AVENUE, DAVENPORT, IA 52807-7002 (319) 887-1462

PURCHASE ORDER

TWINING OFFICE SUPPLY
700 BROWN STREET
DAVENPORT IA 52802-4566

Purchase Order No.: ~~416221~~ 416368
Date: ~~July 10~~ January 20, 19--
Terms: 2/10, n,30
Shipped Via: Wayne Express

Quantity	Description/Stock Number	Price	Per	Total
~~10~~ 15 bx	File Folders--862-380-41	~~14.88~~ 15.10	bx	~~148.80~~ 226.50
12 dz	Pencils--862-T-860	1.39	dz	16.88
~~10~~ 12 dz	Razorpoint Pens--862-SW-BK	8.88	dz	~~88.80~~ 106.56
2 dz	Markers--862-04467	7.49	dz	14.98
10 bx	Staples--862-467	.71	bx	7.10
				~~269.26~~ 372.02

By ______________________

Document 8
Report

> OLIVIA REINHOLD
> IPC Supervisor
>
> Please prepare a final copy of this report. Insert the following items:
>
> Report Title: **DESKTOP PUBLISHING**
>
> Side Headings:
> Paragraph 3, **Hardware Requirements**
> Paragraph 4, **Software Requirements**
>
> Key **REFERENCES** a QS below the last line of body copy; begin list QS below head.
>
> "Desktop Publishing Drives a High-Tech Company." Modern Office Technology, May 1988, 80-88.
>
> Lloyd, Julian. "Desktop Publishing." Office Guide, July 1988, 62-63.
>
> Metzner, Kermit. "Desktop Publishing: Pretty as a Picture." Office Systems 88, March 1988, 33-38.
>
> OR

Desktop publishing (DTP), according to Metzner (1988, 34), allows in-house production of high-quality output that almost looks typeset. ~~reported Metzner (1988, 34).~~ Some of the benefits of in-house production include faster turnaround time, lowered production costs, increased control over the publication process and improved layout and design (Modern Office Technology, 1988, 80).

Although most automated companies own some of the components required for DTP, some hardware and software additions and/or modifications are usually necessary.

According to Lloyd (1988, 62-63, the hardware requirements include a personal computer with at least 512K of random-access memory (RAM) and graphics capability. He further indicates that a mouse, although optional is helpful. A mouse is described by Metzner (1988, 34) as a hand held device attached to the computer; it is used by moving the device around on a hard surface to reposition images and arrows or other indicators as well as to activate commands. The additional hardware required is a laser printer.

As a minimum, two kinds of software are needed for a DTP project. Ideally, an integrated program is used to create a document before it is transferred to the DTP program.

(continued, p. 393)

63b (continued)

words

Table 1
Two-Column Table with Main Heading
half sheet; CS: 12; SS column entries with DS below heading

OTHER OFTEN MISSPELLED WORDS		6
installation	previously	11
judgment	prior	14
monitoring	pursuant	18
opportunity	received	22
permanent	recommendation	27
personnel	reference	31
participants	similar	35
patient	successful	39
possibility	sufficient	43

Table 2
Two-Column Table with Main, Secondary, and Column Headings and Source Note
half sheet; CS: 8; DS all lines

∧	insert
sp	spell out
∾	transpose

TEMPORARY

MOST WANTED WORKERS 6

% of Companies Hiring 12

Job Clasification	%	20
Clercial/receptionist	87	25
Secretarial/word processing	75	31
Accounting/finacial	52	36
Data procesing	30	39
Engineering	14	42

________________ 46

Source: USA Today, April 24 1989. 55

Table 3
Three-Column Table with Multiple Headings and Source Note
full sheet; CS: 8; DS all lines

TOP TEN TV STARS 3

At Television's 50th Anniversary 10

No.	Star	Show	15
1	Johnny Carson	The Tonight Show	22
2	Lucille Ball	I Love Lucy	27
3	Jackie Gleason	The Honeymooners	34
4	Walter Cronkite	CBS Evening News	41
5	Sid Caesar	Your Show of Shows	47
6	James Arness	Gunsmoke	52
7	Mary Tyler Moore	Mary Tyler Moore Show	60
8	Bill Cosby	The Cosby Show	66
9	Carroll O'Connor	All in the Family	73
10	Milton Berle	Texaco Star Theater	81

____________ 84

Source: People Weekly, Extra, 1989. 92

226b-229b (continued)

Document 4
Report

> OLIVIA REINHOLD
> IPC Supervisor
>
> Please prepare this document as a report to accompany the memo from Mr. Chaney. Insert the following items:
>
> Report Title: LASER PRINTERS
>
> Side Headings:
> Paragraph 2, **Key Features of Laser Printers**
>
> Paragraph 3, **Major Advantages of Laser Printers**
>
> Key **REFERENCES** a QS below the last line of body copy; begin list a QS below head.
>
> OR

Key features and major advantages of laser printers should be given careful consideration when a new ~~one~~ printer is selected. #2 Some of the key features of laser printers are ~~discussed~~ identified by Hart (1988, 49, 51). They ~~are~~ include the ~~ability~~ capacities to print a wide range of fonts and type faces, to combine text and graphics, and to print "an entire page at a time, rather than character by charater or line by line" (Hart, 1988, 51). These capabilities offer ~~many~~ several printing advantages.

~~The~~ three major advantages of using laser printers are desktop-publishing capability, high-speed printing and high-quality printing. With desk top publishing, many companies have substantially reduced printing costs while maintaining high quality publications. And with an output speed of ten pages per minute, an acceptable office standard reported by Brindza (1988, 106), a large volum e of work can be processed ~~printed~~ by one printer.

Brindza, Stephen. "Advancing Technology Hones in on Printing." Modern Office Technology, October 1988, 102-106.

Hart, Roger. "Computer Printers: How to Choose One." Office Systems 88, October 1988, 48-52.

Documents 5 and 6
Tables

> OLIVIA REINHOLD
> IPC Supervisor
>
> This table was received from the Accounting Department with directions to prepare the table once with columns 1-4, including totals, and a second time with columns 1-3 and 5, omitting totals.
>
> Main Heading: NET CHANGES IN INCOME
>
> Secondary Heading: FY 1990-FY 1991
>
> Please DS each table on a full sheet.
>
> OR

Product Group	FY-1990	FY-1991	$ Change	%
Hardware	$3,636,482	$4,100,236	$463,754	12.8
Software	121,~~421~~ 386	166,281	44,~~860~~ 895	~~36.9~~ 37.0
Printware	56,223	41,862	(14,361)	-25.5
Instructoin	89,248	104,286	15,038	16.8
Supplies	21,224	27,864	6,640	31.3
Consulting	47,863	66,291	18,428	38.5
Total	$3,972,~~461~~ 426	$4,506,820	$534,~~359~~ 394	

64a ▶ 6 Conditioning Practice

each line twice SS (slowly, then faster); if time permits, two 1′ writings on line 4

alphabet	1	Al criticized my six workers for having such quick tempers on the job.
figures	2	Add 14 meters 25 centimeters, 89 meters 36 centimeters, and 70 meters.
fig/sym	3	Both start today (6/7): Tina Ho at $421.89/wk.; Vic Kuo at $10.53/hr.
speed	4	It is the wish of all of us to lend a hand to the visitor to the city.

| 1 | 2 | 3 | 4 | 5 | 6 | 7 | 8 | 9 | 10 | 11 | 12 | 13 | 14 |

64b ▶ 9 Check Keyboarding Skill: Straight Copy

1. Take a 1′ writing on each ¶; find *gwam;* circle errors.
2. Take a 3′ writing on the two ¶s combined; find *gwam;* circle errors.
3. If time permits, take an additional 1′ writing on each ¶ to build speed.

all letters used | A | 1.5 si | 5.7 awl | 80% hfw

	gwam 3′	5′
As you build your keying power, the number of errors you make is	4	3
not very important because most of the errors are accidental and inci-	9	5
dental. Realize, however, that documents are expected to be without	14	8
flaw. A letter, report, or table that contains flaws is not usable	18	11
until it is corrected. So find and correct all of your errors.	22	13
The best time to detect and correct your errors is while the copy	27	16
remains in the machine or on a monitor. Therefore, just before you	31	19
remove the copy from the machine or screen, proofread it and correct	36	21
any errors you have made. Learn to proofread carefully and to correct	40	24
your errors quickly. This is the way to improve your productivity.	45	27

gwam 3′ | 1 | 2 | 3 | 4 | 5 |
gwam 5′ | 1 | 2 | 3 |

64c ▶ 35 Check Formatting Skill: Tables

2 half sheets, 1 full sheet; DS all lines; correct errors

Table 1
Table with Main and Secondary Headings and Source Note

half sheet; CS: 18

		words
ENLISTED WOMEN IN UNIFORM		5
(Percent of Each Service Branch)		12
Air Force	13.2%	15
Army	11.0%	17
Navy	9.3%	19
Marines	5.1%	22
______		26
Source: Dept. of Defense, 1988.		32

Tables 2 and 3 are on p. 114.

226a-229a ▶ 5 (daily) Conditioning Practice

Key the lines at least twice a day to ensure that your equipment is working properly.

alphabet 1 Zack, be a good fellow and keep quiet as you relax to enjoy his movie.
figures 2 Of the 647 seniors and 893 juniors, 1,250 attended the prom last week.
fig/sym 3 List your expenses: taxi $59, air fare $260, mileage $37 (148 miles).
speed 4 Their visit may end the problems of the firm and make us a big profit.

| 1 | 2 | 3 | 4 | 5 | 6 | 7 | 8 | 9 | 10 | 11 | 12 | 13 | 14 |

226b-229b ▶ 45 (daily) Document Processing

Documents 1 and 2
Letters LP pp. 5-7

OLIVIA REINHOLD
IPC Supervisor

Process these letters for **Ms. Diane A. Palmer, Learning Center Director.** Provide missing letter parts, including a subject line. Use the date of **January 16, 19—** and the information below.

Mr. Reginald R. Gates
Office Manager
Tucker and James Trucking
2000 Adams Street
Davenport, IA 52803-8115

(A) **Document Maker**
(B) **February 10, 16, and 24**

Mrs. Doris C. Johnson
Administrative Vice President
Miller Construction Co.
750 North Colfax Avenue
Minneapolis, MN 55405-1004

(A) **Project Manager**
(B) **February 11, 17, and 25**

OR

Recently you expressed an interest in receiving information about our (A) Instructional Program for next month. We now have three sessions scheduled and hope that your new users of (A) will be able to participate in one of them.

The dates are (B) from 1:30 p.m. to 4:30 p.m. with an optional two-hour open lab following. All sessions will be held in our Learning Center at this location. All instructional materials will be provided; however, participants may wish to bring their (A) Operator's Manuals if they have already purchased the software.

The cost of this instructional program is $50 per person or $40 per person if three or more from your company register. The enclosed registration form should be completed and returned in time for us to receive it at least two days prior to the training session your users wish to attend. If you have questions, call me at (319) 887-1462.

Document 3
Simplified Memo plain paper

OLIVIA REINHOLD
IPC Supervisor

Key this memo to **All Sales Representatives** from **Thomas Chaney, Sales Manager,** whose secretary is ill. Date it **January 16, 19—.** OR

The enclosed report about laser printers ~~should~~ will be helpful to you when working with clients who should be thinking about updating their printers. ~~Although~~ Even though clients may not have mentioned the need for a new printer, simply describing the ~~main~~ key features and major advantages of a laser may cause your clients to start thinking about one.

I suggest that you give a copy of this report to every client who does not already have a laser printer. ~~It's~~ It is a good introductory sales piece.

I am sending a supply of about 100 copies. ~~If~~ When you need more, let me know.

64c (continued)

Table 2
Two-Column Table with Multiple Headings and Total Line
full sheet; CS: 8

HOW FAMILIES SPEND THEIR INCOME		words
(Showing Percent of Total)		6
		12
Item	%	15
Housing	30.3	17
Transportation	21.2	21
Food	14.8	23
Insurance and Retirement Plans	9.4	31
Apparel, Services	5.1	35
Savings	4.3	38
Other	10.2	41
Total	100.0	44

Table 3
Three-Column Table from Rough Draft with Source Note
half sheet; CS: 6; recall proofreader's marks below

∧	insert
sp	spell out
ℓ	delete and close

WORD SKATING CHAMPIONS — 6

Year	Men	Women	words
1985	Aleksandr Fadev, USSR	Katerina Witt, E. Germany	22
1986	Brian Boitano USA	Debbi Thomas, USA	31
1987	Bryan Orser, Can.	Katarina Vitt, E. Gerany	41
1988	Brian Boitano, USA	Katarina Witt, E. Germany	51
1989	Kurt Browning, Canada	Midori Ito, Japan	60

________________ 64

Source: The World Almanac 1990. — 74

ENRICHMENT ACTIVITY: Language Skills

Capitalization, Number Expression, and Word Choice

LL: 60 spaces; LS: DS

1. Read and key each line, making needed changes in capitalization, number expression, and word choice.

2. Check accuracy of work with your teacher; rekey any line that contains errors in rule applications.

1 if your going for a new goal, chose the goal with care.
2 they are do hear in an our for the banquet honoring athletes.
3 we must choose cheerleaders from only fifteen applicants.
4 i no your hear earlier then necessary; in fact, so am i.
5 mr. wojcik lead the choir in 4 of my favorite songs.
6 its their wish to live on cypress avenue in new britain?
7 your very fortunate to have mary ann for a sister.
8 if its up to me, i say let's go four the winning field goal.
9 i went to salem on monday; than on friday i went to boston.
10 we waited hear for half an our to here president bush speak.

UNIT 53 LESSONS 226 – 229
Information Processing Center

Production Goals

1. To follow carefully the standard formatting guides for processing documents.

2. To produce high-quality documents by proofreading and correcting all errors.

3. To work efficiently in completing the various documents assigned.

Documents Processed

1. Letters in Block Format with Open Punctuation

2. Simplified Memorandums

3. Unbound Report with Internal Citations

4. Tables with Blocked Column Headings

5. Purchase Order

MIDWESTERN OFFICE PRODUCTS: INFORMATION PROCESSING CENTER

Before beginning the documents on pages 390-394, read the copy at the right. When planning the assigned documents, refer to the formatting guides given here to refresh your memory about proper formatting and spacing of documents.

Work Assignment

Your first assignment with Midwestern Office Products is in the Information Processing Center (IPC) where you will work under the direction of Ms. Olivia M. Reinhold, the IPC supervisor. All documents that you process will be assigned by Ms. Reinhold and will be returned to her for approval before they are sent to the originator.

Along with specific document formatting guidelines, Ms. Reinhold gives you the following information and instructions.

The documents that you will process will be from handwritten and rough-draft copy, typewritten copy, and boilerplate. You may need to supply letter parts that have not been provided by the document originator, and you will have to correct language-skills errors that have not been marked for correction.

Unless otherwise instructed, use the formats described in the Guide to Document Formats.

Guide to Document Formats

Letters--Block Format, Open Punctuation

Stationery: letterheads.
SM (side margins): short, 2″; average, 1½″.
PB (page beginning): short, line 18; average, line 16.
Letter parts: all begin at LM (left margin).
LS (line spacing): QS below date and complimentary close; DS below other parts.
Attention line: first line of address.
Subject line: DS below salutation, ALL CAPS.
Enclosure notation: DS below reference initials.
Copy notation: DS below reference initials or below enclosure notation when used.

Envelope (Large #10)

Address placement: 5 spaces left of center.
Format: ALL CAPS, no punctuation.

Memorandums--Simplified

Stationery: plain sheets.
SM: 1″.
PB: line 10.
Memo parts: all begin at LM.
LS: QS below date and last line of body; DS below other parts.

Tables

LS: DS (body may be SS), including space above and below 1½″ divider line separating body and source note; underline last figure above totals.
CV (center vertically): calculate PB by subtracting lines used from lines available and dividing by 2; disregard fraction; if even number results, space down that number of lines; if odd number results, use next lower number and space down that number of lines.
CS (columnar spacing): 6 to 20 (even number).
CH (center horizontally): backspace from center once for every 2 strokes of longest line of each column and once for every 2 intercolumn spaces. Set LM (if the equipment you are using has an automatic centering feature, use it to determine the LM setting). From LM space forward once for each stroke in longest line of column plus once for each space in intercolumn. Set tab and continue spacing forward to set remaining tabs.
Column heads: blocked at LM and tabs.

Reports--Unbound

Stationery: plain sheets.
References: internal citations.
SM: 1″.
BM (bottom margin): 1″.
PB (first page): line 10, 10-pitch; line 12, 12-pitch.
PB (second and succeeding pages): line 6, page number. line 8, text.
LS: QS below main or secondary head; DS text.

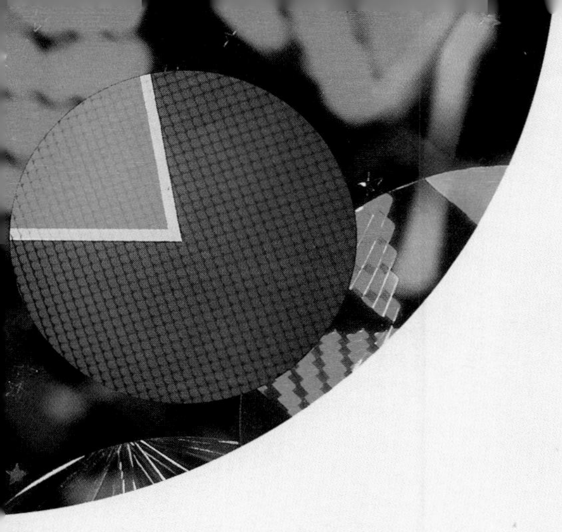

UNIT 12 LESSONS 65 – 67
Improve Keyboarding/Language Skills

Learning Goals

1. To improve keying technique.
2. To improve keying speed.
3. To improve keying accuracy.
4. To review/improve language skills.

Format Guides

1. ***Paper guide*** at *0* (for typewriters).
2. LL: 70 spaces for drills and ¶s.
3. LS: SS drills; DS ¶s.
4. PI: 5 spaces for ¶s.

Lesson 65 *Keyboarding/Language Skills*

LL: 70
LS: SS

65a ▶ 6 Conditioning Practice

each line twice SS (slowly, then faster); if time permits, two 1′ writings on line 4

alphabet 1 With quick jabs and deft parries, a young boxer amazed several people.
figures 2 Yuki keyed 51 letters, 84 envelopes, 37 tags, 92 labels, and 60 cards.
fig/sym 3 He's given me the numbers and prices: #16392, $48.30; #14593, $75.95.
speed 4 It is their duty to sign the amendment if he is to handle the problem.

| 1 | 2 | 3 | 4 | 5 | 6 | 7 | 8 | 9 | 10 | 11 | 12 | 13 | 14 |

65b ▶ 14 Improve Language Skills: Word Choice

1. Study the spelling/definitions of the words in the color block at right.

2. Key line 1 (the **Learn** line), noting the proper choice of words.

3. Key lines 2-3 (the **Apply** lines), choosing the right words to complete the lines correctly.

4. Key the remaining lines in the same way.

5. Check your accuracy; rekey lines containing word-choice errors.

to (prep/adj) used to indicate action, relation, distance, direction

too (adv) besides; also; to excessive degree

two (pron/adj) one plus one in number

sew (vb) to fasten by stitches

so (adj/conj) in the same manner or way; in order that; with the result that

sow (vb) to plant seed; scatter; disperse

Learn 1 Is it too late for the two of us to go to the two o'clock movie today?
Apply 2 I am (to, too, two) give everyone (to, too, two) cupfuls of beef soup.
Apply 3 We are going (to, too, two) the opera; Stan is going, (to, too, two).

Learn 4 He can sew the bags so that we can use them to sow the grass seed.
Apply 5 I can have them (sew, so, sow) the oats if you say (sew, so, sow).
Apply 6 The design is intricate, (sew, so, sow) I can't (sew, so, sow) it now.

65c ▶ 13 Improve Keyboarding Technique: Response Patterns

1. Key each line twice SS (slowly, then faster); DS between 6-line groups.

2. If time permits, take a 1′ writing on each of lines 3, 6, and 9; find *gwam* on each; compare rates.

letter response
1 were pump edge join gave milk bear pink fact upon draw jump ever union
2 red ink | get him | draw up | bad milk | gave him | draw upon | ever join | beat him
3 As we are aware, my union drew upon a few area data in a gas tax case.

word response
4 with they them make than when also work such form then wish paid their
5 rich girl | pays half | they also | busy firm | auto fuel | turn down | city panel
6 I paid the busy girls to make the six bus signs for the big city firm.

combination response
7 the pin | big ads | aid him | for oil | got you | oak bed | tie pin | and him | pay up
8 fuel test | busy area | city cars | held fast | then join | when safe | both serve
9 John is to sign the card and join the union with the rest of the crew.

| 1 | 2 | 3 | 4 | 5 | 6 | 7 | 8 | 9 | 10 | 11 | 12 | 13 | 14 |

LESSONS 226 – 250

PHASE 10

MIDWESTERN OFFICE PRODUCTS: COOPERATIVE WORK EXPERIENCE

You have been hired by Midwestern Office Products to work half days in a cooperative work experience program. Midwestern sells a wide range of automated office equipment, software, and printware. In addition, the company offers consulting services in selecting office systems and determining office layout. Midwestern also offers hands-on instruction in its Learning Center.

During the cooperative work experience, you will work first in the Information Processing Center (IPC) to become familiar with the kinds of documents processed by the company. Following that experience, you will work in the Sales Department replacing an employee who quit. You will also be asked to work in the Executive Office when the work load there becomes excessive. In these assignments, you will produce letters, reports, tables, and forms that require editing and revising to correct errors.

Throughout this work experience, you will continue to receive in-school instruction and drills to improve document processing productivity and language-skill development. In addition, you will learn to prepare employment documents and will take tests to establish your employability as an office worker.

65d ▶ 17 Check/Improve Keyboarding Skill

1. Take a 1′ writing on ¶ 1; find *gwam*.

2. Add 2-4 *gwam* to the rate attained in Step 1, and note quarter-minute checkpoints from the table below.

3. Take two 1′ guided writings on ¶ 1 to increase speed.

4. Practice ¶s 2 and 3 in the same way.

5. Take a 3′ writing on ¶s 1-3 combined; find *gwam* and circle errors.

6. If time permits, take another 3′ writing.

gwam	¼′	½′	¾′	1′
24	6	12	18	24
28	7	14	21	28
32	8	16	24	32
36	9	18	27	36
40	10	20	30	40
44	11	22	33	44
48	12	24	36	48
52	13	26	39	52
56	14	28	42	56

all letters used | A | 1.5 si | 5.7 awl | 80% hfw

	gwam 3′	5′
What is a job? In its larger sense, a job is a regular duty, role,	5	3
or function that one performs for pay. Therefore, when you apply for	9	6
and accept a job, you accept responsibility for completing a series of	14	8
specified tasks such as record keeping, word processing, and data entry.	19	11
What is a career? A career is a broad field in business, profes-	23	14
sional, or public life that permits one to progress in successive steps	28	17
up the job ladder. Whatever the tasks performed, one may have a career	33	20
in law, in health services, in education, or in business, for example.	37	22
It should be very clear that a career may include many jobs, each	42	25
with different ability requirements. Realize, however, that many of the	47	28
jobs leading to increasing success in most careers are better done with	51	31
greater ease by people who have built a high level of keying skill.	56	34

gwam 3′ | 1 | 2 | 3 | 4 | 5
5′ | 1 | 2 | 3

Lesson 66 Keyboarding/Language Skills

LL: 70
LS: SS

66a ▶ 6 Conditioning Practice

each line twice SS (slowly, then faster); if time permits, two 1′ writings on line 4

alphabet 1 Jan was very quick to fix many broken zippers for the bright children.

figures 2 The shipment included 162 sofas, 179 lamps, 104 desks, and 385 chairs.

fig/sym 3 Order the roll-top desks (57″ × 26″ × 48″) from Hermann's for $391.50.

speed 4 Rick may wish to go downtown by bus to pay a visit to a busy rug firm.

| 1 | 2 | 3 | 4 | 5 | 6 | 7 | 8 | 9 | 10 | 11 | 12 | 13 | 14 |

66b ▶ 14 Improve Language Skills: Word Choice

1. Study the spelling/definitions of the words in the color block.

2. Key the **Learn** lines as shown; key the **Apply** lines using the proper words to complete them correctly.

3. Check your accuracy; rekey lines containing word-choice errors.

buy (n/vb) a bargain; to purchase; to acquire

by (prep/adv) close to; via; according to; close at hand; at/in another's home

vary (vb) change; make different; diverge

very (adj/adv) real; mere; truly; to a high degree

Learn 1 She stopped by a new shop on the square to buy the new CD album.
Apply 2 We are to go (buy, by) bus to the ski lodge to (buy, by) ski togs.
Apply 3 Did you (buy, by) the new novel (buy, by) Margaret Atwood?

Learn 4 Marquis said it is very important that we vary our attack.
Apply 5 The (vary, very) nature of skill is to (vary, very) the response.
Apply 6 As you (vary, very) input, you get (vary, very) different results.

225b (continued)

Document 3
Invoice
LP p. 219
Prepare an invoice from the information at the right.

words

CENTRAL COMPUTER SUPPLIES
210 Lincoln Street Columbia, SC 29201-1342
Tel: (803) 991-3582 FAX: (803) 892-4974

INVOICE

PEOPLE'S HOME SAVINGS ASSN — Date: September 19, 19-- 9
3287 RIVER DRIVE — Customer Order No.: 5X43-2 13
COLUMBIA SC 29201-1342 19

Terms	Shipped Via	Our Order No.	Date Shipped	words
3/10, n/30	*Ruby Transport*	D-75-466	*9/20/--*	27

Quantity	Description/Stock No.	Unit Price		Amount		words
6	Computer Dustcover {C12B-878}	7	95	*47*	*70*	36
1	CPU Floor Stand {C12B-852}	50	95	*50*	*95*	44
6	Screen Filter {C12B-874}	45	45	*272*	*70*	53
4	Keyboard Storage Drawer {C12B-897}	82	95	*331*	*80*	63
2	Cable Manager {C12B-861}	37	95	*75*	*90*	72
				779	*05*	74
	Sales Tax			*46*	*74*	78
				825	*79*	80

Document 4
Invoice
LP p. 219
Prepare an invoice from the information at the right.

Document 5
Invoice
LP p. 221
Use the information below and on the purchase order you prepared in Document 2 to process an invoice. Address it to
ADVERTISING SPECIALISTS
2065 ARTHUR AVENUE
TROY MI 48083-2502
Date it **July 25, 19--.** Add 6% sales tax of **$9.98.** Use our order no. **936-81-A.** Use ship date of **7/23/--.**
Total words: 80
If you complete Documents 1-5 before time is called, start over. Use LP p. 221.

DELRAY TIRE & AUTO CENTER
155 Erie Street Marquette, MI 49855-1317 (616) 342-9185

INVOICE

EVERETT CONSTRUCTION CO — Date: October 1, 19-- 8
1079 ALTAMONT STREET — Customer Order No.: A-54-92 12
MARQUETTE MI 49855-4945 19

Terms	Shipped Via	Our Order No.	Date Shipped	words
5/10, n/30	Customer Pick Up	2245-12	9/25/--	28

Quantity	Description/Stock No.	Unit Price		Amount		words
4	Treadloc Truck Tires {95-a65921t}	105	99	423	96	38
4	All-Terrain *Truck* Tires {95-A58312C}	49	99	199	96	48
1	Ace Heavy-Duty Bat*t*ery {28-A9609B} *9*	59	99	59	99	59
				683	*91*	61
	Sales Tax			*41*	*03*	65
				724	*94*	66

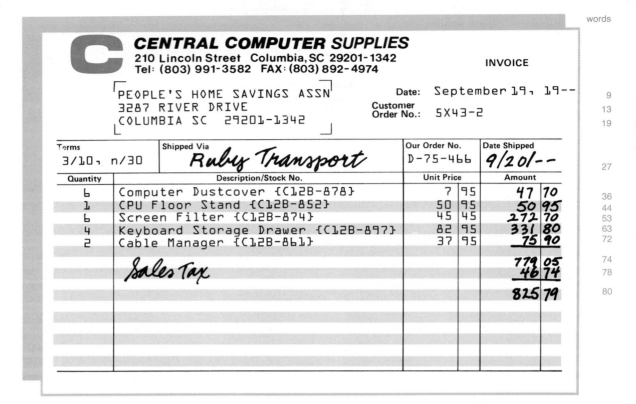

66c ▶ 13 Improve Keyboarding Technique

1. Key each line twice SS; DS between 2-line groups.

2. Take a 1′ writing on each of lines 2, 4, 6, 8, and 10.

Space bar (quick down-and-in thumb motion)

1 All the men on the quay may go by bus to the town on the lake to work.
2 Jan may do key work for the six men on the audit of the big city firm.

Shift keys (finger reaches to shift keys)

3 Spiro and Jacki left with Epson and Lana for a trip to Padua and Rome.
4 Mars leaves for Bora Bora in March; Nancy goes to Lake Worth in April.

Adjacent-key reaches (fingers curved and upright)

5 Luis was the last guy to be weighed in before stadium practice opened.
6 We are to open a shop by the stadium to offer the best sporting goods.

Long direct reaches with same finger (quiet hands and arms)

7 Myra broke my gym record to receive a bronze medal at the county meet.
8 Eunice brought a recorder to music hall to record my recital of hymns.

Balanced-hand sentences (word response)

9 Both of them may also wish to make a formal bid for the big auto firm.
10 I wish to do the work so the girls may go with them to make the signs.

| 1 | 2 | 3 | 4 | 5 | 6 | 7 | 8 | 9 | 10 | 11 | 12 | 13 | 14 |

66d ▶ 17 Check/Improve Keyboarding Skill

1. Take a 1′ writing on ¶ 1; find *gwam.*

2. Add 2-4 *gwam* to the rate attained in Step 1, and note quarter-minute check points from the table below.

3. Take two 1′ guided writings on ¶ 1 to increase speed.

4. Practice ¶s 2 and 3 in the same way.

5. Take a 3′ writing on ¶s 1-3 combined; find *gwam* and circle errors.

6. If time permits, take another 3′ writing.

gwam	¼′	½′	¾′	1′
24	6	12	18	24
28	7	14	21	28
32	8	16	24	32
36	9	18	27	36
40	10	20	30	40
44	11	22	33	44
48	12	24	36	48
52	13	26	39	52
56	14	28	42	56

all letters used | A | 1.5 si | 5.7 awl | 80% hfw |

	gwam 3′	5′
In deciding upon a career, learn as much as possible about what	4	3
individuals in that career do. For each job class, there are job re-	9	5
quirements and qualifications that must be met. Analyze these tasks	13	8
very critically in terms of your personality and what you like to do.	18	11
A high percentage of jobs in major careers demand education or	22	13
training after high school. The training may be very specialized, re-	27	16
quiring intensive study or interning for two or more years. You must	32	19
decide if you are willing to expend so much time and effort.	36	21
After you have decided upon a career to pursue, discuss the choice	40	24
with parents, teachers, and others. Such people can help you design a	45	27
plan to guide you along the series of steps required in pursuing your	49	30
goal. Keep the plan flexible and change it whenever necessary.	54	32

gwam 3′ | 1 | 2 | 3 | 4 | 5 |
5′ | 1 | 2 | 3 |

225b ▶ 45 Evaluate Production Skill: Business Forms

LP pp. 217-221

Time Schedule

Plan and prepare .... 5′
Timed production........30′
Proofread; compute *n-pram*.....10′

1. Arrange materials for ease of handling.

2. Format and key Documents 1-4 for 30′. Proofread and correct errors before removing each form from the machine.

3. After time is called (30′), proofread again and circle any uncorrected errors. Compute *n-pram*.

Document 1
Purchase Requisition

LP p. 217

Prepare a purchase requisition from the information at the right.

words

ADVERTISING SPECIALISTS
2065 ARTHUR AVENUE | PHONE: (313) 485-6091
TROY, MI 48083-2502 | FAX: (313) 485-5575

PURCHASE REQUISITION

Deliver to: Sean Curry — Requisition No. M-25-J 4
Location: Mailroom — Date July 9, 19-- 8
Job No. M-170-J — Date Required August 1, 19-- 13

Quantity	Description	words
6 rolls	Mailroom Tape, 2" X 60 yds.	20
7 boxes	Packing List Tape Pads	26
2 rolls	Filament Tape, ½" X 36 yds.	34
3 boxes	Self-Seal Mailers, 10½" X 16"	42
4 boxes	Clasp Envelopes, 9" X 12"	49

Requisitioned by: John Assini 51

Document 2
Purchase Order

LP p. 217

Prepare a purchase order from the information at the right.

ADVERTISING SPECIALISTS
2065 ARTHUR AVENUE | PHONE: (313) 485-6091
TROY, MI 48083-2502 | FAX: (313) 485-5575

PURCHASE ORDER

D&F OFFICE SUPPLIES
46500 NEWTON STREET
WAYNE MI 48188-1630

Purchase Order No.: B-4932-6 2
Date: July 11, 19-- 9
Terms: 5/10, n/30 15
Shipped Via: Harper Express 22

Quantity	Description/Stock Number	Price		Per	Total		words
6 rolls	Mailroom Tape (3750)	3	19	ea	19	14	31
7 boxes	Packing List Tape Pads (824-P)	6	09	bx	42	63	42
2 rolls	Filament Tape (898)	2	99	ea	5	98	50
3 boxes	Self-Seal Mailers (18-288)	21	25	bx	63	75	60
4 boxes	Clasp Envelopes (37790)	8	69	bx	34	76	71
					166	26	72

By ______________________

Documents 3-5 are on page 387.

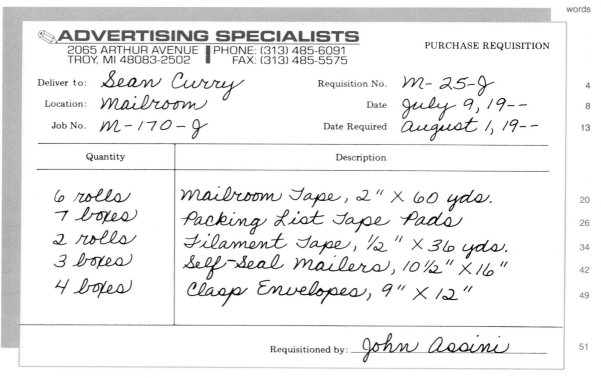

67a ▶ 6 Conditioning Practice

each line twice SS (slowly, then faster); if time permits, two 1′ writings on line 4

alphabet 1 The blitz vexed the famous quarterback whose game plan just went awry.

figures 2 Today we keyed 40 letters, 15 reports, 369 orders, and 278 statements.

fig/sym 3 Make finger reaches (hands quiet) to key 303#, 126.95%, and $1.475.98.

speed 4 He may hand me the clay and then go to the shelf for the die and form.

| 1 | 2 | 3 | 4 | 5 | 6 | 7 | 8 | 9 | 10 | 11 | 12 | 13 | 14 |

67b ▶ 14 Improve Language Skills: Word Choice

1. Study the spelling/definitions of the words in the color block.

2. Key the **Learn** lines as shown; key the **Apply** lines using the proper words to complete them correctly.

3. Check your accuracy; rekey lines containing word-choice errors.

passed (vb) past tense of *pass;* already occurred; gave an item to someone

past (adv/adj/prep/n) gone or elapsed; time gone by; moved by

some (n/adv) unknown or unspecified unit or thing; to a degree or extent

sum (n/vb) the whole amount; the total; to find a total; summary of points

Learn 1 In the past we passed the church before we marched past the library.

Apply 2 As we (passed, past) in our tests, we filed (passed, past) the teacher.

Apply 3 In the (passed, past) month, I have (passed, past) up two new jobs.

Learn 4 The problem was to find the sum, but some of the students couldn't.

Apply 5 "In (some, sum)," she said, "both ideas are true to (some, sum) degree."

Apply 6 I bought (some, sum) pears and apples for the (some, sum) of $2.30.

67c ▶ 13 Improve Keyboarding Speed: Skill Transfer

LL: 60 spaces; LS: DS

1. Take a 1′ writing on each ¶; find *gwam* on each.

2. Compare the *gwam* figures to identify the two slower ¶s.

3. Take two more 1′ writings on each of the two slower ¶s, trying to equal your *gwam* on the fastest ¶.

4. Take another 1′ writing on each ¶; find *gwam* on each.

Goals
¶ 2: 80% of ¶ 1 *gwam*
¶ 3: 90% of ¶ 1 *gwam*

Each ¶ is of average difficulty. Differences in speed, therefore, should result from the form in which the copy is presented:
- straight copy
- rough-draft copy
- script copy

gwam 1′ | 2′

As you prepare for your chosen career, try to talk with 11 6
as many individuals as possible who are in that career. If 23 12
you exhibit interest in the tasks these people perform on a 35 18
regular basis, they will answer questions and volunteer in- 47 24
formation that is hard to obtain in any other way. In this 59 30
continuing process, you may acquire vital job leads. 69 35

Whether you must ~~have to~~ earn money or not, make part-time or 11 40
summer work a part of your career plan. A carefully chosen 22 46
work experience can offer opportunities ~~many chances~~ to meet workers in 34 52
your career field and to observe firsthand ~~directly~~ many of the activi- 47 58
ties and features of the jobs related to that field. You can 59 64
make such work a valuable career learning experience. 70 70

Do not expect your first position to be near the top of 11 75
your chosen career ladder. Although you may not be required 23 81
to begin at the very bottom rung, realize that you have to 35 87
demonstrate your capability of performing at a higher level 47 93
before you will be placed there. To advance in your chosen 59 99
career, you must gain related experience of increasing value. 71 105

224b (continued)

Table 3
4-Column Table
Key the table at the right; DS body; CS: 6 between Columns 1 & 2; 10 between Columns 2 & 3; 6 between Columns 3 & 4.

words

MARCH BIRTHDATES 3

(Includes Employees as of 2/15/--) 10

Employee	Birthdate	Employee	Birthdate	25
Eleanor Byer	3/2/42	Jordan Brown	3/15/51	33
Royce McKnight	3/2/35	Nydia Ros	3/17/64	41
Judith Zupi	3/4/55	Kasi Jamshidi	3/24/70	49
Michele Linmar	3/5/68	Paul Lang	3/25/57	57
Sandy Testa	3/7/32	Brett Medich	3/29/49	65
Anna Alams	3/9/45	Ryan Notaro	3/31/62	73

Table 4
3-Column Table with Source Note
Key the table at the right; DS body; CS: 10.

OLDEST U.S. COLLEGES AND UNIVERSITIES 8

Name	Location	Year	15
Harvard University	Cambridge, Mass.	1636	23
William and Mary College	Williamsburg, Va.	1693	32
Yale University	New Haven, Conn.	1701	40
Princeton University	Princeton, N.J.	1746	48
Columbia University	New York, N.Y.	1754	56
University of Pennsylvania	Philadelphia, Pa.	1756	66
Brown University	Providence, R.I.	1764	74
Rutgers University	New Brunswick, N.J.	1766	83
Dartmouth College	Hanover, N.H.	1769	90

____________________ 94

Source: The World Book Encyclopedia. 106

Lesson 225 Evaluation: Business Forms

225a ▶ 5 Conditioning Practice

each line twice SS (slowly, then faster); if time permits, take 1′ writings on line 3

alphabet 1 Marji plans to study her new notes before taking the next civics quiz.
figures 2 I would like to have 875-4210 or 875-3690 for my new telephone number.
symbols 3 Practice the percent (%), asterisk (*), dollar ($), and ampersand (&).
speed 4 The busy fieldhand kept the fox in a pen to keep it cozy and in sight.

| 1 | 2 | 3 | 4 | 5 | 6 | 7 | 8 | 9 | 10 | 11 | 12 | 13 | 14 |

67d ▶ 17 Check/Improve Keyboarding Skill

1. Take a 1′ writing on ¶ 1; find *gwam.*

2. Add 2-4 *gwam* to the rate attained in Step 1, and note quarter-minute checkpoints from the table below.

3. Take two 1′ guided writings on ¶ 1 to increase speed.

4. Practice ¶s 2 and 3 in the same way.

5. Take a 3′ writing on ¶s 1-3 combined; find *gwam* and circle errors.

6. If time permits, take another 3′ writing.

gwam	1/4′	1/2′	3/4′	1′
24	6	12	18	24
28	7	14	21	28
32	8	16	24	32
36	9	18	27	36
40	10	20	30	40
44	11	22	33	44
48	12	24	36	48
52	13	26	39	52
56	14	28	42	56

all letters used | A | 1.5 si | 5.7 awl | 80% hfw |

	gwam 3′	5′
For many people in the early part of the century, staying in the	4	3
same job with a single company or institution for their entire produc-	9	5
tive lives was not too uncommon. Now it is thought that many fledgling	14	8
workers will switch jobs several times in their working lifetimes.	18	11
The pace of change in the national job arena today requires that	23	14
all people prepare themselves to move upward or outward in the same com-	27	16
pany or from firm to firm. Such moves demand widened experience and	32	19
education. Often the moves result in better pay and benefits.	36	22
So do not envision your diploma or your initial job as the end of	40	24
anything. Recognize that they are merely milestones in the ongoing	45	27
process of preparing for a richer, more responsible life. Living is a	50	30
process of becoming rather than a state of being.	53	32

gwam 3′ | 1 | 2 | 3 | 4 | 5
gwam 5′ | 1 | 2 | 3

ENRICHMENT ACTIVITY: Language Skills Checkup

LL: 70 spaces
LS: SS; DS between groups

1. Lines 1-7: As you key each line, select the words that correctly complete the sentence.

2. Lines 8-14: As you key each line, supply capitalization where needed.

3. Lines 15-20: As you key each line, express numbers correctly.

1 He (passed, past) the ball just as the receiver ran (passed, past) me.
2 (Its, It's) up to them to (do, due) the work required to win the prize.
3 She is (to, too, two) small (to, too, two) play on the varsity squad.
4 We (sew, so, sow) seed in the fall (sew, so, sow) we have early grass.
5 They want (vary, very) much to (buy, by) a new car (buy, by) spring.
6 More (than, then) an (hour, our) passed before the bus arrived.
7 (Choose, Chose) the right one, since (your, you're) the leader.

8 ms. barnes visited the eiffel tower in paris when she was in france.
9 the senior class will have its prom at the skirvin hotel this fall.
10 maria, frederic, and joanna comprise this year's prom committee.
11 on labor day we had a picnic in sloan park, followed by a ball game.
12 "how often," she asked, "do you watch the san diego chargers on TV?"
13 did you write the check to stephen p. kendall, d.d.s.?
14 we took wilshire boulevard to the beverly wilshire hotel yesterday.

15 15 members of the Drama Club attended the meeting; 4 did not.
16 She took the eight thirty a.m. shuttle; I met her at Gate twenty-nine.
17 Kenney Center is at One 4th Street; Keyes Tower, at 4 Kyles Lane.
18 Your article will appear on pages three and four of the next issue.
19 I answered Questions 1-10 on page nine and Questions 1-5 on page 18.
20 The committee met in Room ten at three p.m. on November fifteenth.

224a ▶ 5 Conditioning Practice

each line twice SS (slowly, then faster); if time permits, take 1′ writings on line 2

alphabet 1 Patrick will come back to judge the quality of the next seven waltzes.

figures 2 Tina surveyed 3,657 women, 2,980 men, and 1,940 children last January.

fig/sym 3 Buy 13 color #620-X monitors and 9 #478-A CPU's and get a 5% discount.

speed 4 Their city auditor may fish off the dock at the lake by the cornfield.

| 1 | 2 | 3 | 4 | 5 | 6 | 7 | 8 | 9 | 10 | 11 | 12 | 13 | 14 |

224b ▶ 45 Evaluate Production Skill: Tables

Time Schedule
Plan and prepare .... 5′
Timed production .... 30′
Proofread; compute *n-pram* .... 10′

1. Arrange 4 full sheets for ease of handling.

2. Format and key Documents 1-4 for 30′. Proofread and correct errors before removing each table from the machine.

3. After time is called (30′), proofread again and circle any uncorrected errors. Compute *n-pram.*

Table 1
3-Column Table with Total Line
Key the table at the right; DS; CS: 10.

			words
TEN LARGEST AREA ADVERTISING AGENCIES			8
Ranked by Millions of Dollars in Billings			16
Name	Billings	Employees	25
Carlson Advertising	$118.5	202	32
Robert Harn Agency	104	158	37
HARR Advertising	55.8	95	42
Rendar-Gazdacko	21.~~0~~9	25	47
Crea, Peake, & Weisz Inc.	16.4	36	54
Sundy Group	13.5	35	58
Park/Vladnoski	13.3	24	62
DeMark Communications	12	42	68
Cavicchia Group	11.1	27	73
Abdel Kamal Agency	10	18	80
Total	$375.6	662	84

Table 2
4-Column Ruled Table
Key the table at the right; DS body; CS: 6.

PRINTING BIDS RECEIVED				5
For 19-- Sales Catalog				9
				22
Firm	Contact	Telephone	Bid	27
				39
DataPrint	John Wolff	221-3300	$30,970	47
Beyer Printing	Sig Beyer	829-6143	29,450	56
Typeset Press	E. V. Henry	247-7000	29,250	64
Reed & Park	A. J. Reed	682-3633	28,540	72
Publisher's Choice	Bob Arch	241-8200	27,985	81
Copy Mate	Val Mejeas	243-8010	27,750	88
VIP Press	Peg Scott	362-6700	26,450	95
				107

UNIT 13 *LESSONS 68 – 69*

Prepare for Measurement

Learning/Review Goals

1. To improve keyboarding skills.
2. To review/improve language skills.
3. To review formatting guides and procedures for letters, memos, tables, reports and outlines.
4. To demonstrate skill in formatting letters, memos, tables, reports and outlines.

Format Guides

1. ***Paper guide*** at *0* (for typewriters).
2. LL: 70 spaces for drills and ¶s; as required for document formats.
3. LS: SS drills; DS ¶s; as required for document formats.
4. PI: 5 spaces for ¶s and reports.

Lesson 68 *Prepare for Measurement*

LL: 70
LS: SS

68a ▶ 5 Conditioning Practice

each line twice SS (slowly, then faster); if time permits, rekey line 4

alphabet 1 Five excellent joggers pounded quickly along the beach in a warm haze.
figures 2 They replaced at cost 50 plates, 78 knives, 194 forks, and 362 spoons.
fig/sym 3 The Roe & Son check, dated May 17, should be $45.39 instead of $62.80.
speed 4 She may cycle to the city to go to the ancient chapel by the big lake.

| 1 | 2 | 3 | 4 | 5 | 6 | 7 | 8 | 9 | 10 | 11 | 12 | 13 | 14 |

68b ▶ 15 Improve Language Skills: Word Choice

1. Study the spelling/definitions of the words in the color block at right.
2. Key line 1 (the **Learn** line), noting the proper choice of words.
3. Key lines 2-4 (the **Apply** lines), choosing the right words to complete the lines correctly.
4. Key the remaining **Learn/Apply** lines in the same way.
5. Key the **Review** lines, inserting the proper words to complete each sentence correctly.
6. Check your accuracy; rekey lines containing word-choice errors.

their (pron) belonging to them

there (adv/pron) in or at that place; word used to introduce a sentence or clause

they're (contr) a contracted form of *they are*

raise (vb/n) to lift up; to collect; an increase in amount, as of wages

rays (n) beams of energy or light; lines of light from a bright object

raze (vb) to tear down; to demolish

Learn 1 They're to be there to present their plans for the new building.
Apply 2 Were you (their, there, they're) for the fireworks display?
Apply 3 Do you think (their, there, they're) going to elect her as mayor?
Apply 4 In (their, there, they're) opinion, the decision was quite unfair.

Learn 5 The rays of the sun caused the flowers to raise their heads.
Learn 6 If we raise the price, will they raze the old building this month?
Apply 7 The (raise, rays, raze) of the sun will (raise, rays, raze) the fog.
Apply 8 After they (raise, rays, raze) the gym, work on a new arena can begin.

Review 9 (Your, You're) to (choose, chose) two of the (for, four) gifts.
Review 10 Is it (to, too, two) late for us to (vary, very) the choices?
Review 11 If you are taller (than, then) I am, why do (your, you're) clothes fit me?
Review 12 They are (do, due) in an (hour, our), and I (know, no) they'll come.

68c ▶ 30 Selective Review: Document Formats

plain full sheets

Review the formatting guides on p. 68, p. 76, and p. 105.

Letters/Memos

Make a list of the problems and page numbers given below:

pp. 69-70, 39c-40c, model
pp. 73-74, 41c-42c, model
pp. 77-78, 43c, model

Tables

List the problems and page numbers given below.

p. 106, 58b, Drill 2
pp. 106-107, 58c, model
p. 112, 63b, Table 3

Select the formats you need most to review. Review the format features given in the unit introductions. Then format and key selected documents from your list. Correct all errors.

223b (continued)

words

and Lake Ontario. As the huge sheets of ice melted, the 85
meltwater from the glaciers helped fill the basins. 96

Physical Feature 103

Size. The Great Lakes have a combined area of 94,510 162
sqaure miles (244,780 square kilometers). Lake Superior, 173
the largest of thqe lakes, is only slightly smaller than 185
Maine; and Lake Ontario, the smallest of the lakes, is 196
about the size of New Jersey. 202

Elevation. The lakes vary quite a bite in elevation. 214
Lake Superior, the highest, lies 600 feet (183 meters) 225
above sea level, while Lake Ontario, the lowest, lies just 236
245 feet (75 meters) above sea level. There is a 325-foot 248
difference in elevation between lakes Erie and Ontario. 260
Most of the water from the lakes drains into the St. 270
Lawrence River, which flows into the Atlantic Ocean. 281

Depth. The depth of the Great Lakes varies widely. 294
The deepest, Lake Superior is 1,333 feet (406 meters) deep. 306
Lake Erie, the shallowest, is only 210 (64 meters) deept. 319
Connecting Waterways 327

Three sets of locks and canals make it possible 336
for ships to sail from one Great Lake to another and to the 352
Atlantic Ocean, so they can access any port in the world. 366
The canals and the waterways they connect are listed here. 379

1. Welland Canal--connects Lake Erie and Lake Ontario. 390

2. Soo Canals--connect Lake Superior and Lake Huron. 401

3. St. Lawrence Seaway--connects Lake Ontario with
the Atlantic Ocean. 416

Significance of the lakes 426

The five Great Lakes and the canals that link them to- 437
gether make up the most important inland waterway in North 449
America. They provided the transportatin systme needed to 463
turn the Great Lakes region into one of the most impoortant 474
industrial areas in the United States. 481

Although the Great Lakes were all formed by glacial 113
activity during the same period, they are quite 123
different from one another. The irregular 132
movement of the glaciers created variations in the 142
size, elevation, and depth of the lakes. 150

Document 3
Leftbound Report
Reformat Document 2 as a leftbound report.

69a ▶ 5 Conditioning Practice

each line twice SS (slowly, then faster); if time permits, rekey line 4

alphabet 1 Jacki saw five prime quail and two big foxes down by the old zoo lake.

figures 2 We had 36 work tables, 247 office chairs, and 85 office desks in 1990.

fig/sym 3 The bookcase (36″ × 59″ × 14½″) is on sale at the Mart for $178.50.

speed 4 The busy visitor may work with usual vigor to form a key social panel.

| 1 | 2 | 3 | 4 | 5 | 6 | 7 | 8 | 9 | 10 | 11 | 12 | 13 | 14 |

69b ▶ 10 Check Keyboarding Skill: Straight Copy

1. Take two 3′ writings on the 3 ¶s combined; find *gwam* and circle errors on each writing.
2. Record the *gwam* and number of errors on the better writing.
3. If time permits, take a 1′ writing on each ¶ to improve speed.

all letters used | A | 1.5 si | 5.7 awl | 80% hfw

	gwam 3′	5′
A job description is a formal statement of the duties performed by	4	3
a worker. It may include both quality and quantity factors. The job	9	5
description is used to select new workers and place them in jobs that	14	8
best fit their abilities. A brief summary of the job description may	18	11
be given to people who show interest in working for a company.	23	14
A performance appraisal form is a formal method of assessing the	27	16
performance of workers. It defines each level of excellence a person	32	19
may reach. It then lists in major groups the duties workers in a job	36	22
class perform. The supervisor rates the person on each duty, using a	41	25
scale of one to five, with a rating of three representing the standard.	46	27
A job description and an appraisal form may have a section on work	50	30
habits: attitude on the job, working well with others, proper use of	55	33
time, skill in writing and speaking, and initiative. When a job is done	60	36
equally well by two workers, the one who shows better work habits and	64	39
attitudes will usually get the prized promotion or pay increase.	69	41

gwam 3′ | 1 | 2 | 3 | 4 | 5 |
5′ | 1 | 2 | 3 |

69c ▶ 35 Selective Review: Document Formats

plain full sheets

Review the formatting guides on p. 92, p. 96, and p. 102.

Reports

Make a list of the problems and page numbers given below.

pp. 93-95, 51d, model
p. 96, 52c

Outline

Note the problem and page number given below.

p. 102, 56c, Outline 1

Select the formats you need most to review. Review the format features given in the unit introduction. Then format and key selected documents from your list. Correct all errors.

223a ▶ 5 Conditioning Practice

each line twice SS (slowly, then faster); if time permits, take 1′ writings on line 4

alphabet	1	Jamie expects a high score on every big law quiz if he keeps studying.
figures	2	Mary sold 105 shirts, 28 belts, 94 sweaters, 36 suits, and 47 jackets.
fig/sym	3	Policy #31-407-A paid $26.97 interest and a $47.38 dividend on 3/5/91.
speed	4	The dorm official may name six sorority girls to visit the big social.

| 1 | 2 | 3 | 4 | 5 | 6 | 7 | 8 | 9 | 10 | 11 | 12 | 13 | 14 |

223b ▶ 45 Evaluate Production Skill: Memos/Reports

Time Schedule

Plan and prepare .... 5′
Timed production .... 30′
Proofread; compute *n-pram* .... 10′

1. Arrange 4 full sheets and LP p. 215 for ease of handling.

2. Format and key Documents 1-3 for 30′. Proofread and correct errors before removing each document from the machine.

3. After time is called (30′), proofread again and circle any uncorrected errors. Compute *n-pram.*

Document 1
Simplified Memo

LP p. 215

Key the copy at the right as a simplified memo.

words

January 14, 19-- Hilary L. Tribuzio, Marketing Director 11
SUBJECT: GREAT LAKES COPY FOR PRODUCT BROCHURE 19

¶ Here is the first draft of the copy on the Great 29
Lakes. Review and return it to me with any 37
changes you recommend. I need it by January 21 47
in order to complete the brochure describing our new 58
schooner by the date you specified. ¶ I agree 67
with you that general interest topics like this can 77
be included in sales brochures when appropriate. 87
This topic should be of special interest to our cus- 97
tomers since most of them sail their schooners on 107
the Great Lakes. ¶ You should consider placing in 117
your next brochure an article on the canals that 127
connect the lakes. 131

Elena J. Harris, Communications Group xx Enclosure 141

Document 2
Unbound Report

Key the copy at the right and on p. 383 as an unbound report.

THE GREAT LAKES 3

QS

The five GReat Lakes were formed ~~formed~~ more than 250,000 13
years ago during the Ice Age. ~~A~~ Large glaciers moved south across the 27
land of what is now called the Great Lakes region. The thick 40
glaciers gouged the land as ~~their way down~~, scooping out weak rock ~~as~~ 52
they moved, to form the five basins which now hold ~~form~~ the Great 62
Lakes--Lake Michigan, Lake Erie, Lake Superior, Lake Huroin, 74

UNIT 14 LESSONS 70 – 72
Measure Keyboarding/Formatting Skills

Measurement Goals

1. To demonstrate that you can key for 3′ on straight-copy material of average difficulty at an acceptable speed and within an error limit specified by your teacher.

2. To demonstrate that you can format and key letters, memos, reports, and tables according to standard formatting guides and with errors corrected.

Format Guides

1. ***Paper guide*** at *0* (for typewriters).

2. LL: 70 spaces for drills and ¶s; as formats require for letters, memos, reports, and tables.

3. LS: SS drills; DS ¶s; as formats require for letters, memos, reports and tables.

4. PI: 5 spaces when appropriate.

Lesson 70 *Measure Letter/Memo Skills*

LL: 70
LS: SS

70a ▶ 5 Conditioning Practice

each line twice SS (slowly, then faster); if time permits, a 1′ writing on line 4

alphabet	1	Barth was given a big prize for completing six quick high jumps today.
figures	2	The inventory includes 96 pamphlets, 1,827 books, and 3,450 magazines.
fig/sym	3	The #329 item is sold by Janoch & Co. for $875.46 (less 10% for cash).
speed	4	The key to proficiency is to name the right goals, then work for them.

| 1 | 2 | 3 | 4 | 5 | 6 | 7 | 8 | 9 | 10 | 11 | 12 | 13 | 14 |

70b ▶ 10 Check Keyboarding Skill: Straight Copy

1. Take two 3′ writings on ¶s 1-3 combined; calculate *gwam* and circle errors on each writing.

2. If time permits during the next unit, take additional 3′ writings on the combined ¶s to improve your skill.

all letters used | A | 1.5 si | 5.7 awl | 80% hfw |

	gwam 3′	5′
Workers on the job have to plan their workdays and organize their	4	3
work so that all duties are done in a timely fashion. As a result,	9	5
much is being said about teaching students to prioritize work. The	13	8
truth is that novice office workers have only limited opportunities to	18	11
set their own priorities; rather, priorities are often set for them.	23	14
For example, in a word processing center a supervisor receives the	27	16
work from various document writers. He or she then assigns the work to	32	19
keyboard operators on the basis of their work loads and in the sequence	37	22
of immediacy of need. Even a private secretary is often told by the	41	25
"boss" which work is urgent and which may not be needed immediately.	46	28
As workers develop on the job and are given a greater variety of	50	30
tasks to perform, the need to set priorities increases. By then, how-	55	33
ever, they will have learned through their supervisors which types of	60	36
tasks take priority and which ones can be put off. Realize that pri-	64	39
orities grow out of the immediacy or timeliness of need.	68	41

gwam 3′ | 1 | 2 | 3 | 4 | 5 |
5′ | 1 | 2 | 3 |

222b (continued)

words

Letter 2
LP p. 211
modified block format with indented ¶s, mixed punctuation; address envelope

September 13, 19-- Ms. Roberta L. Davis 212 Seventh 11
Street Bangor, ME 04401-4447 Dear Ms. Davis: 20

¶ Thank you for conducting the "Personal Productivity" 31
seminar for the executive secretaries and administra- 41
tive assistants at Berger Insurance Company last week. 53
¶ I have reviewed the results of the evaluation com- 62
pleted by the participants for our training and develop- 73
ment staff. Without exception, the participants ranked 85
each topic as being relevant or highly relevant to their 96
needs. The topic pertaining to dealing with inter- 106
ruptions received the highest ranking. 114
¶ You should also know that almost all participants 124
rated your presentation style and materials as very 134
good or excellent. Most stated they wanted you 144
back for another seminar. 149

Sincerely, Mrs. Susan L. Delfiore President xx 159
c Mr. L. James Walter, Training Director 167/179

Letter 3
LP p. 213
simplified format; address envelope

Letter 4
plain full sheet
Format Letter 3 in modified block format, mixed punctuation, and address it to
Mr. Samuel T. Ataliotis
820 West Hollis Street
Nashua, NH 03062-3599
Supply other letter parts as needed.
Total words: 132

October 31, 19-- MR ANDREW W HENDERSON 1008 ELM STREET 11
MANCHESTER NH 03101-1716 DAMAGED VALUE PLUS CARD 21

Your Value Plus electronic banking card was found in the au- 33
tomatic teller ~~when it was used on October 29, 19--~~ at Landmark's ~~the~~ 39
Granite Street branch. Apparently, your card ~~it~~ was not returned ~~retained~~ because 53
it was ~~of~~ damaged while being used on October 29. ~~during the transaction.~~ ¶ Since the card ~~it~~ will not ~~longer~~ 67
operate an automatic teller ~~the machine~~ any more, it must be replaced. We have 81
ordered a new card, and you will receive it in the mail with in 93
② (sp) weeks. ¶ You will be able to use ~~take advantage of~~ this conve- 102
nient form of banking again as soon as you receive ~~have~~ your replacement card. 117

MISS TRUDI A. PITTS, BRANCH MANAGER xx 125/138

70c ▶ 35 Check Formatting Skill: Letters/Memos

1 letterhead (LP p. 79); plain full sheets; correction supplies

Document 1
Personal-Business Letter

Format and key the letter on a plain full sheet. Use block format; LL: 60 spaces; PB: line 14. Correct errors.

words

2274 Cogswell Road | El Monte, CA 91732-3846 | December 3, 19-- | Mrs. Alice 14
M. Wiggins | 11300 Lower Azusa Road | El Monte, CA 91732-4725 | Dear Mrs. 28
Wiggins 30

Thanks to you and other PTA members who brought guests, our November 18 44
meeting was a tremendous success. Dr. Gibson was overwhelmed by the 58
high level of interest in computer literacy shown by parents of our students. 74

You will be pleased to know that two of the guests you brought have now reg- 89
istered to become regular PTA members. The total new-member registra- 103
tion was nine. 106

The other officers of the El Monte PTA join me in appreciation of the active 121
role you are taking this year. 128

Cordially yours | Ms. Laura J. Marsh 134

Document 2
Business Letter

Format and key the letter on a letterhead. Use block format; use the *Letter Placement Guide* on p. 76 for margins and date placement. Correct errors.

December 4, 19-- | Mr. Duane R. Burk, Office Manager | Huesman & Schmidt, 14
Inc. | 662 Woodward Avenue | Detroit, MI 48226-1947 | Dear Mr. Burk 27

Miss Chun and I certainly enjoyed our discussions with you last week. We 41
are highly pleased that you have given us an opportunity to work with you to 57
maximize your office space. 63

Based upon your plan to regroup certain personnel, Miss Chun is reworking 77
her design to accommodate the changes. That work should be completed 91
next week. At that time we shall also have a firm bid to show you. 105

Would next Friday at ten o'clock be a convenient time for us to show you the 121
new plans? If not, please suggest another date and time. 132

Sincerely yours | Virgil P. Thompson | Assistant Sales Manager | xx (105) 145

Document 3
Simplified Memo

Format and key the simplified memo on a plain full sheet. SM: 1″; PB: line 10. Correct errors.

Date: **December 4, 19--**
Addressee: **Vicente W. Lugo**
Subject: **NEW SERVICE CONTRACT FOR OFFICE EQUIPMENT**
Writer: **Danielle E. Bogarde**
Reference: **your initials**

opening lines 15

(¶) We have just signed a new service contract with the 25
Lee & Perin Company. Henceforth, they will clean, service 37
and repair all our keyboarding and word processing 48
equipment. 50
(¶) L&P has asked me to notify all supervisors that only 61
L&P personnel should do internal cleaning or make repairs 72
on any typewriter, computer, or word processor. When service 85
is required, please call 521-8590 to make your request. 96
(¶) Make sure everyone under your supervision knows 106
about this change. 110

closing lines 114

Document 4

If time remains after completing Document 3, begin rekeying Document 1.

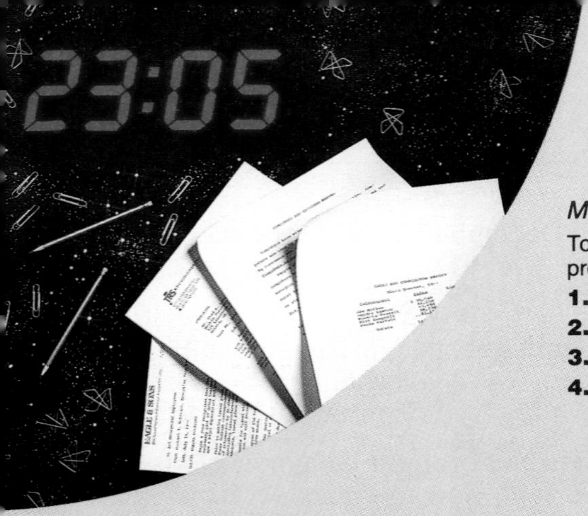

UNIT 52 LESSONS 222 – 225
Evaluate Document Processing Skills

Measurement Goals

To demonstrate your knowledge and skill in processing

1. Letters
2. Memos and reports
3. Tables
4. Business Forms

Format Guides

1. Paper guide at *0* (for typewriters).
2. LL: 70 spaces for drill copy; as needed for documents.
3. LS: SS drill lines; as needed for documents.
4. PI: 5 spaces, unless otherwise directed.

Lesson 222 — *Evaluation: Letters in Various Formats*

222a ▶ 5 Conditioning Practice

each line twice SS (slowly, then faster); if time permits, take 1′ writings on line 1

alphabet 1 Merv saw my new pilot quickly taxi a jet to the zone by the big field.
figures 2 Their soccer league had 3,650 boys and 2,478 girls in the 1991 season.
fig/sym 3 Expenses increased $82,965 (5%) and net profit decreased $31,470 (6%).
speed 4 The busy neighbor may fix the rifle, bugle, and cycle for the visitor.

| 1 | 2 | 3 | 4 | 5 | 6 | 7 | 8 | 9 | 10 | 11 | 12 | 13 | 14 |

222b ▶ 45 Evaluate Production Skill: Letters

LP pp. 209-213
plain full sheet

Time Schedule
Plan and prepare .... 5′
Timed production ....30′
Proofread; compute *n-pram* ....10′

1. Arrange materials for ease of handling.
2. Format and key Letters 1-4 for 30′. Proofread and correct errors before removing each letter from the machine.
3. After time is called (30′), proofread again and circle any uncorrected errors. Compute *n-pram.*

Letter 1
LP p. 209
block format, open punctuation; address envelope

words

April 15, 19-- Mr. Joseph P. Taylor Taylor's Plumbing and Heating 98 Buell 15
Street Burlington, VT 05401-3805 Dear Mr. Taylor Subject LEASE RE- 27
NEWAL FOR 98 BUELL STREET PROPERTY 34

Enclosed are two copies of your new lease for the property you now lease 48
from Associated Estates Corporation. 56

The enclosed lease is identical to the present one which expires on May 15, 71
19--, except that the new monthly rent ($555.50) has been substituted for 86
the current one ($505). You were notified of this 10 percent increase in my 101
letter of March 15. 105

Before April 30, please return one signed copy of the lease with your signa- 120
ture notarized. Retain the other copy for your files. If you need more in- 135
formation before you sign this lease, call Mrs. Harriet Jamison at 279-4698. 151

Sincerely ASSOCIATED ESTATES CORPORATION Ms. Maryanne E. Shade- 163
Minor Lease Renewal Manager xx Enclosures postscript If you pay the 175
rent for one year before May 15, 19--, you will receive an 8.5 percent dis- 190
count. The discount conditions are the same as those in your current lease. 205/**224**

71a ▶ 5 Conditioning Practice

each line twice SS (slowly, then faster); if time permits, a 1′ writing on line 4

alphabet	1	Monkeys in the quaint park watched a fat lizard devour six juicy bugs.
figures	2	The telephone number for your 120 N. Lotus Drive location is 378-4569.
fig/sym	3	The rates varied from 15 1/2% to 17 1/4% on loans from $98 to $36,500.
speed	4	Kay may make an authentic map of the ancient city for the title firms.

| 1 | 2 | 3 | 4 | 5 | 6 | 7 | 8 | 9 | 10 | 11 | 12 | 13 | 14 |

71b ▶ 45 Check Formatting Skill: Reports

plain full sheets; correction supplies

Document 1
2-Page Unbound Report with Enumerated Items

Format and key the copy at right and on p. 125. Place the reference list on the second page. Make all changes marked in the source document and correct all errors.

Note: Before removing a page from your machine or screen, make a final check for errors and correct any that you may have overlooked.

words

CARE OF WORD PROCESSING EQUIPMENT 7

In the [era] ~~days~~ of manual typewriters, [keyboard operators] ~~typists~~ often cleaned, 20
oiled, adjusted[,] and repaired thier [own] machines. Manufacturers [and vendors] of 36
electronic keyboarding/word processing devices [today] recommend that 50
only professionally trained service people atempt to make [internal] ad- 64
justments and repairs (IBM Operators Guide, 1988, iii). 80

BEcause modern equipment uses sofisticated technology, 91
waranties may be revoked if [untrained] people attempt to correct malfunc- 105
tions. Some [maintenance] contracts become void if equipment damage results 120
from attempts of ownres [or operators] to adjust[,] [repair, or install] internal parts. 137

The operator's guide that acompanies [new] equipment usually 149
contains a statement about equipment care. [and maintenance.] 161

Care of typewriters. 169

1. If a dust cover is available[,] cover the typewriter when it is not being used. [for extended periods.] 180 189

2. Dust the area around the typewriter [at least] once a week. 202

3. Clean the printing head [(daisy wheel or element)] periodically using a vendor-reccommended cleaner. 218 223

4. Clean the [outer] surfaces (housing and keyboard) ofthe typewriter as needed to remove fingerprints, stains, and dust. Do not use water, alcohol, or thinners; use only vendor-recommended products. 234 246 256 263

5. [When] ~~If~~ equipment doesnot function, be sure [it is] ~~it's~~ properly plugged in and turned on before calling a service/maintenance representative. Call your maintenance vendor whena bona fide malfunction occurrs; do not attempt to make internal repairs yourself. 275 286 297 308 314

(continued, p. 125)

221d ▶ 10
Measure Keyboarding Skill

1. A 3′ writing on both ¶s; calculate *gwam;* circle errors.
2. A 5′ writing on both ¶s; calculate *gwam;* circle errors.

all letters used | A | 1.5 si | 5.7 awl | 80% hfw |

gwam 3′ | 5′

Taking a major test or examination is very similar to playing an 4 3 46
important game. In both situations, you must control your anxiety level 9 6 49
if you want to achieve the best results. Most people find an increased 14 8 52
anxiety level before a game or test to be normal and helpful. It is im- 19 11 55
portant, however, that the heightened anxiety does not negatively affect 24 14 58
your ability to concentrate on the task at hand. You must focus all 28 17 61
your thoughts and energy on the test questions or game action and not 33 20 63
on the final results to have a good performance. 36 22 65

Another similarity is the need for preparation before taking a test 41 24 68
or playing a game. Coaches and players know they must develop a game 45 27 71
strategy and practice it repeatedly if they expect to achieve desired 50 30 74
results. Similarly, test takers must realize the importance of good 55 33 76
planning and studying. They must plan what, when, where, and how they 59 36 79
will study for a test and then execute the plan. A good routine to fol- 64 39 82
low is to begin studying well in advance of the test and to leave time 69 41 85
for relaxation and reflection before the test is taken. 73 44 87

gwam 3′ | 1 | 2 | 3 | 4 | 5
gwam 5′ | 1 | 2 | 3

221e ▶ 15
Prepare for Measurement

LP p. 207; correct errors

Document 1
Purchase Order
Key the purchase order shown at the right.

Document 2
Invoice
Prepare an invoice from the purchase order at the right. Address it to
SHAEFER RENTALS
1600 MARKET STREET
SAN FRANCISCO CA 94105-2186
Date it **September 23, 19--.**
Date Shipped: **9/22/--**
Add 6% sales tax and compute a new total.
Use our order no. **543-85**
Total words: 79

words

To: PARK'S BUSINESS PRODUCTS — Purchase Order No.: B-45987-A 7
5704 HOLLIS STREET — Date: September 5, 19-- 14
OAKLAND CA 94608-2514 — Terms: 5/15, n/30 21
Shipped Via: Terner Express 24

Quantity	Description/Stock Number	Price	Per	Total	words
5	Adjustable Hole Punch (P-435)	10.95	ea	54.75	33
4	Office Shear--10″ (S-189)	10.85	ea	43.40	42
10	Push Pins (R-726)	.69	pk	6.90	49
3	Desk Stapler (X-705)	20.95	ea	62.85	56
3	Staples (X-605)	3.55	bx	10.65	63
3	Staple Remover (X-814)	2.75	ea	8.25	72
				186.80	73

71b (continued)

words

2 315

DS The ~~above~~ foregoing guides will help you attain long life and 326
satisfactory performance from electronic typewriters. 337

Care of Computers 344

5 sp Dusting, cleaning, and covering suggestions for computers 356
are the same as for typewriters. Some procedures apply more 368
specifically to computers: (Oliverio and Pasewark, 1988, 194). 380

1. Be sure all components are properly installed, properly 392
interconnected, and plugged into wall outlets. 402

\# 2. Be sure all components are turned off before plugging 414
them into or unplugging them from wall outlets. 423

3. Clean disk drive heads periodically by using a cleaning 435
disk as prescribed by your vendor. 443

4. Do not remove the housing of the CPU to adjust or install chips, 456
boards, or other electronic devices. 464

5. Keep electronic hardware/software in a cool, dry place 476
that is free of magnetic fields. 483

6. When malfunctions occur, call your service/mainten- 493
ance person; do not attempt to make repairs yourself. 504

REFERENCES 507

IBM Operator's Guide. International Business Machines Corporation, 524
1988. 526

Oliverio, Mary Ellen, and William R. Pasewark. The Office: 540
Procedures and Technology. Cincinnati: South-Western 556
Publishing Co., 1988. 560

Document 2
Title Page
Format and key a title page for the report on a plain full sheet. Use **your name** and **school name** and the **current date.** Correct errors.

Document 3
If time remains after completing Document 2, begin rekeying Document 1.

Lesson 72 — Measure Centering/Table Skills

LL: 70
LS: SS

72a ▶ 5 Conditioning Practice

each line twice SS (slowly, then faster); if time permits, a 1′ writing on line 4

alphabet 1 Brave jockeys and large quarter horses whiz past farmers in box seats.

figures 2 Your Order No. 648 calls for 103 chairs, 29 typewriters, and 75 desks.

fig/sym 3 She wired them $365 on May 29 for the items ordered on Invoice #40187.

speed 4 Cy may be the right man to blame for the big fight in the penalty box.

| 1 | 2 | 3 | 4 | 5 | 6 | 7 | 8 | 9 | 10 | 11 | 12 | 13 | 14 |

221a ▶ 5 Conditioning Practice

each line twice SS (slowly, then faster); then a 1′ writing on line 4

alphabet 1 Pamela will acquire three dozen red vinyl jackets for the big exhibit.
figures 2 My teacher plans to have 75 test items from pages 289-306 for Unit 41.
symbols 3 Mai-Ling practiced the symbols $, ″, %, &, and # in class on 10/25/91.
speed 4 The rich widow is to endow the sorority chapel on a visit to the city.

| 1 | 2 | 3 | 4 | 5 | 6 | 7 | 8 | 9 | 10 | 11 | 12 | 13 | 14 |

221b ▶ 10 Check Language Skills

plain full sheet

1. The memorandum at the right contains errors in spelling, grammar, and punctuation.

2. Key the memo in simplified format. Use **today's date;** address it to **William A. Kurtz, Advertising Manager.** Use **AUTHORIZATION TO ADVERTISE** as the subject; **Leon H. Johnson, Marketing Vice President,** as the writer. Add other memo parts as needed. Correct errors as you key.

words

opening lines 16

Enclosed is the approved advertizing copy for 25
the new line of bridle gowns we are to begin sailing 36
next month. I have authorized $15,000 for the adver- 46
tisements in this series. The controller has been 56
instructed to transfer $15,000 from my contingency 67
account to your advertizing account. 74
Please note that I have indicated that bowled 83
print is to be used to emphasise the deference 93
among the knew line and the old line. The ad 102
is too be run everyday for one week and is too 111
be placed in the daily and weakly news papers 120
so it will be scene by a divers audience. 129

closing lines 140

221c ▶ 10 Improve Keyboarding Speed

1. Each line once as shown; push for speed.

2. A 1′ writing on each of lines 8, 10, and 12; calculate *gwam* on each writing.

home/3d rows
1 set pay | low tide | jury duty | quit work | high speed | just that | good futures
2 Pete said he will work at the pet store this week for his two sisters.

home/1st rows
3 mad dash | can call | hand ax | lack cash | sand bags | black flag | sad jazz band
4 Hannah and Lana have a small ax, half a banana, a fan, and a gas mask.

3d/1st row emphasis
5 may cut | buy ten | fix bike | new tire | quit my | be quiet | no review | rezone it
6 Vi is quite sure now is the time to rezone every zoo in the community.

stroke response
7 my mom | my dad | at noon | sad pup | was brave | look up | hilly knoll | water pump
8 You saw my only pony pull a garage cart uphill at a fast average rate.

word response
9 do half | fix it | pay me | got it | when the | both bowls | giant dog | penalty box
10 The proficient man is to fix the lane signs when down by the big lake.

combination response
11 no risks | get up | data base | name it | signal them | average pay | minimum wage
12 The city auditor reacted to the abstract statement with a good answer.

| 1 | 2 | 3 | 4 | 5 | 6 | 7 | 8 | 9 | 10 | 11 | 12 | 13 | 14 |

72b ▶ 10 Check Language Skills

LL: 70 spaces; LS: DS

Key each line, making needed changes in capitalization, number expression, and word choice.

1 b. j. goodman moved from 2277 arbor lane to 910 beverly circle.

2 the cod package was received at two ten p.m. on february tenth.

3 we took the paddlewheel Delta Queen down the ohio to louisville.

4 after you have past st. louis, you still have a long drive to dallas.

5 dr. kenz is attending an ama convention in san juan, puerto rico.

6 the bedford bid is forty-five dollars more then the kaplan bid.

7 if their going with us to boston, they should be hear by now.

8 he asked, "is labor day always the first monday in september?"

9 she said that their was to much rain last week to sew the wheat.

10 hartwell corporation had it's sales conference in colorado springs.

11 of the twelve branch offices, only too failed to increase sales.

12 the quotation can be found in section 4, page 67, lines 14-16.

13 the new foundation will raze the floor by four and a half inches.

14 we worked 4 ours a day at markum's during the christmas rush.

15 the queen city club is the site for they're valentine's day party.

72c ▶ 35 Check Formatting Skill: Centering/Tables

plain full sheets for all tables; correction supplies; LS: DS

Document 1
Announcement

plain full sheet; center announcement horizontally and vertically; correct errors

words

ANNUAL PTA BAZAAR 4

Saturday, February 13, 19-- 9

10 a.m. to 3 p.m. 13

Central High School Gymnasium 19

FLEA MARKET, FOOD, BEVERAGES, PRIZES 26

Admission $1.00 29

Proceeds Go to Senior Prom Fund 36

Documents 2, 3, and 4 are on p. 127.

220b ▶ 10
Language Skills: Word Choice

1. Study the spelling and definition of the words.

2. Key the line number (with period); space twice, then key the **Learn** sentence, noting the correct use of the words.

3. Key the line number (with period); space twice, then key the **Apply** sentences DS, selecting the word in parentheses that makes each sentence correct.

explicit (adj) expressed with precision; clearly defined

implicit (adj) implied or understood although not directly expressed

foul (adj) spoiled; rotten; putrid

fowl (n) any bird used as food or hunted as game

Learn 1. My nod gave implicit agreement; Joe gave explicit agreement.
Apply 2. By starting to weed, she expressed an (explicit/implicit) desire to help.
Apply 3. Please give me (explicit/implicit) directions the next time I need help.

Learn 4. The fowl had a foul odor because it was not refrigerated properly.
Apply 5. Jim, Tom, and Sheila plan to serve (foul/fowl) at the picnic.
Apply 6. Be careful you do not eat (foul/fowl) chicken on the camping trip.

220c ▶ 10
Improve Keyboarding Control

each line twice SS (slowly, then faster); DS between 6-line groups

adjacent keys
1 are oil her pot cash copy rent void past port true worth liquid tickle
2 were there | avoid action | either term | report copy | new trade | fruit juices
3 Sam heard the cheer on the radio as the extra point kick hit the post.

direct reaches
4 many vice cent fund album enemy music brown hence forum manual produce
5 much music | check payment | specific fund | forum audiences | anybody special
6 My music album and brown manual will have a special price at my forum.

one-hand words
7 ace hop bet nil ward lump face puny wear upon treat imply weave poplin
8 are you | best car | extra crew | only hill | water pump | safe starts | was jolly
9 Loni, my greatest pupil, stressed care after my data base was created.

shift keys
10 Pam Sis Zoe Lars Mary Rory Paula Alena Nancy Bobbi Hazel Winnie Vivian
11 Spring Garden | Alabama City | Five Points | Howley Lake | Happy Jack McDowell
12 Will, Mary, Enos, Ozzie, Von, and Karla went to Lower Kalskag, Alaska.

220d ▶ 25
Prepare for Measurement

plain full sheets; correct errors

Document 1
Table with Source Note

Key the table at the right; CS: 8

Document 2
Table with Totals

Rekey Document 1; CS: 12; add amounts in each column; key the total for each column.

Total words: 82

Document 3
Table with Rules

Rekey Document 2; CS: 10; add horizontal rules.

Total words: 122

If necessary, see p. 351.

words

Crestwood Realty Company 5
Commercial Property Division 11

Property	Assessed Value	Property Tax Paid	words
			13
			27
517 Locust Place	$ 75,000	$ 12,754	34
5 Merchant Plaza	~~45,000~~ 49,765	9,650	41
St. Clair Building	109,550	14,975	49
~~Eger~~ Edgar Medical Center	83,600	12,875	56
Allison Park Center	64,500	10,450	64

______ 67

Source: 19-- Property Tax Invoices. 74

72c (continued)

Document 2
Two-Column Table with Secondary Heading
plain full sheet; CS: 12; center horizontally and vertically; correct errors

		words
NOISE LEVEL OF SELECTED SOUNDS		6
(Measured in Decibels)		11
Gun Muzzle Blast	140	15
Auto Horn	115	18
Chainsaw	100	20
Truck Traffic	90	24
Typewriter	60	27
Whisper	30	29

Document 3
Two-Column Table with Columnar Headings and Source Note
plain full sheet; CS: 12; center horizontally and vertically; correct errors

		words
CELLULOID PRESIDENTS		4
(Those Most Often Portrayed in Movies)		12
Name	Times	16
Abraham Lincoln	134	20
Ulysses S. Grant	44	24
George Washington	34	28
Theodore Roosevelt	23	33
Franklin D. Roosevelt	23	38
Thomas Jefferson	18	42
____________		46
Source: Guinness Book of Movie Facts		59
and Figures, 1988.		65

Document 4
Three-Column Table with Columnar Headings and Source Note
plain full sheet; CS: 8; center horizontally and vertically; correct errors

			words
CHANGES IN WEEKLY BASE SALARIES			6
(Based on 5% Increase in Cost of Living)			15
Job Title	Current	New*	23
Clerical Assistant I	$210	$221	29
Clerical Assistant II	250	263	35
Secretary I	270	284	39
Secretary II	320	336	44
WP Specialist	295	310	48
Administrative Assistant	350	368	55
____________			58
*Rounded to nearest dollar.			64

219c ▶ 35
Prepare for Measurement

plain full sheets; correct errors

Document 1
Unbound Report

Key the copy at the right as a 2-page unbound report. Use **FINDLEY HIGH SCHOOL BUSINESS CLUB ACTIVITIES** as the title.

Document 2
Simplified Memo

Use the material at the right to key a 2-page memo in simplified format to **Evelyn W. Lane, Principal.** The memo is from **Hazel W. Woodley, Business Club Advisor.** Use the title of the report as the subject; use today's date. Eliminate the side headings but retain the paragraph headings. Add this copy as the last paragraph.

May I have your written authorization that the Business Club can conduct these projects. I would like to have your response within ten days so I will have an answer before the club's next meeting.

```
Evelyn Lane
Page 2
Current date
```

Second-Page Heading (begin on line 6)

Document 3
Leftbound Report

Begin rekeying Document 1 as a 2-page leftbound report. Prepare a title page showing that the report was prepared by the **Findley High School Business Club.**

words

The members of the Findley High School Business Club met last week 22
and decided to conduct the projects listed below. Please consider this docu- 38
ment as the club's request for permission to organize and conduct these 52
projects during this school year. The proposed projects will publicize the 67
business education program to students, parents, and other members of the 82
community that Findley High School serves. In addition, they will bring 97
recognition to current business education students. 107

<u>Fall Semester Projects</u> 116

The following projects have been suggested for the fall semester. These 131
projects will help to draw students' attention to the business education pro- 146
gram early in the school year. 152

<u>Poster contest</u>. The club will sponsor a poster contest in late September 170
to recruit new members into the Business Club. The posters will be dis- 184
played throughout the high school building and the winner will receive a 199
coupon good for two dinners at George's Family Restaurant. 211

<u>Open house</u>. Club members will participate in the Business Education 227
Department's Fourth Annual Open House. The members will 1. Greet the 241
guests at the main entrance. 2. Escort the guests to the Business Education 256
Department where the program will be held. 3. Demonstrate the computer 271
hardware and software that is used in the business classes. 4. Serve re- 286
freshments in the hall outside the accounting classroom. 297

<u>Spring Semester Projects</u> 307

During the spring semester, Business Club members will conduct activi- 321
ties designed to advertise the business education program to the community 336
outside the school. The following projects have been proposed. 349

<u>Mall exhibit</u>. Senior and alumni club members will staff an exhibit booth 366
at Findley Shopping Mall during the two weeks preceding course selection at 381
the high school. The exhibit will focus on what is learned in business 396
classes and opportunities for business education graduates. 408

<u>Radio talk show</u>. The Business Club officers will appear on "High School 425
Perspectives," a weekly talk show on WDCF. The show will focus on the 440
business education curriculum, the cooperative education program, and the 454
activities of the Business Club at Findley High School. 466

<u>Career day</u>. Club members will assist the faculty with the career day 482
program for junior high students. A member will "shadow" each junior high 497
student who tours the Business Education Department to explain the advan- 511
tages of business courses and the activities of the department. 524

Lesson 220 *Keyboarding/Prepare for Measurement*

220a ▶ 5
Conditioning Practice

each line twice SS (slowly, then faster); then a 1′ writing on line 4

alphabet	1	Buzz likely will be the paid judge for the exclusive quarter-mile run.
figures	2	Harry can call Darlana at 375-4901 on Monday or 268-9103 on Wednesday.
shift lock	3	She will learn COBOL and BASIC in C1201 and PASCAL and MUMPS in C1301.
speed	4	The men may focus on their work if they are apt to make a tidy profit.

| 1 | 2 | 3 | 4 | 5 | 6 | 7 | 8 | 9 | 10 | 11 | 12 | 13 | 14 |

UNIT 15 LESSONS 73 – 75
Keystone Recreation Center (An Office Job Simulation)

Learning Goals

1. To learn to transfer your keying, formatting, and language skills to a realistic office setting.

2. To learn to format mailing-list index cards and file-folder labels as processed in a business office.

3. To learn to process a series of related documents (errors corrected) in orderly fashion with minimum assistance.

Documents Processed

1. Mailing-List Index Cards
2. "Form" Letters with Variables
3. File-Folder Labels
4. Summary of Talk in Report Format
5. Simplified Memo with Table

KEYSTONE RECREATION CENTER (An Office Job Simulation)

Before you start to process the documents on pp. 129-131, read the *Work Assignment* and study the *Standard Formatting Guides* given at right. When planning documents, refer to the *Standard Formatting Guides* again to refresh your memory.

Work Assignment

You have been hired as a part-time office assistant at Keystone Recreation Center.

Keystone Recreation Center (KRC) is located at the edge of Woodward Park on the Arkansas River in West Tulsa, Oklahoma. KRC offers recreational and educational programs for children, teenagers, and adults of all ages.

The center is organized and operated by the following people:

Mr. Morgan W. Lindsay, Director
Mrs. Doris L. Moon, Associate Director
Ms. Elva Mae Simms, Assistant Director of Child Programs
Mr. Jason B. Appel, Assistant Director of Teenager Programs
Mrs. Joyce M. Dempsey, Assistant Director of Adult Programs

As an office assistant, you will work in the office of Mrs. Doris L. Moon. Your primary responsibility is to process letters, memos, reports, and other documents for various members of the staff. A few of the documents--index cards and file-folder labels, for example--must be completed on a typewriter rather than a word processor. In addition, you may be asked to answer the telephone, copy and file correspondence and other records, and enter data into a computer.

Your keyboarding teacher has verified that you know how to format standard documents in the basic styles used by Keystone Recreation Center: letters in block format, reports in unbound format, memos in simplified format, and announcements and tables centered on full and half sheets.

To assist you in formatting documents, Mrs. Moon gives you *Standard Formatting Guides*. When unfamiliar tasks are assigned, she will give special instructions.

Standard Formatting Guides

Letters

1. Process letters on KRC letterheads; use block format with open punctuation.
2. Use 1½" SM.
3. Place date on line 16.
4. QS between the date and letter address and between complimentary close and keyed (printed) name of writer. DS between all other letter parts.

Memos

1. Process memos on plain paper; use simplified format.
2. Use 1" SM.
3. Place date on line 10.
4. QS between date and name(s) of addressee(s) and between last line of message and keyed (printed) name of writer. DS between all other memo parts.

Announcements and Tables

1. Process announcements on half sheets; process tables on full sheets.
2. DS all lines of announcements and tables unless otherwise directed. Center both types of documents horizontally and vertically. An even number of spaces between columns is preferred.

Reports

1. Use unbound format for all reports:
   SM: 1"
   PB: line 10 in pica (10-pitch)
   line 12 in elite (12-pitch)
   Bottom Margin: at least 1"
2. QS between title and report body; DS between all other lines of reports, including side headings. SS enumerated items but DS between items and above and below the series.
3. Place page numbers on line 6 at the RM of all pages except the first, which is not numbered. DS and continue the report body on line 8.

218c ▶ 25 Prepare for Measurement

2 plain full sheets; LP p. 205; correct errors.

Letter 1
Modified Block Format

Key the letter at the right in modified block format, indented ¶s, and mixed punctuation. If necessary, see p. 136.

Letter 2
Simplified Block Format

Rekey Letter 1 in simplified block format. If necessary, see p. 308.

Letter 3
Block Format

LP p. 205
or executive-size stationery

Rekey Letter 1 in block format, open punctuation. Omit the subject line and company name. If necessary, see p. 308.

words

Current date Mrs. Sheila T. Rapowski Beta Safe & Lock 3684 Berger 14
Avenue St. Louis, MO 63109-1101 Dear Mrs. Rapowski Subject YOUR 26
HELP IS NEEDED 29

(¶ 1) For over fifty years, Scientific Products has manufactured many prod- 42
ucts designed to satisfy special needs of customers. 53

(¶ 2) On the enclosed survey are several short questions that will allow you 67
to tell us your feelings about products we are currently considering. The 82
survey requires only a few minutes to complete and can be returned to us in 97
the enclosed postage-paid envelope. 105

(¶ 3) Please respond so that we will have your input when we determine the 119
future products to manufacture to meet your special needs. Your response 133
will be kept confidential, and we will not place your name on mailing lists we 149
share with other firms. 154

Sincerely SCIENTIFIC PRODUCTS Ms. Linda L. Kugas, President xx 167
Enclosure postscript The enclosed coin is a token of our appreciation. We 180
hope it will brighten the day of a small child you know. 191

Lesson 219 Keyboarding/Prepare for Measurement

219a ▶ 5 Conditioning Practice

each line twice SS (slowly, then faster); then a 1′ writing on line 4

alphabet 1 A jazz player acquired six or seven big weekend dates from his agents.
figures 2 Jan's 67 stores in 19 states gave discounts of 20, 35, and 48 percent.
shift keys 3 I may visit Perry, Columbus, Langley, Wooster, and South high schools.
speed 4 Six girls may visit the city to see the giant robot make an auto body.

| 1 | 2 | 3 | 4 | 5 | 6 | 7 | 8 | 9 | 10 | 11 | 12 | 13 | 14 |

219b ▶ 10 Language Skills: Word Choice

1. Study the spelling and definition of the words.

2. Key the line number (with period); space twice, then key the **Learn** sentence, noting the correct use of the words.

3. Key the line number (with period); space twice, then key the **Apply** sentences DS, selecting the word in parentheses that makes each sentence correct.

divers (adj) various; several; sundry

diverse (adj) distinct in kind; disparate; unlike

everyday (adj) suitable for ordinary days or routine occasions

every day (adj & n) each and all days without exception

Learn 1. The twins had diverse opinions about divers items of clothing.
Apply 2. The yearbook should include (divers/diverse) pictures of the soccer team.
Apply 3. The (divers/diverse) positions of the two boys led to the debate.

Learn 4. See if Marilyn can wear everyday clothing to the office every day.
Apply 5. He is to practice keying straight copy (everyday/every day).
Apply 6. I think I have established an (everyday/every day) routine.

73a-75a ▶ 5
Machine Check

each line twice *daily* to see that equipment is working properly

alphabet 1 Jacques has asked to be given one week to reply to this tax quiz form.

figures 2 Raul must study Section 2, pages 75-190, and Section 4, pages 246-380.

fig/sym 3 The new rate on Glenn & Taylor's $2,856 note (due 4/13/97) is 10 1/2%.

speed 4 Jo may sign the usual form by proxy if they make an audit of the firm.

| 1 | 2 | 3 | 4 | 5 | 6 | 7 | 8 | 9 | 10 | 11 | 12 | 13 | 14 |

73b-75b ▶ 45 (daily)
Document Processing Work Assignments

Documents 1-2
Mailing-List Index Cards

LP p. 81

Mrs. Moon asks you to prepare mailing-list index cards for two new members, using the format guides and model index card shown at right.

Index Card Format Guides

1. On line 2, 3 spaces from left edge of card, key the name in index order (surname, first name, middle initial). Key a courtesy title (Miss, Ms., Mrs., Mr.) in parentheses after the middle initial.

2. DS; key the name (in address order) and address in USPS style.

3. DS; key the phone number.

4. DS; key the Group information.

```
Hummingbird, George C. (Mr.)          line 2
DS
MR GEORGE C HUMMINGBIRD
4265 S PEORIA AVENUE
TULSA OK  74105-1844
DS
(918) 541-8255
DS
Group:  Senior Adult

3 spaces
```

New Members

Mr. and Mrs. Jacob N. Ishimura
4510 S. Lewis Avenue
Tulsa, Oklahoma 74105-2845
(918) 541-2665
Group: Young Adult

Miss Ramona L. Ogilvie
1748 S. Harvard Avenue
Tulsa, Oklahoma 74112-3810
(918) 871-3628
Group: Upper Teenager

Documents 3-4
"Form" Letters

LP pp. 83-86

Mrs. Moon asks you to process "form" letters (copy at right) to the new members (Documents 1-2). By using the variables below, you will tailor each letter to fit its addressee(s). Use the **current date** and supply an appropriate **salutation** and **complimentary close.** Don't forget to add **reference initials** and an **enclosure notation.**

Document 3 Variables

V 1: **Ishimura address**
V 2: **young adult**
V 3: **young men and women**
V 4: **couples**
V 5: **Mrs. Joyce M. Dempsey Assistant Director**

Document 4 Variables

V 1: **Ogilvie address**
V 2: **upper teenager**
V 3: **high school students**
V 4: **young people**
V 5: **Mr. Jason B. Appel Assistant Director**

("Mr." on envelope only.)

(V 1)

Here is your Keystone Recreation Center (KRC) Membership Card. You should bring it along each time you visit the center. This card identifies you as a member in good standing and is your entree to all regular and special (V 2) activities.

You have joined a stimulating group of (V 3). I'm sure KRC membership will mean a lot to you, as it has to so many other (V 4). Do take full advantage of it during the coming year. Use the enclosed "Activity Schedule" to remind you of the wide variety of activities that awaits you at Keystone Recreation Center.

I hope to see you here often. Why not stop by my office the next time you come in; perhaps I can answer any questions you may have about the many programs we have planned for you.

(V 5)

Documents 5, 6, 7, and 8 are on pp.130-131.

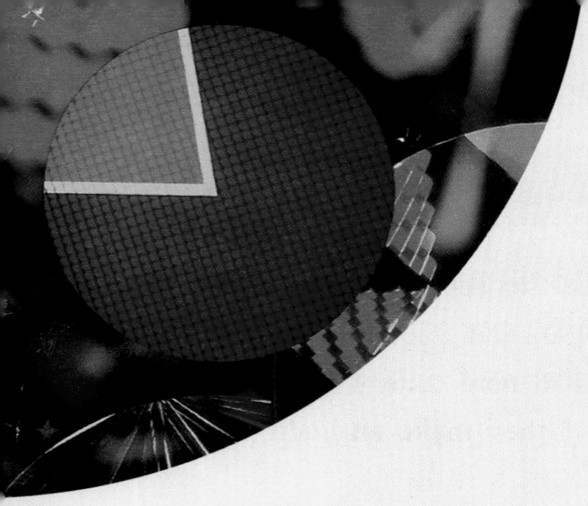

UNIT 51 *LESSONS 218 – 221*
Extend and Measure Keyboarding/Language Skills

Learning Goals

1. To improve basic skills in keyboarding, word choice, and document production.
2. To prepare for measurement of skills in language usage; in keying straight copy; and in preparing letters, memos, reports, tables, invoices, and purchase orders.

Format Guides

1. Paper guide at *0* (for typewriters).
2. LL: 70 spaces for drill copy; as needed for documents.
3. LS: SS drill lines; DS ¶s; or as directed within an activity.
4. PI: 5 spaces, unless otherwise directed.

Lesson 218 *Keyboarding/Prepare for Measurement*

218a ▶ 5 Conditioning Practice

each line twice SS (slowly, then faster); then a 1′ writing on line 4

alphabet 1 Drew thought a jinx had kept them from solving the big puzzle quickly.
figures 2 The association had 7,863 members in 62 chapters in 45 states in 1990.
shift keys 3 Ms. Eppots asked to see Mary, Rob, Janis, Zoe, and Naomi before class.
speed 4 Lana sat by the aisle with them for the sorority ritual at the chapel.

| 1 | 2 | 3 | 4 | 5 | 6 | 7 | 8 | 9 | 10 | 11 | 12 | 13 | 14 |

218b ▶ 20 Improve Keyboarding Skill: Guided Writing

1. A 3′ writing on ¶s 1-2 combined; calculate *gwam.*
2. A 1′ writing on ¶ 1; calculate *gwam* to establish your base rate.
3. Add 2-6 words to Step 2 *gwam;* use this as your goal rate.
4. Take three 1′ speed writings on ¶ 1, trying to reach your quarter-minute checkpoints as the guides (¼, ½, ¾, time) are called.
5. Follow Steps 2-4 for ¶ 2.
6. Repeat Step 1. Compare *gwam* on the two 3′ writings.
7. Record on LP p. 3 your better 3′ *gwam.*

all letters used | A | 1.5 si | 5.7 awl | 80% hfw |

	gwam 3′	5′	
Have you ever paused to consider how you can improve your ability	4	3	37
to take quizzes, tests, and examinations? You should realize that you	9	5	39
can improve your performance by improving your test-taking ability.	14	8	42
One thing you can do is to understand that good performance does not	18	11	45
mean that you must receive the highest score in your group. Rather, it	23	14	48
means that you should score at the highest level you can.	27	16	50
Test results generally can be improved if you become concerned,	31	19	53
positive, and realistic about major tests and follow improvement strate-	36	22	56
gies. If you are concerned about your results, you are likely to be	41	24	58
motivated to do your best. If you have a positive attitude, you are	45	27	61
likely to learn from the strengths and weaknesses that test scores can	50	30	64
reveal. If you are realistic, you are likely to set proper goals and	55	33	67
be able to achieve them.	56	34	68

gwam 3′ | 1 | 2 | 3 | 4 | 5 |
gwam 5′ | 1 | 2 | 3 |

73b-75b (continued)

Documents 5-6
File-Folder Labels

LP p. 81

Mrs. Moon asks you to prepare file-folder labels for the new members. She gives you format guides and a model to help you. Use the mailing-list index cards for information.

Label Format Guides

1. On line 1 below the rule, 3 spaces from the left edge, key the name (surname, first name, middle initial) and title in ALL CAPS, no punctuation.

2. Key the city, state, and ZIP Code on the next line; key the street address on the third line.

```
HUMMINGBIRD GEORGE C MR
Tulsa, OK  74105-1844
4265 S. Peoria Avenue
```

Document 7
Talk Summary in Report Format

Mrs. Moon asks you to prepare for Mr. Lindsay the summary of a talk he gave at our recent seminar for adult members and their guests. Mrs. Moon suggests that you use standard unbound report format. Mr. Lindsay requested two photocopies of the final draft. Mrs. Moon asks you to watch for and correct any unmarked errors as well as the marked ones and those you make as you key.

BASIC FITNESS

FIVE STEPS TO PHYSICAL AND MENTAL ~~HEALTH~~

Human beings are both body and mind--flesh and spirit. What ever our personnel definition of "soul" it is quiet clear that our minds and bodies are intricately interrelated. The health of the one effects the well being of the other. Let us look then at some ways of "keeping body and sould together"--healthfully

and mental

The basic steps to physical fitness listed here are feew and with a bit of self discipline, not difficult to take.

Consume

1. ~~Eat~~ the right kinds and amounts offood and drink.
2. Engage daily in appropriate forms of bodily exercise.
3. Relax the mind and body with plenty of ~~rest~~, sleep.
4. Keep yourself clean. inside and out.

5. Engage in a wide vareity of ~~interests~~, activities.

and most

Consume the right amounts of food drink. ~~Nearly all~~ of us eat too much of to few different kinds of food. We gorge ourselves with French fries, double decker sandwiches, and pizza--washing them down with cola and other carbonated sugar waters. We eat more then we need and "justify" it by saying "waste not, want not." Is it better, however, for food to go to waist than to waste? Eat according to a plan, rather than according to habit: Try a new food each weak and learn to choose foods that are rich in protien, vitamins, and minerals, avoiding those that are high in fat, salt and sugar.

daily bodily

Engage in appropriate forms of exercise. Office workers are a sedentary lot. Teh only exercise many of us get during the day is the short walks we take to and from coffee breaks and lunch. Evven worse our at home exercise often consists of littel more than trips to the refrigerator and, for some, the TV and CD player controls. Most people say they can't afford a health club. The truth is, sedentary office workers can't afford not to. Unless you discipline your self to a daily exercise routine, such as those outlined in popular physicial fitness books, you should discipline your pocket book to a health or recreation club membership.

to join

(continued, p. 131)

213b-217b (continued)

LP p. 203

Document 11
Reservation Form

Mr. Quinnones: Here is a reservation form that needs to be keyed before I sign and distribute it.

CLEARVIEW MANOR

CLEARVIEW MANOR CONFERENCE CENTER
ROOM/FACILITY RESERVATION FORM

COMPLETE THIS FORM in full and give it to the marketing manager at least two weeks prior to the event date(s).

Direct all inquiries to the marketing manager, (717) 226-5435.

1) Name of Group: Quadcore Computer Systems, Inc.

2) Group Contact: Miss Andrea L. Norman   3) Phone number (717) 543-6060

4) Number of People Expected: 28   Date of Event May 17-20, 19--

5) Description of Event: Seminar: Maintenance Management with Microcomputer LANs

6) Special Preparations:

- ☒ Maintenance (specify): classroom-style setup for 28
- ☒ Resort Lodging: block reserve 28 rooms (evenings of 5/17-5/19)
- ☒ Food service: lunch to be served each day
- ☒ Audio-Visual: overhead projector/screen; flip chart; VCR/monitor
- ☒ Security: open seminar room at 8:30 a.m.; lock at 5:30 p.m.
- ☒ Other: 4 tables at front of room for microcomputers

7) Room/Facility	Date	Time
Right Suite-seminar	May 17-20	8:30 a.m. to 5:30 p.m.
Left Suite-lunch	May 17-20	12 noon to 1 p.m.
Entrance Suite-reception	May 17	8 p.m. to 10:30 p.m.
		to
		to

8) Reservation Requested By (signature): ____________________

9) Department: Marketing   Date: March 3, 19--

NOTE: Please report any changes to the operations manager.

Date Received: ____________ Operations Manager: ____________

APPROVED: ☐   *DENIED:* ☐

COMMENTS: ____________________

73b-75b (continued)

Relax the mind and body with plenty of rest. How much sleep does the average working person require? Some has facetiously anwserd, "Five minutes more." All people don't require the same amount of sleep but seven to eight hours is a good rule of thumb. It is desirable, too, that they be the same hours every night. And if you are one of those people who needs "five minutes more," get them by going too bed earlier instaed of getting up latter!

Keep youself clean--inside and out. Cleanliness may not be next to godliness, but its close. Water, soap, shampoo, antiperspirant, dentifrice, and other toiletries are to inexpensive not to be used by every one as insurance against being personally offensive. And don't put off frequent trips to the laundry, dry cleaner, and shoe repair shop. Clothes do not make the person; but clean, well-maintained clothes reflect her or his self concern.

Engage in a wide variety of interests. With todays increasing leisure time, we are no longer concerned with the "all work and no play" adage. But we are concerned with the kinds of liesure activity in which people engage in. Too many of us have become spectators rather than participants. We over use one or two kinds of recreation: TV or movies or reading or musical tapes/disks. Diversify your recreational activities. Develop some interests that reqiure you to take action for others as well with others.

These five steps, easily taken will go far in helping you improve your physical and mentel fitness.

Document 8
Simplified Memo with Table

Mrs. Moon asks you to process for her signature the attached memorandum. She gives you these notes:

Date: **Current**
Addressee: **All KRC Assistant Directors**
Subject: **EVENT SCHEDULE FOR MARCH**

Mrs. Moon points out that a table in an SS document should be SS. She tells you to be alert to possible unmarked errors in the rough-draft copy and asks that you make 5 photocopies.

The following events are scheduled to take place during the month of March.

Adult Ping Pong Tournament	March 4
Young Adult Marathon	March 8
Lower Teen Basketball Play-off Game	March 10
Upper Teen Basketball Play-off Game	March 16
Children's Arts/Crafts Show	March 17
Young Womens Softball Opening Game	March 20
Young Men's Baseball Opening Game	March 25
Young Adult Racquet ball Tournament	March 27

Please prepare bulletin board announcements and plan a publicity campaign to promote the event(s) for which you are responsible. Keep in mind that we want to attract as many members and freinds to these events as possible.

Let's plan to meet next Thursday at 2 a.m. to discuss your promotion plans.

213b-217b (continued)

Dining facilities. The Center is prepared to provide an elegant cuisine of fine dining, informal buffets, nutritious snacks and diet menus for a few to thousands. The ~~Center's~~ master chef can provides many choices from ~~its~~ standard breakfast, lunch, dinner, and reception menus or will be happy to discuss special ~~requests.~~

General Information. The Conference Center staff can provide special requests for such things as entertainment, unusual decorations, and theme parties or meetings. Courier service can be provided for pickup or deliver of materials shipped via the rapid delivery services. Personnel for collecting tickets or staffing registration and information tables can also be provided ~~upon request.~~ ~~Pennsylvania State Tax~~ is percent and will be added to all accounts. In addition, a gratuity of 15 percent will be charged on all food and beverage service.

Mr. Quinnones: Add these paragraphs to the end of the report in the order they are numbered. I have taken them from existing brochures.

Travel Information

Clearview Manor is easily accessible by automobile or plane. If you are driving, you should use Exit 44 on Interstate 80 and follow the directional signs to Clearview Manor. If you are flying, use the Wilkes-Barre/Scranton Airport. Airport limousine, taxi, or automobile rental services are conveniently available.

Lodging. Every room at Clearview Manor is spacious and professionally furnished with two double beds, a sofa, a table, and two chairs. Each room is equipped with a direct-dial telephone system, a safe, a refrigerator, color TV featuring cable and movie stations, and AM & FM radio with built-in alarm clock.

The Resort

Clearview Manor's resort facilities provide everything necessary to make your stay pleasant and memorable. The resort offers top-quality accommodations, exceptional dining experiences, and a wide variety of entertainment and activities to choose from.

Recreational facilities. There's always something to do at Clearview Manor. Golf is available at the Manor's 18-hole golf course, and tennis can be played on the two indoor or five outdoor courts. Squash and racquetball can be played on air-conditioned indoor courts. In addition, resort guests can swim indoors or outdoors, and walk, jog, or hike for miles on well-marked trails. During the winter, guests can ski cross country on well-patrolled trails, ride for miles on a snowmobile, or skate on the indoor or outdoor rinks.

Dining and entertainment. Clearview Manor's popular Top-of-the-Mountain restaurant is known for its continental cuisine and quality service. The Top of the Mountain is open 7 days a week for breakfast, lunch, and dinner. The adjoining Manor Lounge is perfect for a relaxing conversation after a busy day. Later in the evening it's just the place to enjoy the greatest names in entertainment, which Clearview Manor provides each night of the week.

Skill Comparison: Sentences

LL: 70 spaces; LS: SS; DS between groups

1. Key lines 1, 3, 5, 7, and 9 at your own pace to master keystroking patterns.

2. Key a 1′ writing on line 2 to establish a goal rate.

3. Key a 1′ writing on each of lines 4, 6, 8, and 10; calculate *gwam* on each.

4. Compare rates on the 5 timed writings.

5. Key additional 1′ writings on each of the slower lines.

balanced-hand words	1	if he but own held firm sign visit girls profit height entitle visible
	2	The men may visit the ancient town by the lake when he signs the form.
double-letter words	3	all too off zoo good food door hall keep small issue sorry allow shall
	4	All seem to meet my new speed goal; few will keep within three errors.
combination response	5	six you the joy for are also best such only form wear work union title
	6	Only six of them serve on the wage panel for the oil union in my town.
adjacent-key words	7	as buy saw top try pod fort post ruin owes coin dare glass opens moist
	8	We are going to post top scores at the regional meet and at the state.
long-reach words	9	my sun ice mug sum gym sect nice curb bran must cent under bring curve
	10	Myra served a number of guests a mug of iced punch after the gym meet.

| 1 | 2 | 3 | 4 | 5 | 6 | 7 | 8 | 9 | 10 | 11 | 12 | 13 | 14 |

Timed Writing: Paragraphs

1. Take a 1′ writing on ¶ 1; calculate *gwam*. Add 2-4 words to set a new goal rate.

2. Take two 1′ writings on ¶ 1 at your new goal rate, guided by a ¼′ call of the guide.

3. Key ¶ 2 in the same way.

4. Key a 3′ or a 5′ writing on ¶s 1-2 combined; calculate *gwam;* circle errors.

5. If time permits, key additional 1′ writings on each ¶ for speed or for control, according to your needs.

all letters used | A | 1.5 si | 5.7 awl | 80% hfw

	gwam 3′	5′
Your basic keying skill will continue to grow during the process-	4	3
ing of letters, memos, and reports. It is a good idea, however, to	9	5
return from time to time to straight-copy materials for special skill-	14	8
building drill. Even if keying speed does not transfer at a high level	18	11
to document production, the production skill will be limited unless	23	14
your keying skill is high. Work on both as often as possible.	27	16
Another way to improve production speed is to give special atten-	31	19
tion to quickening the spacing between document parts so that more of	36	22
your time is spent in keying copy. Make this a major goal in the days	41	24
ahead. How you spend your time between completing one document and	45	27
starting another is of utmost importance, also. Realize this now and	50	30
attempt to reduce the time you spend between one problem and the next.	55	33

gwam 3′ | 1 | 2 | 3 | 4 | 5 |
gwam 5′ | 1 | 2 | 3 |

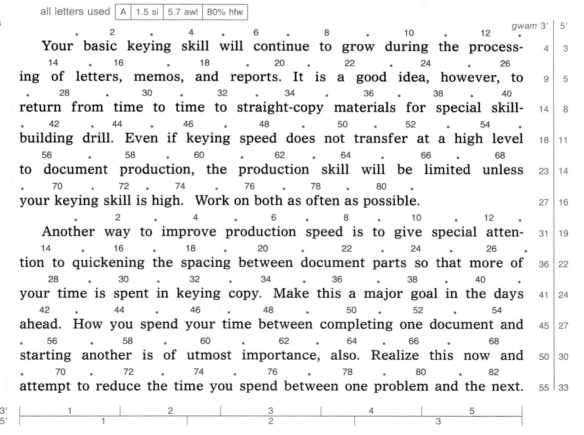

213b-217b (continued)

Document 10
Unbound Report

Mr. Quinnones: I have made some revisions to the first-draft brochure copy you formatted for me. Prepare another draft in unbound report form. I have added some information at the end to be included in this draft.

CONFERENCE CENTER

CLEARVIEW MANOR

Located 2,000 feet high on 2,700 acres of beautiful Pocono Mountainside, the Clearview Manor is a unique learning, meeting, training, and resort facility for business and professional groups. Located two miles west of Mt. Pocono on Route 314, Clearview Manor provides an opportunity for groups to combine excellent conference facilities with outsanding resort faciltes and activities.

The Conference Center

The Center has large and small meeting rooms with up-to-date computer and communication capabilities, spacious exhibit area, and elegant dining areas which provide the necessary flexible space to meet the needs of every group from five to five hundred.

Meeting rooms. With nearly 6,000 square feet of meeting room space, the Conference Center is a perfect choice for meetings. The meeting rooms can be divided into eight separate, completely soundproof meeting areas for groups ranging from 18 to 75. If larger areas are required, the space can be divided to handle two large groups--one at 376 and another at 262.

Exhibit area. The Conference Center can accomodate approximately 100 exhibitors in an unobstructed area of 15,00 square feet. Each exhibitor can access alternating current, three-phase 60-cycle, 120/208-volts or 120-volt, single-phase current for both light and power cirucits. Telephone, computer, radio, braodcast cable and closed circuit television connections can be made. Delivery can be made through a roll-up door 10 feet high by 11 feet wide from a straight and level delivery drive.

(continued, p. 372)

LESSONS 76 – 100

PHASE 4 IMPROVE KEYBOARDING, FORMATTING, AND LANGUAGE SKILLS

In the 25 lessons of Phase 4, you will:

1. Refine technique patterns.
2. Improve basic keyboarding and language skills.
3. Improve skill on rough-draft and script copy.
4. Improve formatting and production skill on memos, letters, reports, and tables.
5. Learn to format in modified block style.
6. Apply formatting skills to process a series of documents for a simulated real estate office.
7. Measure and evaluate document processing skills.

213b-217b (continued)

Document 8
Invoice

LP p. 199

Mr. Quinnones: Here is a handwritten copy of the invoice we will send to the mathematics conference speaker who had us key and print a handout for his session. Everything you need is on the form except the cost of your time. You will have to multiply your time by $14.00 per hour to get the processing cost. Round your time to the nearest quarter hour to compute the cost. Once you have the cost, complete the extensions as needed.

CLEARVIEW MANOR | P.O. Box A, Pocono Manor, PA 18349-2010, (717) 225-9988

INVOICE

DR RICHARD K SIMMS
BECKLEY COLLEGE
WASHINGTON PA 15301-4211

Date: *Current*
Customer Order No.: *via phone*

Terms	Delivery	Our Order No.	Event Date
30 days	*client pick up at manor*	*1101*	*current*

Quantity	Service/Product	Unit Price		Amount	
	Per hour report processing fee (3 pages)	*14*	*00*		
450	*Per page duplicating fee*		*04*	*18*	*00*
	Total				

Document 9
News Release

LP p. 201

Mr. Quinnones: I made this draft on my typewriter at home. Please format it as a news release. State that it is for immediate release and name me as the contact person.

POCONO MANOR, PA, (current month, day, year). Clearview Manor, one of the oldest resort hotels and conference centers in the Pocono Mountains, is expanding its conference center facilities. Construction ~~isxscheduledxtoxwillxtoxbeginxwithxaxmonthxonxa~~ of this new addition will provide ~~modern,xxupxtoxdate~~ flexible space for meetings, banquets, and exhibits.

The addition will be made at the north end of the ~~present~~ existing conference center ~~and~~ near the present executive dining room area. ~~MrxxThomasxRxxQuinnones~~ Ms. Helen T. Caldwell, conference center director, said that the ~~addition~~ facility will provide Clearview Manor with an additional 3,000 square feet of space. She stated, "The architects have designed the facility in such a manner that we can convert ~~fromxanxopen~~ within a matter of minutes from a completely open space to six fully-equipped individual meeting rooms."

Mulaney ~~and~~ Associates, Inc., ~~are~~ is serving as the architectural firm and Baumann Brothers is the general contractor. ~~ItxisxestimatedxexpectedxthatThe~~ The facility will be ready for use within five months. Mr. Thomas R. Quinnones, the marketing manager, is ~~nowxaccepting~~ already scheduling groups into the new space. He said, "We are finding that this additional space is in high demand by the many groups who use the resort and conference center facilities at Clearview Manor."

###

UNIT 16 LESSONS 76 – 81
Improve Letter/Memo Formatting Skills

Learning Goals

1. To review/improve letter and memo formatting skills.
2. To learn to format business letters in modified block style.
3. To check/improve language skills.

Format Guides

1. Paper guide at *0* (for typewriters).
2. LL (line length): 70 spaces for drills and ¶s; as specified in placement table for letters, p. 76; 1″ margins for memos.
3. LS (line spacing): SS drills, letters, and memos; DS ¶s.
4. PI (paragraph indention): 5 when appropriate.

Lesson 76 *Keyboarding Skills/Letters*

76a ► 5 Conditioning Practice

each line twice SS (slowly, then faster); DS between 2-line groups; as time permits, rekey selected lines

alphabet 1 Mr. Zahn will ask very specific questions before judging the exhibits.

figures 2 Only 32 of the 64 computers were replaced in 1990 with the B758 model.

space bar 3 It may not be too late for him to bake the cake in time for the party.

speed 4 The formal social for the visitor is to be held in the ancient chapel.

| 1 | 2 | 3 | 4 | 5 | 6 | 7 | 8 | 9 | 10 | 11 | 12 | 13 | 14 |

76b ► 10 Check Keyboarding Skill: Straight Copy

1. A 3′ writing on ¶s 1-3 combined; find *gwam*, circle errors.
2. A 1′ writing on each ¶; find *gwam*, circle errors.
3. Another 3′ writing on ¶s 1-3 combined, find *gwam*, circle errors.
4. Record your better 3′ rate for comparison in 81b, page 143.

Additional Skill Building

As time permits during the unit

1. Take a series of 1′ *guided* writings on each of the 3 ¶s using the plan given on p. 38.
2. Take additional 3′ writings to check skill increases.

all letters used | A | 1.5 si | 5.7 awl | 80% hfw |

	gwam 3′	5′
People in business are concerned about what is communicated by the	4	3
written word. As they write memos, letters, and reports, they may plan	9	6
for the content but may not plan for the image of the message. Experts,	14	8
however, realize that neglecting the way a document looks can be costly.	19	11
Many times a written piece of correspondence is the only basis on	23	14
which a person can form an impression of the writer. Judgments based on	28	17
a first impression that may be formed by the reader about the writer	33	20
should always be considered before mailing a document.	36	22
The way a document looks can communicate as much as what it says.	41	25
Margins, spacing, and placement are all important features to consider	46	27
when you key a document. A quality document is one that will bring the	50	30
interest of the reader to the message rather than to the way it appears.	55	33

gwam 3′ | 1 | 2 | 3 | 4 | 5 |
5′ | 1 | 2 | 3 |

213b-217b (continued)

3. The chart's third column can be used to explain that the meter is the basic unit used to measure length and that other units are ~~either~~ parts ~~of a meter~~ or multiples of a meter. The chart ~~orders~~ lists the units of measurement from the smallest to the largest.

4. The third column can also be used to show students how they can convert from one metric unit to another by moving the decimal point in the meter measurement to the left to convert to smaller units or to the right to convert to larger units.

5. The last column of the chart can be used to establish the relationship between ~~various~~ selected metric and English ~~units of~~ measurements units.

Summary

The metric system of measurement must be taught along with the English system. It is a system that can be presented in an understandable manner if the teacher establishes goals and uses good examples, illustrations, and applications to present the content. The chart is an example of an illustration that can ~~be easily~~ be used easily to enhance learning.

DS

---

make superscript. (If not possible, make it "1.##")

1 Roswell E. Fairbank, Robert A. Schultheis, and Raymond M. Kaczmarski, Applied Business Mathematics, ~~Thirteenth Edition,~~ (Cincinnati: South-Western Publishing Co., 1990), p. 167. 13th ed.

Document 7
Table

Mr. Quinnones: Format and key the price list to accompany the composite menu you completed. Use **(Proposed Prices, May through October, 19--)** as the secondary heading.

CLEARVIEW MANOR PRICE LIST*

Meal No.	Breakfast	Luncheon	Dinner
1	$ 6.95	$ 8.95	$ 14.25
2	6.25	9.25	15.50
3	10.95	8.95	15.95
4	6.95	10.50	17.75
5	8.25	7.95	19.50
6	6.35	9.50	18.95

---

* Prices do not include 6% tax and 15% gratuity.

76c ▶ 35
Review Document Formatting Skill: Letters

3 plain full sheets

Letter 1
Personal-Business Letter

Format and key in block style the letter shown at the right. Use a 60-space line; place date on line 16. (See p. 70 for model.) Correct any errors you make as you key.

words

3716 Rangely Drive | Raleigh, NC 27609-4115 | October 14, 19-- | Mr. Robert C. 15
Johnson | Wayler Insurance Company | 206 Polk Street | Raleigh, NC 27604- 28
4120 | Dear Mr. Johnson | Subject: INFORMATION ON CAREER OPPORTUNITIES 40

Please send me information on career opportunities available with Wayler 55
Insurance Company in the administrative services area. As part of a class 70
assignment, I will be giving an oral report on a company for which I would 85
be interested in working. Wayler Insurance is an impressive company, and 99
I would like to do the report on career opportunities with your firm. 114

The report needs to address job titles, job requirements, educational require- 129
ments, salary, and opportunities for advancement. Any information that you 144
are able to provide on these areas will be greatly appreciated. 157

Sincerely | Richard B. Lyons | xx 163

Placement Note

Use the Letter Placement Guide on page 76 to determine margins and dateline placement for business letters in this unit. The number of words in the body is indicated by the number in parentheses at the end of each letter.

Letter 2
Business Letter

Format in block style with open punctuation the letter shown at the right. Correct any errors you make as you key.

October 20, 19-- | Mr. Richard B. Lyons | 3716 Rangely Drive | Raleigh, NC 14
27609-4115 | Dear Mr. Lyons 19

Wayler Insurance Company is always interested in potential employees. We 34
hope that you will consider us once you are graduated. 45

As you will see from reading the information which is enclosed, we have 59
different levels of administrative support positions in our company. Job ti- 75
tles, job requirements, educational requirements, and starting salaries are 90
included for each level. Our company philosophy is to reward loyal employees; 106
therefore, we like to promote from within when qualified employees are avail- 121
able. We also reimburse employees for additional job-related schooling 135
completed during their employment. 142

If you need further information or would like one of our administrative sup- 157
port supervisors to talk with your class, please call us. (words in body: 149) 169

Sincerely yours | Robert C. Johnson | Customer Relations Director | xx | Enclosure 184

Letter 3
Business Letter

Format in block style with open punctuation the letter shown at the right. Use the address and date given in Letter 2. Use an appropriate salutation. Correct any errors you make as you key.

opening lines 19

Robert Johnson, our director of customer relations, indicated that you are 34
interested in career opportunities with Wayler Insurance Company in the 48
administrative support services division. He asked me to provide you with 63
additional information. 69

As word processing supervisor, I have the opportunity to interview and test 84
many applicants. We are looking for applicants with excellent communi- 98
cation and keyboarding skills. Both are extremely important skills for indi- 113
viduals to possess in order to be an asset to our organization. Any course you 129
take to enhance these skills will increase your marketability. 142

If you would like to visit our word processing center before giving your re- 157
port, please let me know. You can telephone me at 833-7291. (149) 169

Sincerely yours | Mrs. Mary A. Worthington | Word Processing Supervisor | 183
xx | c Robert C. Johnson 187

Additional excerpt from CLEARVIEW MANOR DOCUMENT PROCESSING MANUAL:

To hang-indent: For each enumerated item, key the number and period and space twice. Set a tab stop at the point where the first letter of the first word will be keyed. For lines that follow, tab over so that each line begins flush under the first letter of the first word in the line above.

Goals of the Instruction

Students must ~~be required to~~ complete a series of learning activities which will enable them to

1. Understand, read, write, and pronounce the basic metric measures for length, wieght, and capacity.
2. Add, subtract, multiply, and divide metric measurements.
3. Convert from one metric unit to another.
4. Solve problems that use metric measurements.
5. ~~To~~ convert commonly used metric measures to English mfasures and vice versa.

DS between items

Instructional Strategies

To accomplish the learning goals, a variety of learning ~~activities~~ aids such as charts, oral and written exercises, and word problems can and should be used extensively in the learning process. The chart is an excellent learning resource which can be used to accomplish many of the objectives.

Charts. The chart below is an example of how ~~the~~ basic metric units of length can be presented in visual form. A similar chart for weight and capacity could be developed.

METRIC UNITS OF LENGTH

Unit	Abbreviation	Equivalent in Meters	Common English Equivalents
Millimeter	mm	0.001 m	-----
Centimeter	cm	0.01 m	1 foot = 30 cm
Decimeter	dm	0.1 m	-----
Meter	m	1 m	1 yard = .9 m
Dekameter	dam	10 m	-----
Hectometer	hm	100 m	-----
Kilometer	km	1000 m	1 mile = 1.6 km

Using the Chart. The chart above can be used in numerous ways to accomplish the instructional objectives.

1. The first column of the chart can be used for an oral exercise in which students are asked to pronounce each ~~of~~ unit of measurement.

2. The second column of the chart can be used to show students the ~~metric~~ abbreviations ~~and that they are written in lowercase letters.~~ for metric units, which are always shown in lowercase letters.

(continued, p. 369)

77a ▶ 5 Conditioning Practice

each line twice SS (slowly, then faster); DS between 2-line groups; if time permits, rekey selected lines

alphabet 1 Jack answered many questions about the exact value of each topaz ring.

figures 2 On Monday, November 14, 1988 I bought pattern numbers 32A57 and 60B94.

fig/sym 3 The 1987 cost ($414) was 15 percent greater than the 1982 cost ($360).

speed 4 The neighbor's dog was with the girl by the big sign in the cornfield.

| 1 | 2 | 3 | 4 | 5 | 6 | 7 | 8 | 9 | 10 | 11 | 12 | 13 | 14 |

77b ▶ 35 Learn to Format Letters in Modified Block Format

plain full sheet; correct errors

1. Read the information at the right and study the model letter on page 137 illustrating modified block format (blocked paragraphs) with mixed punctuation.

2. Key the model letter using the Letter Placement Guide on page 76 to determine correct side margins and placement. The body of the letter contains 173 standard 5-stroke words.

3. Key letter again, but address it to

Mr. Karl M. Bedford
Berwick Drilling Co.
1088 Windsor Avenue
Waco, TX 76708-9316

4. Indent the subject line and ¶s and change "blocked" to "indented" in the subject line.

5. For the first two lines, substitute the following:

This letter is arranged in modified block format with indented subject line and paragraphs. Another difference *(continue lines)*.

Modified Block Letter Format

"Modified Block" simply means that the block format has been *modified;* that is, the date and the closing lines (complimentary close, writer's name, and writer's job title or department) start at the horizontal center of the paper instead of at the left margin. Modified block format may have either blocked (p. 137) or indented (see model at right) paragraphs.

Open and Mixed Punctuation

A letter in modified block format may be keyed with either open or mixed punctuation. In *open punctuation,* no punctuation follows the salutation or the complimentary close. In *mixed punctuation,* a colon follows the salutation and a comma follows the complimentary close.

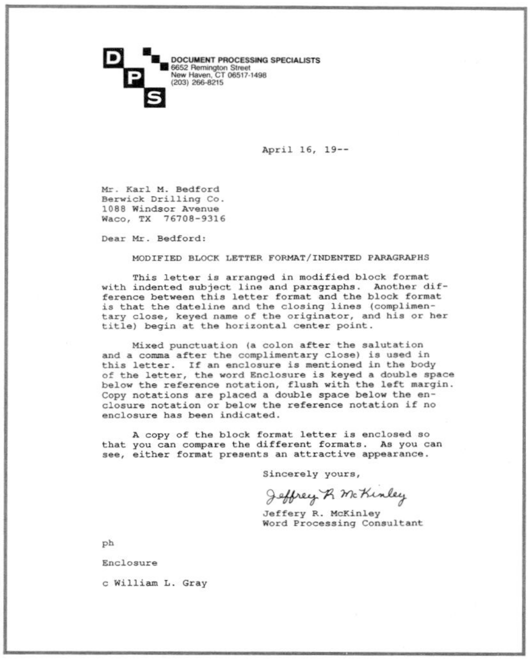
DOCUMENT PROCESSING SPECIALISTS
6652 Remington Street
New Haven, CT 06517-1498
(203) 266-8215

April 16, 19--

Mr. Karl M. Bedford
Berwick Drilling Co.
1088 Windsor Avenue
Waco, TX 76708-9316

Dear Mr. Bedford:

MODIFIED BLOCK LETTER FORMAT/INDENTED PARAGRAPHS

This letter is arranged in modified block format with indented subject line and paragraphs. Another difference between this letter format and the block format is that the dateline and the closing lines (complimentary close, keyed name of the originator, and his or her title) begin at the horizontal center point.

Mixed punctuation (a colon after the salutation and a comma after the complimentary close) is used in this letter. If an enclosure is mentioned in the body of the letter, the word Enclosure is keyed a double space below the reference notation, flush with the left margin. Copy notations are placed a double space below the enclosure notation or below the reference notation if no enclosure has been indicated.

A copy of the block format letter is enclosed so that you can compare the different formats. As you can see, either format presents an attractive appearance.

Sincerely yours,

Jeffrey R. McKinley

Jeffery R. McKinley
Word Processing Consultant

ph

Enclosure

c William L. Gray

77c ▶ 10 Check Language Skills: Capitalization

SS sentences; DS between 5-line groups

1. Key line number (with period); space twice, then key the sentence, supplying the needed capital letters.

2. If time permits, key the sentences again to increase decision-making speed.

1. sacred heart hospital is located on madison or monroe street.
2. reno, las vegas, and sparks are the largest cities in nevada.
3. is your dental appointment with dr. hall in november or december?
4. the next phi beta lambda meeting will be wednesday, september 12.
5. my favorite holidays are thanksgiving day and the fourth of july.

6. mr. jay told us to key lines 7, 8, and 9 on page 20 of lesson 9.
7. aaa must be the abbreviation for american automobile association.
8. the next commencement address will be given by president miller.
9. is mt. rushmore located in south dakota or in north dakota?
10. alex and damion both live in mead hall on lincoln boulevard.

11. mary will arrive this wednesday at noon on american airlines.
12. the california angels beat the new york yankees on friday night.
13. the secretary for future business leaders of america is oki saga.
14. the steam engine played a major part in the industrial revolution.
15. yellowstone lake and jackson lake are both located in wyoming.

213b-217b (continued)

Document 5
Table

Mr. Quinnones: The catering manager has given me these three menu cards. Format all three of them on one full sheet. Use **CLEARVIEW MANOR MENUS** as the main heading and **(Proposed for May through October, 19--)** as the secondary heading. **Breakfast** is to be the 1st column heading; **Luncheon** the 2d; **Dinner** the 3d. Key the numbers after the meals because they will be used to prepare a price list.

Keep the composite menu until I give you the price list to key. When both are completed, fasten them together with the menu on top of the price list.

Breakfast	Luncheon	Dinner
Scrambled Eggs served with choice of Bacon, Ham, or Sausage --1	Baked Stuffed Chicken Breast with Sauce Poulette --1	Broiled Breast of Chicken a la Kiev with Sauce Supreme --1
French Toast served with choice of Bacon, Ham, or Sausage --2	Marinated London Broil with Deluxe Mushroom Sauce --2	Baked Stuffed Center-Cut Pork Chop with ~~Deluxe~~ Mushroom Sauce --2
Breakfast Steak with Scrambled Eggs --3	Broiled Fillet of Lemon Sole ~~with Lemon Butter~~ --3	Broiled Fillet of Boston Scrod --3
Corned Beef Hash with Scrambled Eggs --4	Open-Faced Prime Rib of Beef Sandwich --4	Broiled ~~Jumbo~~ Shrimp Stuffed with Crabmeat --4
Eggs Benedict --5	Braised Swiss Steak--5	Prime Rib of Beef--5
~~Blueberry~~ Banana Pancakes --6	Steak Sandwich --6	Veal Marsala --6

Document 6
Report

Mr. Quinnones: Here is a copy of a report that Dr. Richard Simms, a speaker at tomorrow's math teacher conference, faxed to us. He needs us to process a final copy and print 150 copies of it. Dr. Simms has asked that the enumerations be keyed in the hang-indent style. With this exception, use the usual report format. Be sure to record your time on the log so we can bill him for your time.

Note: Dr. Simms does not want us to prepare a reference page for this report.

A NEED TO KNOW METRICS

QS

DS ~~There is a need~~ Today students need to learn two systems of measurements--the metric system which is used throughout the world and the English or Customary system which is the most often-used system in the United States. /1/ ← make this superscript without diagonals if possible.

Rationale for the Instruction

Instruction relating to the basic components of the metric system must be included in the curriculum of our nation's schools because all people must have an understanding of the metric system to function in today's society. Metrics are everywhere! Automobile engines, soft drink containers, ~~medicine~~, nutrition information listed on food packages, jean and sizes, (film), and most of the nuts ~~and~~ bolts and screws ~~which are~~ used to assemble products imported to the United States are examples of common items which are measured in metric units.

(continued, p. 368)

DOCUMENT PROCESSING SPECIALISTS
6652 Remington Street
New Haven, CT 06517-1498
(203) 266-8215

			words in parts	total words
Dateline	April 16, 19--	Line 16 QS; operate return 4 times to quadruple-space (3 blank lines)	3	3
Letter address	Miss Linda S. LaValley		8	8
	Vermillion Paper Products		13	13
	5067 Blackstone Lane		17	17
	Hartford, CT 06108-4913 DS		22	22
Salutation	Dear Miss LaValley: DS		26	26
Subject line	MODIFIED BLOCK LETTER FORMAT/BLOCKED PARAGRAPHS DS		10	36
Body of letter	This letter is arranged in modified block format with		20	46
	blocked paragraphs. The only difference between this		31	57
	letter format and the block format is that the date-		41	67
	line and the closing lines (complimentary close, keyed		52	78
	name of the originator, and his or her title) begin at		63	89
	the horizontal center point. DS		69	95
	Mixed punctuation (a colon after the salutation and a		80	106
	comma after the complimentary close) is used in this let-		91	117
	ter. If an enclosure is mentioned in the body of the		102	128
	letter, the word Enclosure is keyed a double space below		114	140
	the reference notation, flush with the left margin. Copy		125	151
	notations are placed a double space below the enclosure		136	163
	notation or below the reference notation if no enclosure		148	174
	has been indicated. DS		152	178
	A copy of the block format letter is enclosed so that		163	189
	you can compare the different formats. As you can see,		174	200
	either format presents an attractive appearance. DS		184	210
Complimentary close	Sincerely yours, QS		3	213
	Jeffrey R. McKinley			
Keyed name	Jeffrey R. McKinley		7	217
Official title	Word Processing Consultant DS		13	223
Reference notation	ph DS		13	223
Enclosure notation	Enclosure DS		15	225
Copy notation	c William L. Gray DS		19	229

Shown in pica type
1½" side margins
camera reduced

Modified Block with Blocked Paragraphs and Mixed Punctuation

213b-217b (continued)

Document 3
Table

Mr. Quinnones: Key this table of room sizes. We will use the information in this format until the new brochure is printed, if it is approved.

CLEARVIEW MANOR

CONFERENCE CENTER ROOM SIZES

(Ceiling Height is 10')

Areas	Dimensions L x W	Banquet Seating	Theatre Seating	Classroom Seating*
Left Suite	31' x 20'	50	72	48
Center Suite	56' x 54'	250	376	244
Right Suite	31' x 18'	40	60	36
Entrance Suite	28' x 40'	90	130	84
Board Room	26' x 16'	N/A	N/A	18
Exhibit Area	146' x 110'	(Space for ~~300~~ 100 exhibitors.)		

* Tables: 2' wide, 6' long; upholstered chairs: 22" wide.

Document 4
Letters

LP pp. 193-197

Mr. Quinnones: Send this letter to each of the three people whose business cards are given at the right. The information you need is supplied on each card.

Note: Use these Code numbers: **p366.4a, p366.4b, p366.4c.**

Wednesday, June 6, 19--

Helen T. Wilde, Ph.D.
Executive Director
(914) 753-2285

Eastern Economic Association
98 Highview Avenue
New Rochelle, NY 10801-5316

Thursday, May 3, 19--

Mrs. Emma T. Zappalo

LANDMARK DEVELOPERS
103 Vine Street
Shamokin, PA 17872-5533

Telephone: **(717) 362-9462**
Telecopier: **(717) 391-5555**

Monday, May 21, 19--

SCIENTIFIC RESEARCH, INC.

David F. Moore
Sales Manager
(301) 654-9278

500 Gorusch Ave.
Baltimore, MD
21218-3549

Thank you for selecting Clearview Manor for your function scheduled for (day, month, year).

Enclosed are two copies of the contract. After reviewing the contract, sign one copy and return it to me. Keep the other copy for your records. You must return the signed contract within ten days to guarantee the dates and facilities.

As indicated in the contract, you can choose to revise your food service guarantees up to 48 hours prior to the event. If the Catering Department does not receive a revised guarantee from you, the information in the contract will be used.

If I can be of further assistance to you, please call me. Clearview Manor's Operating Manager will call you about three weeks before your function to finalize all the arrangements.

78a ▶ 5 Conditioning Practice

each line twice SS (slowly, then faster); DS between 2-line groups; if time permits, rekey selected lines

alphabet 1 Pamela Jaworski inquired about the exact size of the very large house.

figures 2 Flight 687 from Boston will arrive at 10:45 a.m. on May 29 at Gate 13.

fig/sym 3 The 5% sales tax on Order #394 is $16.80; for Order #202 it is $17.50.

speed 4 The haughty man may signal with a giant emblem or with the usual sign.

| 1 | 2 | 3 | 4 | 5 | 6 | 7 | 8 | 9 | 10 | 11 | 12 | 13 | 14 |

78b ▶ 7 Formatting Drill: Modified Block Letter

plain paper; 1½" SM

1. Two 1′ writings in modified block format on opening lines (date through ¶ 1) of letter on p. 137. Concentrate on correct placement of letter parts.

2. Two 1′ writings in modified letter format on closing lines (¶ 3 through copy notation) of letter on p. 137. If you finish before time is called, DS and begin again. Stress correct placement of letter parts.

78c ▶ 28 Format Letters in Modified Block Format

Letter 1 -- Business Letter

plain paper; modified block format, blocked ¶s; open punctuation; correct errors

words

February 21, 19-- 4

Mr. Seth J. Johnson 8
Jones & Bartells 11
Accounting Associates 15
2893 Frederick Avenue 20
Princeton, NJ 07067-3093 25

Dear Mr. Johnson 28

Is your company interested in participating in 38
our high school's chapter of Future Business 47
Leaders of America Career Day? It will be held 56
on Friday, March 22, from 9 a.m. to 3 p.m. 65

The purpose of Career Day is to provide a forum 75
for chapter members to become acquainted with 84
occupations they are interested in pursuing. 93
Many members are interested in the field of 102
accounting. It would be great to have Jones & 112
Bartells Accounting Associates be one of the 121
firms representing this dynamic area. 128

If you are interested, please let me know by 137
March 1. One of our members will telephone 146
you with the details of the day's activities. (128) 155

Sincerely 157

Jonathan R. Coggins 161
President 163

xx 164

c Ms. Charla G. Oaks, Advisor 170

Letter 2 -- Personal-Business Letter

plain paper; modified block format, indented ¶s; mixed punctuation; 60-space line; correct errors

words

3988 Bancroft Court 4
Roswell, GA 30075-9082 9
July 2, 19-- 11

Attention Software Manager 16
Fehr Computer Products 21
829 Silverwood Drive 26
Atlanta, GA 30349-4217 30

Ladies and Gentlemen: 35

"QUALITY SYSTEM" WP SOFTWARE

Last week when I was in Atlanta, I purchased
the "Quality System" word processing software
package from your store. Today when I tried 68
to use the software, I found that there was no 77
user's manual included. 82

Please send me a copy of the manual as soon 91
as possible so that I will be able to install the 101
software and start using it. I've enclosed a copy 111
of the receipt which contains the identification 121
numbers for the software. (84) 126

Sincerely yours, 130

Mrs. Carla A. Cerone 134

Enclosure 136

Letter 3 is on p. 139.

213a-217a ▶ 5 (daily)
Conditioning Practice

Key the lines as many times as you can in 5′ at the beginning of each work session during the simulation.

alphabet 1 I will need a pretty gift box for the quartz clock I have to send Jim.

figures 2 A school received 8,032 applications for 4,675 freshmen spots in 1989.

fig/sym 3 Jan said, "Buy Model #3746 or #1098 at a 25% discount at Frey & Sons."

speed 4 Diane and my busy neighbor may dismantle the shanty on the big island.

| 1 | 2 | 3 | 4 | 5 | 6 | 7 | 8 | 9 | 10 | 11 | 12 | 13 | 14 |

213b-217b ▶ 45 (daily)
A Document Processing Simulation

Work Assignment: As you complete each document in this simulation, record the information required on the Document Processing Log on LP p. 191 (or use one that your supervisor has provided).

Document 1
Letter

Mr. Quinnones: Here is a draft of a letter we can send to people who request information about our facilities. Prepare a formatted copy on plain paper so I can review it again. Use today's date, the name and business address given below, an appropriate salutation and complimentary close, and my name and title.

Mrs. Susan L. Kellog
M. S. Kuga Company
620 Harvey Avenue
Pontiac, MI 48053-2913

Thank you for inquiring about holding a conference at Clearview Manor. Enclosed is a packet of information which describes the meeting, exhibit hall, resort, and recreational facilities.

Clearview Manor Conference Center is well equipped with state-of-the-art audiovisual and videotaping technology, complete computer compatibility, excellent food service, and a professional staff to provide needed assistance and service.

Please review the packet. If you need additional information about the facilities or want to discuss available dates, please call or write me.

Document 2
Memo

Mr. Quinnones: Process this memo from me to **Ms. Caldwell.** Use her full name and title and supply all other parts of the memo.

During the past few months, it has become apparent to me and to others who have contact with prospective clients that the brochure we use to describe the Conference Center must be revised. This need is evident because we are getting numerous questions about the center's capability to handle groups planning to do extensive videotaping or use computers in a classroom setting.

I would like to have your approval to revise the brochure to include information about these and other features missing from the present brochure and then seek prices to print the revised brochure in four colors.

We will not need to pay a professional typesetter because we will be able to format the copy using the new desktop publishing software that will be installed in the very near future.

78c (continued)

Letter 3
Business Letter

plain paper; modified block format; blocked ¶s; open punctuation; correct errors

Address letter to:

Mr. Jonathan R. Coggins
FBLA President
Lincoln High School
5987 Plymouth Drive
Princeton, NJ 07065-8172

Date the letter February 26 and supply an appropriate salutation.

words

opening lines 28

¶ Thank you for your invitation. Jones + Bartells Asso- 39
ciates would be delighted to take part in the career 49
day being sponsored by your FBLA Chapter. 58
¶ This time of year is very busy for accounting firms. 69
However, we will be able to have one of our partners attend 81
during the morning and another in the afternoon. Miss 92
Kathleen Cruz will be there from 9 a.m. to 1 p.m. and Mr. Jay 104
Lorentz will be there for the remainder of the day. 115
¶ Please call Miss Cruz and Mr. Lorentz to finalize 125
the arrangements. Their business cards are enclosed. (110) 135
Sincerely / Seth J. Johnson, CPA / Partner in Charge / xx / 146
Enclosures / c Kathleen A. Cruz / Jay P. Lorentz 155

78d ▶ 10 Improve Language Skills: Word Choice

1. Study the spelling and definition of each word.

2. Key the line number (with period), space twice, then key the **Learn** sentence; key the **Apply** sentences in the same format, selecting the correct word in parentheses to complete the sentences.

3. DS between three-line groups.

want (vb) need, desire; as a noun, lacking a required amount

won't (vb) will not

peak (n) pointed end; top of a mountain

peek (vb) to glance or look at for a brief time

Learn 1. If they want additional supplies, won't Dr. Greenawalt contact us?
Apply 2. Each (want, won't) was evaluated in terms of the actual cost involved.
Apply 3. If you (want, won't) be leaving until Sunday, you can go to the game.

Learn 4. If you peek around the corner, you will see the mountain peak.
Apply 5. The (peak, peek) of the iceberg was about to disappear from view.
Apply 6. The instructor told the students not to (peak, peek) at the keyboard.

Lesson 79 Modified Block Letters/Language Skills

79a ▶ 5 Conditioning Practice

each line twice SS (slowly, then faster); DS between 2-line groups; if time permits, rekey selected lines

alphabet 1 Robert kept examining the size and quality of the very choice jewelry.
figures 2 He scored 94, 75, 82, 64, and 100 on the quizzes for an average of 83.
shift keys 3 Why are Mary and Kathy going to Chicago on Labor Day for eight months?
speed 4 The eight giant signs are downtown by the city chapel by the big lake.

| 1 | 2 | 3 | 4 | 5 | 6 | 7 | 8 | 9 | 10 | 11 | 12 | 13 | 14 |

UNIT 50 LESSONS 213 - 217
Clearview Manor (A Document Processing Simulation)

Learning Goals

1. To apply previously learned keyboarding, formatting, and language knowledge and skills at levels expected of a document processor in an entry-level position.
2. To produce in usable form a variety of business documents within a reasonable time when given minimal directions and supervision.

Documents Processed

1. Modified Block Letters
2. Simplified Memo
3. Tables
4. Leftbound and Unbound Reports
5. Business Forms
6. News Release

CLEARVIEW MANOR: A DOCUMENT PROCESSING SIMULATION

Before you begin processing the documents in this simulation, read carefully the information at the right.

Make notes of any formatting guides that you think will save time during the completion of the documents.

Daily Work Plan

Conditioning practice .... 5′
Document processing .... 45′

Work Assignment

You have just been employed as a Document Processor I in the Conference Center of Clearview Manor. Located in the Pocono Mountains in Pennsylvania, Clearview Manor is a well-known resort/conference center with outstanding meeting, exhibit, and recreational facilities.

The primary functions of the Conference Center staff are to

1. Promote the conference center as a place where businesses and professional associations can hold conferences, seminars, etc.
2. Assist clients in designing event activities to take full advantage of the facilities.
3. Work closely with clients during the event to ensure that their needs are met.

The Conference Center director, Ms. Helen T. Caldwell, is ultimately responsible for all functions of the center. The following people report to her. The marketing manager, Mr. Thomas R. Quinnones, is responsible for securing clients for the conference center. The operations manager, Ms. Anne Wells-Baker, works with clients during events. The catering manager, Mr. Bill Timbly, is responsible for all food and beverages served during events.

Your supervisor is Mr. Quinnones, the marketing manager. Most of the work he gives you will be in handwritten or draft form. Information about each document you process should be recorded on the Document Processing Log on LP p. 191, or the one provided by your supervisor.

Follow these procedures in completing the Document Processing Log sheet. In the **Code** column, record the textbook page number, followed by a period and the document number--for example, **p365.1**. In the **Originator** column, enter the name of the person who originated the document and his or her department--for example, **Quinnones/Marketing**. Indicate the type of document in the **Document** column: form, letter, memo, etc. Use the codes listed on the log sheet to indicate the type of source copy in the **Input** column.

In the **Time In** column, record the exact starting time; when the document is complete or when work is interrupted for more than 10′, record the exact ending time in the **Time Out** column. (Incomplete documents that are "logged out" must be "logged in" again when processing resumes.) Determine the time required (in minutes) to process each document (**Time** column). Count each line regardless of length; enter the number in the **Lines** column.

The following excerpts from the Document Processing Manual should be helpful to you in formatting and processing documents. You may also rely on other desk resources such as *Century 21 Keyboarding, Formatting, and Document Processing,* Fifth Edition.

Excerpts from CLEARVIEW MANOR DOCUMENT PROCESSING MANUAL

Interoffice correspondence is processed in simplified memorandum format on plain paper. Final copies of letters are prepared on Clearview Manor letterhead; draft copies are done on plain paper. The preferred letter format is modified block with blocked paragraphs and open punctuation. All correspondence is keyed on a 6½″ line (SM: 1″); use the current date. You are to supply your reference initials and notations for any copies, attachments, or enclosures.

Tables are keyed DS and centered vertically and horizontally on plain full sheets. CS: an even number of spaces.

Reports are prepared on plain paper. Use leftbound format unless otherwise specified. Footnotes are used for references and explanatory notes.

News releases are prepared on letterhead and are formatted as shown in Unit 44, *Century 21 Keyboarding, Formatting, and Document Processing,* Fifth Edition.

Proofread and correct each document carefully before you begin a new one. Check keyed numbers with the numbers in the source document. Include proofreading and correction time as part of the time you spend completing a document before you record the ending time on your log sheet.

79b ▶ 35
Format Letters in Modified Block Style

3 plain sheets; correct errors

Letter 1
Business Letter

modified block, open punctuation; blocked ¶s

Date: March 1, 19--
Address letter to:

Mr. Morris E. Young
904 Beatrice Street
Titusville, FL 32780-8192

Salutation: Dear Mr. Young

words

opening lines 19

¶ Walstrom Industries has informed us that you have 29
accepted a position in their accounting department 39
and soon will be moving to Rockville. Congratula- 49
tions and best wishes. 54

¶ Our bank has designed a packet of information to help 65
new citizens in the community become acquainted with 75
the local area. The packet includes a map of the city, housing 88
and rental guides, and a brochure that highlights upcoming 100
cultural and civic events. This material will provide you 112
with information that will make relocating a little easier. 124

¶ Once you arrive in Rockville, we would appreciate having 135
the opportunity to discuss ways that the First National Bank 147
of Rockville can accommodate your banking needs. (139) 157

Sincerely | Ms. Marge L. Bowman | Customer Service | xx | Enclosures 169

Learn to "make" an exclamation mark (!)
If your machine has an exclamation mark key, the left little finger is used to strike it. To "make" the !:

Strike ' (apostrophe); backspace and strike . (period).

Letter 2
Business Letter

modified block, mixed punctuation; indented ¶s

Learning cue: To place a table within the body of a letter, follow these guidelines.

1. DS above and below the table; SS the body of the table.
2. Clear all tab stops.
3. Determine and set the tab stop for each column of the table. (The table must be centered within the margins of the letter.)

Letter 3
Business Letter

Reformat Letter 2 to:

Miss Michelle L. Mistle
2840 Ardwick Drive
Rockville, MD 20852-4127

Change the certificate number to B-2995 and the value of the certificate to $2,646.16 on the letter to Miss Mistle.

March 1, 19-- | Mr. Cody G. Sykes | 625 Pacific Avenue | Rockville, MD 20853- 14
3107 | Dear Mr. Sykes: 19

How quickly time passes! It seems like only yesterday that you renewed 33
your 24-month certificate of deposit (B-2987) with our bank. On March 15 it 49
will again mature. 53

For your convenience we processed the certificate so that it would be re- 67
newed automatically for the same time period at the current market rate. If 83
we do not hear from you prior to the maturity date, your certificate will be 98
renewed at 7.5 percent for the next two years. The value of your certificate 114
as of March 15, will be $1,323.08. 121

Should you wish to have the certificate renewed for a longer period of 135
time at a higher interest rate, we can also do that. The time periods and cur- 151
rent interest rates are as follows: 158

36-month certificate	7.8 percent	165
48-month certificate	8.1 percent	172
60-month certificate	8.4 percent	178

Call or stop in if you decide to go with a longer period for your certificate. 194
We appreciate your patronage and look forward to assisting with your bank- 209
ing needs in the future. (193) 214

Sincerely, | Mrs. Eiko R. Kimura | Investments | xx 223

Lesson 212 Prepare for a Simulation

212a ▶ 5 Conditioning Practice

each line twice SS (slowly, then faster); DS between 2-line groups; if time permits, take 1′ writings on line 4

alphabet	1	Cody will acquire six blue jackets to give as door prizes to freshmen.
figures	2	I will fly 3,670 miles in May, 2,980 miles in June, and 1,450 in July.
fig/sym	3	Cookbook prices increased 14% from 7/1/89 to 6/30/90 in 25 bookstores.
speed	4	Claudia, the girl with the rifle, saw six turkeys by the lake at dusk.

| 1 | 2 | 3 | 4 | 5 | 6 | 7 | 8 | 9 | 10 | 11 | 12 | 13 | 14 |

212b ▶ 10 Improve Keyboarding Skill

1. Key a 1′ timed writing on each ¶.

2. Key a 5′ timed writing on ¶s 1-2 combined; find *gwam;* circle errors.

all letters used | A | 1.5 si | 5.7 awl | 80% hfw |

	gwam 1′	5′	
Efficiency is one word that you probably have heard repeatedly.	13	3	46
At home your parents have probably told you to use your time in an effi-	27	5	49
cient manner so you can study, do your household chores, and still have	42	8	52
time to play or relax. Most of your teachers have probably encouraged	56	11	55
you to arrange your work area in an orderly manner so you can utilize	70	14	58
your study time efficiently. If you have a part-time job, your super-	84	17	60
visor has likely stressed the importance of being efficient when com-	98	20	63
pleting the tasks assigned to you.	105	21	65
Efficiency is a quality that you can improve. You can improve it	13	24	67
by doing required tasks with a minimum waste of time and effort. Most	27	26	70
people improve efficiency by keeping their work area in order so sup-	41	29	73
plies can be easily retrieved when needed. Another way to improve it is	56	32	76
to try to be accurate. By being accurate, you will not need to repeat	70	35	79
work because of undetected errors. Also, you will be more efficient if	84	38	81
you don't think endlessly before making a decision. Rather, get the	98	41	84
facts you need, consider all the possibilities, and then make a decision.	113	44	87

gwam 1′ | 1 | 2 | 3 | 4 | 5 | 6 | 7 | 8 | 9 | 10 | 11 | 12 | 13 | 14 |
gwam 5′ | 1 | 2 | 3 |

212c ▶ 35 Prepare for a Simulation

In the simulation in Unit 50, you will process a variety of documents similar to those you have done during the school term.

1. List the page numbers below and review the Formatting Guides for

Letters: pp. 275 and 318
Memos & News Releases: p. 325
Reports: p. 281
Tables: p. 288

2. Prepare a list of the documents at the right. From this list, choose and practice selected documents before you start Unit 50.

List of Documents

Letter (plain paper)
p. 276, 155b, Letter 2

Memo (plain paper)
p. 332, 192b, Document 1

News Release (plain paper)
p. 330, 190b, News Release 1

Report (plain paper)
p. 284, 160b, Document 1

Tables (plain paper)
p. 292, 165c, Table 4
p. 349, 202c, Table 2

79c ▶ 10 Check Language Skills: Number Expression

SS sentences; DS between groups of sentences

Key line number (with period); space twice, then key the sentence, supplying the correct form of number expression. If time permits, key the sentences again to increase decision-making speed.

1. About 2/3's of the senior class attended the last forum.
2. The bank was on the corner of 3rd Avenue and 35th Street.
3. Almost 50 of our former students passed the CPA exam last May.
4. Only 2 of the fifteen applicants applying for the job will be hired.
5. The President will address the nation on Monday, June 5, at 6:10 p.m.

6. The office of Baxter & Jones is located at Six McKinley Avenue.
7. Of Mathew's twenty hits, eight of them were for extra bases.
8. Twelve of the computers arrived on Monday; 12 arrived on Wednesday.
9. There were six seniors, 12 juniors, and 15 sophomores at the dance.
10. Rules 7-10 are presented in Chapter four; Rules 11-13 in Chapter 5.

11. The new baby was twenty-one inches long and weighed 7 lbs. 12 oz.
12. Fifteen of the delegates voted for Johnson; twenty voted for Lopez.
13. The instructor had to replace seven of the 25 computer diskettes.
14. The address of the New York Historical Society is 1 State Street.
15. The publishing company plans for Volume Two to be finished by May 5.

Lesson 80 — *Simplified Memos/Language Skills*

80a ▶ 5 Conditioning Practice

each line twice SS (slowly, then faster); DS between 2-line groups; if time permits, rekey selected lines

alphabet 1 Morgan Sanchez was frequently invited to exhibit her artwork in Japan.

figures 2 We purchased 3,148 of her 7,260 shares on Thursday, December 15, 1990.

fig/sym 3 Frederick & Gilbertson paid me $635,000 for the 460 acres on 12/17/89.

speed 4 She may make us visit the big chapel in the dismal city on the island.

| 1 | 2 | 3 | 4 | 5 | 6 | 7 | 8 | 9 | 10 | 11 | 12 | 13 | 14 |

80b ▶ 25 Recall Document Processing Skills: Simplified Memo

Memo 1

plain full sheet

Format and key the memo given at the right. (See p. 74 for an example of simplified memo format.) Correct any errors you make as you key.

words

November 4, 19-- 3

All Employees 6

PROFESSIONAL DEVELOPMENT SEMINARS 13

The company is implementing a new program for professional development 27
this year. Every employee will be given one day off to attend one of the 42
company-sponsored professional development seminars. 53

Tentative topics for this year's seminars are the value of leadership, im- 67
proving oral communication skills, integrated software applications, and 82
stress management. Indicate your preference for each of the seminars on 97
the attached form by placing #1 by your first choice, #2 by your second 111
choice, and so forth. 116

We will try to accommodate everyone's first or second choice. The more 130
popular programs will be offered twice during the year in an effort to con- 145
trol the number of participants at each seminar. 155

Sophia Ramirez, Personnel 160

xx 161

Enclosure 162

Memo 2 is on p. 142.

211b (continued)

Document 2
Purchase Order

DELTA MORTGAGE CORPORATION

1590 CLIFTON AVENUE, COLUMBUS, OH 43202-1704 (614) 345-0001

PURCHASE ORDER — words

SIMMON'S OFFICE FURNITURE
43 CORTLAND STREET
DETROIT MI 48203-3598

Purchase Order No.: T-4587-2 — 2
Date: March 5, 19-- — 10 14
Terms: 10/30, n/90 — 21
Shipped Via: Wilson Shipping — 24

Quantity	Description/Stock Number	Price		Per	Total		words
1	Executive Pedestal Desk (E4-1230)	390	00	ea	390	00	34
1	Walnut Credenza (E4-1230-1)	375	00	ea	375	00	44
1	Executive Swivel Tilt Chair (E4-1330)	430	00	ea	430	00	55
3	Guest Conference Chair (E4-1420)	286	00	ea	858	00	66
2	25" Deep File Cabinet (F1-2125)	151	00	ea	302	00	77
					2355	00	79

By ____________________

Document 3
Invoice

PARK'S BUSINESS PRODUCTS

5704 Hollis Street Oakland, CA 94608-2514 (415) 227-9009

INVOICE

WESTERLY MANUFACTURING
7301 FULTON STREET
HOUSTON TX 77022-4498

Date: August 3, 19-- — 8
Customer Order No.: O-6538-T — 11 18

Terms	Shipped Via	Our Order No.	Date Shipped	words
5/30, n/60	Reliable Transit	LT-5009-Z	8/1/--	27

Quantity	Description/Stock No.	Unit Price		Amount		words
15	Card File (X8-5363)	6	29	94	35	34
1	Literature Rack (T5-LRF56)	184	00	184	00	43
1	Time Card Rack (T5-RRF95)	55	25	55	25	51
10	Multi-Pack File Labels (F1-437)	3	89	38	90	61
50	Interior Folders (F1-384)		13	6	50	70
				379	00	71
	Sales Tax (6%)			22	74	78
				401	74	79

Document 4
Reformat the invoice in Document 3, making these changes.

Change our order number to **LT-5011-Y**. Change the order for **Item F1-437** from 10 to **20** at **$3.59 each**. Make all necessary changes to extensions and totals.

80b (continued)

Memo 2
plain full sheet

1. Format and key the memo at high speed.
2. Proofread and mark copy for correction using proofreader marks.
3. Rekey the document; correct errors.

words

November 4, 19-- 3

Accounting Department 8

SELECTION OF NEW ACCOUNTING DEPARTMENT MANAGER 17

As most of you have heard by now, last week Marsha Mobley announced her 32
intent to retire at the end of this year. In keeping with company policy, 47
President Norwood prefers to have the position filled by a current employee. 62

If you are interested in applying for the position, submit an updated resume 78
and letter of application to the personnel office before November 21. It is 93
our intent to have the position filled by December 1, so that the new man- 108
ager will have the opportunity of working with Ms. Mobley for a month be- 122
fore she retires. 126

Sophia Ramirez, Personnel 131

xx 132

80c ▶ 10 *Improve Language Skills: Word Choice*

Study the spelling and definition for each word. Read the **Learn** sentence. Key the **Learn** sentence and the **Apply** sentences (select the proper word in parentheses to complete the sentence correctly).

lie (n) an untrue or inaccurate statement; as a verb, to rest or recline

lye (n) a strong alkaline solution

flew (vb) to move through the air

flue (n) a channel in a chimney

Learn 1. Jeffrey told a lie about how the lye stained our brand new carpet.
Apply 2. They told one (lie, lye) after another just to protect themselves.
Apply 3. Did you ask the owner how much (lie, lye) is needed in the solution?

Learn 4. The bird flew to the chimney where it made a nest in the flue.
Apply 5. The blocked (flew, flue) in the chimney was the cause of the problem.
Apply 6. The only time Mary (flew, flue) to New York, the plane was hijacked.

80d ▶ 10 *Improve Keyboarding Skill: Straight Copy*

1. Take a 1′ writing on the ¶; find *gwam*.
2. Add 4-6 words to your *gwam;* divide the new rate by 4 to determine the number of words you must key each 15″ to reach your new goal rate.
3. Note where you must be in the copy at the end of 15, 30, 45, and 60″ to reach new goal.
4. Take a 15″ timing, trying to achieve your goal.
5. Take a 30″ timing, trying to reach your goal each 15″.
6. Take a 45″ timing.
7. Take a 60″ timing, trying to maintain your goal rate.
8. Repeat this activity as time permits.

all letters used	A	1.5 si	5.7 awl	80% hfw

Year after year employers express their desire to hire employees who have strong communication skills. Those with the ability to organize and deliver ideas in written or oral form become an asset to their firms; those who do not have this ability quickly become a liability. If you plan on entering the job market in the near future, you will want to refine these skills so that you will be an asset rather than a liability.

211a ▶ 5 Conditioning Practice

each line twice SS (slowly, then faster); DS between 2-line groups; if time permits, take 1′ writings on line 2

alphabet 1 Fog is a major hazard for the very swift bird Kal acquired in Phoenix.

figures 2 She wrote checks 398-429 in May, 430-457 in June, and 458-461 in July.

fig/sym 3 The next junior/senior prom can be at 7:35-10:50 p.m. on 4/29 or 6/18.

speed 4 The man got six bowls, eight forks, and a few big pans for the social.

| 1 | 2 | 3 | 4 | 5 | 6 | 7 | 8 | 9 | 10 | 11 | 12 | 13 | 14 |

211b ▶ 45 Measure Document Production Skill: Forms

Time Schedule

Plan and prepare .... 5′
Timed production ....30′
Proofread; circle errors............ 7′
Compute *n-pram*.................... 3′

1. Arrange supplies and LP pp. 183-187.

2. When directed to begin, key for 30′ from the following documents, correcting all errors neatly. Proofread before removing the documents from the machine.

3. Compute *n-pram* for the 30′ writing.

4. Turn in all documents completed in the order shown.

Document 1
Purchase Requisition

Documents 2-4 are on page 362.

words

DELTA MORTGAGE CORPORATION

1590 CLIFTON AVENUE, COLUMBUS, OH 43202-1704 (614) 345-0001

PURCHASE REQUISITION

Deliver to: Janet Mc Clellan — Requisition No. A-1547-J 5
Location: Suite 355 — Date March 2, 19-- 10
Job No. A-636 — Date Required March 25, 19-- 14

Quantity	Description	words
1	Executive Pedestal Desk	19
1	Walnut Credenza	23
1	Executive Swivel Tilt Chair	29
3	Guest Conference Chair	34
2	25" Deep File Cabinet	39

Requisitioned by: Heather Bowles 41

81a ▶ 5 Conditioning Practice

each line twice SS (slowly, then faster); DS between 2-line groups; if time permits, rekey selected lines

alphabet 1 Jackson believed he might maximize profits with a quality sales force.

figures 2 Jo's social security number, 504-18-2397, was recorded as 504-18-2396.

fig/sym 3 Invoice #689 (dated 10/24) for $3,575 was paid on Tuesday, November 1.

speed 4 Their neighbor may dismantle the ancient ricksha in the big cornfield.

| 1 | 2 | 3 | 4 | 5 | 6 | 7 | 8 | 9 | 10 | 11 | 12 | 13 | 14 |

81b ▶ 10 Check Keyboarding Skill: Straight Copy

1. A 3′ writing on ¶s 1 and 2 combined; find *gwam;* circle errors.

2. A 1′ writing on each ¶; find *gwam;* circle errors.

3. Another 3′ writing on ¶s 1 and 2 combined; find *gwam;* circle errors.

4. Compare the better 3′ rate with the rate recorded for 76b, page 134. How much did your rate improve?

all letters used | A | 1.5 si | 5.7 awl | 80% hfw |

	gwam 3′	5′
A firm interested in improving both the quality and quantity of the	5	3
documents produced by the office staff may want to consider the latest	9	6
word processing equipment now on the market. Word processing equipment	14	8
which was too expensive in the past is now affordable for even the small-	19	11
est office. This is due in large part to the vast strides that have been	24	14
made in the field of computer technology.	27	16
The advanced packages of word processing software turn a computer	31	19
into a word processor which has most of the features of the more advanced	36	22
word processing equipment. It is now a simple job to review and edit	41	24
letters, reports, and tables on a computer. Insert, move copy, replace,	45	27
and delete are common features of most packages. This has made the job	50	30
of an office worker in many organizations much easier than it used to be.	55	33

gwam 3′ | 1 | 2 | 3 | 4 | 5 |
5′ | 1 | 2 | 3 |

81c ▶ 10 Improve Language Skills: Word Choice

Study the spelling and definition for each word. Read the **Learn** sentence. Key the **Learn** sentence and the **Apply** sentences (select the proper word in parentheses to complete the sentence correctly).

adapt (vb) to make fit; adjust

adept (adj) thoroughly proficient; expert

air (n) the look, appearance or bearing of a person

heir (n) one who inherits or is entitled to inherit money

Learn 1. Once he was able to adapt the form, he became adept with it.
Apply 2. Yoko will (adapt, adept) the house plans to take care of your concerns.
Apply 3. Juan was very (adapt, adept) at working with the integrated software.

Learn 4. Rebecca felt the heir to the throne possessed a certain air about him.
Apply 5. Martin always displayed an (air, heir) of importance when in public.
Apply 6. As (air, heir) to the entire fortune, she will someday be very rich.

209c (continued)

Document 2
Invoice
Prepare the invoice shown at the right. Proofread; circle errors.

Document 3
Invoice
Reformat the invoice of Document 2, making these changes.

Change the quantity of **Color Film ASA 1000** from 24 to **18**, **Color Film ASA 400** from 12 to **24**, and drop the Black and White Film from the invoice. Compute new extensions, totals, and taxes as needed.

PARK'S BUSINESS PRODUCTS
5704 Hollis Street Oakland, CA 94608-2514 (415) 227-9009

INVOICE

words

MARY WELLS STUDIO
20497 TILLMAN AVENUE
LONG BEACH CA 90746-3515

Date: November 5, 19-- 7
Customer Order No.: MW-101-N 11

18

Terms	Shipped Via	Our Order No.	Date Shipped	words
10/10, n/30	Overland Transit	2-66-1A	11/5/--	27

Quantity	Description/Stock No.	Unit Price		Amount		words
2	Prefix Dater {R1-16P}	14	95	29	90	35
1	Numbering Machine {RL-RN57}	44	95	44	95	44
12	Black and White Film {M5-159}	3	14	37	68	52
24	Color Film ASA 1000 {M5-156}	6	11	146	64	61
12	Color Film ASA 400 {M5-155}	5	37	64	44	71
				323	61	73
	Sales Tax {6%}			19	42	79
				343	03	80

Lesson 210 Review: Forms Processing

210a ▶ 5 Conditioning Practice

each line twice SS (slowly, then faster); DS between 2-line groups; if time permits, take 1′ writings on line 3

alphabet 1 Vicki expects to question dozens of boys and girls for the major show.
figures 2 Al's agent needs to sell 43 tables, 59 beds, 187 chairs, and 206 rugs.
fig/sym 3 The stopwatch (#34-908) and pedometer (#21-756) are on sale this week.
speed 4 My neighbor and the girl are to visit an ancient chapel on the island.

| 1 | 2 | 3 | 4 | 5 | 6 | 7 | 8 | 9 | 10 | 11 | 12 | 13 | 14 |

210b ▶ 45 Build Sustained Document Processing Skill: Forms

Time Schedule
Plan and prepare .... 5′
Timed production ....30′
Proofread; circle errors............ 7′
Compute *n-pram*.................... 3′

1. Make a list of documents to be formatted/processed:
page 357, 207c, Document 2
page 358, 208c, Document 2
page 360, 209c, Document 2
page 360, 209c, Document 3

2. Arrange supplies and LP pp. 179-183.

3. When directed to begin, key for 30′ from the list of documents, correcting all errors neatly. Proofread before removing the documents from the machine.

4. Compute *n-pram* for the 30′ period.

5. Turn in documents in the order listed in Step 1.

81d ▶ 25
Document Processing Skills: Letters and Memos

2 letterheads
LP pp. 11-13
or plain full sheets

Use Letter Placement Guide on p. 76, if necessary; correct errors.

Document 1
Business Letter

block format; open punctuation

words

Current date | Mrs. Jacki Babcock | 1390 Wilcox Avenue | Los Angeles, CA 14
90028-4130 | Dear Mrs. Babcock 20

We hope you and your family are enjoying the living room furniture you 34
purchased at Wilson's Department Store. Oakwood is an excellent line of 49
furniture that should last for many years. If, however, there is any reason 64
you are not pleased with the furniture, let us know. We will take the neces- 79
sary steps to guarantee your satisfaction. 88

Wilson's has been in business for over 100 years because of satisfied cus- 103
tomers. We are committed to keeping customer satisfaction high by offer- 117
ing quality goods and services at reasonable prices. 128

We appreciate our loyal customers and hope you will remain one of them. 142
Please let me know when we can be of further service. (133) 153

Sincerely yours | Miss Phyllis B. Clayborn | Furniture Consultant | xx 166/**179**

Document 2
Business Letter

modified block format, blocked ¶s; mixed punctuation

Current date | Ms. Beverly J. Lorenzo | 308 Paseo El Greco | Anaheim, CA 14
92807-8030 | Dear Ms. Lorenzo: 20

Discussing your dining room furniture needs with you yesterday was enjoy- 34
able. I checked with the department manager, and the next shipment of 48
furniture should arrive within a few weeks. Eight new styles of dining room 64
sets were ordered. When the shipment arrives, I will call you. 77

In the meantime, you may be interested in looking over the brochures of 91
dining room furniture that are enclosed. If there is a set which is of particu- 107
lar interest to you, we could order it for you. About four weeks are required 123
for delivery. You would be under no obligation to buy the set if it does not 138
meet your expectations when it arrives. As I indicated, Wilson's Department 154
Store is committed to customer satisfaction. 163

I look forward to working with you to assure that you will become one of 178
Wilson's satisfied customers. If you have any questions about any of the 192
furniture you looked at yesterday, please call me at 836-4829. (183) 205

Sincerely, | Miss Phyllis B. Clayborn | Furniture Consultant | xx | Enclosures 219/**232**

Document 3
Simplified Memo

standard format and placement (see p. 74 if necessary)

Current date | Adrian S. Comstock | OFFICE TECHNOLOGY SYMPOSIUM 12

Information on the "Fifth Annual Office Technology Symposium" is enclosed. 28
I attended last year's symposium and found it very beneficial. Since we 42
have been allocated money for upgrading the word processing department, I 57
plan to attend again this year. 64

There is enough money in the budget to pay the expenses for two people to 78
attend. Since you will be involved in upgrading the word processing center, 94
you may be interested in attending. If you are, please let me know before 109
the end of the month so I can make the necessary arrangements. 122

Harriet D. Steinman | xx | Enclosure 128/**137**

209a ▶ 5 Conditioning Practice

each line twice SS (slowly, then faster); DS between 2-line groups; if time permits, take 1′ writings on line 2

alphabet 1 Biggi excluded a very quick jaunt to the new zoo from my travel plans.

figures 2 You can find answers to the 150-point test on pages 8, 32, 46, and 79.

fig/sym 3 Runner #3019 was first (49 min.) and runner #687 was second (52 min.).

speed 4 The rifleman saw my hand signal to go right at the fork by the shanty.

| 1 | 2 | 3 | 4 | 5 | 6 | 7 | 8 | 9 | 10 | 11 | 12 | 13 | 14 |

209b ▶ 15 Improve Tabulating Technique

LL: 70 spaces

1. Clear tab stops.
2. Starting at the left margin, set 4 tab stops 11 spaces apart.
3. Key the copy once, tabulating from column to column.
4. Take as many 2′ writings as time permits to improve tabulating skills.

					gwam 2′	
$102.93	84%	#7560	(100)	$22.77	3	28
$609.87	79%	#8096	(806)	$76.80	6	31
$534.12	43%	#5124	(341)	$42.51	9	34
$394.01	38%	#9183	(471)	$72.03	12	37
$389.21	76%	#1602	(278)	$40.57	16	40
$354.12	24%	#3476	(208)	$96.87	19	43
$268.40	19%	#7351	(862)	$53.79	22	47
$145.67	29%	#6708	(541)	$27.03	25	50

209c ▶ 30 Format/Process Invoices

LP pp. 177-179

Document 1
Invoice
Prepare the invoice shown at the right. Follow placement/spacing guides shown in color. Proofread; circle errors.

words

PARK'S BUSINESS PRODUCTS
5704 Hollis Street Oakland, CA 94608-2514 (415) 227-9009

INVOICE

Tab → CENTURY PRODUCTIONS INC
1661 EAST 32D STREET
LONG BEACH CA 90807-5291

Tab ↓ Date: October 21, 19-- 8
Customer Order No.: AP-1659-T 13

20

Terms	Shipped Via	Our Order No.	Date Shipped	words
6/10, n/30	Safeway Shipping, Inc.	2-44-7A	10/20/--	30

Quantity	Description/Stock No.	Unit Price		Amount		words
1	Electronic Postal Scale (PS2PR)	299	95	299	95	40
2	Electric Sharpener (KP33-BG)	49	95	99	90	49
5	Double Desk Set (N1-5201)	57	00	285	00	57
24	Drafting Pencil (N5-5007)		61	14	64	66
500	Envelopes 9" x 12" (P2-S28)		07	35	00	76
				DS		
				734	49	77
	Sales Tax (6%)			44	07	83
				DS		
				778	56	84

Approximate center; Set tab 1 or 2 spaces from rule; Indent 3 spaces; Tab; Tab

Documents 2 and 3 are on page 360.

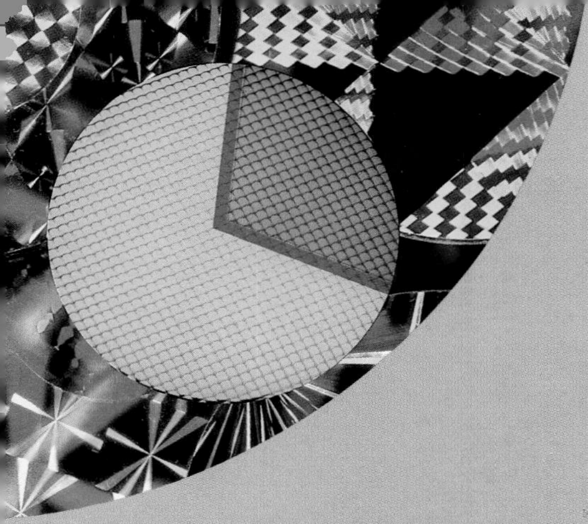

UNIT 17 LESSONS 82 – 83
Improve Keyboarding and Language Skills

Learning Goals

1. To improve/refine technique and response patterns.
2. To increase speed on straight copy.
3. To improve language skills.

Format Guides

1. Paper guide at *0* (for typewriters).
2. LL: 70 spaces.
3. LS: SS drills; DS ¶s.
4. PI: 5 spaces.

Lesson 82 *Keyboarding/Language Skills*

82a ▶ 5 Conditioning Practice

each line twice SS (slowly, then faster); DS between 2-line groups; if time permits, rekey selected lines

alphabet	1	The vast Cox farm was just sold by the bank at quite an amazing price.
figures	2	Their firm constructed 340 of the 560 new homes between 1987 and 1992.
fig/sym	3	Martin paid Invoice #382 ($56.79 with a 5% discount) with Check #1084.
speed	4	The girls and the maid may go downtown to pay for the six giant signs.

| 1 | 2 | 3 | 4 | 5 | 6 | 7 | 8 | 9 | 10 | 11 | 12 | 13 | 14 |

82b ▶ 15 Improve Keyboarding Skill: Skill Comparison

1. A 30″ writing on each line; find *gwam* on each. 1′ *gwam* × 2
2. Compare rates.
3. Another 30″ writing on each line; try to increase speed.

balanced-hand	1	He is apt to make the men go to the island for the coalfish and clams.
double letters	2	Kellee saw three little rabbits hopping between rows looking for food.
3d row	3	Three of our territory reporters were told to type their trade report.
adjacent-key	4	Every owner was there to report the trade union's prior point of view.
outside reach	5	Paula Quixote won all six top prizes last season for her zealous play.
one-hand	6	Polly saw a few deserted cats on a battered crate in a vacated garage.
shift-keys	7	Janie saw Karen, Lauren, Ellen, and Claudia while she was in Columbus.
figures	8	Her phone number is 836-9572; her address is 3014 Jefferson Boulevard.

| 1 | 2 | 3 | 4 | 5 | 6 | 7 | 8 | 9 | 10 | 11 | 12 | 13 | 14 |

82c ▶ 10 Improve Language Skills: Verbs

LL: 70-spaces; SS with DS between 2-line groups

1. Read and key the **Learn** sentences (with number and period), noting how the rule has been applied.
2. Key each **Apply** sentence using the correct verb shown in parentheses.
3. If time permits, key the **Apply** lines again at a faster speed to quicken decision-making skill.

SINGULAR VERBS

Use a singular verb with a singular subject.

Learn 1. The mail carrier has not delivered today's mail.
Learn 2. She has already completed her solo.
Apply 3. An outstanding executive assistant (is, are) difficult to find.
Apply 4. He (has, have) been accepted at Harvard.

Use singular verbs with indefinite pronouns (each, every, any, either, neither, one, etc.) used as subjects.

Learn 5. Every employee is expected to attend the exquisite awards banquet.
Learn 6. Everyone has been given permission to attend the game.
Apply 7. Each person (has, have) his/her own ideas on the subject.
Apply 4. Neither one of the gymnasts (is, are) very good.

208c ▶ 35
Format/Process Purchase Orders

LP pp. 173-175

Document 1
Purchase Order
Prepare the purchase order shown at the right. Follow placement/spacing guides shown in color. Proofread; circle errors.

DELTA MORTGAGE CORPORATION

1590 CLIFTON AVENUE, COLUMBUS, OH 43202-1704 (614) 345-0001

PURCHASE ORDER — words

Tab

WEBSTER'S OFFICE PRODUCTS
4646 WEST BROAD STREET
COLUMBUS OH 43228-1687

Purchase Order No.: AQ-4931 (Tab) 2
Date: July 24, 19-- 10
Terms: 5/10, n/30 14 21
Shipped Via: Ohio Express 24

Quantity	Description/Stock Number	Price		Per	Total		words
6	Stackable printer stand (F5-16)	49	95	ea	299	70	34
6	Underdesk keyboard drawer (F5-58)	34	98	ea	209	88	44
1	Printer sound shield (F5-50)	199	00	ea	199	00	54
25	17" binder racks (E4-501)	3	95	ea	98	75	63
2	Data racks (E4-502)	195	00	ea	390	00	71
2	Set of casters (E4-519)	30	00	set	60	00	81
					1257	33	83

LM (Quantity column); Approximate center; Set tab 1 or 2 spaces from rule; Tab; Tab

By ____________________

Document 2
Purchase Order
Prepare the purchase order as you did in Document 1. Add the figures in the total column and enter the total under the column.

Document 3
Purchase Order
Rekey the purchase order of Document 2, making the following changes.

Increase the order for **Glue stick** by 5 (use the same unit price but calculate a new total). Add to the order **10 rolls** of **Transparent tape** (Stock no. **A8-176**) at **$1.47 per roll.** Compute new totals as needed.

DELTA MORTGAGE CORPORATION

1590 CLIFTON AVENUE, COLUMBUS, OH 43202-1704 (614) 345-0001

PURCHASE ORDER

SCHRIBNER'S OFFICE SUPPLIES
281 HAMILTON STREET
HARTFORD CT 06106-2989

Purchase Order No.: AB-1076 2
Date: March 2, 19-- 10
Terms: 2/10, n/30 14 21
Shipped Via: Air Express 23

Quantity	Description/Stock Number	Price		Per	Total		words
1	Secretarial handbook (B5-46)	10	95	ea	10	95	33
1	ZIP Code directory (B5-478)	5	95	ea	5	95	41
5	Glue stick (C1-175)		89	ea	4	45	48
2	Flowchart template (D2-548)	4	50	dz	9	00	60

By ____________________

82d ▶ 8 Improve Technique: Numbers and Tabulator

LL: 70 spaces; CS: 4; key the drill twice (slowly, then faster); correct any errors you make as you key; if time permits, rekey lines

Concentrate on figure location; quick tab spacing; eyes on copy.

2831	4094	9018	9335	7481	3042	4402	10297	34783
7609	5961	3137	192	9366	3149	7215	41234	66552
9078	8272	463	8656	5438	476	321	79809	12676
6562	3735	6555	7051	1017	2022	8797	8458	93081

82e ▶ 12 Improve Keyboarding Skill: Straight Copy

1. A 3′ writing on ¶s 1-2 combined; find *gwam*, circle errors.
2. A 1′ writing on ¶ 1, then on ¶ 2; find *gwam* and circle errors on each.
3. Another 3′ writing on ¶s 1-2 trying to increase your *gwam* by 2 *wam* over first 3′ writing.
4. Record your best 1′ and 3′ writing for use in 83b.

all letters used | A | 1.5 si | 5.7 awl | 80% hfw |

	gwam 3′	5′
If you are planning to purchase a computer, you should consider the	5	3
hard disk drive feature which is available on many computers. This	9	5
feature increases the flexibility of the unit as well as the storage	14	8
space. The amount of added storage depends on the type of hard disk	18	11
purchased, but the amount can increase by the equivalent of several dozen	23	14
floppy disks. Those who use the hard disk enjoy better response time.	28	17
One concern with the hard disk is that it is quite sensitive and can	32	19
be damaged. Any information stored on the hard disk should be copied on	37	22
to a floppy disk for backup purposes. Having the second copy will assure	42	25
that important information is not lost if damage to the hard disk should	47	28
take place. Computer users often forget to make a second copy until	52	31
important information is lost from the hard disk.	55	33

gwam 3′ | 1 | 2 | 3 | 4 | 5 |
5′ | 1 | 2 | 3 |

Lesson 83 Keyboarding Technique/Language Skills

83a ▶ 5 Conditioning Practice

each line twice SS (slowly, then faster); if time permits, rekey selected lines

alphabet 1 Mr. Garvey told Jay to pick up six dozen roses for the awards banquet.

figures 2 Gains of 5.09 and 6.15 the last two days put the Dow Jones at 1842.37.

one-hand 3 After I averaged my art grades, I sat defeated in my car in my garage.

speed 4 They may blame the six girls for the problem with the neighbor's auto.

| 1 | 2 | 3 | 4 | 5 | 6 | 7 | 8 | 9 | 10 | 11 | 12 | 13 | 14 |

83b ▶ 10 Improve Keyboard Skill: Straight Copy

1. Two 1′ writings on ¶ 1 of 82e above. Strive to increase rate recorded previously for 82e by 4 *wpm*.
2. Repeat Step 1 using ¶ 2.
3. A 3′ writing using both ¶s.
4. Determine 3′ *gwam* and record.

207c (continued)

Document 2
Purchase Requisition
Prepare the purchase requisition shown at the right. Proofread; circle errors.

Document 3
Purchase Requisition
Repeat the purchase requisition of Document 2, making the following changes. Increase the order for **Glue stick** by 5. Add to the requisition **10 rolls** of **Transparent tape.**

words

DELTA MORTGAGE CORPORATION

PURCHASE REQUISITION

1590 CLIFTON AVENUE, COLUMBUS, OH 43202-1704 (614) 345-0001

Deliver to: Barbara Merkitz — Requisition No. R-4975 — 5

Location: Building 5, Room 315 — Date March 1, 19-- — 12

Job No. 9854-BM — Date Required March 21, 19-- — 16

Quantity	Description	words
1	Secretarial handbook	21
1	ZIP Code directory	25
5	Glue stick	28
2	Flowchart template	32

Requisitioned by: Samuel Gillespie — 35

Lesson 208 Language Skills/Purchase Orders

208a ▶ 5 Conditioning Practice

each line twice SS (slowly, then faster); DS between 2-line groups; if time permits, take 1′ writings on line 3

alphabet 1 Becky Gazeto is not exempt from equal justice if she violated the law.
figures 2 Eastern College has 5,789 boys and 6,431 girls in 20 different majors.
fig/sym 3 My new house (267-A Westbury Drive) was appraised at $153,400 in 1989.
speed 4 Eight was the divisor for half of the problems Al did on the city bus.

| 1 | 2 | 3 | 4 | 5 | 6 | 7 | 8 | 9 | 10 | 11 | 12 | 13 | 14 |

208b ▶ 10 Language Skills: Word Choice

1. Study the spelling and definitions of each pair of words.
2. Key the **Learn** line, with the number and period, noting the proper use of the often confused words.
3. Key the **Apply** lines, with the number and period, using the word that completes each sentence correctly.

decree (n) an authoritative order; edict
degree (n) a unit division of a temperature scale
deference (n) courteous respect
difference (n) the fact, condition, or degree of being different

Learn 1. When it is over 80 degrees, we give a decree for air conditioning.
Apply 2. The principal gave the (decree/degree) to stop running in the corridors.
Apply 3. My guess is that today's temperature is six (decrees/degrees) higher.

Learn 4. Joe and Si's age difference may explain the deference Joe gets.
Apply 5. The (deference/difference) between Jim and Harry is like day and night.
Apply 6. It was out of (deference/difference) that I opened the door for my guests.

83c ▶ 15
Improve Keyboarding Technique

1. Key each line twice.

2. Take three 1′ writings on line 3; first for accuracy, then for speed, then again for accuracy.

3. Repeat Step 2 for lines 6 and 9.

Shift keys

1 Donald, Tom, Jan, and I all live on Park Haven Court, two blocks away.
2 We have visited Alabama, Kansas, Colorado, Maine, Florida, and Hawaii.
3 Mark Wolterman, president of Sparks Electric, lives near Jasmine Lane.

Space bar

4 Jane will go to the city next week to buy trees for our moms and dads.
5 Chi may be in town next week to see his aunt and uncle for a few days.
6 They may be able to fix only seven of the ten tires by noon on Friday.

Balanced-hand sentences

7 To the right of the dismal shanty is a small cornfield with six foals.
8 Their tutor may go with them when they go to the city for the bicycle.
9 The ivory box with the shamrock and iris is by the door of the chapel.

| 1 | 2 | 3 | 4 | 5 | 6 | 7 | 8 | 9 | 10 | 11 | 12 | 13 | 14 |

83d ▶ 10
Improve Techniques: Numbers/Tabulation

LL: 70 spaces; CS: 4

1. Key copy given at the right. Correct any errors you make as you key.

2. Take two 1′ writings.

			words
802 Crawley Road	Odessa, FL 33556-9512	(813) 920-7447	11
3173 Murphy Drive	Memphis, TN 38106-1001	(901) 454-6954	22
1049 Sunny Vale Lane	Madison, WI 53713-3358	(608) 266-6782	34
22 West 12th Street	Cincinnati, OH 45210-6904	(513) 512-5674	46
1908 Association Drive	Reston, VA 22091-1591	(703) 860-4977	58
1834 W. Southern Avenue	Mesa, AZ 85202-4867	(602) 833-3469	70

83e ▶ 10
Improve Language Skills: Verbs

LL: 70 spaces; SS with DS between line groups

1. Read the first rule.

2. Key the **Learn** sentences below it (with number and period), noting how the rule has been applied.

3. Key the **Apply** sentences using the correct verb shown in parentheses.

4. Practice the other rules in the same way.

5. If time permits, key the **Apply** lines again at a faster speed to quicken decision-making skills.

SINGULAR VERBS (continued)

Use a singular verb with singular subjects linked by *or* or *nor.* Exception: If one subject is singular and the other is plural, the verb agrees with the closer subject.

Learn 1. Either my mother or father was invited to the opening ceremony.
Learn 2. Neither Mr. Puleo nor the word processing operators have the manual.
Apply 3. Either Eric or Marsha (has, have) the blueprints.
Apply 4. Neither the editor nor the authors (is, are) aware of the deadlines.

Use a singular verb with a singular subject that is separated from the verb by phrases beginning with *as well as* and *in addition to.*

Learn 5. The report as well as the letters has to be finished before noon.
Apply 6. The advisor as well as the officers (is, are) going to attend the meeting.

Use singular verbs with collective nouns (committee, team class, jury, etc.) if the collective noun acts as a unit.

Learn 7. The finance committee has the April budget.
Learn 8. The parliamentary procedure team is going to perform on Friday.
Apply 9. The board (is, are) going to discuss that issue next week.
Apply 10. The staff (wants, want) to be in charge of the banquet.

207b ▶ 15 Improve Keyboarding Skill

1. Three 1′ writings on ¶ 1; find *gwam;* circle errors.
2. Practice ¶ 2 in the same way.
3. Two 3′ writings on ¶s 1-2 combined; find *gwam;* circle errors.

all letters used | A | 1.5 si | 5.7 awl | 80% hfw

gwam 1′ | 3′

Simply stated, self-esteem is the feeling you have about yourself. 14 | 5
If you feel good about yourself, you are likely to have a high degree of 28 | 9
self-esteem. If you feel bad about yourself, you are said to have a low 43 | 14
degree of self-esteem or self-respect. It is important that you have 57 | 19
the highest possible level of self-esteem because it influences the per- 71 | 24
sonality you exhibit and the quality of life you will likely experience. 86 | 29
It is equally important that you realize that you can increase your de- 100 | 33
gree of self-esteem by knowing more about yourself and your values. 114 | 38

If you place a high level of importance on achieving a particular 13 | 42
objective and are unable to attain that objective, you could have a 27 | 47
problem with self-esteem. One way to keep a high level of self-esteem 41 | 52
is to think about successful experiences that make you feel good about 55 | 56
yourself rather than just failures that have a tendency to lower self- 69 | 61
esteem. Even though you are likely to experience failure at times, it 83 | 66
is important for your self-esteem that you learn from rather than dwell 98 | 71
on the negative aspects of your failures. 106 | 73

gwam 1′ | 1 | 2 | 3 | 4 | 5 | 6 | 7 | 8 | 9 | 10 | 11 | 12 | 13 | 14
3′ | 1 | 2 | 3 | 4 | 5

207c ▶ 30 Format/Process Purchase Requisitions

LP pp. 171-173

Document 1
Purchase Requisition
Prepare the purchase requisition shown at the right. Follow placement/spacing guides shown in color. Proofread and circle errors.

words

DELTA MORTGAGE CORPORATION

PURCHASE REQUISITION

1590 CLIFTON AVENUE, COLUMBUS, OH 43202-1704 (614) 345-0001

LM — Tab

Deliver to: Juanita Salinas — Requisition No. A25497B — 5

Location: Gateway Two — Date July 23, 19-- — 10

Job No. C-500t — Date Required August 8, 19-- — 14

Quantity	Description	words
6	Stackable printer stand	20
6	Underdesk keyboard drawer	26
1	Printer sound shield	30
25	17" binder handles	35
2	Data racks	38
2	Set of casters	41

LM; Approximate center; Set tab 2 spaces from rule

Requisitioned by: Mary Bellino — 44

Documents 2 and 3 are on page 357.

UNIT 18 LESSONS 84 – 87

Improve Report Formatting Skills

Learning Goals

1. To review/improve report formatting knowledge and skills.

2. To improve keyboarding skills on straight copy, script copy, and rough-draft copy.

3. To improve language skills (verbs).

Format Guides

1. Paper guide at *0* for typewriters.

2. LL: 70 spaces for drills and ¶s; as required for documents.

3. LS: SS drills; as required for documents.

4. PI: 5 spaces.

FORMATTING GUIDES: UNBOUND REPORTS

THE CHANGING OFFICE

A secretary returning to an office job after a 25-year absence would have a difficult time coping with the changes that have taken place during that time. Changing technology would best describe the challenges facing today's office worker. Two "buzzwords" which are currently being used in the office are electronic desktop publishing and electronic mail.

Electronic Desktop Publishing

Desktop publishing is the process of integrating text and graphics by utilizing computer software to produce professional-looking documents without using professional services. According to Winsor (1987, 29):

> Desktop publishing has a bright future. . . . Desktop publishing enables people and businesses to develop their own brochures, newsletters, and other documents at a fraction of the cost and time expended sending the work out to a professional graphics studio.

Since today's firms are more concerned than ever about creating the proper image, it is expected that a greater number of firms will turn to desktop publishing to enhance their images.

Electronic Mail

The second "buzzword" being used extensively in the modern office is electronic mail (E-mail). E-mail is the sending, storing, and delivering of written messages electronically. Reiss and Dolan (1989, 529) identify two categories of electronic mail services:

1. In-house electronic mail. (E-mail which is run on a firm's computer system.)

2

2. Commercial electronic mail. (E-mail which is supplied by organizations such as General Electric Information Services and MCI Communication.)

Summary

Desktop publishing and electronic mail are but two of the changes which are shaping the future of information processing. Each year new technology enhances the ability of office personnel to produce quality information in less time.

REFERENCES

Reiss, Levi, and Edwin G. Dolan. Using Computers: Managing Change. Cincinnati: South-Western Publishing Co., 1989.

Winsor, William M. "Electronic Publishing: The Next Great Office Revolution." The Secretary, June/July 1987.

Margins

Top First Page	Place main heading on line 10 (pica/10 pitch) line 12 (elite/12 pitch)
Second Page	line 6
Side	1″ left and right
Bottom	At least 1″ on all pages

Spacing

Reports are usually double-spaced, but may be single-spaced if desired. Whether double- or single-spaced, the paragraphs are indented five spaces.

Single-space quoted material of four or more lines. Indent the quoted material five spaces from the left margin; block the lines at that point. The right margin for quoted material remains at one inch. Double-space above and below the quoted material.

Indent enumerated items five spaces from the left margin; block the lines at that point. The right margin for enumerated items remains at one inch. Single-space individual items; DS between items as well as above and below a series of items.

Page Numbers

The first page may be numbered, but it need not be. The number, if used, is centered on line 62 from the top edge of the sheet. For the second page and subsequent ones, place the page number on line 6 from the top edge approximately even with the right margin. Leave a DS below the page number; begin the first line of the report body on line 8.

Headings and Subheadings

Main heading. Center the main heading in ALL-CAPS over the line of writing. Quadruple-space (QS) below it. A QS is 2 DS or 4 SS.

Side headings. Begin side headings at the left margin. DS above and below them. Capitalize the first letter of the first word and all other main words in each heading. Underline side headings.

Paragraph headings. Begin paragraph headings at the same point other paragraphs of the report begin. Capitalize the first letter of the first word only, underline the heading, and follow the heading with a period.

Documentation (Textual Citation)

References used to give credit for quoted or closely paraphrased material may be cited in parentheses in the report body. This form of documentation is known as a textual or internal citation. (Footnotes are presented in Phase 5.)

Textual citations should include the name(s) of the author(s), the date of the referenced publication, and the page number(s) of the material cited (Roberts, 1992, 275). When the author's name is used in the text introducing the quotation, only the year of publication and the page number(s) appear in parentheses: Roberts (1992, 275) said that . . . .

All references cited are listed alphabetically by author surnames on the last page of the text or at the end of the report (often on a separate page) under the heading REFERENCES or BIBLIOGRAPHY. The reference page has the same top and side margins as the first page of the report. Each reference is single-spaced with a double space between references. The first line of each reference begins at the left margin; all other lines are indented five spaces from the left margin.

UNIT 49 LESSONS 207 – 212
Format/Process Business Forms

Learning Goals

1. To develop skill in formatting purchase requisitions, purchase orders, and invoices.
2. To improve tabulating skills.
3. To improve language skills.

Format Guides

1. Paper guide at *0* (for typewriters).
2. LL: 70 spaces.
3. LS: SS sentence drills; DS ¶s; as needed for problems.
4. Tab sets: 5 spaces for ¶ indention; as needed for problems.

FORMATTING GUIDES: BUSINESS FORMS

Purchase Requisition
A form used by an employee to request the purchasing department to order items such as supplies, equipment, or services.

Purchase Order
A form used by the purchasing department of one company to order merchandise or services from another company.

Invoice
A form used by one company to bill a person or another company for services or merchandise purchased from the company that sends the invoice.

Guides for Formatting Business Forms

1. Set left margin and tab stops for the items to be keyed in the columns so the items (except the items keyed under the description head) are approximately centered under the form's column headings. The description column items should begin 1 or 2 spaces to the right of the vertical line.

2. When appropriate, use these margin and/or tab stops to begin lines to be keyed in the heading portion of the business form. For example, the address lines on many forms can begin at the tab stop set for the description column.

3. SS the items to be keyed in the column beginning a double space below the horizontal rule under the column headings.

4. When amounts in a column are totalled, underline the amount for the last item; then DS and key the total. Business forms can have totals keyed with or without commas separating thousands and hundreds.

5. Forms are often mailed in window envelopes (see RG 7). Caution must, therefore, be taken to ensure that the address is formatted and keyed so it will be seen in the envelope's "window."

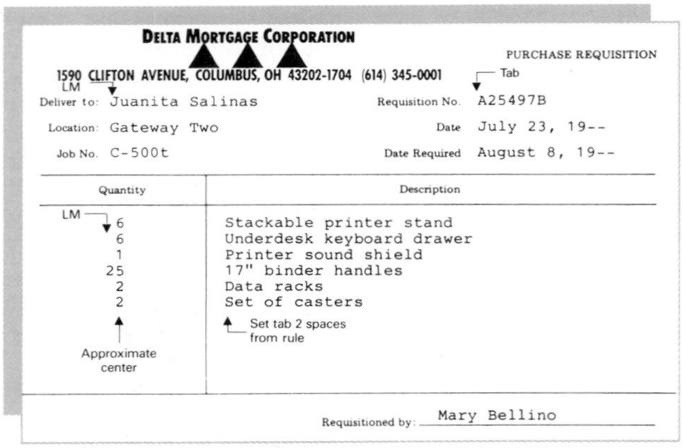
DELTA MORTGAGE CORPORATION
1590 CLIFTON AVENUE, COLUMBUS, OH 43202-1704 (614) 345-0001
PURCHASE REQUISITION

Deliver to: Juanita Salinas — Requisition No. A25497B
Location: Gateway Two — Date July 23, 19--
Job No. C-500t — Date Required August 8, 19--

Quantity	Description
6	Stackable printer stand
6	Underdesk keyboard drawer
1	Printer sound shield
25	17" binder handles
2	Data racks
2	Set of casters

Requisitioned by: Mary Bellino

Formatted Purchase Requisition

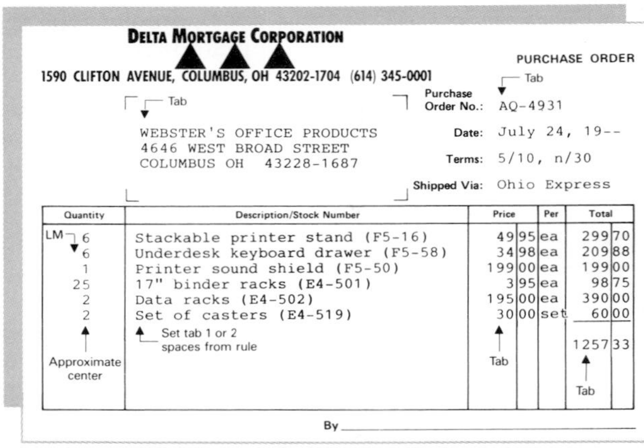
DELTA MORTGAGE CORPORATION
1590 CLIFTON AVENUE, COLUMBUS, OH 43202-1704 (614) 345-0001
PURCHASE ORDER

WEBSTER'S OFFICE PRODUCTS
4646 WEST BROAD STREET
COLUMBUS OH 43228-1687

Purchase Order No.: AQ-4931
Date: July 24, 19--
Terms: 5/10, n/30
Shipped Via: Ohio Express

Quantity	Description/Stock Number	Price	Per	Total
6	Stackable printer stand (F5-16)	49 95	ea	299 70
6	Underdesk keyboard drawer (F5-58)	34 98	ea	209 88
1	Printer sound shield (F5-50)	199 00	ea	199 00
25	17" binder racks (E4-501)	3 95	ea	98 75
2	Data racks (E4-502)	195 00	ea	390 00
2	Set of casters (E4-519)	30 00	set	60 00
				1257 33

By

Formatted Purchase Order

Lesson 207 Keyboarding Skills/Purchase Requisitions

207a ▶ 5 Conditioning Practice

each line twice SS (slowly, then faster); DS between 2-line groups; if time permits, take 1′ writings on line 2

alphabet 1 Peggy and Kami will enjoy a quiet, lazy bath after very hard exercise.

figures 2 Dave has 9,687 names and 12,534 addresses stored on one 80-track disk.

fig/sym 3 My electric bill was $135.98 (up 6%); my gas bill was $92.47 (up 10%).

speed 4 The auditor for a sorority cut by half the big goal for the endowment.

| 1 | 2 | 3 | 4 | 5 | 6 | 7 | 8 | 9 | 10 | 11 | 12 | 13 | 14 |

84a ▶ 5 Conditioning Practice

each line twice SS (slowly, then faster); DS between 2-line groups; if time permits, rekey selected lines

alphabet 1 Dr. Zisk told us to keep quiet just before the physics exam was given.

figures 2 Jason hit .418 in May, .257 in June, .360 in July, and .409 in August.

space bar 3 If I can find the parts for the old car, it will be quite easy to fix.

speed 4 The ornament on their oak mantle is a small antique ivory lamb or cow.

| 1 | 2 | 3 | 4 | 5 | 6 | 7 | 8 | 9 | 10 | 11 | 12 | 13 | 14 |

84b ▶ 35 Format and Key Unbound Report

Document 1
Report from Rough Draft

1. Review the formatting guides for unbound reports on page 148.

2. Format the report in unbound style. Do not correct your errors as you key.

3. When you finish, proofread your copy, mark it for correction, and prepare a final copy, all errors corrected.

Recall: Indent the quotation 5 spaces to the right of the left margin; let the line run full to the right margin. DS above and below the quotation.

words

THE CHANGING OFFICE 4

A secretary returning toan office job after a a 25 year 15
~~leave of~~ absence would have a difficult time coping with the 25
changes that have taken place during that time. Changing 37
technology would best describe the challenges facing today's 49
office worker. Two "buzzwords" which are currently bieng 61
used in the office are ~~electronic~~ desktop publishing and 72
electronic mail. 76

Electronic Desktop Publishing 88

Desktop publishhng is the process of integrating text 98
and graphics by utilizing computer soft ware to produce 109
profession-looking documents without using profesional ser- 122
vices. According to Winsor: 130

> Desktop publishing has bright future. . . . Desktop 141
> publishing enables people and businesses to develop their 153
> own broqures, newsletters, and other documents at a frac- 164
> tion of the cost and time expended sending the work out 175
> to a professional graphics studio. 183

Since todays firms are more concerned than ever about 194
creating the proper image, it is exptected that greater num- 206
ber of firms will turn to publishing to enhance their image. 220

Electronic Mail 226

The second "Buzz word being used extensively in the modern 238
office is electronic mail (E-mail). E-mail is the sending 250
storing, and deliver of message electronically. ~~According~~ 262
~~to~~ Reiss and dolan (1989, 529) identify two categories of 273
electronic mail services: 279

1. In-house electronic mail. (E-mail which is run on 290
a firm's computer system.) 295

(continued, p. 150)

206b (continued)

Table 2
3-Column Table with Multiple-Line Column Headings and Source Note
DS body; CS: 6 spaces

words

LAND VEHICULAR TUNNELS IN U.S. 6

(Over 5,000 Feet in Length) 12

Name	Location	Length in Feet	words
			13
			21
E. Johnson Memorial	Colorado	8,959	28
Eisenhower Memorial	Colorado	8,941	35
Allegheny	Pennsylvania	6,070	41
Liberty Tubes	Pennsylvania	5,920	48
Zion National Park	Utah	5,766	54
East River Mountain	West Virginia & Virginia	5,412	64
Tuscarora	Pennsylvania	5,326	70

______________ 74

Source: *The World Almanac*. 82

Table 3
4-Column Table from Revised Copy
DS body; decide spaces between columns

BUSINESS EXPENSE SUMMARY 5
(Renato Huarte) DS 8

Quarter	Travel	Meals	Lodging	words
				19
First	$325.65	$175.69	$300.50	26
Second	294.58	225.43	124.47	32
Third	437.95	175.48	256.45	37
Fourth	371.57	202.87	76.77	49
Total	$1,429.75	$960.71	$677.22	56

Table 4
Table with Horizontal and Vertical Rules
DS body; decide spaces between columns; insert horizontal and vertical rules

Table 5
Reformat Table 3; DS body; CS: 10 spaces; add horizontal rules

Table 6
Reformat Table 2; DS body; decide spaces between columns; add horizontal rules

INVENTORY REPORT OF DISCONTINUED APPLIANCES 9

(Number of Units Remaining) 14

Appliance	Last Month	This Month	words
			27
			34
			47
Microwave oven--M-010-B	135	101	53
Dishwasher--D-320-A	25	20	59
Videocassette recorder--C-005-A	142	123	67
Refrigerator--R-279-C	47	29	73
Portable television--T-863-A	107	83	80
Electric hair dryer--D-539-C	127	101	88
			101
Total	583	457	104
			116

84b (continued)

words

2. Commercial electronic mail. (E-mail which is supplied by organizations such as General Electric Information Services and MCI Communication.) 301 318 324

Summary 327

Desktop publishing and electronicmail are but 2 of the changes which are shaping the future of information processing. Each year new technology enhanes the ability of personnel to produce information in less time. 339 351 364 374

Document 2
Reference List

Center the word REFERENCES on line 10 (pica) or line 12 (elite); key the list.

Winsor, William M. "Electronic Publishing: The Next Great Office Revolution." <u>The Secretary</u>, June/July 1987. 14 28

Reiss, Levi and Edwin G. Dolan. <u>Using Computers: Managing Change</u>. Cincinnati: South-Western Publishing Company, 1989. 46 57 59

84c ▶ 10 *Improve Language Skills: Verbs*

LL: 70 spaces; SS with DS between line groups

1. Read the first rule.
2. Key the **Learn** sentences below it (with number and period), noting how the rule has been applied.
3. Key the **Apply** sentences (with number and period), using the correct word shown in parentheses.
4. Practice the next rule in the same way.
5. If time permits, key the **Apply** lines again at a faster speed to quicken decision-making skill.

SINGULAR VERBS (continued)

> Use singular verbs with the pronouns *all* and *some* (and with fractions and percentages) when used as subjects if their modifiers are singular. Use plural verbs if their modifiers are plural.

Learn 1. Some of the research is finished.
Learn 2. All of the girls were planning to attend the banquet.
Apply 3. All of the wood (is, are) stacked behind the garage.
Apply 4. Some of the clothes (was, were) purchased in Paris.

> Use a singular verb when *number* is used as the subject and is preceded by *the,* however, use a plural verb if *number* is preceded by *a.*

Learn 5. The number of students who are passing the CPA exam has not decreased.
Learn 6. A number of women have volunteered to assist with the project.
Apply 7. A number of clients (has, have) complained about our service.
Apply 8. The number of students representing our district (is, are) excellent.

Lesson 85 *Report with a Table*

85a ▶ 5 *Conditioning Practice*

each line twice SS (slowly, then faster); DS between 2-line groups; if time permits, rekey selected lines

alphabet 1 For the next two weeks you could save the big quilts for major prizes.
figures 2 Kane received 1,845 votes; Kennedy, 973 votes; and Mertins, 602 votes.
fig/sym 3 Their bill came to $68.19 ($47.63 for paper and $20.56 for envelopes).
speed 4 Their neighbor on the cozy island is the chair of the sorority social.

| 1 | 2 | 3 | 4 | 5 | 6 | 7 | 8 | 9 | 10 | 11 | 12 | 13 | 14 |

205b ▶ 45
Sustained Production: Tables with Leaders and Horizontal and Vertical Rules

Time Schedule
Plan and prepare .... 5′
Timed production .... 30′
Proofread/circle errors.......... 7′
Compute *n-pram*................. 3′

1. Make a list of tables to be processed:
page 348, 201c, Table 2
page 349, 202c, Table 1
page 351, 203d, Table 3
page 352, 204c, Table 3

2. Arrange supplies: full sheets, correction materials, list, etc.

3. When directed to begin, key for 30′ the listed tables. Correct errors neatly. Proofread each table carefully before removing it from the machine. If you finish before time is called, key as much of the two tables identified below as you can in the time remaining.
page 348, 201c, Table 1
page 349, 202c, Table 2

4. Compute *n-pram* and then turn in the tables arranged in the order given in Step 1.

Lesson 206 — Evaluation: Table Processing

206a ▶ 5
Conditioning Practice

each line twice SS (slowly, then faster); DS between 2-line groups; if time permits, take 1′ writings on line 3

alphabet 1 Maja was to have five pens and extra clips in a kit for your big quiz.
figures 2 Sandy was 25 years old when she moved to 4360 Rosegarden Road in 1987.
fig/sym 3 She arrived at 12:47 a.m. on Flight #860 (Gate 38) with 59 classmates.
speed 4 Pam kept the big emblem in a fir box by the enamel bowls on the shelf.

| 1 | 2 | 3 | 4 | 5 | 6 | 7 | 8 | 9 | 10 | 11 | 12 | 13 | 14 |

206b ▶ 45
Measure Production: Tables

Time Schedule
Plan and prepare .... 5′
Timed production .... 30′
Proofread/circle errors.......... 7′
Compute *n-pram*................. 3′

Supplies: full sheets and correction materials

Procedures: Key the tables on this and the next page for 30′. Proofread each table carefully before removing it from the machine. Correct errors neatly.

Table 1
Table with Leaders
DS body; CS: 20 spaces between columns 1 & 2 and 4 spaces between columns 2 & 3

Tables 2-6 are on p. 354.

SWIFT CONSTRUCTION (4)
(New Building Plans for 19-- Catalog) (11)

Building Plan	Code	Price	words
			21
Traditional Log Home	SCP025	$25.00	33
Stackwood Barn	SCP015	15.00	45
Earth-Sheltered Home	SCP020	17.50	57
Little Red Barn	SCP031	12.50	68
Family-Sized Storm Shelter	SCP033	17.50	80
Backyard Multi-Rec Set	SCP038	5.00	92
Multipurpose Greenhouse	SCP022	10.00	104
Multi-Use Workbench	SCP039	5.00	116
Special Dollhouse	SCP040	7.50	127
Solar Greenhouse	SCP010	15.00	139
Heavy-Duty Garden Cart	SCP035	10.00	151

85b ▶ 35
Format and Key Unbound Reports

Document 1
Unbound Report with a Table

Format and key the copy shown at the right as an unbound report. Correct the errors marked in the copy and any you make as you key.

Learning cue: To place a table within the body of a report, follow these guidelines:

1. DS above and below the table; SS the body of the table.

2. Clear all tab stops.

3. Determine and set the tab stop for each column of the table. (The table must be centered within the margins of the report.)

4. After completing the table, reset the tab stop for paragraph indention before keying the remainder of the report.

words

LISTENING 2

One of the most *critical* ~~important~~ skills that an individual 12
acquires ~~possesses~~ is the skill of communicatnig. Studdies indicate 24
that a person spends 70-80 percent of *his/her* ~~their~~ time communicat- 36
ing. *Nixon and West (1989, 28) give the following* ~~A~~ break down for the average individual of ~~the~~ time 55
spent communicating ~~includes (Bell, 1987, 8)~~: 60

Writing	*9%*	62
Reading	*16%*	64
Speaking	*30%*	67
listen*ing*	*45%*	70

Since *almost half* ~~most~~ of the time spent communicating is spent listen- 83
ing, it is important to overcome any barriers that obstruct 95
our ability to listen and to learn new ways to improve our 107
listening ability. 111

Barriers to Listening 119

Anything that interferes with our ability to listen *is* ~~can~~ 130
~~be~~ classified as a barrier to listening. Barreirs that 141
obstruct our ability to listen can be divided into two basic 153
categories--external and internal barriers. 162

Internal Barriers. Internal barriers are those *barriers* that 178
deal with the mental or psychologcal aspects of listening. 190
The perception of the importance of the message, the emo- 202
tional state, and the tuning in and out of the speaker by 213
the listener are *a few* examples of internal barriers. 224

External Barriers External barriers are barriers other 239
than those that deal *with* the mental and psychological make up of 252
the listener that tend tokeep the listener from devoting *full* at- 265
tention to what is being said. Telephone interruptions, 277
uninvited visitors, noise, and the physical environment are examples 290
of external barriers. 295

(continued, p. 152)

204c ▶ 35
Format/Process Tables with Horizontal and Vertical Rules

full sheets; correct errors

Table 1
Table with Horizontal Rules
DS body; decide spaces between columns

Subentries are indented 3 spaces.

			words
BOYCE UNIVERSITY ENROLLMENT REPORT			7
			19
College	Last Year	This Year	25
			37
Arts and Sciences			40
Commuting students	3,658	3,767	46
Resident students	5,220	5,324	52
Business			54
Commuting students	4,791	5,030	60
Resident students	5,768	5,998	66
Education			68
Commuting students	1,236	1,310	75
Resident students	987	1,056	81
			92

Table 2
Table with Horizontal and Vertical Rules
SS body; decide spaces between columns; box the table by inserting vertical lines between columns

Table 3
Reformat Table 1; SS body within each college group; DS between the college groups. Using the two totals given below, add a total line to the table.
Last year's total: **21,660**
This year's total: **22,485**
Total words: 108

				words
NOTABLE BUSINESS EQUIPMENT INVENTIONS				8
(From 1642 to 1899)				12
				24
Invention	Date	Inventor	Nationality	31
				44
Adding machine	1642	Pascal	French	51
Calculating machine	1833	Babbage	English	59
Typewriter	1867	Sholes	U.S.	65
Stock ticker	1870	Edison	U.S.	71
Telephone	1876	Bell	U.S.-Scottish	77
Cash register	1879	Ritty	U.S.	83
Fountain pen	1884	Waterman	U.S.	90
Ballpoint pen	1888	Loud	U.S.	96
Tape recorder	1899	Poulsen	Danish	102
				115
Source: The World Almanac.				124

Lesson 205 Review: Table Processing

205a ▶ 5
Conditioning Practice

each line twice SS (slowly, then faster); DS between 2-line groups; if time permits, take 1′ writings on line 3

alphabet 1 That expensive black racquet is just the wrong size for many children.
figures 2 Linda has 72 blue, 68 yellow, 49 red, 30 green, and 15 orange marbles.
fig/sym 3 Norman was born 7/10/42, Mary was born 9/3/46, and I was born 5/15/48.
speed 4 The ensign works with the official to right the problem with the dock.

| 1 | 2 | 3 | 4 | 5 | 6 | 7 | 8 | 9 | 10 | 11 | 12 | 13 | 14 |

words

Ways to Improve Listening _DS_ 305

 Barriers to listening can be overcome ; However, it 316

does take a conscientious effort on the part of the 326

listener. A ~~good~~ *stet* listener will try to maintain eye contact 338

with the speaker and work to avoid tuning the speaker out. Removing as many 353

external distractions as possible is another means for 364

improving listening. 369

 Listening is also improved by directing attention to 379

the message rather than ~~on~~ *to* the speaker./ *appearance and mannerisms* Focusing on the 396

main points being made by the speaker and taking notes, if 408

(Rader and Kurth, 1988, 417-419)

appropriate, are ways of directing attention to the message. 427

Document 2
Reference Page
Review, if necessary, the arrangement of references in the model on page 148; then prepare a reference page.

Document 3
Title Page
Using your name, school, and the current date, prepare a title page for your report. Refer to page 96 for illustration.

Nixon, Judy C., and Judy West. "Listning--The New Com- 14

 petency. The Balance Sheet, January/February 1989, 27-29 29

Rader, M.H., and Linda A. Kurth. *Business* 40

Communication for the Computer Age. South- 55

Western Publishing Company, Cincinnati, 1988. 63

85c ▶ 10
Improve Language Skills: Verbs

LL: 70 spaces; SS with DS between line groups

1. Read the first rule.

2. Key the **Learn** sentences below it (with number and period), noting how the rule has been applied.

3. Key the **Apply** sentences (with number and period), using the correct word shown in parentheses.

4. Practice the next rule in the same way.

5. If time permits, key the **Apply** lines again at a faster speed to quicken decision-making skill.

PLURAL VERBS

Use a plural verb with a plural subject (noun or pronoun).

Learn 1. The three pictures have been framed.
Learn 2. They are going to ask you to present the award.
Apply 3. The napkins (is, are) on the counter.
Apply 4. New desks (has, have) been ordered.

Use plural verbs with compound subjects joined by *and*.

Learn 5. Tom and Sue are in charge of the program.
Learn 6. Mr. Miller and his wife have already registered to vote on Monday.
Apply 7. My dog and your cat (has, have) been digging in Mrs. Chi's garden.
Apply 8. The treasurer and the secretary (is, are) planning to attend.

203d (continued)

Table 2
3-Column Table with Multiple-Line Column Headings
DS body; CS: 8 spaces

Table 3
Reformat Table 2; decide spaces between columns; convert the multiple-line headings into single-line headings as follows.
Column 2: **Birth Date**
Column 3: **Birth Place**

NOTABLE ENTERTAINERS 4

ENTERTAINER	BIRTH DATE	BIRTH PLACE	words
			7
			15
Steve Allen	12/26/21	New York, NY	22
Chevy Chase	10/8/43	New York, NY	29
Bill Cosby	7/12/37	Philadelphia, PA	36
Jose Feliciano	9/10/45	Lares, Puerto Rico	45
Michael Jackson	8/29/58	Gary, IN	51
Paul Newman	1/26/25	Cleveland, OH	58
Tom Selleck	1/29/45	Detroit, MI	64

Lesson 204 Tables with Horizontal/Vertical Rules

204a ▶ 5 Conditioning Practice

each line twice SS (slowly, then faster); DS between 2-line groups; if time permits, take 1′ writings on line 2

alphabet 1 Chad thought Pamela's long joke about the next quiz wasn't very funny.
figures 2 Bill is to read pages 271-305 for history and pages 69-84 for English.
fig/sym 3 Mary bought 30 (15%), David bought 78 (39%), and Lynn bought 92 (46%).
speed 4 The busy maid is to rush the cocoa to the eight men on the dorm panel.

| 1 | 2 | 3 | 4 | 5 | 6 | 7 | 8 | 9 | 10 | 11 | 12 | 13 | 14 |

204b ▶ 10 Learn to Format Tables with Horizontal and Vertical Rules

Study the illustration at the right, observing the spacing between the keyed copy and the rules. Then key the table on a full sheet; DS body; CS: 8 spaces. Use the vertical spacing format guides to key the horizontal rules. Begin each rule at the beginning of the first column and end each aligned with the final stroke in the last column. Remove the page and, using a pen (preferably black ink), draw vertical rules at the midpoint between columns.

Note: When formatting tables with horizontal rules, the most error-free method of vertical spacing is to set the machine for single spacing and return twice for double-spaced entries.

THIRD QUARTER SUBSIDIARY PERFORMANCE
DS
(In Millions of Dollars)
SS

Subsidiary	Total Assets	Net Income
Emerald Isle	129.754	1.477
Century Savings & Loan	217.748	2.006
TGP Transportation	304.127	3.032
Reeves Manufacturing	93.373	1.233
Total	745.002	7.748

(Spacing guides: DS above headings, SS below; DS before first entry; SS after last entry; DS before Total, SS after.)

86a ▶ 5 Conditioning Practice

each line twice SS (slowly, then faster); DS between 2-line groups; if time permits, rekey selected lines

alphabet 1 Kevin justified his low quiz score by explaining his unusual problems.
figures 2 She accumulated 2,453 miles in June, 989 in July, and 1,706 in August.
shift keys 3 Ms. Nancy Slater and Mr. Robert Siverson will arrive on Monday, May 1.
speed 4 Diana and the visitor can handle the problems of the eighth amendment.

| 1 | 2 | 3 | 4 | 5 | 6 | 7 | 8 | 9 | 10 | 11 | 12 | 13 | 14 |

86b ▶ 32 Format and Key an Unbound Report with Internal Citations and References

Document 1
Unbound Report

1. Format the copy as an unbound report; correct any errors you make as you key.

2. Prepare a reference page on a separate sheet; correct all errors.

words

STUDENT ORGANIZATIONS 4

Student organizations play a vital role in the 14
educational process of students. Students who 23
participate in such organizations are given op- 32
portunities to test the concepts they were taught 42
in the formal classroom environment. Two such 52
organizations that are widely recognized in the 61
business education field are Future Business 70
Leaders of America and Business Professionals 80
of America (formerly called Office Education 89
Association). 92

Future Business Leaders 101

Future Business Leaders of America is a vo- 109
cational association that helps students bridge 119
the gap between the classroom and the business 128
world. Two of the major goals outlined in the 138
Future Business Leaders of America Handbook 147
(1985, 5) are as follows: 152

1. Develop competent, aggressive business 161
leadership. 163
2. Create more interest in and understand- 172
ing of American business enterprise. 179

Business leadership. Students have the oppor- 192
tunity to develop leadership skills by serving 201
as officers, attending conferences, working with 211
businessmen and businesswomen in the com- 219
munity, and participating in competitive events 229
sponsored by the organization. The organiza- 238
tion's strong emphasis on community service 246
provides another avenue for the development 255
of leadership skills. 260

Business enterprise. A greater understanding 273
of business enterprise is gained by students as 282
they participate in chapter projects dealing with 292
this important subject. These projects give stu- 302
dents experiences in learning more about the 311
operation of business enterprise in America. 320

Business Professionals of America 334

Business Professionals of America is another 343
vocational business and office education pro- 351
gram for students interested in developing per- 361
sonal, leadership, and office skills. According 370
to Goodman (1987, 11), the executive director 380
of the organization for 1987-88, the goal of the 389
organization has been to promote leadership 398
and professionalism among students in order 407
to prepare them for satisfying and successful 416
careers in the business world. 423

The two goals, developing business leadership 432
and understanding business enterprise, empha- 441
sized by FBLA are also emphasized by Business 450
Professionals of America. They, too, have pro- 459
grams designed to provide students with the op- 468
portunity to develop their leadership skills and 478
to foster a greater understanding of the role of 488
the entrepreneur in the free enterprise system. 498

REFERENCES 500

Future Business Leaders of America Handbook. 518
Reston, Virginia: FBLA-PBL, Incorporated, 526
1985. 528

Goodman, Dorothy M. "A New Image for Our 536
Organization," 1987-88 Chapter Handbook, 549
Columbus, Ohio: Office Education Associa- 557
tion, 1987. 559

203a ▶ 5 Conditioning Practice

each line twice SS (slowly, then faster); then a 1′ writing on line 4

alphabet 1 Mindy requires size six or seven jackets for both perky girls to wear.
figures 2 My order for 1,475 boxes and 3,690 bags was shipped by truck on 12/28.
fig/sym 3 He took the monitor (#3246-B), CPU (#784-9B), and keyboard (#05-61-B).
speed 4 My antique dish in the hall in the downtown chapel is authentic ivory.

| 1 | 2 | 3 | 4 | 5 | 6 | 7 | 8 | 9 | 10 | 11 | 12 | 13 | 14 |

203b ▶ 7 Improve Language Skills: Word Choice

1. Study the spelling and definition of each pair of words.
2. Key the **Learn** line, with the number and period, noting the proper use of the often confused words.
3. Key the **Apply** lines, with the number and period, using the word that completes each sentence correctly.

bridal (adj) of or pertaining to a bride or a wedding

bridle (n) a harness fitted about a horse's head, used to restrain or guide

cooperation (n) working together toward a common end

corporation (n) a business enterprise chartered by the state with its own rights, privileges, and liabilities

Learn 1. The riding instructor gave a bridle as a bridal gift to Sue and Tom.
Apply 2. The photographer took three pictures of the (bridal/bridle) party.
Apply 3. The trainer had a difficult time putting the (bridal/bridle) on the colt.

Learn 4. The cooperation of the workers made the corporation successful.
Apply 5. Most businesses depend on (cooperation/corporation) to get things done.
Apply 6. The (cooperation/corporation) has an elected board of directors.

203c ▶ 8 Recall Procedures for Centering Column Headings

CS: 8 spaces

Key the drills as directed below.
Drill 1: Center by column entries.
Drill 2: Center by column headings.
Drill 3: Center by longest item in each column, whether a heading or an entry.

Drill 1	Director	Gross	Net
	Saundra Murphy	$1,482.95	$1,284.25
Drill 2	Automobile	Body Style	Engine Size
	Apollo	Sedan	4.2 L
Drill 3	Business Name	City	Employees
	Hoppe, Inc.	Baltimore	201

203d ▶ 30 Format/Process Tables with Column Headings of Variable Lengths

full sheets; correct errors
References: p. 288, RG 11

Table 1
Table Centered by Longest Item in Column (Whether Entry or Column Heading)
DS body; CS: 8 spaces

QUALITY TEAM LEADERS — words 4

Leader	Department	Extension	words
			15
Thomas Broggi	Planning	8475	20
Elizabeth Pyncheski	Personnel	8299	27
Gerri Holmes-Ray	Accounting	8344	34
Karen Stoverton	Marketing	8070	40
Juan Hernandez	Transportation	8765	47
Vera Senti	CIS	8432	51
Randi Welesko	Advertising	8279	57
Pat Zimwalt	Purchasing	8645	63

86c ▶ 13
Improve Language Skills: Verbs

LL: 70 spaces; SS with DS between line groups.

1. Read the first rule.
2. Key the **Learn** sentences below it (with number and period), noting how the rule has been applied.
3. Key the **Apply** sentences (with number and period) using the correct word shown in parentheses.
4. Practice the other rules in the same way.
5. If time permits, key the **Apply** lines again at a faster speed to quicken decision-making skill.

OTHER VERB GUIDES

If there is confusion whether a subject is singular or plural, consult a dictionary.

Learn 1. The data presented in your report are confusing.
Learn 2. Several alumni are invited to this year's commencement activities.
Learn 3. The analyses completed by Mrs. Carter are excellent.
Apply 4. The same criteria (has, have) been used in the past.
Apply 5. The analysis (is, are) very extensive.

When used as the subject, the pronouns *I, we, you,* and *they,* as well as plural nouns, require the plural verb *do not* or the contraction *don't.*

Learn 6. They do not want to become involved with the project.
Learn 7. The plans don't include a private office for the manager.
Apply 8. I (don't, doesn't) agree with the report you submitted.
Apply 9. The reviews (don't, doesn't) look very promising.

When used as the subject, the pronouns *he, she, it,* as well as singular nouns, require the singular verb *does not* or the contraction *doesn't.*

Learn 10. She doesn't want the office layout changed.
Learn 11. The price does not include the software.
Apply 12. It (don't, doesn't) concern me; you take care of it.
Apply 13. The job (don't, doesn't) require shorthand.

Lesson 87 — *Report with Long Quotation and Numbered List/Language Skills*

87a ▶ 5
Conditioning Practice

each line twice SS (slowly, then faster); DS between 2-line groups; as time permits, rekey selected lines

alphabet 1 Everyone except Zelda Jenkins will be required to go to the math fair.
figures 2 Jo's Nursery sold 370 trees and 458 shrubs between May 29 and June 16.
fig/sym 3 The checks written on 8/4 ($81.52) and 9/3 ($68.70) were not recorded.
speed 4 The box with the emblem of the bugle is on the mantle by the fishbowl.

| 1 | 2 | 3 | 4 | 5 | 6 | 7 | 8 | 9 | 10 | 11 | 12 | 13 | 14 |

87b ▶ 10
Improve Language Skills: Word Choice

Study the definition and spelling of each word. Note how it is used in the **Learn** sentence. Key the **Learn** sentence and the **Apply** sentences (with number and period) selecting the proper word in parentheses to complete the sentence correctly.

die (vb) to pass from physical life
dye (n) a soluble or insoluble coloring matter
peace (n) a state of tranquility or quiet
piece (n) a part of a whole

Learn 1. He will die when he sees the color of the dye they plan to use.
Apply 2. The (die, dye) they ordered will arrive in time to meet their needs.
Apply 3. Before I (die, dye) I want to see Austria, Germany, and Switzerland.

Learn 4. If you want peace, Brad, you better save him a piece of your cake.
Apply 5. She was about to give him a (peace, piece) of her mind when he hung up.
Apply 6. He was at (peace, piece) with himself after passing his written exams.

202b ▶ 10 Learn to Format Tables with Leaders

full sheet; DS body; decide spaces between columns; insert leaders as shown

To align leaders

Key the first line of the first column; space once; note the position of the printing point indicator or cursor (on an odd or even number); key a period, then space alternately across the line stopping 2 or 3 spaces before the next column. On lines that follow, align the periods with those in line 1. Leave at least one blank space before keying the first period in the leader on a line.

RADIO STATION FORMATS

Classical music	WKTC-AM
Country music	WYRM-FM
News and weather	WNWZ-AM
Rock music	WZZR-FM
Talk show	WXRE-AM

202c ▶ 35 Format/Process Tables with Leaders and Column Headings

full sheets unless otherwise directed; correct errors

Table 1
2-Column Table with Leaders

DS body; decide spaces between columns; insert leaders

CELTIC REDS EXECUTIVE BOARD — words 6

Office	Incumbent	words
		12
President	Huerta Perez	22
President-elect	Frank Linberg	33
First Vice President	Josephine Luiz	44
Second Vice President	Karen Appelt	54
Corresponding Secretary	Rodney Luther	65
Recording Secretary	Barbara Miller	76
Historian	John Tomczak	86
Past President	Robert O'Hare	97

Table 2
3-Column Table with Leaders and Totals

DS body; CS: 16 spaces between columns 1 & 2; 6 spaces between columns 2 & 3; insert leaders between columns 1 & 2

Note: Do not key leaders in the *Total* line.

SCHOLARSHIP FUND DRIVE — 5

(Status report--End of fourth Quarter) — 12

Donor	Pledge	Paid	words
			19
Scott Twinskey	$250	$105	29
Mary Rob-Yates	360	200	36
Sam bukitsch	170	75	43
Jeanne Batz	380	240	51
Juan Salazar	240	90	58
richard Simms	190	60	66
Alberti Alvarez	300	180	73
chun Wau Wacker	250	75	80
T. G. Bailey	400	160	91
Total	$2,450	$1,185	96

Table 3

Reformat Table 1 on a half sheet, long edge at top; DS body; decide spaces between columns. Change the name of the Second Vice President from **Karen Appelt** to **Elizabeth Austin.**

87c ▶ 35
Format and Key an Unbound Report

Document 1
Unbound Report with Long Quotation and Numbered List

Format and key the copy as an unbound report. Correct all errors you make as you key.

words

TAXES 1

Americans are taxed in order to raise revenues to finance governmental 15
activities. Taxation has never been popular. Much time and energy have 30
been devoted by the legislature trying to devise a system that requires 44
everyone to pay his/her fair share. Taxes are generally based on the bene- 59
fits received and/or on the ability to pay. Two of the most common revenue 74
raising taxes are the personal income tax and the sales tax. 87

Personal Income Tax 95

The personal income tax is the tax individuals are required to pay on 109
their earnings. Employers deduct this tax from employees' paychecks. 123
When employees file their income tax returns, they will either receive a 137
refund for any excess which has been paid or they will have to pay the bal- 152
ance due. 154

> Personal income taxes have been the Federal Government's largest single 169
> source of revenue and a major source of state revenues as well. On the 183
> federal level, the personal income tax is a graduated tax, which means 198
> the more you make, the higher the percentage of your income you pay in 213
> taxes (Rachman and Mescon, 1987, 529). 220

With the Tax Reform Act of 1986, the highest tax an individual will pay is 235
33 percent. The amount an individual pays changes with each tax reform. 249
In the past, the top tax rate has been as high as 70 percent (Anrig, 1988, 56). 266

Sales Taxes 270

The sales tax is another tax with which most people are familiar. It is a 285
tax that is added to the retail price of goods and services. Two examples of 301
this type of tax are as follows: 308

1. General Sales Tax. The general sales tax is a tax levied by most states 323
on goods and services. The amount of tax and the specific goods and ser- 337
vices that are taxed varies by state. 345

2. Excise Tax (Selective Sales Tax). The excise tax is a state tax levied 360
against specific items. Examples of items with an excise tax include to- 375
bacco, alcoholic beverages, and gasoline. 383

While the income tax is a tax based on the individual's ability to pay, the 398
general sales tax and the excise tax are based on benefits received. For 413
example, taxes collected on gasoline are used for highways. Individuals 428
purchasing gasoline are those who benefit from the construction and mainte- 443
nance of highways. 446

Document 2
Reference List

Format and key the reference list on a separate sheet. Correct any errors you make as you key.

Document 3
Title Page

If time permits, prepare a title page using your name, school, and current date.

REFERENCES 2

Anrig, Greg, Jr. "Making the Most of 1988's Low Tax Rate." Money, Febru- 18
ary 1988, 56-57. 21

Rachman, David J., and Michael H. Mescon. Business Today. New York: 38
Random House, 1987. 42

201c ▶ 25 *Recall Basic Table Format*

full sheets; correct errors
References: p. 288, RG 11

Table 1
3-Column Table with Totals
DS body; CS: 6 spaces

			words
PROPERTY VALUES			3
<u>Property</u>	<u>This Year</u>	<u>Last Year</u>	14
Scrubbs Ranch	$ 1,355,750	$ 1,308,457	23
State Street	754,900	749,500	29
Westlake Mall	5,387,000	5,401,750	36
Airport Complex	7,980,250	6,906,900	43
Center City	2,450,500	2,250,750	54
Total	$17,928,400	$16,617,357	60

Table 2
3-Column Table with Source Note
SS body; decide spaces between columns

Table 3
Reformat Table 2; DS body; decide a different number of spaces between columns

SOME ENDANGERED MAMMALS			5
<u>Mammal</u>	<u>Scientific Name</u>	<u>Historic Range</u>	19
Bobcat	Felis rufus escuinapae	Central Mexico	28
Cheetah	Acinonyx jubatus	Africa to India	37
Gorilla	Gorilla gorilla	Central & West Africa	46
Giant panda	Ailuropoda melanoleuca	China	54
Gray whale	Eschrichtius robustus	North Pacific Ocean	65
Leopard	Panthera pardus	Africa & Asia	72
Tiger	Panthera tigris	Asia	78
____________________			81
Source: U.S. Fish and Wildlife Service, U.S. Interior Department.			95

201d ▶ 8 *Language Skills: Word Choice*

1. Study the spelling and definition of each pair of words.

2. Key the **Learn** line, with the number and period, noting the proper use of the often confused words.

3. Key the **Apply** lines, with the number and period, using the word that completes each sentence correctly.

berth (n) a built-in bed on a ship or vehicle
birth (n) the act or condition or being born
bold (adj) fearless; courageous
bowled (vb) knocked over with something rolled

Learn 1. The cat's birth unexpectedly took place in the ship's upper berth.
Apply 2. The farmer is planning for the (birth/berth) of a foal next month.
Apply 3. The cost of the cruise includes a cabin with two (births/berths).

Learn 4. The bold little boy bowled a strike to win the game.
Apply 5. I am seeking a (bold/bowled) hiker to climb the mountain with me.
Apply 6. We (bold/bowled) three games before going to the movies on our last date.

Lesson 202 *Tables with Leaders and Totals*

202a ▶ 5 *Conditioning Practice*

each line twice SS (slowly, then faster); DS between 2-line groups; if time permits, take 1′ writings on line 3

alphabet 1 Jake will buy a very good quality zinc from the experts at the stores.
figures 2 The license plate numbers for her cars are 247951, 836067, and 443086.
fig/sym 3 Leah just renewed Policies #23-4598-623 (auto) and #35-9107-44 (home).
speed 4 My field hand saw the small dirigible signal the men in the cornfield.

| 1 | 2 | 3 | 4 | 5 | 6 | 7 | 8 | 9 | 10 | 11 | 12 | 13 | 14 |

UNIT 19 LESSONS 88 – 89
Improve Keyboarding and Language Skills

Learning Goals

1. To refine keyboarding technique and response patterns.
2. To increase speed and improve accuracy on straight copy.
3. To review/improve language skills.

Format Guides

1. Paper guide at *0* (for typewriters).
2. LL: 70 spaces for drills, language skills, and timed writings.
3. LS: SS drills and language skills; DS ¶s.
4. PI: 5 spaces.

Lesson 88 — *Keyboarding Technique/Language Skills*

88a ▶ 5
Conditioning Practice

each line twice SS (slowly, then faster); as time permits, rekey selected lines

alphabet 1 Jacob was quite puzzled when Mr. Grifey told us to take the exam over.
figures 2 There are 1,503 engineering majors; 879 are males and 624 are females.
fig/sym 3 My 1992 property tax increased by 6.75% ($241); I paid $3,580 in 1991.
speed 4 Helen owns the six foals and the lame cow in the neighbor's hay field.

| 1 | 2 | 3 | 4 | 5 | 6 | 7 | 8 | 9 | 10 | 11 | 12 | 13 | 14 |

88b ▶ 10
Improve Technique: Numbers

Beginning at the left margin, set 3 tab stops according to the key beneath the lines. Key the lines twice (slowly, then faster), tabbing from column to column.

04/15/49	(715) 809-4657	$1489.88	4:06 a.m.
11/23/63	(803) 629-9879	$ 38.27	10:25 p.m.
01/25/67	(343) 821-4546	$ 638.79	10:57 a.m.
12/17/64	(609) 459-6093	$ 6.86	7:45 p.m.
02/28/54	(302) 905-1756	$2788.25	12:29 a.m.
05/21/34	(786) 965-7489	$ 302.97	12:37 p.m.

KEY | 8 | 10 | 14 | 10 | 8 | 10 | 10 |

88c ▶ 10
Improve Language Skills: Pronoun Agreement

LL: 70 spaces; SS with DS between line groups

1. Read the first rule.
2. Key the **Learn** sentences below it (with number and period), noting how the rule has been applied.
3. Key the **Apply** sentences (with number and period) using the correct pronoun shown in parentheses.
4. Practice the second rule in the same way.
5. If time permits, key the **Apply** lines again at a faster speed to quicken decision-making skill.

PRONOUN AGREEMENT

> Pronouns (I, we, you, he, she, it, their, etc.) agree with their antecedents in person (i.e., person speaking—first person; person spoken to—second person; person spoken about—third person).

Learn 1. Kay said, "I will see the play when I finish my project." *(1st person)*
Learn 2. When you are finished with your homework, turn it in. *(2d person)*
Learn 3. Janet said that she would host the party at her home. *(3d person)*
Apply 4. The executives who saw the plans said (he/she, they) were pleased.
Apply 5. After you get in shape, (one's, your) level of energy increases.
Apply 6. "(I/She) want to revise the schedule before I leave the office."

> Pronouns agree with their antecedents in gender (masculine, feminine, and neuter).

Learn 7. Rebecca will recite her part after the introductions. *(feminine)*
Learn 8. The tree lost its leaves before the end of October. *(neuter)*
Apply 9. Each female will be given a rose as she receives (her, its) diploma.
Apply 10. The ball bounced strangely before (he, it) whizzed past the outfielder.

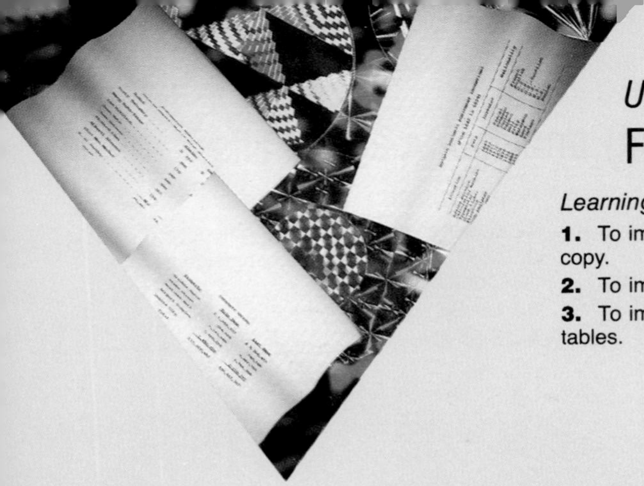

UNIT 48 LESSONS 201 – 206
Format/Process Tables

Learning Goals

1. To improve keyboarding skill on straight copy.
2. To improve statistical keyboarding skill.
3. To improve skill in formatting/processing tables.

Format Guides

1. Paper guide at *0* (for typewriters).
2. LL: 70 spaces.
3. LS: SS sentence drills; DS ¶s; as directed for problems.
4. Tab sets: 5 spaces for ¶s; as needed for problems.

Lesson 201 *Tables with Totals and Source Notes*

201a ▶ 5 Conditioning Practice

each line twice SS (slowly, then faster); DS between 2-line groups; if time permits, take 1′ writings on line 2

alphabet 1 Jeb asked him a very zany question before each good example was given.
figures 2 My daughter will arrive on Flight 906 at Gate 35 on 12/18 at 4:37 p.m.
fig/sym 3 Ray sold 56 new advertisements ($13,780) between 12/14/91 and 1/30/92.
speed 4 Eight busy men may fix the penalty box when they visit the city field.

| 1 | 2 | 3 | 4 | 5 | 6 | 7 | 8 | 9 | 10 | 11 | 12 | 13 | 14 |

201b ▶ 12 Improve/Check Keyboarding Skill: Statistical Copy

1. Two 1′ writings on each ¶; find *gwam,* circle errors.
2. One 3′ writing on ¶s 1-3 combined; find *gwam,* circle errors.

all letters used | A | 1.5 si | 5.7 awl | 80% hfw |

gwam 1′ | 3′

The two professors who are taking 35 students to study in foreign 13 4
countries met with the parents of the students on the night of Febru- 27 9
ary 19 in Room 612. The major purpose of the meeting was to give infor- 41 14
mation to the parents of the students who were to study from March 15 55 18
to May 15 in Florence, Italy, and Vico Morote, Switzerland. 68 23

Every parent was informed that the group would be required to leave 14 27
O'Hare Airport (Chicago) on All World Flight #908 on the evening of 27 32
March 15. Flight #908 will go directly to Milan, Italy, where the group 42 36
will stay the first evening. After the trip to Milan, the students will 56 41
be taken to Florence where they will study until April 30. 68 45

On May 1 every student and teacher will take an express train to 13 50
Vico Morote, Switzerland, where they will remain until May 15. When class 27 54
is over on May 15, every student will take an overnight express 41 59
train to Frankfurt, Germany, for return on All World Flight #47. Flight 55 64
#47 is to land at O'Hare early in the evening on May 16. 67 68

gwam 1′ | 1 | 2 | 3 | 4 | 5 | 6 | 7 | 8 | 9 | 10 | 11 | 12 | 13 | 14 |
3′ | 1 | 2 | 3 | 4 | 5 |

88d ▶ 10
Improve Technique: Keystroking and Response Patterns

LL: 70 spaces

1. Lines 1-3: each word 3 times (slowly, faster, top speed); when bell rings, complete word, return, and continue.

2. Lines 4-6: each phrase 3 times (slowly, faster, top speed); when bell rings, complete word, return, and continue.

3. Lines 7-9: each sentence 3 times (slowly, faster, top speed).

Goal: High-speed keyboarding response (think and key each word or word group as a whole).

Emphasize fast finger reaches with hands quiet, wrists low and relaxed.

balanced-hand words

1 to end cow dog eye apt for cue ham ivy bug may men rug toe cut bus six
2 corn bush idle paid rush torn auto duty form work hair wish lamb world
3 giant field right rocks focus amend blend cycle ivory snake their girl

Emphasize high-speed phrase response.

balanced-hand phrases

4 paid for it | fix it | go to work | go with them | sign the title | their island
5 their own problems | if they go | when she paid | the right box | turn signals
6 haughty neighbor | small cubicle | bushel of corn | giant firm | to the end of

Emphasize high-speed, word-level response; quick spacing.

balanced-hand sentences

7 I paid the man by the dock for the six bushels of corn and the turkey.
8 Diana and Vivian kept the food for their fish by the antique fishbowl.
9 Did the haughty girls pay for their own gowns for the sorority social?

| 1 | 2 | 3 | 4 | 5 | 6 | 7 | 8 | 9 | 10 | 11 | 12 | 13 | 14 |

88e ▶ 15
Check/Improve Keyboarding Skill

1. A 1′ writing on ¶ 1; find *gwam*.

2. Add 2-4 *gwam* to the rate attained in Step 1, and note quarter-minute checkpoints from table below.

3. Take two 1′ guided writings on ¶ 1 to increase speed.

4. Practice ¶ 2 in the same way.

5. A 3′ writing on ¶s 1 and 2 combined; find *gwam* and circle errors.

6. If time permits, take another 3′ writing.

Quarter-Minute Checkpoints

gwam	1/4′	1/2′	3/4′	1′
32	8	16	24	32
36	9	18	27	36
40	10	20	30	40
44	11	22	33	44
48	12	24	36	48
52	13	26	39	52
56	14	28	42	56
60	15	30	45	60
64	16	32	48	64

all letters used | A | 1.5 si | 5.7 awl | 80% hfw

	gwam 3′	5′
Many options are available for people to ponder as they invest their	5	3
money. Real estate, savings accounts, money market accounts, bonds, and	9	6
stocks are but a few of the options that are open to those who wish to	14	9
invest their extra money. Several factors will determine which type of	19	11
investment a person will choose. These factors pertain to the expected	24	14
rate of return, the degree of liquidity desired, and the amount of risk a	29	17
person is willing to take.	30	18
An investor who seeks a high rate of return and who is willing to	35	21
take a high degree of risk often considers the stock market. Stock mar-	40	24
kets or stock exchanges are organizations that bring investors together	44	27
to buy and sell shares of stock. Stock represents a share in the owner-	49	30
ship of a company. Since more risk is associated with an investment that	54	33
has a high rate of return, judgment must be exercised by those thinking	59	35
about the purchase of stock.	61	37

gwam 3′ | 1 | 2 | 3 | 4 | 5 |
gwam 5′ | 1 | 2 | 3 |

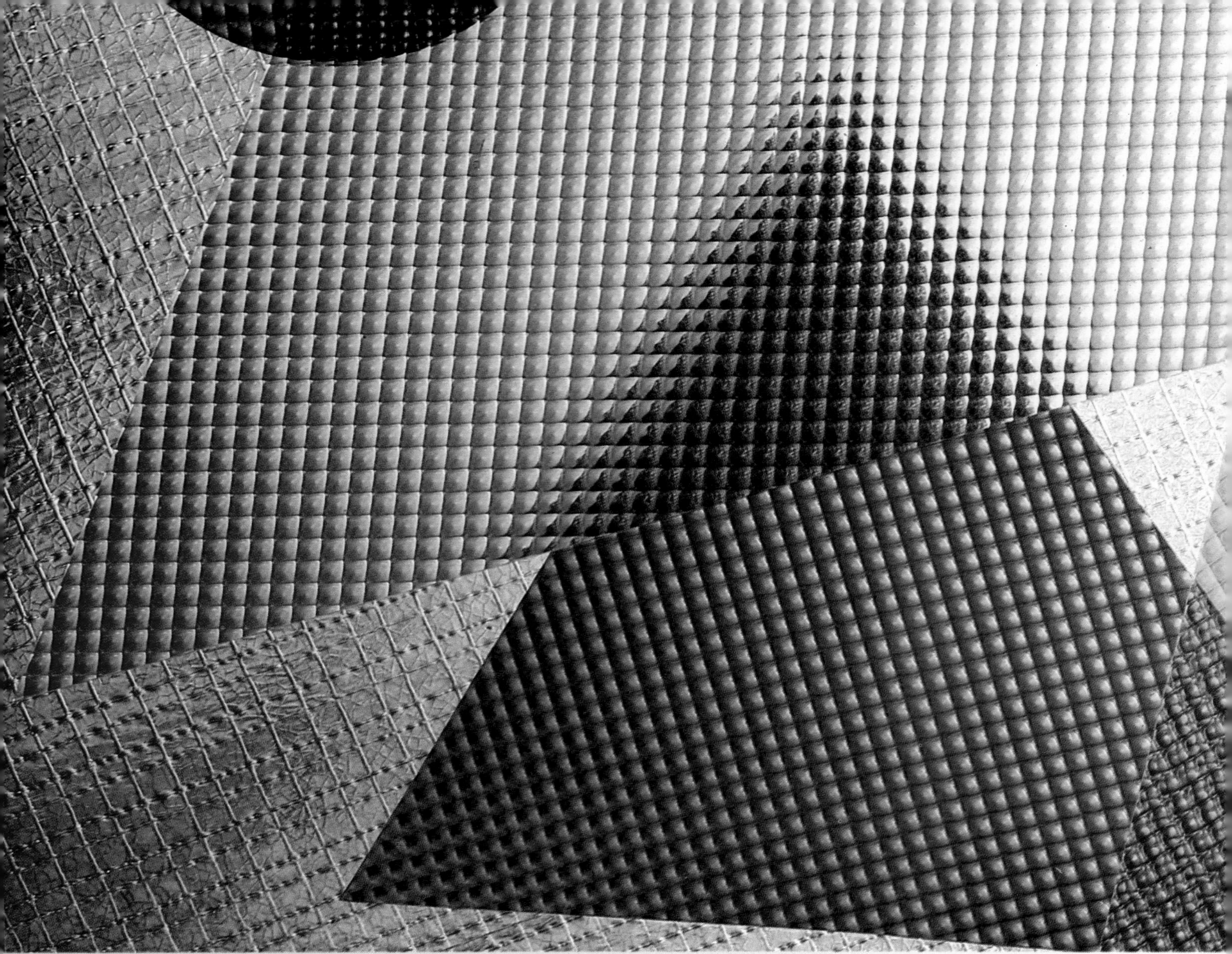

LESSONS 201 – 225

PHASE 9

EXTEND STATISTICAL DOCUMENT PROCESSING SKILLS

Keyboard operators in most offices must be able to prepare statistical documents with a high level of proficiency. This phase is designed to help you develop this important job qualification. After intensive practice in formatting and processing tables and forms, you will apply those skills in an office job simulation which imitates the work of a real office.

Specifically, Phase 9 (Lessons 201-225) will help you:

1. Develop your ability to work with minimum directions and to use your decision-making skills.
2. Increase your table processing skills.
3. Improve your skill in processing purchase requisitions, purchase orders, and invoices.
4. Apply your skills in a simulated office position where you will process a variety of documents typical of those used in modern offices.
5. Improve your language and composition skills.

89a ▶ 5 *Conditioning Practice*

each line twice (slowly, then faster); as time permits, repeat selected lines

alphabet 1 Mozambique was the place Karen most enjoyed visiting in exotic Africa.

figures 2 South High School had 350 graduates in 1986 and 284 graduates in 1987.

fig/sym 3 Order #3845-6079 was damaged during shipment by J&B Express on May 21.

speed 4 The lame lapdog may wish to dognap on the burlap by the antique chair.

| 1 | 2 | 3 | 4 | 5 | 6 | 7 | 8 | 9 | 10 | 11 | 12 | 13 | 14 |

89b ▶ 8 *Improve Techniques: Return/Tab Keys*

LL: 50 spaces; set a tab 15 spaces to the right of center

1. Key the lines given at the right. Concentrate on correct techniques for return and tab keys.

2. Take two 30″ writings; work for speed.

3. Take three 1′ writings; try to increase amount keyed with each writing.

Emphasize quick return and start of new line.

			gwam 1′
Yellowstone	Tab	Wyoming	4
Yosemite	Tab	California	8
Glacier	Tab	Montana	11
Rocky Mountain	Tab	Colorado	16
Grand Canyon	Tab	Arizona	20
Zion	Tab	Utah	22

89c ▶ 15 *Improve Technique: Response Patterns*

each line 3 times (slowly, faster, top speed); as time permits, repeat selected lines

Goal: To reduce time interval between keystrokes (read ahead to anticipate stroking pattern).

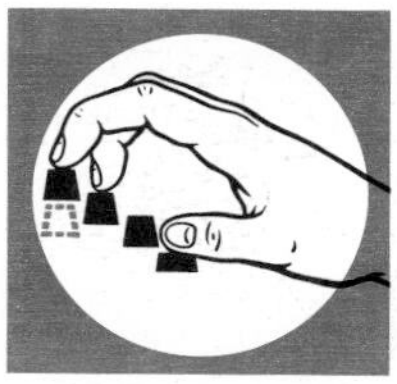

Finger reaches, quiet hands

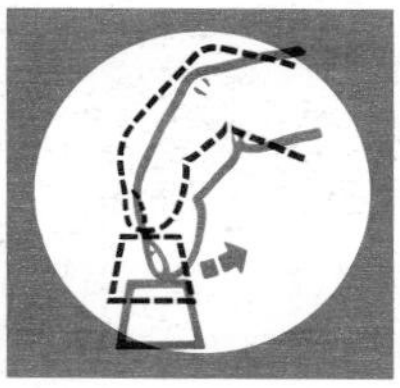

Snappy keystroking

Quick spacing

Emphasize curved, upright fingers; finger-action keystroking.

one-hand words

1 my beg oil sat joy car him add ink egg inn far ill few mom set pup bed

2 best hymn acre join face milk draw pull edge upon wage only tact knoll

3 onion weave union beads pupil defer holly erase imply serve jolly gate

Emphasize independent finger action; quiet hands.

one-hand phrases

4 in my bag | at ease | be at my | bad debt | grade on my test | you better beware

5 a nylon vest | bad career start | pink kimono | average grades | minimum taxes

6 bad start | a red taffeta dress | you deserve better | only awards | on a date

Emphasize continuity; finger-action with fingers close to keys.

one-hand sentences

7 After a decrease in oil tax rates, we agreed on a greater oil reserve.

8 In my opinion, my award was based on my grade average on my art tests.

9 Jim agreed on decreased cab fare rates after gas taxes were decreased.

| 1 | 2 | 3 | 4 | 5 | 6 | 7 | 8 | 9 | 10 | 11 | 12 | 13 | 14 |

200b (continued)

Document 4
News Release
LP p. 147
Key the document given at the right as a news release for release immediately. The contact will be **Megan Ryan, (401) 896-3175.**

words

heading 8

OMAHA, NE, September 20, 19--. Sweeping changes in the executive staff of 23
the Forum Group have been announced by Harvey E. Jamison, president and 37
chief executive officer. "These changes," according to Jamison, "are par- 52
tially the result of a reorganization designed to invigorate and stimulate the 68
activities and growth of the Group." 75

Alyce T. Higgins, formerly president of Continental Business Enterprises, 91
has been named executive vice president for marketing, replacing Matthew 105
W. Columbo, who retired on September 1. Higgins, a graduate of the Wharton 120
School of Business, will also serve as a member of the executive committee. 135

J. Robert Schmitt has been appointed a senior vice president and general 150
counsel. A former director of the Alliance Foundation, Schmitt has prac- 164
ticed law for more than 20 years and is the senior partner in the firm of 179
Schmitt, Solomon, and DeVito. 185

Katherine P. Quinn, currently a senior vice president, has been promoted to 200
the position of executive vice president for operations. In this position, she 216
will direct the overall operations of the Group worldwide. Quinn has held 231
several administrative and executive positions in the Forum Group over the 246
past 18 years. ### 250

Document 5
Formal Memorandum
LP p. 149
Key the document shown at the right as a formal memorandum. List the enumerated items in ¶ 3.

TO: All Managerial Employees FROM: Michael T. Robinson, Executive 11
Vice President DATE: July 19, 19-- SUBJECT: TRAVEL POLICIES 20

Eagle & Sons recognizes that the costs related to travel are a necessary part 36
of doing business. At the same time, travel costs are a major expenditure 51
and must be effectively controlled. 58

Prior to making travel plans, alternatives must be considered. These include 74
correspondence (including overnight mail), exchange of information by 88
facsimile transmission, and telephone calls (including teleconferencing). If 103
these alternatives are inadequate, travel plans should be made. 116

Requests for travel will be submitted to the director of administration and 132
will include the following: 1. Purpose of the travel, including a justification 144
for not using alternative means. 2. Specific destination, with preference 159
for mode of transportation and hotel or motel accommodations. 3. Dates 174
and desired times of departure and return. 183

Upon approval, all travel arrangements will be made by the travel coordina- 197
tor in the administration office. The most efficient mode of travel that meets 213
the needs of the individual will be selected. Hotel/motel reservations will be 229
made at a convenient location. 235

Care should be taken to incur the lowest possible costs. Meal costs are lim- 250
ited to the actual cost plus tip. Entertainment costs are limited to meals un- 266
less approval for more lavish entertainment has been approved in advance. 281

Upon return, a request for reimbursement for any costs incurred should be 296
submitted to the finance office. Receipts must be provided for each item 311
except for minor costs such as tips and local telephone calls. The adminis- 326
tration office is responsible for the supervision of these policies to insure 341
compliance by all employees. xx 348/**355**

89d ▶ 10
Improve Language Skills: Pronoun Agreement

LL: 70 spaces; SS with DS between line groups

1. Read the first rule.
2. Key the **Learn** sentences below it (with number and period), noting how the rule has been applied.
3. Key the **Apply** sentences (with number and period) using the correct pronoun shown in parentheses.
4. Practice the second rule in the same way.
5. If time permits, key the **Apply** lines again at a faster speed to quicken decision-making skill.

PRONOUN AGREEMENT (continued)

> Pronouns agree with their antecedents in number (singular or plural).

Learn 1. Timothy bought his new car in Atlanta early last month. *(singular)*
Learn 2. The members made plans for their next convention. *(plural)*
Apply 3. The boys must finish (his, their) game before noon.
Apply 4. The dog had (its, their) chain caught on the fence.

> When a pronoun's antecedent is a collective noun, the pronoun may be either singular or plural, depending on the meaning of the collective noun.

Learn 5. The Board of Directors has completed its meeting. *(acting as a unit)*
Learn 6. The Board of Directors have their own offices. *(acting individually)*
Apply 7. The Executive Committee presented (its, their) plan to the members.
Apply 8. The Executive Committee will give (its, their) reports on Friday.

89e ▶ 12
Improve/Check Keyboarding Skill

1. A 3′ writing on ¶s; find *gwam*.
2. Add 3 *gwam* to the rate attained in Step 1.
3. Take a 1′, 2′, and 3′ writing, trying to achieve the goal established in Step 2 for each writing.

all letters used | A | 1.5 si | 5.7 awl | 80% hfw

	gwam 3′	5′
The requirements of today's secretary are changing. The ability to	5	3
use a computer or a word processor is a major skill now required for	9	5
office support personnel by a sizeable number of firms. This is a trend	14	8
expected to continue with an even greater emphasis on computer usage in	19	11
the future. This will make it more critical than ever for those pursuing	24	14
a position in this field to have an excellent keyboarding skill in order	29	17
to make the best use of the costly equipment.	32	19
A student deciding on a career in this field will also find that the	36	22
role assumed by many office support staff members is that of an assistant	41	25
to a person at the management level. More and more of the titles used in	46	28
offices of today reflect this trend. It is quite common now for a secre-	51	31
tarial position to have a title of an administrative assistant or an	56	33
executive assistant. A college degree for positions such as these, how-	60	36
ever, may be stipulated.	62	37

gwam 3′ | 1 | 2 | 3 | 4 | 5
5′ | 1 | 2 | 3

200b (continued)

words

Reservations have been made for you during your stay in New Haven at the 163
Peachtree Plaza Hotel effective July 31. If you have any questions prior to 179
the orientation program, please call Mrs. Madison. 189

We are looking forward to your joining us in a long and mutually beneficial 204
association as the regional director of the Island Division. 217

Sincerely yours Keith T. Kona, President xx Enclosure 227/**241**

Document 2
Simplified Block Letter
LP p. 145
List the enumerated items in ¶ 1.

July 14, 19-- MS LINDSAY M SAXE CHAIRPERSON ELECTRONICS TRADE 12
SHOW SAXE RESEARCH ASSOCIATES INC 351 FIFTH AVENUE NEW YORK 24
NY 10118-7820 EVALUATION OF PANEL DISCUSSION 34

Thank you, Lindsay, for sending me the evaluation sheets completed by those 49
who attended the panel discussion of "The Electronic Office--Today and To- 63
morrow," at the Electronics Trade Show. My administrative assistant has 78
reviewed the evaluation sheets and has provided the following conclusions. 93
1. Ms. Yoko Lee's presentation was given an average rating of 8.2. Most 108
of the comments about her presentation were favorable, although a few 122
participants indicated they had difficulty understanding her. This may have 137
been caused by the poor quality of the amplification system. 2. Dr. Ira 152
Colton's presentation was given an average rating of 6.1. Many people noted 167
that he spoke very rapidly and was difficult to follow. 3. Mrs. Lila T. 182
Alverez received an average rating of 9.4. Many enthusiastic comments 196
were made about her account of the worldwide information processing sys- 211
tem she recently completed. 216

There were no unfavorable comments about the physical arrangements ex- 230
cept for the projection of slides. Many people complained that they were un- 245
able to read some of the slides from the back of the room. In future shows, 261
speakers should be advised that because of the size of the conference rooms, 276
large lettering on all visual aids is a must. 286

It was a pleasure working with you on this trade show. I hope these evalua- 301
tions will be helpful in planning for next year's show. 312

KEITH T. KONA, PRESIDENT xx 317/**324**

Document 3
Simplified Memo
plain full sheet

DATE: July 15, 19-- TO: Keith T. Kona, President SUBJECT: ORIENTATION 11
FOR CARLOS T. BOLIVAR 15

Carlos T. Bolivar, who was recently selected to be the regional distributor of 31
our Island Division, has informed me that because of a previous commitment, 46
he will not be able to travel to New Haven for the two-week orientation pro- 61
gram we have scheduled for him beginning on August 1. 72

At Mr. Bolivar's request, I have rescheduled his orientation program to be- 87
gin on August 15. Attached is a revised itinerary for Mr. Bolivar, which has 102
also been provided to all personnel involved in his orientation program. The 118
Peachtree Plaza has been notified that Mr. Bolivar will not arrive until 133
August 14, and the hotel has made the change in his reservations. 146

Jessica C. Madison, Director of Marketing xx Attachment 157

Documents 4 and 5 are on p. 345.

UNIT 20 LESSONS 90 – 93

Improve Table Formatting Skills

Learning Goals

1. To review and improve table formatting skills.
2. To maintain and improve techniques and basic skills.
3. To improve language skills.

Format Guides

1. Paper guide at *0* (for typewriters).
2. LL: 70 spaces for drills, language skills, and timed writings.
3. LS: SS drills and language skills; DS ¶s; as directed for tables.
4. PI: 5 spaces.

Lesson 90 Two-Column Tables/Language Skills

90a ▶ 5 Conditioning Practice

each line twice SS (slowly, then faster); DS between 2-line groups; if time permits, rekey selected lines

alphabet 1 They are moving to a new development just back of the Vasquez complex.

figures 2 Between 1987 and 1992 there were 203,564 recorded births in our state.

fig/sym 3 The balance due on Account #2849 after the 10% down payment is $3,756.

speed 4 The proficient auditor was in dismay due to the problem with an audit.

| 1 | 2 | 3 | 4 | 5 | 6 | 7 | 8 | 9 | 10 | 11 | 12 | 13 | 14 |

90b ▶ 10 Recall Centering Skills

half sheet, long edge at top; correct any errors you make as you key

1. Review horizontal and vertical centering procedures on page RG 10.
2. DS copy; center problem vertically and each line horizontally.

DRUGS: FACTS OR FICTION

January 23, 19--

3:30 p.m.

High School Gymnasium

Sponsored by:

McNamara Drug Treatment Center

90c ▶ 20 Recall Table Formatting

2 half sheets; DS all lines; format the tables given at the right and on page 161, long edge at top; correct any errors you make as you key

Table 1
Two-Column Table with Main Heading

CS (column spacing): 14

		words
COMMONLY MISSPELLED WORDS		5
absence	arrangements	9
academic	audit	12
access	authorized	16
already	benefits	19
alternative	calendar	24
appreciate	commission	28

199c ▶ 15 Measure Basic Keyboarding Skills

Take two 5′ writings on the ¶s at the right. Record *gwam* and errors on the better writing.

all letters used | A | 1.5 si | 5.7 awl | 80% hfw

gwam 1′ | 5′

Policies and procedures are set up by the managers of a business 13 | 3
to promote efficiency. A policy is considered to be a decision that 27 | 5
is made in advance, since it provides a guide or rule of action that 41 | 8
can be used to solve problems that arise frequently. To be effective, 55 | 11
a policy must be written in a clear, concise manner and, of the utmost 69 | 14
importance, be understood by all. Procedures are more specific and 83 | 17
set forth the exact steps to be taken in implementing policies. 95 | 19

Policies are used by managers as aids in making decisions at all 108 | 22
levels of a business. Policies promote efficiency since they save a 122 | 24
great deal of time, provide ready solutions to many day-to-day prob- 136 | 27
lems, and allow managers to do their jobs with more freedom of action. 150 | 30
Care must be taken to insure that policies are fair and accord equi- 164 | 33
table treatment to all employees. Further, all policies must be re- 177 | 35
viewed on a regular basis and revised when needed to meet all new or 191 | 38
changing conditions. 195 | 39

Many of the tasks performed by people in a business setting are 208 | 42
standard or routine in nature. To save time and to promote efficiency, 222 | 44
an organization may specify a set of step-by-step procedures for per- 236 | 47
forming these routine tasks. These procedures are almost always writ- 250 | 50
ten and are included in a manual for training and reference purposes. 264 | 53
If, on the job, you learn these procedures quickly and employ them in 278 | 56
order to produce work of high quality, you will be well on your way 292 | 58
to success. 294 | 59

gwam 1′ | 1 | 2 | 3 | 4 | 5 | 6 | 7 | 8 | 9 | 10 | 11 | 12 | 13 | 14
gwam 5′ | 1 | 2 | 3

200b ▶ 45 Measure Document Production Skills

Key the documents on this page and pages 344 and 345 for 30 minutes. Correct all errors.

Time Schedule

Plan and prepare .... 5′
Timed production ....30′
Proofread; compute *n-pram* .....10′

Document 1
Letter on Executive-Size Stationery

LP p. 143, block format; open punctuation

words

July 11, 19-- Mr. Carlos T. Bolivar 1100 Ponce De Leon Avenue San Juan, 14
PR 00907-3385 Dear Mr. Bolivar 21

It is a pleasure for me to welcome you formally to the executive group of 36
Alpha Electronics, Inc. You were selected from a group of five highly quali- 51
fied individuals to be the regional distributor in our Island Division, which 66
includes Puerto Rico and the U.S. Virgin Islands. 77

As a regional distributor, you will work under the direct supervision of 91
Jessica C. Madison, director of marketing, in accordance with the policies 106
and standard operating procedures established by our executive group. 120

We have scheduled a two-week orientation program for you in New Haven 134
beginning on Monday, August 1. A copy of your itinerary is enclosed. 149

(continued, p. 344)

90c (continued)

Table 2
Three-Column Table with Main Heading
CS: 8

			words
OTHER COMMONLY MISSPELLED WORDS			6
addition	fiscal	maintenance	12
approximately	foreign	material	18
especially	implementation	means	25
expenditures	industrial	maximum	31
facilities	initial	minimum	36
faculty	limited	mortgage	41

90d ▶ 10 *Improve Language Skills: Commas*

LL: 70 spaces; SS with DS between groups

1. Read the first rule.

2. Key the **Learn** sentences below it (with number and period), noting how the rule has been applied.

3. Key the **Apply** sentences (with number and period), supplying the needed commas.

4. Read and practice the other rules in the same way.

5. If time permits, key the **Apply** sentences again to increase decision-making speed.

COMMA

Use a comma after (a) introductory words, phrases, or clauses and (b) words in a series.

Learn 1. If you finish your homework, you may go to the play with Mary.
Learn 2. We will play the Tigers, Yankees, and Indians on our next home stand.
Apply 3. The next exam will cover memos simple tables and unbound reports.
Apply 4. When she came to visit Jo brought Dave Rob and Juanita with her.

Do not use a comma to separate two items treated as a single unit within a series.

Learn 5. Her favorite breakfast was bacon and eggs, muffins, and juice.
Apply 6. My choices are peaches and cream brownies and strawberry shortcake.
Apply 7. She ordered macaroni and cheese ice cream and a soft drink.

Use a comma before short, direct quotations.

Learn 8. The announcer said, "Please stand and welcome our next guest."
Apply 9. The woman asked "What time does the play begin?"
Apply 10. Sachi answered "I'll be in Chicago."

90e ▶ 5 *Improve Technique: Response Patterns*

Key each line twice.

Technique hints:

1. Keep fingers curved and upright.

2. Use quick, snappy keystroking.

3. Space quickly after each word.

Fingers curved and upright

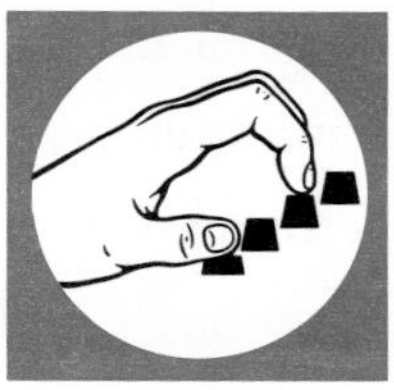

Use quick, snappy keystroking

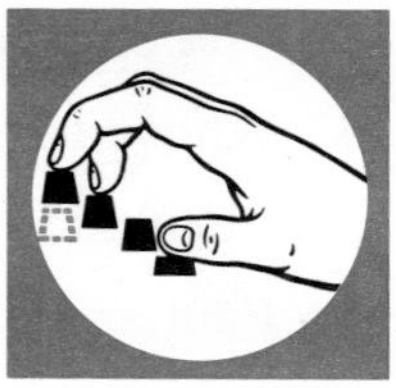

Space quickly after each word

letter 1 In my opinion, Dave agreed on estate taxes only after we defeated him.
word 2 She and the neighbor may go downtown to sign the form for the auditor.
combination 3 Helen started to work on the audit after they paid their estate taxes.

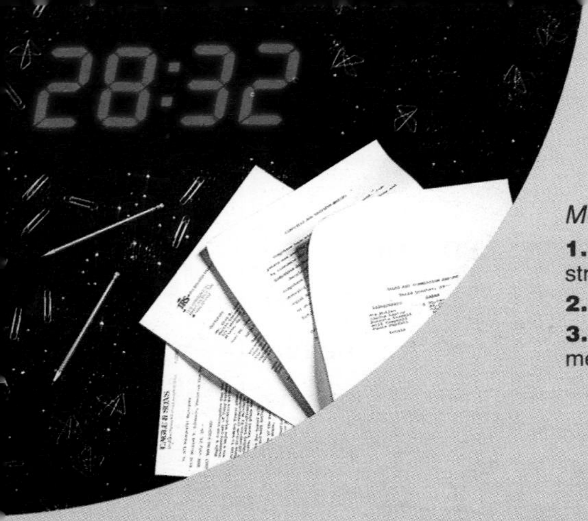

UNIT 47 *LESSONS 199 - 200*

Measure Basic Language/Production Skills

Measurement Goals

1. To measure your speed and accuracy on straight-copy material.

2. To measure your communication skills.

3. To measure your ability to produce documents neatly and correctly.

Machine Adjustments

1. Paper guide at *0* (for typewriters).

2. LL: 70 spaces for drills, paragraphs, and Language Skills activity; as directed or necessary for documents.

3. LS: DS sentences and timed writings; space problems as directed or as necessary.

Lessons 199-200 *Language/Production Skills*

199a-200a ▶ 5 (daily) Conditioning Practice

each line twice SS (slowly, then faster); if time permits, take 1′ writings on line 1

alphabet 1 Duke may vote for any major law liberalizing changes in export quotas.

figures 2 Ken bowled 197, 209, and 237, but May's scores were 198, 235, and 246.

fig/sym 3 The tax was 3% in 1974, 5.2% in 1983, 5.6% in 1987, and 10.2% in 1991.

speed 4 She did fix the dual signals to make the big sign to downtown visible.

| 1 | 2 | 3 | 4 | 5 | 6 | 7 | 8 | 9 | 10 | 11 | 12 | 13 | 14 |

199b ▶ 30 Evaluate Language Skills

1. In each sentence at the right, items have been underlined. The underlines indicate that there *may* be an error in spelling, punctuation, capitalization, grammar, or word/figure usage.

2. Study each sentence carefully. Key the line, with the number and period. If an underlined item is incorrect, correct it as you key the sentence. Also, correct any keyboarding errors you may make.

1. "After you finish," he said, "Take the form to the Personel office."
2. Keep in mind: the committee will explore the matter farther.
3. Their's a new shop on 6th Avenue that sells VCR cassettes.
4. Almost 60% of the men in the neighborhood voted "yes."
5. Neither Diane nor Mary are planning to go to the movie.
6. Maria_our supervisor_will attend the meeting, too.
7. We will schedule you're program over the next two year period.
8. Its my opinion that we will not receive our benifits this week.
9. Angela's and Lisa's report was very well done.
10. The panel reccomended that we accept the lowest bid.
11. The time past quickly as we entered the systom into the computer.
12. The comission on teen problems will make it's findings public.
13. The corparate officers will meet in the executive dining room.
14. Whose responsible for the maintanance of the facsimile machine?
15. Chris did better than me with 5 Bs on her report card.
16. Paul and Jess left for the new boy's club imediately after lunch.
17. In 1991_472 employees enrolled for health care under policy 645820.
18. The magazine, "Computer Monthly," offers many intresting articles.
19. We're planning too leave on Friday for the spring festival.
20. Tina Jones' test scores make her elligible for a scholarship.

91a ▶ 5 Conditioning Practice

each line twice SS (slowly, then faster); DS between 2-line groups; if time permits, rekey selected lines

alphabet	1	Making a yearly budget was a very unique experience for Jonathan Zorn.
figures	2	There were 386 blue, 274 green, and 159 yellow lights on the 10 trees.
fig/sym	3	Computer Model #364-A8 sells for $1,250; Model #364-A7 sells for $995.
speed	4	I may work with the city on their problems with the city turn signals.

| 1 | 2 | 3 | 4 | 5 | 6 | 7 | 8 | 9 | 10 | 11 | 12 | 13 | 14 |

91b ▶ 27 Recall Table Formatting

1 half sheet; 2 full sheets; DS all lines; format the tables given at the right; block column headings; correct errors

Table 1
Table with Main and Column Headings
half sheet; CS: 14

EXECUTIVE OFFICERS		words
		4
Position	Name	9
Chief Executive Officer	Donald Espinosa	17
Chairperson of the Board	Alice Gomory	25
Chief Financial Officer	Gregg Foster	32
Senior Vice President	Michael McCoskey	40
Vice President	Mary Whitney	45
Treasurer	Nancy Schneider	50

Table 2
Table with Main and Column Headings with Source Note
full sheet; CS: 18

1983-1989 WORLD SERIES CHAMPIONS		words
		7
Team	Year	10
Baltimore (AL)	1983	14
Detroit (AL)	1984	18
Kansas City (AL)	1985	22
New York (NL)	1986	26
Minnesota (AL)	1987	30
Los Angeles (NL)	1988	34
Oakland (AL)	1989	38
______________		41
Source: World Almanac.		48

Table 3
Table with Main, Secondary, and Column Headings with Total Line
full sheet; CS: 14

UNITED WAY		words
		2
(July Donations)		6
Company	Amount	11
Gunderson Construction Company	$1,500	19
Lakeview Data Products	1,500	25
Wilkerson Automotive	1,000	30
First National Bank	500	35
Bates Photography	400	40
Krause Associates	250	45
Anderson's Home Furnishings	200	53
Total	$5,350	56

195b-198b (continued)

Document 7
Unbound Report

plain full sheets

Mrs. Dunn: Josef Tuberski, an administrative assistant in the guest facilities branch, is helping to prepare a brochure about the corporation. He has requested that we key his first draft as an unbound manuscript.

Follow the instructions he has given on the bottom of his draft and be on the lookout for unmarked errors.

Log #157

FIVE STAR CORPORATION--A ~~STUDY IN~~ MODEL OF SUCCESS

For more than (40) sp years, the Five Star Corporation has set the ~~standards~~ pace for the hospitality/travel industry through a program of expansoin and improvement to meet the ~~demands~~ needs of our guests world wide. The corporation is dedicated to ~~further~~ growth and improvement to ensure that it remains in the forfront of the industry.

The Five Star Corporation ~~has~~ consists of the following four major components, which are distinct and serve diverse needs.

The Five Star hotels serve large metropolitan areas with accommodations for individuals and groups. There is ~~today~~ now at least one Five Star Hotel in every city in the (U.S.) sp with a population of 300,000 or more

The Five Star logo is famous throughout the United States and Europe and represents first class acommodations at reasonable rates. At the end of ~~the previous~~ last year, there were 806 Five Star Inns, for a total of more than 150,000 rooms. Since the beginning of this year, 16 new inns have ~~been built~~ opened in the (U. S.) sp alone.

A few hotels in the Five Star family have been ~~named~~ designated as plazas. These are deluxe facilities with spacious meeting rooms. Future plazas are planned in coordinination with ~~huge~~ large shopping malls in metropolitan ~~areas~~ centers. Construction on Five Star Plazas is currently under way in New Orleans and Seatle.

Located in ~~prominent~~ popular tourist areas, suites meet our guests' needs for extended visits. The suites feature eficiency units with complete kitchens, lounge areas, and sleeping acommodations for as many as eight ~~persons~~ people. The suites have been very populer with families on vacation and profesional people on ~~long~~ extended stays.

Please move ¶4 ahead of ¶3 and add these side headings:

¶3 Five Star Inns

¶4 Five Star Hotels

¶5 Five Star Plazas

¶6 Five Star Suites

91c ▶ 10
Improve Language Skills: Punctuation

LL: 70 spaces; SS with DS between groups

1. Read the first rule.
2. Key the **Learn** sentence below it (with number and period), noting how the rule has been applied.
3. Key the **Apply** sentences (with number and period), supplying the needed commas.
4. Read and practice the other rules in the same way.
5. If time permits, key the **Apply** sentences again to increase decision-making speed.

COMMA (continued)

Use a comma before and after word(s) in apposition.

Learn 1. Jan, the new reporter, has started working on the next newsletter.
Apply 2. Our branch manager Carmen Jackson will be here tomorrow.
Apply 3. The editor Jason Maxwell said several changes should be made.

Use a comma to set off words of direct address.

Learn 4. If I can be of further assistance, Mario, please let me know.
Apply 5. Finish this assignment Martin before you start on the next one.
Apply 6. I would recommend Mr. Clinton that we cancel the order.

Use a comma to set off nonrestrictive clauses (not necessary to the meaning of the sentence); however, do not use commas to set off restrictive clauses (necessary to the meaning of the sentence).

Learn 7. The manuscript, which I prepared, needs to be revised.
Learn 8. The manuscript that presents banking alternatives is now available.
Apply 9. The movie which was on the top ten list was very entertaining.
Apply 10. The student who scores highest on the exam will win the scholarship.

91d ▶ 8
Check/Improve Keyboarding Skill: Straight Copy

1. Take a 1′ writing.
2. Take another 1′ writing starting at the place where you stopped after the first 1′ writing.
3. Take another 1′ writing starting at the place where you stopped after the second 1′ writing.
4. Take a 3′ writing trying to go beyond your last stopping point. Determine your *gwam*.

all letters used | A | 1.5 si | 5.7 awl | 80% hfw

	gwam 3′	5′
The value of an education has been a topic discussed many times with	5	3
a great deal of zest. The value is often measured in terms of costs and	9	6
benefits to the taxpayer. It is also judged in terms of changes in the	14	9
individuals taking part in the educational process. Gains in the level	19	11
of knowledge, the development and refinement of attitudes, and the	24	14
acquiring of skills are believed to be crucial parts of an education.	28	17
Education is a never-ending process. A person is exposed to formal	33	20
and informal education throughout his or her life. Formal learning takes	38	23
place in a structured situation such as a school or a college. Informal	42	25
learning occurs from the experience gained from daily living. We are	47	28
constantly educated from all the types of media with which we come in	52	31
contact each day as well as by each person with whom we exchange ideas.	57	34

gwam 3′ 1 2 3 4 5
5′ 1 2 3

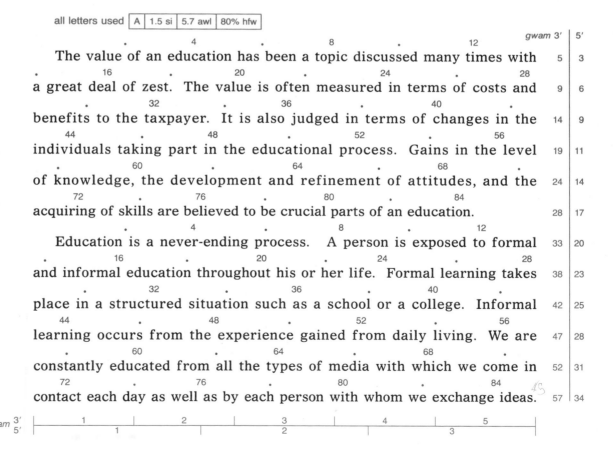

195b-198b (continued)

Documents 3 and 4
Letters from Boilerplate

LP pp. 139-141

Mrs. Dunn: Mark F. Schwartz, national coordinator for group facilities, requests that we prepare Form Letter 12, dated **April 18,** for the addressees below. Insert the appropriate information as shown.

Letter 1

Mrs. Rita C. Smith
President
Flower Clubs of America
P.O. Box 3870
Little Rock, AR 72203-1440

(A) **Mrs. Smith** (B) **December of this year** (C) **Dallas Central Five Star** (D) **March of next year**

(Log #124)

Letter 2

Mr. Louis F. DiAngelo
Executive Director
National Greentree Association
401 Sixth Avenue
Des Moines, IA 50309-5901

(A) **Mr. DiAngelo** (B) **January of next year** (C) **Boston Five Star Plaza** (D) **April of next year**

(Log #125)

Document 5
Table

plain full sheet

Mrs. Dunn: Denise T. Brach, an assistant marketing manager, requests that we key the table at the right, making the changes marked.

(Log #136)

Document 6
Table

plain full sheet

Mrs. Dunn: Ms. Brach requests that we prepare a table showing occupancy rates for both February and March. Head the second column **February** and the third column **March.**

(Log #148)

FORM LETTER 12

RESERVATIONS FOR GROUP FACILITIES

Thank you, (A), for your inquiry regarding the availability of group facilities in (B) at the (C).

We are very sorry indeed that the facilities you desire are completely booked through (D). Reservations for conventions, banquets, meetings, and other large events are usually made at least a year in advance. Planning for these events takes considerable time and coordination to ensure that they are successful.

Enclosed is a pamphlet showing the group facilities that are available at the (C). May we arrange to serve your organization at a later date? If you wish to discuss your special event, simply call 1-800-219-4600 and one of our service representatives will be happy to assist you.

MARK F. SCHWARTZ, NATIONAL COORDINATOR FOR GROUP FACILITIES

OCCUPANCY RATE FOR THE MONTH OF ~~FEBRUARY~~ MARCH

Northeastern Division

Location	Rate
Albany Five Star Motel	~~71%~~ 72%
Atlantic City Five Star Casino Plaza	~~79%~~ 83%
Baltimore Harbor Five Star Hotel	~~68%~~ 71%
Boston Five Star Plaza	~~79%~~ 85%
Buffalo Five Star Motel	~~83%~~ 81%
New Bedford Five Star Ocean Motel	~~64%*~~ 61%*
New York Central Five Star Hotel	~~81%~~ 84%
New York Downtown Five Star Hotel	~~72%~~ 75%
Philadelphia Five Star Hotel	~~70%~~ 73%
Pittsburgh Five Star Hotel	~~66%~~ 71%
Portland (Maine) Five Star Motel	~~63%~~ 71%

*Rate affected by major road construction.

92a ▶ 5 Conditioning Practice

each line twice SS (slowly, then faster); DS between 2-line groups; if time permits, rekey selected lines

alphabet	1	Marquis Becks enjoyed expanding his vast knowledge of Arizona history.
figures	2	Games of 36, 28, 24, and 21 gave Brian a 1990 season average of 27.25.
fig/sym	3	Stone Realty sold the houses on Lots #3 & #6 for $87,950 and $104,200.
speed	4	The proficient man was kept busy with the problem with the city docks.

| 1 | 2 | 3 | 4 | 5 | 6 | 7 | 8 | 9 | 10 | 11 | 12 | 13 | 14 |

92b ▶ 35 Improve Table Formatting Skill

3 full sheets, format the tables given at the right; correct any errors you make as you key

Table 1
Three-Column Table with Blocked Column Headings and Total Line
CS: 8; DS table

MARCH SALES

Sales Manager	Territory	Sales	words
			2
			14
Diane Aldredge	Connecticut	$204,500	21
Marcia Kelly	Maine	135,200	27
Ruth Peterson	Massachusetts	125,000	34
Rebecca Johnston	New Hampshire	135,800	42
Orlando Martinez	New York	172,900	48
Jonathan Akervik	Rhode Island	88,200	56
Roger McDonald	Vermont	115,200	64
Total Sales		$976,800	69

Table 2
Three-Column Table with Blocked Column Headings and Notation
CS: 8; DS table

Table 3
Three-Column Table with Centered Column Headings and Footnote
Reformat Table 2; SS; CS: 10

HAMBURG SCHOOL OF BALLET ITINERARY 7

19-- Summer Tour* 11

Sponsor	City	Date	
			17
Boston Ballet	Boston	June 4	24
Ballet Academy of Miami	Miami	June 11	32
Dallas Ballet Academy	Dallas	June 18	39
Ruth Page Foundation	Chicago	June 25	47
Northwest Ballet	Minneapolis	July 1	54
Colorado Ballet Center	Denver	July 8	61
Dancers' Stage Company	San Francisco	July 15	70
Pacific Northwest Ballet	Seattle	July 22	79

______________ 82

*Leave for Boston on June 1; return to Hamburg on July 27. 94

Learning cue: To center column headings shorter than column entries, follow these steps:

1. Determine placement of columns in usual way.
2. From column starting point, space forward once for each two strokes in longest entry. From this point, backspace once for each 2 strokes in column heading.
3. Key and underline column heading.

195b-198b **(continued)**

Time. Enter the exact time, in minutes, that was required to complete the document.

~~Total~~ Lines. Indicate the total lines in the document. Count each line regardless of length (including any titles or subtitles). Count three lines for the opening lines of ~~a~~ letters and memos and three lines for the closing lines. Count four lines for all letter envelopes and one line for all COMPANY MAIL envelopes.

Document 2
Simplified Memorandum
plain full sheet
Mrs. Dunn puts on your desk the note shown at the right.

4/17/-- Log #108

Please key the following as a simplified memorandum for my signature to Michael C. Beauvais, Supervisor, Data Processing, with a subject, "~~Word~~ Document Processing Log Sheets."

As agreed during our meeting with Ms. Maguire on March 30, we will begin the work measurement program in the Document Processing Center on May 1. The weekly ~~Word~~ Document Processing Log Sheets, separated by operator, will be forwarded to the Data Processing Center on the Monday following the week in which the work was performed. ¶ As we agreed, you will provide me with a weekly and monthly report, by operator, which will show the total time, the total weighted lines keyed, and the average (mean) weighted lines per hour. Copy will be weighted as indicated below.

SS

Copy	Weight
Boilerplate (B)	1.0
Handwritten (S)	1.3
Rough Draft (RD)	1.6
Statistical (STAT)	2.0

92c ▶ 10
Improve Language Skills: Punctuation

LL: 70 spaces; SS with DS between line groups

1. Read the first rule.

2. Key the **Learn** sentences below it (with number and period), noting how the rule has been applied.

3. Key the **Apply** sentences (with number and period), supplying the needed commas.

4. Read and practice the other rules in the same way.

5. If time permits, key the **Apply** sentences again to increase decision-making speed.

COMMA (continued)

Use a comma to separate the day from the year and the city from the state.

Learn 1. On July 4, 1776, the Declaration of Independence was signed.
Learn 2. The next convention will be held in New Orleans, Louisiana.
Apply 3. Kingsborough Community College is located in Brooklyn New York.
Apply 4. Abraham Lincoln was born on February 12 1809 in Kentucky.

Use a comma to separate two or more parallel adjectives (adjectives that could be separated by the word "and" instead of a comma).

Learn 5. The angry, discouraged teacher felt she had been betrayed.
Learn 6. Sara opened the door and found a small brown box. *(comma cannot be used)*
Apply 7. Karen purchased a large antique desk at the auction on Friday.
Apply 8. Ms. Sawyer was an industrious dedicated worker for our company.

Use a comma to separate (a) unrelated groups of figures which come together and (b) whole numbers into groups of three digits each. Note: Policy, year, page, room, telephone, and most serial numbers are keyed without commas.

Learn 9. Before 1995, 1,500 more employees will be hired by our firm.
Learn 10. The serial number on the television in Room 1338 is Z83251.
Apply 11. The telephone number listed on Policy #39445 is 834-8822.
Apply 12. During the summer of 1990 32980 policyholders submitted claims.

Lesson 93 — *Centered Column Headings/Language Skills*

93a ▶ 5
Conditioning Practice

each line twice SS (slowly, then faster); DS between 2-line groups; if time permits, rekey selected lines

alphabet 1 Max would ask very specific questions before analyzing the job issues.
figures 2 Test scores of 84, 93, 75, 62, and 100 gave Marcia an average of 82.8.
fig/sym 3 Jane wrote Checks #807 & #794 for $1,650.03 and $212.50, respectively.
speed 4 He owns both the antique bottle and the enamel bottle on their mantle.

| 1 | 2 | 3 | 4 | 5 | 6 | 7 | 8 | 9 | 10 | 11 | 12 | 13 | 14 |

93b ▶ 10
Improve Language Skills: Word Choice

1. Study the spelling and definition of each word.

2. Key the line number (with period), space twice, then key the **Learn** sentence; key the **Apply** sentences in the same format, selecting the correct word in parentheses to complete the sentences.

3. DS between three-line groups.

done (adj) brought to an end; through	**seam** (n) the joining of two pieces
dun (vb) to make demands for payment	**seem** (vb) to give the impression of being

Learn 1. When he is done with the big job, we can dun him for payment.
Apply 2. Carol planned to (done, dun) Tim every week until the bill was paid.
Apply 3. When you are (done, dun) with the project, please hand it in.

Learn 4. If I putty the seam using the same color, it will seem much smaller.
Apply 5. Does it (seam, seem) to be about the same size as the one we replaced?
Apply 6. The (seam, seem) should hold until we are able to buy a new connection.

195a-198a ▶ (daily)
Conditioning Practice

each line twice SS (slowly, then faster); if time permits, take 1′ writings on line 1

alphabet 1 Jerry criticized queries we have been making on the six final reports.

figures 2 Please ship Orders 1271, 3965, 6238, and 0845 by parcel post tomorrow.

fig/sym 3 Ship us 60 reams of 20# 8 1/2″ × 11″ paper (Stock #943) at $2.75 each.

speed 4 If the men work with proficiency, the big coalfield may make a profit.

| 1 | 2 | 3 | 4 | 5 | 6 | 7 | 8 | 9 | 10 | 11 | 12 | 13 | 14 |

195b-198b ▶ 45 (daily)
Document Processing

Document 1
Formal Memorandum

LP p. 137

Mrs. Dunn: Please key this material as a formal memorandum for my signature. Address it to **all keyboard operators.** Date the memo **April 16** and use the subject **DOCUMENT PROCESSING LOG.** Log the document in your Document Processing Log on LP p. 135, or your supervisor will provide your Document Processing Log sheet.

Log #101

~~Beginning June~~ Effective May 1, 19--, all operators will ~~keep~~ maintain a weekly ~~Word~~ Document Procesing Log Sheet (lc). The ~~information given~~ data below will be entered on the Log sheet for each document ~~you~~ process~~.~~ed.

Document code. The suprevisor will log-in each document by placing a Code (lc) Number (lc) ~~which will be placed~~ in the upper right-hand corner. In correspondance, the ~~log~~ code number will be keyed following the operator's initials; in all other documents, it will be placed a DS (sp) below the last line.

Originator. The word originator of the document will be identified by name and dept. (sp), ~~i.e.,~~ e.g., "Carter/Sales."

Document. The document will be identified by ~~sort~~ type: letter, memo, report, table, form, etc.

Input. The form in which the document was recieved will be indicated as RD (rough draft), S (handwritten), ~~P~~ B (boilerplate), or STAT (statistical).

Time in. ~~Indicate~~ Enter time work on document was ~~received~~ begun.

Time out. ~~Indicate~~ Enter time document was ~~finished~~ completed. If work on a document is ~~delayed~~ interrupted for more than ten minutes, complete the information for the document on the log sheet and re-enter it when work is ~~begun~~ continued.

(continued, p. 339)

93c ▶ 35 *Improve Table Formatting Skill*

3 full sheets; format the tables given at the right; DS all lines; correct any errors you make as you key

Table 1
Table with Centered Column Headings

CS: 6; center column headings over columns

words

19-- SPRING RECRUITMENT *Schedule* 7

Martin Bartlett 10

University	Date	Area of Specialization	
			27
San Diego *State* University	March 3	Marketing	36
Arizona State University	March 10	Management Information	47
University of Colorado	March 10 *7*	Management Information	58
University of Kentucky	March 24	*Management*	67
Tennesses *e* State *University*	March 31	Accounting	76
Florida A & M	April 7	Marketign	83
Duke University	April 14	Accounting	90

Table 2
Table with Centered Column Headings

CS: 8; center column headings over columns

Table 3

Reformat Table 2. Alphabetize the table by name of national park; CS: 12; use the copy you keyed for Table 2 to mark for alphabetizing.

National Parks 3

(Established 1872-1917) 8

National Park	*State*	*Year*	
			18
Yellowstone	*Wyoming*	*1872*	23
Sequoia	*California*	*1890*	28
Yosemite	*California*	*1890*	33
Mount Rainier	*Washington*	*1899*	39
Crater Lake	*Oregon*	*1902*	44
Wind Cave	*South Dakota*	*1903*	49
Mesa Verde	*Colorado*	*1906*	54
Glacier	*Montana*	*1910*	58
Rocky Mountain	*Colorado*	*1915*	64
Hawaii Volcanoes	*Hawaii*	*1916*	70
Lassen Volcanic	*California*	*1916*	76
Mount McKinley	*Alaska*	*1917*	82

______________ 85

Source: Encyclopedia Americana. 96

UNIT 46 *LESSONS 195 – 198*
Five Star Corporation (A Simulation)

Learning Goals

1. To become familiar with the procedures followed in a typical document processing center.

2. To improve your ability to process documents from unarranged, rough-draft, and script copy.

3. To improve your ability to read and follow directions and to detect and correct unmarked errors.

Documents Processed

1. Formal Memorandum
2. Simplified Memorandum
3. Letters from Boilerplate
4. Tables
5. Report

FIVE STAR CORPORATION: A DOCUMENT PROCESSING CENTER SIMULATION

Work Assignment

You have been hired as a keyboard operator in the headquarters of the Five Star Corporation, operators of motels and hotels throughout the continental United States and Europe. The headquarters is located at 200 West Washington Street, South Bend, Indiana 46601-7230.

You will work in the Document Processing Center under the direction of Mrs. Diane C. Dunn, supervisor of the center, who reports to Ms. Margaret L. Maguire, chief of administration.

You will prepare a variety of documents prepared in handwritten or rough-draft form by executives or word originators. You will also key form letters from boilerplate (standardized paragraphs or letters). Documents dictated by executives are transcribed by word processing specialists in the center.

Five Star has established standard formatting procedures that specify the formats for letters, memos, reports, and tables. Excerpts from these procedures follow. As part of your orientation, Mrs. Dunn asks you to study these procedures carefully.

Standard Formatting Procedures

Documents are prepared in the following formats unless the originator indicates otherwise. Correct any errors you make as you prepare a document in final form. Correct any unmarked errors made by the originator in spelling, punctuation, grammar, etc.

Letters. Letters are keyed in the simplified block style, using a standard 6″ line with the date on line 12, regardless of the length of the letter. Except for rough drafts, key letters on letterhead stationery. Use current date if one is not specified and use your initials as reference.

Simplified memos. Simplified memos are keyed on plain paper in block format, using a standard 6″ line with the date on line 10. QS below the date and the last paragraph of the body. DS below other parts of the memo and between paragraphs. Use current date if one is not specified and use your initials as reference.

Formal memos. Formal memos are keyed on forms with printed headings in block format, using a standard 6″ line with the heading information at the same point as the left margin. DS below the heading information, between paragraphs, between the last line and your initials, and between your initials and any notation, such as "Attachment."

Reports. Reports are always prepared in unbound format, using a standard 6″ line, with the PB (page beginning) on line 10 (pica, 10-pitch) or line 12 (elite, 12-pitch). QS below titles; DS other parts, including the spacing above and below a divider line between the report and a reference notation, if one is used.

Tables. Tables are centered on the page vertically and horizontally. All headings are centered, including columnar headings. Use DS throughout the table, except when the tabular items are SS. DS below the last line of the table; key the divider line; DS below the divider line; key the source note. (SS a source note that consists of two or more lines.)

UNIT 21 LESSONS 94 – 98

Ritter Realty Company (An Office Job Simulation)

Learning Goals

1. To experience the keyboarding activities of an executive assistant in a real estate office.

2. To improve your document processing skills by keying from unarranged, rough-draft, and script source documents.

Documents Processed

1. Simplified memorandums.
2. Letters in block format.
3. Centered announcement.
4. Tables with centered headings.
5. Report in unbound format.
6. Reference page of a report.

RITTER REALTY COMPANY (An Office Job Simulation)

Before you begin the jobs on pages 168-173, read the copy at the right. When planning the assigned jobs, refer to the formatting guides given here to refresh your memory about the proper formatting and spacing of documents.

Work Assignment

You have been hired to work as an executive assistant for Ritter Realty Company. You will work for the Branch Manager, Ms. Jessica Sampson.

Each year Ritter Realty sponsors a Parade of Homes. The Parade of Homes is a showing open to the general public of newly constructed homes which feature the latest innovations in the housing industry. This year the company will be inviting former clients to attend a private showing prior to the Parade of Homes. Most of the documents that you will process this week will be about the Parade of Homes and the private showing. The work will include the processing of memos, tables, letters and a report.

Written instructions for each job assigned are given by Ms. Sampson. Use the date included on the instructions for all correspondence requiring a date. Ms. Sampson likes all her letters signed as follows:

Sincerely

Ms. Jessica A. Sampson
Branch Manager

Ms. Sampson has given you a copy of "A Quick Guide to Document Formats" which summarizes the basic features of formats used by Ritter Realty Company. Refer to this guide as needed when processing the various documents.

You will supply appropriate parts of documents when necessary. You will use your own initials for reference.

If Ms. Sampson's directions and the "Quick Guide" summary are not sufficiently detailed, use what you have been taught when making formatting decisions. In some cases, you are expected to correct undetected errors in grammar or punctuation that have been overlooked by Ms. Sampson.

You are expected to produce error-free documents, so proofread and correct your work carefully before presenting it for Ms. Sampson's approval.

A QUICK GUIDE TO DOCUMENT FORMATS

Use the following quick reference as a guide to formatting and spacing documents.

Memos

Stationery: plain sheets
Side margins: 1″
Format: simplified
Spacing: QS below date and last paragraph. DS below other parts of memo and between paragraphs.
Date: line 10 from top of paper
Subject: ALL CAPS

Letters

Stationery: letterheads
Side margins: short, 2″; average 1½″
Spacing: SS with DS between paragraphs
Format: block with open punctuation
Date: short, line 18; average, line 16

Tables

Stationery: plain full sheets
Placement: centered
Vertical spacing: DS throughout
Horizontal spacing: 6-10 spaces between columns (Use an even number)

Reports

Stationery: plain sheets
Format: unbound with internal citations
Side margins: 1″
Top margin: line 10, 10-pitch; 12, 12-pitch
Bottom margin: at least 1″
Spacing: DS text; SS quotations and lists
References: on separate sheet

194a ▶ 5 Conditioning Practice

each line twice SS (slowly, then faster); if time permits, take 1′ writings on line 3

alphabet 1 Anna may be required to organize the complex work of the vast project.
figures 2 The test scores were: 19, 24, 32, 46, 50, 57, 68, 70, 83, 91, and 96.
fig/sym 3 Sue's note read, "Profits of Erb & Lee Co. rose 8.3% to $627,195,420."
speed 4 The girl did sign both of the proxy forms for the auditor of the firm.

| 1 | 2 | 3 | 4 | 5 | 6 | 7 | 8 | 9 | 10 | 11 | 12 | 13 | 14 |

194b ▶ 20 Improve Language Skills: Proofread/Correct

1. In each sentence, items have been underlined. The underlines indicate that there *may* be an error in spelling, punctuation, capitalization, grammar, or in the use of words or figures.

2. Study each sentence carefully. Key the sentence (with number and period). If an underlined item is incorrect, correct it as you key the sentence. Also, correct any keyboarding errors you may make.

3. Check your work with your teacher; then rekey any sentences in which you made errors.

1. He said, "it is apparant that you did not read the lable."
2. "It is my beleief," he said, "That we must make a total commitment."
3. My neice visited these foreign countries, England, Spain, and Italy.
4. Keep in mind: guesswork is no substitute for good jugement.
5. A new version of The Taming of the Shrew is all ready in rehearsal.
6. Jane is an assistent to president Marks, not his Secretary.
7. The town counsel will meet in room 302 at 4 o'clock.
8. We must analize the questionaire on womens' rights very carefully.
9. Does the new rules on insurence supercede the old ones?
10. Have the committee filed it's report on the personel office?
11. Each of the men have benefitted from their experience.
12. There were thirty five occurrences of vandalism this month.
13. The restarant is located on 5th avenue near the labratory.
14. In March the morgage rate rose to 11 percent.
15. Bess's report card showed she achieved all most all As.

194c ▶ 10 Improve Keystroking Skills: Figures and Symbols

1. Take four 1′ writings on each ¶5.

2. Strive for accuracy, especially when keying the figures and symbols.

gwam 1′

Borrowing money can be very expensive. If, for example, you bor- 13
row $2,000 at 8% interest and agree to pay it back in 15 monthly in- 27
stallments, you will pay $147 per month or a total of $2,205 (including 41
$205 in interest). The annual percentage rate, though, is actually 55
15%. An interest rate of "only" 1 1/2% per month equals an annual rate 69
of 18%. 70

The mortgage interest on a house may be greater than the original 13
cost of the house. A 20-year, 10% mortgage on $75,000 will require a 27
monthly payment of $727.50 or a total of $174,600 ($727.50 × 12 × 20). 42
A 30-year mortgage under the same terms would cost $660 a month or a 55
total of $237,600--$63,000 more than the 20-year mortgage. 67

194d ▶ 15 Improve Basic Keyboarding Skills

1. Take two 1′ writings on each ¶ of 193c, p. 335.

2. Take one 5′ writing on the three ¶s combined.

Goal: Improved speed and accuracy.

94a–98a ▶ 5 (daily)

Conditioning Practice

each line twice SS (slowly, then faster); DS between 2-line groups

alphabet 1 Stacks of judo magazines were piled very high on the exquisite tables.

figures 2 By 6:45 p.m. on May 28 the men had branded all but 19 of the 730 cows.

double letters 3 good need meet been issue happy letter effect accept dollars committee

speed 4 Enrique may wish he had vigor when he duels with the haughty neighbor.

| 1 | 2 | 3 | 4 | 5 | 6 | 7 | 8 | 9 | 10 | 11 | 12 | 13 | 14 |

94b–98b ▶ 45 (daily)

Work Assignments

Jobs 1-3

Message from JESSICA SAMPSON

Key the attached memos.

The first memo goes to All Agents. Use PARADE OF HOMES SCHEDULE for the subject line.

The second memo goes to Mary Carlson, Sales Agent. Use REFRESHMENTS FOR PARADE OF HOMES as the subject line.

The third memo goes to John Morgan, Broker. Use ELECTRONIC MAIL as the subject line. JS 5/12

The response from former home buyers who are interested in the private showing of this year's Parade of Homes has been excellent. Meeting with past customers to determine if we can be of further assistance to them with their housing requirements is a real opportunity for us. All of the individuals invited have been in their present homes for over five years and may be ready to consider the purchase of a new home.

Michi will be coordinating schedules for the two days of the private showing. We should have your schedule ready within the next two or three days. A meeting will be held on May 20 at 8:30 a.m. to discuss specific details for the Parade of Homes.

Mary, last month when we were discussing some of the details for the Parade of Homes private showing, you indicated that you would be willing to handle the arrangements for refreshments. I would like to take you up on that offer if it still stands.

Please stop by my office sometime this week so that we can discuss a few of the specifics.

John, the information on electronic mail you brought back from the convention in Miami was intriguing. When you have a few minutes, stop by my office and let's discuss the applications that you think may be of value to our office.

193c ▶ 15 Improve Basic Keyboarding Skills

Take two 5′ writings on the ¶s. Record *gwam* and errors.

all letters used | A | 1.5 si | 5.7 awl | 80% hfw

	gwam 1′	5′	
A procedure is simply a series of steps which are followed in a	13	3	60
regular or definite order to achieve a desired goal. In an office,	26	5	63
standardized procedures are set up to insure that work is done in an	40	8	66
orderly and efficient manner. Procedures are of special help to the	54	11	68
employee on the job since, once the procedure is learned, the work can	68	14	71
be done quickly with less effort. A procedure for processing written	82	16	74
documents is an important element in the success of any office.	95	19	77
Although the procedure for the processing of documents differs	13	21	79
from office to office, there are several major steps. The first step	27	24	82
is the creation of the author's original material, which is known as	40	27	85
input. Input may be in written, rough draft, or dictated form. The	54	30	87
next step is to key the material which, when printed, is known as out-	68	33	90
put. In many offices, the first time a document is keyed it is done as	83	35	93
a rough draft since, without question, changes will be made.	95	38	95
After the author has made the final corrections and changes in the	13	41	98
document, it is then produced in final form. It is at this point that	28	43	101
the advantages of a word processor are most evident. Instead of keying	42	46	104
the entire document again, the operator merely recalls the material	56	49	107
from computer memory, keys the necessary changes and then simply gives	70	52	109
the instructions to the printer to make a hard copy on paper. The final	84	55	112
step is to transmit the document to the person for whom it is intended.	99	58	115

gwam 1′ | 1 | 2 | 3 | 4 | 5 | 6 | 7 | 8 | 9 | 10 | 11 | 12 | 13 | 14 |
5′ | 1 | 2 | 3 |

193d ▶ 10 Improve Keystroking Skills: Figures

Key each sentence twice *by touch.* If time permits, repeat sentences in which you made errors in figures.

1 Line items 2, 7, 9, 10, 28, 34, 59, and 63 must be ordered by July 15.
2 Please check paragraphs 4.1, 6.8, 7.3, 10.5, and 19.2 of the contract.
3 There are 246 seats in Room 201, 319 in Room 415, and 170 in Room 582.
4 Floppy disks 2506, 3718, 4923, 5701, and 6849 were not filed properly.
5 Prescription 16590 was renewed on June 3; 28374 was renewed on June 5.
6 Certificates 6390-167, 7428-936, and 8541-020 will mature on March 17.
7 On August 1 my office phone will be 389-6452; my home phone, 876-2103.
8 Her checking account number is 6418293045; savings account, 590376128.

| 1 | 2 | 3 | 4 | 5 | 6 | 7 | 8 | 9 | 10 | 11 | 12 | 13 | 14 |

Message from JESSICA SAMPSON

Key the document as an unbound report. The material should answer some of the questions that first-time home buyers often ask. The two inserts are attached. Key the references on a separate page. JS 5/13

Insert A

Rate	*Monthly Payment*
8.0%	$ 7.34
9.0	8.05
10.0	8.78
11.0	9.53
12.0	10.29
13.0	11.07

Insert B

1. Loan origination fees
2. Mortgage insurance application fee
3. Appraisal fee
4. Credit report fee
5. Loan discount (points)

HOME MORTGAGES

Many types of creative financing for home loans are offered by financial institutions. However, the two most common
types of mortgages are the fixed-rate mortgage and the
adjustable-rate mortgage. DS

Fixed-Rate Mortgage # The intrest rate of a fixed-rate mortgage
remains the same for the duration of the loan. Even if eco-
n omic conditions change, the interest rate cannot be adjusted.
this can be an advantage or disadvantage, depending on whether
interest rates are increas~~ed~~ ing or decreasing. The table below
(Wyllie, 1988, 301) illustratse the amount of a monthly mortgage payment on a 30 year loan per $1,000 borrowed. For example, ~~The~~ month-
ly payment for a $50,000 loan for 30 years at 10 percent would
be $439 ($8.78 x 50 = $439).

Insert A

One percentage point can # make a sizable difference in the amount
paid each month. It is to a borrowers advantage to check with
several financial institutions to find the best interest rate available.
When analyzing interest rates, how ever, a buyer should keep in
mind that there are variable closing costs ~~attached~~ associated with securing a loan. These costs may include the following:

Insert B

Adjustable-Rate Mortgage

Another common type of morgage offered by most financial
institutions is the adjustable rate mortgage.

An adjustable-rate mortgage is a loan with an interest rate
that can be adjusted up or down an agreed-upon number of times
during the life of the loan. The interest rate is usually tied
to changes in a monetary index, such as the interest rates on
U.S. Treasury securities or the rates financial institutions
must pay their depositors or investors. (Green, 1988, 441)

REFERENCES

Wyllie, Eugene ~~E~~ D., et al. Consumer Economics. 11th ed. Cincinnati: South-Western Publishing Company, 1988. tr

Green D. Hayden. Consumers in the Economy. 2nd ed. Cincinnati: South-Western Publishing Co., 1988.

UNIT 45 LESSONS 193 – 194

Improve Keyboarding/Language Skills

Learning Goals

1. To improve your basic keyboarding skills with emphasis on figures and symbols.
2. To increase your keystroking speed and to improve your accuracy on straight copy.
3. To improve your communications skills.

Format Guides

1. Paper guide at *0* (for typewriters).
2. LL: 70 spaces.
3. LS: SS sentence drills with a DS between sets; DS paragraph writings; DS language skill sentences.
4. PI: 5 spaces when appropriate.

Lesson 193 *Keyboarding/Language Skills*

193a ▶ 5 Conditioning Practice

each line twice SS (slowly, then faster); if time permits, take 1′ writings on line 3

alphabet 1 Julio Vasquez asked for views on bylaws that experts are recommending.
figures 2 Her book, published in 1990, has 658 pages, 230 pictures, and 74 maps.
fig/sym 3 Ship 1,850 computer chips (Catalog #738924) to Black & Co. on July 16.
speed 4 Their neighbor did the field audit for them and it may make them rich.

| 1 | 2 | 3 | 4 | 5 | 6 | 7 | 8 | 9 | 10 | 11 | 12 | 13 | 14 |

193b ▶ 20 Improve Language Skills: Commonly Confused Words

1. Study the spelling and definitions of the words.
2. Key the line number (with period); space twice, then key the **Learn** sentence, noting the correct use of the words.
3. Key the line number (with period); space twice, then key the **Apply** sentences DS, selecting the word in parentheses that makes each sentence correct.

way (n) a course or route
weigh (vb) to determine heaviness

conscious (adj) aware; felt or perceived
conscience (n) sense of moral goodness

heard (vb) perceived by the ear
herd (n) a group of animals of one kind

accede (vb) to express approval or consent
exceed (vb) to extend beyond or surpass

discreet (adj) careful or prudent
discrete (adj) separate or distinct

minor (adj) lesser, smaller, or secondary
miner (n) one who digs or excavates

Learn 1. On our way to the depot, we can weigh the package.
Apply 2. He lost his (way, weigh) on his trip to the city.
Apply 3. How much did the football player (way, weigh)?

Learn 4. I was conscious of the fact that he had a guilty conscience.
Apply 5. In good (conscience, conscious), I cannot agree to the changes.
Apply 6. Is she (conscience, conscious) of the bad feeling between them?

Learn 7. We heard the herd of deer in the forest.
Apply 8. The tour group saw a (heard, herd) of elephants in Kenya.
Apply 9. We (heard, herd) the noise of the zoo animals.

Learn 10. Did they accede to our request to exceed the budget?
Apply 11. If you agree to the proposal, I will (accede, exceed) the point.
Apply 12. He will (accede, exceed) his authority if he fires my assistant.

Learn 13. As a unique, discrete unit, we should be discreet when we speak.
Apply 14. We use a set of (discreet, discrete) symbols for this computer program.
Apply 15. He was not very (discreet, discrete) when he gave us the confidential data.

Learn 16. The miner made a minor adjustment to his headlamp.
Apply 17. Did the (minor, miner) locate a vein of coal?
Apply 18. We made only (minor, miner) changes in the report.

94b–98b (continued)

Job 5
LP pp. 19-23

Message from JESSICA SAMPSON

Here are the names of three more clients that Jeff Grayson would like invited to the private showing. A copy of the original letter is attached. Key a letter to each client for me to sign.

Mr. and Mrs. Chi Shen
1288 Paramount Lane
Houston, TX 77067-4310

Ms. Marjorie S. Butler
3198 Rosedale Circle
Houston, TX 77004-7120

Mr. Kevin N. King
2982 Spring Field Road
Houston, TX 77062-1312

JS 5/14

May 1, 19--

Mr. and Mrs. Jason R. Walton
1825 Victoria Drive
Houston, TX 77022-1903

Dear Mr. and Mrs. Walton

The 19-- Parade of Homes will be held June 7-21. This year we are planning something new. A limited number of our previous home buyers from Ritter Realty are being invited to participate in a private showing prior to the public opening of the Parade of Homes.

The private showing will give Ritter Realty agents the time needed to point out the many fine features of the quality homes being shown this year and to answer any questions you may have. With so many people taking part in the Parade of Homes, it is difficult to give our preferred customers the attention they deserve during the days the homes are shown to the public.

If you are interested in this free showing, sign and return the enclosed card. We look forward to showing you the outstanding homes built for this year's home show.

Sincerely

Jessica A. Sampson

Ms. Jessica A. Sampson
Branch Manager

xx

Enclosure

Job 6
LP p. 25

Message from JESSICA SAMPSON

Please send the attached letter to

Mr. Nelson C. Decker
Lakeside National Bank
2310 North Main Street
Houston, TX 77009-4612

JS 5/14

Here is a copy of an article ~~which~~ on streamlining the mortgage process which may be of interest to you. ~~from~~ It appeared in the April issue of <u>Mortgage Banking</u>. ~~It has~~ Several good suggestions for ways of cutting the time between the application ~~date~~ and ~~the~~ closing dates are presented. ¶ As I mentioned to you last week, we have recently had several customers who ~~are~~ were quite concerned about the length of time that ~~it is currently taking~~ was required for the processing of their loans. I will be interested in your reaction to the article. Sincerely,

192b (continued)

words

Document 2
Formal Memo

1. Key the copy given at the right as a formal memo to **All Word Processing Operators,** from **Kelly T. Rice, Chief of Document Processing.** Date the memo **July 8, 19--** with the subject **Care of Floppy Disks.**

2. List the enumerated items.

Note: The memos will be sent in reusable interoffice envelopes that do not require keyed addresses.

opening lines 22

A few unfortunate accidents have occurred during the past several weeks 36
which have caused the loss of important documents stored on 5 1/4" floppy 51
disks. These accidents were caused primarily by improper handling of the 66
disks. When using floppy disks, follow these basic rules. 78

1. Except when in use, keep the disks in their protective covers and store 93
them in the plastic boxes provided. Never cover disks with heavy objects. 108
2. When using the disks, do not touch the surface. Hold the disks gently by 124
the edges and insert them into the disk drives carefully. Under no circum- 138
stances attempt to force the disks into the drive. 3. Keep disks away from 154
metal or magnetized items. This includes paper clips and scissors. 4. Use 169
only felt markers to write on the label of a disk. If you use a ballpoint pen 185
or attempt to erase a label, you can ruin the disk. 5. Food of any kind, if 201
spilled on a disk, may ruin the disk. It is for this reason that eating in the 217
document processing room is forbidden. 225

Please keep these simple precautions in mind. Remember, pages of informa- 239
tion are stored on one floppy disk--information which can be lost in a second 255
by improper handling. 260

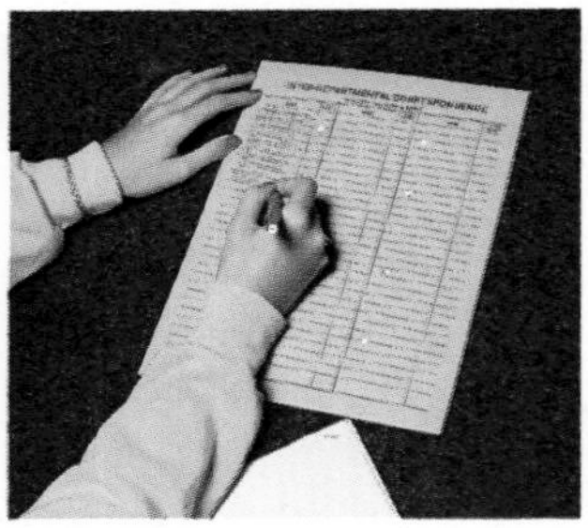

Reusable Company Mail Envelope

Document 3
News Release

Key the copy given at the right as a news release for release **Immediately** with **Elizabeth P. McNeil 401-896-3275** as the contact.

opening lines 9

(¶ 1) OMAHA, NE, September 16, 19--. At the annual meeting of the Forum 22
Group stockholders on September 15, Harvey E. Jamison, president and 36
chief executive officer, announced that ground-breaking ceremonies for a 51
new multipurpose corporate complex will be held October 1 on a site adja- 65
cent to Carter Lake in East Omaha. 72

(¶ 2) The corporate complex will include a ten-story office building and a ten- 87
story building with 240 condominium units. Connecting the two buildings 102
will be an enclosed mall with three department stores, 60 smaller shops, and 117
a recreational center with a complete health spa. Estimated cost of the com- 132
plex is $1.5 billion. 137

(¶ 3) The construction of this new multipurpose complex reflects a strong 150
corporate position in international commerce and increased growth. In this 166
fiscal year, the Forum Group expects a growth rate of 40% which it hopes to 181
sustain into the next decade. 187

(¶ 4) "Forum Park will be open within two years," Mr. Jamison announced, 200
"and will be the first complex in the United States to provide combined fa- 215
cilities for working, living, and recreation." ### 225

Document 4
News Release

Key the news release in Document 3 again with the following changes.

1. Eliminate the final sentence of ¶ 2.

2. In place of the final sentence of ¶ 2, substitute the copy in ¶ 4.

3. As the final ¶, key the material at the right.

Document 4 word count 215

(¶ 5) The plans for the construction of the complex were greeted with great 229
enthusiasm by the stockholders, who gave Mr. Jamison a standing ovation 244
upon the completion of his announcement. 253

94b–98b (continued)

Job 7

Message from JESSICA SAMPSON

Key the listing of homes that will be in this year's Parade of Homes. Use Parade of Homes for the main heading and June 7-21, 19--, as the secondary heading. Center column headings. JS 5/14

Location	Builder	Price
3885 Wimbledon Lane	Brock Construction	$ 133,000
3892 Glencliffe Lane	Murphy Homes Inc.	95,000
114 Fernbrook Lane	J & P Construction	215,000
803 Ashmore Drive	Berry & Sons Construction	149,000
5574 Blue Hills Road	Homes by Makely	99,000
4348 Mossridge Drive	Valleyview Home Builders	105,000
3872 Glencliffe Lane	Dalton & James Realty	91,000
120 Fernbrook Lane	Your Home Builders	175,000

Job 8

Message from JESSICA SAMPSON

Key the attached information in announcement form on a full sheet of paper. You decide on the layout; you've done a very nice job with previous announcements. The eight builders are listed with some of the other documents I've given to be keyed. Make sure to list them in alphabetical order. JS 5/15

19-- Parade of Homes
June 7-21
Monday - Friday 5 p.m. to 9 p.m.
Saturday & Sunday 10 a.m. to 6 p.m.
Featuring homes built by
(List the eight homebuilders in alphabetical order)
Sponsored by Ritter Realty Company

Job 9
LP p. 27

Message from JESSICA SAMPSON

Please send the attached letter to

Mr. and Mrs. Paul Taylor
1320 Lorl Lane #3
Odgen, UT 84404-4396

JS 5/14

Dear Mr. and Mrs. Taylor:

Rebecca Smithson, personnel manager of Tyson Production Company, informed me that you have accepted a position with them and will be moving to Houston the first part of July. I know you will enjoy living in this area.

A copy of the "Movers Guide" published by our real estate company is enclosed. It is designed to give helpful hints on making the move as painless as possible. We hope you will find it useful as you organize for the move to Texas.

If we can be of assistance to you in locating a place to rent or a home to purchase, please telephone our office.

Sincerely, Enclosure

Lesson 191 Sustained Production: Memorandums/News Releases

191a ▶ 5 Conditioning Practice

each line twice SS (slowly, then faster); DS between 2-line groups; if time permits, take 1′ writings on line 3

alphabet 1 Philip may serve freshly squeezed orange juice at breakfast next week.
figures 2 The show can be seen at 2:30 p.m. and 6:45 p.m. on May 17, 18 and 19.
fig/sym 3 Is the Model #5436 Printer (Serial #48391) listed at $1,325 or $2,790?
speed 4 She may go with us to the civic hall downtown for a world title fight.

| 1 | 2 | 3 | 4 | 5 | 6 | 7 | 8 | 9 | 10 | 11 | 12 | 13 | 14 |

191b ▶ 45 Sustained Production: Memos/News Releases

LP pp. 125-127
plain full sheets
Refer to Time Schedule in 192b.

1. Make a list of documents to be processed, including any special instructions.

p. 326, 188b, Memo 2, *except* change the name "Omnibus" to "Jupiter" each time it appears.
p. 328, 189b, Memo 2, *except* key the table SS.
p. 328, 189b, Memo 3
p. 330, 190b, News Release 2

2. Arrange letterheads and plain paper for efficient handling.

3. Work for 30′ when directed to begin. Correct errors as you key. Proofread each document before removing it from the machine.

4. Compute *n-pram;* turn in documents in the order given in Step 1.

Lesson 192 Evaluate Memorandums/News Releases

192a ▶ 5 Conditioning Practice

each line twice SS (slowly, then faster); DS between 2-line groups; if time permits, take 1′ writings on line 1

alphabet 1 Vicky and Jay requested boxes of many sizes filled with writing paper.
figures 2 Please correct the errors on pages 3, 6, 8, 9, 21, 46, 50, 73, and 82.
symbols 3 The ratings are: Superior (****); Good (***); Fair (**); or Poor (*).
speed 4 An amendment to the audit may entitle the girls to the rich endowment.

| 1 | 2 | 3 | 4 | 5 | 6 | 7 | 8 | 9 | 10 | 11 | 12 | 13 | 14 |

192b ▶ 45 Measure Production Skills: Memos/News Releases

LP pp. 129-133
plain full sheets

1. Arrange letterheads and plain full sheets for efficient handling.

2. Key for 30′ the documents below and on p. 333. Correct errors neatly; proofread each document before you remove it from the machine.

3. After timed production, proofread and circle any errors you may have missed.

4. Compute *n-pram.*

Time Schedule

Plan and prepare .... 5′
Timed production .... 30′
Proofread; compute *n-pram* .. 10′

Document 1
Simplified Memorandum

Key the copy given at the right as a simplified memo.

Documents 2, 3, and 4 are on p. 333.

words

June 16, 19-- Paul A. Williams, President PLANNING CONFERENCE AGENDA 14

As you requested, the agenda for the Planning Conference to be held on 28
June 25 has been changed. The report SEASONAL CHANGES which was 41
scheduled for 10:15 a.m. has been eliminated as well as the MANAGERIAL 55
EFFICIENCY report scheduled for 1:30 p.m. Instead, a report entitled THE 70
ENVIRONMENTAL IMPACT OF PROJECT 209A will be presented by John R. 83
Day, the project engineer, at 10:15 a.m. At 1:30 p.m., Marjorie K. Lamont, 98
director of human relations, will discuss EXECUTIVE STRESS. 111

Your closing remarks at the conference are now scheduled for 3:15 p.m., to 126
be followed by general comments from participants who will suggest areas 140
for future discussion. A revised copy of the agenda for this conference is 155
attached. 158

Robert E. Pitts, Administrative Assistant xx Attachment 169

94b–98b (continued)

Job 10

LP p. 29

> **Message from JESSICA SAMPSON**
>
> *Please send the attached letter to*
>
> JS 5/15
>
> Mr. Charles L. Atkins
> 1241 Warren Drive
> Denver, CO 80221-7463

Dear Mr. Atkins

It appears as though you would fit in very nicely with the "Ritter Realty Team." Your resume looks very impressive, and your references all speak very highly of you.

As you know from speaking with John Morgan about two weeks ago at the convention in Miami, we are looking for a person from outside the area who can bring in new ideas and who has been successful in the promotion and sales area. Your background shows a strength in both of these areas.

Would you be available to spend a day with us in Houston during the week of May 26-30 to discuss the position? I will call next week to determine your availability and to make arrangements for your visit.

Job 11

> **Message from JESSICA SAMPSON**
>
> *Please key the attached Parade of Homes schedule for Roxanne Davis.*
>
> JS 5/16

SCHEDULE FOR ROXANNE DAVIS

Client	Phone	Time
June 5		
Mr. and Mrs. Dave Johnson	836-4877	10 a.m.
Dr. and Mrs. Reed Kurth	839-8125	
Ms. Patricia Hansen	823-1143	1 p.m.
Mr. and Mrs. Scott Jones	834-1935	
Dr. Faye Snell	839-7680	4 p.m.
Mr. and Mrs. Timothy Reedsberg	823-4676	
Mr. and Mrs. Karl Hallie	836-2908	7 p.m.
Mr. and Mrs. Gregory Haas	823-1298	
June 6		
Mr. Jerry Sawyer	823-1095	10 a.m.
Mr. and Mrs. Jason Walton	836-6547	
Mr. Robert Todd	839-7231	1 p.m.
Miss Sandra Kurtz	836-3452	
Ms. Gretchen Kuehn	823-9876	
Mr. and Mrs. Barry Bauer	839-2349	4 p.m.
Dr. and Mrs. Ronald Baker	823-1520	7 p.m.
Miss Tami Seymour	836-4822	

FORUM GROUP

Suite 82, Forum Building
5800 Dodge Center
Omaha, Nebraska 68132-6459

401-896-3000

words

News Release

For Release: Upon receipt 3
Contact: Christine M. O'Ryan 7
401-896-3175 QS 9

OMAHA, NE, March 21, 19--. The Forum Group, the holding com- DS 21
pany for the Forum Insurance Companies of North America with $1.8 34
billion in assets, has filed today a registration statement with 47
the Securities and Exchange Commission for the proposed sale of 60
$10 million of cumulative convertible preferred stock. 71

This offering will consist of 500,000 shares of preferred 83
stock with a liquidation value of $20 per share, which will be 95
convertible into the Forum Group's common stock. The company will 109
not be empowered to redeem the shares for the first three years 122
with funds raised at a lower cost than that of the new preferred. 135
The shares will otherwise be redeemable from the time of issuance 148
at a premium initially equivalent to the dividend rate and declin- 161
ing to redemption at $20 per share after eight years. The divi- 174
dend rate, offering price, and conversion ratio on the preferred 187
stock will be determined at the time of offering. 197

The brokerage firm of Houseman & Fields, Inc., will manage 209
the offering which is expected the latter part of April. DS 220

221

Model News Release

Job 12
LP pp. 31-35

Message from JESSICA SAMPSON

Three more clients have accepted invitations to the private showing. Send a copy of the attached letter using the information provided below.

Mr. and Mrs. Mark O'Mara
1583 Nassau Bay Drive
Houston, TX 77058-2196

Ms. Kathy S. Ristow
1418 Rainwood Drive
Houston, TX 77079-3170

Mr. and Mrs. Juan Cruz
4573 Red Maple Drive
Houston, TX 77064-4407

Mark Grayson will show Mr. and Mrs. O'Mara and Ms. Ristow the homes on Saturday, June 6, at 7 p.m. Mathew Sparks will show Mr. and Mrs. Cruz the homes on Friday, June 5, at 1 p.m.

JS 5/16

May 16, 19--

Mr. and Mrs. Jason R. Walton
1825 Victoria Drive
Houston, TX 77022-1903

Dear Mr. and Mrs. Walton

We are pleased to have you take part in our private showing of the homes that will be in this year's Parade of Homes. The eight homes you will see combine quality construction, professional decorating, and exclusive landscaping to make this year's show the best ever.

I have made arrangements with (AGENT'S NAME) to show you the homes. Please meet (HIM/HER) at our office at (TIME) on (FRIDAY/SATURDAY), June (5/6). It will take approximately two hours to visit the homes.

I am looking forward to hearing your comments about the homes after the showing. If you have any questions prior to the showing, please telephone me.

Sincerely

Jessica A. Sampson

Ms. Jessica A. Sampson
Branch Manager

xx

c (NAME OF AGENT)

190a ▶ 5 Conditioning Practice

each line twice SS (slowly, then faster); DS between 2-line groups; if time permits, take 1′ writings on line 3

alphabet 1 Have Jo fix the bad wiring and synchronize the company clocks quickly.
figures 2 Paragraphs 39.1, 47.2, 50.8, and 60.1 of the bylaws were added June 8.
fig/sym 3 Taxes rose 5.4% in 1983, 7.6% in 1985, 10.1% in 1987, and 12% in 1991.
speed 4 When the men turn the dials, they may fix the problem with the signal.

| 1 | 2 | 3 | 4 | 5 | 6 | 7 | 8 | 9 | 10 | 11 | 12 | 13 | 14 |

190b ▶ 45 Format News Releases

LP pp. 119-123

News Release 1

1. Study the information on formatting a news release on p. 325.

2. Note the format of the model news release on p. 331.

3. Prepare a copy of the model news release on p. 331.

News Release 2

Key copy given at the right as a news release for release **Immediately** with **David C. Taylor 401-896-3286** as the contact; make the changes as marked.

words

opening lines 8

OMAHA, NE, June 30, 19--. Harvey E. Jamison, president 19
and chief executive officer of the Forum Group, announced 31
today the merger of the ~~firm's~~ company's import-export sub- 41
sidiary, Intercon, Inc., with the Boston-~~located~~ based Atlan- 52
tis Group. In exchange for Intercon, Inc., the Forum Group 63
will ~~attain~~ receive 50% of the ~~ownership~~ equity in the ex- 71
panded Atlantis Group. 77

"With the merger, the Atlantis Group will rank ~~in~~ among 87
the top three import-export ~~outfits~~ companies in the United 98
States," said Jamison. "More importantly," he ~~said~~ added, 108
"this merger provides a unique opportunity for the Forum 120
Group to ~~enlarge~~ expand its international ~~potential~~ opera- 128
tions and capabilities." 133

T. Harlan Mayer, the ~~present~~ current president of the 142
Atlantis Group, will retire on September 1 of this year. 154
His ~~job~~ position will be assumed by Marian C. Bodner, who 164
is ~~currently~~ presently the executive vice president of Martin 175
Industries Inc., another ~~part~~ subsidiary of the Forum Group. 186
The replacement for Bodner will be ~~divulged~~ announced at a 196
later date. ### 199

News Release 3

Key copy given at the right as a news release for release on **July 16, 19--** with **Lisa T. Cole 401-896-3289** as the contact.

opening lines 8

(¶ 1) OMAHA, NE, July 14, 19--. A historic agreement has been made with 21
the Republic of China by the Forum Group, according to Harvey E. Jamison, 36
president and chief executive officer of Forum. Under the agreement, Forum 51
will open a branch office in Tianjin as the initial step in establishing a series 68
of centers to serve business interests throughout China. 79

(¶ 2) Charles C. Goldsmith, currently the assistant director of Forum's Inter- 94
national Trade Division, will head the Forum office in Tianjin. His immediate 109
assistant will be Paul Yi Chung. Born in China, Mr. Chung became a citizen 125
of the United States in 1962. He is a graduate of Williams Academy and the 140
Wharton School of Business, University of Pennsylvania. Mr. Chung has held 155
numerous high-level managerial positions during the past ten years and most 170
recently served as president of America-Pacifico, Ltd., a firm which special- 185
izes in trade with Far and Middle Eastern countries. 196

(¶ 3) Until appropriate office facilities can be established in Tianjin, the 210
Forum Group will be located in Hong Kong at 80 Moody Road, Kowloon City 225
Centre. It is anticipated that the Tianjin office will open in December of 240
this year. ### 243

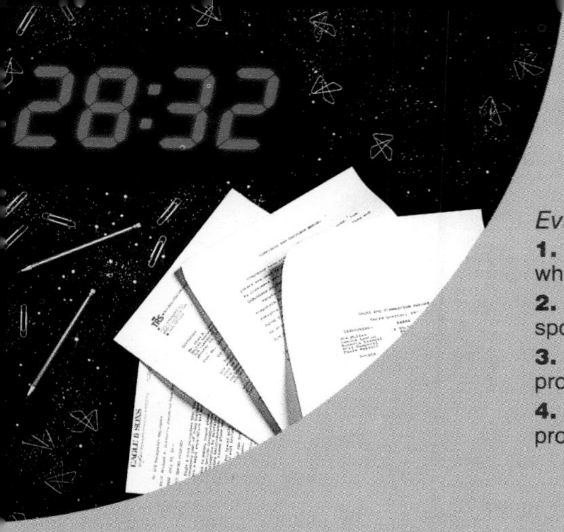

UNIT 22 LESSONS 99 – 100

Evaluate Keyboarding/Document Processing Skills

Evaluation Goals

1. To measure the speed and accuracy with which you key straight-copy material.

2. To evaluate your ability to process correspondence in proper formats.

3. To evaluate your ability to process tables in proper format.

4. To evaluate your ability to process reports in proper format.

Format Guides

1. Paper guide at *0* (for typewriters).

2. LL: 70-space line for drills and ¶s; as appropriate for documents.

3. LS: SS drills; DS ¶s; as required by document formats.

4. PI: 5 spaces for ¶s; as appropriate for document formats.

Lesson 99 — Evaluate Formatting Skills: Letters, Memos, and Tables

99a ▶ 5 Conditioning Practice

each line twice SS (slowly, then faster); DS between 2-line groups; if time permits, rekey selected lines

alphabet 1 Their equipment manager always kept an extra five dozen jumper cables.

figures 2 The total attendance for 1992 was 87,653, about a 40 percent increase.

fig/sym 3 The desk (#28A935) and chair (#73Z146) are usually sold for over $700.

speed 4 Sue owns the wheelchair in the shanty at the end of the big cornfield.

| 1 | 2 | 3 | 4 | 5 | 6 | 7 | 8 | 9 | 10 | 11 | 12 | 13 | 14 |

99b ▶ 45 Evaluate Formatting Skills

Time Schedule

Plan and prepare .... 5′
Document processing ...... 30′
Proofread; compute *n-pram* .... 10′

2 letterheads
LP pp. 41-43
2 plain full sheets

Document 1
Business Letter

Format the letter in block style with open punctuation. Use the Letter Placement Guide on p. 76 to determine margins and dateline placement.

Correct any errors you make as you key; proofread and correct any remaining errors before removing the document from the machine or screen. Address an envelope.

words

April 20, 19--/ Mr. Martin J. Pasquez/ Human Resource Manager/ 12
Murphy Enterprises/ 2950 Freedom Drive/ Charlotte, NC 28208- 24
2389/ Dear Mr. Pasquez/ Subject: JUNE SEMINAR 33

¶ Here is the information on our seminar being held June 5-9. 45
The seminar on "Quality Circles" is excellent for companies that 58
are interested in involving employees in decision making. 70

¶ Companies that implement quality circles have found that em- 82
ployee morale is increased, human relations among employees 94
are improved, and employee potential is maximized. These are 106
just a few of the extra benefits derived from using quality 118
circles. The main benefit is more profits from increased productivity. 133

¶ More information about the seminar is enclosed. We always en- 145
joy working with employees from Murphy Enterprises. (122) 156
Sincerely/ Ms. Jacqueline C. Bennett/ Seminar Coordinator/ 167
xx/ Enclosure/ c Mark J. Harada 173/**194**

KRĀEBIN INDUSTRIES

3875 SUGAR RIDGE DRIVE ROANOKE, VA 24018-2419

words

May 5, 19-- QS 2

All Department Chiefs DS 7

INSTALLATION OF COMPUTER AND PERIPHERALS DS 15

In accordance with the terms of our contract with Allied Business 28
Machines, installation of the Omega VI mainframe computer will 41
begin on June 1 and will be completed no later than June 16. A 54
systems check will begin immediately after installation; it is 66
scheduled to be completed by June 23. DS 74

Concurrent with the installation of the Omega VI, peripheral equip- 87
ment in the form of terminals and fax machines will be installed 100
in major departments of the company as shown below. DS 111

Department	Peripherals	words
Administration	6 terminals	125
	1 fax machine	128
Purchasing	1 fax machine	133
Marketing	2 terminals	137
	1 fax machine	140
Research and Engineering	2 terminals	148
	1 fax machine	150
Production	1 terminal DS	155

Please inform all of your employees of these plans so that they 168
will understand exactly what is taking place. A series of ori- 180
entation sessions for all employees regarding the purpose and use 193
of the computer and peripheral equipment will be conducted by the 206
Training Section. Schedules of these sessions will be published 219
by the Administration Department in the very near future. QS 231

A. Maynard Kelton, Executive Vice President DS 240

xx 240

Simplified Memorandum

99b (continued)

Document 2
Simplified Memo
plain full sheet
Format and key the memo in simplified style.

words

April 21, 19-- Mark McGinnis INFORMATION MANAGEMENT SALARIES 12

Attached is the inform ation you requested on salaries for 24
various field in the Information Management area. I have 36
listed the titles as well as the locations of the firms ad- 50
vertising the positions. This information was gathered from 63
the careers section of Computer Focus. 73

The range was $21,200 to $48,500. This should give you some 88
idea of the salary level you will need to offer for the the 99
two new positions in our information management department. 112
Let me know if there is further information that I can pro- 123
vide to asist in filling these position. 132

Courtney Williams Attachment xx 138

Document 3
Table
Format and key the table on a full sheet. Center column headings and leave 8 spaces between columns.

Document 4
Rekey Document 1. Address letter to:

Miss Michelle R. Gordon
Management Systems, Inc.
2845 Finch Street
Stamford, CT 06905-6384

Address an envelope.

INFORMATION MANAGEMENT SALARY Ranges 7

April 15, 19-- 10

Job Title	Location	Salary	22
Business Systems Analyst	Atlanta, GA	$45,000	32
Computer Analyst	Brooklyn, NY	48,500	41
Data Processing Manager	St. Louis, MO	32,000	50
Data Base Analyst	Houston, TX	48,000	57
Program Analsyt	Raleigh, NC	37,000	64
Senior Program Analyst	New Orleans, LA	40,000	73
Software Consultants	Detroit, MI	32,760	81
Support Systems Engineer	Portland, OR	32,200	90
Systems Analyst	Los Angeles, CA	36,000	98

101
Source: Computer Focus, February 20, 19--. 113

189a ▶ 5 Conditioning Practice

each line twice SS (slowly, then faster); DS between 2-line groups; if time permits, take 1′ writings on line 3

alphabet 1 Pam made the objective of the exercises clear by giving a weekly quiz.
figures 2 The population of the town rose from 75,204 in 1980 to 83,564 in 1990.
fig/sym 3 On 8/16/90, we sold 1,320 shares of Gee & Gee stock at $47.50 a share.
speed 4 Their firm goal is to visit the city and to fight the rigid amendment.
| 1 | 2 | 3 | 4 | 5 | 6 | 7 | 8 | 9 | 10 | 11 | 12 | 13 | 14 |

189b ▶ 45 Format Simplified Memorandums

plain full sheets

Memo 1

1. Study the information on formatting a simplified memo on p. 325.

2. Note the format of the model memo on p. 329.

3. Prepare a copy of the model memo on p. 329.

Memo 2

1. Format and key the rough-draft copy as a simplified memo dated **May 9, 19--,** to **All Division Chiefs** with the subject **COMPUTER ORIENTATION SESSIONS** for the signature of **Sarah T. Burton, Chief of Administration.**

2. Key the schedule as a table (DS) with the headings Department and Time and Date.

3. Make changes as marked.

words

opening lines 12

During the installatoin of the Omega VI main frame computer and peripherals, 28
a series of orientations sessions for employees will be led conducted by the 42
training section, by department, in accordance with the following schedule. 57

Administration, 9:30 a.m.-11:30 a.m., May 16; Purchasing, 78
1:30 p.m.-3:30 p.m., May 16; Marketing, 9:30 a.m.-11:30 a.m., 90
May 18; Research and Engineering, 1:30 p.m.-3:30 p.m., May 18; 102
Production, 9:30 a.m.-11:30 a.m., May 19. 110

All meetings will be held in room 102 of the Administration 122
Office. Building Please ask all employees to be prompt. Paper and 135
pencils for taking notes will be provided. 143

closing lines 152

Memo 3

Format and key the copy as a simplified memo; check the figures carefully.

May 20, 19-- Paul A. Williams, President PRELIMINARY FINANCIAL FIGURES 14

Preliminary figures for the fiscal year ended April 30 indicate that net sales 30
for the year reached $67,160,000--an increase of 12% over the previous year. 46
Net income for this year totalled $1,679,000 or $.80 per common share. Total 61
assets at year's end are estimated to exceed $48,600,000. 73

Shares of common stock outstanding at the end of the fiscal year numbered 88
exactly 2,098,750 with 970,451 shareholders of record. Shares of the Cumu- 103
lative Preferred $5 stock totalled 845,000 with 1,746 shareholders of record. 118

Based on these preliminary figures, it is recommended that we declare a 133
cash dividend of $.32 per share of common stock. This will reflect our 147
growth during this fiscal year and will represent an increase of $.10 over the 163
previous year's dividend. 168

Elizabeth D. McNamara, Treasurer xx 175

100a ▶ 5
Conditioning Practice

each line twice SS (slowly, then faster); DS between 2-line groups; if time permits, rekey selected lines

alphabet	1	Judy quickly spent all her extra money on a new puzzle before leaving.
figures	2	Order No. 78966 was for 140 disks, 30 printer ribbons, and 25 manuals.
fig/sym	3	March sales ($366,680) were 24% higher than February sales ($295,700).
speed	4	The big social for their neighbor may also be held in the city chapel.

| 1 | 2 | 3 | 4 | 5 | 6 | 7 | 8 | 9 | 10 | 11 | 12 | 13 | 14 |

100b ▶ 10
Evaluate Keyboarding Skills: Straight Copy

1. A 3′ writing on ¶s 1-3 combined; find *gwam*, circle errors.

2. A 1′ writing on ¶ 1; then a 1′ writing on ¶ 2; find *gwam* and circle errors on each.

3. Another 3′ writing on ¶s 1-3 combined; find *gwam*, circle errors.

4. Record on LP p. 3 your best 3′ *gwam*.

all letters used | A | 1.5 si | 5.7 awl | 80% hfw |

	gwam 3′	5′
Firms that plan to operate at a profit must employ people who are	4	3
willing to work as a team to achieve goals. Various management styles	9	5
have been used in the past to achieve company goals. These range from an	14	8
autocratic style where decisions are made by one person to a democratic	19	11
style where decisions are made by a group of employees. The team method	24	14
of decision making has become more accepted by many firms.	28	17
One of the more democratic forms of management that is becoming	32	19
quite popular is the quality circles concept. Employees are invited to	37	22
participate as part of a team to make decisions and deal with the problems	42	25
related to their jobs. The idea behind quality circles is to have the	47	28
workers who are most familiar with the job make all of the decisions	51	31
directly related to it rather than those who are further removed.	56	33
Research shows that employees who feel they are a valuable part of	60	36
a company team are more satisfied with their jobs. The end result of	65	39
job satisfaction is a higher level of achievement. Of course, a higher	70	42
achievement level means more profit for a firm and more benefits to the	74	45
worker. Because of the recent success of quality circles, more firms are	79	48
using this approach to help maximize employee output.	83	50

gwam 3′ | 1 | 2 | 3 | 4 | 5 |
5′ | 1 | 2 | 3 |

EAGLE & SONS

2299 Seward Highway ▪ Anchorage, Alaska ▪ 99503-4100

INTERоFFICE MEMORANDUM

words

TO: Warren E. Latouch, Director of Administration 9

FROM: Carla M. Boniface, Chief of Personnel 17

DATE: May 2, 19-- 19

SUBJECT: Employee Evaluation Program DS 25

As the company continues to expand, it is desirable that we estab- 38
lish an effective program for evaluating the performance of all 51
our employees. A sound evaluation program offers many advantages 64
to both the company and our employees, including the following: DS 77

1. Assists employees in judging their own value and accomplish- 89
ments. Ratings should include strong points as well as short- 102
comings, with suggestions for improvement. DS 110

2. Provides managers with information which they may use to de- 123
termine promotions or lateral reassignments in order to make the 136
most effective use of each employee's abilities. DS 146

3. Provides a basis for determining increases in compensation or 159
for bonus payments to reward the most efficient employees. DS 171

4. Requires supervisors to analyze the work done by their subor- 184
dinates and to recognize the contribution they make in the accom- 197
plishment of their mutual objectives. DS 205

5. Promotes an atmosphere of mutual respect and teamwork among 217
supervisors and employees. DS 223

6. Provides an evaluation of the effectiveness of other personnel 236
programs such as recruitment, selection, orientation, and training. DS 250

It is essential that clear-cut policies be established for this 263
new evaluation program. To insure success, the objectives of the 276
program must be clearly established, thoroughly understood, and 289
fully accepted by all concerned. A recommended plan of action to 302
accomplish these objectives is attached. DS 311

As a matter of priority, I recommend that the establishment of a 324
program to evaluate employee performance be placed on the agenda 337
of the executive committee for consideration at the earliest pos- 349
sible date. DS 352

xx DS 353

Attachment 355

Formal Memorandum

100c ▶ 35 Evaluate Formatting Skills: Reports

Time Schedule
Plan and prepare .... 4′
Document processing ...... 25′
Proofread; compute *n-pram* .... 6′

3 plain full sheets

Document 1
Unbound Report

Format and key the material given at the right as an unbound report. Correct any errors you make as you key. Before removing each page from the machine or screen, proofread and correct any remaining errors.

Document 2
Reference Page

Prepare a reference page for the report using the following information.

Cherrington, David J. The Work Ethic. New York: AMACOM Division of the American Management Association, 1980.

Manning, George, and Kent Curtis. Morale: Quality of Work Life. Cincinnati: South-Western Publishing Co., 1988.

Document 3
Title Page

Prepare a title page for the report using your **name, school,** and **current date.**

words

WORK--TODAY AND YESTERDAY *QS* 5

Even though there are those who question the degree of 16
existence ofthe american work ethic, most americans still 28
believe it exists in the U.S. today. Included as part of 41
this work ethic is the belief that: 49

1. Workers should take pride in their work and do 59
their jobs well. 63

DS 2. Employees should have feelings of commitment and 73
loyalty to their profession, their company, and their work 85
group. 87

DS 3. People should acquire wealth through honest labor 97
and retain it through thrift and wise investments 108
(Cherrington, 1980, 20).

Regard less of whether the American Work Ethic has or 118
has not changed over the years, work and how it is viewed 130
have changed. Because of technology, jobs are less physical 142
and more mental than ever before. Worker expectations of 154
jobs ~~has~~ *have* also changed. Jobs are no longer viewed as simply 166
a means of putting food on the table. Such things as job 178
satisfaction and employee morale are now extremely important 190
to employees as well as employers. 197

Job Satisfaction 204

Today's employees are more concerned about job satis- 214
faction than ever before. The emphasis ~~following the~~ 222
~~depression which was~~ placed on income and job security *during and following the depression* has 237
been replaced by an emphasis on job satisfaction. This is 249
directly related to an affluent society with many *well-paying* jobs 262
available. As a result, *qualified* workers can now be more selective 276
in choosing jobs that offer ~~intrinsic rewards~~ *personal fulfillment*. 286

Employee Morale 292

With research indicating a direct relationship between 303
job performance and *employee* morale, employers are *continually evaluating* ~~taking a long look~~ 318
~~to determine how~~ *ways in which employee* morale can be increased. Maning and Curtis 332
(1988, 71) believe morale energizes people and brings out 343
the best in their job performance. They define morale as 355
being a person's attitude toward the ~~work~~ *stet* experience. The 376
job itself, the work group, managment practices, and econom- 388
ic rewards are included as part of this work experience. 390

188a ▶ 5 Conditioning Practice

each line twice SS (slowly, then faster); if time permits, take 1′ writings on line 4

alphabet 1 Mickey will award six prizes for jet travel at the gala banquet today.
figures 2 Stocks rose 48.1 points on June 29 but dropped 57.6 points on June 30.
fig/sym 3 They made payments of $349.25, $412.73, $507.80, $614.06, and $789.25.
speed 4 The auditor may suspend the fight for the title to the ancient chapel.

| 1 | 2 | 3 | 4 | 5 | 6 | 7 | 8 | 9 | 10 | 11 | 12 | 13 | 14 |

188b ▶ 45 Format Formal Memorandums

Memo 1
Formal Memo
LP p. 113

1. Study the information about formal memos on p. 325.
2. Note the format of the model memo on p. 327.
3. Prepare a copy of the model memo on p. 327.

Memo 2
Formal Memo
LP p. 115

Key the memo shown at the right.

Memo 3
Formal Memo
LP p. 117

Key the memo at the right again, but each time the name "Omnibus" appears, change it to "Omicron."

Note: The global search and replace feature on a word processor permits the operator to instruct the machine to change a word automatically wherever it appears in a document.

Note: If you do not have Lab Pac (LP) pages to use for the formal memo, follow these guidelines.

1. Set side margins at 1″.
2. Beginning on line 10, key each heading flush with the left margin.
3. Space twice after the colon and key the information following each heading.

words

TO: ~~Mrs.~~ Sharon C. Gross, Manager, Information Systems FROM: 9
Brandon L. London, Communications Chief DATE: September 14, 20
19-- SUBJECT: Word Processing Systems 26

As you ~~directed~~ requested in your memo (sp) of September 2, my staff 38
and I have been ~~looking into~~ investigating word processing systems for use 50
in our secretaail pool. Within the price guides lines you estab- 63
lished, we examined and tested six systems. After careful 75
~~thought~~ consideration, we concluded that the Omnibus System ~~is best.~~ will best meet our needs. 91

The Omnibus has dual disk drives with 526K expandable memory. Automatic features of 108
the Omnibus include automating c centering, underlining, ~~and~~ 118
decimal tabulation, and carrier return. 127

Among the desirable ~~aspects~~ features of the Omnibus are a 60,000- 138
word dictionary which automatically checks the spelling of 150
words and a "save" ~~feature~~ mechanism which prevents the loss of stored data 163
in the event of a power failure. Best of all, the Omnibus 175
is truly "user friendly." There are no ~~arduous~~ difficult commands to 188
learn since all instructions ~~used~~ are given in simple words. 199

We strongly reccommend that ~~consideration~~ approval be given for 209
the purchase of six Omnibus Systems for installation at the 221
~~soonest.~~ earliest possible date. 225

xx 226/**237**

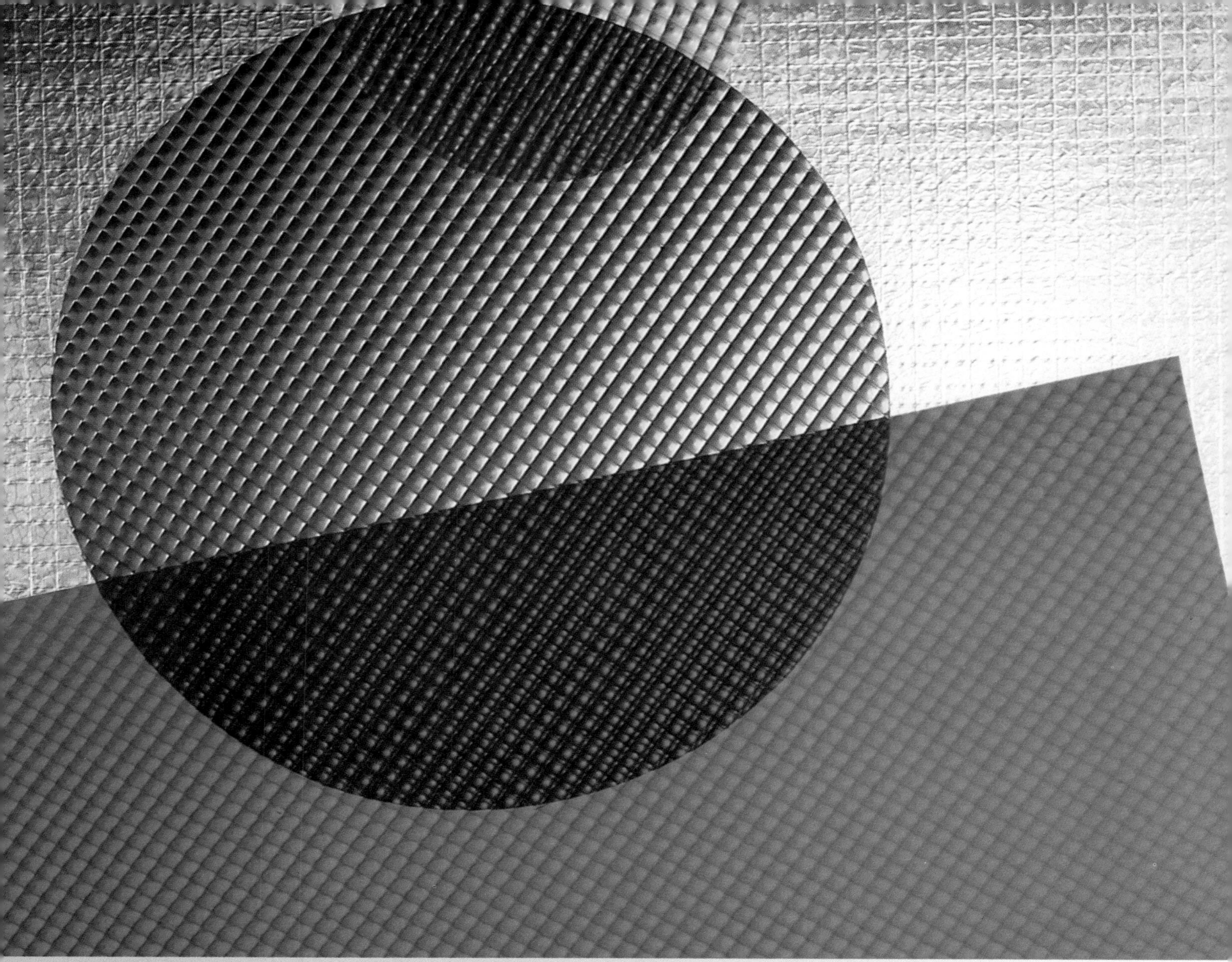

LESSONS 101 – 125

PHASE 5 EXTEND DOCUMENT PROCESSING SKILLS

Phase 5 continues the emphasis on improving keyboarding and document processing skills. The lessons are designed to help you:

1. Further refine keyboarding techniques as you apply your keyboarding skill.

2. Improve and extend document formatting skills on simple and complex tables, reports containing footnotes or endnotes, and letters in block and modified block formats.

3. Increase language-skill competency.

4. Increase keyboarding speed and control.

5. Improve proofreading competency.

6. Improve skill in keying from rough-draft and script copy.

UNIT 44 LESSONS 188 – 192

Learn to Format Memorandums and News Releases

Learning Goals

1. To learn/review how to format a formal memorandum.
2. To learn/review how to format a simplified memorandum.
3. To learn how to format a news release.
4. To build production skill on memorandums and news releases.

Format Guides

1. Paper guide at *0* (for typewriters).
2. LL: 70 spaces for drill copy; as directed or required for documents.
3. LS: SS drill lines with DS between 2-line groups; space documents as directed or required.
4. PI: 5 spaces, when a document format requires indention.

FORMATTING GUIDES: MEMORANDUMS/ NEWS RELEASES

Interoffice Memorandums

Interoffice memorandums are used to convey information among people *within* a firm. The address, personal titles (Mr., Mrs., Miss, Ms.), salutation, and complimentary close are omitted. Memorandums may be prepared in a formal or a simplified format.

Formal format. Formal memorandums are prepared on full- or half-sheet forms with preprinted headings (see model memo on p. 327). They are keyed in block format with 1″ side margins. The headings **TO:**, **FROM:**, **DATE:**, and **SUBJECT:** are printed in the left margin. The data to be inserted begins two spaces to the right of the headings, which should be at the margin stop set for a 1″ left margin.

The headings are double-spaced (DS), and a DS separates the last heading line from the message. The body is single-spaced (SS) with a DS between paragraphs. The operator's initials are placed at the left margin a DS below the message. If there are any attachments to the memo, the notation "Attachments" is placed a DS below the operator's initials.

Simplified format. Simplified memorandums are prepared on plain paper or on company letterhead (see model memo on p. 329). These memorandums do not include preprinted headings. Simplified memos are prepared in block format with 1″ side margins and are formatted as follows.

Date: plain paper, line 10; letterhead, a DS below the letterhead.

Addressee's name: on the 4th line space (QS) below the date. The name may be followed on the same line by a job title or department name.

Subject: in ALL CAPS a DS below the addressee's name.

Body: a DS below the subject line; single-spaced (SS) with a DS between paragraphs.

Writer's name: on the 4th line space (QS) below the last line of the body of the memo.

Operator's initials: a DS below the writer's name.

Attachments (if any)**:** a DS below the operator's initials. Some firms prefer the use of the word "Enclosures," which is handled in the same way.

News Releases

News releases announce items of special interest to newspapers and other news media. The release is usually prepared on letterhead with the words "News Release" printed at the left and the words "For Release:" and "Contact:" at the right (see model release on p. 331).

Side margins of 1″ are used. Paragraphs are double-spaced (DS) and indented five spaces. The time of release is placed two spaces to the right of "For Release:" and the name and telephone number of the person to contact for additional information is keyed two spaces to the right of "Contact."

The body of the release (which always begins with the city, state, and date) begins a quadruple space (QS) below the heading information. The symbols ### are centered a double space (DS) below the last line to indicate the end of the release.

UNIT 23 LESSONS 101 – 103

Extend Keyboarding and Language Skills

Learning Goals

1. Improve and assess keyboarding techniques.
2. Improve and assess keyboarding speed and control (accuracy).
3. Improve language skills.

Format Guides

1. Paper guide at *0* (for typewriters).
2. LL: 70 spaces.
3. LS: SS word and sentence drills; DS ¶s; or space as directed within an activity.
4. PI: 5 spaces for ¶s.

Lesson 101 *Keyboarding/Language Skills*

101a ▶ 5 Conditioning Practice

each line twice SS (slowly, then faster); DS between 2-line groups; if time permits, rekey selected lines

alphabet 1 Vera quickly justified the six itemized party food bills while dining.
figures 2 He flew 3,250 miles on Monday, 1,896 on Tuesday, and 475 on Wednesday.
adjacent keys 3 The loud voices from Drew's radio in the atrium were from a new opera.
speed 4 An off-duty ensign got sick with the toxic virus and was to go to bed.

| 1 | 2 | 3 | 4 | 5 | 6 | 7 | 8 | 9 | 10 | 11 | 12 | 13 | 14 |

101b ▶ 5 Improve Language Skills: Semicolon

LL: 70-spaces; SS with DS between 3-line groups

1. Read and key the **Learn** sentence (with number and period), noting how the rule has been applied.
2. Key the **Apply** sentences (with numbers and periods), using the correct punctuation.
3. If time permits, key the **Apply** lines again at a faster speed to quicken decision-making skill.

Use a semicolon to separate two or more independent clauses in a compound sentence when the conjunction is omitted.

Learn 1. Eve Harris must enjoy dancing; she goes to every dance at South High.
Apply 2. Tom was worried about the engine noise he went to see his mechanic.
Apply 3. Joe is an excellent student he reads every chance he gets.

Use a semicolon to separate independent clauses when they are joined by a conjunctive adverb (however, therefore, consequently, etc.)

Learn 4. We waited in line for an hour; however, the movie was worth the wait.
Apply 5. Al is a good speaker therefore, he receives invitations to speak.
Apply 6. Ed will not be president furthermore, he will not accept any office.

101c ▶ 10 Improve Response Patterns

Key each line twice SS; DS between 2-line groups; then 1′ writings as time permits on lines 2, 4, and 6.

Adjacent keys

words 1 same suit cure spot sale foil other prior worthy fields opened quickly
sentences 2 Open bidding on truck tires will suit the clerk's priority quite well.

Direct reaches

words 3 much race cent fund worthy music union checks fifty zebra great length
sentences 4 Eight special loans in the large green manuals depend on mutual funds.

One-hand words

words 5 race upon sage yolk refer union vases zebra wages tested uphill veered
sentences 6 Ted's greatest starts in regatta races were based on a steadfast crew.

| 1 | 2 | 3 | 4 | 5 | 6 | 7 | 8 | 9 | 10 | 11 | 12 | 13 | 14 |

187b (continued)

Document 2
Electronic Message

plain paper
PB: line 7; LL: 60

Key *only* the data that would be entered by the sender and would appear on the screen. If you make an error, backspace and strike the correct key.

Total words: 118

```
login:  WTaylor
password:  CEO
Mon Apr 20 09:35:26 EST 1992
mail
To:  FJenkins
Subject:  Net Sales in the Omaha Region

A review of the quarterly reports from our branch offices
indicates that there may be some difficulties in the Omaha
regional office.  Net sales in that region are down almost
19 percent when compared with sales during the same period
last year.

Will you please study the quarterly report from Omaha and,
if necessary, contact Thomas Kelly, the regional chief, to
determine why there has been such a drastic drop in sales.

Please give me a report on this matter no later than 1600
hours on Friday of this week.

end-of-file
What next?  send
logout
```

Document 3
Letter with Special Features

LP p. 109
SM: 1″; PB: line 12

1. Key the letter in block format, open punctuation, for the signature of **Martin M. Stern, Trust Officer.**

2. Send the letter by **REGISTERED MAIL.** Provide an appropriate salutation and complimentary close. Correct errors.

3. Center the list of note numbers. Use the company name in the closing lines: **FRANKLIN NATIONAL BANK.** List the enclosures and indicate that a copy of the letter has been sent to **D. Elaine Hawkins.**

Document 4
Letter with Special Features

LP p. 111
SM: 1″; PB: line 12

1. Key the letter in Document 3 to

Adams Legal Associates
33 St. James Avenue
Boston, MA 02116-5348

to the attention of **Jessica T. Parsons.** In ¶ 2, change the name of the executor to **Ms. Parsons.**

2. Add a subject line: **ESTATE OF MURRAY T. MILES;** do *not* include the company name in the closing lines and do *not* send a copy of the letter to **D. Elaine Hawkins.**

words

November 10, 19-- Mrs. Melissa F. Rowland 628 Cambridge Street Boston, 17
MA 02134-7490 24

At the direction of D. Elaine Hawkins, attorney-at-law, I am releasing to you 40
the following U.S. Treasury Notes which are enclosed. Each note has a face 55
value of $10,000. 59

7456901 60
7935462 62
8054095 63

These notes are a part of the estate of Murray T. Miles and have been held in 79
trust by us. As executor of the estate, Mrs. Rowland, it will be your respon- 94
sibility to have the notes registered with the U.S. Treasury Department in 109
the names of the beneficiaries. 116

Under Probate Court Order No. 56230 of October 30, you are now authorized 131
to control the accounts, both savings and checking, on deposit with us in the 146
name of the decedent. Will you please complete and sign the enclosed signa- 161
ture cards prior to making any demands on these accounts. 173

closing lines 200/**217**

101d ▶ 30 Assess/Improve Keyboarding Speed/Accuracy

1. A 1′ writing on each ¶ for speed; find *gwam* on each writing.

2. A 1′ writing on each ¶ for control; circle errors on each writing.

3. A 3′ writing on ¶s 1-3 combined; find *gwam*, circle errors.

4. Record your 3′ *gwam* to compare with your 3′ *gwam* in 103c.

Skill Building

1. Set a goal of greater speed or fewer errors; if you made 6 or more errors on the 3′ writing, work for control; otherwise, work for speed.

2. Take two 1′ writings on each of the 3 ¶s trying to increase speed or reduce errors, according to your goal.

3. Take a 5′ writing on ¶s 1-3 combined; find *gwam*, circle errors.

4. Record your 5′ *gwam* to compare with your *gwam* in 103c.

all letters used | A | 1.5 si | 5.7 awl | 80% hfw |

	gwam 3′	5′	
A word processing system is an excellent tool which young people	4	3	43
can use to develop their writing skills. When young people use such a	9	5	45
system to prepare papers for school or other purposes, the final copy	14	8	48
produced is likely to reflect their finest efforts because of the amazing	19	11	51
ease with which draft copies can be altered time after time.	23	14	54
Two basic functions of word processing systems that make it quite	27	16	56
easy to change writing are called insert and delete. These functions	32	19	59
permit the operator to add or take out a single space or character or an	37	22	62
entire word, sentence, paragraph, or document within a short period of	41	25	65
time with a great deal of ease.	44	26	66
When large amounts of material are moved from one place to another,	48	29	69
copied to another place, or deleted from the document, the word processor	53	32	72
often just marks the beginning and ending of the text to be moved, cop-	58	35	75
ied, or deleted. To do this, the person operating the system may use a	63	38	78
special function key to mark the material at the proper points.	67	40	80

gwam 3′ | 1 | 2 | 3 | 4 | 5 |
gwam 5′ | 1 | 2 | 3 |

Lesson 102 Keyboarding/Language Skills

102a ▶ 5 Conditioning Practice

each line twice SS (slowly, then faster); DS between 2-line groups; if time permits, rekey selected lines

alphabet 1 Buffi was told to try to keep singing until her next major vocal quiz.

fig/sym 2 Tony Mason had 702 points, 451 rebounds, and 436 assists from '88-'91.

adjacent keys 3 Sam has to avoid a higher rent policy if he hopes to have more action.

speed 4 Their proficient robot with a giant hand and eye can fix the problems.

| 1 | 2 | 3 | 4 | 5 | 6 | 7 | 8 | 9 | 10 | 11 | 12 | 13 | 14 |

102b ▶ 20 Improve Keyboarding Skill: Timed Writing

1. Two 1′ writings on each ¶ in 101d, above; find *gwam* on each writing.

2. A 3′ writing on ¶s 1-3 combined; try to equal your best 1′ rate in Step 1.

3. A 5′ writing on ¶s 1-3 combined; find *gwam*, circle errors.

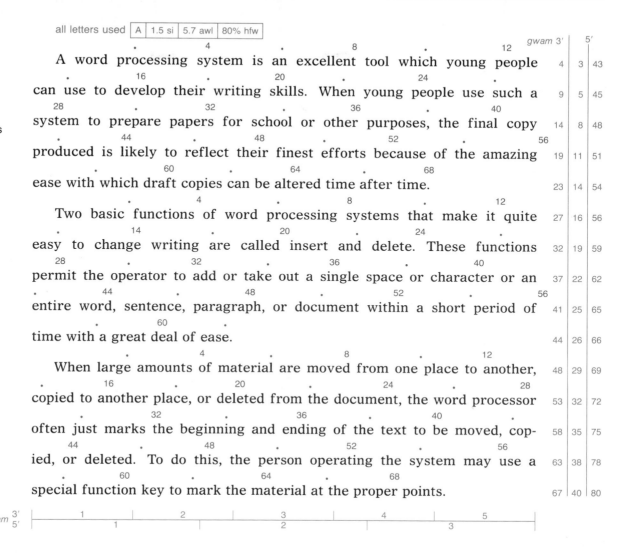

Lesson 186 Sustained Production: Messages with Special Features

186a ▶ 5 Conditioning Practice

each line twice SS (slowly, then faster); DS between 2-line groups; if time permits, take 1′ writings on line 1

alphabet 1 We have begun a check of quarterly expenses itemized in their journal.

figures 2 Check all of the memos filed under 215.39, 480.76, 583.19, and 679.20.

fig/sym 3 Acme computers (Model 286327) are listed at $945, less a 10% discount.

speed 4 Andy may work with a neighbor and me to dismantle and fix the bicycle.

| 1 | 2 | 3 | 4 | 5 | 6 | 7 | 8 | 9 | 10 | 11 | 12 | 13 | 14 |

186b ▶ 45 Sustained Production: Messages with Special Features

LP pp. 101-105
or plain full sheets

Time Schedule
Plan and prepare .... 5′
Timed production ....30′
Proofread; compute *n-pram* .....10′

1. Make a list of messages to be processed:

p. 319, 183b, Letter 2
p. 321, 184b, Message 1
p. 322, 185b: Send letter to

Miss Suzie F. Lee
62 Exeter Street
Boston, MA 02116-4120

using the following information.

(A) **six-month**
(B) **643910**
(C) **November 21**
(D) **$2,104.96**
(E) **Boston**
(F) **563-7000**

2. Arrange letterheads and plain paper for efficient handling. Address envelopes.

3. Work for 30′ when directed to begin. Proofread each letter carefully before removing it from the machine. Correct errors neatly. If you finish before time is called, begin with Letter 1 and rekey on plain sheets as much as possible in the time remaining.

4. Compute *n-pram;* turn in messages arranged in the order given in Step 1.

Lesson 187 Evaluate Messages with Special Features

187a ▶ 5 Conditioning Practice

each line twice SS (slowly, then faster); DS between 2-line groups; if time permits, take 1′ writings on line 4

alphabet 1 He examined previous job analyses to standardize sequences of working.

figures 2 Line item 14 on page 27 indicates we produced 590,386 units in August.

fig/sym 3 Send 80 5″ × 3″ (12.7 × 7.6 cm) and 90 6″ × 4″ (15.2 × 10.1 cm) cards.

speed 4 The proficient handiwork of both girls may entitle them to the profit.

| 1 | 2 | 3 | 4 | 5 | 6 | 7 | 8 | 9 | 10 | 11 | 12 | 13 | 14 |

187b ▶ 45 Measure Production Skills: Messages with Special Features

LP pp. 107-111
or plain full sheets

Time Schedule
Plan and prepare .... 5′
Timed production ....30′
Proofread; compute *n-pram* .....10′

Documents 2, 3, and 4 are on p. 324.

1. Make a list of the variables as listed below for Document 1 addressed to

Mr. Ralph J. Devins
16 Franklin Lane
Duxbury, MA 02332-6075

Variables: (A) **one-year**
(B) **754029**
(C) **November 15**
(D) **$5,781.19**
(E) **Duxbury**
(F) **876-8830**

2. Arrange letterheads and plain sheets for efficient handling.

3. Key for 30′ the documents given here and on p. 324. Proofread and correct each document carefully *before* you remove it from the machine or screen.

4. After the timed production, proofread and circle any errors you may have missed.

5. Compute *n-pram.*

Document 1
Form Letter

LP p. 107; LL: 1½″ margins;
PB: line 14
Date: November 1, 19--

1. Using the list of variables you made in Step 1 at the left, key the form letter given on p. 322 in modified block format with indented paragraphs.

2. Use open punctuation.

3. Supply an appropriate salutation and complimentary close.

4. Correct errors made as you key.

102c ▶ 5 Improve Language Skills: Semicolon

LL: 70 spaces; SS with DS between 3-line groups

1. Read and key the **Learn** sentence (with number and period), noting how the rule has been applied.

2. Key the **Apply** sentences (with numbers and periods), using the correct punctuation.

3. If time permits, key the **Apply** lines again at a faster speed to quicken decision-making skill.

SEMICOLON

Use a semicolon to separate a series of phrases or clauses (especially if they contain commas) that are introduced by a colon.

Learn 1. The dates are as follows: May 1, 1982; May 5, 1987; and May 6, 1991.
Apply 2. The cities are as follows: Ada, OH Muncie, IN and Tampa, FL.
Apply 3. The teams include the following: Reds, Area I and Lions, Area II.

Place the semicolon *outside* the closing quotation mark; the period and comma, *inside* the closing quotation mark.

Learn 4. Miss Enders said, "Begin right away"; Ms. King said, "Wait a minute."
Apply 5. Mrs. Hart said, "Print your answers;" I said, "I need a pencil."
Apply 6. Kathy's topic was "It All Starts Here;" Sandy's was "I Can Do It".

102d ▶ 20 Improve Skill Transfer: Script Copy

1. Two 1′ writings on each ¶ for speed; find *gwam* on each writing.

2. One 1′ writing on each ¶ for control; circle errors on each writing.

3. One 3′ writing on ¶s 1-3 combined; find *gwam;* circle errors. If you finish before time is called, start over.

all letters used | A | 1.5 si | 5.7 awl | 80% hfw

	gwam 1′	3′
Ethical conduct is a subject which has received a great	11	4
deal of attention in recent years. Many businesses have de-	23	8
veloped written codes and have taken steps to ensure that em-	36	12
ployees of the business and the public are aware of these	47	16
codes. Making people aware of the codes is a company's way	59	20
of renewing its commitment to ethical practice.	69	23
A major purpose of a code of ethics is to relay a com-	11	27
pany's values and business standards to all its workers. Each	24	31
worker must realize he or she is required to apply these stan-	36	35
dards in all relations with co-workers, potential and current	49	39
customers and suppliers, and the public at large.	59	43
Employees must be able to combine personal standards with	12	47
those of the business to adhere to the code. This mixture is	24	51
important because each job has an ethical aspect and each em-	36	55
ployee has a responsibility to carry out the functions of the	49	59
job in an ethical and proper manner.	56	61

185a ▶ 5 Conditioning Practice

each line twice SS (slowly, then faster); if time permits, take 1′ writings on line 1

alphabet 1 Jose Ruiz quickly taped very wild shows for a big festival next month.

figures 2 Send 15 copies of Form 6749, 20 copies of 8159, and 30 copies of 8321.

symbols 3 Use the "and" sign (&) in company names: C & D Autos; Sheehan & Sons.

speed 4 Did the maid mend the pale paisley formal gown for the sorority girls?

| 1 | 2 | 3 | 4 | 5 | 6 | 7 | 8 | 9 | 10 | 11 | 12 | 13 | 14 |

185b ▶ 45 Format Form Letters

LP pp. 95-99
modified block format with indented ¶s; open punctuation; SM: 1½″; PB: line 14

1. Key the form letter given at the right below, dated **October 30, 19--**, to the persons listed below.

2. Provide an appropriate salutation and complimentary close. The letters will be signed by **Sara C. Mills, Senior Vice President.**

3. Insert the personalized data in the appropriate spaces; correct errors.

Form Letters

The letter below is an example of a form letter (also known as boilerplate). These letters are used when the same information is sent to many individuals. The letter can be "personalized" or "customized" by inserting the appropriate information in the blank spaces. The blanks are identified by letter or number so that the operator can quickly identify the information to be inserted.

On an electronic typewriter with memory, a form letter can be stored, retrieved when needed, and programmed to stop at the appropriate places so that the operator can insert the personalized data.

When prepared on a word processor or computer, the form letter can be stored on one disk and the personalized data on a separate disk. The word processor or computer can then be programmed to merge the text and the personalized information automatically. This procedure is known as document assembly or text merging.

Letter 1
Ms. Maria C. Fuentes
1501 Bay Avenue
Chelsea, MA 02150-4362
(A) **six-month** (B) **4057128**
(C) **November 15** (D) **$10,052.48**
(E) **Chelsea** (F) **452-6010**

Letter 2
Mrs. Rachel F. Stein
1605 Cheney Place
Lowell, MA 01851-9501
(A) **one-year** (B) **5057124**
(C) **November 20**
(D) **$11,562.37** (E) **Lowell**
(F) **565-4910**

Letter 3
Mr. Sean F. Reilly
10 Tremont Street
Boston, MA 02108-6107
(A) **30-month** (B) **6948239**
(C) **November 17** (D) **$6,157.44**
(E) **Boston** (F) **563-7000**

words

opening lines 19

Our records indicate that your Franklin (A) certificate #(B) is due to mature 37
on (C). As you consider your reinvestment options, there are many ways 53
Franklin can help you to make the most of your money. 64

You can reinvest your funds totalling (D) in principal and accrued interest in 81
another certificate at the rate in effect on the day your present certificate 96
matures. Franklin offers a wide range of certificates with terms from 111
30 days to 10 years at attractive rates compounded daily. 122

If you wish to learn more about the many savings and investment opportuni- 137
ties we can offer you or if you have any questions concerning your account, 152
please call our (E) office at (F). 161

Don't delay. Prompt action on your part will insure that your funds will con- 177
tinue to earn high interest rates in the months and years ahead. 190

closing lines 201/**212**

103a ▶ 5 Conditioning Practice

each line twice SS (slowly, then faster); DS between 2-line groups; if time permits, rekey selected lines

alphabet	1	Jerry met his quota for seventy new wax paper and zip-lock bag orders.
figures	2	I have sold 48 hot dogs, 35 hamburgers, 72 candy bars, and 1960 sodas.
adjacent keys	3	I hope the new report on the point of the poem will be done next week.
speed	4	The girls in the sorority dorms pay for the autobus to go to the town.

103b ▶ 8 Improve Keyboarding Skill: Guided Writings

1. Two 1′ writing; find *gwam.*
2. Add 4 words to better rate; determine 15″ goals.
3. Two 30″ writings; try to reach your 15″ goals.
4. Two 1′ writings; try to reach your 15″ goals for the entire minute.

all letters used | A | 1.5 si | 5.7 awl | 80% hfw

Most codes of ethics require workers to sign an itemized statement each year to certify they are handling business in an ethical and just way. The statement usually deals with conflicts of interest which may arise when, for example, a worker accepts an unjust cash payment, favor, or present from someone who is doing or wishes to do business with the company.

103c ▶ 14 Measure Keyboarding Skill: Straight Copy

1. Two 3′ writings; find *gwam,* circle errors on each writing.
2. One 5′ writing; find *gwam,* circle errors. **Goal:** To maintain 3′ rate for 5′.
3. Record better 3′ rate and the 5′ rate.
4. Compare these rates with those you recorded in 101d.

all letters used | A | 1.5 si | 5.7 awl | 80% hfw

	gwam 3′	5′	
Appearance, which is often defined as the outward aspect of someone	5	3	43
or something, is quite important to most of us and affects just about	9	6	46
every day of our lives. We like to be around people who and things which	14	8	48
we consider attractive. Because of this preference, appearance is a	19	11	51
factor in almost every decision we make.	22	13	53
Appearance often affects our selection of food, the place in which	26	16	56
we live, the clothes we purchase, the car we drive, and the vacations we	31	19	59
schedule. For example, we usually do not eat foods which are not visu-	36	21	61
ally appealing or buy clothing that we realize will be unattractive to	40	24	64
others who are important to us.	43	26	66
Appearance is important in business. People in charge of hiring	47	28	68
almost always stress the important of a good appearance. Your progress	52	31	71
in a job or career can be affected by how others judge your appearance.	57	34	74
It is not uncommon for whose who see but do not know you to evaluate	61	37	77
your abilities and character on the basis of your personal appearance.	66	40	80

```
login:  MBurns
password:  Goodguy
Mon Nov 9 13:47:58 EST 1992
mail
To:  CMiller, RPolk
Subject:  Revision of Personnel Handbook

Recent changes have been made in the laws regarding fair and
equitable treatment of employees regardless of race, sex,
religion, or age.  As a result, we must review our Personnel
Handbook and make necessary changes.

Please review the new regulations which are located in Data
Base Files 231.2 and 247.5 in preparation for a conference
in my office at 1500 hours on November 23.

end-of-file
What next?  send
logout
```

Electronic Message

Lesson 184 Electronic Messages

184a ▶ 5 Conditioning Practice

each line twice SS (slowly, then faster); if time permits, take 1′ writings on line 1

alphabet 1 Five boys and six girls worked hard to equip and customize the jalopy.

figures 2 Model No. 539077 will be manufactured in sizes 10, 12, 14, 16, and 18.

fig/sym 3 The invoice shows that Brogan & Co. shipped #869 on 3/24/91, not #570.

speed 4 Blanche kept both of the keys to the auto with the maps of the island.

| 1 | 2 | 3 | 4 | 5 | 6 | 7 | 8 | 9 | 10 | 11 | 12 | 13 | 14 |

184b ▶ 45 Format Electronic Messages

Note: A "data base" is an electronic encyclopedia in which important information is stored in computer memory.

Message 1
LP p. 91
PB (page beginning): line 7;
LL: 60 spaces

1. Key the electronic message shown above. If you make an error, backspace and strike the correct key.

2. When you have completed the message, refer to the directions on p. 318. Underline, in pencil, those prompts which were provided by the system; circle the prompts the sender used; and draw a line through the item which, although keyed, would not appear on the screen.

For those using plain paper:
Key the electronic message above exactly as shown, including the prompts provided by the system. Then follow the directions given in Step 2.

Message 2
LP p. 93
PB: line 7; LL: 60 spaces

1. Assume that you have received the electronic message above and find that you have another meeting scheduled at 1500 hours on November 23.

2. Compose a reply to MBurns. Use your name to login and a nickname as the password. Prompt the system to mail a message to MBurns with the subject: Meeting to Revise Personnel Handbook.

3. In the message, tell MBurns that you have an important meeting of the Executive Committee at 1500 hours on November 23 and will not be able to attend his conference to discuss changes in the Personnel Handbook. Ask him if he can set another date and time.

4. Close the message (end-of-file), instruct the system to send it, and then logout.

5. If you make an error, backspace and strike the correct key.

For those using plain paper:
Key the prompts as shown in the model above as you compose the message to MBurns. Follow the directions given in Steps 2 through 6.

103d ▶ 5 Improve Language Skills

LL: 70 spaces; SS with DS between 3-line groups

1. Read and key the **Learn** sentence (with number and period), noting how the rule has been applied.
2. Key the **Apply** sentences (with numbers and periods), using the correct punctuation.
3. If time permits, key the **Apply** lines again at a faster speed to quicken decision-making skill.

EXCLAMATION POINT

> Use an exclamation mark after emphatic exclamations and after phrases and sentences that are clearly exclamatory.

Learn 1. Kevin yelled excitedly, "Whew, what a run!"
Apply 2. As we reached the top, Kim said breathlessly, "What a pretty view."
Apply 3. At halftime, Jeffry said with enthusiasm, "What an exciting game."

QUESTION MARK

> Use a question mark at the end of a sentence that is a direct question; however, use a period after a request that appears in the form of a question.

Learn 4. Do you know how to move text within a document?
Learn 5. Will you stay after class to help me with my assignment.
Apply 6. Will you try to find the book for me by tomorrow.
Apply 7. Did you stay awake during the late movie.

103e ▶ 18 Improve Skill Transfer: Rough Draft

1. Two 1′ writings on each ¶ for speed; find *gwam* on each writing.
2. One 1′ writing on each ¶ for control; circle errors on each writing.
3. One 3′ writing on ¶s 1-3 combined; find *gwam;* circle errors. If you finish before time is called, start over.

all letters used | A | 1.5 si | 5.7 awl | 80% hfw

	gwam 1′	3′
Reputation is the image people have aobut your stan-	11	4
dards of conduct; your ethical and morale principals. Most	22	7
people think that a good reputation is needed to succeed in	35	12
any job; and it is therefore one of the most importnat per-	47	16
sonal assets you can acquire in your life.	56	19
A good reputation is a valued asset that requires time,	11	22
effort, and discipline to develop and project. A bad reputa-	24	26
tion can be a longterm liability established in a short time	38	31
period. It can be a result from just one misdeed and can be a	48	34
heavy burden to carry throughout life.	56	37
It is important to realize that most of you have an op-	11	41
portunity to develope and protect the reputation you want.	22	45
You have many chioces to make which will destroy or enhance	34	49
the image you want to extned. The choices are hard; and hon-	47	53
esty, loyalty, and dedicatoin are most often involved.	58	56

gwam												
3′	1	2	3	4	5	6	7	8	9	10	11	12
5′		1			2			3			4	

REVERE SILVERSMITHS

1242 Delaware Avenue • Buffalo, NY 14209-6358 • (716) 438-7400

		words in parts	total words
	February 8, 19-- DS	3	3
Mailing notation	CERTIFIED DS	5	5
Attention line	Attention Mr. Arnold Bishop	10	10
	King Department Store	15	15
	800 Broad Street	19	19
	Chattanooga, TN 37402-1905 DS	24	24
	Ladies and Gentlemen DS	29	29
Subject line	SILVER FOR WEDDINGS DS	<u>32</u>	32
	We are pleased to announce a special sale of silver items espe-	12	45
	cially for weddings. The sale includes personal gift items for	25	58
	attendants such as money clips and perfume bottles as well as tra-	38	71
	ditional gift items for the bride and groom. You will find an	51	83
	interesting array of merchandise in the enclosed catalog. DS	63	95
	As one of our preferred customers, we are offering you a special	76	108
	discount of 10% on all silver wedding items ordered no later than	89	121
	April 15. This discount is in addition to the regular discounts	102	134
	we offer for payment of invoices within 10 or 30 days. DS	113	145
	The enclosed special order blank identifies you as a preferred	126	158
	customer. After you have reviewed the outstanding bargains we	138	171
	offer, complete the order blank and return it without delay. Miss	152	184
	Marylou Simpson of our Shipping Department has been alerted to	164	197
	process your order immediately upon receipt. DS	<u>173</u>	205
	Sincerely DS	2	207
Company name in closing lines	REVERE SILVERSMITHS QS	6	211
	E. Martin Bronson		
	E. Martin Bronson	10	215
	Sales Manager DS	12	218
	mb DS	13	218
Listed enclosures	Enclosures SS	15	221
	Catalog	17	222
	Special Order Blank DS	21	226
Copy notation	c Marylou Simpson DS	24	230
Postscript	If you need additional order blanks, please call my office and we	38	243
	will mail them to you promptly.	44	249

Letter with Special Features

UNIT 24 LESSONS 104 – 106

Extend Letter Processing Skills

Learning Goals

1. To improve skill in processing block and modified block format letters using open or mixed punctuation.
2. To improve skill in processing letters with special features.
3. To use the ALL CAP, unpunctuated format for formatting letter and envelope addresses.

Format Guides

1. Paper guide at *0* (for typewriters).
2. LL: 70 spaces, or as directed.
3. LS: SS word and drill lines; space letters as directed.
4. PI: 5 spaces, when appropriate.

Lesson 104 *Processing Letters*

104a ▶ 5 Conditioning Practice

each line twice SS (slowly, then faster); DS between 2-line groups; as time permits, rekey selected lines

alphabet 1 Gwen's six jumpers quickly seize every chance to practice before dawn.
fig/sym 2 Sam will pay $1,954 for the 16-MHz EP/37 PC which is 80286-compatible.
shift key 3 Tom and Jim wanted LT/PCs; Sue wanted the WO/PC with a Q-Tron printer.
speed 4 They may do the handiwork for the panel with the usual vigor and rush.

| 1 | 2 | 3 | 4 | 5 | 6 | 7 | 8 | 9 | 10 | 11 | 12 | 13 | 14 |

104b ▶ 15 Composing Letter Formatting Features

Read the questions at the right. Compose a complete sentence answer for each. If needed, refer to Letter Formatting Guide on p. 76. Number your answers as you key them. SS the lines of answers; DS between answers. X-out or strike over keyboarding errors you may make as you compose.

1. How many words may be in the body of an average-length letter?
2. How wide (in inches) should the left margin be for a long letter?
3. How wide (in pica spaces) should the left margin be for a short letter?
4. On what line should the date be keyed for a short letter?
5. What punctuation style uses a colon after the salutation?
6. What letter part follows the last line of the letter body?
7. What salutation is used if the letter is addressed to a company?
8. How many lines below the dateline should the letter address be keyed?
9. What letter part follows the writer's title?
10. How wide (in elite spaces) should the left margin be for an average-length letter?

104c ▶ 15 Format Short Letters

plain full sheets

Letter 1--Block format, open punctuation; do not correct errors; use proofreader's marks to identify errors.

Letter 2--Modified block format; mixed punctuation; do not correct errors; use proofreader's marks to identify errors.

Letter 3--Prepare a copy of Letter 1 from the rough-draft copy. Correct all errors.

words

February 10, 19--| Ms. Jane Z. Cawlfield | Sales Representative | Micro-World, 15
Inc. | 89 - 54th Street, SW | Grand Rapids, MI 49508-5699 | Dear Ms. Cawlfield 29

The business teachers at South High are pleased that you will speak at a 44
school-wide assembly on March 3, 19--, from 1:30 to 2:30 p.m. 56

Your presentation on how computers are used in local business and industry 71
will be of great benefit. Further, more students may see the wisdom of de- 86
veloping keyboarding and computer application skills after listening to what 102
you say. 104

Sincerely | Miss Thelma C. Scott | Department Head | xx 113

183a ▶ 5 Conditioning Practice

each line twice SS (slowly, then faster); if time permits, take 1′ writings on line 1

alphabet	1	Vic asked him to take the job of awarding prizes for quality exhibits.
figures	2	Items 72, 465, 825, 934, 1068, and 1739 were removed from the catalog.
fig/sym	3	Their 1987 rates ranged from 6 3/4% to 10 1/5% (an average of 8 1/2%).
speed	4	If the firm pays half of the penalty, the men may also pay their half.

| 1 | 2 | 3 | 4 | 5 | 6 | 7 | 8 | 9 | 10 | 11 | 12 | 13 | 14 |

183b ▶ 45 Format Letters with Special Features

Letter 1
plain paper

1. Study the guides on p. 318 for formatting letters with special features.

2. Key the letter on p. 320 with 1″ side margins, and key the date on line 12. Correct errors.

Letter 2
LP p. 89
block format; SM: 1″; PB: line 14

1. Key the letter shown at the right. Use open punctuation.

2. Send the letter by **SPECIAL DELIVERY** to the attention of **Miss Rose M. Chan** with the subject line: **YOUR ORDER 45821A.** Provide an appropriate salutation and complimentary close. Correct errors.

Letter 3
plain paper
SM: 1″; PB: line 14

1. Key the letter at the right in modified block format, open punctuation. Provide an appropriate salutation and complimentary close. Correct errors.

2. Use the company name in the closing lines: **ASSOCIATION OF OFFICE MANAGERS,** list the enclosures, and indicate that a copy of the letter has been sent to **Mrs. Carla F. Fernandez.**

3. Add the following postscript: **If you have received these publications previously, please accept these copies with our compliments.**

words*

March 28, 19-- Bronson Jewelers, Inc. 702 Broadway Street Denver, CO 23
80203-4117 33

The silver ornaments you ordered on February 15 have been delayed because 48
the special silver alloy required for these ornaments has not been received 63
from our supplier. We now anticipate that the silver will be received no 78
later than April 10. 82

Normally, a special order of this nature requires at least ten days to process. 98
In view of the situation, however, we will expedite the manufacture of your 114
ornaments and will complete your order in a maximum of five days after 128
receipt of the silver. 133

Thank you for your patience in this matter. If all goes well, we will ship 148
your ornaments by air express no later than April 15. 159

Ms. Lisa T. Scott 164
Marketing Manager 168/**190**

September 26, 19-- Mr. Frank P. Dalton 90 Spring Street Portland, ME 14
04101-7430 19

It has come to my attention that several of the publications you ordered in 34
August may not have arrived as yet. According to the enclosed copy of your 50
order, Items 3765A, 4890B, and 5021X have not yet been shipped. 63

Normally, orders received by the Association of Office Managers are pro- 77
cessed within 10 days of receipt. Because of a computer problem, however, 92
it appears that some orders in August may not have been completed. 105

A copy of Item 3765A is enclosed. Copies of 4890B and 5021X will be sent 120
priority mail within the next few days by Mrs. Carla F. Fernandez, chief of 135
special orders. 139

We appreciate your interest in our publications and thank you for your 153
patronage. 155

Brian E. Miller 168
Director of Publications 204/**216**

***Note:** Words in letter parts added to the letter are included in the word count at the right of the letter.

104d ▶ 15 Process Average-Length Letters

plain full sheets

supply appropriate salutations; correct all errors

Letter 1--modified block format with indented ¶s; mixed punctuation

Letter 2--Reformat Letter 1 using block format; open punctuation. Address letter to

Dr. Martin K. Jobbs
Superintendent
Highland School District
1727 Hurd Drive
Irving, TX 75038-4309

words

May 10, 19--|Mrs. Donna W. Wells|School Board President|Highland School District|1727 Hurd Drive|Irving, TX 75038-4309|Dear Mrs. Wells 27

Computer literacy is an important concern that I believe should be addressed by the Highland School District. It is important to our students while in school and will be even more important to them upon graduation. 71

The level of computer literacy varies with the grade level of the student. At the elementary level it may involve the use of tutorial software to improve learning. For high school students it may mean the use of word processing, spreadsheet, database, and other software. For all students it should include the ability to operate the keyboard by touch. 142

I hope the recently appointed curriculum committee will put improving computer literacy at the top of its priority list. 167

Sincerely|Robert L. Harris, President|Instantcare Health Services|xx 180

Lesson 105 Processing Letters

105a ▶ 5 Conditioning Practice

each line twice SS (slowly, then faster); DS between 2-line groups; if time permits, rekey selected lines

alphabet 1 Gwen just froze the bread, chickens, pork, veal, quiche, and six yams.

figures 2 Sheila was told to call Ruth around 5:30 p.m. at 264-8498 or 264-7130.

shift key 3 Fred O'Barsky plans to advertise on WPCI-TV and KWPA-AM/FM this month.

speed 4 An auditor on the panel did not sign a key element of the small audit.

| 1 | 2 | 3 | 4 | 5 | 6 | 7 | 8 | 9 | 10 | 11 | 12 | 13 | 14 |

105b ▶ 15 Preapplication Drill: Formatting Letter Parts

2 plain full sheets
LL: 1½" SM
PB: line 16

1. Review the block format model letter on p. 78.
2. On a full sheet and at the signal to begin, space to line 16 and key the opening lines of Drill 1.
3. After keying the salutation, return 12 times and key the closing lines.
4. Complete Drill 2 in the same way after reviewing the modified block format model letter on p. 137.
5. Do not correct errors.

Drill 1: Block format; open punctuation

March 10, 19--
QS

Attention Mr. John P. Steffan
Stocker & Juarez, Inc.
430 Branner Street, SE
Topeka, KS 66607-1899
DS
Ladies and Gentlemen
DS
AGREEMENT #97-1253-46-AA

Space down 12 times (using INDEX or RETURN) to allow for body of letter.

Sincerely yours
DS
K & N SALES AND SERVICE
QS

Mrs. Marianne A. Perez, Director
DS
pjc
DS
pc Betty M. Gleaner

Drill 2: Modified block format; mixed punctuation

April 30, 19--
DS
REGISTERED MAIL
DS
Mr. Edwin H. Whitman
Greene Trucking Co.
3200 Grand Street
Wichita, KS 67218-2923
DS
Dear Mr. Whitman:

Space down 12 times (using INDEX or RETURN) to allow for body of letter.

Sincerely,
QS

Ms. Sue P. Mori, Manager
DS
upj
DS
Enclosure
DS
Will you need a hotel room for three evenings?

UNIT 43 LESSONS 183 – 187

Learn to Format Messages with Special Features

Learning Goals

1. To learn how to process letters with special features.

2. To learn how to process form letters with variables.

3. To learn how to format messages to be sent by electronic mail.

4. To build production skill on messages with special features.

Format Guides

1. Paper guide at *0* (for typewriters).

2. LL: 70 spaces for drill copy; as directed for documents.

3. LS: SS drill lines with a DS between groups; space documents as directed or required.

4. PI: 5 spaces, when appropriate.

FORMATTING GUIDES: MESSAGES WITH SPECIAL FEATURES

ASSOCIATION OF OFFICE MANAGERS
538 JUNIPER CIRCLE GOLDEN, CO 80403-6249 (303) 930-7749

September 26, 19--

Mr. Frank P. Dalton
90 Spring Street
Portland, ME 04101-7430

Dear Mr. Dalton

It has come to my attention that several of the publications you ordered in August may not have arrived as yet. According to the enclosed copy of your order, Items 3765A, 4890B, and 5021X have not yet been shipped.

Normally, orders received by the Association of Office Managers are processed within 10 days of receipt. Because of a computer problem, however, it appears that some orders in August may not have been completed.

A copy of Item 3765A is enclosed. Copies of 4890B and 5021X will be sent priority mail within the next few days by Mrs. Carla F. Fernandez, chief of special orders.

We appreciate your interest in our publications and thank you for your patronage.

Sincerely yours

ASSOCIATION OF OFFICE MANAGERS

Brian E. Miller

Brian E. Miller
Director of Publications

xx

Enclosures
Order
Item 3765A

c Mrs. Carla F. Fernandez

If you have received these publications previously, please accept these copies with our compliments.

Letter with Special Features

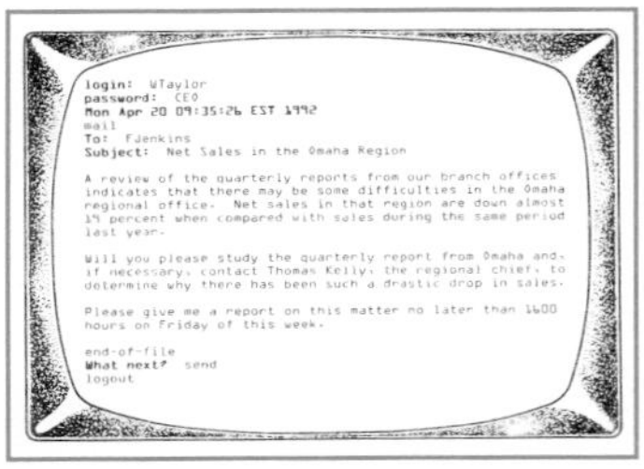

Electronic Mail

Letters with Special Features

Features which serve special purposes may be used in a letter as follows.

Mailing notations. A mailing notation such as CERTIFIED MAIL or SPECIAL DELIVERY is placed at the left margin a DS below the date, followed by a DS.

Attention line. The attention line is used to call the letter to the attention of a specific person, department, or job title (Attention Ms. Barr). It is keyed as the first line of the address.

Subject line. A subject line identifies the content of the letter and may be placed at the left margin, indented as the ¶s, or centered a DS below the salutation.

Company name in closing lines. A company name is keyed in ALL CAPS a DS below and aligned under the complimentary close, followed by a QS.

Listed enclosures. Enclosures are placed at the left margin a DS below the reference initials. Key the word "Enclosures" and then list each enclosure below SS, three spaces from the left margin, or key a colon after the word "Enclosures," space twice, and list each enclosure one beneath the other.

Copy notation. A copy notation is indicated with a "c" for either a carbon copy or a photocopy, and is placed at the left margin a DS below the reference initials (or enclosures), followed by the person's name. If more than one name is shown, list them SS one under the other or on the same line separated by a comma.

Postscript. A postscript is a message added at the end of a letter. It is placed a DS below the last reference line in the same manner as the ¶s in the body of the letter. (The abbreviation P.S. is no longer widely used.)

Electronic Mail

Electronic mail is any method of communication that involves sending text or facsimiles of documents electronically. E-Mail can be transmitted from one computer to another in the same system.

There are many different mail systems, and few of them use exactly the same procedures in processing electronic mail. Most systems provide or respond to "prompts" which indicate information required or action to be taken.

The steps below illustrate, in a general way, a simple E-Mail system. (See illustrative screen on page 321.) The system prompts are shown in italics.

1. The system prompts the sender to *login* which may be done by entering the sender's first initial and last name: "MBurns."

2. The sender is then prompted to enter his or her *password*. This may be any combination of characters or a nickname, such as "Goodguy." For security reasons, the password, when keyed, does not appear on the screen.

3. The system now shows the day, date, and time of login: "Mon Nov 9 13:47:58 EST 1992." Note: For time, the 24-hour clock is used in which the hours are numbered from 0100 (1 a.m.) to 2400 (midnight). 13:47:58, therefore, is 1:47 and 58 seconds p.m.

4. The sender then keys in a prompt, such as *mail*, to indicate that he/she wishes to send a message.

5. The system prompts *To* and the sender indicates the name or names: "CMiller, RPolk."

6. The system then prompts *Subject* and the sender enters the subject of the message: "Revision of Personnel Handbook."

7. After the message has been keyed, the sender enters *end-of-file*.

8. The system then prompts *What next?* The sender can now edit the message, delete it, or send it by keying *send*.

9. To complete the session, the sender enters *logout* to log off the system.

105c ▶ 30
Reinforce Letter Processing Skills

LP pp. 55-59

correct errors; address envelopes

Letter 1
modified block format; mixed punctuation

words

March 3, 19--|Attention Miss Terry L. Ely|Valley Area High School|375 14
Baker Street|Jamestown, NY 14701-7598|Ladies and Gentlemen:|SUBJECT: 26
ADVANCED STANDING CREDIT FOR CYNTHIA BAXTER 35

Ms. Cynthia Baxter, a Valley Area High School senior, completed an ad- 49
vanced standing examination at Jamestown Business Institute (JBI) last 63
week at the freshman orientation session. 72

As a result of Cynthia's high school data processing studies, she is able to be- 88
gin her JBI computer studies at the intermediate level. In addition, she will 103
receive three credits toward a degree. 111

I want to congratulate Cynthia and her data processing teacher for their out- 127
standing accomplishments in the data processing area. (102) 138

Sincerely,|Robert L. Carr|Admission Counselor|xx|pc Dr. Ray M. Ness 151/**170**

Letter 2
block format; open punctuation

Letter 3
Reformat Letter 1 using block format and open punctuation.

Letter 4
Use plain full sheet and reformat Letter 2 using modified block format with indented ¶s and open punctuation.

March 5, 19--|Attention Nursing Director|Computer Institute|960 Pembroke 15
Street|New Rochelle, NY 10801-3127|Ladies and Gentlemen 26

Enclosed is a signed copy of the Memorandum of Understanding agreement 40
between Computer Institute and New Rochelle Health Systems. As requested, 55
I have retained a copy for my files and am forwarding one copy to you. 70

If you have any questions regarding this agreement, please call me. (57) 83

Sincerely|NEW ROCHELLE HEALTH SYSTEMS|Fred F. Valdez|President|xx| 97
Enclosure|I will mark my calendar to remind me to contact you in 90 days to 112
discuss extending the agreement for another six months. 123/**142**

Lesson 106 Processing Letters

106a ▶ 5
Conditioning Practice

each line twice SS (slowly, then faster); DS between 2-line groups; if time permits, rekey selected lines

alphabet 1 A new expert may organize both journal displays quickly for the event.
fig/sym 2 D & L Shops cashed in Policy #2847-08 for $15,986 on October 30, 1991.
shift key 3 T. J. Wurtz expects S & L Co. to merge with ROBO, a subsidiary of TMW.
speed 4 Make the panel suspend the pay of their city officials as the penalty.

| 1 | 2 | 3 | 4 | 5 | 6 | 7 | 8 | 9 | 10 | 11 | 12 | 13 | 14 |

106b ▶ 5
Improve Language Skills: Word Choice

1. Study the spelling and definition of each word.

2. Key the line number (with period), space twice, then key the **Learn** sentence; key the **Apply** sentences in the same format, selecting the correct word in parentheses to complete each sentence.

dual (adj) composed of two parts; double

duel (n) a struggle between two contending persons, groups, or ideas

fair (adj) just, equitable, visually beautiful or admirable

fare (n) a transportation charge

Learn 1. The duel between Jim and Harry served a dual purpose.
Apply 2. The unions' (dual, duel) may affect taxes for trucks with (dual, duel) axles.

Learn 3. Mary Ann thought the taxi fare was not fair for such a short trip.
Apply 4. I paid the (fare, fair) and then sat back to enjoy the (fare, fair) sky.

182a ▶ 5 Conditioning Practice

each line twice SS (slowly, then faster); DS between 2-line groups; if time permits, take 1′ writings on line 3

alphabet 1 Jen is working very hard to examine and publicize quotes from my book.

figures 2 The group will meet on June 28 to discuss Articles 10, 36, 75, and 94.

fig/sym 3 Of Lot #4763A, 25% (180 units) was rejected at a total cost of $2,390.

speed 4 If they wish me to do so, I may rush the hen turkeys and ducks by air.

| 1 | 2 | 3 | 4 | 5 | 6 | 7 | 8 | 9 | 10 | 11 | 12 | 13 | 14 |

182b ▶ 20 Improve Language Skills: Proofread/Correct

1. In each sentence at the right, items have been underlined. The underlines indicate that there *may* be an error in spelling, punctuation, capitalization, grammar, or word/figure usage.

2. Study each sentence carefully, then key the line (with number and period). If an underlined item is incorrect, correct it as you key the sentence. Also, correct any keyboarding errors you may make.

1. She said, "the committee did not follow it's agenda."
2. There will be adequate accomodations in our office in the south.
3. You're Doctor reported that nearly 1/2 of the group has the virus.
4. The delegates at the womens' conference past the rules unanimously.
5. Neither man are elligible to be chief of the personel division.
6. He declared; "The employee don't want to make a serious commitment."
7. At an apropriate time, we will review the book "Office Automation."
8. In my judgement, Joe was quite adapt in his work, he was fast to.
9. The pole showed that about 6% of the participants were absent.
10. We thought it was a posibility that Adams's study would win.
11. Prier to the meeting, we must impliment project X for there benefit.
12. In the absence of the jury panal, the Judge reviewed the calender.
13. Each of the men have their annual commission reports to prepare.
14. The subject of the correspondance was the currant 5 year plan.
15. Pursuent to her memo, new carpet was layed in rooms 986 and 1,020.

182c ▶ 10 Improve Keystroking Skills: Figures and Symbols

Take four 1′ writings on each ¶. Work for accuracy, especially when keying figures/symbols.

gwam 1′

The Consumer Price Index (CPI) measures changes in our buying power. 14
For comparison purposes, the cost of 400 items in 1967 was used as the 28
base and given a value of 100. Prices are collected monthly in 85 areas 43
from over 25,000 tenants, 20,000 owners, and about 32,400 establishments. 57

As an historic example, the CPI in 1980 was 246.8--an increase of 13
146.8% since 1967. In 1986, the CPI was 331.1--an increase of 84.3% 27
in just 6 years. In terms of dollars, the items that cost $100 to buy 41
in 1967 rose to $331.10 in 1986--an increase of 231.1%. 52

gwam 1′ | 1 | 2 | 3 | 4 | 5 | 6 | 7 | 8 | 9 | 10 | 11 | 12 | 13 | 14 |

182d ▶ 15 Improve Basic Keyboarding Skills

1. Two 1′ writings on each ¶ of 181c, p. 316. Find *gwam* and circle errors on each.

2. One 5′ writing on the three ¶s combined. Find *gwam* and circle errors; record scores.

Goals: To increase speed on 5′ writing by at least 2 *gwam* with fewer errors when compared with 181c.

106c ▶ 40
Reinforce Letter Processing Skills

LP pp. 61-67
or plain full sheets
correct errors; address envelopes

Letter 1
block format; open punctuation

Use ALL CAP, unpunctuated format for letter address. If necessary, refer to formatting guide on p. 83.

Letter 2
Reformat Letter 1 using modified block format, open punctuation. Do not use ALL CAP, unpunctuated format for the letter address.

words

April 10, 19-- | Attention Mrs. Luze L. Sanchez | Compuworks | 7110 Claasen Ave- 15
nue | Cleveland, OH 44105-5023 | Dear Mrs. Sanchez | SUBJECT: GRADUATE 28
FOLLOW UP QUESTIONNAIRE 33

It hardly seems possible that six months have passed since Maria Deucsh 47
began working for your company as a word processor. 58

As you may recall, our department tries to find out how graduates of Central 73
High School perform in the business world. We gain valuable information 88
from these studies which enables us to evaluate the success of our program 103
and helps us keep the content of our courses current and relevant. In addi- 118
tion, it provides us with employment information we can pass on to our 132
students. 134

Would you have Maria's supervisor complete the enclosed questionnaire so 149
we can learn about Maria's progress and other items pertaining to Central 164
High. Please return the questionnaire in the enclosed envelope. 177

Thank you; we look forward to placing some of our other graduates with 191
Compuworks. (160) 194

Sincerely yours | Ronald W. Thomas, Jr. | Business Department Chair | xx | 207
Enclosures | pc Guidance Office | If you could use a student on a co-op assign- 222
ment, please call me. 226/**243**

Letter 3
Modified block format with indented ¶s, mixed punctuation.

Use ALL CAP, unpunctuated format for letter address. Address letter to

Attention Office Ed. Dept.
Woodward High School
101 Ash Street
San Diego, CA 92101-3096

Letter 4
Reformat Letter 3 using block format, open punctuation.

Use ALL CAP, unpunctuated format for letter address. Address letter to

Attention Office Ed. Dept.
Central High School
1707 Wood Street
Oakland, CA 94607-2514

Supply appropriate salutation; change copy notation to "c Principal."

Ladies & Gentlemen

address 18

April 10, 19-- / SUBJECT: KEYBOARDING COMMITTEE MEETING 31

¶ The Keyboarding Task Force will meet at the San Diego 42
Airport Hotel at 10:00 a.m. on Wednesday, April 15, 19--. 53
¶ Please plan to join us so we can review the sur- 63
vey results relating to the need for touch keyboarding 74
skills in various occupational fields. A copy of the 84
results are enclosed. 89
¶ A quick review of the data reveals that respondents 99
from many different occupational areas indicate a 109
need for employees to have touch keyboarding skills 120
to operate computer keyboards efficiently and effectively. 132
Once confirmed, this finding can be the basis for the con- 143
clusion that each student, regardless of expected career, 155
should learn touch keyboarding in school. (132) 163

Yours truly, / Ms. Elisa T. Witt / Task Force Chair / XX / 173
Enclosure / c Dr. Geoff W. Hurd, Principal / We'll have 184
a "Dutch Treat" lunch at the hotel. 191/**209**

181c ▶ 15 Improve Basic Keyboarding Skills

Take two 5′ writings on the ¶s at the right. Record *gwam* and errors.

Note: In the broadest sense, the word *telecommunications* describes the transmission of data by any electronic means. A computer can send messages to other computers provided that the computers are on the same network or system.

all letters used | A | 1.5 si | 5.7 awl | 80% hfw

	gwam 1′	5′	
In the field of word processing, there are a number of levels of	13	3	61
jobs. A trainee, for example, is an entry-level position which calls	27	5	63
for good keyboarding and communications skills. The person must also be	42	8	66
able to follow directions, have the ability to use reference materials	56	11	69
of many kinds, and get along well with others. A trainee must be pre-	70	14	72
pared to produce documents in the proper format, to proofread all work	84	17	75
carefully, and to maintain a record of production each day or week.	97	19	77
A word processing operator is the next step up in the organiza-	13	22	80
tion. An operator is one who has been on the job a year or two and is	27	25	83
able to key text-editing functions quickly in order to turn out many	41	28	86
types of documents. A word processing specialist, on the other hand,	55	30	88
is one who can format, revise, and produce complex papers such as long	69	33	91
technical or scientific reports from many sources. Further, a special-	83	36	94
ist may process mail by means of a telecommunications system.	95	39	96
A word processing supervisor must be a very versatile person. He	13	41	99
or she must have the ability to make work schedules, assign work to the	28	44	102
operators, keep in touch with users, check all work for errors, keep a	42	47	105
record of work completed, and make changes in procedures when they are	56	50	108
needed. A word processing manager, at the top level, must plan, orga-	70	53	111
nize, control, and direct the overall activities of the center to insure	85	55	113
that all work is accomplished in a timely and efficient manner.	97	58	116

gwam 1′ | 1 | 2 | 3 | 4 | 5 | 6 | 7 | 8 | 9 | 10 | 11 | 12 | 13 | 14 |
5′ | 1 | 2 | 3 |

181d ▶ 10 Improve Keystroking Skills: Figures

Key each sentence twice *by touch.* Proofread and circle errors; then repeat the sentences in which you made the most errors in figures, if time permits.

1 The special committee will meet on May 14, 17, 19, 25, 26, 28, and 30.
2 Please correct the errors on pages 10, 61, 94, 105, 127, 132, and 189.
3 On June 28, we made 5,714 units, but on June 29 made only 3,806 units.
4 Place these figures in Column 1: 987, 1,605, 2,734, 3,806, and 5,192.
5 In 1987, they had only 2,653 employees; in 1989, 7,146; today, 10,540.
6 Locate cars with serial numbers 16328, 20597, 37546, 48190, and 52460.
7 Items 639510, 748029, 762513, 842501, and 963874 are not now in stock.
8 The population of the city grew from 934,575 to 1,860,273 in 20 years.

| 1 | 2 | 3 | 4 | 5 | 6 | 7 | 8 | 9 | 10 | 11 | 12 | 13 | 14 |

UNIT 25 *LESSONS 107 – 113*

Extend Table Processing Skills

Learning Goals

1. To improve skill in centering material horizontally and vertically on paper of different sizes.
2. To improve skill in formatting tables with single- and multiple-line headings, source notes, and totals.
3. To improve language-skill ability.

Format Guides

1. Paper guide at *0* (for typewriters).
2. LL: 70-space line, or as directed.
3. LS: SS word and drill lines; space tables as directed.
4. PI: 5 spaces, when appropriate.

FORMATTING GUIDES: TABLES

Table Spacing Summary

Double-Space (DS):

1. Below all heading lines.
2. Above and below column headings.
3. Column entries when so directed.
4. Above and below source note ruling separating column entries from source notes.
5. Above column TOTALS, when used.

Single-Space (SS):

1. Column entries when so directed.
2. Multiple-line column headings.

Vertical Placement

Step 1: Count all lines to be used in table (including all blank line spaces).

Step 2: Subtract this figure from total lines available on sheet. **Note.** Most machines have six line spaces to the vertical inch; therefore, paper 8½″ × 11″ has 66 vertical line spaces (11 × 6).

Step 3: Divide remainder by 2 to determine the number of the line on which to key the main heading. If a fraction results, disregard it. If the number that results is

EVEN, space down that number from the top;

ODD, use next lower even number.

Note. This means that the main heading of a table will always begin on an even number.

Horizontal Placement of Columns Using Backspace-from-Center Method

Step 1: Move margin stops to ends of scale and clear all tab stops.

Step 2: From the horizontal center of sheet, backspace once for each 2 strokes in the longest line in each column (carry over to the next column any extra stroke at the end of a column but ignore any extra stroke at the end of the last column); then backspace once for each 2 spaces to be left between columns. **Note.** As center point of paper 8½″ wide, use 42 for pica; 51 for elite.

Step 3: Set left margin stop at point where backspacing ends.

Step 4: From the left margin stop, space forward once for each stroke in the longest line in the first column, and once for each space to be left between the first and second columns. Set a tab stop at this point for the start of the second column. Continue procedure for any additional columns.

Spacing Between Columns

As a general rule, leave an even number of spaces between columns (4, 6, 8, 10 or more).

Column Headings

When used, column headings are often centered over the longest line in the column. When the column heading is the longest line in the column, other lines are centered under it.

lines used			
1		REGISTERED STUDENTS	
2			
3		Course	
4	Name	Number	Code
5			
6	Mary Jones	E101	3T
7			
8	Charles Harris	E106	7P
9			
10	Mark Stevens	G205	4C
11			
12	Sue Booth	A443	1W
13			
14	________________		
15			
16	Source: Registrar, July 15, 19--.		

If a table has single- and multiple-line headings (see model above), the bottom line of each multiple-line heading is placed on the same line as the single-line headings. The lines of multiple-line headings are single-spaced.

Horizontal/Vertical Placement with a Word Processor/Computer

Horizontal. Word processors/computers usually have a function which can be used to simplify horizontal centering. You should refer to the *User's Manual* to see how this function works on your equipment. On most, a trial line (consisting of the longest line in each column plus the spaces between the columns) is keyed on the screen before or after a center function is used. After the trial line is keyed and centered, set left margin or tab stop at the beginning of each column. Delete the trial line; then key the table using the margin and tab stops.

Vertical. If your equipment has a vertical centering function key, refer to your *User's Manual* to see how it works. If not, determine the vertical line on which the last line of the table ends after it is keyed. Subtract this line number from the lines on the paper and divide the answer by 2. If necessary, round this answer to the next lower even number and then insert this number of blank lines above the first line of the table.

UNIT 42 LESSONS 181 – 182

Improve Keyboarding and Language Skills

Learning Goals

1. To improve basic keyboarding skills with emphasis on figures and symbols.
2. To increase keystroking speed and to improve accuracy on straight copy.
3. To improve communications skills.

Format Guides

1. Paper guide at *0* (for typewriters).
2. LL: 70 spaces for drills, paragraphs, and language skills.
3. LS: SS sentence drills with DS between sets; DS paragraph writings; DS language skill sentences.

Lesson 181 *Keyboarding and Language Skills*

181a ▶ 5 Conditioning Practice

each line twice SS (slowly, then faster); if time permits, take 1′ writings on line 3

alphabet 1 Jacques knew I might receive sizable rebates for taxes paid last year.
figures 2 Stereo music can be heard on 82.1, 96.5, 104.3, and 105.7 on the dial.
fig/sym 3 Costs in 1990 (based on final reports) rose $147,865 or 23% over 1989.
speed 4 The cubicle held a giant map of the world and a big map of the Orient.

| 1 | 2 | 3 | 4 | 5 | 6 | 7 | 8 | 9 | 10 | 11 | 12 | 13 | 14 |

181b ▶ 20 Improve Language Skills: Commonly Confused Words

1. Study the spelling and definitions of each pair of words.
2. Key the **Learn** line (with number and period) noting the proper use of the often confused words.
3. Key the **Apply** lines (with number and period), choosing the word that completes the sentence correctly.

disburse (vb) to pay out
disperse (vb) to cause to break up

emerge (vb) to become evident
immerge (vb) to plunge oneself into something

recent (adj) the very near past
resent (vb) to feel displeasure

elusive (adj) tending to evade grasp or pursuit
illusive (adj) misleading or deceptive

precede (vb) to go or come before
proceed (vb) to go on or to continue

ware (n) manufactured items or goods
wear (vb) to bear or to have on the person

Learn 1. The crowd will disperse when we disburse the paychecks.
Apply 2. We can (disburse, disperse) free samples at the meeting.
Apply 3. The chemicals will cause the oil slick to (disburse, disperse).

Learn 4. A clean boy may emerge if Andrew will immerge himself in the bath.
Apply 5. The swimmers like to (emerge, immerge) themselves in the pool.
Apply 6. As the facts (emerge, immerge), the truth will become evident.

Learn 7. Did Mark resent the remarks made at the recent meeting?
Apply 8. Jessica was elected mayor during the (recent, resent) election.
Apply 9. Arturo may (recent, resent) the terms of the contract.

Learn 10. An illusive tip misled me in my search for the elusive men.
Apply 11. Scientists searched years for the (elusive, illusive) virus.
Apply 12. The magician performed several amazing (elusive, illusive) acts.

Learn 13. If they precede us, we will not proceed with the parade.
Apply 14. After a short break, we will (precede, proceed) with the meeting.
Apply 15. He earned the right to (precede, proceed) them at the ceremony.

Learn 16. The wares at the bazaar were mostly items that people wear.
Apply 17. Did she (wear, ware) a wig for her role in the play?
Apply 18. A favorite birthday (wear, ware) for a man is a necktie.

107a ▶ 5 Conditioning Practice

each line twice SS (slowly, then faster); DS between 2-line groups; if time permits, rekey selected lines

alphabet 1 Seven new boys qualified through expert knowledge of jazz dance music.

figures 2 Ms. Tedd excluded Chapters 19 and 20, pages 378 to 465, from the exam.

shift lock 3 SWOPWO will buy one LM-PC at AABSCO rather than a PC-WEX from WEYSCOT.

speed 4 She bid on the field by the lake as the right land for the big chapel.

| 1 | 2 | 3 | 4 | 5 | 6 | 7 | 8 | 9 | 10 | 11 | 12 | 13 | 14 |

107b ▶ 6 Improve Language Skills: Word Choice

1. Study the spelling and definition of each word.
2. Key the line number (with period), space twice, then key the **Learn** sentence; key the **Apply** sentence in the same format, selecting the correct word in parentheses to complete each sentence.

beat (vb) to strike repeatedly; to defeat

beet (n) the name of a plant with a dark-red root

basis (n) the fundamental ingredient of anything

bases (n) plural for base or basis

Learn 1. I beat the drum loudly when my canned beets won first prize.
Apply 2. Carter High (beat, beet) Dennison High for the championship.
Apply 3. Mary wanted Jim to plant at least four rows of (beats, beets).

Learn 4. The basis of good base stealing is fast speed and accurate timing.
Apply 5. The (basis, bases) of his argument is not supported by facts.
Apply 6. The runner missed first and second (basis, bases) while running.

107c ▶ 6 Preapplication Drill: Backspace and Tab Keys

1. Center each of lines 1-4 horizontally.
2. Key lines 5-6, tabbing from one column to the next. For pica machines, set left margin stop at 15 and tab stops at 31, 48, and 64. For elite machines, set left margin stop at 23 and tab stops at 39, 56, and 72.
3. Do not correct errors.

Backspace Key Drill:

1 Angela L. Robinson
2 Rogelio M. Rodriquez
3 James P. Feltenberg
4 Margaret H. Breedlove

Tab Key Drill:

5	10,432	in case	lay by	blazon
6	57,986	it will	my box	amazed
7	24,103	on base	do cut	benzol
8	97,856	no case	an elf	cozily

107d ▶ 10 Review Horizontal Placement of Tables

1. Study horizontal placement procedures on p. 188.
2. Center horizontally on a full sheet the table at the right; DS data; CS: 6 between longest items in columns; PB: line 26; correct errors.

COMMONLY MISSPELLED WORDS			words
			5
activities	necessary	professional	12
address	offered	reason	17
decision	participation	representative	24
entry	position	schedule	29
experience	premium	supervisor	35
important	procedure	transportation	42

180b (continued)

words

We cordially invite the managers in your various branch offices to attend 161
this informative and instructive seminar. Simply have your administrative 176
assistant complete the enclosed form giving the names and titles of the indi- 191
viduals who will attend each of the seminars, and return it to me no later 206
than May 10. 209

Sincerely yours Christina F. LaMonica Director of Public Relations xx 223
Enclosure 225/**246**

Letter 2
Simplified Block Letter

LP p. 79

Prepare the letter shown at the right in the simplified block format. List the enumerated items.

September 8, 19-- MS LINDSAY M SAXE CHAIRPERSON ELECTRONICS TRADE 13
SHOW SAXE RESEARCH ASSOCIATES INC 351 FIFTH AVENUE NEW YORK 25
NY 10016-7820 SECOND ANNUAL ELECTRONICS TRADE SHOW 36

As Chairperson of the panel discussion "The Electronic Office--Today and 50
Tomorrow," to be presented at the Electronics Trade Show next June 12 to 14, 66
I have chosen the following individuals to be panel members. 1. Ms. Yoko 81
Lee, assistant director of the Atlantic Institute, has had 15 years of expe- 96
rience in word processing, office automation, and information process- 109
ing. During that time, she has held positions in research, product planning 125
and design, training, marketing, and managing information systems. 2. Dr. 140
Ira Colton, senior associate of Colton, Rollins & Schmitt, Inc., has been 155
involved with electronics in the business office for more than 18 years. 170
As a consultant, he has assisted federal agencies and Fortune 500 corpo- 184
rations in designing integrated information systems, installing electronic 199
equipment, and developing specialized software to meet specific and unique 214
requirements. 3. Mrs. Lila T. Alverez, information systems officer at Elec- 229
tronics International, Ltd., has recently completed the installation of a world- 245
wide information system which links all elements of Electronics Interna- 259
tional on three continents. Mrs. Alverez earned her doctorate at MIT and has 275
written and lectured extensively on electronics in the office. 288

Each of the panel members will speak for 20 minutes, leaving 30 minutes for 303
questions from the audience. With panel members of such high caliber, I 317
feel certain that this panel discussion will be an exciting and informative one. 334

KEITH T. KONA, PRESIDENT xx 339/**363**

Letters 3 and 4
Letters from Form Paragraphs

LP pp. 81-83

1. Prepare letters for Mr. Scott's signature in block format with open punctuation from form ¶s on p. 312.

2. Place current date on line 16 and use side margins of 1½".

3. Provide an appropriate salutation and complimentary close.

4. Copy the addresses and ¶ numbers in Letters 3 and 4 for the letters you are to format.

Letter 3
Prepare letter to
Miss Jennifer T. Franklin
577 Memorial Drive
Boston, MA 02139-4051
Use ¶s 1.1 (product: ABC ARRAY), 2.2, and 3.1.
Total words: 187/**200**

Letter 4
Prepare letter to
Mr. David C. Adams
2330 Alamo Street
Dallas, TX 75201-6452
Use ¶s 1.3 (name: Elizabeth Reita; product: IDEALWORD), 2.1, and 3.3.
Total words: 174/**185**

Center

			words
TALL BUILDINGS IN CHICAGO line 22			5
DS			
Listed by Height in Feet and Meters			12
DS			
<u>Building</u>	<u>Feet</u>	<u>Meters</u>	20
DS			
Sears Tower	1,454	443.470	25
Amoco	1,136	346.480	29
John Hancock Center	1,127	343.735	36
Water Tower Place	859	261.995	42
First National Bank	852	259.860	48
Three First National Plaza	775	236.375	56
DS			
____________ 1½"			60
DS			
Source: <u>The World Almanac</u>.			68

Table on a Full Sheet

107e ▶ 23
Format Three-Column Tables

plain full sheets, short edge at top; correct errors

Table 1
Format model table above; DS data; CS: 6 between longest items in columns; block column headings.

Table 2
Format table at the right; DS data; CS: 8 between longest items in the columns; block column headings.

			words
Tall Buildings in New York City			6
Listed by Height in Feet and Meters			14
<u>Building</u>	<u>Feet</u>	<u>Meters</u>	21
World Trade Center	1,350	411.750	28
Empire State (without TV tower)	1,250	381.250	37
Chrysler	1,046	319.030	41
American International	950	289.750	48
40 Wall Tower	927	282.735	53
Citicorp Center	914	278.770	59
____________			63
Source: <u>The World Almanac</u>.			72

Lesson 179 — Review Special Letters

179a ▶ 5 Conditioning Practice

each line twice SS (slowly, then faster); if time permits, take 1′ writings on line 4

alphabet 1 Jane found that good executives were able to analyze problems quickly.

figures 2 Of the 18,907 computers, 16,853 were accepted and 2,054 were rejected.

fig/sym 3 Read pages 245-306 in Infosystems by Ray & Dorr (Third Edition, 1987).

speed 4 The rich men may wish to amend the title of the firm when they own it.

| 1 | 2 | 3 | 4 | 5 | 6 | 7 | 8 | 9 | 10 | 11 | 12 | 13 | 14 |

179b ▶ 45 Sustained Production: Special Communications

letterheads, LP pp. 69-75
plain full sheets

Time Schedule
Plan and prepare .... 5′
Timed production .... 30′
Proofread; compute *n-pram* .... 10′

1. Make a list of letters to be processed:
p. 310, 177b, Letter 2
p. 309, 176b, Letter 1
p. 309, 176b, Letter 2
p. 312, 178b, Letter 2

2. Arrange letterheads and plain paper for efficient handling.

3. Key the documents for 30′ when directed to begin. Proofread each letter carefully before removing it from the machine. Correct errors neatly. Address envelopes. If you finish before time is called, begin with Letter 1 and rekey on plain sheets as many documents as possible in the time remaining.

4. Compute *n-pram:*
total words − penalty* / time (30′)
*penalty is 15 words for each uncorrected error.

5. Turn in letters arranged in the order given in Step 1.

Lesson 180 — Evaluate Special Communications

180a ▶ 5 Conditioning Practice

each line twice SS (slowly, then faster); rekey selected lines if time permits

alphabet 1 Shares of the Wexcom stock took a sizable jump in quite heavy trading.

figures 2 The panel met on June 1, 24, 27, and 30 and on July 5, 6, 7, 8, and 9.

fig/sym 3 Ross & Lawler offered a discount of $437 (10% and 2%) on Order #56891.

speed 4 The visitor to the island paid for a ruby and a pair of antique bowls.

| 1 | 2 | 3 | 4 | 5 | 6 | 7 | 8 | 9 | 10 | 11 | 12 | 13 | 14 |

180b ▶ 45 Measure Production Skills: Special Communications

letterheads, LP pp. 77-83
plain full sheets
Refer to Time Schedule in 179b.

1. Arrange letterheads and plain sheets for efficient handling.

2. Key for 30′ the letters below and on page 314. Correct errors neatly; address envelopes. Proofread each letter carefully *before* you remove it from the machine. If you finish before time is called, begin with Letter 1 and rekey on plain sheets as many letters as possible in the time remaining.

3. After the timed production, proofread and circle any errors you may have missed; compute *n-pram.*

Letter 1
Letter on Executive-size Stationery
LP p. 77
modified block format, open punctuation

words

April 24, 19-- Mr. Michael C. Evans Vice President CMC Industries, 13
Inc. Suite 6452 World Trade Center New York, NY 10048-3326 Dear 26
Mr. Evans 28

Alpha Electronics is offering a one-day seminar entitled "Analyzing Informa- 43
tion Needs" for managers at all levels. This seminar will be held in several 59
Eastern cities during the month of June. 67

The first meeting will be held in Philadelphia at the William Penn Room of 82
the International Inn on June 6. On June 13, the seminar will be held in the 98
Crystal Suite of the Boston Concord Shelley Hotel. The seminar will be re- 113
peated in the Rodney Room of the Concord Hotel in Wilmington, Delaware, 127
on June 20 and in the Petite Ballroom of the Chatham Hotel in Baltimore, 142
Maryland, on June 27. 146

(continued, p. 314)

108a ▶ 5 Conditioning Practice

each line twice SS (slowly, then faster); DS between 2-line groups; if time permits, rekey selected lines

alphabet 1 Jackie Wadman's next goal is to qualify for the event's bronze trophy.

figures 2 There were 12,087; 9,365; and 8,401 fans at the last three home games.

symbols 3 Jane practiced keying *, /, and — on Monday; %, $, and # on Wednesday.

speed 4 Lay the clamshell at the end of the rug on the big shelf at the right.

| 1 | 2 | 3 | 4 | 5 | 6 | 7 | 8 | 9 | 10 | 11 | 12 | 13 | 14 |

108b ▶ 7 Preapplication Drill: Center Column Headings Over Columns

Use the procedure in the color block at the right to center each of the column headings over the longest entry in its column. Key the headings and entries on a drill sheet; DS between heading and entry; SS the entries; CS: 8 between longest items in the columns; do not correct errors.

Center Column Headings (When Column Heading is not Longest Line)

1. Identify the longest entry in each column.

2. Find center point of entry by spacing forward once for every two characters and spaces. If a stroke is left over at the end of the item, do not space forward for it.

3. From the center point of the longest column entry backspace once for every two characters and spaces in the column heading. Begin the heading where the backspacing ends.

Name	Class	Position
Harry Aine	Junior	Tackle
Tom Burrell	Sophomore	Flanker
Bill Casey	Senior	Linebacker

108c ▶ 38 Format Tables with Centered Headings

center all headings

Table 1

plain full sheet, short edge at top; DS data; CS: 8 between longest items in columns; do not correct errors

SUE TOTH'S 19-- PAYROLL DEDUCTIONS 7

Deduction	Amount	words
		15
Federal Income Tax	$11,070.68	21
State Income Tax	1,305.43	26
City Income Tax	652.72	31
Social Security Tax	3,131.70	37
Disability Insurance	37.68	43
Pension Plan	2,916.60	48
Medical & Dental Insurance	441.95	55

Table 2

plain full sheet, short edge at top; DS data; CS: 8 between longest items in columns; correct errors

Table 3

Reformat Table 1 on a half sheet, long edge at top; arrange deductions in alphabetical order; SS data; CS: 12 between longest items in columns; correct errors.

POPULATION PROJECTIONS FOR SELECTED COUNTRIES 9

Reported in Millions for Years 2000 and 2025 18

Country	2000	2025	words
			26
Canada	29.4	34.4	30
China: Mainland	1,255.7	1,460.1	37
France	57.1	58.5	41
Japan	127.7	127.6	45
Mexico	109.2	154.1	49
Soviet Union	314.8	367.1	55
United Kingdom	56.2	56.4	61
United States	268.1	312.7	66

______________________ 70

Source: Population Division of United Nations. 79

178a ▶ 5 Conditioning Practice

each line twice SS (slowly, then faster); if time permits, take 1′ writings on line 4

alphabet	1	Jack said he filled the boutique with bizzare and very expensive gems.
figures	2	Note carefully the footnotes on pages 19, 32, 46, 57, 68, 83, and 107.
fig/sym	3	Barr & Derry paid the balance ($852.93) on September 6 by Check #7410.
speed	4	Ruth paid for both of the mementos of their visit to the ancient city.

| 1 | 2 | 3 | 4 | 5 | 6 | 7 | 8 | 9 | 10 | 11 | 12 | 13 | 14 |

178b ▶ 45 Learn to Produce Letters from Form Paragraphs

LP pp. 63-67

1. Prepare form letters below in block format, open punctuation to be signed by Jan T. Scott, Chief, Software Division.

2. Use current date (on line 16) and 1½″ side margins. Supply an appropriate salutation and complimentary close; address envelopes; circle errors.

Letter 1
Prepare letter to

Miss Rose T. Chase
223 W. Jefferson Street
Louisville, KY 40202-3001

Use ¶s 1.2 (product: IDEALWORD), 2.1, and 3.3.
Total words: 177/**190**

Letter 2
Prepare letter to

Mr. John P. Powers
913 Main Street
Kansas City, MO 64105-2750

Use ¶s 1.1 (product: DB III), 2.3, and 3.1.
Total words: 191/**203**

Letter 3
Prepare letter to

Ms. Nicole P. White
129 Madison Avenue
Memphis, TN 38103-3475

Use ¶s 1.3 (name: David Mays; product: ABC ARRAY), 2.2, and 3.2.
Total words: 179/**191**

¶ 1.1 At a recent trade show, you requested that we provide additional information about (insert product). We are pleased that our demonstration at the show prompted you to write for more information.

¶ 1.2 Thank you for your recent letter requesting information about (insert product). We are always pleased to receive requests of this nature which reflect an interest in one of our products.

¶ 1.3 We are pleased to learn that (insert name) suggested that you write to us about (name of product). It is always satisfying to learn that we have been recommended by one of our customers.

¶ 2.1 IDEALWORD 2.1 is one of the most advanced word processing programs available. In addition to the usual editing functions, IDEALWORD includes a thesaurus, spell checking, and outlining features. It also permits you to create personalized letters, forms, and tables, and to merge text through automated routines. Of paramount importance, IDEALWORD 2.1 is flexible, speedy, and easy to learn.

¶ 2.2 ABC ARRAY is a spreadsheet program which offers a great deal more than automatic calculations. Templates are included which permit you to perform typical data processing tasks such as analyzing, projecting, and forecasting statistical data. For greater flexibility, individual cells can be moved from one location to another and entire rows and cells can be rearranged. For ease of comprehension, the data can be displayed as charts and graphs.

¶ 2.3 DB III is a data base program which opens up the world of information to you. With DB III you can create files, store and retrieve data, and build reports quickly by following a few simple directions. If you want information on a specific topic, simply key in the topic and the computer will conduct an electronic search. The Structured Query Language (SQL) incorporated into DB III permits you to interface with different programs and systems to broaden your data base.

¶ 3.1 Thank you for your inquiry. If you would like any additional information, please call or write us and we will be happy to provide it.

¶ 3.2 If you would like a demonstration of this program, please call us at 1-800-555-7400 and we will be pleased to arrange it.

¶ 3.3 Your inquiry has been forwarded to our regional representative in your area who will call you in a few weeks to see if we can be of any further service.

109a ▶ 5 Conditioning Practice

each line twice SS (slowly, then faster); DS between 2-line groups; if time permits, rekey selected lines

alphabet 1 Quen said subzero weather may crack six big joints in the paved floor.
figures 2 They delivered 9,821 subcompact; 6,704 mid-size; and 395 luxury autos.
fig/sym 3 At 2:45 p.m., Teams #9 & #7 (Court 3-5) and #6 & #10 (Court 1-8) play.
speed 4 The neighbor burns wood and a small bit of coal to make a giant flame.

| 1 | 2 | 3 | 4 | 5 | 6 | 7 | 8 | 9 | 10 | 11 | 12 | 13 | 14 |

109b ▶ 7 Assessing Table Formatting Skills

Follow directions at the right.

1. Move margin stops to ends of line-of-writing scale.
2. Clear all tab stops.
3. At signal to begin, format and key as much of the model table on p. 190 as you can in 5′ (plain full sheet, short edge at top; DS data; CS: 10).
4. When time is called, determine errors and verify accuracy of settings for the left margin and tab stops.

109c ▶ 18 Format Tables

plain full sheets, short edge at top; center all headings; correct errors

Table 1
DS data; CS: 8 between longest items in columns

Learning cue: Align numbers at the right or at the decimal point if one is used.

		words
SNOWIEST PLACES IN U.S.		5
Annual Average Snowfall		10
City and State	Amount	20
Stampede Pass, Washington	36.04 feet	27
Valdez, Alaska	24.59 feet	32
Mt. Washington, New Hampshire	20.74 feet	41
Blue Canyon, California	20.27 feet	48
Yakutat, Alaska	17.37 feet	53
Marquette, Michigan	10.14 feet	59
Sault St. Marie, Michigan	9.6 feet	67
______________		70
Source: National Climatic Data Center.		78

Table 2
DS data; CS: 8 between longest items in columns

Learning cue: To indicate a total, underline the last entry the full length of the total figure; DS; key the total figure.

			words
TRI-VALLEY RECREATION CLUB			5
Comparison of Estimated and Actual Incomes			14
Income Source	Est.	Actual	25
Membership Dues	$11,050	$12,370.50	32
Court Fees	15,300	14,210.75	38
Weight Room Fees	3,750	4,010.25	45
Swimming Pool Fees	2,500	2,650.00	52
Instruction & Other	3,750	3,981.45	62
(Indent 5 spaces) Totals	$36,350	$37,222.95	68

Communication Concepts Inc.

178 S. Prospect Avenue ■ San Bernardino, CA 92410-4567 ■ (714) 586-7934 4 4

words in parts | total words

Dateline September 15, 19-- QS line 12

MISS MICHELLE T LAWSON 8 8
DEL AMO SECRETARIAL SERVICE 14 14
21200 HAWTHORNE AVE 18 18
LOS ANGELES CA 90058-2820 DS 23 23

Subject line SIMPLIFIED BLOCK LETTER FORMAT DS 29 29

Body of letter This letter illustrates the features that distinguish the 12 41
Simplified Block Letter format from the standard block format. DS 24 54

1. The date is placed on line 12 so that the letter address 37 66
will show through the window of a window envelope when used. DS 49 78

2. The letter address is keyed in the style recommended by 61 90
the U. S. Postal Service for OCR processing: ALL-CAP letters 73 103
with no punctuation. Cap-and-lowercase letters with punctua- 85 115
tion may be used if that is the format of the addresses stored 98 127
in an electronic address file. Personal titles may be omitted. DS 111 140

3. A subject line replaces the traditional salutation which 123 153
some people find objectionable. The subject line may be keyed 136 165
in ALL-CAP or cap-and-lowercase letters. A double space is 148 177
left above and below it. DS 153 182

4. The complimentary close, which some people view as a need- 165 195
less appendage, is omitted. DS 171 200

5. The writer's name is placed on the fourth line space below 184 213
the body of the letter. The writer's title or department name 196 226
may appear on the line with the writer's name or on the next 208 238
line below it. The signature block may be keyed in ALL-CAP or 221 250
cap-and-lowercase letters. DS 227 256

6. A standard-length line is used for all letters. A six-inch 239 269
line is a common length (60 pica or 10-pitch spaces; 72 elite 252 281
or 12-pitch spaces). DS 256 286

The features listed and illustrated here are designed to bring 269 298
efficiency to the electronic processing of mail. QS 278 308

Omit complimentary close *Maria T. Lopez*

Writer's name and title MRS. MARIA T. LOPEZ, DIRECTOR DS 6 314

Reference notation tms 7 314

shown in pica type
six-inch line

Simplified Block Letter

109d ▶ 7 Preapplication Drill: Center Column Headings Over Columns

Use the procedure in the color block at the right to center each column heading over the longest entry in the column. Key the headings and entries on a drill sheet; DS between heading and first entry; SS the entries; CS: 8 between longest items in columns.

Center Column Headings (When Column Heading is Longest Line)

1. Set the left margin and tab stops for columns.
2. Key the column headings; DS.
3. Find center point of first column heading by spacing forward once for every two characters and spaces. If a stroke is left over at the end of the heading, do not space forward for it.
4. Identify the longest line in the column entries.
5. From the center point of the heading, backspace once for every two characters and spaces in the longest entry (drop leftover or extra stroke). Set new tab where backspace stops.
6. Repeat Step 2 through 4 for each remaining column.

Atlantic Division	Central Division	Pacific Division
Boston	Detroit	Phoenix
Philadelphia	Chicago	San Diego
Washington	St. Louis	Portland

109e ▶ 13 Format Tables with Long Column Headings

plain full sheets; short edge at top; center all headings; correct errors

Table 1
DS data; CS: 10 between longest items in columns

Table 2
Reformat Table 1; SS data; CS: 8 between longest items in columns.

LOCAL FM RADIO STATIONS

Call Letters	Dial Location	Telephone No.	words
			5
			21
WYTP	88.3	918-3637	26
WLTK	91.5	321-5422	32
WBZS	100.7	879-7090	37
KLPM	102.5	273-6401	43
WMEZ	104.3	521-4343	49
WLQP	106.7	988-9889	54
WQRS	106.9	343-7899	60
WEAS	107.9	314-5454	65

Lesson 110 Processing Tables

110a ▶ 5 Conditioning Practice

each line twice SS (slowly, then faster); DS between 2-line groups; if time permits, rekey selected lines

alphabet 1 This weekly journal gives exact sizes of old boat and plane equipment.

figures 2 I know the ZIP Code plus 4 for 49-13th Street is listed as 92057-1683.

fig/sym 3 The 72″ × 96″ tablecloth will cost $84.63 less discounts of 10% & 15%.

speed 4 The soggy field by the city dog kennels was good for a big tug of war.

| 1 | 2 | 3 | 4 | 5 | 6 | 7 | 8 | 9 | 10 | 11 | 12 | 13 | 14 |

110b ▶ 10 Format Tables with Centered Column Headings

plain full sheet; short edge at top; DS data; CS: 6 between longest items in columns; centered headings; correct errors

RETURNING VARSITY LETTERMEN ROSTER

Name	Sophomore	Junior	Senior	words
				7
				19
Jim Alvarez			X	22
Tom Beatty		X		25
David Dow		X		28
Fred Litteri	X			32
Sam Selkski			X	36
Pietro Thoeni		X		39
Tim Wemblack			X	43
Raul Waurez			X	46
Earl Zetz	X			52
Totals	2	3	4	57

177a ▶ 5 Conditioning Practice

each line twice SS (slowly, then faster); if time permits, take 1′ writings on line 4

alphabet 1 Zack may request we adjust gross profits on big items except vehicles.
figures 2 In June, 5,498 units were processed; in July, 7,215; in August, 8,603.
fig/sym 3 The balance (as of May 1, 1991) was $36,450,700 -- an increase of 28.6%.
speed 4 To the dismay of the girls, he kept the key to the shanty by the lake.

| 1 | 2 | 3 | 4 | 5 | 6 | 7 | 8 | 9 | 10 | 11 | 12 | 13 | 14 |

177b ▶ 45 Learn to Format Simplified Block Letter

Letter 1
plain full sheet

1. Study the formatting guides for the Simplified Block Letter on p. 308 and the model letter on p. 311.

2. Key the Simplified Block Letter on p. 311 in the proper format.

3. Proofread; circle errors; check copy for correct format.

Letter 2
LP p. 59

1. Key the letter shown at the right in the Simplified Block Letter format. List the enumerated items.

2. Proofread; circle errors; check copy for correct format.

words

July 5, 19-- GLOBAL SALES INC 33 BROAD STREET NW ATLANTA GA 30303- 13
2108 ZEUS FACSIMILE MACHINE 19

When you want to send a document quickly, why spend hours at a cost of 33
dollars when you can send the document in minutes for a few cents with a 48
ZEUS Facsimile Machine. Consider these facts. 1. The ZEUS can transmit 63
documents, including drawings and photographs, at the speed of light any- 77
where in the country or the world--wherever there is a telephone. As a 91
multipurpose machine, the ZEUS can receive as well as transmit messages. 106
2. You can transmit documents to just one person or location or to almost 121
100 addressees simultaneously. 3. The ZEUS is small enough to set on a 136
desktop and merely plugs into the nearest electrical outlet and telephone 151
line. 4. Personnel can be trained to use the ZEUS in just a few minutes. 166
5. Errors in messages are completely eliminated. The document received 180
is an exact copy of the document transmitted. 6. Continuous (24-hour) op- 195
eration is possible which solves communications problems caused by the dif- 210
ferences in time throughout the country and the world. 221

Let us show you how you can save time and money with a ZEUS Facsimile 235
Machine. Call Lisa Dent at 555-7442 for a demonstration in your office. 250

JAMES M. TAYLOR, SALES DIRECTOR xx 257/**269**

Letter 3
LP p. 61

1. Key the letter shown at the right in the Simplified Block Letter format.

2. Proofread; circle errors; check copy for correct format.

July 1, 19-- MISS JULIA C REED DIRECTOR OF ADMINISTRATION JOHN- 12
SON & SONS INC 120 EAST HANCOCK AVENUE ATHENS GA 30601-1203 25
JANUS OPTICAL CHARACTER READER 31

For years, the United States Postal Service has been able to process mail with 47
phenomenal speed through the use of Optical Character Readers (OCR) 60
to scan ZIP Codes. Using OCR equipment, banks process checks and deposit 75
slips electronically by "reading" magnetic ink characters to sort the docu- 90
ments and post all necessary data to the proper account. 101

Thanks to the JANUS Optical Character Reader, you too can process docu- 115
ments with great speed. The JANUS has the ability to read printed or type- 130
written characters from almost any document. In a matter of minutes, the 145
JANUS will "read" and enter a document into a word processor for revision 160
or storage. Think of the time and money this can save. 171

The JANUS Optical Character Reader can be installed in minutes. For a 185
demonstration of this machine, simply call Jeff Barnes at 555-7430 to arrange 201
for a demonstration in your office at your convenience. 212

JAMES M. TAYLOR, SALES DIRECTOR xx 219/**241**

110c ▶ 10
Preapplication: Formatting Multiple-Line Column Headings

1. If needed, review 108b, p. 191 and 109c, p. 192 (centering column headings).

2. Center each of the lines in the multiple-line headings in Drill 1 over the longest entry in its column. Key the headings and entries on a drill sheet; DS between last line of heading and first entry; DS the entries; CS: 8; do not correct errors.

3. Complete Drill 2 in the same manner.

Learning Cues:

1. Multiple-line headings are single-spaced, and the bottom line has an underscore as long as the longest line in the heading.

2. When a table contains single-line column headings and column headings of two or more lines, the bottom line of the multiple-line heading is placed on the same line as the single-line heading(s).

Drill 1

Fruit Sold	Vegetables Sold	Meat Bought
Bananas	Peas	Beef
Apples	Corn	Pork
Pears	Beans	Lamb

Drill 2

Date of Purchase	Number	Sale Price
5/1/91	95	$11,650
7/9/91	101	11,425
9/5/91	77	11,875

110d ▶ 25
Process Tables with Multiple-Line Column Headings

center all headings; correct errors

Table 1
plain full sheet; short edge at top; DS data; CS: 8 between longest items in columns

words

CELLULAR TELEPHONES 4

End-of-Month Clearance Sale 10

Cellular Telephone	Regular Selling Price	Clearance Price	words
			16 / 29
TEC P-9100	$1,699.99	$888.88	35
TEC P-9110	1,999.99	999.99	42
Rawlins CP-1000	1,549.99	825.88	49
Rawlins CP-2000	1,749.99	925.88	57
Cellatel 380	1,224.99	749.99	63
Cellatel 480	1,924.99	974.99	70
Carfone XT	1,399.99	649.99	77
Carfone ST	1,599.99	848.88	83
Carfone ZT	1,799.99	949.88	89

Table 2
plain full sheet; short edge at top; DS data; CS: 8 between longest items in columns

Table 3
Reformat Table 2 on a half sheet; long edge at top; SS data; CS: 8 between longest items in columns.

MONEY MARKET FUNDS 4

Percents for Week Ending May 30, 19-- 11

Fund	Average Annual Yield	Change from Last Week	words
			16 / 27
AAPMny	8.35	−.02	32
ActAsMny	7.64	.01	37
AlexGrn	7.52	—	42
CDAMny	8.44	.01	47
Lndpt	8.23	.06	52
MPS Life	7.90	−.03	57
NassCash	8.31	.16	62
VenPe	6.86	−.12	67
WllngHS	7.89	.06	72
XtrMny	6.98	−.04	76

176a ▶ 5 Conditioning Practice

each line twice SS (slowly, then faster); if time permits, take 1′ writings on line 4

alphabet 1 James quickly analyzed and reviewed the usage of the complex keyboard.
figures 2 The pamphlet published in 1991 has 432,500 entries and 6,870 pictures.
fig/sym 3 The discount on Invoice #3196-91V should be $171.22 (4% of $4,280.50).
speed 4 Rosie may go with them by bus to the city and to the dock by the lake.

| 1 | 2 | 3 | 4 | 5 | 6 | 7 | 8 | 9 | 10 | 11 | 12 | 13 | 14 |

176b ▶ 45 Learn to Format Letters on Executive-size Stationery

LP pp. 53-57

1. Study and follow the formatting guides for executive-size stationery on p. 308.

2. Use modified block format, open punctuation, for Letters 1 and 2; address envelopes; circle errors.

Letter 1
Key the first letter in the proper format.

Letter 2
Key the script letter with a date of May 20, 19-- to

Mr. Arthur T. Ashby
58 Marietta Street N.W.
Atlanta, GA 30303-1248

for the signature of Lee T. Levy, executive vice president. Use an appropriate salutation and complimentary close.

Letter 3
Rekey Letter 2 in block format, open punctuation to

Mrs. Keith C. Thomas
260 Peachtree Street N.E.
Atlanta, GA 30303-1020

for the signature of Mr. Levy. Use an appropriate salutation and complimentary close.

words

September 1, 19-- Mr. Samuel T. Ortega, President Ortega Office Machines 15
Distributors, Inc. 210 St. James Avenue Boston, MA 02116-4985 Dear 28
Mr. Ortega 30

Are you interested in becoming a regional distributor for a new word proces- 46
sor we are currently developing? Tentatively called the TELEWRITER, this 60
word processor will extend beyond the current state-of-the-art machines and 76
will offer features never before found in a low-cost machine. 88

The TELEWRITER will be a lightweight, portable machine with a detachable 103
keyboard and a combined CRT and printer. The printer will utilize inter- 117
changeable daisy wheels which will permit the use of many type styles. With 133
the built-in software, most operators will be able to perform basic editing 148
functions at high rates of speed after an hour of training. There are no com- 163
plex codes or commands to memorize. 171

We plan to introduce this machine at the National Office Systems Confer- 185
ence to be held in New York in April of next year. If you are interested in be- 201
coming the distributor of this machine in the New England area, please 215
write to Ms. Joan Winston, our sales manager, at the address above. 229

Sincerely yours Mrs. Jessica C. Madison Director of Marketing xx 241/**263**

opening lines 20

(¶1) As one of our favored customers, you are cordially 30
invited to attend a special preview of our exhibit at 41
the American Electronics Trade Show to be held at The 52
Omni June 10-12. (¶2) Your preview will begin at 6:30 p.m. 63
on June 9 in the V.I.P. Lounge. After the reception, you 75
will view our presentations of the new JANUS Optical 85
Character Reader and the amazing new ZEUS Facsimile 96
Machine. (¶3) So that we may complete our plans, will 106
you please call my executive assistant, Frank King, 116
at 555-7484 and let him know if you can join us. 126

closing lines 137/**150**

111a ▶ 5 (daily) Conditioning Practice

each line twice SS (slowly, then faster); DS between 2-line groups; if time permits, rekey selected lines

alphabet 1 Eight quick joggers wanted very badly many prizes and expensive gifts.

figures 2 Nearly 250 pupils and 146 adults attended the game which we won 97-83.

long words 3 The administrative manager will purchase seven bidirectional printers.

speed 4 Nancy is to make an official bid for title to the authentic dirigible.

| 1 | 2 | 3 | 4 | 5 | 6 | 7 | 8 | 9 | 10 | 11 | 12 | 13 | 14 |

111b ▶ 7 Improve Language Skills: Word Choice

1. Study the spelling and definition of each word.
2. Key the line number (with period), space twice, then key the **Learn** sentence; key the **Apply** sentence in the same format, selecting the correct word in parentheses to complete each sentence.

plain (adj) with little ornamentation or decoration
plane (n) an airplane or hydroplane
pole (n) a long, slender rounded piece of wood or other material
poll (n) a canvassing of persons to analyze public opinion

Learn 1. The seat in the plane was covered with plain beige cloth material.
Apply 2. I will wear my (plain, plane) suit on the (plain, plane) next week.

Learn 3. The young person taking the poll was near the corner light pole.
Apply 4. A recent (pole, poll) showed a need for a new basketball (pole, poll).

111c ▶ 8 Measure Basic Skill: Straight Copy

1. One 5′ writing; find *gwam*.
2. Proofread; circle errors.
3. Record *gwam* rate.

all letters used | A | 1.5 si | 5.7 awl | 80% hfw |

	gwam 3′	5′	
Character is often described as a person's combined moral or ethical	5	3	44
strength. Most people think it is like integrity which is thought to	9	6	47
be a person's ability to adhere to a code or a set standard of values.	14	8	49
If a person's values are accepted by society, others are likely to view	19	11	52
her or him as having a somewhat high degree of integrity.	23	14	55
You need to know that character is a trait that everyone possesses	27	16	57
and that it is formed over time. A person's character reflects his or	32	19	60
her definition of what is good or just. Most children and teenagers mold	37	22	63
their character through the words and deeds of parents, teachers, and	42	25	66
other adults with whom they have regular contact.	45	27	68
Existing character helps mold future character. It is important to	50	30	71
realize that today's actions can have a lasting effect. For that reason,	54	33	74
there is no better time than now to make all your words and deeds speak	59	36	77
favorably. You want them to portray the things others require of people	64	38	79
who are thought to possess a high degree of character.	68	41	82

gwam 3′ | 1 | 2 | 3 | 4 | 5 |
gwam 5′ | 1 | 2 | 3 |

UNIT 41 *LESSONS 176 – 180*

Learn to Format Special Communications

Learning Goals

1. To learn how to process letters on executive-size stationery.

2. To learn how to format and process a Simplified Block Letter.

3. To learn how to produce form letters from form paragraphs.

4. To build production skill on special communications.

Format Guides

1. Paper guide at *0* (for typewriters).

2. LL: 70 spaces for drill copy; as directed for documents.

3. LS: SS drill lines with DS between groups; space documents as directed or required.

STANDARD FORMATTING GUIDES: SPECIAL COMMUNICATIONS

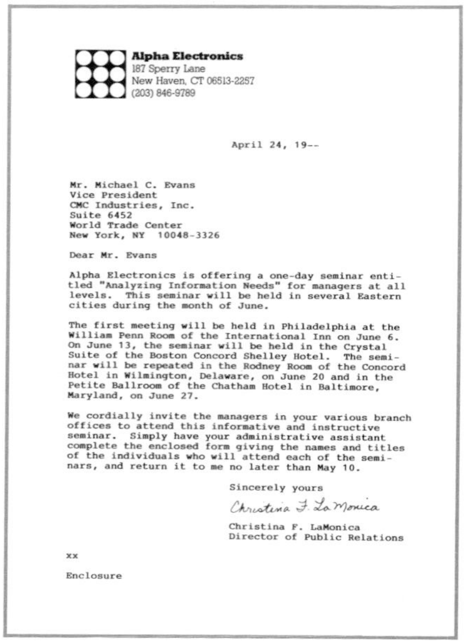

Alpha Electronics
187 Sperry Lane
New Haven, CT 06513-2257
(203) 846-9789

April 24, 19--

Mr. Michael C. Evans
Vice President
CMC Industries, Inc.
Suite 6452
World Trade Center
New York, NY 10048-3326

Dear Mr. Evans

Alpha Electronics is offering a one-day seminar entitled "Analyzing Information Needs" for managers at all levels. This seminar will be held in several Eastern cities during the month of June.

The first meeting will be held in Philadelphia at the William Penn Room of the International Inn on June 6. On June 13, the seminar will be held in the Crystal Suite of the Boston Concord Shelley Hotel. The seminar will be repeated in the Rodney Room of the Concord Hotel in Wilmington, Delaware, on June 20 and in the Petite Ballroom of the Chatham Hotel in Baltimore, Maryland, on June 27.

We cordially invite the managers in your various branch offices to attend this informative and instructive seminar. Simply have your administrative assistant complete the enclosed form giving the names and titles of the individuals who will attend each of the seminars, and return it to me no later than May 10.

Sincerely yours

Christina F. LaMonica

Christina F. LaMonica
Director of Public Relations

xx

Enclosure

Executive-size letter 7¼″ × 10½″

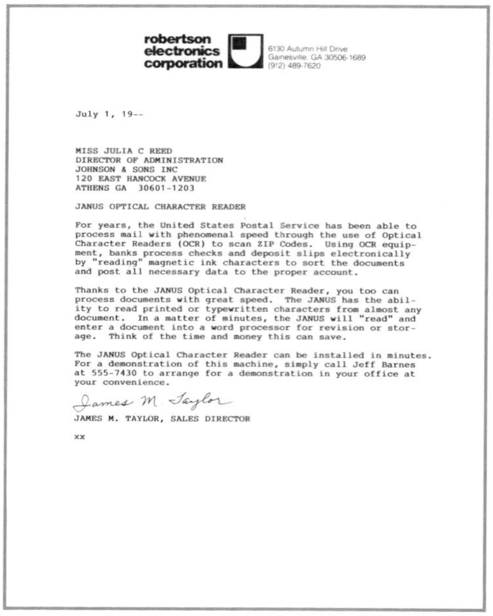

robertson electronics corporation
6130 Autumn Hill Drive
Gainesville, GA 30506-1689
(912) 489-7620

July 1, 19--

MISS JULIA C REED
DIRECTOR OF ADMINISTRATION
JOHNSON & SONS INC
120 EAST HANCOCK AVENUE
ATHENS GA 30601-1203

JANUS OPTICAL CHARACTER READER

For years, the United States Postal Service has been able to process mail with phenomenal speed through the use of Optical Character Readers (OCR) to scan ZIP Codes. Using OCR equipment, banks process checks and deposit slips electronically by "reading" magnetic ink characters to sort the documents and post all necessary data to the proper account.

Thanks to the JANUS Optical Character Reader, you too can process documents with great speed. The JANUS has the ability to read printed or typewritten characters from almost any document. In a matter of minutes, the JANUS will "read" and enter a document into a word processor for revision or storage. Think of the time and money this can save.

The JANUS Optical Character Reader can be installed in minutes. For a demonstration of this machine, simply call Jeff Barnes at 555-7430 to arrange for a demonstration in your office at your convenience.

James M. Taylor

JAMES M. TAYLOR, SALES DIRECTOR

xx

Simplified Block Letter

Standard Formatting Guides

Executive-size Stationery (7¼″ × 10½″)

Format. Any letter format may be used.

Margins. 1″ side; at least 1″ bottom

Dateline. Line 12

Spacing. QS below dateline and complimentary close; DS above and below salutation, above complimentary close, below name of sender or title of writer, and above and below any special parts.

Simplified Block Letter

Dateline. Line 12

Letter Address. ALL CAPS with no punctuation

Format. Block

The salutation and complimentary close are omitted. A subject line in ALL CAPS is always included. Writer's name and title are keyed in ALL CAPS.

Margins. 6-inch line (12-72+, 10-pitch; 15-87+, 12-pitch)

Spacing. QS below date; DS above and below subject line; QS below letter body; DS between special parts.

Form Letters

A standardized letter that can be sent to numerous addressees is known as a form letter or "boilerplate." A form letter (or paragraphs which can be used to make up a letter) can be stored in memory on a diskette or an electronic typewriter and retrieved when needed. Address lists can be stored on the same diskette or on a separate diskette. Through text merging, a form letter and the addresses can be merged to provide an original letter to each addressee.

Format. Any letter format can be used.

111d ▶ 30 Process Complex Tables on Special-Size Paper

Table 1
Study the information at the right and the model table on p. 197. Then, key the model table as illustrated using a half sheet, short edge at top; DS date; CS: 4 between longest items in columns; correct errors.

Centering on Special-Size Paper

To find horizontal center of special-size paper:

1. Note on line-of-writing or format scale the scale reading at the left edge and at the right edge of the sheet.

2. Add the two figures.

3. Divide the total by 2.

4. The resulting figure is the horizontal center point of the paper--the point from which to backspace to center copy.

On a half sheet of paper, short edge at the top:

1. There are 51 vertical line spaces available for keying.

2. The horizontal center is:
28 for pica (10-pitch)
33 for elite (12-pitch)

Table 2
half sheet, short edge at top; DS data; CS: 6 between longest items in columns; correct errors

		words
NEUROPSYCHIATRIC CLINIC INCOME REPORT		8
For Quarter Ending March 30, 19--		14
Area	Sales	21
Psychiatric Services	$ 14,320.40	28
Sleep Disorder Medicine	1,610.85	35
Anxiety Disorders	2,753.25	40
Drug and Alcohol Addiction	20,248.35	48
Stress Management Classes	11,795.00	55
Psychological Testing	17,455.90	61
Neuroelectrodiagnostics	3,944.00	68
Eating Disorders	14,987.00	73
Weight Loss Groups	25,210.50	79
Weight Gain Groups	11,100.90	87
Total Income	$123,426.15	93

Table 3
half sheet, short edge at top; DS data; CS: 6 between longest items in columns; correct errors

			words
EAST COAST AIRLINE TICKET INCOME			7
(In Millions of Dollars)			11
	Current	Next	14
Airport	Year	Year	22
Atlanta, GA	$ 3	$ 3.3	27
Baltimore, MD	2.5	3	32
Boston, MA	2.75	3.1	36
Charleston, SC	1.12	1.41	42
Charleston, WV	.6	.85	48
Hartford, CT	1.78	1.9	53
Miami, FL	3.25	3.3	57
Newark, NJ	3.01	3.21	62
Philadelphia, PA	2.87	2.98	69
Savannah, GA	.98	1.05	76
Total Income	$21.86	$24.1	82

Table 4
plain full sheet, long edge at top; DS data; CS: 10 between longest items in columns

TUITION INCOME				3
For Fiscal Year Ending June 30, 19--				10
	This	Last	%	15
Department	Year	Year	Change	28
Accounting	$ 96,948	$ 89,052	8.9	36
Administrative Management	25,548	22,939	11.4	45
Business Teacher Education	14,750	14,180	4	54
Communications & English	124,654	126,958	−1.8	64
Computer Information Systems	44,563	48,675	−8.4	74
Economics & Finance	35,980	34,540	4.2	82
Management & Marketing	112,274	108,541	3.4	91
Quantitative & Natural Sciences	95,613	94,590	1.1	101
Social Sciences	113,542	115,652	−1.8	113
Totals	$663,872	$655,127	1.3	120

LESSONS 176 – 200

PHASE 8

ENHANCE SKILL IN DOCUMENT PROCESSING

Employees in a modern office are called upon to prepare many different kinds of communications. In Phase 8, you will learn how to prepare some special communications, including memorandums and letters with special features. At the same time, special drills are included to increase your efficiency at the keyboard and to improve your communications skills.

Specifically, the objectives of Phase 8 are as follows:

1. To develop skill in formatting special communications, including memorandums and letters with special features.

2. To improve your ability to plan, organize, and prepare communications quickly and efficiently.

3. To increase your basic keyboarding and language skills.

Approximate Center

words

OFFICE SPACE RENTALS line 12 — 4

DS

Availability & Cost as of May 21, 19-- — 12

DS

Building	Square Footage	Rent per Square Foot	words
			15 / 27
USP Tower	332,000	$23.50	33
One Court Centre	132,000	18.00	40
PTN Building	41,673	19.50	46
Detroit Plaza	None	20.25	52
Lee Plaza	300,000	22.50	57
Riverfront Center	109,000	21.75	64
Four Steel Plaza	40,000	24.25	71
State Bank Building	7,756	17.50	78
Fifth Avenue Place	14,000	19.00	86
Corporate Tower	51,666	20.50	92

DS (after column headings)

Table on Special-Size Paper

175a ▶ 5 Conditioning Practice

each line twice SS (slowly, then faster); DS between 2-line groups; if time permits, rekey selected lines

alphabet	1	Mary's five quaint, prized jugs and their six bowls broke into pieces.
fig/sym	2	Di (5/19/74) is my oldest sister; Lea (6/30/82) is my youngest sister.
one hand	3	Barbara beat Garrett in a debate on greater taxes on assessed acreage.
speed	4	He may sign the usual form by proxy if they make an audit of the firm.

| 1 | 2 | 3 | 4 | 5 | 6 | 7 | 8 | 9 | 10 | 11 | 12 | 13 | 14 |

175b ▶ 9 Evaluate Straight-Copy Skill

1. Take a 5′ writing on the ¶s at the right.
2. Find *gwam* and number of errors.
3. Record score on LP p. 4.

all letters used | A | 1.5 si | 5.7 awl | 80% hfw |

	gwam 1′	5′	
Many people support the notion that a worker with a healthy body and	14	3	44
mind is a valued worker. Healthy employees often have a greater chance	28	6	47
for professional growth, produce more on the job, are happier with their	43	9	49
lives, and are likely to be more successful than those who are in poor	57	11	52
physical health or are not mentally alert.	65	13	54
If you want to have a healthy body, you should try to perform appro-	79	16	57
priate activities during your leisure time or try to find ways to enhance	94	19	60
the level of your physical activity during your regular school day or	108	22	62
workday. Brisk walking is a great way to bring exercise into daily ac-	122	24	65
tivities with amazing ease and quick results.	131	26	67
Fast walks from your home to the bus stop, from the bus stop to your	145	29	70
class, or from one class to another are very good ways to reap the bene-	159	32	73
fits of exercise while you carry out your daily routine. Doing isometric	174	35	76
exercises as you study, read, or watch television will produce excellent	189	38	79
results. You should, of course, do only exercises that will not disrupt	203	41	82
others.	205	41	82

gwam 1′ | 1 | 2 | 3 | 4 | 5 | 6 | 7 | 8 | 9 | 10 | 11 | 12 | 13 | 14 |
5′ | 1 | 2 | 3 |

175c ▶ 36 Evaluate Document Processing Skills: Leftbound Report

Time Schedule

Plan and Prepare .... 3′
Timed Production .... 25′
Proofread/Compute *n-pram* ...... 8′

3 full sheets; correct errors

Document 1

Reformat the report in 174c as a leftbound report; but instead of using footnotes for documentation, use the endnotes shown at the right. Place them on a separate page.

Proofread and correct each page before removing a page from the machine or screen.

After you compute *n-pram*, turn in your work in document number order.

	words
ENDNOTES	2
[1]The New Encyclopaedia Britannica, 15th	16
ed., 1985, s.v. "Tariffs."	22
[2]Philip Kotler, Marketing Essentials, (Engle-	35
wood Cliffs, New Jersey: Prentice-Hall, Inc.,	44
1984), p. 428.	47
[3]Albert Giordano, Concise Dictionary of	59
Business Terminology, (Englewood Cliffs, New	72
Jersey: Prentice-Hall, Inc., 1981), p. 53.	81

112a-113a ▶ 5 (daily)
Conditioning Practice

each line twice SS (slowly, then faster); DS between 2-line groups; if time permits, rekey selected lines

alphabet 1 Maxine and Peggy requested that a dozen wives join the breakfast club.

figures 2 I answered 4,978; Sidney answered 5,102; the correct answer was 5,360.

fig/sym 3 Both courses (#23-981 & #45-760) meet every Tuesday night at 6:30 p.m.

speed 4 The ensign is to make a turn to the right when the signal is in sight.

| 1 | 2 | 3 | 4 | 5 | 6 | 7 | 8 | 9 | 10 | 11 | 12 | 13 | 14 |

112b ▶ 5
Improve Language Skills: Word Choice

1. Study the spelling and definition of each word.

2. Key the line number (with period), space twice, then key the **Learn** sentence; key the **Apply** sentence in the same format, selecting the correct word in parentheses to complete each sentence.

idle (adj) inactive

idol (n) one that is adored

leased (vb) to grant use or occupation of under contract in exchange for rent

least (adj) lowest in importance or rank

Learn 1. Tom Smith's newest singing idol was idle last week due to illness.
Apply 2. During my (idle, idol) time, I read the biography of my (idle, idol).

Learn 3. The fact that he leased his new automobile is least important.
Apply 4. The (leased, least) apartment is the (leased, least) of his concerns.

112c-113c ▶ 40/45 (daily)
Process Tables

Use the time remaining in this period and in the next period to complete as many documents on pp. 198-200 as you can; center headings; correct errors.

Document 1

plain full sheet, short edge at top; DS data; CS: 6 between longest items in columns

RICHMOND SALES OFFICE DIRECTORY

Name	Position	Extension	words
			6
			18
Bill Adair	Marketing Manager	8341	26
Patricia Aley	Marketing Representative	8378	35
Walter Barnett	Service Representative	8278	44
Russell Fosia	Office Manager	8279	51
Louis Glumac	Marketing Representative	8342	60
Joy Hovanik	Administrative Specialist	8377	69
Denise Summerville	Service Representative	8276	79
Susan Vold	Marketing Representative	8228	87
Lena Wahl	Customer Service	8328	94
Janice Williamson	Administrative Specialist	8376	104

Document 2

plain full sheet, short edge at top; DS data; CS: 8 between longest items in columns

THINGS TO KNOW 3

Alaska and Western Canada 8

Location	Capital	Area in Square Kilometers	words
			11
			26
Alaska	Juneau	1,518,778	31
Alberta	Edmonton	644,392	38
British Columbia	Victoria	930,533	46
Manitoba	Winnipeg	548,497	52
Northwest Territories	Yellowknife	3,246,404	62
Saskatchewan	Regina	570,271	68
Yukon Territory	Whitehorse	478,036	77

______________ 80

Source: American Automobile Association Tourbook. 106

Document 3 is on p. 199.

174c (continued)

words

Document 1
Unbound Report with Footnotes
2 full sheets; correct errors as you key; proofread and make any additional corrections before removing a page from the machine or screen

INTERNATIONAL TRADE 4

A Report on Common Trade Restrictions 12

It is important that employees of companies that market goods in foreign 26
markets have a basic understanding of restrictions a nation can impose to 41
reduce or eliminate goods being imported into the country. 53

Common Trade Restrictions 63

Before marketing goods to a foreign country, the exporting company 77
should know the trade restrictions it is likely to face. 88

Tariff. The most common device a government uses to restrict trade 103
between its nation and another is the tariff. 112

> A tariff is a tax levied upon goods as they cross national boundaries 126
> usually by the government of the importing country. The words tariff, 141
> duty, and customs are generally used interchangeably. Tariffs may be 155
> levied either to raise revenue or to protect domestic industries.[1] 168

Quota. A quota is used by governments to set a limit on the amount of 183
goods that can be imported in certain product categories. "The purpose of 198
the quota is to conserve on foreign currency and protect local industry and 214
employment."[2] 217

Other Trade Restrictions 226

Although the foregoing restrictions are the most commonly used, nations 241
can discourage international trade through other means. 252

1. Reducing the amount of foreign currency available to buy imports 266
and setting exchange rates at levels that make imports more costly. 280

2. Using nontariff barriers, such as discriminating against the bids of 294
certain exporting countries or setting high product standards. 307

3. Establishing an embargo to eliminate imports coming into the coun- 321
try. Giordano defines embargo as "a government order stopping the im- 335
port or export of a particular commodity or commodities."[3] 346

____________________ 350

[1]The New Encyclopaedia Britannica, 15th ed., 1985, s.v. "Tariffs." 370

[2]Philip Kotler, Marketing Essentials, (Englewood Cliffs, New Jersey: 388
Prentice-Hall, Inc., 1984), p. 428. 396

[3]Albert G. Giordano, Concise Dictionary of Business Terminology, 417
(Englewood Cliffs, New Jersey: Prentice-Hall, Inc., 1981), p. 53. 430

Document 2
Bibliography
full sheet, correct errors

Document 3
If time permits, reformat Document 1 as an unbound report with internal citations; prepare a REFERENCE list on the last page of the report text; correct errors.

BIBLIOGRAPHY 3

Giordano, Albert G. Concise Dictionary of Business Terminology. Englewood 26
Cliffs, New Jersey: Prentice-Hall, Inc., 1981. 36

Kotler, Philip. Marketing Essentials. Englewood Cliffs, New Jersey: 54
Prentice-Hall, Inc., 1984. 60

"Tariffs." The New Encyclopaedia Britannica. Vol. 26. Chicago: Encyclo- 81
paedia Britannica, Inc., 1985, 430. 88

words

112c-113c (continued)

Document 3

plain full sheet, short edge at top; DS data; CS: 8 between longest items in columns

Document 4

Reformat Document 3 on a half sheet, long edge at top; SS data; CS: 6 between longest items in columns.

EMPLOYEE TUITION REIMBURSEMENT REPORT 8

As of Second Quarter Ended May 31, 19-- 16

Name	First Quarter	Second Quarter	All Previous Quarters	words
				23 / 38
Elaine Wilson	$ 430	$ 860	$ 5,655	47
Jean Baker	325	—	1,870	52
Surin Bajwa	890	445	4,286	57
Frances Danoff	1,115	575	8,760	64
Dolores Foseco	145	290	870	70
Cory Gentile	—	450	450	75
Cynthia Kernohan	925	470	10,270	82
Dennis Massoni	—	1,010	1,010	88
Carl Schweiger	840	—	15,780	95
Sun Yoko	750	750	2,250	99
Carla Stevens	1,400	1,400	8,400	110
Totals	$6,820	$6,250	$59,601	118

Document 5

plain full sheet, long edge at top; DS data, CS: 8 between longest items in columns

Document 6

Reformat Document 5 on a half sheet, short edge at top; DS data; CS: 4 between longest items in columns.

OFFICE SUPPLIES 4

Proposed Spring Sale Prices 9

Item	Regular Price	Sale Price	Discount Rate	words
				14 / 26
Correction Fluid	$ 1.59	$ .89	44%	34
Tape Dispenser	4.87	1.79	63%	40
Copyholder	16.95	10.99	35%	45
List Finder	16.95	12.69	25%	51
Desk Tray	4.00	1.89	53%	56
Letter Opener	.80	.59	29%	62
Desk Stapler	21.95	5.99	73%	68

Document 7

plain full sheet, long edge at top; DS data; CS: 10 between longest items in columns

NORTH BEDFORD HIGH LADY PANTHERS 6

Section 7-AAAA Basketball Results 13

Opponent*	W-L	Score	Top Scorer	Top Rebounder	words
					31
BLACKLICK	W	65-54	Stellar	Swalga	38
Forest Hills	L	70-61	Stellar	Swalga	45
Central	W	74-49	Montgomery	Birch	52
BELLWOOD	W	64-56	Swalga	Swalga	58
PANTHER VALLEY	W	69-64	Stellar	Birch	65
McKinley	L	65-59	Birch	Domack	71
FOREST HILLS	W	66-64	Domack	Lewis	78
CENTRAL	W	85-71	Montgomery	Birch	84
Bellwood	W	62-58	Lewis	Swalga	90
Panther Valley	L	65-60	Swalga	Domack	98
McKINLEY	W	73-68	Stellar	Lewis	104

______________ 108

*Home games in ALL CAPS. 112

Document 8 is on p. 200.

173c (continued)

Document 3
4-Column Table with Multiple-Line Column Headings

full sheet, short edge at top; DS data; CS: 4; center column headings; correct errors

Document 4

Reformat Document 1, p. 303, on a half sheet, short edge at top; DS data; CS: 4; center column headings; correct errors

	words
COLLEGE OF BUSINESS	4
Expenditure Comparison	9

Department	Last Year	This Year	Percent Difference	words
				12
				24
Accounting	$ 512,789	$ 537,614	4.84	33
Administrative Management	325,827	341,906	4.93	42
Business Teacher Education	85,401	89,723	5.06	52
Computer Information Systems	317,962	345,098	8.53	62
Economics and Finance	217,906	237,458	8.97	71
Logistics Management	95,763	102,948	7.5	79
Marketing	410,216	395,978	−3.48	85
Management	728,364	750,912	3.09	92
Sport Management	72,165	74,943	3.84	99
Quantitative Methods	174,269	193,058	10.78	112
Totals	$2,940,662	$3,069,638	4.38	121

Lesson 174 Evaluate Report Processing Skills

174a ▶ 5 Conditioning Practice

each line twice SS (slowly, then faster); DS between 2-line groups; if time permits, rekey selected lines

alphabet 1 Jean may use twelve quart tins for packaging the extra zucchini bread.

symbols 2 Here & Now (Vol. 17, No. 12) was rated the #1 magazine in a 1992 poll.

first row 3 Vance named his baby Zina, Ben named his Maxine, and I named mine Nan.

speed 4 Their field hand works in the cornfield down by the lake by the docks.

| 1 | 2 | 3 | 4 | 5 | 6 | 7 | 8 | 9 | 10 | 11 | 12 | 13 | 14 |

174b ▶ 9 Evaluate Language Skills

As you key each sentence, with the number and period, correct errors in spelling and word usage. Correct keying errors you find or make. DS between sentences.

1. She is confidant she will be aloud to buy the stationary this year.
2. They were adviced to paint a picture of a sandy desert on the canvass.
3. Your overdo for sum good weather to pour concrete at a job sight.
4. I wont be build for the flew cleaning until he halls away the durt.
5. I aloud the hiring of for workers to expand the personal role.

174c ▶ 36 Evaluate Document Processing Skills: Unbound Report

Time Schedule

Plan and Prepare .... 3′
Timed Production ....25′
Proofread/Compute *n-pram* ...... 8′

1. Process the copy on p. 305 as an unbound report with footnotes.

2. If time permits, format a bibliography page from the report's footnotes.

3. Proofread/correct errors as you key.

4. Compute *n-pram* and turn in your work in document number order.

112c-113c (continued)

Document 8

LP p. 69 or
plain full sheet

1. Use block format; open punctuation.

2. Supply **current date.**

3. Address letter to
Ms. Leona X. Wilhite
High Point High School
335 Tryon Road
Raleigh, NC 27603-3595

4. Address an envelope.

Learning Cue: Center the table within the margins of the letter. DS above and below the table and below the column headings; SS the column entries. Leave an even number of spaces between columns. The table may be indented an equal number of spaces from the left and right margin settings.

words

opening lines 20

Dear Ms. Wilhite 23

You should be proud that your business English classes at 35
High Point have decided to participate in the Learning Cen- 46
ter's competitive spelling ~~competition.~~ event 53

As you know, the purpose of this year's competition is to 65
improve every student's ability to spell correctly those 76
words which are commonly misspelled in business communica- 88
tions. A secondary purpose is to give recognition to stu- 99
dents who can spell with 100% accuracy the words which will 111
be included on a 100-item list at the end of the program. 123

Since a complete listing of each weeks words will not be 134
available until early next month, I am sending you the words 147
for the first three weeks. 152

Week 1	Week 2	Week 3	
			162
function	interest	analysis	167
manufacturing	presently	attention	174
provisions	production	capacity	180
administrative	registration	closing	187
distribution	technical	division	194
paragraph	together	entitled	199

Good luck to you and your students. We are proud that we can 212
sponsor such a valuable program and pleased that you are able 224
to participate in it. (205) 228

Sincerely 230

Harry L. Connors 234
Education Liasion 237

xx 238/**254**

ENRICHMENT ACTIVITY: Improve Basic Skill: Statistical Copy

1. Select a goal: Accuracy--Reduce errors by one on each writing; Speed--Increase *gwam* by 3 on each writing.

2. Take three 3′ writings; determine errors and *gwam.*

all letters used | A | 1.5 si | 5.7 awl | 80% hfw |

gwam 1′ | 3′

The sales report for the quarter ending September 31 indicated that 14 | 4
sales for Easy-Korec Blue Correctable Film ribbon (Stock #B193) were 27 | 9
down by 40% while sales of all other ribbons were up by an average of 41 | 14
15%. To boost sales of B193 ribbons, the selling price will be reduced 56 | 19
during the next quarter from $7.50 to $4.49 per ribbon (a 40% discount). 71 | 24
Also, a four-color display board emphasizing that the B193 ribbon can be 85 | 28
used as a replacement ribbon for TJK-133 and XRT-159 will be available 100 | 33
to all salespersons in the region. 106 | 35

gwam 1′ | 1 | 2 | 3 | 4 | 5 | 6 | 7 | 8 | 9 | 10 | 11 | 12 | 13 | 14
3′ | 1 | 2 | 3 | 4 | 5

173a ▶ 5 Conditioning Practice

each line twice SS (slowly, then faster); DS between 2-line groups; if time permits, rekey selected lines

alphabet 1 Margy expected pop quizzes on the new books and five journal articles.
fig/sym 2 Tom's cancelled checks (#398 & #401) showed he paid for Model #25-769.
shift lock 3 MRS. MARY SMITH, 1234 BAKER ROAD, ALIQUIPPA, PA 15001, is to be added.
speed 4 To their dismay, the townsman kept the fox and the dog in the kennels.

| 1 | 2 | 3 | 4 | 5 | 6 | 7 | 8 | 9 | 10 | 11 | 12 | 13 | 14 |

173b ▶ 9 Evaluate Language Skills

As you key the ¶, correct errors in punctuation, capitalization, number expression, and correct any keying errors you find or make.

in 2 weeks it will be announced that professor tom wargo will visit 4 cities in the ussr to lecture to university students. professor wargo author of friendship among nations will be accompanied on the 2 week tour by his wife 2 daughters and 3 sons. the wargo family plans to leave the usa on thanksgiving and return in time for the professor to administer final exams at evergreen university.

173c ▶ 36 Evaluate Document Processing Skills: Tables

Time Schedule

Plan and Prepare .... 3′
Timed Production .... 25′
Proofread/Compute *n-pram* ...... 8′

Document 1
3-Column Table with Block Column Headings

half sheet, long edge at top; DS data; CS: 8; correct errors

			words
FIVE MAJOR BATTLES OF THE CIVIL WAR			7
		Estimated	9
Battle	State	Casualties	18
Gettysburgh	Pennslyvania	40,000	24
Seven Days	Virginia	36,000	30
Petersbur	Virginia	30,000	35
Chickamuaga	Georgia	28,500	41
The Wilderness	Virginai	28,000	47
______________			51
Source: The World Book Encyclopedia.			63

Document 2
3-Column Table with Centered Column Headings

full sheet, short edge at top; SS data; CS: 6; correct errors

Documents 3 and 4 are on p. 304.

			words
SALES AND COMMISSION REPORT			6
Third Quarter, 19--			10
Salesperson	Sales	Commission	21
Jim Mullen	$ 35,540	$ 7,108	27
Sandra Lawton	41,250	8,250	32
Roberta Tessell	53,680	10,736	39
Bill Campbell	34,230	6,846	44
Paula Perfett	47,116	9,423	52
Totals	$211,816	$ 42,363	58

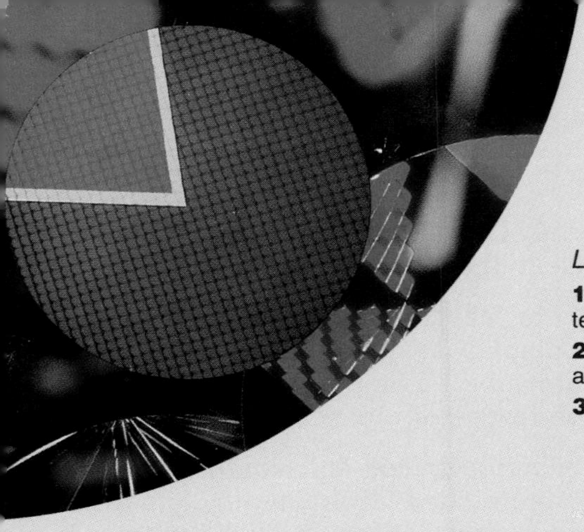

UNIT 26 *LESSONS 114 – 116*

Extend Keyboarding, Language, and Composing Skills

Learning Goals

1. To improve and assess keyboarding techniques.
2. To improve and assess keyboarding speed and control.
3. To improve language and composing skills.

Format Guides

1. Paper guide at *0* (for typewriters).
2. LL: 70-space line.
3. LS: SS word and sentence drills; DS ¶s; or space as directed within an activity.
4. PI: 5 spaces, when appropriate.

Lesson 114 *Keyboarding/Language Skills*

114a ▶ 5 Conditioning Practice

each line twice SS (slowly, then faster); DS between 2-line groups; if time permits, rekey selected lines

alphabet 1 Buzz expects to take his good vehicle for quick journeys on warm days.

fig/sym 2 I made Check #948 payable to O'Hare & O'Brien for $156.07 on April 23.

shift key 3 Flo Pritts told Mary White and Glenn Nance to meet her at Hall & Sons.

speed 4 Their men are in good shape to box with vigor to the end of the fight.

| 1 | 2 | 3 | 4 | 5 | 6 | 7 | 8 | 9 | 10 | 11 | 12 | 13 | 14 |

114b ▶ 5 Improve Language Skills: Apostrophe

1. Read and key the **Learn** sentence (with number and period), noting how the rule has been applied.
2. Key the **Apply** sentences (with numbers and periods), using the correct punctuation.
3. If time permits, rekey the **Apply** lines at a faster speed.

Use an apostrophe as a *symbol* for *feet* in billings or tabulations, or as a symbol for minutes. (Quotation marks may be used to signify inches or seconds.)

Learn 1. I was able to install five 2″ × 4″ × 8′ studs in 10′ 30″.

Apply 2. The 6 ft. 2 in. man scored a basket every 2 min. and 30 sec.

Apply 3. I ordered 2 in. × 4 in. × 12 ft. boards 30 min. ago.

Use an apostrophe as a symbol to indicate the omission of letters or figures (as in contractions).

Learn 4. Mary better not register for more than five classes in winter '94.

Apply 5. It's a car that is very similar to the 55 Chevy.

Apply 6. We plan to study the 72 flood at two oclock this afternoon.

114c ▶ 10 Improve Keyboarding Technique: Letter Emphasis

each line 3 times (slowly, then faster, then in-between rate for control)

Goal: To keep hands quiet with keystroking action limited to the fingers.

Emphasize: Continuity and rhythm with curved, upright fingers.

a After Alana and Anna ate the pancakes, each had an apple and a banana.

b Barb became the best batter by being best at batting big rubber balls.

c Cris can use pictures of a raccoon, cactus, and cacao in the calendar.

d Did Red declare he was a decoy doing deep runs to defeat the defenses?

e Ed, Eve, and Keene were elected to chaperone every late evening event.

f Fred figures fifty fast rafts floated from Fairfax to Fordstaff Falls.

g Gregg and George glanced at the gaggle of geese going over the garage.

h His healthy habits and high hopes help him through hot hockey matches.

i I think he will insist on sliding down the icy path five or six times.

172c (continued)

words

Document 1
Letter

LP p. 37 or full sheet

block format; open punctuation; proofread/correct errors; process envelope

Current date Dr. Henrietta L. Mateer California College of Business 2806 15
Belden Street Sacramento, CA 95815-1731 Dear Dr. Mateer 26

I'm sending your official membership certificate for the Society for Super- 41
visors and Curriculum Developers. Please display it in your office or 55
classroom so other educators and administrators will identify you as par- 70
ticipating in an organization that is shaping the future of our schools. 85

As a new member in the Society, you will receive a free subscription to 99
Leadership in the Nation's Schools, which is published each month, Sep- 120
tember through May. Members receive a large discount on texts that the 134
organization publishes each year. Further, as a member you will be able 149
to register for next year's conference at a reduced rate. 161

I'm glad that you have decided to join the Society for Supervisors and 175
Curriculum Developers, and I hope you will be an active member. (161) 181

Sincerely Ms. Martha E. Ipolito Executive Director xx Enclosure 200/**220**

Document 2
Formal Memo

LP p. 39 or full sheet

Note: If you are using a plain sheet, refer to the note on p. 277 for help in setting up the form.

heading 24

TO:	Jim Kohl, Information Management Director	FROM:	Angela Roski, Vice President for Administration
DATE:	Current date	SUBJECT:	ACCESS RIGHTS

You are authorized to give Ray Allan access to these files on the NuTech com- 39
puter system: GET.BIO.DATA, CLASS.ROST, GRADES, and LOCATE. 51

Mr. Allan is authorized to access this information on the terminal in his office. 68
His authorization is limited to access; he is not permitted to change or print 84
the information stored in the files. 91

Please make the necessary changes to the security program so Ray will be 106
able to access this material beginning on the first of next month, the effec- 121
tive date of his promotion to director of nursing certification. 134

xx 135/**153**

Document 3
Simplified Memo

full sheet

proofread/correct errors

Document 4
Letter

Reformat Document 1 on a plain sheet as a modified block letter with mixed punctuation; proofread/correct errors.

Current date Editorial Staff and Managers APPOINTMENT OF ASSOCIATE 14
EDITOR 15

I am pleased to announce that Jane L. McManis has accepted an offer to join 30
the International Association of Facility Managers as associate editor for the 46
publication, Managing Facilities. 57

Ms. McManis brings to our association a wealth of experience in facilities 72
management. She has managed seven theaters for Cinimex, Inc., in Pensa- 86
cola, Florida; the Dayton Civic Center in Dayton, Ohio; and the Preston Hotel 102
and Conference Center in Dallas, Texas. Jane was graduated from Orlando 116
College where she studied management and communications. She has taught 131
facilities management courses at three colleges. 141

Ms. McManis will begin her editorial duties at the beginning of the month and 157
will be located in the office next to mine. 166

Leona Q. Swartz, Editor xx 171

114d ▶ 30 Assess/ Improve Keyboarding Speed and Control

1. A 1′ writing on each ¶ for speed; find *gwam.*

2. A 1′ writing on each ¶ for control; circle errors.

3. A 3′ writing on ¶s 1-3 combined; find *gwam;* circle errors.

4. Record your 3′ *gwam* to compare with your 3′ *gwam* in 116d.

Skill Building (as time permits)

1. Set a goal of speed or control. If you made 6 or more errors on the 3′ writing, work for control; otherwise, work for speed.

2. Take two 1′ writings on each ¶ trying to increase speed or reduce errors according to your goal.

3. Take a 5′ writing on ¶s 1-3 combined; find *gwam;* circle errors.

4. Record your 5′ *gwam* to compare with your *gwam* in 116d.

all letters used | A | 1.5 si | 5.7 awl | 80% hfw |

	gwam 3′	5′	
The computer is an amazing machine. It is amazing because of the	4	2	38
many things it does, the speed at which it does its operations, and the	9	6	42
degree of accuracy it maintains. In short, the computer is one of man-	14	8	44
kind's most important inventions and a resource that seems to be every-	19	11	47
where and do everything.	20	12	48
Computers are used by students in many classes. They are used by	25	15	51
people who work in health, law, farming, and athletics to record, keep,	30	18	54
and process data. Rock stars use them to run concerts and to write music.	35	21	57
Computers run and work on assembly lines and are used to design many con-	40	24	60
sumer goods.	40	24	60
Computers have changed extensively in the short period they have	45	27	63
existed. Early ones had to be kept in special areas and run by trained	50	30	66
personnel. Today, young children use them to learn or for play. The	54	33	69
jumbo, slow computers of yesteryear have given way to the small, quick	59	35	71
computers in use today.	61	36	72

gwam 3′ | 1 | 2 | 3 | 4 | 5 |
5′ | 1 | 2 | 3 |

Lesson 115 Keyboarding/Language/Composing Skills

115a ▶ 5 Conditioning Practice

each line twice SS (slowly, then faster); DS between 2-line groups; if time permits, rekey selected lines

alphabet 1 The Arizona firm will quote a very good price for the jet's black box.

figures 2 Of the 13,748 people who entered this year's 10k race, 9,652 finished.

shift key 3 The North-Side Vikings beat the Ipseyville Knights on Tuesday evening.

speed 4 Profit is no problem for the sorority social when it is held downtown.

| 1 | 2 | 3 | 4 | 5 | 6 | 7 | 8 | 9 | 10 | 11 | 12 | 13 | 14 |

115b ▶ 20 Improve Keyboarding Skill: Timed Writing

1. Take two 1′ writings on each ¶ of 114d, above; find *gwam* on each writing.

2. Take a 3′ writing on ¶s 1-3 combined; try to equal your best 1′ *gwam* in Step 1.

3. Take a 5′ writing on ¶s 1-3 combined; find *gwam;* circle errors.

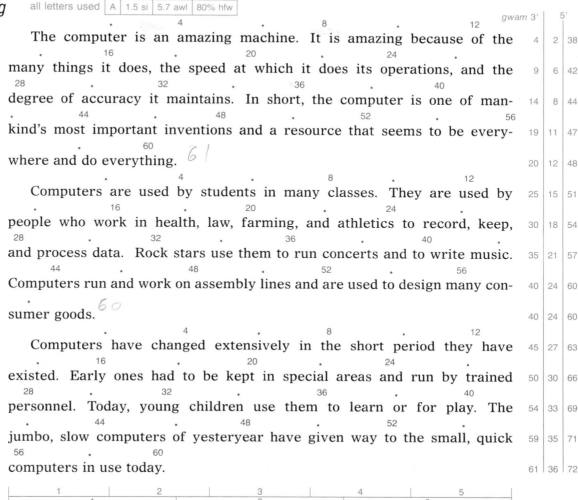

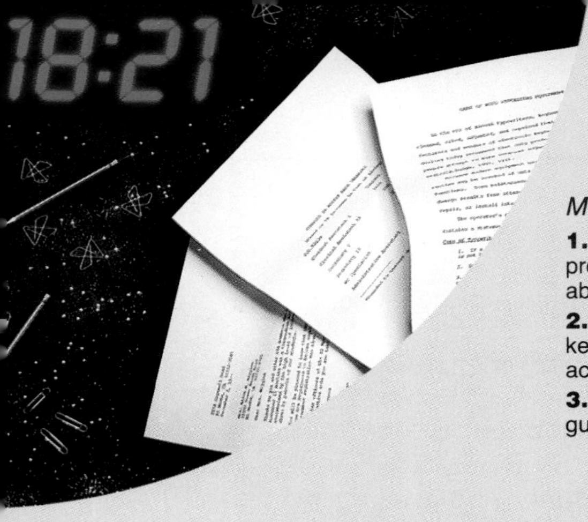

UNIT 40 LESSONS 172 – 175

Evaluate Keyboarding/Document Processing Skills

Measurement Goals

1. To measure/evaluate your competency in processing letters, reports, and tables in acceptable format under time pressure.

2. To measure the speed at which you can key straight copy with a reasonable degree of accuracy.

3. To evaluate your ability to apply your language skills as you key.

Format Guides

1. Paper guide at *0* (for typewriters).

2. LL: 70 spaces for drills and paragraphs.

3. LS: SS drill lines; DS ¶s; space documents as directed.

4. PI: 5 spaces, unless otherwise indicated.

Lesson 172 Evaluate Correspondence Processing Skills

172a ▶ 5 Conditioning Practice

each line twice SS (slowly, then faster); DS between 2-line groups; if time permits, rekey selected lines

alphabet 1 The fight crowd began to exit quickly just as the prize sum was given.

figures 2 The truck with License No. A987-135 is assigned to Space 240 in Lot 6.

long words 3 Two new software packages from nuSofttech are protechNet and safeWork.

speed 4 A key goal of the sorority tutor is to shape or form the right theory.

| 1 | 2 | 3 | 4 | 5 | 6 | 7 | 8 | 9 | 10 | 11 | 12 | 13 | 14 |

172b ▶ 9 Evaluate Straight-Copy Skill

1. Take a 5′ writing on the ¶s at the right.

2. Find *gwam* and number of errors.

3. Record score on LP p. 4.

all letters used | A | 1.5 si | 5.7 awl | 80% hfw |

	gwam 1′	5′	
A job description often lists the education, training, experience,	13	3	41
and personal qualities required of people who hold the job being de-	27	5	44
scribed. A job description is commonly used to list the major functions	42	8	47
of a job and to outline the main duties the person in the job should be	56	11	50
able to perform in a suitable fashion.	64	13	51
Another major function of a job description is to specify the rela-	77	15	54
tionship of the job to other jobs in the business. To do this, the job	91	18	57
description should have a section that names the supervisor of the job	106	21	60
being described and lists the jobs supervised by the person in the job	120	24	62
being described.	123	25	63
It is important that all jobs be analyzed from time to time because	137	27	66
many jobs are likely to change. They change because the duties of the	151	30	69
job often change. Some are dropped and other duties are added. If	164	33	71
changes in a job occur and the job description is not revised, the job	179	36	74
description becomes obsolete because its information is not correct.	192	38	77

gwam 1′ | 1 | 2 | 3 | 4 | 5 | 6 | 7 | 8 | 9 | 10 | 11 | 12 | 13 | 14 |
5′ | 1 | 2 | 3 |

172c ▶ 36 Evaluate Document Processing Skills: Letters/Memos

Time Schedule

Plan and Prepare .... 3′
Timed Production .... 25′
Proofread/Compute *n-pram* ...... 8′

Format and key as many of the letters/memos on p. 302 as you can in 25′.

Compute *n-pram* and turn in your work arranged in document number order.

n-pram =
wds. keyed − (10 × errors) ÷ 25′

115c ▶ 5 Improve Language Skills: Apostrophe

1. Read and key the **Learn** sentence (with number and period), noting how the rule has been applied.

2. Key the **Apply** sentences (with numbers and periods), using the correct punctuation.

3. If time permits, rekey the **Apply** lines at a faster speed.

Use an apostrophe *plus s* to form the plural of most figures, letters, and words (6's, A's, five's). In market quotations, form the plural of figures by the addition of *s* only.

Learn 1. Your d's look like 4's. Chicago Growth Fund 89s are due in 2007.
Apply 2. Reprint all ts, fs, and gs. Buy Prospect 7s this coming month.
Apply 3. He consistently keyed %s as 5s, $s as 4s, and *s as 8s.

To show *possession,* use an apostrophe *plus s* after (1) a singular noun and (2) a plural noun which does not end in *s.*

Learn 4. The children's toys were expensive, but the boy's clothes were not.
Apply 5. We went to the mens store on the left to buy a mans suit.
Apply 6. Marys new coat was found in the womens locker room.

115d ▶ 10 Improve Keyboarding Technique: Letter Emphasis

each line 3 times (slowly, faster, then in-between rate for control)

Goal: To keep hands quiet with keystroking action limited to fingers.

Emphasize: Continuity and rhythm with curved, upright fingers.

j Jed just objected to taking Jim's jeans and jogging jersey on the jet.
k Karl kept Kay's knicknack in a knapsack in the keel of the knockabout.
l All small holes in the lane to the left of my dwelling will be filled.
m Myra meets my mama most mornings at the mall during the summer months.
n Nora's niece and nephew can be tended by only one new nanny on Monday.
o One of four officers opposed opening more offshore moorings for boats.
p Pam's playful puppy pulled the paper wrapping off the apple and pears.
q Quinten quit questioning the requirements for bouquets at the banquet.
r Rory and Larry arrived from a rough carriage ride over the rural road.

115e ▶ 10 Compose at the Keyboard

1. Compose a paragraph describing the most memorable thing that happened to you last year.

2. Jot down the thoughts you want to relate, arrange them in a logical sequence, and then compose your paragraph from your notes.

3. Review your composition; use proofreader's marks to indicate the changes you want to make.

4. Save the copy for Lesson 116.

Lesson 116 Keyboarding/Language/Composing Skills

116a ▶ 5 Conditioning Practice

each line twice SS (slowly, then faster); DS between 2-line groups; if time permits, rekey selected lines

alphabet 1 Fay Bok's new zoo job requires her to do seven or eight complex tasks.
fig/sym 2 The cost of Model #40-79 is $352 plus 6% sales tax and 18% excise tax.
shift key 3 Dana, Jerry, and Fred plan to see the movie, Let Janis Lead the Games.
speed 4 The official goal of the spa downtown is to get my body in good shape.

| 1 | 2 | 3 | 4 | 5 | 6 | 7 | 8 | 9 | 10 | 11 | 12 | 13 | 14 |

116b ▶ 10 Compose at the Keyboard

1. Retrieve the revised copy you prepared in 115e, above.

2. Review the copy once more, marking any additional changes you want to make.

3. Key a final draft of your paragraph with 1½" side margins and "A Most Memorable Thing" as a title; DS the ¶.

Job 6
**Reference Page, Title Page,
and Table of Contents**

Message from
SUSAN DEMMET

*Process the reference page
as the last page of the report; prepare a title page
using my name and position
and the club name. Lastly,
prepare a table of contents
using all side and para-
graph headings.* SD

Job 7
Table

Message from
SUSAN DEMMET

*Here's a promotion schedule
from last year. Process one
for this year by making
these changes.*

*1. Add TENTATIVE to the
heading.*
*2. Change Actual to Esti-
mated.*
*3. Add 1 day to each June
date.*
*4. Change Calendar to
Umbrella.*
5. Increase $ amount by 5%.
*6. Do not use horizontal
lines except to underline
column heads and to place
divider line properly.* SD

Job 8
Memo

Message from SD
SUSAN DEMMET

*Prepare this memo that
I composed at my typewriter.
Address it to all staff; use
PLAYER APPEARANCE
GUIDELINES as the subject.*

REFERENCES

Bullaro, John J., and Christopher R. ~~Edgington~~ Edginton.
 <u>Commercial Leisure Services</u>. New York: ~~MacMill~~ Mac-
 millan Publishing Company, 1986.

Lewis, Guy, and Herb Appenzeller, eds. <u>Successful Sport Man-
 agement</u>. Charlottesville, VA: ~~LawxPublishers~~ The
 Michie Company, 1985.

Rudolph, Barbara. "Bonanza in the Bushes." <u>Time</u>, 1 August
 1988, 38-39.

PROMOTION SCHEDULE FOR MAY, JUNE, AND JULY 19--

Date	Promotion	Actual Cost to Club	Item to Be Given to
May 5	Bat Night	$6,000	All fans under 16
May 18	Sportsbag Day	None*	First 5,500 fans
June 15	Cap Night	$5,000	All fans
June 30	Calendar Day	None*	All fans
July 15	Jersey Day	$3,000	First 5,500 fans

*Sponsor pays for promotion item.

To avoid ~~mostxof~~ last year's problems relating to player appearances that ~~caused~~ resulted in confusion, embarrassment,
and ~~bad~~ poor public relations, please follow these guidelines when you ~~axexasked~~ receive a request for a player appearance.

1. All player appearance requests must be made in writing ~~a
minimum~~ at least ~~10~~ ten days in advance of the appearance date.

2. ~~Check~~ Refer to the Player Appearance Chart to determine
if a player (or the player requested) is available.

3. Once a player's availability has been confirmed, complete ~~anxAppe~~ Player Appearance Form. Send two copies of
this form to the player (one ~~isxto~~ mailed to his home and
~~the~~ another delivered to him via interoffice mail). Send
the third copy to me; keep the fourth copy for your files.

4. Call the player making the appearance the day before the
appearance date to remind him of his commitment and to give
him information about the people he is to meet.

5. After the appearance, call the group to find out if they
were satisfied with the appearance, and then relay these
comments to the player who made the appearance.

116c ▶ 10 Improve Keyboarding Technique: Letter Emphasis

each line 3 times (slowly, faster, then in-between rate for control)

Goal: To keep hands quiet with keystroking action limited to the fingers.

Emphasize: Continuity and rhythm with curved, upright fingers.

s Susanne sat still as soon as Suno served his sushi and sashimi dishes.
t Ted took title to two tiny cottages the last time he went to the city.
u Uri usually rushes uptown to help us unload the sugar from the trucks.
v Vera voted to review the vivid videos during her visit to the village.
w Walter was waving wildly when the swimmers were wading into the water.
x Tax experts explain that we are exempt from the existing excise taxes.
y Your young boys yearn to go yachting each year on my big yellow yacht.
z Zeno puzzled over a zany zealot who seized a bronze kazoo at a bazaar.

116d ▶ 20 Measure Keyboarding Skill: Straight Copy

1. Two 3′ writings; find *gwam*, circle errors on each.

2. Two 5′ writings; find *gwam*, circle errors on each.

Goal: to maintain 3′ rate for 5′.

3. Record better 3′ and better 5′ *gwam*.

4. Compare these rates with those achieved in 114d.

Skill Building (as time permits)

1. Set a goal of speed or control: If you made 6 or more errors on the 3′ writings, work for control; otherwise, work for speed.

2. Take two 1′ writings on each ¶ trying to increase speed or reduce errors according to your goal.

3. Take a 5′ writing on ¶s 1-3 combined; find *gwam*, circle errors.

4. Record your 5′ *gwam* if it exceeded the 5′ rate attained earlier in the lesson.

all letters used | A | 1.5 si | 5.7 awl | 80% hfw

	gwam 3′	5′	
Being able to communicate well is one of the leading keys to the	4	3	43
success of any business. Information must move outside a business and	9	5	45
up, down, and sideways within a business so people can use acquired	14	8	48
facts to make good decisions. The report is one medium that a business	18	11	51
can use to relay information in internal and external directions.	23	13	53
A business report is generally thought to be a written message that	27	16	56
is used to make business decisions. To be of value, the message must be	32	19	59
based on factual information rather than fancy and should be presented	37	22	62
in a format that is easy to read, consistent in style, neat, and free of	42	25	65
keying and language skills errors.	44	27	67
Business reports can be done in many formats. Informal ones can	49	29	69
utilize a letter or memo style. Progress, proposal, annual, or other	53	32	72
major reports are often done in a formal style. These formal reports	58	35	75
have a required style for margins, spacing, and headings and often have	63	38	78
parts such as a title page, a table of contents, and an abstract.	67	40	80

gwam 3′ | 1 | 2 | 3 | 4 | 5
gwam 5′ | 1 | 2 | 3

167b-171b (continued)

Specific promotions

The ideas mentioned below are based on listings in Lewis and Appenzeller (1985, 164-168) and an article that appeared in Time (Rudolph, 1987, 38-39).

Good fans. Since fans in the good category are not likely to be as near their satiation point as those in the avid and best categories, most of this year's promotion efforts will aim at this group. The efforts include continuation of the product give-away promotions allready in place, the addition of quasi-price promotions (2for 1's, half price days, ladies days), and special attractions (fireworks, circus acts, party).

Avid fans. While most of the promotions targeted for the good fans will also work for avid fans, a new multiple-ticket plan will be started help move the avid fans to the higher group. This plan will be named theGOLDen 25" and will allow fans to buy season tickets for 25 games. The only restriction on choice is that the tickets purchased must include at least one game with each opponent.

Best fans. Increasing the games attended is the primary objective for fans in the best fans category. To help accomplish the goal, 30 free parking passes will be given to a person ordering two season tickets this coming year. In addition, season ticket holders will be given speical discounts on extra tickets purchased during the season.

Conclusion

If the marketing efforts result in the addition of 25,000 fans, the GOLD will have made a good market better. This better base will provide the financial base needed to field a competitive team in a first-rate facility.

116e ▶ 5 Improve Language Skills: Apostrophe

1. Read and key the **Learn** sentence (with number and period), noting how the rule has been applied.

2. Key the **Apply** sentences (with numbers and periods), using the correct punctuation.

3. If time permits, rekey the **Apply** lines at a faster speed.

> To *show possession,* use an apostrophe *plus s* after a proper name of one syllable that ends in *s.*

Learn 1. I will buy Tom Ross's watch if it is for sale soon.
Apply 2. Did you see Susan Chris' shoes or Tom Bess' hat near the table?
Apply 3. I just learned Tom Sams' and Rita Tess' books were found.

> To *show possession,* use *only* an apostrophe after (1) plural nouns ending in *s* and (2) a proper name of more than one syllable which ends in *s* and *z.*

Learn 4. The boys' teacher will help with Thomas' science project.
Apply 5. The ladies watches were found in Douglas Variety Store.
Apply 6. Leon Contos's agenda for the officer's meeting was clear.

ENRICHMENT ACTIVITY: Improve Keyboarding and Composing Skills

Improve Keyboarding Skill: Speed-Forcing Drill

1. Each line twice at top speed; then:

2. In each set, try to complete each sentence on the call of 15″, 12″, or 10″ timing as directed. Force speed to higher levels as you move from line to line.

3. Move from Set 1 to Set 2 to Set 3 as you are able to complete the lines in the time allowed.

4. Two 1′ speed-forcing timings on lines 1e, 2e, and 3e. Compare rates.

5. Take additional 1′ timings on the sentence or sentences on which you made your lowest rate(s).

		gwam 15″	12″	10″
	Set 1: High-frequency balanced-hand words emphasized.			
1a	**The girl will hand the sorority emblem to the visitors.**	44	55	66
1b	**The handyman is to go to the field to cut ivy for the bowls.**	48	60	72
1c	**Their goal is to surprise the four city officials during a visit.**	52	65	78
1d	**Eight girls in the dorm lend a hand to the maid to keep the dorm cozy.**	56	70	84
	Set 2: High-frequency combination-response patterns emphasized.			
2a	**Nancy was at the dorm cafe by six p.m. to eat with him.**	44	55	66
2b	**The abstract is to be added to the formal report we drafted.**	48	60	72
2c	**The extra pupil is to join me by the pool to work on fast starts.**	52	65	78
2d	**My dad attested that the barber paid the wage tax to the city auditor.**	56	70	84
	Set 3: High-frequency one-hand words emphasized.			
3a	**Bret saw fast deer retreat after Johnny started uphill.**	44	55	66
3b	**My pupil asserts that great debates are based only on facts.**	48	60	72
3c	**Lilli Mull addressed my pupils on minimum state tax rates on gas.**	52	65	78
3d	**In my opinion, only a few eager pupils read texts on careers in trade.**	56	70	84

| 1 | 2 | 3 | 4 | 5 | 6 | 7 | 8 | 9 | 10 | 11 | 12 | 13 | 14 |

Compose at the Keyboard

1. Compose a paragraph describing an accomplishment of yours of which you are proud.

2. Jot down the thoughts you want to relate, arrange them in a logical order, and then compose your paragraph from your notes.

3. Review your composition, use proofreader's marks to indicate the changes you want to make.

4. Process a final copy.

focus makreting efforts on existing customers first. . . . Internal marketing has shown to be cheaper and more effective at increasing total attendance and/or participation levels. In turn, more satisifed existing customers attract more non consumers so that internal marketing has added benefits (Lewis and Appenzeller, 1985, 174).

An important aspect of internal marketing is that it relies on making existing fans who are good fans into avid fans, making avid fans into our best fans, and maintaining the fans who will not or cannot increase their attendance. Madison GOLD will still need to attract some new fans who will attend a few games during the season.

<u>Madison GOLD Fans</u>

<u>Existing attendance</u>. Based on the information we have garnered during the past three years, it has been determined that Madison GOLD fans fall into the following categories:

Fan Category	No. of Fans in Category	Average No. of Games Attended	Computed Total Attendance
Best Fans	500	23	11,500
Avid Fans	1,050	14	14,700
Good Fans	14,500	3.5	50,750
Computed Total Attendance			76,950

<u>Projected Attendance</u>. The following methods can be used to increase attendance for coming season.

1. "Move" 10% of the avid fans into the best fans category; move 5% of the good fans into the avid category; and attract new fans to replace those who are "moved" or stop attending.

2. increase the average number of games attended in each category by 10%.

If these goals can be realized, the total attendance in would climb almost 25 percent to 95,928, as shown in the table below.

Fan Category	No. of Fans in Category	Average No. of Games Attended	Computed Total Attendance
Best Fans	605	25.3	15,306
Avid Fans	1,775	15.4	27,335
Good Fans	14,500	3.675	53,287
Computed Total Attendance			95,928

(continued, p. 299)

UNIT 27 LESSONS 117 – 122

Extend Report Formatting Skills: Leftbound Reports

Learning Goals

1. To learn to format and process leftbound reports with footnotes and endnotes.
2. To learn to format and process leftbound reference lists (bibliographies) and title pages.
3. To improve language-skill competency.

Format Guides

1. Paper guide at *0* (for typewriters).
2. LL: 70 spaces for drills; as required for documents.
3. LS: SS drills; as required for documents.
4. PI: 5 spaces for ¶s and documents.

FORMATTING GUIDES: LEFTBOUND REPORTS WITH FOOTNOTES AND ENDNOTES

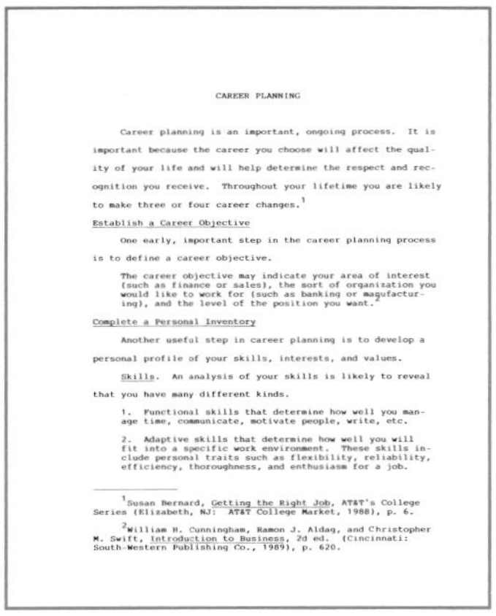

CAREER PLANNING

Career planning is an important, ongoing process. It is important because the career you choose will affect the quality of your life and will help determine the respect and recognition you receive. Throughout your lifetime you are likely to make three or four career changes.[1]

Establish a Career Objective

One early, important step in the career planning process is to define a career objective.

The career objective may indicate your area of interest (such as finance or sales), the sort of organization you would like to work for (such as banking or manufacturing), and the level of the position you want.[2]

Complete a Personal Inventory

Another useful step in career planning is to develop a personal profile of your skills, interests, and values.

Skills. An analysis of your skills is likely to reveal that you have many different kinds.

1. Functional skills that determine how well you manage time, communicate, motivate people, write, etc.

2. Adaptive skills that determine how well you will fit into a specific work environment. These skills include personal traits such as flexibility, reliability, efficiency, thoroughness, and enthusiasm for a job.

[1] Susan Bernard, Getting the Right Job, AT&T's College Series (Elizabeth, NJ: AT&T College Market, 1988), p. 6.

[2] William H. Cunningham, Ramon J. Aldag, and Christopher M. Swift, Introduction to Business, 2d ed. (Cincinnati: South-Western Publishing Co., 1989), p. 620.

Leftbound Report

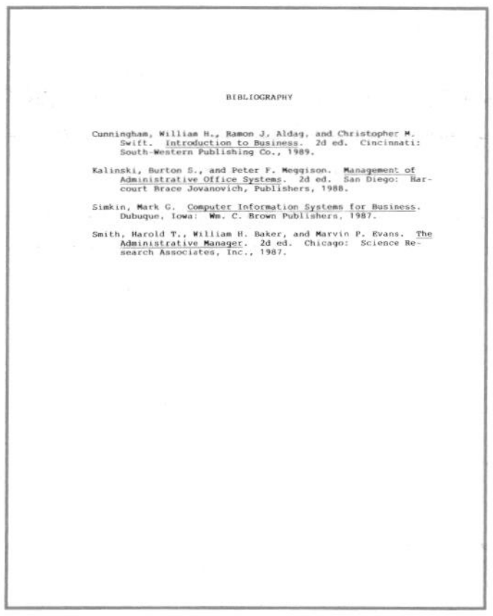

BIBLIOGRAPHY

Cunningham, William H., Ramon J. Aldag, and Christopher M. Swift. Introduction to Business. 2d ed. Cincinnati: South-Western Publishing Co., 1989.

Kalinski, Burton S., and Peter F. Meggison. Management of Administrative Office Systems. 2d ed. San Diego: Harcourt Brace Jovanovich, Publishers, 1988.

Simkin, Mark G. Computer Information Systems for Business. Dubuque, Iowa: Wm. C. Brown Publishers, 1987.

Smith, Harold T., William H. Baker, and Marvin P. Evans. The Administrative Manager. 2d ed. Chicago: Science Research Associates, Inc., 1987.

Leftbound Bibliography

Many business reports, as well as personal/professional ones, are bound at the left margin. When reports are leftbound, an additional half inch is left at the left side for binding; thus, the left margin is 1½ inches wide (15 pica or 10-pitch spaces; 18 elite or 12-pitch spaces). The right margin is 1 inch wide as in unbound reports.

Vertical placement and spacing is the same as for unbound reports.

Margins Leftbound and Unbound Reports

Top	Place main heading on line 10 (pica) line 12 (elite)
Side	1½″ left and 1″ right margins for leftbound 1″ left and right margins for unbound
Bottom	At least 1″ on all pages

Headings and Subheadings

Main heading. Center the main heading in ALL CAPS over the *line of writing;* leave a quadruple space (QS) below it.

To find the center of the line of writing, add the readings at the left and right margins on the line-of-writing or format scale and divide the total by 2.

pica (10-pitch): $(15 + 75) \div 2 = 45$
elite (12-pitch): $(18 + 90) \div 2 = 54$

Backspace from these points to center titles and headings in leftbound reports.

Side headings. Begin side headings at left margin, underline, and capitalize the first letter of all main words. DS above and below side headings.

Paragraph headings. Begin paragraph headings at paragraph indention point, underline and follow by a period. Capitalize the first letter of only the first word.

Documentation (Footnotes)

When material is quoted or closely paraphrased, the source is indicated by keying a footnote reference number a half space *above* the line of writing immediately after the quoted material and a correspondingly numbered footnote at the foot of the page (separated from last line of text by a 1½″ underline).

```
. . . electronic mail."¹  Special forms

may be used for formatting such mail.

________________

     ¹S. H. VanHuss and W. R. Daggett, Jr.,
Electronic Information Systems (Cincinnati:
South-Western Publishing, Co., 1990), p. 308.
```

For equipment that does not permit half spacing, keying the reference figure *on* the line of writing immediately preceded and followed by a diagonal is acceptable.

```
   . . . electronic mail."/1/  Special forms
```

Separate the footnote divider rule from the report body by a DS; DS below the divider rule to begin the footnote.

Indent each footnote 5 spaces and SS it; DS between footnotes. If your equipment can raise figures, key the figure in the footnote a half space *above the line of writing.* If your equipment cannot raise figures, key the figure in the footnote *on the line of writing* followed by a period and two spaces.

In planning footnote placement, allow at least a 1″ bottom margin below footnotes on all pages except the last. On the last page, the dividing line and footnotes may begin a DS below the last line of text *or* be placed at the bottom of the page with at least 1″ of white space in the bottom margin.

Number footnotes consecutively throughout a report, and place each footnote on the same page as its in-text reference figure.

Page Numbers

The first page need not be numbered, but it may be. When numbered, center the number on line 62. For the second page and subsequent pages, place numbers on line 6 approximately even with the right margin.

Radio Station WMMG Pregame Party. Station WMMG will provide free refreshments (soft drinks and hot dogs), a disc jockey, and music from 6:00 p.m. to 7:00 p.m. before an August game. The date will be selected by mid-July and WMMG will publicize the party and the game.*

Additional Efforts

The marketing staff will continue to plan promotional events for strategic times in the season. These events will be consistent with the objectives of the marketing plan that we discussed and is almost ready for distribution.

---

*The decision is being delayed until mid-July so we can determine the date that our nearest competitor in the standings will be playing us at home.

Job 5
Report with Internal Citations

Message from SUSAN DEMMET

Here's the most recent draft of the marketing strategy report I have cut and pasted together. Process a final draft for me.

SD

A MARKETING STRATEGY

strategy QS extensive statistical

This marketing plan is based upon the marketing staff's

analysis of (1) the responses to surveys which have been com-

7,500

pleted by over 500 fans during each of the last three years and (2) the information availiable as a result of the data base information system instaled two years ago. It uses a

an innovative The plan

marketing orientation where "the commercial leisure service business adjusts its products and services to meet the needs of the customer" rather than the traditional selling orientation that focuses "on products or services that the business produces," (Bullaro, 1986, 212).

the

and Edginton

Assumptions

The plan has been constructed upon the following assumptins:

1. Madison Gold is a mature sports organization with an established base market.

2. Madison Gold's marketing strategy should be based on the results of the market research conducted from 1989-1991.

can

3. Existing fans will account for the majority of increases in attendance in the next three-year periodd.

Internal Marketing DS recommends

The staff believes that internal marketing as described in Lewis and Appenselder (1985, 157-175) should be adopted

during the next three years. Internal marketing is a technique used to

117a ▶ 5 Conditioning Practice

each line twice SS (slowly, then faster); DS between 2-line groups; if time permits, rekey selected lines

alphabet 1 Maxim just now realized his favorite racquet broke from rough playing.
fig/sym 2 My Policy #49-3816 for $75,000 will mature 20 (twenty) years from now.
figures 3 Flight 1089 leaves at 8:45 p.m. while Flight 2496 leaves at 10:37 p.m.
speed 4 They are to fix the problem with the right signal so it works at dusk.

| 1 | 2 | 3 | 4 | 5 | 6 | 7 | 8 | 9 | 10 | 11 | 12 | 13 | 14 |

117b ▶ 5 Improve Language Skills: Word Choice

1. Study the spelling and definition of each word.
2. Key the line number (with period), space twice, then key the **Learn** sentence; key the **Apply** sentences in the same format, selecting the correct word in parentheses to complete each sentence.

loan (n) a sum of money lent at interest

lone (adj) companionless; solitary

lessen (vb) to cause to decrease; to make less

lesson (n) something to be learned; a period of instruction; a class

Learn 1. The lone transaction in our department today was the loan he made.
Apply 2. I gave him a (loan, lone) so he could buy the (lone, loan) car on the lot.
Apply 3. The (loan, lone) person in the lobby wanted to make a (loan, lone).

Learn 4. This lesson will lessen the time it takes you to do the job.
Apply 5. My failure to listen will (lessen, lesson) what I can learn from this (lessen, lesson).

117c ▶ 10 Preapplication Drill: Formatting Footnotes

1. Review Formatting Guides for leftbound reports with footnotes on p. 206.
2. Set margins for a leftbound report (1½" left and 1" right margin).
3. Leaving a bottom margin of about 1", determine the line on which to begin keying the material at the right.
4. Key the last two lines of text and the footnotes in correct format.

```
        key to financial control.1  A budget is often created on the
                                                              DS
margin 1½"  basis of past experience.2                                1"
                                      DS
dividing line 1½"  ___________________
                                      DS
             1Burton S. Kaliski and Peter F. Meggison, Management of
        Administrative Office Systems, 2d ed.  (San Diego:  Harcourt
        Brace Jovanovich, Publishers, 1988), p. 447.
                                                   DS
             2Richard M. Hodgetts and Donald F. Kurato, Effective
        Small Business Management, 3d ed.  (San Diego:  Harcourt Brace
        Jovanovich, Publishers, 1989), p. 265.
```

117d ▶ 30 Format Leftbound Report with Footnotes

plain full sheet; correct errors

1. Study again, if necessary, the Formatting Guides on p. 206. Note in the model report on p. 208 how the formatting and spacing guides are applied.

Note. The model report is shown in pica (10-pitch) type, camera reduced. If you are keying in elite (12-pitch) type, your line endings will be different from those in the model but the vertical spacing will be the same.

2. Key the model report, following the formatting and spacing annotations shown on it.

Footnote Placement Hints: Typewriter

1. Make a light pencil mark at the right edge of the paper 1" from the bottom.

2. As you key each footnote reference number in the body of the report, make another pencil mark ½" above the previous one. This will help you reserve about 3 line spaces for each footnote. (If you have a page line gauge, such as the one on LP p. 5, use it.)

Job 4
Report

Message from SUSAN DEMMET

Mary processed this draft for me to review before she left. I reviewed it; it looks good. You will have to find and correct spelling and keying errors; I didn't mark them when I reviewed the report. Also do the following:

1. Key GOLD in all caps when it refers to the baseball club.

2. Delete WMMG Radio from the sponsor list in paragraph 2.

3. Key "giveaway" as "give-away" when it appears in paragraph 5.

4. Key "homerun" as two words in paragraph 6.

5. Place each explanatory note at the bottom of the page on which it appears.

SD

SPECIAL PROMOTIONS -- A PROGRESS REPORT
as of December 31, 19--

The marketing staff has lined up numerous promotions that should promote the Madison Gold Baseball Club and increase attendance at home games this coming season.

Preseason Promotions

Pocket schedules. Sponsors have been lined up to pay for, print, and distribute over one million pocket schedules, starting late January. The sponsors are Parkway Autos, Taco Haven, First City Bank, WMMG Radio, Scanlon Soft Drinks, Foodmarket, and local Quick Stop Marts.

Promotional video. A vidoetape of highlights from last year's season has been produced under the direction of Promo Video, Inc., and is available for distribution to professional, civic, and other community groups.*

GOLD Caravan. Players and other field personnel are scheduled to participate in the Gold Caravan during the month of January. Appearances are scheduled in over 45 stores within a 50-mile radius of Madison.

In-Season Promotions

Giveaway promotions. The giveaway items and schedule for May, June, and July will be finalised by the middle of January. Five such events are planned for this threemonth period, and four more are to be planned for the remainder of the season.

Chili homeruns. If one of our players hits a homerun in the ninth inning, the Chili Palace will give a free bowl of chili to everyone with a valid ticket stub from the game.

GOLD Program certificates. One of the players will autograph 15 programs before each game, and certificates from local restaurants will be awrded to those having autogrphed programs.

Special Promotions

Madison Area Chamber of Commerce Family Night. For $25 the Gold offers a mail order package of four tickets, soft drinks, hot dogs, and one parking pass. The Chamber prints and distributes coupons that publicize the game and offer.

Little League Night. The Gold offers community Little League associations discounted tickets good for admission, hot dog, and soft drink, provided the association places a minimum order of 100 tickets. Each league will promote the offer to its players.

Senior Citizen GOLD Cards. The Gold provides senior citizens with wallet-size GOLD cards that entitle them to a 10% discount on up to four tickets for each game and free parking in Lot A at day games. The Madison Senior Citizen Association will promote this offer to all of its members in a February mailing.

---

*Six copies of the 30-minute videotape are available for distribution; two copies always will be kept for staff to use.

MONEY MANAGEMENT line 10 pica line 12 elite

QS

Money is a resource you must learn to manage wisely so you can buy the goods and services you need and have some money left to do things you find enjoyable and worth doing. DS

A Budget DS

One way to help balance your income and expenses is to prepare a budget. A budget is an itemized spending plan that enables you to set priorities for the money that remains after you have accounted for your fixed expenses.[1] Also, a budget helps you develop effective money management habits. DS

1½" left margin

Prepare a Budget DS

1" right margin

To prepare a budget for a month, list in one column the sources of your money and note when you expect it. Include gifts you will receive, interest from your savings account, allowances, and wages and tips you earn. In another column, identify what you want to save and list the amounts for fixed expenses--the cost of the "must buys." DS

Indent quotations 5 spaces from left margin.

> After you include all your fixed expenses, total each column and subtract the monthly amounts from your monthly income in the first listing you made. That will give you what you have left for comforts, self-improvements, and luxuries.[2] DS

_______________ DS

[1]Robert K. Gerver and Richard J. Sgroi, Dollars and Sense (Cincinnati: South-Western Publishing Co., 1989), p. 500. DS

[2]Caroline Reynolds, Dimensions in Professional Development, 3d ed. (Cincinnati: South-Western Publishing Co., 1988) p. 301.

1 line 62

(at least 1" bottom margin)

Leftbound Report with Footnotes

167b-171b (continued)

Job 2
Table

Message from SUSAN DEMMET

Please prepare a final copy of the GOLD Caravan schedule from the rough draft at the right while I compose a letter to send with it.

SD

MADISON GOLD CARAVAN SCHEDULE*

January 15 and 16, 19--

January	Time	Location	Store
15	~~11:45 a.m.~~ [1:00 p.m.]	Green City Mall	~~Harvey's~~ [Altmants]
15	4:00 p.m.	Crestmont Village	The Sport Spot
15	7:30 p.m.	East Shopping Mall	Everetts
16	~~1:00 p.m.~~ [11:30 a.m.]	Five Points	Athlete's Wear
16	2:30 p.m.	Westend Village	Oscar's Corner
16	5:45 p.m.	High Point Center	~~The Wilson Co.~~ [D & J Clothing]
16	~~7:45~~ [8:00] p.m.	Southland Mall	Big League's

---

*The members ~~of the~~ caravan are Manager, Al S. Rojah and players, Chuck H. Mravic [Mravic] and Jim R. Alberti. The driver is Ted S. Botts. [SS]

Job 3
Letters
LP pp. 27-31

Message from SUSAN DEMMET

Here's a rough-draft copy of a letter that will be sent to the manager and players taking part in the caravan on January 15 and 16. Their names are listed at the bottom of the Caravan schedule.

Prepare a letter and envelope for each; date each letter January 6. The addresses are as follows:

Manager:
609 Menees Lane
Madison, TN 37115-5807

Chuck:
317 Adair Road
Jackson, TN 38305-2912

Jim:
6700 Forest Road
Columbus, GA 31907-3011

SD

Dear ______________:

The ~~itinerary~~ schedule for this month's Gold Caravan has been set for January 15 and 16, the two days you have agreed to represent the ~~club~~ GOLD baseball team. I have neclosed [enclosed] a copy of the schedule for the two days ~~so you can see the~~ and have listed the locations [and stores at which] you will appear.

Please ~~report come to~~ be in my office by ~~11:30~~ 11:15 a.m. on January 15 so we can have a ~~short~~ luncheon meeting to review the purpose of the [public appearances] ~~caravan~~ and the schedule.

We ~~plan to~~ will all leave the stadium in one car at 12:30 [p.m.] to drive to the first [location] ~~appearnace~~.

Sincerly

118a ▶ 5 Conditioning Practice

each line twice SS (slowly, then faster); DS between 2-line groups; if time permits, rekey selected lines

alphabet 1 Jeb, Dom, and I favor analyzing the weekly exchange prices frequently.

fig/sym 2 The agreement (#19-723) must state that Payment #48 is $506; not $312.

figures 3 I hope to bus 67 players, 140 band members, 23 teachers, and 598 fans.

speed 4 Diane and she may visit the ancient city chapel when they are with us.

| 1 | 2 | 3 | 4 | 5 | 6 | 7 | 8 | 9 | 10 | 11 | 12 | 13 | 14 |

118b ▶ 10 Check Language Skills

plain full sheet; LL: 70

As you read and key the ¶, correct any errors in capitalization, spelling, word choice, punctuation, etc., that you find. If you make any errors as you key, correct those also. Check work with your teacher.

The result's of Glenn Adam's pole of members of the teenagers' Club served as the bases for the dezision to reserve space on john jones' Best of the '90s tour. The usual fair fore this tur is $395.95, however the Clubs' fair will be at leased 20% lower. The club's fair is lower becuase john jones has an idol dual-engine plain which can fly Club member's to Buffalo, New York, Erie, Pennsylvania, and Dayton, Ohio tomorrow. Plan to be at the air port at 7:45 am, the plain leafs at 8;15 am.

118c ▶ 35 Process a Leftbound Report with Footnotes

plain full sheets; PI: 5; DS the body; correct unmarked as well as marked errors and errors you make as you key

Recall Hints

1. Refer to proofreader's marks on RG 10 as needed.
2. Review formatting features for leftbound reports, p. 206.
3. The left margin for long quotations is at the paragraph indention point. Long quotations are single-spaced.
4. Footnotes go on the same page as the footnote reference number is keyed.
5. Plan to end the page so there is at least 1″ of white space for the bottom margin.
6. The dividing line is 1½″ in length.

words

Career Planning 3

Career planning is an important, ong(o)ing process. It is 15
important because the career you ~~follow~~ (choose) will affect ~~your~~ (the) 26
quality of (your) life and will help determine the respect and 38
recognition you ~~will~~ recieve. Throughout your lifetime you 49
are likely to make (three or four) career changes ~~times~~.[1] 59

Establish a Career Objective 71

One (early,) important ~~and early aspect of~~ (step in the) ~~career~~ (start) planning (process) is to 83
define ~~a~~ (your) career objective. 89

> The career objective may indicate your area of interest 101
> (such as finance or sales), the sort of organization 111
> you would like to work for (such as banking or manufac- 122
> turing), and the level of the position you want.[2] 132

Complete a Personal Inventory 144

Another useful step in ~~the~~ career planning is to devel- 154
op a personal profile of your skills, values and interests. 166

(continued, p. 210)

167a-171a ▶ 5 (daily)
Conditioning Practice

each line twice SS (slowly, then faster); DS between 2-line groups; if time permits, rekey selected lines

alphabet 1 Jun quickly wrapped the five dozen big macaroons and the six cupcakes.

fig/sym 2 Ben sold 132 at $34 less 15%; 98 at $87 less 20%; & 56 at $76 less 8%.

shift key 3 RLS is pushing Part #196-74 for their PC's named QuikNet and QuikWork.

speed 4 The giant icicle did melt in the big right hand of the ensign on duty.

| 1 | 2 | 3 | 4 | 5 | 6 | 7 | 8 | 9 | 10 | 11 | 12 | 13 | 14 |

167b-171b ▶ 45 (daily)
Simulation: Madison GOLD

Study the information on p. 293 before starting the simulation and refer to it as needed throughout the processing of the jobs in this unit. Correct any errors you make.

While Miss Ross is on vacation, Ms. Demmet will give you instructions for the following jobs.

Job 1
Letters

LP pp. 21-25

Message from SUSAN DEMMET

Mary Ross was unable to send letters to the three people named on the cards clipped to the bottom of the letter at the right.

Use the letter at the right and the information on the cards to prepare a letter for each person. Use January 5 for the date; insert the appropriate ad size in the body of the letter.

SD

Madison GOLD is pleased to report that sales of its program book, GOLD Program, have increased in each of the last five seasons. Another increase is predicted for the coming season since the club expects to draw fans in record numbers.

A copy of the (ad size) page advertisement you placed in last year's program is enclosed for you to review. If you want to change your ad, revise the enclosed copy or send new copy.

Write the ad size you want in the upper left corner of the copy you return; you will receive an invoice in February. The prices for the ads are listed below.

Ad Size	Rate
Quarter Page	$ 125
Half Page	225
Full Page	400

Madison GOLD appreciates your support and is pleased that the GOLD Program helps promote your business.

Henry L. Yu
West Chevrolet
207 Mann Road
Madison, TN 37115-4219
Quarter-page ad

Mary T. Salter-Day
Valley Office Supplies
501 Marthonna Road, N
Madison, TN 37115-4507
Full-page ad

James E. Covic
C & F Construction
625 Vista Drive
Memphis, TN 38114-2323
Half-page ad

118c (continued)

Self-Check Questions

1. Do you know where you will end the first page? If not, plan ahead at this time and then check your page-ending mark or line indicator as you near the bottom of the page.

2. Do you know where the page number is keyed on the second page? If not, refer to p. 206.

3. Are you maintaining a correct right margin? If not, you should divide words according to the word division rules you have learned.

4. Do you recall that when an enumeration exceeds one line, the second and all succeeding lines begin under the number. If several lines are needed to key the enumeration(s), the left margin should be reset until the enumeration(s) is keyed.

words

Skills. An analyses of your skills is likely to reveal 179
that your have different kinds of skills. 186

1. Functional skills that determine how well you 196
manage time, communicate, motivate people, write, etc. 208

2. Adaptive skills that determine how well you will 218
fit into a specific work environment. These skills include 230
personal traits such as flexibility, realiability, ef- 241
ficeincy, thoroughness, and enthusiasm for the job. 251

3. Technical skills or work content skills that are 260
required to perform a specific job. These skills may 271
include keyboarding, accounting, computer operation, 285
and language arts skills.3 291

Interests. "Interests refer to the things that you 303
like or dislike."4 By listing and analyzing them you should 315
be able to identify a desirable wrok environment. For exam- 327
ple, your list is likely to indicate if you like to work 338
with things or people, work along or with others, lead or 349
follow others, being indoors or outdoors. 358

Values. These are your priorities in life and you 370
should identify them early so you can pursue a career which 382
will enhance your ability to achieve them. Some of the more 394
obvious considerations include the importance you place on 404
family, security, wealth, prestige, creativity, power, inde- 416
pendence, and glamour. 421

_______________ 425

1Susan Bernard, Getting the Right Job, A T & T's Col- 439
lege Series (Elizabeth, NJ: AT&T College Market, 1988), p. 451
2. 452

2William H. Cunningham, Ramon J. Aldag, and Christopher 463
M. Swift, Introduction to Business, 2d ed. (Cincinnati: 479
South-Western Publishing Co., 1989), 620. 488

3Adele Scheele, "Deciding What You Want To Do", Busi- 500
ness Week Careers, 1988 ed., 7. 511

4Bernard, Getting the Right Job, 1-2. 523

5Cunninham, Introduction to Business, p. 617. 537

UNIT 39 LESSONS 167 – 171

Madison GOLD Baseball Club (An Office Simulation)

Performance Goals

To demonstrate your ability to integrate the knowledge and skills reviewed and acquired in Phase 7.

1. Processing letters, reports, and tables.

2. Detecting language-skills and keyboarding errors.

3. Making decisions in appropriate situations.

Documents Processed

1. Letters/Simplified Memorandum

2. Tables

3. Report with Explanatory Notes

4. Report with Internal Citations

5. Reference Page, Title Page, and Table of Contents

MADISON GOLD BASEBALL CLUB: AN OFFICE SIMULATION

Unit 39 (Lessons 167-171) is designed to give you the kinds of experiences you are likely to have when you are working in an office. Assume you are enrolled in a second-year document processing course at your high school and have been doing general office work for Madison GOLD Baseball Club (the official corporate name) as a participant in your school's cooperative education program. Madison GOLD is a minor league baseball team in Madison, Tennessee. You have been answering the telephone, filing, photocopying, and processing routine letters, reports, and tables for various people since you started your co-op education assignment.

Miss Mary L. Ross (the full-time secretary assigned to Ms. Susan M. Demmet, Director, Promotions and Marketing) is scheduled for vacation this coming week, and you have been asked to do Miss Ross's work while she is away. Ms. Demmet is glad to have you because her colleagues have spoken highly of the quality of your work and your work ethic and habits. You are eager to have this assignment because it could lead to a full-time position when you are graduated, if you show that you can perform well.

Since this is the off-season for baseball, most of the activities in the Promotions and Marketing area focus on promoting next year's team and schedule.

Specific promotional activities include such things as having members of Madison GOLD Baseball Club remain active in the communities from which the Club draws its fans; developing marketing strategies; planning specific promotions for the upcoming season and planning various other activities designed to enhance the image of the baseball team so attendance can be increased in the coming season.

You are familiar with the general office policies, procedures, and routines used by the Club. To help you learn the specific preferences of Susan Demmet, her secretary left you these directions and tips. Follow the guidelines below. If a formatting guide is not given, use your previously acquired knowledge to decide the format features for a document.

Correspondence

1. Prepare all letters in block format with open punctuation; supply an appropriate salutation and complimentary close (if you cannot determine the appropriate title for a woman, use Ms.); use your reference initials; supply enclosure and copy notations as needed.

2. Prepare memorandums in simplified style with appropriate margins and vertical line spacing.

Tables

1. Center all tables horizontally and vertically on full sheets.

2. Determine the number of spaces to leave between columns and whether items within a column should be single- or double-spaced.

3. Center all headings.

Reports

1. Reports should be formatted as unbound.

2. Cited works should be formatted as internal citations with references.

Other

1. Be particularly alert to correct errors in punctuation, capitalization, spelling, word usage, and consistency (for example, "GOLD" appears in all caps when referring to the baseball team).

2. Susan Demmet always uses the title "Ms." before her name and her position title in the letters she sends. Also, she insists that you use the personal titles of the people to whom she sends letters.

Lesson 119 Leftbound Report with Footnotes/Bibliography

119a ▶ 5 Conditioning Practice

each line twice SS (slowly, then faster); DS between 2-line groups; if time permits, rekey selected lines

alphabet	1	Max will authorize me to get quality products from major bike vendors.
fig/sym	2	Each computer desk (42″ wide × 36″ long × 27″ high) will cost $158.90.
figures	3	Mary served 138 donuts, 279 danish, 60 cupcakes, and 45 elephant ears.
speed	4	They are proficient for the quantity and rigor of work they are to do.
		| 1 | 2 | 3 | 4 | 5 | 6 | 7 | 8 | 9 | 10 | 11 | 12 | 13 | 14 |

119b ▶ 35 Process a Leftbound Report with Footnotes/Bibliography

words

Document 1 — Leftbound Report with Footnotes
leftbound; DS; correct errors; review format features on p. 206 if necessary

words

COMPUTERS AND DECISION MAKING 6

Computers have widespread use in today's 14
world. Computers are used by workers who pro- 23
duce goods and services and by consumers who 32
use goods and services. 37

Computers in Business 46

People who pursue a career in business will 55
learn that computers have helped reduce the 64
cost of and time devoted to managing and pro- 73
cessing information. Computers have had no 81
equal for computing, classifying, sorting, mov- 91
ing, editing, or storing information. 99

New Uses 102

Computers have been used to provide "the 110
right information to the right manager at the 119
right time in a cost-effective manner."[1] This 129
use is taking on a new dimension as other in- 138
novative computer applications are introduced. 147
The new use is to provide top-level managers 156
with resources to improve decision making. 165
Three such resources are decision support sys- 174
tems, expert systems, and decision modeling. 184

Decision support systems. Decision support 197
systems are computer applications which sup- 206
port the decision-making process in a business. 216

Decision support systems allow managers 224
to ask a series of "what if" questions about 233
business problems. With a decision support 242
system, a manager and computer essen- 249
tially engage in a dialogue. That is, the 258
manager sits at the microcomputer and asks 266
a series of questions to which the computer 275
responds. The computer does not make a 283
decision; instead, it provides information 292
which the manager can use for decision 299
making.[2] 301

Expert systems. Expert systems are com- 312
puter applications which "store knowledge about 322
a given subject in a data base."[3] The knowledge 332
stored is the data and decision rules pertain- 341
ing to a specialized knowledge area a nonex- 350
pert needs to be able to perform at the level 359
comparable to that of an expert in that knowl- 368
edge area. 370

Decision modeling. The term decision mod- 382
eling refers to computer applications designed 392
to free managers from having to make routine 401
decisions. A computer model "is designed to 410
behave as the decision maker behaves."[4] Once 419
the model meets accuracy standards of the 427
decision maker, it then becomes the decision 436
maker's replacement. 441

These computer applications are significant 450
enhancements to the functions of the computer, 459
and they are likely to become more prevalent 468
as a means to improve decision making.[5] 478

________________ 482

[1]Mark G. Simkin, Computer Information 494
Systems for Business (Dubuque, Iowa: Wm. C. 507
Brown Publishers, 1987), p. 305. 513

[2]William H. Cunningham, Ramon J. Aldag, 521
and Christopher M. Swift, Introduction to 533
Business, 2d ed. (Cincinnati: South-Western 544
Publishing Co., 1989), pp. 69-70. 551

[3]Burton S. Kalinski and Peter F. Meggison, 559
Management of Administrative Office Systems, 577
2d ed. (San Diego: Harcourt Brace Jovanovich, 586
Publishers, 1988), p. 507. 592

[4]Cunningham, Introduction to Business, p. 70. 606

[5]Harold T. Smith, William H. Baker, and 614
Marvin P. Evans, The Administrative Manager, 628
2d ed. (Chicago: Science Research Associates, 638
Inc., 1987), p. 67. 642

165c (continued)

Table 3

Format on full sheet; DS data; CS: 6; center headings; correct errors.

Learning cue: To indicate a total, underline the last entry the full length of the total figure; DS; key the total figure.

				words
THIRD QUARTER ANALYSIS				5
	Cost of	Operating	Operating	10
Department	Goods Sold	Expenses	Profits	25
Hardware	$ 3,758	$ 2,753	$ 1,655	33
Lawn & Garden	5,785	4,595	1,858	39
Toys	2,987	1,758	1,369	44
Clothing	15,878	6,549	7,337	50
Appliances	7,650	2,876	4,735	60
Totals	$36,058	$18,531	$16,954	68

Table 4

Format on full sheet; DS data; CS: 6; center headings; correct errors.

				words
CHEMICAL ELEMENTS				4
(Discoveries Since 1950)				9
Chemical		Atomic	Year	13
Element	Symbol	Weight	Discovered	21
Hahnium	Ha	262	1970	25
Rutherfordium	Rf	261	1969	30
Lawrencium	Lr	260	1961	35
Nobelium	No	258	1958	39
Mendelevium	Md	258	1955	44
Fermium	Fm	257	1953	48
Einsteinium	Es	254	1952	53
Californium	Cf	251	1950	58
________________				61
Source: The World Almanac.				70

Lesson 166 Sustained Document Processing: Tables

166a ▶ 5 Conditioning Practice

each line twice SS (slowly, then faster); DS between 2-line groups; if time permits, rekey line 3

alphabet 1 Visitors did enjoy the amazing water tricks of six quaint polar bears.

figures 2 Bea Day flew 3,580 miles in January, 1992 and 4,976 in December, 1991.

symbols 3 I used the search/locate key to find each @, #, &, and * in my report.

speed 4 Lena is proficient when she roams right field with such vigor and pep.

| 1 | 2 | 3 | 4 | 5 | 6 | 7 | 8 | 9 | 10 | 11 | 12 | 13 | 14 |

166b ▶ 45 Sustained Table Processing

format/key each table as directed; proofread; correct errors

Time Schedule

Plan and Prepare .... 5′
Timed Production .... 35′
Proofread/Compute *n-pram* ..... 5′

1. Make a list of the tables to be processed:

p. 289, 163d, Table 1
p. 290, 164b, Table 1
p. 290, 164b, Table 3
p. 291, 165c, Table 1
p. 292, 165c, Table 3

2. Arrange paper and correction materials for efficient handling.

3. At the signal to begin, process as many tables as you can in 35′. Correct errors as you key. Proofread each table before removing it from machine.

4. Determine *n-pram;* turn in tables in the order given in Step 1.

3 line 6

BIBLIOGRAPHY line 10 pica line 12 elite

QS

Cunningham, William H., Ramon J. Aldag, and Christopher M. Swift. Introduction to Business. 2d ed. Cincinnati: South-Western Publishing Co., 1989. DS

Kalinski, Burton S., and Peter F. Meggison. Management of Administrative Office Systems. 2d ed. San Diego: Harcourt Brace Jovanovich, Publishers, 1988. DS

Simkin, Mark G. Computer Information Systems for Business. Dubuque, Iowa: Wm. C. Brown Publishers, 1987. DS

Smith, Harold T., William H. Baker, and Marvin P. Evans. The Administrative Manager. 2d ed. Chicago: Science Research Associates, Inc., 1987.

1½" left margin

1" right margin

119b (continued)

Document 2 — Bibliography
plain full sheet; SS entries with a DS between; correct errors
Key model bibliography above.

Top margin: line 10 pica; line 12 elite
Side margins: left, 1½" right, 1"
Bottom margin: at least 1"

Learning Cues
1. Key page number on line 6 at the right margin.
2. ALL CAP heading.
3. Begin first line of each entry at left margin; indent remaining lines 5 spaces.
4. SS each entry; DS between entries.

Lesson 120 — Leftbound Report with Endnotes

120a ▶ 5 Conditioning Practice

each line twice SS (slowly, then faster); DS between 2-line groups; if time permits, rekey selected lines

alphabet 1 Jo quickly sighted seven African whydahs by the bear complex at the zoo.
fig/sym 2 Here are my latest costs: #621-3A, $54; #908/5, $76; and #56-89, $38.
figures 3 Janice ordered 27 pants, 36 skirts, 50 belts, 48 socks, and 19 shirts.
speed 4 A problem for the ill ensign was to focus on the rigor of the rituals.

| 1 | 2 | 3 | 4 | 5 | 6 | 7 | 8 | 9 | 10 | 11 | 12 | 13 | 14 |

120b ▶ 45 Learn to Format a Leftbound Report with Endnotes

plain full sheets; leftbound report format; correct errors

1. Format the leftbound report given on p. 213. DS the body of the report.
2. Raise the endnote reference numbers or use /1/ if your equipment cannot raise the reference numbers.

Learning Cues: Endnotes
Endnotes are keyed on a separate sheet of paper which follows the last page of the report. They are arranged in the same order as footnotes.

In endnotes, the reference number is either *elevated* or is placed *on the line and followed by a period.* Vertical spacing is the same as for a reference page.

164c ▶ 5 Improve Language Skills: Word Choice

1. Study the spelling and definitions of each pair of words.

2. Key the **Learn** line with the number and period, noting the proper use of the often confused words.

3. Key the **Apply** line, choosing the words that complete each sentence correctly.

confidant (n) one to whom secrets are confided

confident (adj) having assurance or certainty, as of success

envelop (vb) to surround; encircle

envelope (n) a flat, folded paper container for a letter

Learn 1. Ada is confident that her confidant will protect the mission's goals.
Apply 2. The (confidant/confident) is not (confidant/confident) in his ability.

Learn 3. The wrapper was placed so it would envelop the stack of envelopes.
Apply 4. Jim's large hand could (envelop/envelope) the small (envelop/envelope).

Lesson 165 Tables

165a ▶ 5 Conditioning Practice

each line twice SS (slowly, then faster); DS between 2-line groups; if time permits, rekey line 3

alphabet 1 Zeb checked the liquid oxygen just before moving down the sizable pad.
figures 2 Deb's new stock fell 4.50 points to 86.75 on Tuesday, August 31, 1992.
long words 3 An electronic time sheet can be used in project-oriented environments.
speed 4 The visitor also saw six big turkeys in the field by the lake at dusk.

| 1 | 2 | 3 | 4 | 5 | 6 | 7 | 8 | 9 | 10 | 11 | 12 | 13 | 14 |

165b ▶ 5 Reinforce Formatting of Multiple-Line Column Headings

1. Multiple-line column headings are SS and the last line of each heading should be keyed on the same horizontal line.

2. Center the multiple-line column headings by longest item, whether it is one of the column-heading lines or column-entry lines. Key the first line of the headings on line 12 on a half sheet of paper, short edge on top; SS data; CS: 6; do not correct errors.

Distribution Center	Center Manager	Quota Last Year
East	Mary McKaiser	125,000
South	Tom Ridgewood	97,000

165c ▶ 40 Processing Tables

Table 1

Format on full sheet; DS data; CS: 8; center headings; correct errors.

Table 2

Reformat Table 1 on half sheet, long edge at top; SS data; CS: 6; center headings; correct errors; arrange lakes in order of size, listing the one with the largest area first, the second-largest area second, etc.

Table 3 and Table 4 are on p. 292.

THE GREAT LAKES (words: 3)

Great Lake	Length (miles)	Breadth (miles)	Area (Square Miles)	words
				8
				22
Erie	241	57	32,630	26
Huron	206	183	74,700	30
Michigan	307	118	67,900	35
Ontario	193	53	34,850	39
Superior	350	160	81,000	44

____________ 48

Source: The World Almanac. 55

120b (continued)

words

NETWORKING--A STATUS REPORT 6

The purpose of this report is to inform you 14
of the status of the project to network the micro- 24
computers assigned to the Public Relations and 34
Advertising departments. 39

Decisions Made 45

Based on the recommendations made in Mr. 53
John Boyer's report,[1] it has been decided to in- 63
stall a star network: 67

> One of the most popular ways of creating 75
> local area networks is with physical coaxial 84
> and a host computer. The cables physically 93
> connect to the central host computer and 101
> thus "hardwire" the network. This is often 110
> called a star network because workstation 119
> connections (nodes) radiate from the host 127
> computer like the many points of a star.[2] 136

The decision has been made to network 25 144
computers, 5 printers, and a scanner; to pur- 153
chase a higher level graphics package; and to 162
delay adding an electronic mail system. 170

Current Activities 178

The director of computing is seeking prices 186
on the following items which are needed to in- 196
stall the network. 200

1. Network software, network cards, active 208
and passive hubs, cabling, etc. 215
2. Network versions of existing word pro- 223
cessing, desktop publishing, data base, and 232
spreadsheet applications software packages. 241
3. Graphics software which will run on the 250
network. 252
4. A microcomputer capable of serving as 260
the host computer on the network. 267
5. Furniture to accommodate the equipment 276
which will be purchased. 281

Advantages and Disadvantages 293

Advantages. The chief advantage of net- 303
working is that the department's 25 micro 311
users will share computer files, software pack- 320
ages, a scanner, and computer printers.[3] 329
Sharing will improve the quantity and quality 338
of the documents and presentations. 346

Disadvantages. One drawback to network- 356
ing is the large initial investment in hardware 366
and software that must be made. Another 374
relates to security in that a "greater effort to 384
protect the system and its sensitive file infor- 393
mation"[4] will need to be taken. 400

ENDNOTES 402

[1]John A. Boyer, "Networking--A Preliminary 410
Report," (Pittsburgh: Office Network Consul- 419
tants, Inc., 1990), p. 5, photocopied. 427

[2]Mark G. Simkin, Computer Information 439
Systems for Business (Dubuque, Iowa: Wm. C. 452
Brown Publishers, 1987), p. 161. 459

[3]"The Future, According to Wang," The 467
Office, June 1988, p. 40. 474

[4]Simkin, Computer Information Systems for 488
Business, p. 163. 493

Lessons 121-122 Leftbound Report with Endnotes/Title Page

121a-122a ▶ 5 (daily) Conditioning Practice

each line twice SS (slowly, then faster); DS between 2-line groups; if time permits, rekey selected lines

alphabet 1 Viki will begin to expedite the zone office's major quarterly reports.

fig/sym 2 Catalog item #9087 will cost Anessi & Co. $432.65 (less 10% for cash).

figures 3 The team averages 28,915 fans per game in a stadium that seats 34,760.

speed 4 The toxic gas odor in the air did make the girls sick when they slept.

| 1 | 2 | 3 | 4 | 5 | 6 | 7 | 8 | 9 | 10 | 11 | 12 | 13 | 14 |

121b-122b ▶ 45 (daily) Format Leftbound Report with Endnotes/Title Page

plain full sheets; correct errors

1. Format and key the report with endnotes presented on the next two pages in leftbound format.

2. Use the report title, your name, your school's name, and current date to prepare a title page in leftbound format.

Note: If your equipment permits you to raise the reference numbers, raise them; otherwise, place the reference numbers on the line preceded and followed by diagonals: /1/.

163e ▶ 5 Improve Language Skills: Word Choice

1. Study the spelling and definitions of each pair of words.

2. Key the **Learn** line with the number and period, noting the proper use of the often confused words.

3. Key the **Apply** line with the number and period, choosing the words that complete the sentence correctly.

canvas (n) a heavy, coarse, tightly woven fabric

canvass (vb) to conduct a survey on a given topic; to poll

cereal (n) an edible grain, such as wheat, corn, or oats

serial (adj) of, forming, or arranged in a series

Learn 1. The man waiting near the canvas awning was to canvass all walkers.
Apply 2. I will (canvas/canvass) all designers on the use of (canvas/canvass) as a wall covering.

Learn 3. Serial numbers are assigned to farmers who grow grain for cereal.
Apply 4. Each box of (cereal/serial) had a different (cereal/serial) number.

Lesson 164 Tables

164a ▶ 5 Conditioning Practice

each line twice SS (slowly, then faster); DS between 2-line groups; if time permits, rekey line 3

alphabet 1 Gwen moved quickly to pack the extra dozen lanyards Freda just bought.
figures 2 The library has 95,468 books, 1,209 periodicals, and 3,735 references.
3d row 3 Porter worked quietly to prepare to fire the pretty pottery for Terry.
speed 4 When the auditor works in the city, he is to handle their big problem.

| 1 | 2 | 3 | 4 | 5 | 6 | 7 | 8 | 9 | 10 | 11 | 12 | 13 | 14 |

164b ▶ 40 Processing Tables: Various Paper Sizes (Centered Column Heads)

Table 1
Format on full sheet; DS data; CS: 10; correct errors.

Table 2
Reformat Table 1 on half sheet, long edge at top; SS data; CS: 6; do not correct errors.

			words
PRINCIPAL RIVERS OF THE WORLD			6
River	Continent	Kilometers	16
Nile	Africa	6,680	20
Amazon	South America	6,400	25
Yangtze	Asia	5,800	29
Hwang	Asia	4,873	32
Zaire	Africa	4,700	36
Amur	Asia	4,500	39
____________			43
Source: Collier's Encyclopedia.			54

Table 3
Format on full sheet; DS data; CS: 12; correct errors.

Learning cue: Add the line-of-writing scale readings at the left and right edges of the paper and divide the sum by 2 to determine the center point.

Table 4
Reformat Table 3 on half sheet, short edge at top; DS data; CS: 4; do not correct errors.

Learning cue: The line of underscores indicating total should be as long as the longest item in the column.

			words
MARY MORRIS' TEACHING ASSIGNMENT			7
(Fall 19-- Semester)			11
Course	Credits	Enrollment	21
Accounting I	1	28	24
Business Law	.5	24	28
Computer Applications	.5	20	34
Document Processing I	1	32	39
Document Processing I	1	29	44
Study Hall	---	45	49
Totals	4	178	52

121b-122b (continued)

words

A COURSE PROPOSAL 4

The business education faculty has voted 12
unanimously to propose that a one-semester 20
desktop publishing (DTP) course be added to 29
the curriculum next fall. The course could be 39
an elective course for all students who have 48
completed the existing word processing or 56
business computer applications courses. 64

Rationale for the Course 74

Desktop publishing is one of the fastest- 82
growing computer applications because its use 91
saves businesses money and reduces the time 100
required to create professional-looking docu- 109
ments and presentation graphics.[1] Because of 118
this increased use and the resulting demand for 128
employees who can use DTP software, the busi- 136
ness education faculty has a responsibility to 146
teach students about this technology.[2] 154

In addition to learning DTP applications, stu- 163
dents will apply their writing, problem-solving, 173
decision-making, and creativity skills as they 182
prepare text, plan graphics, and lay out the 191
various documents they have to process in the 200
course.[3] 202

Course Description 210

Desktop publishing provides students with 218
an opportunity to learn about desktop publishing 228
and how to use DTP software. Students write 237
text, plan graphics, and design document layout 246
for various business documents. Experience 255
with laser printers and scanners is also acquired. 266
Being a competent user of word processing 274
and graphics software is a prerequisite for the 284
course. 285

Course Objectives 292

Students who complete the desktop publish- 301
ing course will: 304

1. Understand what desktop publishing is, 313
the benefits of desktop publishing, and how 322
desktop publishing works.[4] 327

2. Have gained "hands on" experience using 336
a microcomputer, desktop publishing soft- 344
ware, a laser printer, and a scanner. 352

3. Have designed and created newsletters, 360
certificates, business cards, letterheads, re- 369
port covers, fliers, and directories which are 379
used extensively in business. 385

words

4. Understand the desktop publishing field 394
and know of the employment opportunities 402
in the field. 405

Teaching/Learning Strategies 416

Readings, lectures, demonstrations, and 424
class discussions will be used for about 25 per- 434
cent of the class time to accomplish the course 443
objectives relating to acquisition of knowledge 453
and understanding. Students will spend the re- 462
maining class time applying what they have 471
learned. During this time, they will use DTP 480
and other software which supports DTP to pro- 489
duce the required documents. 495

Teaching/Learning Resources 506

Recommendation. It is recommended that 517
this course be taught in a classroom with micro- 526
computers, printers, and at least one scanner 536
on a network. Furthermore, it is recommended 545
that section enrollment not exceed 25 students 554
and that each student have a microcomputer 563
workstation. 566

If this recommendation is accepted, the fol- 574
lowing equipment will be needed: 581

1. Twenty-seven 80286 microcomputers (25 589
for students, 1 for the teacher, and 1 to be 598
used as the file server on the network). 607
Each with two floppy disk drives, one fixed 616
disk, graphics board, one serial port, one 624
parallel port, LAN board, and enhanced 632
keyboard. 634

2. Twenty-four black and white monochrome 643
monitors with video adapters. 649

3. Three VGA color monitors with VGA 657
video adapters. 660

4. Twenty-six mouse units. (A mouse unit 669
is a handheld pointer used to manipulate the 678
cursor on the microcomputer monitor.) 685

5. One desktop, flatbed design scanner with 694
interface kit and scanner software. 702

6. Three laser printers with 8½″ × 11″ paper 711
tray. 712

Cost and location. It is estimated that it 725
will cost no more than $15,000 to upgrade the 734
hardware and software in one of the existing 743
microcomputer classrooms to meet the specifi- 752
cations needed to offer this desktop publish- 760
ing course. The faculty recommends that the 769

163a ▶ 5 Conditioning Practice

each line twice SS (slowly, then faster); DS between 2-line groups; if time permits, rekey line 3

alphabet	1	This bright jacket has an amazing weave and is of exceptional quality.
figures	2	Flight 679 will leave on Runway 28 at 10:45 p.m. with 13 crew members.
shift key	3	Mary Smith, Robert Kwon, and F. T. Pax work for MacDougal & O'Connell.
speed	4	Iris held half the land for the endowment for the ancient city chapel.

| 1 | 2 | 3 | 4 | 5 | 6 | 7 | 8 | 9 | 10 | 11 | 12 | 13 | 14 |

163b ▶ 15 Processing Tables: Blocked Column Headings

Table 1

Format on full sheet; DS data; CS: 8; block column headings; correct errors.

Table 2

Reformat Table 1 on half sheet, long edge at top; SS data; CS: 6; block column headings; correct errors.

Learning cue: Key $ beside the first number in column (and with total figure in column, if used) in a position so it is one space to the left of the largest number in the column.

BUSINESS EDUCATION BUDGET — words 5

Fiscal Year Starting June 1, 19-- — words 12

Account Name	Budget	words
		20
Dues and Subscriptions	$ 225	26
Supplies General	975	32
Instructional Equipment	24,637	36
Instruction Supplies	2,450	43
Other Services	1,895	48
Faculty Salaries	110,139	53

163c ▶ 5 Formatting Column Headings

1. Review centering of column headings in formatting guides on p. 288.
2. Center the column headings and entries at the right by the longest line, whether heading or entry. Key the headings on line 12 on a half sheet of paper, long edge at top; CS: 6; DS data; do not correct errors.

Model Number	Capacity	Cost
625.348	Low	$347.99
625.3481	Medium	374.65
625.34811	High	396.44

163d ▶ 20 Processing Tables: Centered Column Headings

Table 1

Format on full sheet; DS data; CS: 6; correct errors.

Table 2

Reformat Table 1 on half sheet, long edge at top; SS data; CS: 8; arrange column entries in alphabetical order by subject; do not correct errors.

ANN MAY'S SUBJECT SCHEDULE — words 5

Subject	Period	Room	words
			13
Business Dynamics	1	East-118	19
World History	2	South-135	24
Algebra	3	West-126	28
English Composition	4	North-109	34
Physical Education	5	North-Gym	40
Document Processing II	6	East-114	47
Science and Technology	7	West-129	54

121b-122b (continued)

words

computing resources in Room 101 be upgraded 778
and used and that the room be named the Business 787
ness Technologies Computer Laboratory. When 796
completed, this room will be able to support in- 805
struction which utilizes word processing, data 815
base, graphics, spreadsheet, and communica- 823
tions computer software packages. 830

Evaluation and Grading 839

Students will be evaluated according to their 848
performance on written examinations, the qual- 857
ity and quantity of documents produced, and 866
classroom participation. Written examinations 876
will be given near the end of each grading 884
period, unannounced quizzes will be given pe- 893
riodically during each grading period, and re- 902
quired documents will be due throughout the 911
course. Grades will be computed based on the 920
following weighting: 924

1. Desktop publishing documents--50%. 932
2. Unannounced quizzes--10%. 939
3. Written examinations--30%. 945
4. Classroom participation--10%. 952

Conclusion 956

The business education faculty believes that 965
the desktop publishing course must be added to 975
the curriculum so the department can continue 984
to equip graduates with up-to-date skills and 993
knowledge they need to enter and perform well 1002
in the business world. 1007

Truly, desktop publishing is a technology 1015
whose time has come. It will have a signifi- 1024
cant impact on the way information is handled 1033
and presented and will become a productivity 1042
tool in most businesses. And, like all present 1052
computer applications in business education, 1061
the teaching of desktop publishing is being de- 1070
fined by those business teachers who are will- 1079
ing to experiment, test, fail periodically, and 1089
try again.[5] 1091

ENDNOTES 1093

1. Michael Antonoff, "Setting Up for Desk- 1102
top Publishing," Personal Computing, July 1987, 1115
p. 76. 1116

2. Janice Schoen, Henry and Heide R. 1124
Perrault, "Guidelines for Choosing and Using 1133
Desktop Publishing Software," Instructional 1144
Strategies, Winter 1989, p. 1. 1153

3. Rose Mary Wentling, "Desktop Publish- 1161
ing: A New Approach," Business Education 1173
Forum, March 1989, p. 29. 1179

4. Wentling, pp. 27-28. 1184

5. Wentling, p. 28. 1188

ENRICHMENT ACTIVITY: *Timed Writing*

1. Take two 5′ writings; find *gwam* on each.
2. Proofread and circle errors on each.
3. Record better *gwam* rate.

all letters used | A | 1.5 si | 5.7 awl | 80% hfw

gwam 3′ | 5′

There are few job skills more important than being able to present 4 | 3 | 43
your ideas clearly. This skill is needed when you are speaking to your 9 | 6 | 46
boss, co-workers, or customers. If you cannot present your ideas in a 14 | 8 | 48
skillful manner, you will not be able to establish the trust, credi- 19 | 11 | 51
bility, or rapport needed to be a valued worker. 22 | 13 | 53

Fortunately, there are techniques and strategies that you can use 26 | 16 | 56
to improve your skills in this area. Many of them are easy to under- 31 | 19 | 59
stand and can be controlled by you when you are speaking. First, you 36 | 21 | 61
should make eye contact with the person who is listening because the 40 | 24 | 64
contact suggests that you express a sincere interest in the listener. 45 | 27 | 67

The volume of your voice is also critical. You should always speak 50 | 30 | 70
loud enough to be heard but not so loud as to make the listener uncom- 54 | 33 | 73
fortable. Also, the volume of your voice should be varied. You should 59 | 35 | 75
talk louder than required to emphasize major points and talk softer than 64 | 38 | 78
usual at some points to encourage listening. 67 | 40 | 80

gwam 3′ | 1 | 2 | 3 | 4 | 5
gwam 5′ | 1 | 2 | 3

UNIT 38 LESSONS 163 – 166

Assess/Improve Table Processing Skills

Learning Goals

1. To assess and reinforce knowledge of table format.
2. To improve ability to process tables.
3. To improve language-skill competency.

Format Guides

1. Paper guide at *0* (for typewriters).
2. LL: 70 spaces or as directed.
3. LS: SS word and drill lines; or as directed within an activity; space tables as directed.
4. CS: (columnar spacing) as directed.

FORMATTING GUIDES: TABLES

Full sheet

CHEMICAL ELEMENTS

(Discoveries Since 1950)

Chemical Element	Symbol	Atomic Weight	Year Discovered
Hahnium	Ha	262	1970
Rutherfordium	Rf	261	1969
Lawrencium	Lr	260	1961
Nobelium	No	258	1958
Mendelevium	Md	258	1955
Fermium	Fm	257	1953
Einsteinium	Es	254	1952
Californium	Cf	251	1950

Source: The World Almanac.

Half sheet, long edge at top

THE GREAT LAKES

Great Lake	Length (Miles	Breadth (Miles)	Area (Square Miles)
Superior	350	160	81,000
Huron	206	183	74,700
Michigan	307	118	67,900
Ontario	193	53	34,850
Erie	241	57	32,630

Source: The World Almanac.

Half sheet, short edge at top

BUSINESS EDUCATION BUDGET

Fiscal Year Starting June 1, 19--

Account Name	Budget
Dues and Subscriptions	$ 225
Faculty Salaries	110,139
General Supplies	975
Instructional Equipment	24,637
Instructional Supplies	2,650
Other Services	1,895

To format tables, you must know how to center vertically and horizontally.

Vertical Centering (top to bottom)

Tables are keyed on sheets so that the top and bottom margins are approximately equal. Approximately half of the lines of the table are placed above vertical center and approximately half are placed below the vertical center.

To determine the line on which to key the main heading, take the following steps:

1. Count the total lines needed in the table, including internal blank line spaces.

2. Subtract the total lines needed from lines available (66 for full sheet; 33 for half sheet, long edge at top; 51 for half sheet, short edge at top).

3. Divide the remainder by 2 to determine the number of the line on which to start. If a fraction results, disregard it. If an even number results, space down that number of lines from the top edge of the paper. If the number is odd, use the next lower number.

By dropping fractions and using even numbers, tables are placed a line or two above the exact center--in what is called "reading position."

Horizontal Centering (side to side)

Tables should be placed horizontally so that an equal number of blank spaces appears in the left and right margins. Half the number of characters and spaces in the lines of the table should be to the left of the horizontal center point of the paper, and half should be to the right of the horizontal center point.

Spacing between columns of tables varies, depending upon the number of columns to be centered. For ease of centering, leave an even number of spaces between columns. Use these steps to center horizontally:

1. Clear all margin and tab stops.

2. To find exact horizontal center, add the typewriter or format scale reading at the left and right edges of the paper and divide the total by 2.

3. Backspace from center point once for every 2 strokes in the longest item of each column, whether the longest item is a column heading or column entry. Carry over to the next column any extra stroke at the end of a column but ignore any extra stroke at the end of the last column. Then backspace once for every 2 spaces between columns. Set left margin stop.

4. Space forward once for each stroke in the longest item in the first column plus once for each space between Columns 1 and 2. Set a tab stop at this point for Column 2; continue the procedure for the remaining columns.

Centering Column Headings

Take the following steps to center column headings over their respective columns.

Note: When backspacing or spacing forward in the following procedures, do not backspace or space forward for any odd or leftover stroke at the end of any column entry or column heading.

When Column Heading is Shorter than Longest Column Entry

1. Determine the center point of the column by spacing forward once for every 2 characters and spaces in the longest column entry.

2. From the center point of the longest entry, backspace once for every 2 characters and spaces in the column heading.

3. Begin keying the column heading where the backspacing stops.

When Column Heading is Longer than Any Column Entry

1. Determine the center point of the column heading by spacing forward once for every 2 characters and spaces in the column heading.

2. From the center point of the column heading, backspace once for every 2 characters and spaces in the longest column entry.

3. The longest column entry should begin where the backspacing ends. Reset tab stop at this or other appropriate point to key the column entries.

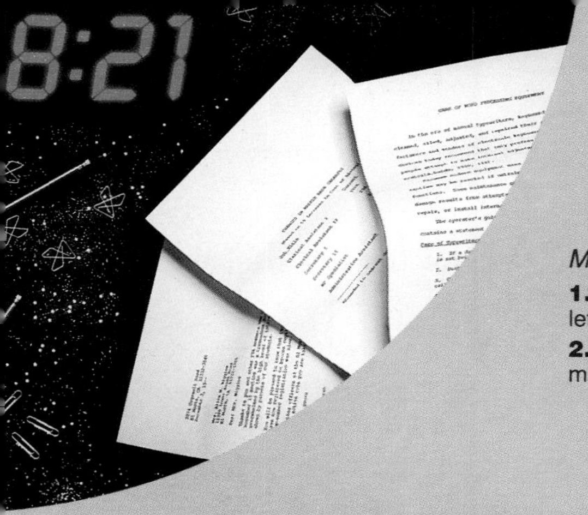

UNIT 28 LESSONS 123 – 125

Evaluate Letter, Report, and Table Processing Skills

Measurement Goals

1. To evaluate your ability to process tables, letters, and reports in correct format.

2. To measure your ability to key straight-copy material.

Format Guides

1. Paper guide at *0* (for typewriters).

2. LL: 70 spaces for drills and ¶s; as required for documents.

3. LS: SS drills; DS ¶s; as required for tables, letters, and reports.

4. PI: 5 spaces for ¶s and documents.

Lesson 123 *Evaluate Straight-Copy/Letter Processing Skills*

123a ▶ 5 *Conditioning Practice*

each line twice SS (slowly, then faster); DS between 2-line groups; if time permits, rekey lines 2 and 3

alphabet	1	Jim wants both freshmen guards to execute the zone press very quickly.
figures	2	They won the last three games by scores of 135-117; 102-94; and 80-76.
fig/sym	3	Ed called (505) 257-5980 before 1:15 p.m. and 413-6766 after 4:15 p.m.
speed	4	Pamela may name an official tutor to work for the widow and eight men.

| 1 | 2 | 3 | 4 | 5 | 6 | 7 | 8 | 9 | 10 | 11 | 12 | 13 | 14 |

123b ▶ 8 *Evaluate Straight-Copy Skill*

1. A 5′ writing on all ¶s.

2. Determine *gwam* and number of errors.

3. Record *gwam* and errors to compare with 124c and 125b.

all letters used | A | 1.5 si | 5.7 awl | 80% hfw |

	gwam 3′	5′	
A business is an entity that uses investment money, raw materials,	4	3	41
and/or labor to make a profit or offer a service to consumers. The	9	5	43
success of the business depends to a large extent on the management	14	8	46
skills of the people who start, organize, and operate the business.	17	10	48
The owners are certain to earn profits if the business is successful.	22	13	51
All businesses should try to improve society. They can do this	26	16	54
by selling quality products and services that are valued and demanded.	31	19	57
A thriving business can be a way for a worker to earn an income, gain	36	22	60
security, and grow as a person and as a professional. Also, a dutiful	41	24	62
business can help by aiding civic affairs.	44	26	64
In our country's economic system, the public plays a major part in	48	29	67
determining which businesses will be successful and which ones will not.	53	32	70
The public gets this critical part because it has the freedom to choose	58	35	73
to buy or not to buy the goods and services that businesses bring to the	63	38	76
marketplace.	63	38	76

gwam 3′ | 1 | 2 | 3 | 4 | 5 |
gwam 5′ | 1 | 2 | 3 |

161c-162b (continued)

words

of this material will be based on the work of 662
Manning and Curtis who concluded: 669

> There is no universally effective style of 678
> leading and following. Sometimes it is best 687
> for the leader to tell subordinates what to 695
> do; sometimes it is best for leaders and sub- 704
> ordinates to make decisions together; and 713
> sometimes it is best for the subordinates to 722
> direct themselves.[3] 726

____________________ 730

[3]George Manning and Kent Curtis, <u>Leader-</u> 739
<u>ship</u> (Cincinnati: South-Western Publishing Co., 749
<u>1988</u>), p. 56. 752

Document 2
Bibliography

1. Review formatting guides for preparing a bibliography on p. 281 and RG 9.

2. Format the references shown at the right as the bibliography for Document 1.

words

BIBLIOGRAPHY 3

Manning, George, and Kent Curtis. <u>Leadership</u>. Cincinnati: South-Western 20
Publishing Co., 1988. 24

Ray, Charles, and Janet Palmer. <u>Office Automation: A Systems Approach</u>. 47
Cincinnati: South-Western Publishing Co., 1987. 57

Reynolds, Caroline. <u>Dimensions in Professional Development</u>. 3d ed. 78
Cincinnati: South-Western Publishing Co., 1987. 88

Stout, Vickie Johnson, and Edward A. Perkins, Jr. <u>Practical Management</u> 107
<u>Communication</u>. Cincinnati: South-Western Publishing Co., 1987. 122

Documents 3 and 4
Title Page and Table of Contents

1. Review the formatting guides on p. 281 for preparing a title page and a table of contents.

2. Prepare a title page for Document 1; use your name, school, and today's date.

3. Prepare a table of contents for Document 1. Use side and ¶ headings as entries; insert leaders by alternating periods and spaces, noting whether the first period is on an odd or even space.

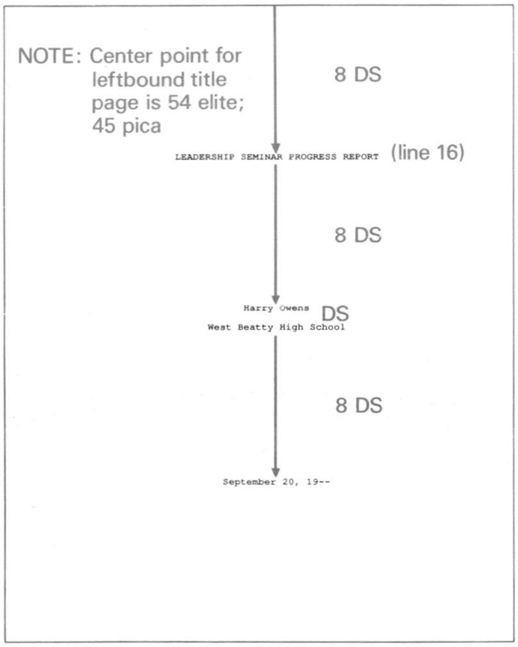

Leftbound title page

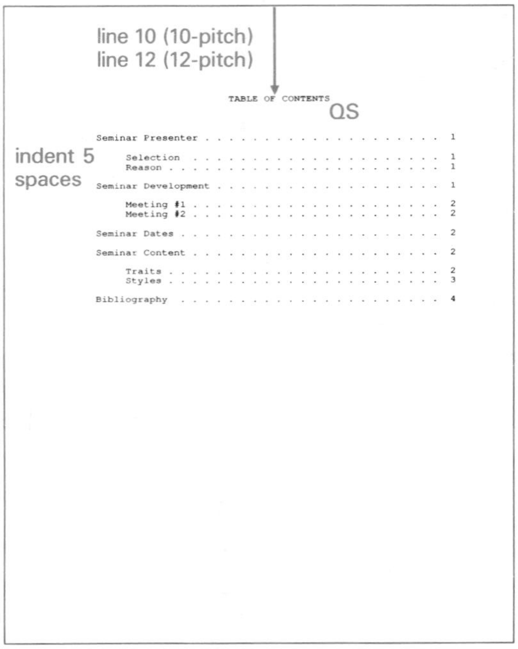

Leftbound table of contents

Document 5
Topbound Report

Topbound reports differ from unbound reports in only two ways: (1) the first item keyed on each page is 2 lines lower than for unbound reports; (2) page numbers are centered at the bottom of the page on line 62.

1. Reformat Documents 1-4 as a topbound report. Begin text on
line 12, pica (10 pitch)
line 14, elite (12 pitch).

2. On page 2, begin text on
line 10, pica (10 pitch)
line 10, elite (12 pitch).

3. Center page numbers on line 62 from top edge of the paper.

4. Begin title, bibliography, and contents pages 2 line spaces lower than for unbound reports to allow for binding.

123c ▶ 37
Evaluate Letter Processing Skills

Time Schedule
Plan and prepare .... 4′
Document processing .... 25′
Proofread/compute *n-pram* ... 8′

1. Arrange materials for ease of handling.
(LP pp. 75-79 and one plain full sheet)

2. Format and key Documents 1-4 for 25′. Proofread and correct errors before removing paper from machine.

3. After time is called, proofread again and circle any uncorrected errors. Compute *n-pram.*

Document 1
Short Letter

block format; open punctuation; address envelope

Document 2
Average Letter

modified block format; block ¶s; mixed punctuation; address envelope

Date the letter **May 27, 19--.** Address the letter to

Attention Customer Relations
Haynes and Jones, Inc.
1697 Wilson Avenue
Ames, IA 50010-5365

Close the letter

Henrietta J. Hadley, M.D.

xx

Enclosure

Add the following postscript:

I have bought many other electronic appliances from your store; this is the first time I have been dissatisfied.

Document 3 is on p. 218.

words

May 15, 19--|Mr. Gene M. Sakely|Highlands High School|700 Elm Street| 14
Muncie, IN 47302-2346|Dear Mr. Sakely 22

Thank you for inviting me to the "Career Planning" conference that was held 37
at your school last week. The session topics were relevant and all the pre- 52
senters were excellent. 57

The panel of recent graduates was the highlight of the day for me. Their 72
remarks on college studies and the first few months of employment were 86
very enlightening. 90

The conference will benefit my students, too, because it provided me with 105
information about careers I can share with them. 115

Sincerely|Ms. Anita B. Redacki|Business Educator|xx|c Dr. Geraldine W. 129
Greene, Principal 132/**148**

---

words

opening lines 21

Ladies and Gentlemen: 25
Enclosed is a copy of my receipt for the stereo sys- 36
tem I purchased at your East Mall store. The system 46
includes an AM/FM radio, cassette player/recorder, 56
compact disc player, and two speakers. 64
I am very satisfied with the system except for 74
one of the speakers. It seems that a bass speaker 84
in one of them has developed a small tear which 94
distorts the sound. The salesperson who sold me 103
the system indicated that tears are not covered 113
by the one-year limited warranty. 120
While I suspect the tear was caused by de- 128
fective speaker material, I cannot prove it. I can 139
assure you, however, that it was not a result 148
of unreasonable use or improper care by me. 157
Will you please authorize a new speaker so 165
my patients can enjoy the excellent sound the 175
system produced when it was installed. 182
Sincerely yours, 186

closing lines 216/**234**

161c-162b ▶ 30/45 (daily)
Document Processing: Reports

Use leftbound format for the first four documents below and on p. 287; topbound for Document 5.

Document 1
Leftbound Report with Footnotes

1. Begin formatting the documents below and on p. 287. You will have two class periods to complete them.

2. There are 9 embedded (unmarked) errors in the report body. Find and correct them and any keying errors you may make as you key.

3. When you complete the first 4 documents, assemble them in proper order and then complete Document 5.

words

LEADERSHIP SEMINAR PROGRESS REPORT 7

The development of the leadership seminars 16
for supervisors and first-line managers are pro- 25
gressing on schedule. One seminar will be con- 34
ducted at each of the 4 Indiana plant sights. 44
The primary objective of the seminars is to 53
have the participants understand the following: 62

1. The importance of having leaders at all 71
levels of the corporation. 77

2. The definition of leadership and how 85
leadership traits are developed for use within 94
the corporation and the community. 102

3. That various styles of leadership exist and 111
that there is no one best leadership style. 120

Seminar Presenter 127

Selection. Derme & Associates, Inc., a local 138
consulting firm specializing in career enhanse- 147
ment seminars, has been selected to develop 156
and conduct the four seminars. 163

Reason. One reason for selecting Derme & 172
Associates is that they will develop the content 182
of the seminars around Smith and Baker's defi- 191
nition of leadership,[1] which we want to empha- 200
size with employees. 204

Seminar Development 212

We have had two meeting with representa- 220
tives of Derme & Associates since the signing 229
of the agreement two weeks ago. 236

Meeting #1. This meeting was held so we 246
could learn about the contnet of leadership semi- 256
nars Derme & Associates has presented for 264
other clients. 267

Meeting #2. The specific content for the 278
four seminars was identified at this meeting. 287
Also, it was decided to use the same content for 297
each seminar except for the changes we suggest. 307

______________ 310

[1]Caroline Reynolds, Dimensions in Profes- 322
sional Development, 3d ed. (Cincinnati: South- 332
Western Publishing Co., 1988), p. 278. 340

words

These suggestions will be based on the feedback 349
we get from the participants' evaluations at the 359
end of each seminar. 364

Seminar Dates 369

The first seminar will be on October 15, at 378
the Logansport Plant; the second will be at the 387
Muncie Plant on October 22; the third meets at 397
the Fort Wayne Plant on October 29; and the 405
fourth will be at the Evansville Plant on 414
November 5. The 85 employees who are to at- 422
tend will be notified of the dates and times by 432
the end of this week. Instructions will be 441
given for arranging coverage during the at- 449
tendees' absence. 453

Seminar Content 459

The seminars will focus on leadership traits 468
and styles that are applicable to most work and 478
community environments. 483

Traits. While all seven traits which Stout 493
and Perkins[2] consider important will be in- 501
cluded in the seminars, the following four will 511
be targeted for development emphasis. 518

1. Understanding the feelings, problems, 527
and needs of others. 531

2. Allowing others to particpate in deci- 540
sions that affect them. 544

3. Dealing with others in an objective, un- 553
emotional manner. 557

4. Adapting to a constantly changing envi- 565
ronment. 567

Styles. Styles of leadership ranging from 577
the autocratic to the democratic leader will be 586
presented and then role-played in the semi- 595
nars. It will be emphasized that there is no one 605
best leadership style that all should use. Much 615

______________ 618

[2]Vickie Johnson Stout and Edward A. Perkins, 627
Jr., Practical Management Communication (Cin- 643
cinnati: South-Western Publishing Co., 1987), 652
p. 8. 653

(continued, p. 287)

123c (continued)

Document 3
Long Letter

modified block format; PI: 5; mixed punctuation; use **current date;** use following address in ALL CAP, unpunctuated format

DR FERNANDO L RUIZ
DEAN SCHOOL OF BUSINESS
ELLIS UNIVERSITY
8975 EDEN AVENUE
ST LOUIS MO 63123-3244

Use **OFFICE OF THE FUTURE** as a subject line.

Document 4
Average Letter

If you finish Documents 1-3 before time is called, rekey Document 2 on p. 217 in block format, open punctuation; use plain full sheet.

words

opening lines 27

Our school district is planning to implement an "Office of the Future" 41
program in the business education department. The main purpose of this 56
project is to develop an exemplary business education curriculum and facil- 70
ity which will enable our faculty to prepare students who will work in high- 85
tech environments. 89

To meet this purpose, we need to secure the expertise of various agencies 104
outside the public school sector. Since extensive curriculum revision is likely 120
to be a major part of this project, we request that you appoint three faculty 136
members to serve on a steering committee. They will be joined by five rep- 151
resentatives from business and three of our business education teachers. 166

The first meeting of the steering committee will be scheduled early next 180
month. The meeting will be held in our senior high school and will provide 195
an opportunity for the committee members to meet each other, review our 210
curriculum, and tour the business education facilities. 221

We are looking forward to hearing from you at your earliest convenience 236
and having your college become a partner in this exciting project. 249

Sincerely | Dr. Yolanda K. Degini | Superintendent | xx 259/**279**

Lesson 124 — *Evaluate Report Processing/Straight-Copy Skills*

124a ▶ 5 Conditioning Practice

each line twice SS (slowly, then faster); DS between 2-line groups; if time permits, rekey lines 1 and 4

alphabet 1 Mary's parents will quickly join Geoff to criticize both taxi drivers.
figures 2 Bad weather canceled 35 flights with 2,460 passengers on June 7, 1989.
fig/sym 3 Parsit & Brown received Model #239-089/A with Serial #465-17-40 today.
speed 4 Dirk may hand the girls eight shamrocks when they are at their formal.

| 1 | 2 | 3 | 4 | 5 | 6 | 7 | 8 | 9 | 10 | 11 | 12 | 13 | 14 |

124b ▶ 37 Evaluate Report Processing Skills:

Time Schedule
Plan and prepare .... 4′
Document processing .... 25′
Proofread/compute *n-pram* ... 8′

Document 1
Leftbound Report with Footnotes

Format the document shown at the right and on the next page as a leftbound report with footnotes. Correct errors as you key. Footnotes are listed in the left margin on p. 219.

words

TELECOMMUNICATIONS 4

Every time you speak on the telephone, watch television, or listen to the 19
radio you benefit from telecommunications technology. Similarly, those 33
who use a telephone, microcomputer network, teletypewriter, or facsimile 48
unit to conduct business also benefit from telecommunications.[1] 61

Telecommunications Defined 71

Telecommunications is "a technology that provides for the movement 85
of information between two locations by electronic means."[2] The informa- 99
tion that is transmitted can be sounds, pictures, or data in the form of words 115
and/or numbers.[3] 118

Common Methods of Telecommunicating 133

Telegraph services were the principal means of sending messages quickly 147
between distant points until the 1850's. After the invention of the telephone, 163
it became the chief way to transmit voice messages. Recent developments 178
in computer communications provide new methods of communicating. 191

160b (continued)

words

3. National Health Council, Health Careers Programs, 70 West 40th Street, New York, NY 10018. 456 462

4. American College of Health Care Administrators, P.O. Box 5890, 8120 Woodmont Avenue, Suite 200, Bethesda, MD 20814. 476 486

Document 2
Endnotes Page

Using the same margins as for p. 1 of report, format and key the endnotes on a separate page.

Document 3
Unbound Report with Endnotes

Begin reformatting Document 1 in unbound report format; correct errors you make as you key.

ENDNOTES 2

[1]U.S. Department of Labor, Bureau of Statistics, Occupational Outlook Handbook, 1986-1987 ed. (Washington, D.C.: U.S. Government Printing Office, April 1986), p. 29. 20 37 41

[2]John Stodden, "Ten Best Careers for the '90's," Business Week Careers, 1988 ed., p. 5. 59 63

[3]U.S. Department of Labor, Bureau of Statistics, p. 30. 74

[4]Myron D. Fottler, Robert Hernandez, and Charles Joiner, eds., Strategic Management of Human Resources in Health Services Organizations (New York: John Wiley & Sons, 1988), p. 256. 91 117 125

Lessons 161-162 Reports with Footnotes

161a-162a ▶ 5 (daily) Conditioning Practice

each line twice SS (slowly, then faster); DS between 2-line groups; if time permits, rekey selected lines

alphabet	1	Seven quick scores and five extra points just amazed both weary girls.
figures	2	Call 375-4682, Extension 590, by 9 o'clock to set a 3:15 p.m. meeting.
LOCK	3	The YMCA will give away copies of PLAY TENNIS FOR FUN at today's game.
speed	4	The giant dirigible in the air is to land downtown by the island mall.

| 1 | 2 | 3 | 4 | 5 | 6 | 7 | 8 | 9 | 10 | 11 | 12 | 13 | 14 |

161b ▶ 15 Review Footnote Formatting

1. Review information on formatting footnotes on p. 281.
2. Using the copy shown at the right, determine the line on which to begin keying the last line of the report body to have at least a 1" bottom margin below the last footnote.
3. Set a left margin of 1½" and right margin of 1".
4. Key the last line of report body, dividing line, and footnotes. Use a page line gauge from LP p. 8 or the line indicator on the screen to determine footnote placement.

words

marketability of B.A. degree holders in the marketplace. 12

________________ 16

S. Griffith, "Majors Leen to Business Track" The New York Times, 12 April 1987, Education Life, p. 18. 28 40

Ernest E. Boyer, College:The Undergraduate Experience in America (New York: Harper & Row, 1987), p. 45. 59 72

R. L. Jacobsen, "Group of Executives to Wants Make Liberal Arts Part of the Preparation for Business Careers," The Chronicle of Higher Education, 10 September 1985, p. 42. 83 96 113

124b (continued)

[1]Joyce Kupsch and Sandra Whitcomb, The Electronic Office (Mission Hills, CA: Glencoe Publishing Company, 1987), p. 131.

[2]Arnold Rosen, Telecommunications (San Diego: Harcourt Brace Jovanovich, Publishers, 1987), p. 4.

[3]Thomas Keller and Ernest N. Savage, Administrative Information Systems (Boston: Kent Publishing Company, 1987), p. 68.

[4]Susie H. VanHuss and Willard R. Daggatt, Jr., Electronic Information Systems (Cincinnati: South-Western Publishing Co., 1990), pp. 307-308.

Document 2
Bibliography

Keller, Thomas and Ernest N. Savage. Administrative Information Systems. Boston: Kent Publishing Company, 1987.

Kupsch, Joyce and Sandra Whitcomb. The Electronic Office. Mission Hills, CA: Glencoe Publishing Company, 1987.

Rosen, Arnold. Telecommunications. San Diego: Harcourt Brace Jovanovich, Publishers, 1987.

VanHuss, Susie H. and Willard R. Daggatt, Jr. Electronic Information Systems. Cincinnati: South-Western Publishing Co., 1990.

words

Networking. Networking is a relatively new technology that is rapidly 207
changing the way information can be transmitted from one place to an- 221
other. Networking can link telecommunication equipment (telephones, com- 235
puters, teletypewriters, facsimile units, copiers, etc.) to each other so that 251
information can be transmitted between people in the same office or build- 265
ing or another building in the same or different country. 277

Electronic mail. Electronic mail includes Telex and TWX services, elec- 294
tronic messaging on communicating computer systems, facsimile units, and 309
intelligent copiers and printers. 316

Teleconferencing. VanHuss and Daggatt[4] describe teleconferencing as 333
follows: 335

> Teleconferencing is an electronic meeting of individuals in different lo- 349
> cations.... Teleconferencing is not used very extensively. Perhaps the 365
> major reason is that teleconferencing requires a significant change in the 380
> behavior of those participating. 386

Listed below are three basic forms of telecommunicating which can be 400
used separately or in combination with each other. 411

1. Audio teleconferencing--transmission of voices. 421

2. Written teleconferencing--transmission of keyboarded messages by 435
way of connected computer terminals. 443

3. Video teleconferencing--transmission of still or full motion pictures. 458

Telecommunication Carriers 467

Various carriers are used to telecommunicate information from place to 483
place. Common carriers include telephone wires, coaxial cables, fiber op- 497
tics, microwaves, and satellites. 504

124c ▶ 8 Evaluate Straight-Copy Skill

1. Take a 5′ writing on 123b, p. 216.

2. Determine *gwam* and number of errors.

3. Record *gwam* and errors; compare to scores on 123b.

Lesson 125 — *Evaluate Table Processing/Straight-Copy Skills*

125a ▶ 5 Conditioning Practice

each line twice SS (slowly, then faster); DS between 2-line groups; if time permits, rekey lines 1 and 4

alphabet 1 Becky poured the liquid wax from the old jug into a dozen glass vials.

figures 2 I had 489 points, 160 rebounds, 57 assists, and 36 steals in 24 games.

fig/sym 3 The computers will cost $34,679 (less discounts of 20%, 15%, and 18%).

speed 4 The rich widow and the maid may make the usual visit to the city dock.

| 1 | 2 | 3 | 4 | 5 | 6 | 7 | 8 | 9 | 10 | 11 | 12 | 13 | 14 |

125b ▶ 8 Evaluate Straight-Copy Skill

1. Take a 5′ writing on 123b, p. 216.

2. Determine *gwam* and number of errors.

3. Record *gwam* and errors; compare to scores on 123b and 124c.

160a ▶ 5 Conditioning Practice

each line twice SS (slowly, then faster); DS between 2-line groups; if time permits, rekey selected lines

alphabet 1 Alex passed the major keyboarding quiz when he got back from vacation.
fig/sym 2 Contract #41-23-76C (12/05/92) allowed 30% off on orders over $85,000.
long words 3 Reprographics and telecommunications are office administration topics.
speed 4 Their neighbor may fix the ivory dish and then keep it with the bowls.

| 1 | 2 | 3 | 4 | 5 | 6 | 7 | 8 | 9 | 10 | 11 | 12 | 13 | 14 |

160b ▶ 45 Document Processing: Reports

Document 1
Leftbound Report with Endnotes

1. Review formatting guides for leftbound reports and endnotes on p. 281 and refer to the leftbound models on RG 8.

2. Key the copy shown at the right and on p. 285 in leftbound report format; correct errors.

Note: The report copy contains 4 embedded (unmarked) errors. Locate and correct them as you key.

words

HEALTH SERVICES MANAGEMENT PROGRAM 7

This report gives information on opportunities in health services manage- 21
ment. It is expected that a proposal to have Heritage University develope 36
and offer a health services management curriculum at the undergraduate 50
level will be submitted within six months. 59

Employment Opportunities 69

Places of employment. People who are able to manage health services 87
are needed in a wide variety of work settings. The most common place 101
of employment for these individuals is hospitals, followed by the offices of 116
pyhsicians, dentists, and other health-related practioneers.[1] 129

Employment outlook. Careers in the health-care area are included in the 147
"Ten Best Careers for the '90's."[2] It is expected that the demand for health 163
services managers will be strong as the country's population ages and needs 178
increased health-care services. Also, demand for managers will increase as 193
the providers of health care become more oriented to the bottom line because 209
of competition. 212

Educational Opportunities 222

In 1984, about 100 colleges and unviersities offered bachelor's degree pro- 237
grams in health services administration. About 70 schools had pro- 250
grams leading to the master's degree in hospital or health services 264
administration. . . .[3] 269

Bachelor's degree programs. Health services managers are often re- 287
cruited from the college or university from which they were graduated.[4] In 302
larger hospitals, they are often recruited to fill assistant department head 318
positions. In smaller hospitals, they may be able to enter at the department- 333
head level. 336

Additional Information 345

The organizations listed below will be contacted to gather additional in- 359
formation about academic programs in health services management. These 374
organizations will be asked to recommend a curriculum design expert who 388
could assist in developing the courses in the major. 399

1. American College of Healthcare Executives, 840 North Lake Shore 412
Drive, Chicago, IL 60611. 418

2. Association of University Programs in Health Administration, 1911 432
Fort Meyer Drive, Suite 503, Arlington, VA 22209. 442

(continued, p. 285)

125c ▶ 37 Evaluate Table Processing Skills

Time Schedule

Plan and prepare .... 4′
Document processing .... 25′
Proofread/compute *n*-pram....... 8′

correct all errors

Table 1
plain full sheet; short edge at top; CS: 8; DS data; center all headings

words

FILE RETENTION SCHEDULE 5

Adopted January 19-- 9

File	Years Retained	words
		19
Accounts payable	5	24
Accounts receivable	5	29
Annual reports	permanent	34
Articles of incorporation	permanent	41
Bank statements	7	45
Bids	3	48
Contracts (employee)	permanent	54
General correspondence	3	60

____________________ 63

Source: Administrative Information Systems, 1987. 80

Table 2
plain full sheet; short edge at top; CS: 6; SS data; center all headings

SALES DEPARTMENT BUDGET PERFORMANCE 7

Month Ended July 31, 19-- 12

Expense Item	Budget Allocation	Amount Spent	words
			15 / 28
Salaries	$18,600	$18,450	34
Benefits	4,985	4,857	38
Supplies	1,125	1,250	43
Telephone	650	595	48
Postage	475	515	52
Travel	3,275	3,075	59
Totals	$29,110	$28,742	65

Table 3
plain full sheet; short edge at top; CS: 8; DS data; center all headings

Table 4
If time permits, reformat Table 1 on a half sheet with short edge at top; CS: 6; DS data; center all headings.

Accounting Department 4

Proposed Salary Increases for 19-- 11

Employee	Cost of Living Increase	Merit Increase	New Salary	words
				18 / 34
Sandra Morris	$1,500	$ 900	$ 32,400	42
Jane Raleigh	1,140	1,140	25,080	48
William Bossey	990	792	21,582	55
Rita Perez	945	850	20,695	61
Hiro Hito	930	1,116	20,646	67
Harry Kaskie	500	450	12,950	78
Totals	$6,005	$5,248	$133,353	85

159c (continued)

words

4. If necessary, determine the name and number of the person with whom 305
you are speaking in the event a second call must be made. 316

5. Outline the major points of each call and have all needed reference 331
material at hand before placing a call (Stout and Perkins, 1987, 91). 345

Telephone Procedures 353

Employees must know how to screen calls, transfer calls, and to place 367
callers on hold properly if these calls are to be processed effectively. 382

Screening calls. Callers are screened by identifying who is calling and 399
by asking the purpose of the call so the person answering the call can decide 415
to process the call or transfer it to another person. 426

Transferring calls. Since having calls transferred can be an exasperat- 444
ing experience* for callers, the person transferring the call should be cer- 459
tain the caller is given the correct person on the first transfer. 473

Holding calls. Calls should be placed on hold only when necessary, for 489
short periods of time, and in a courteous manner. If calls need to be put on 505
hold for more than a minute or two, callers should be given the option of 520
being called back (Oliverio and Pasewark, 1988, 638). 531

____________________ 535

*Repeated transfers may be exasperating because callers must explain 548
the purpose of the call each time the call is transferred. 560

Learning cue: A single explanatory note in a report may be indicated by an asterisk with a matching asterisk preceding the note at the foot of the page.
If two or more explanatory notes occur in the report, matching superscript figures are used to number them.

Document 2
Reference Page

1. Reviewing formatting guides for references on p. 281 and the model on RG 8.

2. Format the references shown at the right for Document 1.

REFERENCES 2

Oliverio, Mary Ellen and William R. Pasewark. The Office: Procedures and 23
Technology. Cincinnati: South-Western Publishing Co., 1988. 37

Stout, Vickie Johnson and Edward A. Perkins, Jr. Practical Management 55
Communication. Cincinnati: South-Western Publishing Co., 1987. 71

Tilton, Rita Sloan, J. Howard Jackson, and Estelle L. Popham. Secretarial 88
Procedures and Administration. 9th ed. Cincinnati: South-Western Pub- 108
lishing Co., 1987. 112

Document 3
Leftbound Report

1. Review the guides for leftbound reports on p. 281 and the leftbound models on RG 8.

2. If time permits, begin reformatting Document 1 as a leftbound report, substituting the copy at the right for ¶ 1. (Be sure to center the report heading over the line of writing.)

Spoken communication is powerful because through it 10
images are created, emotions are affected, and listeners 22
respond (Stout and Perkins, 1987, 82). It is important, 33
therefore, that business people use the telephone correctly. 45

LESSONS 126 – 150

PHASE 6 PROCESS SPECIAL DOCUMENTS

In the 25 lessons of Phase 6, you will:

1. Improve basic keyboarding and language skills.
2. Learn to format letters with special features, formal memorandums, forms, and employment documents.
3. Compose at the keyboard.
4. Enhance decision-making skills.
5. Apply formatting skills to process information for a firm that markets computer-aided educational products.
6. Measure and evaluate document processing skills.

159a ▶ 5 Conditioning Practice

each line twice SS (slowly, then faster); DS between 2-line groups; if time permits, rekey selected lines

alphabet 1 Maxim just amazed the partial crowd by kicking five quick field goals.

figures 2 Order 97-341 for 215 Series 068 storm windows was shipped last May 28.

symbols 3 Susan's report had asterisks (*), pound signs (#), and ampersands (&).

speed 4 Claudia did lay the ivory memento and oak ornament by the enamel bowl.

| 1 | 2 | 3 | 4 | 5 | 6 | 7 | 8 | 9 | 10 | 11 | 12 | 13 | 14 |

159b ▶ 5 Improve Language Skills: Word Choice

1. Study the spelling and definitions of each pair of words.
2. Key the **Learn** line with the number and period, noting the proper use of the often confused words.
3. Key the **Apply** line with the number and period, choosing the words that complete the sentence correctly.

forward (adj) going or moving to a position in front

forth (adj) forward in time, place, or order

foreword (n) the preface or introductory pages of a book

fourth (adj) being number four in a countable series

Learn 1. The forward leap of technology was described in the book's foreword.

Apply 2. The (forward/foreword) of the text depicts society's (forward/foreward) trend.

Learn 3. Jim came forth to accept his trophy for finishing in fourth place.

Apply 4. The band marched back and (forth/fourth) during (forth/fourth) period.

159c ▶ 40 Document Processing: Reports

Review the formatting guides for unbound reports on p. 281 and the model report on RG 8.

Document 1
Unbound Report with Internal Citations

1. Format and key the copy given at the right and on p. 283 as an unbound report; DS.
2. Before you remove each page from the machine or screen, proofread it and correct any errors you may have made.

Formatting Enumerations:

1. SS each enumeration; DS between enumerations.
2. Key the number at the ¶ indention point used in the report.
3. Key lines to the right margin of the report.
4. Key the first stroke of "runover" line(s) flush with the number.

words

TELEPHONE SKILLS 3

Next to face-to-face communication, the telephone is the most frequent 18 method of exchanging information in business (Stout and Perkins, 1987, 87). 33 It is important, therefore, that all employees realize that the business will 49 be more successful if every employee can use the phone more efficiently 63 and effectively. 67

Telephone Techniques 75

People who have good telephone techniques can turn complaining callers 89 into satisfied ones; create a very good image for the business with its cus- 104 tomers, clients, and suppliers; and get more done each day because they 118 handle callers effectively and efficiently. 127

Processing incoming calls. Incoming calls should be answered immedi- 146 ately, "before the third ring" (Tilton, Jackson, and Popham, 1987, 287). The 162 employee answering the call should identify himself or herself immediately 177 and speak in a tone that is relaxed and low-pitched. A writing pad should 192 be kept near the phone so that all important parts of the conversation can be 207 recorded. The caller should be thanked at the end of the conversation. 222

Processing outgoing calls. These techniques should be used to improve 241 the process of placing calls: 247

1. Group calls and make them during set times each day to reduce the 261 amount of idle chatter. 266

2. Place calls in order of importance or urgency. 277

3. Identify yourself as the caller as soon as the call is answered. 291

(continued, p. 283)

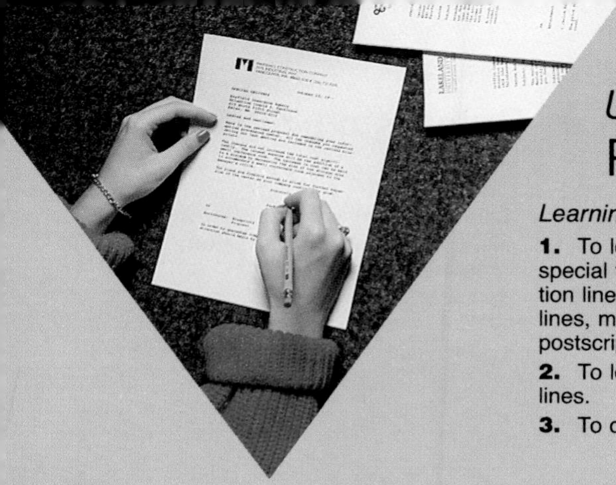

UNIT 29 LESSONS 126 – 129

Process Correspondence with Special Features

Learning Goals

1. To learn to format and process letters with special features such as mailing notation, attention line, subject line, company name in closing lines, multiple enclosures, copy notation, and postscript.

2. To learn to format letter addresses with long lines.

3. To check/improve language skills.

Format Guides

1. Paper guide at *0* (for typewriters).

2. LL: 70 spaces for drills and ¶s; as specified in placement table for letters, p. 76.

3. LS: SS for drill lines and letters, unless otherwise directed.

4. PI: 5 spaces, when appropriate.

FORMATTING GUIDES: CORRESPONDENCE WITH SPECIAL FEATURES

On occasion you will find several special features used in business letters. These features are illustrated in the model letter on page 223. In some cases, alternative formats for special parts are chosen (for example, the subject line may be placed in various positions). The simplest and most efficient formats, however, are illustrated in this unit.

Mailing notations. Mailing notations (REGISTERED, CERTIFIED, SPECIAL DELIVERY or AIRMAIL) begin at the left margin in ALL CAPS a double space below the dateline and a double space above the first line of the letter address. (Note: AIRMAIL is used only on foreign mail.)

Attention line. When an attention line is used in a letter addressed to a company, key it as the first line of the letter and envelope address:

Attention Personnel Officer
InfoMaster Office Equipment, Inc.
3200 Erie Avenue
Cincinnati, OH 45208-2837

When a letter is addressed to a company, the correct salutation is "Ladies and Gentlemen," even though an attention line may name an individual.

Subject line. Place the subject line a double space below the salutation. If the body paragraphs are blocked, block the subject line at the left margin. If the body paragraphs are indented, indent the subject line the same number of spaces or center it. The word "Subject" may be used. If used, follow the word "Subject" by a colon and two spaces before completing the subject line.

Company name. When used, place the company name a double space below the complimentary close in ALL CAPS. QS (quadruple-space) to signature line.

Enclosure notation. Place enclosure (or attachment) notation a double space below reference initials. If multiple enclosures are referred to in the letter, follow the word "Enclosures" with a colon and two spaces and list each enclosure.

Enclosures: Quarterly Report
Travel Expenses

Copy notation. A copy notation indicates that a copy of a letter is being sent to someone other than the addressee. Use "c" followed by the name of the person(s) to receive a copy. Place copy notation a double space below the last line of the enclosure notation or the reference line if there is no enclosure.

c Claudia Gullikson
Dale Ogden
Roberto Griffin

Postscript. A postscript is an additional paragraph that may be added after a letter has been completed. It is the last item in the letter. Begin a postscript a double space below the preceding item. Use the same paragraph format (indented or blocked) as the body paragraphs.

Notes. Long lines in the letter address may be carried to the next line even with the left margin.

In both the letter address and closing lines, professional titles may be placed on the same line as the name separated by a comma or placed on the following line without a comma.

Ms. Karen M. Ming, Executive Director
or
Ms. Karen M. Ming
Executive Director

Use the form which gives the best balance and attractiveness.

When several special features are used in a letter, the dateline may be raised to present a more attractive appearance on the page. Generally, raise the dateline one line for each two special-feature lines used.

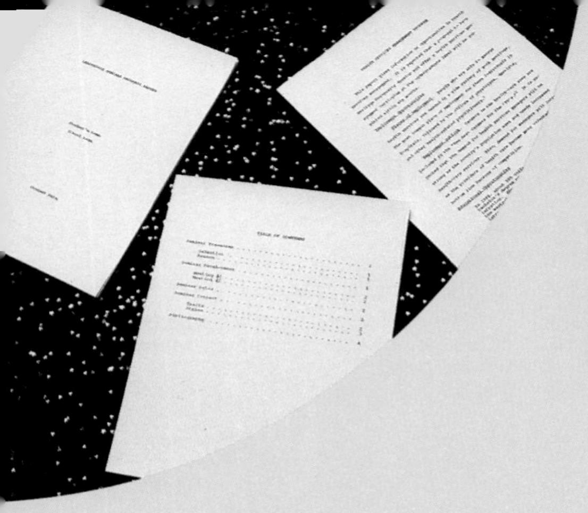

UNIT 37 *LESSONS 159 – 162*

Assess/Improve Report Processing Skills

Learning Goals

1. To improve your ability to produce unbound, topbound, and leftbound reports.

2. To improve your ability to document references by using internal citations/reference page; footnotes/bibliography; and endnotes.

3. To improve language-skill competency.

Format Guides

1. Paper guide at *0* (for typewriters).

2. LL: 70 spaces or as directed in document formatting guide.

3. LS: SS drill lines; DS ¶s; or as directed within an activity.

4. PI: 5 spaces unless otherwise directed.

FORMATTING GUIDES: REPORTS IN UNBOUND, TOPBOUND, AND LEFTBOUND FORMATS

REPORT FORMATS

PLACEMENT/SPACING		UNBOUND		LEFTBOUND		TOPBOUND	
CENTERPOINT:		Pica 42	Elite 51	Pica 45	Elite 54	Pica 42	Elite 51
TOP MARGIN:	FIRST PAGE Place heading on .... QS below heading. No page number is necessary.	line 10	line 12	line 10	line 12	line 12	line 14
	SECOND AND SUCCEEDING PAGES Place page number on ...	line 6 at right margin	line 6	line 6 at right margin	line 6	line 62 bottom center	line 62
	Continue body of report on line	8	8	8	8	10	10
BOTTOM MARGIN:	ALL PAGES	1″ 6 lines	1″	1″ 6 lines	1″	1″ 6 lines	1″
LEFT MARGIN:	ALL PAGES Inches .... Spaces	1″ 10	1″ 12	1½″ 15	1½″ 18	1″ 10	1″ 12
RIGHT MARGIN:	ALL PAGES	All report styles use a 1″ right margin.					
SPACING MODE:		Body of a report is usually DS, but may be SS.					

Footnotes and Explanatory Notes

To find the vertical line space on which to end text on a page with footnotes or explanatory notes, follow these guidelines:

1. Allow 3 lines for divider rule and the blank line space above and below it, 3 lines for each note, and 6 lines for the bottom margin.

2. Subtract the sum of these figures from 66 (number of line spaces on the paper). Text should not be keyed on a line lower than the resulting figure.

After completing the last line of text, DS above and below the 1½″ divider rule. Indent first line of a note 5 spaces and key a superscript number (raised ½ line space). Begin second line and succeeding lines at left margin. SS each note; DS between notes.

On a partially filled page, footnotes may immediately follow the text or may be placed at the foot of the page.

Note: If the equipment cannot print a superscript figure, follow these guidelines:

1. Key the footnote, endnote, or explanatory note reference figure in the text on the line of writing, preceded and followed by a diagonal (/) mark.

2. Key the endnote figure or the footnote or explanatory figure at the bottom of the page on the line of writing indented 5 spaces from the left margin and followed by a period and two spaces.

Reference Page or Bibliography

Use same margins and center point as for first page of report. SS references; DS between them. Begin first line of each entry at left margin; indent second line and succeeding lines 5 spaces.

Endnotes Page

Use same margins and center point as for first page of report. SS endnotes; DS between them. Indent first line of each endnote 5 spaces; key a superscript endnote number. If your equipment cannot print a superscript figure, indent first line of each note 5 spaces; key the note number on line of writing followed by a period and two spaces. Begin second line and succeeding lines of each note at left margin.

Table of Contents

Use same margins and center point as for first page of report. List side and paragraph headings in table of contents (TC). DS side headings beginning at left margin; SS paragraph headings with a DS above and below them. Key page number of TC entry at right margin; connect each entry to its page number by leaders.

Title Page

Use same side margins and center point as for first page of report. Center each line of copy horizontally. Key report title on line 16 in ALL CAPS. Space down 8 DS and key report writer's name. DS and key name of school or department; space down 8 DS and key report date.

SOFTWARE SPECIALISTS
4501 MONARCH STREET • DALLAS, TX 75204-3011
(214) 683-4012

		words in parts	total words
	Line 12 September 16, 19-- DS	4	4
Mailing notation	SPECIAL DELIVERY DS	7	7
	Attention Ms. Dyane E. Ellsworth	14	14
Attention line	Remington Associates	18	18
	784 Winterhaven Drive	22	22
	Mesa, AZ 85203-8563 DS	27	27
	Ladies and Gentlemen: DS	31	31
Subject line	Subject: Desktop Publishing Software DS	8	39
	I enjoyed demonstrating the desktop publishing software	19	50
	to you and members of your department yesterday. You	30	61
	are fortunate to work with such progressive and enthusi-	41	72
	astic individuals.	45	76
	Based on our discussion, I am convinced that your de-	55	86
	partment is ready to move into the area of desktop pub-	66	97
	lishing. The professional image that your company is	77	108
	trying to project will be greatly enhanced through the	88	119
	use of such software.	93	124
	After you have had an opportunity to review the material	104	135
	you received, I would like to discuss further with you	115	146
	and members of your staff the advantages/disadvantages	126	157
	of each package. Before the end of the month, I will	137	168
	call you to arrange a time.	142	173
	Sincerely, DS	4	178
Company name	SOFTWARE SPECIALISTS QS	10	184
	Richard R. Mathews		
	Richard R. Mathews	16	190
	Software Consultant DS	22	196
	xx DS	23	196
Enclosure notation	Enclosures: Price List	28	201
	Brochure DS	29	203
Copy notation	c Gregory P. Schultz DS	34	207
Postscript	Should you have any questions that you would like an-	44	218
	swered prior to our meeting, call me at (813) 839-4899.	55	229

Letter with Special Features

157d ▶ 5 Improve Language Skills: Word Choice

1. Study the spelling and definitions of each pair of words.

2. Key each **Learn** line with the number and period, noting the proper use of the often confused words.

3. Key each **Apply** line with the number and period, choosing the words that complete the sentence correctly.

defer (vb) put off until a future time; postpone

differ (vb) to be unlike or dissimilar

allowed (vb) past tense of allow, which means to let do or happen; permit

aloud (adv) with the voice; orally

Learn 1. Our solutions differ; so we must defer making the decision.

Apply 2. I will (differ/defer) building my model since it (defers/differs) from Jim's.

Learn 3. Lu-yin was allowed to give her response aloud to the class.

Apply 4. Al spoke (allowed/aloud) to each group as soon as he learned he was (allowed/aloud).

Lesson 158 — Sustained Document Processing: Letters and Memorandums

158a ▶ 5 Conditioning Practice

each line twice SS (slowly, then faster); DS between 2-line groups; if time permits, rekey selected lines

alphabet 1 Jerry's big mistake was to list seven dozen xylophones for quick sale.

fig/sym 2 The 6% interest amounted to $190 on account #12-35-470 and #12-48-903.

LOCK 3 Use PAUL ELY of 103 LEMON PLACE in ALL CAPS in the new letter address.

speed 4 If they go to the city and sign the form, I may pay them for the work.

| 1 | 2 | 3 | 4 | 5 | 6 | 7 | 8 | 9 | 10 | 11 | 12 | 13 | 14 |

158b ▶ 35 Sustained Document Processing: Letters and Memorandums

Time Schedule

Plan and prepare .... 3′
Timed production .... 25′
Proofread; compute *n-pram* .... 7′

1. Make a list of documents to be processed:
page 276, 155b, Letter 2
page 278, 156b, Memo 2
page 278, 157b, Memo 1
page 279, 157c, Letter 1

2. Arrange full sheets, formal memo paper from LP p. 11, letterhead from LP pp. 17-19, and correction materials for easy access. Process as many documents as you can in 25′. Proofread and correct before removing each document from the machine.

3. After time is called, proofread document in machine and circle errors.

4. Compute *n-pram;* turn in work arranged in order listed in Step 1.

158c ▶ 10 Paragraph Guided Writing

1. Three 1′ writings for speed with quarter-minute checkpoints noted and guides called on 2nd and 3rd writings (See Table, p. 272).

Goal: 2-6 words faster on each writing.

2. Three 1′ writings for control with quarter-minute checkpoints noted and guides called. Deduct 2-4 words from top speed; then note checkpoints.

Goal: 2 or fewer errors a minute.

all letters used | A | 1.5 si | 5.7 awl | 80% hfw |

gwam 2′

Many office system experts think a sizable number of entry-level 7
office positions in this decade will go unfilled if there is a shortage 14
of qualified workers. They state that to get a position, a person must 21
show a good foundation in basic and technical skills. Employers will 28
hire only those people who can think, read, write, talk, and listen; have 35
balanced their studies with up-to-date technical skills; and show they 42
can relate to people on the job. 46

126a ▶ 5 Conditioning Practice

each line twice SS (slowly, then faster); DS between 2-line groups; if time permits, rekey selected lines

alphabet 1 Just before moving back to Venezuela, they acquired a few exotic pets.
figures 2 The main office was located at 4623 Oxford Drive from 1970 until 1985.
fig/sym 3 You can save 25% ($376.98) by purchasing the 20 desks before March 15.
speed 4 Their neighbors on the island did the handiwork for them at the shanty.

| 1 | 2 | 3 | 4 | 5 | 6 | 7 | 8 | 9 | 10 | 11 | 12 | 13 | 14 |

126b ▶ 25 Format Documents: Letters with Special Features

2 plain full sheets

Review the formatting guides for correspondence with special features on p. 222.

Letter 1 (LL: 1½" SM; line 12)
Format and key the letter on p. 223 in modified block format, giving careful attention to the placement of the special features. Proofread and circle errors. Keep the copy to use as a model in the next lesson.

Letter 2
Rekey the letter on p. 223 in block format with open punctuation. Make the changes listed at the right. Proofread and circle errors.

Addressee:
Ms. Robin A. McIntyre
Mahoney Medical Center
2457 Baltimore Street
Mesa, AZ 85203-6493
Salutation: **Dear Ms. McIntyre**

126c ▶ 10 Check Language Skills: Capitalization

SS sentences; DS between groups of sentences

Key line number (with period); space twice, then key the sentence, supplying the needed capital letters.

If time permits, key the sentences again to increase decision-making speed.

1. dr. dixon indicated he would spend three days in washington, d.c.
2. she will be in orlando on wednesday and in jacksonville on thursday.
3. their convention will be held in april, the week before passover.
4. christmas day is on sunday and new year's eve is on saturday.
5. was the boston tea party part of the american revolution?

6. during june the carne art gallery will display work by botticelli.
7. the art gallery is in king towers, located on hollywood boulevard.
8. ms. j. b. keynes will speak at the next delta kappa gamma meeting.
9. the company president will meet with division managers on friday.
10. mrs. jay told me that president ruiz will be at the board meeting.

11. they will see the grand canyon during their trip to arizona.
12. they hired dr. kellee harper who has a ph.d. in chemistry.
13. greenwich village is located in new york city in manhattan.
14. the two major sponsors were anderson printing and carling realty.
15. one of the world war I treaty signings was held in versailles.

126d ▶ 10 Improve Language Skills: Word Choice

Study the definition and spelling of each word. Read the **Learn** sentence. Key the **Learn** sentence (with number and period) and the **Apply** sentences (with number and period), selecting the proper word in parentheses to complete each sentence correctly.

might (vb) used to express permission, probability, and possibility

mite (n) tiny insects, a very little; bit

accept (vb) to receive, to give approval, to take

except (vb) to exclude

Learn 1. He might be able to exchange the flour containing mites.
Apply 2. It (might, mite) cost more to fix the machine than to replace it.
Apply 3. It was not the first (might, mite) she had found in her food.

Learn 4. I believe they will accept all of the revisions except for Unit 5.
Apply 5. Mary is available every day (accept, except) Friday.
Apply 6. Tom will attend the banquet to (accept, except) the award.

RŌLŌTRON CORPORATION

1351 East Allen Street, Springfield, IL 62703-7988

INTEROFFICE MEMORANDUM

Side margins: 1"

DS (if printed form is used)
Line 10 (if plain paper is used)

words

Date September 8, 19-- QS 4

Addressee Barbara M. Toland, Market Researcher DS 11

Subject DESKTOP PUBLISHING SOFTWARE DS 17

Many vendors have recently introduced desktop publishing (DTP) 29
software that enables operators to integrate text and graphics 42
easier and with more options. DS 48

Body Since your staff uses DTP extensively to create documents for re- 61
search, I want to schedule vendor demonstrations to see if the 74
upgraded versions will better meet your needs. DS 83

In preparation, please have your staff make a list of the require- 96
ments they need from a DTP software package so the vendors can 110
show how their packages meet these needs. QS 117

Gerri S. Yubath

Name of writer Gerri S. Yubath DS 121

Reference initials xx 121

Simplified Memo

157c ▶ 20 Document Processing: Letters

Letter 1

LP p. 15

Format in block style, open punctuation, the letter at the right; correct errors; prepare envelope.

Letter 2

plain full sheet

Format in modified block style, mixed punctuation, the letter at the right. Address the letter to:

Mr. Dwight D. Miller
Architectural Services
70 Ship Street
Providence, RI 02903-4220

Supply an appropriate salutation; correct errors; prepare envelope.

words

September 8, 19-- | Morris Design Group | 1086 Willett Avenue | Providence, 14
RI 02915-2098 | Ladies and Gentlemen 21

Enclosed is an update on the latest version of our personal computer work- 36
station, which is very popular with architects. 46

The ES/10 microcomputer has an 80286 microprocessor, has 3MB of user 59
memory, and comes with advanced color and graphics capabilities. It sup- 74
ports a full-page display monitor and the most sophisticated laser printers 89
and scanners. 92

When combined with state-of-the-art design software, this hardware gives 107
architects an opportunity to use the most advanced technology throughout 121
every phase in the design process. (107) 128

Sincerely | Mrs. Mary Ellen Rosowitz | Sales Representative | xx 140

Enclosure 142/155

127a ▶ 5 Conditioning Practice

each line twice SS (slowly, then faster); DS between 2-line groups; if time permits, rekey selected lines

alphabet 1 Everyone except Jake was amazed by how quickly the fight was finished.

figures 2 The editor made changes on pages 40, 63, 71, 82, and 95 of the script.

fig/sym 3 Their assets ($153,450) were greater than their liabilities ($96,782).

speed 4 The maid paid the men for the work they did on the shanty by the lake.

| 1 | 2 | 3 | 4 | 5 | 6 | 7 | 8 | 9 | 10 | 11 | 12 | 13 | 14 |

127b ▶ 10 Formatting Drill: Letters with Special Features

plain full sheets

1. Two 1′ writings on date through subject line of letter on page 223. Concentrate on correct placement of letter parts.

2. Two 1′ writings on complimentary close through postscript of letter on page 223. Concentrate on correct placement of letter parts.

3. A 3′ writing on correct letter format on the complete letter. Stress correct placement of letter parts.

127c ▶ 25 Improve Formatting Skill: Letters with Special Features

plain full sheets; supply special features as directed; proofread and circle errors

Letter 1
block format; open punctuation

Special Features:
Attention Purchasing Department
Subject: Architecture Designs
Company name in closing lines: **CARLTON PUBLISHING**
Enclosures: Reeves Pamphlet
Blueprint Listing

words

October 13, 19--| Marshall Construction Company| 7695 Industrial Way| 20
Vancouver, WA 98660-3120| Ladies and Gentlemen 35

The 1988 edition of <u>Innovative Home Floor Plans</u> by Bart Reeves and Chan 55
Inoue is no longer in print. <u>Architectural Home Designs for the 1990s</u> is the 79
only publication by Reeves and Inoue we currently have in stock. 92

A pamphlet describing the publication is enclosed. If you decide that you 107
want a copy of the book, return the card which is attached to the pamphlet 122
and the book will be shipped the same day we receive your order. 135

A listing of our current publications that include blueprints of home designs 151
is also enclosed. If you want to review any of the publications on the list, we 167
will be happy to send them to you. (words in body: 140) 174

Sincerely| Ms. Marjorie A. Reynolds| Manager 196/**218**

Letter 2
modified block format; blocked ¶s; mixed punctuation

Special Features:
SPECIAL DELIVERY
Attention Connie L. Parkinson
Enclosures: Blueprints
Proposal
Postscript: **In order to guarantee completion by April 1, 19--, construction should begin by November 1, 19--.**

Letter 3
reformat letter 2 in block format; open punctuation

Special Features:
Company name in closing lines: **MARSHALL CONSTRUCTION COMPANY**
c Barry B. Horn

October 13, 19--| Bayfield Insurance Agency| 415 North Fifth Street| Kelso, 24
WA 98626-4210| Ladies and Gentlemen 31

Here is the revised proposal for remodeling your information processing 46
center. All the changes you requested during our last meeting are included 61
in the revised blueprints. 67

The changes did not increase the total cost significantly. The largest ex- 81
pense will be the addition of a small conference room. The increase in cost 97
can be held to a minimum by decreasing the size of the storage area to ac- 111
commodate a small conference room adjacent to the manager's office. 125

The plans are flexible enough to allow for further expansion of the center as 141
your company continues to grow. (116) 147

Sincerely| Parker A. Dixon| Contractor 182/**205**

156b (continued)

Memo 2

LP p. 11 or plain half sheet

Format and key in formal style the memo shown at the right; correct errors.

words

TO: All Department Heads FROM: Director, Computer Operations 10
DATE: September 7, 19-- SUBJECT: COMPUTER DOWNTIME 17

The Major 9957 computer system will be shut down at 5:30 p.m. on September 15 for 48 hours so we can do preventative maintenance. 32 44

If you need to access its files during this period, you should download the needed files to your microcomputer system. 59 68

xx 68/**74**

156c ▶ 15 Document Processing: Letters

Set margins and determine dateline position by judgment; proofread and correct errors. Review envelope addressing procedures (RG 7). Process envelopes.

Letter 1 LP p. 13

modified block with indented ¶s, mixed punctuation

Letter 2 plain full sheet

Reformat Letter 1 in block style, open punctuation.

words (parts)

September 8, 19-- | Mr. David R. Lundy | X-TRA Corporation | 16606 Grand River Avenue | Detroit, MI 48227-1492 | Dear Mr. Lundy 15 15 / 24 25

The facsimile machine (Model 3540) I purchased from you last May has been out of service on five days during the last month. 15 39 / 25 49

Your service rep responded promptly to each service call, but on three occasions the machine was out of service for more than 24 hours because he could not get parts locally. 40 64 / 56 79 / 60 84

These delays disrupt my business, and I will have to seek service elsewhere if your local inventory is not increased. (84) 76 99 / 84 108

Sincerely | Miss Jeanne L. Dixter | Communication Specialist | xx 12 120 / **137**

156d ▶ 10 Document Processing Drill: Letter Parts

plain full sheets

Use Letter 1, 156c, modified block with indented ¶s, mixed punctuation, to complete the following:

1. Three 1′ writings in letter format on the opening lines and as many of the message lines as you can. Try to improve by 1 or 2 words on each timing.

2. Three ½′ writings in letter format on the last line of the message and closing lines. Try to improve by 1 or 2 words on each timing or complete the timing sooner each time.

3. A 3′ writing on the entire letter. Use a plain full sheet.

Lesson 157 Letters and Memorandums

157a ▶ 5 Conditioning Practice

each line twice SS (slowly, then faster); DS between 2-line groups; if time permits, rekey selected lines

alphabet 1 Seven lions were quietly caught just before they exited the park maze.

figures 2 The March 25, 1993 listing had 87 micros, 14 printers, and 60 copiers.

long words 3 Their powerful minicomputer features parallel processing capabilities.

speed 4 Their men may do the work for us and the city if she pays them for it.

| 1 | 2 | 3 | 4 | 5 | 6 | 7 | 8 | 9 | 10 | 11 | 12 | 13 | 14 |

157b ▶ 20 Document Processing: Simplified Memorandums

Memo 1

plain full sheet

1. Read the information about simplified memos on page 275.

2. Study the model memo on page 279.

3. Process a copy of the model memo on page 279; proofread/correct errors.

Memo 2

plain full sheet

Process a copy of the model memo on page 279 with the following changes.

Change the name/title of the addressee to:

Manual A. Santia
Marketing Promotions

Change "research" in ¶2 to "promotions."

127d ▶ 10 Improve Language Skills: Word Choice

Study the definition and spelling of each word. Read the **Learn** sentence. Key the **Learn** sentence (with number and period) and the **Apply** sentences (with number and period), selecting the proper word in parentheses to complete each sentence correctly.

affect (vb) to influence

effect (n) result; consequence
(vb) to cause; to accomplish

advice (n) opinion; recommendation

advise (vb) to give advice, to recommend

Learn 1. The effect of the recent change will affect our previous decision.
Apply 2. Cutting our staff 25 percent will (affect, effect) employee morale.
Apply 3. What (affect, effect) did the new equipment have on productivity?

Learn 4. If you want my advice, I would advise that you accept the offer.
Apply 5. The only (advice, advise) she offered was to consider all my options.
Apply 6. Mr. Martin will (advice, advise) students on Wednesday mornings.

Lesson 128 Letters with Special Features

128a ▶ 5 Conditioning Practice

each line twice SS (slowly, then faster); DS between 2-line groups; if time permits, rekey selected lines

alphabet 1 Umezaki, the exchange student from Japan, plays racquetball very well.
figures 2 He was born on May 25, 1987, at 4:30 a.m. and weighed just over 6 lbs.
fig/sym 3 The shipping expenses ($29.76) were not included on Invoice #A184-350.
speed 4 The widow of the tax auditor of the firm did handiwork for the chapel.

| 1 | 2 | 3 | 4 | 5 | 6 | 7 | 8 | 9 | 10 | 11 | 12 | 13 | 14 |

128b ▶ 15 Formatting Drill: Letters

plain full sheets; modified block format; open punctuation

1. A 3′ writing on the letter to determine *gwam*.

2. Take three 1′ writings on date through subject line of the letter. If you complete the lines, QS and start over.

3. Take three 1′ writings on the complimentary close through the postscript. If you complete the lines, QS and start over.

4. Take another 3′ writing on the letter. Try to increase your *gwam* by 4-8 words.

gwam 3′

July 5, 19-- SPECIAL DELIVERY Attention Ms. Mary A. Fields Carlson Elec- 5
tronics 897 Rust Street Fairfax, VA 22030-7341 Ladies and Gentlemen 9
Subject: Office Layout Designs 11

(¶ 1) Attached is the information you requested on office layout designs. 16
This plan combines both conventional and open design layouts. The con- 21
ventional layout will isolate some work areas with walls which will pro- 26
vide for the privacy you require. The open portion of the plan allows 30
for flexibility, reduces communication barriers, and better utilizes the 35
available space. 36

(¶ 2) A rough estimate of the cost of the project is also included. I 41
look forward to hearing your branch manager's reaction to your proposal. 45

Sincerely OFFICE CONSULTANTS, INC. Todd P. Harmon Design Consultant xx 50
Attachments: Layout Design Price Estimate c Janice Eastman postscript 54
The price estimate reflects the 15 percent business discount. 58

155d ▶ 5 Reinforce Script-Copy Skill

Three 1′ writings for speed.

Goal: Improve rate by 1 or 2 words with each timing.

Note: If you finish ¶ before time is called, start over.

all letters used | A | 1.5 si | 5.7 awl | 80% hfw | gwam 1′

Applicants who seek a position in an office will be able 11
to increase their chances of getting the position if they can 24
just show that they have qualities for which employers are 36
looking. Applicants should emphasize experiences that show 48
they can work in a group with a great deal of enthusiasm and 60
pride. 61

Lesson 156 Letters and Memorandums

156a ▶ 5 Conditioning Practice

each line twice SS (slowly, then faster); DS between 2-line groups; if time permits, rekey selected lines

alphabet 1 Jaguars very quickly maximize to top speed when faced with big danger.
figures 2 Lenora served 438 hot dogs, 529 donuts, and 1,067 drinks at two games.
shift key 3 The nine vendors are from F & W Products, Cim & Co., and Kwynn & Sons.
speed 4 He or she may work with us to make a profit for the eighty city firms.

| 1 | 2 | 3 | 4 | 5 | 6 | 7 | 8 | 9 | 10 | 11 | 12 | 13 | 14 |

156b ▶ 20 Document Processing: Formal Memorandums

Memo 1

LP p. 9 or plain half sheet

1. Read the information about formal memorandums on p. 275.

2. Process a copy of the memo. Use formal style; block the ¶s; correct errors.

3. Process COMPANY MAIL envelope to:

Jim Torchek, Sales Manager
Sales Department

Note: If you do not have Lab Pac (LP) pages to use for the formal memo, follow these guidelines.

1. Set side margins at 1″.

2. Beginning on line 10, key each heading flush with the left margin.

3. Space twice after the colon and key the information following each heading.

Memo 2 is on p. 278.

words

TO: *Jim Torchek* 2
FROM: *Robert Elfford* 5
DATE: *September 7, 19--* 9
SUBJECT: RESPONSES TO REQUEST FOR QUOTATION (RFQ) 17

Enclosed are the responses to our RFQ from the companies that 29
met the deadline. Note that each addressed the requirements 42
we listed. 44

The enclosed spreadsheet gives each company's price for each 56
unit of equipment listed. I'll send a spreadsheet before 68
the September 14 meeting that shows each company's total 79
prices for all units. 84

xx 84

Enclosure 86

envelope **90**

128c ▶ 30 Build Sustained Document Processing: Letters with Special Features

LP pp. 89-95 or plain full sheets proofread; correct errors

Time Schedule

Plan and prepare .... 4′
Timed production ....20′
Proofread/compute *n-pram* ...... 6′

1. Arrange paper and correction materials for easy access.

2. Make a list of letters to be processed:

page 224, 126b, Letter 2
page 225, 127c, Letter 1
page 225, 127c, Letter 2
page 226, 128b

3. Process as many letters as you can in 20′. Proofread and correct errors as you key.

4. After 20′ timing, proofread again, mark any additional errors not found during keying, and compute *n-pram*.

5. Arrange letters in order listed in Step 2 and turn in work.

n-pram = (total words keyed − penalty*) ÷ time
(*Penalty is 10 words for each uncorrected error.)

Lesson 129 Letters with Special Features/Language Skills

129a ▶ 5 Conditioning Practice

each line twice SS (slowly, then faster); DS between 2-line groups; if time permits, rekey selected lines

alphabet 1 Three dozen packages of equipment were expected to arrive before July.
figures 2 Chapter 20, pages 253-264, of the 1987 edition contains grammar rules.
fig/sym 3 The deductible was changed to $250 on your policy (Q194-837) on May 6.
speed 4 The six haughty men did the work on the bus for the neurotic neighbor.

| 1 | 2 | 3 | 4 | 5 | 6 | 7 | 8 | 9 | 10 | 11 | 12 | 13 | 14 |

129b ▶ 7 Check Language Skills: Number Expression

SS sentences; DS between groups of sentences

Key line number (with period); space twice, then key the sentences, supplying the correct form of number expression.

If time permits, key the sentences again to increase decision-making speed.

1. 10 members of our delegation will not arrive until Friday, June first.
2. Only two of the twelve computers were damaged during shipment.
3. The final exam is scheduled for May 23 at nine a.m. in Room Twelve.
4. 1 office is located at 1 Oak Drive; the other, at 33 Lake Road.

5. The American boxer is five ft 7 in tall and weighs 126 lbs one oz.
6. Please reserve Rooms six and seven for the keyboarding event.
7. The 2 desks were returned to the store located at Six Nyman Drive.
8. Problems six and seven from Chapter twelve are due on Monday, April 5.

9. The bus stops each hour at 5th Avenue and at 75th Street.
10. Exactly 1/2 of the students taking the CPS exam passed.
11. About 50 members voted for Joshua; that is nearly 2/3.
12. Flight eighty-four, the last flight of the day, leaves at nine p.m.

129c ▶ 8 Improve Language Skills: Word Choice

Study the definition and spelling of each word. Read the **Learn** sentence. Key the **Learn** sentence (with number and period) and the **Apply** sentences (with number and period), selecting the proper word in parentheses to complete each sentence correctly.

farther (adv) greater distance

further (adv) additional

threw (vb) past tense of throw

through (prep) passage from one end to another; indicates a period of time

Learn 1. To discuss the matter further, we walked farther down the hall.
Apply 2. The item will be placed on the next agenda for (farther, further) discussion.
Apply 3. Our home is (farther, further) out of town than Jensen's home.

Learn 4. Steve threw the ball through the broken window into the classroom.
Apply 5. Karl drove (through, threw) the tunnel.
Apply 6. When he (threw, through) the bat after striking out, he was ejected.

155a ▶ 5 Conditioning Practice

each line twice SS (slowly, then faster); DS between 2-line groups; if time permits, rekey selected lines

alphabet	1	If Margie has extra help, a jigsaw puzzle can often be solved quickly.
fig/sym	2	BS & Sons used P.O. #708-A to buy 125 chairs (Style LE-64 and SSE-39).
3d row	3	Petite Terry used quite proper etiquette to outwit her poor tired pop.
speed	4	The ivory ornament and paisley handiwork make a rich pair of mementos.

| 1 | 2 | 3 | 4 | 5 | 6 | 7 | 8 | 9 | 10 | 11 | 12 | 13 | 14 |

155b ▶ 30 Document Processing: Letters

Review the formatting guides for letters on p. 275.

Letter 1
Short Letter

plain full sheet

1. Prepare a rough-draft copy in block style, open punctuation.

2. Proofread; identify errors with proofreader's marks; save copy for use in 155c.

Letter 2
Average-Length Letter

plain full sheet

modified block style, mixed punctuation; correct errors

Letter 3

plain full sheet

Reformat Letter 2 using block style, open punctuation; address to:

Mr. James Q. Lento
Qualitech, Inc.
3300 Parallel Avenue
Kansas City, KS 66104-4397

Supply appropriate salutation; correct errors.

	words: parts	total
September 5, 19-- | Mr. Gene L. Howe | ATM Office Supplies | 2300 Mission	14	14
Street | Pasadena, CA 91108-1631 | Dear Mr. Howe	22	23
I want to acknowledge receipt of your response to my Request for Pro-	14	36
posal for 55 microcomputers, 17 laser printers, 2 file servers, and 3 opti-	28	51
cal scanners.	31	54
My staff will consider responses from all companies and make a recommen-	46	68
dation by October 31 so the senior officers can make a decision by Novem-	60	83
ber 15. We plan to purchase no later than November 30. (words in body: 71)	11	94
Sincerely | Richard M. Pugliese | Administrative Manager | xx	22	105

	words: parts	total
September 5, 19-- | Ms. Lynn S. Bost | Office Technology Associates | 615 Miami	15	15
Avenue | Kansas City, KS 66105-2187 | Dear Ms. Bost	24	25
Your presentation at the Cedar Falls Office Systems conference on August 27,	15	40
19-- was excellent. Your expert system for configuring microcomputer net-	30	55
works might be invaluable to my staff as we network the micros in our	44	69
office building.	48	72
As we discussed, I would like you to demonstrate your expert system to my	62	87
staff on September 25, 19--. Please call to confirm this date or to set another	79	103
and to select a time.	83	108
I will have one microcomputer (POS operating system) and a large-screen	98	122
projection device for your demonstration. (106)	106	131
Sincerely | Charles H. Willy | Computer Systems Manager | xx	11	142

155c ▶ 10 Document Processing Drill: Letter Parts

Use the rough-draft copy of Letter 1 prepared in 155b and complete the following:

1. Three 1′ writings in letter format on the opening lines (date through salutation) and as much of the message as time permits. Try to improve by 1 or 2 words with each timing.

2. Three ½′ writings in letter format on the last line of the message and closing lines (complimentary close through initials).

Try to improve by 1 or 2 words each time.

3. A 3′ writing on the entire letter. Use block style, open punctuation, plain full sheet.

129d ▶ 30 Evaluate Document Processing: Letters with Special Features

LP pp. 97-101 or plain full sheets, supply current date, salutation, complimentary close, and special features as directed

Time Schedule
Plan and prepare .... 4′
Timed production .... 20′
Proofread/compute *n-pram* ... 6′

Document 1
modified block format; indented ¶s; mixed punctuation

Special features:
CERTIFIED
Subject: Research on Employee Morale
Company name in closing lines: **THE RESEARCH SPECIALISTS**
Enclosure

Document 2
block format; open punctuation

Special features:
SPECIAL DELIVERY
Company name in closing lines: **WESTRIDGE PUBLISHING, INC.**
Enclosures: Scripts
Brochure

words

Mr. Chad A. Landis | Martin Insurance Company | 726 Lakeshore Drive | Athens, 19
GA 30606-7496 33

Enclosed is our proposal for the research project you would like completed 48
on employee morale. Your decision to hire someone from outside the orga- 63
nization to do the research was a wise one. Our experience has shown em- 77
ployees to be more willing to express their opinions and attitudes to a person 93
from the outside. 97

This research project is designed to address four work-related areas which 112
most frequently influence employee morale. These include economic reward, 127
job satisfaction, co-workers, and management. 136

We are confident that the findings from these four areas will provide your 151
company with the information that you will need to make future decisions on 166
issues related to employee morale. (140) 174

Ms. Erica J. Collins | Research Consultant | xx 191/**211**

Mr. Gordon S. Jennings | Summer Productions, Inc. | 3120 Mount Meeker 20
Road | Boulder, CO 80301-2001 29

Here are copies of the two scripts I discussed with you at the National 43
Theaters Guild Convention in Dallas. Either play would be a good addition 58
to the plays you already have planned for your summer productions. 72

If your goal is to appeal to a younger audience, I would recommend Studio 88
’93. It is a light comedy that we have had excellent feedback on from those 104
who have seen it performed. The other script, 36 Bradford Street, is one of 123
our newest publications. Since it just appeared in print this month, I am not 139
sure what type of audience appeal it will have. From reading it, however, I 154
feel it has great possibilities. 161

The enclosed brochure lists and describes the plays which were most popu- 175
lar last year. If any of these interest you, please let me know. (160) 189

Ms. Melissa M. Masters | Manager | xx | postscript I look forward to attending 215
one of your productions this summer when I am in Boulder. 226/**248**

Document 3
modified block format; blocked ¶s; mixed punctuation

Special features:
Attention Human Resources Director
Subject: Lakeland MBA Program
Enclosures:
MBA Announcement
Information Cards

Document 4
Rekey Document 1 in block format with open punctuation. Do not include the company name in the closing lines.

Griffin Computer Systems, Inc. | 1434 John Hancock Drive | Tallahassee, FL 24
32304-1617 37

The enclosed announcement provides information on the Master of Business 52
Administration degree at Lakeland University. Please share this informa- 66
tion with employees you feel would benefit from completing this program. 81

Lakeland offers a quality MBA program designed to provide advanced and spe- 96
cialized training in management, research, and decision making. Individuals 111
completing the program become more valued employees who generally ad- 125
vance more rapidly in their organizations. 134

Those interested in more details about the program should complete and 148
return one of the cards enclosed with the announcement. (122) 159

Carlos J. Santos | Admissions Director | xx 179/**202**

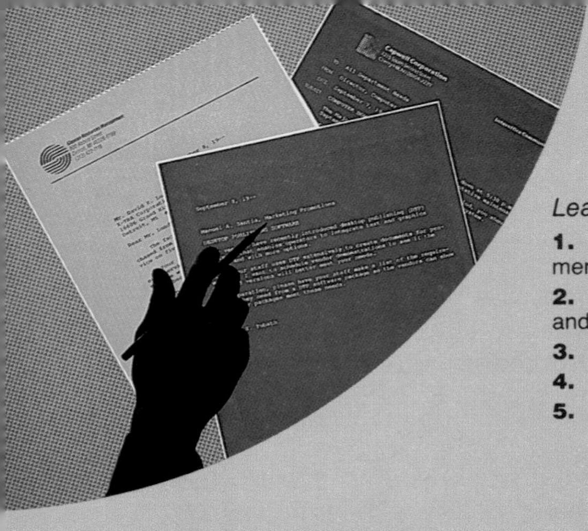

UNIT 36 LESSONS 155 – 158

Assess/Improve Correspondence Processing Skills

Learning Goals

1. To assess/reinforce knowledge of letter and memorandum formats.
2. To improve productivity in processing letters and memorandums.
3. To reinforce production from script copy.
4. To rebuild/extend straight-copy skill.
5. To improve language-skills competency.

Format Guides

1. Paper guide at *0* (for typewriters).
2. LL (line length): 70-space line for sentence and ¶ drills, or as required for documents.
3. LS (line spacing): Single-space (SS) word and sentence drills; double-space (DS) ¶s; or space as directed within an activity.
4. PI (paragraph indent): 5 spaces.

FORMATTING GUIDES: LETTERS AND MEMORANDUMS

Block style letter; open punctuation

Simplified memorandum

Guides for Letters

1. Letter length determines margin stops and date placement. Use the chart below or refer to RG 5 as a guide.

Length	Margins	Dateline
Short	2″	18
Average	1 ½″	16
Long	1″	14

Leave a quadruple space (QS) between the date and the letter address.

2. Include the person's name in the salutation when the letter is addressed to an individual. When a letter is addressed to a company, use the salutation "Ladies and Gentlemen." Use "Dear Sir or Madam" when the letter is addressed to an unidentified person such as "Office Manager." Leave a double space (DS) above and below the salutation.

3. Key the complimentary close a DS below the last line of the message.

4. Key the signer's name a QS below the complimentary close (or the company name if one is used).

5. Key the title of the signer on the line with the name separated by a comma, or on the next line (no comma), depending on the length of both the name and the title.

6. Key reference initials at left margin a DS below the signer's name or title. Use only the keyboard operator's initials (lowercase) when the signer's name is keyed in the closing lines.

7. Key the enclosure notation (if used) at left margin a DS below the reference initials.

8. Key the copy notation "c" a DS below the enclosure notation (or the reference initials if there is no enclosure).

Letter Styles

Block style. *Every* line begins at the left margin. Because of its efficiency, this style is highly recommended.

Modified block style. In this style, the date and the signature block begin at the horizontal center of the paper. (Set a tab stop at the center point to speed processing.)

Paragraphs may be blocked or indented 5 spaces from the left margin.

Punctuation Styles

Open. No punctuation follows the salutation or complimentary close.

Mixed. A colon follows the salutation, and a comma follows the complimentary close.

Either open or mixed punctuation may be used with block or modified block letters. Open punctuation, however, is typically used with block style and often used with modified block style.

Guides for Interoffice Memorandums

Formal style. Formal memos are prepared on full- or half-sheet forms with printed headings. Block style and 1″ side margins are used. The headings (TO:, FROM:, DATE:, and SUBJECT:) are printed in the left margin so that data used after the headings and message align at the 1″ left margin.

Memo headings are double-spaced, and a DS is left between the subject line and the first message line. The message is single-spaced; a DS is left between paragraphs. The keyboard operator's initials are keyed at the left margin a DS below the memo message.

Simplified style. Simplified memos are prepared on plain paper or company letterhead. They contain no preprinted or keyed headings. These memos are prepared in block format with 1″ side margins and follow these format guides:

Date: plain paper, line 10; letterhead, a DS below the last line of letterhead.

Addressee's name: a QS below the date; no personal title precedes name.

Subject: in ALL CAPS or cap-and-lowercase; a DS below the addressee's name.

Body: a DS below the subject line; single-spaced with a DS between paragraphs.

Writer's name: a QS below the last line of message.

Operator's initials: a DS below the writer's name.

Enclosure notation: "Enclosure" or "Attachment" a DS below operator's initials.

ENRICHMENT ACTIVITY: *Skill-Building Drill and Timed Writings*

The two sets of paragraphs on this page are counted internally for 1′ guided and unguided writings. The paragraphs at the bottom of the page are counted for 3′ and 5′ timed writings. They may be used at any time additional drills and/or timed writings are desired.

Straight-Copy Drill

1. A 1′ writing on the ¶ at the top to establish a base rate.

2. Add 4-8 words to base rate to set goal rate. Note quarter-minute checkpoints.

3. Three 1′ writings on the same paragraph, trying to achieve goal rate each quarter minute as guides are called. Set goal rate higher each time the goal is achieved.

4. Three 1′ writings at reduced speed for control (not more than one error a minute).

Note: The same procedure may be used for ¶s 2 and 3 for additional guided writing copy.

Quarter-Minute Checkpoints

gwam	1/4′	1/2′	3/4′	1′
28	7	14	21	28
32	8	16	24	32
36	9	18	27	36
40	10	20	30	40
44	11	22	33	44
48	12	24	36	48
52	13	26	39	52
56	14	28	42	56
60	15	30	45	60
64	16	32	48	64
68	17	34	51	68
72	18	36	54	72
76	19	38	57	76
80	20	40	60	80

Timed Writings

Two 3′ or 5′ writings on the ¶s at the right. Find *gwam* and errors. Record the better of the 3′ and 5′ writings.

all letters used | A | 1.5 si | 5.7 awl | 80% hfw

A basic knowledge of parliamentary procedure is an excellent skill to acquire. Those who possess this skill will be able to put it to use in any organization they belong to that conducts meetings based on parliamentary law. A meeting which is run by this procedure will be conducted in a proper and very orderly fashion. Just as important, the rights of each member of the group are protected at all times.

---

all letters used | A | 1.5 si | 5.7 awl | 80% hfw

	gwam 3′	5′	
More time is devoted to business meetings than ever before. Today a	5	3	48
group rather than an individual is deciding the direction of many organi-	9	6	51
zations. Meetings provide the forum for decisions to be made by a group.	14	9	54
These meetings do not succeed or fail by accident. A successful business	19	12	57
meeting is more likely to occur when advance notice of the time, date,	24	14	60
site, and agenda are provided. The agenda quickly informs the group mem-	29	17	63
bers of the items of business to be conducted at the next meeting. It	34	20	66
allows them to plan and to prepare prior to the time of the meeting.	38	23	68
Even though the decisions are made by a group, the leader of the	43	26	71
group is the key to the success of a meeting. The leader determines when	48	29	74
the meeting starts and when it will conclude, the facilities, the agenda	53	32	77
items to be discussed, and the people to be invited to the meeting.	57	34	80
Effective group leaders strive to start and conclude meetings on time.	62	37	82
They provide members with information on major agenda items prior to the	67	40	85
meeting. They make sure that the meeting site and facilities contribute	72	43	88
to the success of the meeting rather than detract from it.	76	45	91

gwam 3′ | 1 | 2 | 3 | 4 | 5
5′ | 1 | 2 | 3

154d ▶ 5 Improve Language Skills: Word Choice

1. Study the spelling and definitions of each pair of words.

2. Key the **Learn** line, with the number and period, noting the proper use of the often confused words.

3. Key the **Apply** line, with the number and period, using the words that complete the sentence correctly.

complement (n) something that completes or makes up a whole

compliment (n) an expression of praise or congratulation

expend (vb) to use up; consume

expand (vb) to open up or out; enlarge; unfold or extend

Learn 1. Jim's compliment to Mary was that her hat complemented her outfit.
Apply 2. My (complement/compliment) was that Di's blouse is a nice (complement compliment) to her suit.

Learn 3. Al may expend too much time if he tries to expand his sales region.
Apply 4. I will (expand/expend) my display area unless it (expands/expends) too much floor space.

154e ▶ 10 Assess Language Skills: Word Division

1. Review the word-division guides on RG 5.

2. Set left margin at 12; tab stops on 31 and 56; DS.

3. Key the first word at the right beginning at the left margin stop.

4. Tab to first stop and key the word with a hyphen after each syllable.

5. Tab to the second stop and key the word with a hyphen between syllables where the word can be divided without violating any word-division guides.

Example
Column 1: situation
Column 2: sit-u-a-tion
Column 3: situ-ation

radio	spared
reliable	expressive
evacuee	drilling
staffer	occurring
unanimous	well-being
radioactivity	Part #60-798
panning	insufficient

ENRICHMENT ACTIVITY: Assess Language Skills: Spelling, Punctuation, Capitalization, and Composing

1. Proofread each sentence for errors in spelling (lines 1-3), punctuation (lines 4-6), and capitalization (lines 7-9).

2. Key each sentence, with the number and period, correcting the language-skills errors. Also, correct any errors you make while keying.

Spelling

1. Henry Huxster mist the deadline for the reduced fair by three daze.
2. Susan Harris beet the throw to second base by fore steps at leased.
3. The front breaks on my car did not seam write when I tried to stop.

Punctuation

4. Prizes were given to bikers with the top two times: 4′11 and 4′15″.
5. Sue had cheese and crackers peanuts and hot cider at the reception.
6. Ford High had first second and third place finishers in the race.

Capitalization

7. the osa conference is in the desmond building on eighth street north.
8. the senator will speak in spanish on his trip to mexico next january.
9. the answer to problem 2 on test 3 is in lesson 6, unit 7, on page 98.

Composing at the Keyboard

1. Compose at the keyboard in DS format; do not correct language-skills or keying errors; if necessary, x-out errors and continue.

2. Edit your copy; then rekey it in final form on a full sheet. Use a 2″ top margin, 1″ side margins, and DS.

3. Describe the most valuable activity in which you engaged last summer; indicate how it is valuable to you.

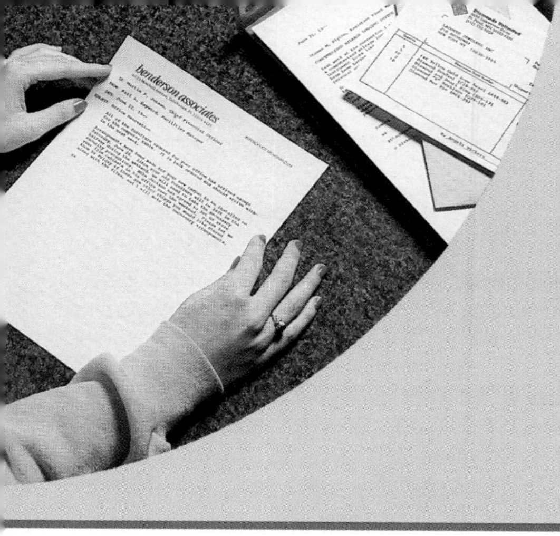

UNIT 30 LESSONS 130 – 134

Process Forms and Special Documents

Learning Goals

1. To learn to format and process formal and simplified interoffice memorandums.

2. To learn to format and process special business forms.

3. To learn to format and process information on ruled forms.

4. To improve language skills.

Format Guides

1. Paper guide at *0* (for typewriters).

2. LL: 70-space lines for drills, ¶s, and language skills; as required for documents.

3. LS: SS drills; DS ¶s; as required by document formats.

4. PI: 5 spaces, when appropriate.

FORMATTING GUIDES: FORMS AND SPECIAL DOCUMENTS

Stratford Manufacturing Company
5410 Redwood Drive, NW, Albuquerque, NM 87120-4130
INTEROFFICE MEMORANDUM

TO: Mark R. Goodwin, Assistant Manager

FROM: Stacey P. McKinney, Marketing Manager

DATE: January 20, 19--

SUBJECT: Western Region Sales Data

Mark, the sales reports that I received yesterday for the fourth quarter indicate that there is a potential problem with the Western Region. The overall sales for that region have been down appreciably during the last two quarters. For the year they are down by almost 15 percent compared to last year.

The reports I receive break down sales only by region. I would like to see sales for each individual state in the region to determine if this is a problem for the entire region or only for one or two states.

Since I am meeting with regional representatives next Monday, I would like to have the information to review this week.

xx

COMPANY MAIL

Mr. Mark Goodwin, Assistant Manager
Marketing Department

Formal Memo and Company Envelope

benderson associates
INTEROFFICE MEMORANDUM

June 12, 19--

Martin F. Jensen, Chief Financial Officer

OFFICE RENOVATION

All of the furniture ordered for your office has arrived except for the computer table. It is back ordered, and it should arrive within the next week.

Arrangements have been made for your new carpet to be installed on Saturday, June 26. Since your old furniture will be left in the hallway during the weekend, we will need to take the necessary security precautions. Mike Jackson has agreed to let you store your file cabinets in his office over the weekend. Please let me know by Friday if there are other things you would like stored along with the files, and I will make the necessary arrangements.

Karl L. Hayward

Karl L. Hayward, Facilities Manager

xx

Simplified Memo

Interoffice Memorandum

Communications within an organization are often formatted as memorandums rather than as letters. Two styles of the interoffice memorandum are commonly used. The *formal memorandum* is processed on a form having special printed headings. The *simplified memorandum* is prepared on plain paper or letterhead without internal headings.

Formatting guides for the interoffice memo are listed below.

1. Use either a full or half sheet.
2. Use block format.
3. Use side margins of approximately 1″.
4. Omit personal titles (Miss, Mr., Ms., Dr., etc.) on memo, but include them on the company envelope.
5. Omit salutation and complimentary close.
6. Use a subject line.
7. SS the body, but DS between ¶s.
8. Use plain envelope with COMPANY MAIL typed in the usual stamp position. Include on the envelope the receiver's personal title, name, and business title; also, include receiver's department (see illustration at left).

Formal memorandum. Begin heading information 2 spaces to the right of printed headings (as shown on page 232). Note that headings are printed in the 1″ left margin so that the lines of the heading data and the message can begin at the 1″ left margin setting. A memo may be sent to more than one individual; if so, each name is included on the same line as the "To:" heading. DS between all parts of the formal memorandum.

Simplified memorandum. Begin the date on line 6 for a half sheet and line 10 for a full sheet. DS between all parts of the simplified memo, *except* below date and the last paragraph of the body. Quadruple-space (QS) below the dateline and below the last paragraph of the body.

Special Forms (See models on pp. 233-234).

Purchase requisitions, purchase orders, invoices, and other similar documents are prepared on printed forms. Although forms vary from company to company, well-designed forms allow the keyboard operator to follow the general guidelines listed below.

1. Set left margin stop so that items are approximately centered in the Quantity column of purchase requisitions, purchase orders, and invoices. (This stop is also used to begin the *Deliver to* block of Purchase Requisitions.)
2. Set a tab stop to begin the Description items of Purchase Requisitions, Purchase Orders, and Invoices 1 or 2 spaces to the right of the vertical rule. Place the address (ALL CAPS) so that it will show through the window of a window envelope.
3. Set a tab stop for keying information in the upper right-hand area of the form (1 or 2 spaces to the right of printed items). This stop may also be used to key items in the Price column, or an additional stop may be set for that purpose.
4. Set additional tab stops for aligning and keying items in remaining column(s).
5. SS column entries, beginning on the first or second space below the horizontal rule under the column headings.
6. If the form has a vertical line to separate dollars and cents in monetary columns, key the cents so they are to the right of the vertical rule. Use of commas to indicate thousands in figure columns is optional.
7. Underline the last figure in the Total column; then, DS before keying the total amount.
8. Tabulate and key across the form rather than keying all items in one column before moving to the next column.

154b ▶ 15 Improve Keystroking Response Patterns

each line twice SS; DS between 2-line groups; as time permits, take a 1′ writing on each of lines 9-12

		Words
letter	1	as no ad up be hop are ink bag kin card hoop dart junk eats noun texts
letter	2	ax oh at in we ilk ate inn bar lip care hull data kiln ewes only vexed
word	3	am and bye doe eke fib irk jay ken lens make name ogle paid quay right
combination	4	ad he in go to hem lop ape rag irk upon fizz veer heir bass giro zebra
		Phrases
letter	5	at ease | join in | ate beef | new facts | no opinion | act better | eager beavers
word	6	lay by | if when | got down | pen pals | rush to | city bus | visit with | by and by
word	7	to own | tow us | paid off | the theory | their goals | naughty man | hand and eye
combination	8	were we | held off | brave men | mangy dog | did better | deserve it | up and down
		Sentences
letter	9	I'll get him a million jolly eager readers after my greatest act ever.
word	10	Keith and the busy girls did make a visit to the tidy chapel downtown.
combination	11	It was great to visit my neighbor and to get to see Zoe, my big puppy.
combination	12	Bret may gas the autobus and cars in the usual cycle at the city pump.

| 1 | 2 | 3 | 4 | 5 | 6 | 7 | 8 | 9 | 10 | 11 | 12 | 13 | 14 |

154c ▶ 15 Assess Straight-Copy Skill

1. Two 5′ writings on ¶s 1-3 combined; find *gwam*, circle errors.
2. Record the better *gwam*.
3. Compare this *gwam* score with the score you recorded in 151d.

all letters used | A | 1.5 si | 5.7 awl | 80% hfw |

	gwam 3′	5′	
A dictionary is a good resource for a secretary and should be part	4	3	40
of every office library. Most secretaries use one to find how words are	9	6	43
spelled, to determine correct definitions of words, and to learn what	14	8	46
part of speech a word can be used as. Another frequent use is to learn	19	11	50
the pronunciation of an unfamiliar word such as zori.	22	13	51
Along with the few major uses listed above, a dictionary can give	27	16	54
secretaries much more. For example, most dictionaries have parts that	31	19	57
list the names of and basic information about famous people and places.	36	22	59
A list of abbreviations used to shorten frequently used words can be	41	25	62
found in quite a few.	42	25	63
In addition to improving spelling skills through dictionary use,	47	28	66
secretaries should know some of the other useful information a dictio-	51	31	68
nary has so they will be able to use it more. Those who know when and	56	34	71
how to use a dictionary will be able to finish most communication tasks	61	37	74
with more speed and accuracy.	63	38	75

gwam 3′ | 1 | 2 | 3 | 4 | 5 |
5′ | 1 | 2 | 3 |

130a ▶ 5
Conditioning Practice

each line twice SS (slowly, then faster); DS between 2-line groups; if time permits, rekey selected lines

alphabet	1	Kay may quit publicizing the major events before the end of next week.
figures	2	Of the 12,874 votes cast, Kern received 6,305 and Bahr received 6,569.
adjacent keys	3	Officers stopped the reception before conditions deteriorated further.
speed	4	The visit by the six sorority girls may be a problem for their mentor.

| 1 | 2 | 3 | 4 | 5 | 6 | 7 | 8 | 9 | 10 | 11 | 12 | 13 | 14 |

130b ▶ 15
Check/Improve Keyboarding Skill

1. A 1′ writing on ¶ 1; find *gwam*.

2. Add 4-8 *gwam* to the rate attained in Step 1, and note quarter-minute checkpoints from table below.

3. Take two 1′ guided writings on ¶ 1 to increase speed.

4. Practice ¶ 2 in the same way.

5. Two 3′ writings on ¶s 1-2 combined; find *gwam* and circle errors.

Quarter-Minute Checkpoints

gwam	1/4′	1/2′	3/4′	Time
24	6	12	18	24
28	7	14	21	28
32	8	16	24	32
36	9	18	27	36
40	10	20	30	40
44	11	22	33	44
48	12	24	36	48
52	13	26	39	52
56	14	28	42	56
60	15	30	45	60

all letters used | A | 1.5 si | 5.7 awl | 80% hfw |

	gwam 3′	5′	
Records are extremely vital for a business enterprise to maintain.	5	3	39
They give executives insight into the day-to-day dealings of a firm.	9	6	42
They also are often the sole basis for executives to make major decisions	14	8	44
on the future direction of a firm. Many different types of documents are	19	11	47
used to record data about a firm. Three such documents that are vital to	24	14	50
the operation of a firm are the purchase requisition, the purchase order,	29	17	53
and the invoice.	30	18	54
A purchase requisition is a document utilized by a firm to request	34	21	57
the purchasing agent to order goods or services. A purchase order is a	39	24	60
document used by the purchasing department of one firm to order goods or	44	26	62
services from another firm. An invoice is a document used by one firm	49	29	65
to bill another firm for goods or services purchased from the firm that	54	32	68
sends the invoice. All three documents will become a record of the	58	35	71
firm's purchasing transactions.	60	36	72

gwam 3′ | 1 | 2 | 3 | 4 | 5 |
gwam 5′ | 1 | 2 | 3 |

130c ▶ 10
Language Skills: Compose at Keyboard

plain full sheet
LL: 70 spaces

1. Compose at the keyboard 1 or 2 paragraphs on one of the questions at the right. DS paragraph(s).

2. Edit your copy, marking corrections and changes to improve sentence structure and organization.

3. Prepare the final copy.

Questions

Who is your favorite singing star? Explain why.

Is an education important? Explain why you believe it is or why you believe it is not.

What qualities do you feel are necessary for a good leader to possess? Why?

153d ▶ 20 Improve Keyboarding Skill: Guided Writing

1. A 3′ writing on ¶s 1-3 combined; find *gwam.*

2. A 1′ writing on ¶ 1; find *gwam* to establish your base rate.

3. Add 2-6 words to Step 2 *gwam;* use this as your goal rate.

4. From the table below, find quarter-minute checkpoints; note these figures in ¶ 1.

5. Take three 1′ speed writings on ¶ 1, trying to reach your quarter-minute checkpoints as the guides (¼, ½, ¾, time) are called.

6. Follow Steps 2-5 for ¶ 2.

7. Take another 3′ writing on ¶s 1-3 combined; find and compare *gwam* with that achieved in Step 1.

8. Record your better 3′ *gwam;* then compare it to the 3′ *gwam* you made in 151b and 151d.

gwam	¼′	½′	¾′	1′
32	8	16	24	32
36	9	18	27	36
40	10	20	30	40
44	11	22	33	44
48	12	24	36	48
52	13	26	39	52
56	14	28	42	56
60	15	30	45	60
64	16	32	48	64
68	17	34	51	68
72	18	36	54	72
76	19	38	57	76
80	20	40	60	80
84	21	42	63	84
88	22	44	66	88
92	23	46	69	92
96	24	48	72	96
100	25	50	75	100

all letters used | A | 1.5 si | 5.7 awl | 80% hfw

	gwam 3′	5′	
Reprographics, a vital part of the information processing field, is	5	3	49
a term that is used to describe all procedures and machines involved in	9	6	52
making multiple copies. It is an area that has undergone many changes	14	8	55
due to the many new machines and procedures that have been introduced.	19	11	58
The vast changes have made it possible for businesses to make copies	23	14	60
easier and faster and for less money than in the past.	27	16	62
Two kinds of equipment are often used to make copies--duplicators	31	19	65
and copiers. Duplicators use stencils or masters to make copies. The	36	22	68
stencils and masters must, of course, be prepared before copies can be	41	25	71
made from them. On the other hand, copiers use an image-forming process,	46	28	74
much like that of a camera, to make an exact copy directly from the	50	30	76
original.	51	31	77
Most copiers use regular or coated paper for the copies. In recent	56	33	80
years, fiber optic copiers have replaced many of the old mechanical	60	36	82
models since they are often small, cost less to run, and are more reli-	65	39	85
able because they have few parts that move. Intelligent copiers that	69	42	88
bring together the power of a computer and the convenience of a copier	74	45	91
have been emphasized in the past few years.	77	46	92

gwam 3′ | 1 | 2 | 3 | 4 | 5 |
5′ | 1 | 2 | 3 |

Lesson 154 — Keyboarding/Language Skills

154a ▶ 5 Conditioning Practice

each line twice SS (slowly, then faster); DS between 2-line groups; if time permits, rekey selected lines

alphabet 1 Five expert judges were asked to quickly analyze both new board games.

fig/sym 2 I should pay $1,825 on Models #04-6 and #73-9 by May 8 to get 15% off.

long words 3 Unexpected fluctuations in work load or personnel affect productivity.

speed 4 Did the big quake on the key island shake the autobus and the visitor?

| 1 | 2 | 3 | 4 | 5 | 6 | 7 | 8 | 9 | 10 | 11 | 12 | 13 | 14 |

INTEROFFICE MEMORANDUM

Stratford Manufacturing Company
5410 Redwood Drive, NW, Albuquerque, NM 87120-4130

2 spaces

words

TO: Mark R. Goodwin, Assistant Manager 7

FROM: Stacey P. McKinney, Marketing Manager 15

DATE: January 20, 19-- 18

SUBJECT: Western Region Sales Data 23

1" ← → 1"

Mark, the sales reports that I received yesterday for the fourth 36
quarter indicate that there is a potential problem with the West- 49
ern Region. The overall sales for that region have been down ap- 62
preciably during the last two quarters. For the year they are 75
down by almost 15 percent compared to last year. 85

The reports I receive break down sales only by region. I would 98
like to see sales for each individual state in the region to de- 110
termine if this is a problem for the entire region or only for 123
one or two states. 127

Since I am meeting with regional representatives next Monday, I 140
would like to have the information to review this week. 151

xx 151/163

Formal Memorandum

130d ▶ 20
Format Documents: Interoffice Memorandums

Document 1
Formal Memorandum
LP p. 103

Review the Formatting Guides for interoffice memorandums and company envelopes on page 230. Format and key the memorandum from the model copy above. Proofread and correct errors. Prepare a company envelope to

Mr. Mark R. Goodwin
Assistant Manager
Marketing Department

Note: If you do not have Lab Pac (LP) pages to use for the formal memos, use plain sheets of paper. Begin on line 10 and set 1" side margins. Key the heading information flush left with the margin. Space twice after the colon and key the information following each heading.

words

words in heading 18

Last week at the convention I picked up the attached brochure on a comput- 33
erized mileage logging device from the exhibit area. This instrument looks 48
like it (might, mite) be the answer to the problems we have been having with 62
company vehicles being used excessively for personal use. 73

In order to determine the (affect, effect) of the device, we are planning to 87
pilot test it in two states from June (threw, through) August. Doing so will 101
provide us with (farther, further) information to make a recommendation to 113
Vice President Dewitz. I believe he will (accept, except) our (advice, ad- 124
vise) regarding its purchase. 130

Please suggest two states in which to pilot test the device--one where the ex- 146
penses appear to be excessive and one where the expenses are below the 160
company average. 164

closing lines 177/**191**

Document 2
Simplified Memorandum
plain full sheet

Format and key the simplified memo above to **Steven M. Blythe, Assistant Fleet Manager,** from **Ramona S. Gonzalez, Fleet Manager.** Date the memo **June 21.**

Supply an appropriate subject line. Select the proper word in parentheses to complete the sentences correctly. Include your reference initials and indicate a copy to **Blake L. Dewitz.** Proofread/correct errors.

Document 3
Formal Memorandum
LP p. 105

Rekey Document 2 as a formal memorandum.

Prepare a company envelope to **Mr. Steven M. Blythe, Assistant Fleet Manager, Transportation.**

152c ▶ 10 Reinforce Word-Division Skills

1. Key in one column the words shown at the right, inserting hyphens between all syllables. Use a 1″ left margin and DS.

2. Review word-division Guides 1-6 on RG 5.

3. In your copy, circle any hyphen that does not violate Guides 1-6.

fitted	selling	benefit
spinner	classes	policies
sunning	actually	association
staffing	manner	evacuation

152d ▶ 15 Improve Script-Copy Skill

Goal: Set a goal of *speed* if you did not exceed 6 errors on the 3′ writing in 152b; *control* if you made more than 6 errors.

1. Take three 1′ writings on each ¶ of 152b, p. 270.

2. Take two 3′ writings on ¶s 1-2 combined; find *gwam* and circle errors.

3. Compare better 3′ *gwam* with 3′ *gwam* recorded in 151b.

4. Record the better *gwam* for use in 153d.

Lesson 153 — *Keyboarding/Language Skills*

153a ▶ 5 Conditioning Practice

each line twice SS (slowly, then faster); DS between 2-line groups; if time permits, rekey selected lines

alphabet	1	Six glazed rolls with jam were quickly baked and provided free to all.
fig/sym	2	The 0-384 MC costs $196.75, and the 300/1200 Baud modem costs $265.89.
shift key	3	Ronald Lee read "A Hard Road" and "Lead Us" for Spanish IV in January.
speed	4	The sixth autobus turns to visit the busy shantytown dock by the lake.

| 1 | 2 | 3 | 4 | 5 | 6 | 7 | 8 | 9 | 10 | 11 | 12 | 13 | 14 |

153b ▶ 10 Reinforce Word-Division Skills

1. Key in one column the words shown at the right, inserting hyphens between all syllables. Use a 1″ left margin and DS.

2. Review word-division Guides 1-9 on RG 5.

3. In your copy, circle any hyphen that does not violate Guides 1-9.

readily	cyclical	wouldn't
comical	self-service	didn't
easily	low-keyed	$535,987
sabbatical	well-mannered	Contract F-23-8765

153c ▶ 15 Assess Keystroking Response Patterns

each line twice SS; DS between 2-line groups; rekey difficult lines as time permits

Words

letter	1	ad in be ho as him age ill awe ion cabs hill daft jink ears milk tarts
letter	2	at my we on ax hip arc imp bad joy cage hook dare join east nook taste
word	3	ye us to so ox nap man lay ken jai ibid corn glem flam envy dory cubit
combination	4	an up by oh it era jam hop gob fad mend moon rich ever pane loll theme

Phrases

letter	5	you are / wade in / trade up / on target / on my raft / fast breeze / fewer awards
word	6	an oak / go half / so sick / make do / lent me / kept down / profit by / such sorrow
word	7	do rush / dial six / sight land / it's downtown / fish and fowl / fuel the flame
combination	8	the men / oak tree / melt down / queue up / right hand / rosy scarf / penalty fees

Sentences

letter	9	Rebecca served plump, sweet plum desserts on my east terraces at noon.
word	10	Diane is due to dismantle the antique chair when it is right to do so.
combination	11	The corn was in the burlap bag and the small beets were in nylon bags.
combination	12	The six beggars deserved a better neighbor than the neurotic busybody.

| 1 | 2 | 3 | 4 | 5 | 6 | 7 | 8 | 9 | 10 | 11 | 12 | 13 | 14 |

131a ▶ 5 Conditioning Practice

each line twice SS (slowly, then faster); DS between 2-line groups; if time permits, rekey selected lines

alphabet 1 The fabulous zoology complex will be located quite near Bjerke Avenue.

figures 2 Of the 830 surveyed, only 256 knew the importance of December 7, 1941.

long reaches 3 The umpire received a number of unusual gifts at the special ceremony.

speed 4 The heir to the endowment may work on the problems with the six firms.

| 1 | 2 | 3 | 4 | 5 | 6 | 7 | 8 | 9 | 10 | 11 | 12 | 13 | 14 |

131b ▶ 10 Improve Language Skills: Word Choice

Study the spelling and definition of each word. Note how it is used in the **Learn** sentence. Key the **Learn** sentence (with number and period) and the **Apply** sentences (with number and period) selecting the proper word in parentheses to complete each sentence correctly.

stationary (adj) fixed; unchanging in condition

stationery (n) paper for writing

weather (n) state of the atmosphere

whether (conj) used to indicate alternatives; if

Learn 1. The stationery is on the stationary cabinet at the front of the room.
Apply 2. Richard will need tools to remove the (stationary, stationery) desks.
Apply 3. The (stationary, stationery) will go on sale this Friday.

Learn 4. The weather will determine whether the meeting has been cancelled.
Apply 5. The (weather, whether) forecast predicts snow before Friday evening.
Apply 6. I am not sure (weather, whether) I will be able to finish the project on time.

131c ▶ 35 Process Special Forms

Review the Formatting Guides for processing purchase requisitions, purchase orders, and invoices on page 230. Proofread carefully and correct errors.

Document 1
Purchase Requisition
LP p. 107

Key purchase requisition as shown at right.

words

OAKRIDGE MEDICAL CENTER
348 New Whitney Street
Boston, MA 02115-8130
(617) 386-3995

PURCHASE REQUISITION

2 spaces

Deliver to: Anne Jackson — Requisition No. B7983 4

Location: Information Processing Center — Date January 13, 19-- 13

Job No. 8729 — Date Required January 30, 19-- 18

Quantity	Description	words
4	Laser Printer Labels	22
5	Laser Printer Paper	27
3	Disk Files	29
10	3 1/2" Disks	33
20	5 1/4" Disks	36

approx. center

2 spaces

Requisitioned by: Martha Landon 39

151c ▶ 10 Reinforce Word-Division Skills

1. Key in one column the words shown at the right, inserting hyphens between all syllables. Use a 1″ left margin and DS.

2. Review the first three word-division guides on RG 5.

3. In your copy, circle any hyphen that does not violate Guides 1-3.

central	furnished	eraser
staged	dozen	obesity
every	began	agency
coverage	universal	obedient

151d ▶ 15 Improve Straight-Copy Skill

Goal: Set a goal of *speed* if you did not exceed 6 errors on the 3′ writing in 151b; *control* if you made more than 6 errors.

1. Take three 1′ writings on each ¶ of 151b. Find *gwam* or circle errors, depending on your goal.

2. Take a 5′ writing on ¶s 1-2 combined. If you finish all copy before time is called, start over. Find *gwam* or circle errors.

3. Record your 5′ *gwam* to compare with your *gwam* in Lesson 154c.

Lesson 152 Keyboarding/Language Skills

152a ▶ 5 Conditioning Practice

each line twice SS (slowly, then faster); DS between 2-line groups; if time permits, rekey selected lines

alphabet 1 Zelda was quite naive to pack the four big boxes with just fresh yams.

figures 2 Try to call me before 10 a.m. at 952-3468; let the phone ring 7 times.

one hand 3 After I stated my opinion based on facts, fewer fees were agreed upon.

speed 4 Elsie and the neighbor got an authentic jai alai title with an emblem.

| 1 | 2 | 3 | 4 | 5 | 6 | 7 | 8 | 9 | 10 | 11 | 12 | 13 | 14 |

152b ▶ 20 Assess Script-Copy Skill

1. Three 1′ writings on each ¶ for speed; find *gwam*.

2. Two 1′ writings on each ¶ for control; circle errors.

3. Two 3′ writings on ¶s 1-2 combined; find *gwam* and circle errors.

Note: If you finish all the copy before time is called, start over.

all letters used | A | 1.5 si | 5.7 awl | 80% hfw |

	gwam 1′	3′
Over the years, keyboard operators have used various meth-	12	4
ods to correct mistakes they made when using manual and elec-	24	8
tric machines. One of the early methods was to use an eraser	36	12
to remove errors from the paper. Other products that have come	49	16
into use in more recent years include correction tape or fluid	62	21
to cover up errors and lift-off tape to take errors from the	74	25
paper.	75	25
Various parts of the typewriter were used to squeeze words	12	29
into less space or spread a word to fill extra space when era-	24	33
sure, cover-up, and lift-off methods were used. When using ma-	37	37
chines that display electronic copy on a screen, workers can	49	41
correct errors just by inserting, deleting, moving, or writing	62	46
over before the final copy is printed on the paper.	72	49

131c (continued)

words

Document 2
Purchase Order
LP p. 107

Key purchase order as shown at right.

OAKRIDGE MEDICAL CENTER
348 New Whitney Street
Boston, MA 02115-8130
(617) 386-3995

PURCHASE ORDER

2 spaces

Purchase Order No.: 826A-38 2

DENTON OFFICE SUPPLY
389 GLENBROOK DRIVE
BIRMINGHAM AL 35213-6487

Date: January 15, 19-- 6 13

Terms: 2/10, n/30 21

Shipped Via: Western Freight 24

Quantity	Description/Stock Number	Price		Per	Total		words
4	Laser Printer Labels (93A391)	7	95	ea	31	80	33
5	Laser Printer Paper (93A592)	49	95	ea	249	75	43
3	Disk Files (29G392)	19	95	ea	59	85	51
10	3 1/2" Disks (18C657)	2	95	ea	29	50	59
20	5 1/4" Disks (18C685)	1	20	ea	24	00	68
↑ approx. center	↑ 2 spaces				394	90	69

By ____________________ 72

Document 3
Invoice
LP p. 109

Key invoice as shown at right.

Document 4
LP p. 109

Repeat Document 3 changing the quantities to 3, 5, 7, 4, 2, and 6. Calculate the total and add 5% sales tax.

The Photo Gallery
5817 Wild Flower Drive Carson City, NV 89701-1901 (702) 325-6715

INVOICE

2 spaces

NATIONAL PHOTOGRAPHY INC
9399 MOUNTAIN VIEW DRIVE
THOUSAND OAKS CA 91320-4311

Date: January 30, 19-- 8

Customer Order No.: AJ-8937 13 21

Terms	Shipped Via	Our Order No.	Date Shipped	words
3/10, n/30	Reed Transit, Inc.	B 388-99	1/30/--	30

Quantity	Description/Stock No.	Unit Price		Amount		words
5	Mini Camera Bag	27	95	139	75	36
3	Shutter Tester	39	95	119	85	42
2	Table Top Viewer	79	50	159	00	50
3	Flash Attachment	93	49	280	47	56
5	Electronic Camera	259	95	1299	75	64
5	Tripod	28	75	143	75	68
↑ approx. center	↑ 2 spaces			2142	57	73
	Sales Tax			107	13	76
				2249	70	77

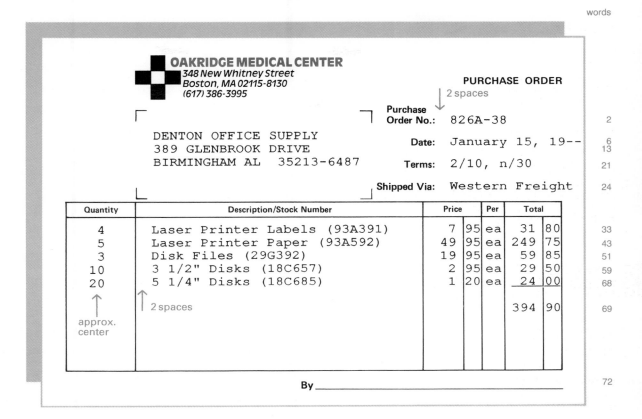

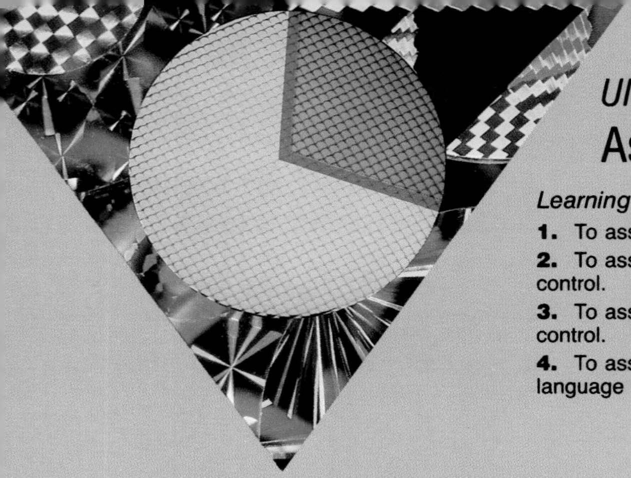

UNIT 35 LESSONS 151 – 154
Assess/Improve Keyboarding and Language Skills

Learning Goals

1. To assess/improve keyboarding techniques.
2. To assess/improve straight-copy speed and control.
3. To assess/improve script-copy speed and control.
4. To assess/improve decision-making and language skills.

Format Guides

1. Paper guide at *0* (for typewriters).
2. LL (line length): 70 spaces.
3. LS (line spacing): Single-space (SS) word and sentence drills; double-space (DS) ¶s; or space as directed within an activity.
4. PI (paragraph indent): 5 spaces.

Lesson 151 *Keyboarding/Language Skills*

151a ▶ 5 Conditioning Practice

each line twice SS (slowly, then faster); DS between 2-line groups; if time permits, rekey selected lines

alphabet	1	Quen packed an extra big jar full of very zesty wild apples for Homer.
figures	2	Order color monitor 4103, printer 278-7, and CPU 3956 for this office.
fig/sym	3	The original PC-409 cost $1,325 while the new clone #6-8 costs $1,187.
speed	4	Pamela got the authentic antique handiwork by the giant island shanty.

| 1 | 2 | 3 | 4 | 5 | 6 | 7 | 8 | 9 | 10 | 11 | 12 | 13 | 14 |

151b ▶ 20 Assess Straight-Copy Skill

1. Three 1′ writings on each ¶ for speed; find *gwam.*
2. Two 1′ writings on each ¶ for control; circle errors.
3. Two 3′ writings on ¶s 1-2 combined; find *gwam,* circle errors.
4. Record your better 3′ *gwam* to compare with your 3′ *gwam* in 153d.

all letters used | A | 1.5 si | 5.7 awl | 80% hfw |

	gwam 3′	5′	
Many aspects of a job present challenges to those who strive to do	4	3	39
their best in all they do. One of the most critical challenges all	9	5	41
workers face is being able to relate well with the many individuals with	14	8	44
whom they have to work. It is common for workers to have daily dealings	19	11	47
with bosses, peers, and subordinates. Also, most workers will interact	24	14	50
with telephone callers and visitors from outside as well as inside the	28	17	53
company.	29	17	53
While it is critical to learn all you can about your job and com-	33	20	56
pany, it is often just as critical to learn about the people with whom	38	23	59
you will work and interact. Frequently you can rely upon experienced	43	26	61
workers for information that will help you analyze the formal structure	47	28	64
of the company and the informal structure the workers bring to the com-	52	31	67
pany. What you learn may help you determine what an employer expects,	57	34	70
likes, or dislikes, and will help you adjust.	60	36	72

gwam 3′ | 1 | 2 | 3 | 4 | 5
5′ | 1 | 2 | 3

132a ▶ 5 Conditioning Practice

each line twice SS (slowly, then faster); DS between 2-line groups; if time permits, rekey selected lines

alphabet 1 Evelyn was just shocked by the extremely crazy sequence of happenings.

figures 2 James drove 487 miles on May 19 and the remaining 356 miles on May 20.

double letters 3 Their committee allocated three million dollars to the school project.

speed 4 My buddy may go with me when I visit the firms with the antique autos.

| 1 | 2 | 3 | 4 | 5 | 6 | 7 | 8 | 9 | 10 | 11 | 12 | 13 | 14 |

132b ▶ 10 Preapplication Drill: Using a Typewriter to Key on Ruled Lines

plain full sheet

1. Strike the underline key to make a line 3 inches long (30 pica spaces; 36 elite spaces).

2. Center and key **your school name** on the line.

3. Study the relationship of the letters to the underline. Only a slight space separates the letters from the underline.

4. Remove the paper from the machine.

5. With a pencil and ruler (or other straight edge), draw 3 horizontal lines 3″ long and approximately ½″ apart.

6. Reinsert and align the paper using the variable line spacer (if your machine has one) and/or the paper release so that only a slight space separates the letters from the underline. Key the information shown at the right on the 3″ lines.

7. Repeat Steps 4-6 but key your name and address on the lines.

```
Roberto Santiago
________________________________

894 Guinevere Drive
________________________________

Spokane, WA  99218-1307
________________________________
```

132c ▶ 25 Key on Ruled and Unruled Forms

Document 1
Index Cards
LP p. 111

1. Key an index card using the information and format illustrated in the model.

2. Using the same format, key index cards for the following information.

Dr. Troy Sheridan
396 Columbia View Drive
Vancouver, WA 98661-2139
(206) 831-2949

Miss Claudia Cepeda
2821 Four Winds Drive N
Salem, OR 97303-4110
(503) 839-4829

```
JORDAN, KELLEE (MS.)

Ms. Kellee Jordan
Liberty Art Gallery
2057 Beacon Street
San Francisco, CA  94131-4130

(414) 326-5610
```

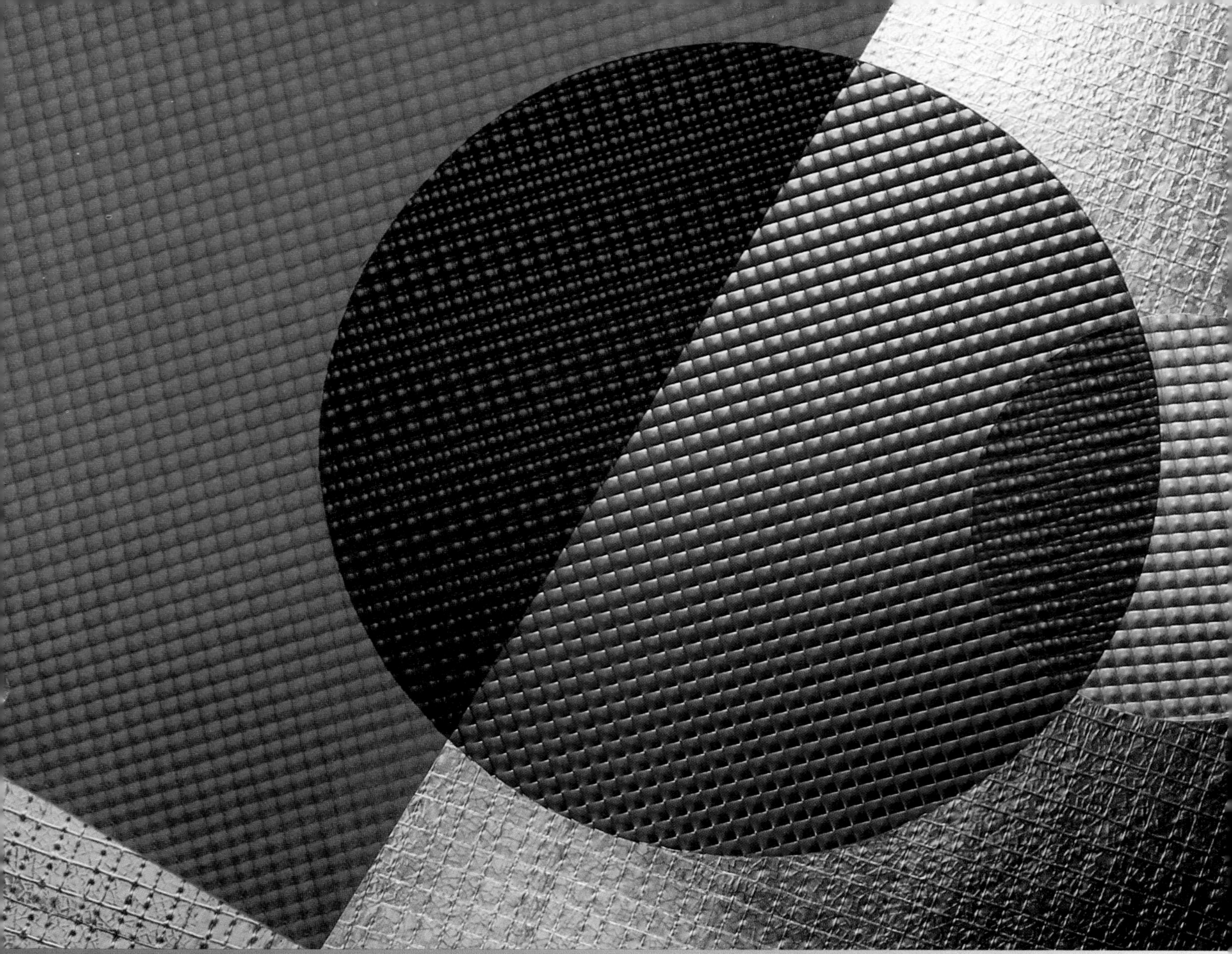

LESSONS 151 – 175

PHASE 7

ASSESS AND IMPROVE KEYBOARDING, FORMATTING, AND DOCUMENT PROCESSING SKILLS

The primary purpose of Phase 7 (Lessons 151-175) is to assess and improve previously learned keyboarding skills. The first unit concentrates on basic keyboarding and language skills. The next three units focus on formatting and processing correspondence, reports, and tables. These units are followed by a simulation designed to integrate keyboarding, formatting, and document processing skills. The last unit in Phase 7 is an evaluation unit.

The learning goals of Phase 7 are to improve the following competencies.

1. Techniques that contribute to keyboarding productivity.
2. Straight-copy keyboarding speed and control.
3. Keyboarding from script and rough-draft copy.
4. Formatting and processing letters, memorandums, reports, and tables.
5. Language skills.
6. Decision-making skills.

132c (continued)

Document 2
Purchase Order
LP p. 113

Prepare a purchase order using the information given at the right and listed below. Correct errors.

Order No.: **8391B**
Date: **February 12, 19--**
Terms: **2/10, n/30**
Ship Via: **McVay Transport**
(total words: 76)

Browning Office Equipment
3338 Creighton Avenue SE
Portland, OR 97267-1498

Quantity	Description/Stock Nos.	Unit Price
3	Microcassette Dictation System (39-69)	489.95
1	Microcassette Transcriber (39-85)	449.95
6	Microcassette Recorder (39-742)	89.95
25	Microcassettes (39-979)	1.95

Rebecca Granger, Purchasing Agent

Document 3
Letter Placement Guide
LP p. 113

Prepare a letter placement guide from the handwritten copy at the right. Correct errors.

LETTER PLACEMENT GUIDE

Letter Classification	5-Stroke Words in Letter Body	Side Margins	Margin Settings		Dateline Position (from Top Edge of Paper)
			Elite	Pica	
Short	Up to 100	2"	24-78*	20-65*	18
Average	101-200	1 1/2"	18-84*	15-70*	16
Long	201-300	1"	12-90*	10-75*	14
Two-Page	Over 300	1"	12-90*	10-75*	14
6" Line	All letters	1 1/4"	15-87*	12-72*	As above

*Plus 3 to 7 spaces for the bell cue — *usually add 5* (see p. 76)

132d ► 10
Improve Language Skills: Word Choice

Study the spelling and definition of each word. Note how it is used in the **Learn** sentence. Key the **Learn** sentence (with number and period) and the **Apply** sentences (with number and period) selecting the proper word in parentheses to complete each sentence correctly.

principal (n) a person in authority; a capital sum

principle (n) a rule

personal (adj) private; individual

personnel (n) employees

Learn 1. Our principal understood the principle of shared governance.
Apply 2. Each management (principal, principle) was presented in the speech.
Apply 3. Mrs. Gilbertson, our (principal, principle), will return on Monday.

Learn 4. The personnel committee took a personal interest in all employees.
Apply 5. The (personal, personnel) director will deal with employee problems.
Apply 6. Rinji felt the problem was too (personal, personnel) to discuss.

150c (continued)

words

armed forces. The person holding the office is ~~also~~ 268
responsible for making treaties, appointing ambassadors, and 280
appointing judges of the Supreme Court. Additional respon- 292
sibilities of the President include giving The State of the 304
Union address, recieving foreign dignitaries, enforcing the 316
laws, and protecting the rights of the citizens of the 327
United States. 330

The role of the President has remained ~~been~~ about the same as 341
when the Constitution was written. However, Davis (1987, 4) states 355
that the responsibilities to fulfill that role have in- 366
creased. 368

No new ¶ Koenig (1986, 14-15) suggests that today's President has the respon- 381
sibility of dealing with: 386

> . . . survival problems in which the very future of the hu- 398
> man race, is at stake; the threat of nuclear weapons tech- 409
> nology; the persistence of war abroad; the remorseless 420
> growth of population, production, and pollution, and their 432
> endangering of the environment; grave unemployment and in- 444
> flation; blighted cities and pervasive poverty and crime; 555
> excessive violations of civil rights and liberties; grossly 467
> inadequate provisions of health services, mass transit, edu- 479
> cation and the care of the elderly. 486

As can be seen from Koenig's ~~the~~ description of the presidential 499
responsibilities ~~outlined by Koenig~~, the President of the 506
United States has a job with many important and varied responsibilities. 519

Document 2
Reference Page

Key a reference page using the information given at the right.

Document 3
Report from Rough Draft

Begin rekeying Document 1 as a leftbound report.

REFERENCES 2

Davis, James W. The American President: A New 18
Perspective. New York: Harper & Row 27
Publishers, 1987. 31

Koenig, Louis W. Chief Executive. 5th ed. San Diego: 45
Harcourt Brace Jovanovich, Inc., 1986. 53

Lesson 133 Business Forms/Composition

133a ▶ 5 Conditioning Practice

each line twice SS (slowly, then faster); DS between 2-line groups; if time permits, rekey selected lines

alphabet 1 Major plans for the next job will be finalized very quickly in August.

figures 2 On January 20, 1990, I moved from 2468 Bay Street to 1357 Lake Street.

space bar 3 She may see us when we go to the big city to pay and to sign the form.

speed 4 Pamela's neighbor is apt to dismantle the small cubicle in the chapel.

| 1 | 2 | 3 | 4 | 5 | 6 | 7 | 8 | 9 | 10 | 11 | 12 | 13 | 14 |

133b ▶ 10 Language Skills: Compose at Keyboard

plain full sheet
LL: 70 spaces

1. Compose at the keyboard 1 or 2 paragraphs on one of the questions at the right. DS paragraph(s).
2. Edit your copy, marking corrections and changes to improve sentence structure and organization.
3. Prepare the final copy.

Questions

If you received a check for $100,000 in the mail today, what would you do with it?

What qualities do you think an employer would be looking for in a prospective employee?

Would you buy a stereo on credit? Explain.

133c ▶ 35 Build Sustained Document Processing: Forms and Special Documents

LP pp. 115-119
company envelopes for formal memos

Time Schedule
Plan and prepare .... 4′
Timed production .... 25′
Proofread, mark errors, and compute *n-pram* .... 6′

1. Arrange forms, supplies, and correction materials for easy access.
2. Make a list of documents to be processed.
page 232, 130d, Document 1
page 232, 130d, Document 2
page 233, 131c, Document 1
page 234, 131c, Document 2
page 234, 131c, Document 3

3. Process as many documents as you can in 25′. Proofread and correct errors as you key.
4. After 25′ timing, proofread again, mark any additional errors not found during keying, and compute *n-pram.*
5. Arrange documents in order listed in Step 2; turn in work.

n-pram = (total words keyed − penalty*) ÷ time
*Penalty is 10 words for each uncorrected error.

Lesson 134 Measure Form Processing Skills

134a ▶ 5 Conditioning Practice

each line twice SS (slowly, then faster); DS between 2-line groups; if time permits, rekey selected lines

alphabet 1 Zachary bought two exquisite paintings of Alaska just before he moved.

figures 2 On March 29 they learned the 7, 1, and 5; on March 30 the 4, 6, and 8.

home row 3 Sally Ash has a faded glass doll. Josh Jakes was a sad lad last fall.

speed 4 The man in the wheelchair was down at the dock with my neighbor's dog.

| 1 | 2 | 3 | 4 | 5 | 6 | 7 | 8 | 9 | 10 | 11 | 12 | 13 | 14 |

134b ▶ 10 Figures and Tab-Key Drill

plain full sheet
LL: 65 spaces
CS: 6
1. Three 1′ writings; find *gwam* on each.
2. Two 2′ writings; find *gwam* on each.

Concentrate on figure locations; quiet hands; quick tab spacing.

							words
1029	3847	5616	2738	4950	1089	4462	7
1392	5705	6783	7887	2954	1036	2198	14
2034	6905	4130	5977	6816	2543	6150	21
2831	9876	4231	9087	5641	8622	3939	28
4705	4507	9988	1055	6436	7221	3470	35
1	2	3	4	5	6	7	

150c ▶ 37
Evaluate Document Processing Skill: Reports

Time Schedule
Plan and prepare .... 4′
Document processing .... 25′
Proofread; compute *n-pram* .. 8′

Document 1
Report from Rough Draft

Format the document shown at the right as an unbound report. Correct your errors as you key.

words

THE PRESIDENT OF THE UNITED STATES 7

The highest elected office in the United States is that 18
of President. The President who is elected by the Citizens 30
of the United States represents all the people. The Presi- 43
dent plays a role in determining the course of direction for 56
the United States under a democratic form of government. 68

Term in Office 73

Since the of the twenty-second amendment to the Con- 86
stitution, the President can serve only two terms. Prior to 98
~~the~~ this amendment the President could serve as long as the 109
people ~~would~~ elect him to the office. FranklinRoosevelt was 121
the last Persident to serve more than two terms. 131

Qualifications 136

The qualifications required for running for the execu- 147
tive office of the United States are out lined in the Con- 158
stitution (article II section 1 paragraph 5). The person 170
must be 35, a natural-born citizen of the United States, and 185
a resident of the United States for ~~the past~~ 14 years. 194

Responsibilities 200

Also outlined in the Constitution (article II, sections 211
2 and 3) are the responsibility of the executive office. 223
The outlined responsibilities are, however, quite general 235
and are often open for interpretation. The Constitution 246
states that the President is the Commander in Cchief of the 258

134c ▶ 35 Measure Document Processing: Forms/Memorandums

Time Schedule
Plan and prepare .... 4′
Timed production .... 25′
Proofread, mark errors, and compute *n-pram* .... 6′

Document 1
Purchase Order
LP p. 119
Prepare a purchase order using the information given at the right.

words

LACONTE JEWELERS INC	Purchase Order No.:	59Z48-3	6
210 BROADWAY	Date:	April 15, 19--	11
NEW YORK NY 10038-7103	Terms:	2/10, n/30	18
	Shipped Via:	Freight Specialists	22

Quantity	Description/Stock No.	Price	Total	words
5	14K Yellow Gold Rope Bezel (A44-98)	95.95/ea	479.75	34
5	Diamond Pendant (C28-95)	149.50/ea	747.50	43
10	Diamond and Pearl Ring (B95-17)	95.00/ea	950.00	54
2	Diamond "V" Necklace (Q39-50)	1250.00/ea	2500.00	65
10	Diamond Bee Pin (M66-29)	249.95/ea	2499.50	77
			7176.75	75

Document 2
Invoice
LP p. 121
Prepare an invoice using the information given at the right. Calculate the final total.

YOUR OFFICE FURNITURE STORE	Date:	June 2, 19--	13
406 MONTGOMERY STREET	Cust. Order No.:	39V881	20
SAN FRANCISCO CA 94104-2486	Terms:	2/10, n/30	22
	Shipped Via:	Bay Shipping	25
	Our Order No.:	B92-8751	26
	Date Shipped:	June 2, 19--	29

Quantity	Description/Stock No.	Price	Total	words
1	Executive Desk (871-56B)	799.95	799.95	37
1	Executive Credenza Bookcase (296-88B)	649.50	649.50	48
1	Printer Stand (391-29C)	399.95	399.95	56
1	Computer Table (218-30C)	359.49	359.49	64
1	Executive Swivel Chair (119-20A)	314.49	314.49	75
			2523.38	77
	Sales Tax		126.17	82

Document 3
Formal Memorandum
LP p. 123
Key a formal memorandum using the information given at the right and the information given below.
To: **Martin F. Jensen, Chief Financial Officer**
From: **Karl L. Hayward, Facilities Manager**
Date: **June 12, 19--**
Subject: **Office Renovation**

Document 4
Simplified Memorandum
plain full sheet
Rekey Document 3 as a simplified memo.

words
words in heading 22

All of the furniture ordered for your office has arrived except for the com- 37
puter table. It is back ordered, and it should arrive within the next week. 53

Arrangements have been made for your new carpet to be installed on Satur- 67
day, June 26. Since your old furniture will be left in the hallway during the 83
weekend, we will need to take the necessary security precautions. Mike 97
Jackson has agreed to let you store your file cabinets in his office over the 113
weekend. Please let me know by Friday if there are other things you would 128
like stored along with the files, and I will make the necessary arrangements. 143

closing lines 144/**159**

149c (continued)

Table 3

center column headings; decide on appropriate number of spaces to leave between columns

Table 4

center column headings; CS: 8

Rekey Table 1 with the names in alphabetical order.

			words
PRESIDENTS OF THE UNITED STATES			6
1923–19--			8
President	Term	Party	18
Calvin Coolidge	1923–1929	Republican	25
Herbert Hoover	1929–1933	Republican	32
Franklin Roosevelt	1933–1945	Democrat	40
Harry Truman	1945–1953	Democrat	46
Dwight Eisenhower	1953–1961	Republican	54
John Kennedy	1961–1963	Democrat	60
Lyndon Johnson	1963–1969	Democrat	67
Richard Nixon	1969–1974	Republican	74
Gerald Ford	1974–1977	Republican	81
Jimmy Carter	1977–1981	Democrat	87
Ronald Reagan	1981–1989	Republican	94
George Bush	1989–	Republican	100
______________			104
Source: Collier's Encyclopedia.			114

Lesson 150 Evaluate Report Processing Skills

150a ▶ 5 Conditioning Practice

each line twice SS (slowly, then faster); DS between 2-line groups; if time permits, rekey selected lines

alphabet 1 **Dr. Joswiak gave both of us excellent marks on the final physics quiz.**

figures 2 **Homes were built at 1683 Kari Road, 2705 Truax Drive, and 49 Oak Lane.**

bottom row 3 **A man and a woman came to exchange a dozen boxes of venison on Monday.**

speed 4 **When I visit the man in the wheelchair, I may go downtown to the firm.**

| 1 | 2 | 3 | 4 | 5 | 6 | 7 | 8 | 9 | 10 | 11 | 12 | 13 | 14 |

150b ▶ 8 Check Straight-Copy Skill

1. Take a 5′ writing on 148b, page 262.

2. Find *gwam* and number of errors.

3. Record score.

UNIT 31 LESSONS 135 – 139

Process Office Employment Documents

Learning Goals

1. To learn/apply guides for preparing a data sheet, application letter, application form, and follow-up letter.
2. To compose and process personal employment documents.
3. To improve language skills through composing activities.
4. To process documents for a simulated employment test.

Format Guides

1. Paper guide at *0* (for typewriters).
2. LL: 70 for drills and language skills activities; as required by document formats.
3. LS: SS for drills and language skills activities; as required by document formats.
4. PI: 5 spaces, when appropriate.

FORMATTING GUIDES: DATA SHEET, APPLICATION LETTER, APPLICATION FORM, AND FOLLOW-UP LETTER

358 Knox Court
Denver, CO 80219-6482
May 15, 19--

Mr. Juan R. Gutierrez
Director of Human Resources
Creswell Manufacturing Co.
8352 West Oxford Avenue
Denver, CO 80236-7483

Dear Mr. Gutierrez:

Ms. Carolyn Baxter, my administrative services instructor, informed me of the secretarial position with your company that will be available June 10. She speaks very highly of your organization. After learning more about the position, I am confident that I am qualified and would like to be considered for the assignment.

Currently I am completing my senior year at Lincoln High School. All of my elective courses have been in the administrative services area. This includes courses in information processing, shorthand, and business procedures. I have a keyboarding skill of 60 words a minute and a shorthand skill of 80 words a minute. The information processing class was taught using computers. We were instructed in word processing, spreadsheet, and data base applications. As an office assistant, I have been able to utilize these skills on the job.

My work experience and school activities have given me the opportunity to work with people to achieve group goals. Participaring in FBLA has given me a better appreciation for the business world.

I would appreciate the opportunity to interview with you to discuss the possibility of employment. You may call me weekdays after 3:30 p.m.

Sincerely,

Leslie-Ann Murphy

Ms. Leslie-Ann Murphy

xx

Enclosure

Application Letter

Employment Documents

Extreme care should be given to the preparation of all employment documents. The data sheet, application letter, and application form are generally the basis of the first impression you make on a prospective employer; they may also determine whether you are invited for an interview.

Prepare application documents on a keyboard with the possible exception of the application form. You may be asked to complete the application form at the time of the interview, in which case it may be prepared with a pen. Always use high-quality paper when preparing your data sheet and application letter. Make sure that each document you prepare is attractively arranged, neat, grammatical, and that it presents both accurate and appropriate information.

Data Sheet

In most cases, a data sheet should be limited to one page. The information presented usually covers five major areas: personal information (your name, address, and telephone number), education, school activities, work experience, and references. It may also include sections listing community activities and hobbies and/or special interests.

Top, bottom, and side margins may vary depending on the amount of information presented. The specific format may also vary with personal preference. In general, the most important information is presented first, which means that a person who has been out of school for several years and has considerable work experience may place that information before educational background information. References, however, are usually the last item on the page. (Always get permission from the individuals you plan to include as references on your data sheet before using their names.)

Application Letter

An application letter should always accompany the data sheet. The letter is formatted as a personal-business letter and should be limited to one page.

The first paragraph of the application letter should indicate the position for which you are applying and how you learned of the position. It is also appropriate to include something positive that you know about the company or someone who works for the company in the opening paragraph.

The next one or two paragraphs are used to convince the reader that you understand the requirements for the position and to explain how your background experiences qualify you for the position for which you are applying. You may do this by elaborating on some of the information on your data sheet and inviting the reader to refer to the enclosed data sheet for additional information.

The final paragraph is used to request an interview. Information is also provided to make it easy for the reader to contact you to make arrangements for the interview.

Follow-Up Letter

Appreciation for an interview is conveyed in a follow-up letter. In addition to thanking the person for the interview, the follow-up letter may also be used to let the interviewer know you are still interested in the job. The letter also may provide any additional relevant information and give positive impressions of the company and/or people you met. To be effective, the letter should be written immediately following the interview. This will increase the likelihood that the interviewer will receive the letter before a decision is made.

149a ▶ 5 Conditioning Practice

each line twice SS (slowly, then faster); DS between 2-line groups; if time permits, rekey selected lines

alphabet 1 Both campus organizations Faye would like to join are quite expensive.

figures 2 You can reach us at 632-5498 before 1 p.m. or at 632-7043 after 1 p.m.

fig/sym 3 The date on the bill (#580A473) from Baxter & Smythe was May 26, 1992.

speed 4 The city official paid the men for the handiwork they did on the dock.

| 1 | 2 | 3 | 4 | 5 | 6 | 7 | 8 | 9 | 10 | 11 | 12 | 13 | 14 |

149b ▶ 8 Check Straight-Copy Skill

1. Take a 5′ writing on 148b, page 262.

2. Find *gwam* and number of errors.

3. Record score.

149c ▶ 37 Evaluate Document Processing Skill: Tables

Time Schedule

Plan and prepare .... 4′
Document processing ....25′
Proofread; compute *n-pram* ..... 8′

4 full sheets; format the tables given at the right; DS all lines; correct errors

Table 1

block column headings; CS: 10

STATE OFFICERS — words 3

Name	Position	Phone	words
			10
Laura Wes^t phal	President	836-4978	17
Josh Rubinstein	Vice President	739-2075	25
Maria Fernandez	Membership Director	684-7825	34
Chris Chan	Secretary	836-2091	40
Mark Stras^s man	Treasurer	235-6511	47
Brett De(lc)Witz	Past President	412-4010	54
Jacqueline McCain	President Elect	633-7189	63

Table 2

center column headings; CS: 8

19-- BANKING INSTITUTE ~~PROGRAM~~ SCHEDULE — words 6

Seminar	Date	Location	words
			17
Game Plans ^for Loan Originators	January 15	Boston	27
Creative Financing	March 16	Chicago	35
Symposimu for Branch Managers	April 20	Portland	44
Todays Automated Banking	June 10	Atlanta	53
Accounting Up date in Banking	August 15	Tuscpon	62
Customer Advertising	October 1	Houston	70
Managing ^Human Resources	November 13	Milwaukee	79

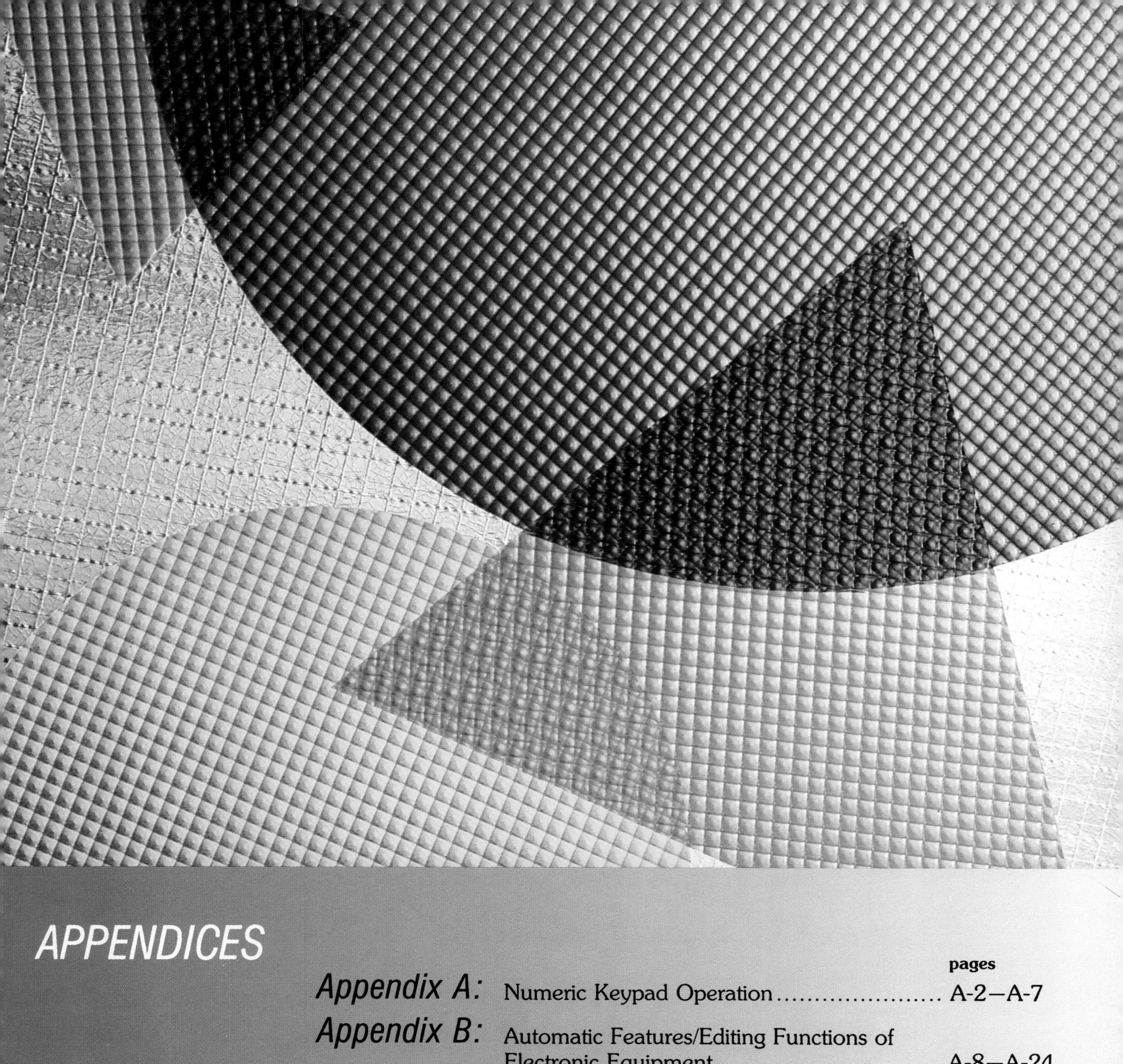

APPENDICES

148c ▶ 37
Evaluate Document Processing Skills: Letters/Memo

LP pp. 147-151

Time Schedule
Plan and prepare .... 4′
Document processing .... 25′
Proofread; compute *n-pram* .. 8′

1. Arrange materials for ease of handling.

2. Format and key Documents 1-4 for 25′. Proofread and correct errors before removing documents from machine.

3. After time is called (25′), proofread again and circle any uncorrected errors. Compute *n-pram.*

Document 1 LP p. 147
block format; open punctuation

Special features:
CERTIFIED
Subject: **19-- Banking Institute Schedule**
c Mark L. Kostner

Document 2 LP p. 149
modified block format; blocked ¶s; mixed punctuation

Insert the following information for the numbers in parentheses: (1) **May** (2) **Houston** (3) **managing human resources** (4) **November 13** (5) **Milwaukee** (6) **Marc Plaza**

Special features:
Company name in closing lines:
BANKING INSTITUTE
c Natasha J. Bartlett
Mark L. Kostner
Postscript: **Will I see you at next week's convention in Hawaii? I'm looking forward to some warmer weather.**

Document 3
Format the document at the right as a simplified memorandum. The document is from you to your teacher. Use the **current date** and **"Report on the Office of the President"** for the subject line.

Document 4 LP p. 151
block format; open punctuation

Rekey Document 2 with the following changes:

Ms. Renae A. Santiago
Suwannee National Bank
5507 Ranchero Road
Tallahassee, FL 32304-9340

(1) **June** (2) **Pittsburgh** (3) **customer advertising** (4) **October 1** (5) **Houston** (6) **Hyatt Regency**

Special features:
same as Document 2; no postscript

---

words

October 13, 19-- | Ms. Natasha J. Bartlett, President | Banking Institute Corpo- 17
rate Office | 628 Nicolet Avenue, N | Chicago, IL 60631-6485 | Dear Ms. 30
Bartlett 39

Attached is a tentative listing of the seminars we plan to offer through the 54
Banking Institute next year. If you would like any of the titles changed be- 69
fore we start promoting the seminars in November, please let me know by 84
October 23. 86

In addition to distributing materials at this year's two remaining seminars, 102
we will be processing a mailing to current members and advertising in two 116
banking publications. Any other suggestions you may have for promoting 131
next year's seminars would be appreciated. Our goal for this coming year is 146
a 20 percent increase in attendance. 154

Sincerely yours | Ryan S. Woodward | Institute Director | xx | Attachment 170/**195**

November 15, 19-- | Mr. Lewis G. Mackenzie | Human Resources Manager | 13
Bank of Nottingham | 1295 Kensington Avenue | Detroit, MI 48230-5286 | Dear 27
Mr. Mackenzie: 30

The seminar you presented last ___(1)___ in ___(2)___ for the Banking Institute on 45
___(3)___ was very well received. Several Institute members have requested 63
that the seminar be offered again this coming year. 74

The seminar is scheduled for ___(4)___ in ___(5)___ at the ___(6)___. Are you available 92
on this date to present the seminar? The honorarium for conducting the 107
seminar has been increased to $1,800. Of course, all your expenses would 122
be paid by the Institute. 127

Please let me know by December 1 whether you will be able to work with us 142
on this year's seminar. 147

Sincerely, | Ryan S. Woodward | Institute Director | xx 160

closing lines 187/**210**

---

opening lines 14

Here is the report on the office of the President of the United States that you 30
assigned last week. The report gives a brief description of the term in of- 45
fice, the qualifications needed to run for the office, and the responsibilities 61
of this very important position. 67

I have also included in the appendix a table of the individuals holding the 83
office since 1923. The table outlines each President's term in office and his 98
party affiliation. 102

I have enjoyed learning more about this important position in our demo- 116
cratic government. Please let me know if you have additional suggestions 131
for improvement. 135

closing lines 140

APPENDIX A
Numeric Keypad Operation

Learning Goals

1. To learn key locations and keyboarding technique on the numeric keypad of a microcomputer.

2. To learn to enter figures rapidly and accurately by touch (without looking).

Practice Procedure

Follow directions given on an instructional diskette for learning key locations and for initial practice. Then return to this book for additional drill and practice.

Use of these activities on word processing software is not recommended.

Activity 1 — *4/5/6/0*

1a ▶ Get Acquainted with Your Data-Entry Equipment

Figure keys 1-9 are in standard locations on numeric keypads of microcomputers (as well as on 10-key calculators).

The zero (0 or Ø) key location may vary slightly from one keyboard to another.

The illustrations at the right show the location of the figure keys on popular makes of microcomputers.

Consult your operator's manual to learn how to correct an error you detect as you enter figures.

Apple IIe numeric keypad

IBM PC

Tandy 1000

1b ▶ Take Correct Operating Position

1. Position yourself in front of the computer just as you do for entering alphabetic copy--body erect, both feet on floor for balance.

2. Place this textbook at the right of the keyboard.

3. Curve the fingers of the right hand and place them on the numeric keypad:
first (index) finger on 4
second finger on 5
third finger on 6
thumb on 0

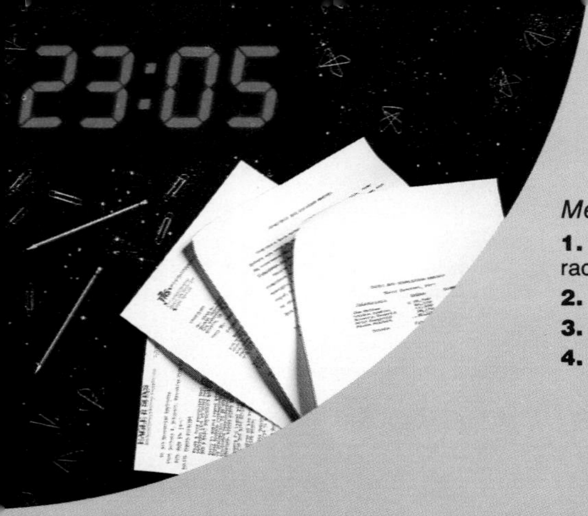

UNIT 34 LESSONS 148 – 150

Evaluate Keyboarding/Document Processing Skills

Measurement Goals

1. To evaluate straight-copy speed and accuracy.
2. To evaluate letter processing skills.
3. To evaluate report processing skills.
4. To evaluate table processing skills.

Format Guides

1. Paper guide at *0* (for typewriters).
2. LL: 70 spaces for drills; as required by document formats.
3. LS: SS for drills; as required by document formats.
4. PI: 5 spaces, when appropriate.

Lesson 148 *Evaluate Letter Processing Skills*

148a ▶ 5 Conditioning Practice

each line twice SS (slowly, then faster); DS between 2-line groups; if time permits, rekey selected lines

alphabet	1	Beatriz might complete five quilting projects by the end of next week.
figures	2	The May 8 test over pages 396-417 had 20 problems worth 5 points each.
space bar	3	Jan and Kay may also bid to work with the men on the map for the city.
speed	4	The girls may go to the social held at the giant chapel on the island.

| 1 | 2 | 3 | 4 | 5 | 6 | 7 | 8 | 9 | 10 | 11 | 12 | 13 | 14 |

148b ▶ 8 Check Straight-Copy Skill

1. A 5′ writing on all ¶s.
2. Determine *gwam* and number of errors.
3. Record score.

all letters used | A | 1.5 si | 5.7 awl | 80% hfw

	gwam 3′	5′	
Something that you can never escape is your attitude. It will be	4	3	45
with you forever. However, you decide whether your attitude is an asset	9	6	48
or a liability for you. Your attitude reflects the way you feel about	14	8	50
the world you abide in and everything that is a part of that world. It	19	11	53
reflects the way you feel about yourself, about your environment, and	23	14	56
about other people who are a part of your environment. Oftentimes, peo-	28	17	59
ple with a positive attitude are people who are extremely successful.	33	20	62
At times we all have experiences that cause us to be negative. The	37	22	64
difference between a positive and a negative person is that the positive	42	25	67
person rebounds very quickly from a bad experience; the negative person	47	28	70
does not. The positive person is a person who usually looks to the	52	31	73
bright side of things and recognizes the world as a place of promise,	56	34	76
hope, joy, excitement, and purpose. A negative person generally has just	61	37	79
the opposite view of the world. Remember, others want to be around those	66	40	82
who are positive but tend to avoid those who are negative.	70	42	84

gwam 3′ | 1 | 2 | 3 | 4 | 5
5′ | 1 | 2 | 3

1c ▶ Enter Data Using Home Keys: 4, 5, 6, 0

1. Turn equipment "on".

2. Curve the fingers of your right hand and place them upright on home keys:
first (index) finger on 4
second finger on 5
third finger on 6
fourth finger on + bar
thumb on 0 or Ø (zero)

3. Using the special ENTER key to the right of the keypad, enter data in Drill 1a as follows:
4 ENTER
4 ENTER
4 ENTER
Strike ENTER

Note: Ignore any decimal (.) or comma (,) that may appear in an entry or total figure.

4. Check TOTAL figure on display screen. It should show 12 on the computer display.

5. If you do not get 12 as the total, reenter the data.

6. Enter and check columns b, c, d, e, and f in the same way.

7. Using the special ENTER key to the right of the keypad, enter data in Drill 2a as follows:
44 ENTER
44 ENTER
44 ENTER
Strike ENTER

8. Check TOTAL figure and reenter data if necessary.

9. Continue Drill 2 and complete Drills 3-5 in a similar manner.

Note: In Drills 4 and 5, strike 0 (zero) with the *side* of your right thumb.

Technique cue
Strike each key with a quick, sharp stroke with the *tip* of the finger; release the key quickly. Keep the fingers curved and upright, the wrist low, relaxed, and steady.

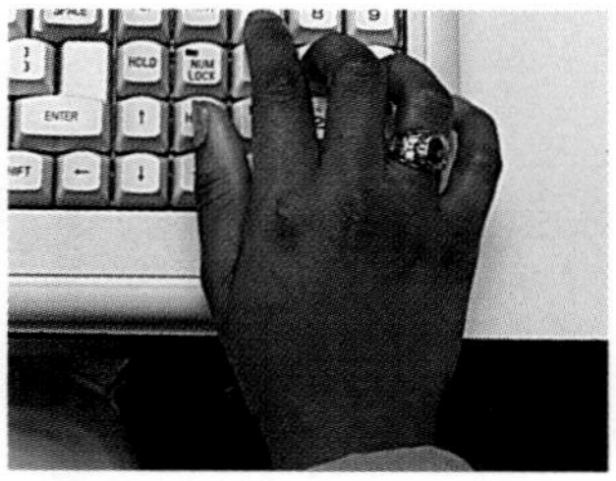

Drill 1

a	b	c	d	e	f
4	5	6	4	5	6
4	5	6	4	5	6
4	5	6	4	5	6
12	15	18	12	15	18

Drill 2

a	b	c	d	e	f
44	55	66	44	55	66
44	55	66	44	55	66
44	55	66	44	55	66
132	165	198	132	165	198

Drill 3

a	b	c	d	e	f
44	45	54	44	55	66
55	56	46	45	54	65
66	64	65	46	56	64
165	165	165	135	165	195

Drill 4

a	b	c	d	e	f
40	50	60	400	500	600
40	50	60	400	500	600
40	50	60	400	500	600
120	150	180	1,200	1,500	1,800

Drill 5

a	b	c	d	e	f
40	400	404	406	450	650
50	500	505	506	540	560
60	600	606	606	405	605
150	1,500	1,515	1,518	1,395	1,815

147c ▶ 35
Reinforce Document Processing Skills: Reports

plain full sheets; correct errors as you key

1. Process the copy at the right as a leftbound report with internal citations. Use **THE JOB INTERVIEW** for the title of the report.

2. Using the information given below, prepare a reference list on a separate sheet.

Reynolds, Caroline. Dimensions in Professional Development. 3d ed. Cincinnati: South-Western Publishing Co., 1988.

Payne, Richard A. How to Get a Better Job Quicker. 3d. ed. New York: NAL Penguin, Inc., 1987.

3. Prepare a title page. Use **your name, your school's name,** and the **current date.**

words

title 4

The result of a successful letter of application and data 15
sheet is an invitation from a employer for a interview. 29
Preparation for the interview is just as important in ob- 40
taining employment as the planning required to prepare an 52
effective application letter and datasheet. 61

The interviewers first impression of the applicant is 72
crucial to the success of the interview. This impression, 84
which may take as little as 60 seconds to form, determines 96
whether the interviewer is interested in learning more about 108
the potential employee. Therefore, the prospective employee 120
must make a special effort to assure a positive first im- 131
pression. Reynolds (229-233, 1988) suggests that in order 143
to make that positive first impression the applicant must be 155
prepared mentally as well as physically. 164

<u>Preparing Mentally</u> 171

Preparing mentally includes learning as much about the 184
Company prior to the interview and anticipating questions 196
that the employer may ask during the interview. The inter- 208
viewee should also plan questions to learn as much as pos- 219
sible about the position and the co. The purpose of the in- 232
terveiw is to provide the interviewer and the interviewee 243
the opportunity to exchange information and to form impres- 255
sions. More information will be exchanged 268
and a better impression made when the interviewee comes to 280
the inter view prepared. 286

<u>Preparing Physically</u> 294

Preparing physically also plays an important part in plan- 305
ning for a successful interview. The interviewee employee 315
should learn about appropriate company dress and grooming 327
standards. The interviewer has to be able to picture the 343
job applicant as person who would fit in well with current 356
employees. Differences in appearance between current em- 369
ployees and the applicant make it difficult for the inter- 380
viewer to picture the aplicant as an employee of their com- 392
pany. 393

references 452

2a ▶ Improve Home-Key Technique

Enter and check the columns of data listed at the right as directed in Steps 1-9 on p. A-3.

a	b	c	d	e	f
4	44	400	404	440	450
5	55	500	505	550	560
6	66	600	606	660	456
15	165	1,500	1,515	1,650	1,466

2b ▶ Learn New Keys: 7, 8, 9

Learn reach to 7

1. Locate 7 (above 4) on the numeric keypad.

2. Watch your index finger move up to 7 and back to 4 a few times *without striking keys.*

3. Practice striking 74 a few times as you watch the finger.

4. With eyes on copy, enter the data in Drills 1a and 1b; check the total figures; reenter data if necessary.

Learn reach to 8

1. Learn the second-finger reach to 8 (above 5) as directed in Steps 1-3 above.

2. With eyes on copy, enter the data in Drills 1c and 1d; check the total figures; reenter data if necessary.

Learn reach to 9

1. Learn the third-finger reach to 9 (above 6) as directed above.

2. With eyes on copy, enter the data in Drills 1e and 1f; check the total figures; reenter data if necessary.

Drills 2-4

Practice entering the columns of data in Drills 2-4 until you can do so accurately and quickly.

Drill 1

a	b	c	d	e	f
474	747	585	858	696	969
747	777	858	888	969	999
777	474	888	585	999	696
1,998	1,998	2,331	2,331	2,664	2,664

Drill 2

a	b	c	d	e	f
774	885	996	745	475	754
474	585	696	854	584	846
747	858	969	965	695	956
1,995	2,328	2,661	2,564	1,754	2,556

Drill 3

a	b	c	d	e	f
470	580	690	770	707	407
740	850	960	880	808	508
704	805	906	990	909	609
1,914	2,235	2,556	2,640	2,424	1,524

Drill 4

a	b	c	d	e	f
456	407	508	609	804	905
789	408	509	704	805	906
654	409	607	705	806	907
987	507	608	706	904	908
2,886	1,731	2,232	2,724	3,319	3,626

2c ▶ Learn to Enter Data with Unequal Numbers of Digits

Enter single, double, and triple digits in columns as shown, left to right. The computer will align the digits automatically.

a	b	c	d	e	f
4	90	79	4	740	860
56	87	64	56	64	70
78	68	97	78	960	900
90	54	64	60	89	67
4	6	5	98	8	80
232	305	309	296	1,861	1,977

146c ▶ 10
Reinforce Language Skills: Word Choice

plain full sheet; LL: 70

As you key each sentence at the right, select the word in each set of parentheses needed to complete each sentence correctly. Key the line number and period; correct errors as you key.

1. (Hear, Here) are the (to, too, two) books that are (do, due) tomorrow.
2. (Its, It's) (to, too) bad you only have (for, four) days of vacation.
3. By (then, than), the (cite, site) you may (choose, chose) could be sold.
4. (Do, Due) you (know, no) what (hour, our) the English class is taught?
5. The company's (lead, led) pipe fittings (passed, past) inspection.

6. If (your, you're) going to (buy, by) the tickets, let me (know, no).
7. (Some, Sum) prices will (vary, very) depending on the day of the week.
8. If you (raise, raze) the rent, the (poor, pour) man will have to move.
9. To learn to (sew, sow) the (right, rite) way, you should take lessons.
10. Take a (peak, peek) at the (knew, new) (stationary, stationery).

11. Do (farther, further) tests to determine the full (affects, effects).
12. You should follow the (principal's, principle's) (advice, advise).
13. The (lessen, lesson) presents the (bases, basis) for decision making.
14. The (plain, plane) (flew, flue) (through, threw) the (air, heir).
15. Dennis did not (accept, except) the results of the latest (pole, poll).

Lesson 147 Reinforce Report Processing Skills

147a ▶ 5
Conditioning Practice

each line twice SS (slowly, then faster); DS between 2-line groups; if time permits, rekey selected lines

alphabet	1	Judge Wirtz quickly thanked both of them for giving excellent reports.
figures	2	The study guides for the next exam are on pages 56, 197, 280, and 304.
shift lock	3	BASIC and COBOL as well as APL, TRAC, and LISP are computer languages.
speed	4	The man with the problems may wish to see the proficient tax official.

| 1 | 2 | 3 | 4 | 5 | 6 | 7 | 8 | 9 | 10 | 11 | 12 | 13 | 14 |

147b ▶ 10
Reinforce Language Skills: Verb Agreement

plain full sheet; LL: 70

As you key each sentence at the right, select the word in parentheses needed to complete each sentence correctly. Key the line number and period; correct errors as you key.

1. The manager (is, are) going to announce the final cuts tomorrow.
2. Almost everyone (is, are) planning to attend the New Year's dance.
3. Either the manager or his secretary (has, have) the purchase orders.
4. The band (has, have) been selected to participate in the parade.
5. The band directors (is, are) going to be meeting in Room 205.

6. The number of individuals buying computers (has, have) increased.
7. Some of the expenses for the banquet (is, are) still being received.
8. Many of the movies about the war (is, are) based on true stories.
9. Neither Alyssa nor Nicole (is, are) aware of the surprise party.
10. The entire department (is, are) going to attend the next meeting.

11. Dean and Tom (has, have) their own computer consulting business.
12. The disks (don't, doesn't) need to be formatted again before using.
13. All of the dinner guests (has, have) already left for the play.
14. A number of changes (has, have) been made in the starting lineup.
15. The manager and the trainers (is, are) meeting with team members today.

3a ▶ Reinforce Reach-Strokes Learned

Enter and check the columns of data listed at the right as directed in Steps 1-9 on p. A-3.

a	b	c	d	e	f	g
44	74	740	996	704	990	477
55	85	850	885	805	880	588
66	96	960	774	906	770	699
165	255	2,550	2,655	2,415	2,640	1,764

3b ▶ Learn New Keys: 1, 2, 3

Learn reach to 1

1. Locate 1 (below 4) on the numeric keypad.

2. Watch your first finger move down to 1 and back to 4 a few times *without striking keys.*

3. Practice striking 14 a few times as you watch the finger.

4. With eyes on copy, enter the data in Drills 1a and 1b; check the total figures; reenter data if necessary.

Learn reach to 2

1. Learn the second-finger reach to 2 (below 5) as directed in Steps 1-3 above.

2. With eyes on copy, enter the data on Drills 1c and 1d; check the total figures; reenter data if necessary.

Learn reach to 3

1. Learn the third-finger reach to 3 (below 6) as directed above.

2. With eyes on copy, enter the data in Drills 1e, 1f, and 1g; check the total figures; reenter data if necessary.

Drills 2-4

Practice entering the columns of data in Drills 2-4 until you can do so accurately and quickly.

Drill 1

a	b	c	d	e	f	g
414	141	525	252	636	363	174
141	111	252	222	363	333	285
111	414	222	525	333	636	396
666	666	999	999	1,332	1,332	855

Drill 2

a	b	c	d	e	f	g
114	225	336	175	415	184	174
411	522	633	284	524	276	258
141	252	363	395	635	359	369
666	999	1,332	854	1,574	819	801

Drill 3

a	b	c	d	e	f	g
417	528	639	110	171	471	714
147	280	369	220	282	582	850
174	285	396	330	393	693	936
738	1,093	1,404	660	846	1,746	2,500

Drill 4

a	b	c	d	e	f	g
77	71	401	107	417	147	174
88	82	502	208	528	258	825
99	93	603	309	639	369	396
264	246	1,506	624	1,584	774	1,395

3c ▶ Enter Data Containing Commas

Enter the data in Columns a-g; check totals; reenter data as necessary.

Note: Even though number data often include commas to separate hundreds from thousands, do not enter them.

a	b	c	d	e	f	g
14	25	36	17	28	39	174
174	285	396	197	228	339	285
1,014	2,025	3,036	9,074	1,785	9,096	1,736
1,740	2,850	3,960	4,714	8,259	6,976	3,982
7,414	8,250	9,636	1,417	2,528	3,639	2,803
753	951	321	283	173	357	196
1,474	2,585	3,696	4,974	5,285	6,398	1,974
2,785	3,896	4,914	8,795	6,836	7,100	8,200
15,368	20,867	25,995	29,471	25,122	33,944	19,350

words

146b ► 35
Reinforce Document Processing Skills: Tables

3 plain full sheets

Tables 1 and 2
Tables with Main, Secondary, and Column Headings

CS: 8; center column headings

Format the tables given at the right; DS all lines; correct errors.

COST OF A $50,000 LOAN 5

15-Year Period 8

Rate	Monthly Payment	Total Repaid	words
			21
9%	$507.50	$ 91,350	26
10%	537.50	96,750	32
11%	568.50	102,330	37
12%	600.50	108,090	43
13%	633.00	113,940	49
14%	666.00	119,880	54
15%	700.00	126,000	60

COST OF A $50,000 LOAN 5

30-year Period 8

Rate	Monthly Payment	Total Repaid	words
			21
9%	$ 402.50	$144,900	26
10%	439.00	158,040	32
11%	476.50	171,540	37
12%	514.50	185,220	43
13%	553.50	199,260	49
14%	592.50	213,300	54
15%	632.50	227,700	60

Table 3
Table with Main and Column Headings with Total Line

Decide on the appropriate number of spaces to leave between columns; center column headings.

SECOND QUARTER SALES, 19-- 5

Employee	April	May	June	words
				14
Edwards, Martin	$ 29,365	$ 26,875	$ 30,650	23
Mahoney, Ryan	24,050	33,195	38,720	30
Merrick, Sheryl	39,540	36,095	37,550	37
North, Annette	16,215	15,385	12,380	44
Reid, Dinah	43,720	38,650	36,380	51
Richardson, Dyan	24,390	26,820	29,650	59
Sheridan, Douglas	19,815	18,790	19,500	66
Soto, Felix	32,100	27,580	30,850	73
Warren, Margo	27,950	35,600	29,380	85
Totals	$257,145	$258,990	$265,060	91

4a ▶ Review Key Locations

Enter and check the columns of data listed at the right as directed in Steps 1-9 on p. A-3.

a	b	c	d	e	f	g
44	55	66	714	414	525	636
14	25	36	825	474	585	696
74	85	96	936	400	500	600
132	165	198	2,475	1,288	1,610	1,932

4b ▶ Improve Keyboarding Facility

Enter the data listed in each column of Drills 1-3; check each total; reenter the data in each column for which you did not get the correct total.

Drill 1

a	b	c	d	e	f	g
14	19	173	1,236	1,714	4,174	4,074
25	37	291	4,596	2,825	5,285	5,085
36	18	382	7,896	3,936	6,396	6,096
74	29	794	5,474	7,414	1,400	9,336
85	38	326	2,975	8,525	2,500	8,225
96	27	184	8,535	9,636	3,600	7,114
330	168	2,150	30,712	34,050	23,355	39,930

Drill 2

a	b	c	d	e	f	g
1	3	40	123	114	1,004	8,274
14	36	50	789	225	2,005	9,386
174	396	70	321	336	3,006	7,494
2	906	740	456	774	7,004	1,484
25	306	360	174	885	8,005	2,595
285	20	850	285	996	9,006	3,686
805	50	960	396	500	5,005	6,006
1,306	1,717	3,070	2,544	3,830	35,035	38,925

Drill 3

a	b	c	d	e	f	g
126	104	107	707	4,400	3,006	1,714
786	205	208	808	5,000	2,005	2,825
324	306	309	909	6,600	1,004	3,936
984	704	407	1,700	7,000	9,006	7,144
876	805	508	2,800	8,800	8,005	8,255
216	906	609	3,900	9,000	7,004	9,366
3,312	3,030	2,148	10,824	40,800	30,030	33,240

4c ▶ Enter Data with Decimals

Enter the data in Columns a-f, placing the decimals as shown in the copy.

a	b	c	d	e	f
1.40	17.10	47.17	174.11	1,477.01	10,704.50
2.50	28.20	58.28	285.22	2,588.02	17,815.70
3.60	39.30	69.39	396.33	3,996.03	20,808.75
4.70	74.70	17.10	417.14	4,174.07	26,909.65
5.80	85.80	28.20	528.25	5,285.08	30,906.25
6.90	96.90	39.30	639.36	6,396.06	34,259.90
24.90	342.00	259.44	2,440.41	23,916.27	141,401.75

145c ▶ 25
Reinforce Document Processing Skills: Letters/Memorandums

plain full sheets; correct errors

Document 1
Letter

Format and key the letter at the right in block format with open punctuation.

words

Current date | Miss Roberta J. Payson | 310 Ledgewood Road | Portland, ME 14
04108-6482 | Dear Miss Payson 20

Here are the two tables that show the cost of a $50,000 home loan. The first 35
table displays various interest rates for a 15-year loan while the second 50
one gives the rates for a 30-year loan. As you can see from the tables, you 66
would decrease your monthly payment by approximately $100 per month 79
by assuming a 30-year loan. The total amount repaid, however, would be 94
considerably more. 98

The tables can also be used to determine the difference between the monthly 113
payments for a fixed mortgage versus the adjustable rate mortgage. Cur- 127
rently our adjustable mortgage rate is 9 percent. As I mentioned yesterday, 142
this type of loan is based on the index tied to the U.S. Treasury securities. 158
The initial rate is guaranteed for two years. At the end of two years the rate 174
can be increased or decreased by two percentage points each year up to a 189
maximum rate of 15 percent. 195

If you have any additional questions about the loans we discussed yesterday, 210
please give me a call. (195) 215

Sincerely | Mark R. Nelson | Loan Officer | xx | Enclosures | c Marshall S. Gagne 229

Document 2
Simplified Memorandum

Format and key the copy at the right as a simplified memorandum. The enclosure will be keyed in Lesson 146.

Document 3
Letter

Rekey 145b in modified block format with indented ¶s and mixed punctuation.

July 7, 19-- | Nichole A. Russell, Marketing Manager | SECOND QUARTER SALES 14
REPORT 16

Here are the sales figures for the second quarter. Overall they represent a 31
7.3 percent increase over the previous quarter and a 3.8 percent increase 46
over the second quarter sales of a year ago. 55

Annette North has given notice that she is resigning effective August 12 to 70
return to school to work on an advanced degree. I believe we should discuss 86
the feasibility of combining her territory with that of Douglas Sheridan. He 101
has indicated a concern about the lack of growth potential in his area. I be- 117
lieve this would be a solution to his concern. He has done a fine job with his 133
current territory, and I agree that there is not much potential for growth. 148

I'll bring additional information about the two territories for discussion at 164
our July 20 meeting. 168

James R. Woodward, District Manager | xx | Enclosure 178

Lesson 146 Reinforce Table Processing Skills

146a ▶ 5
Conditioning Practice

each line twice SS (slowly, then faster); DS between 2-line groups; if time permits, rekey selected lines

alphabet 1 Marjorie quickly realized the beautiful mauve gown was very expensive.

figures 2 After a delay of 45 minutes, Flight 837 left from Gate 26 at 1:09 p.m.

fig/sym 3 My policy (#35-62A-748) with Barnes & Bennett expired on May 30, 1991.

speed 4 They may pay both of us to work for them when they dismantle the dock.

| 1 | 2 | 3 | 4 | 5 | 6 | 7 | 8 | 9 | 10 | 11 | 12 | 13 | 14 |

5a ▶ Review Key Locations

Enter and check the columns of data listed at the right.

a	b	c	d	e	f	g
477	588	707	107	41.6	141.4	936.6
417	528	808	205	52.9	252.5	825.6
717	825	909	309	63.3	393.3	719.4
1,611	1,941	2,424	621	157.8	787.2	2,481.6

5b ▶ Improve Keyboarding Facility

Enter the data listed in each column of Drills 1-4; check each total by entering the data a second time (from bottom to top).

If you get the same total twice, you can "assume" it is correct. If you get a different total the second time, reenter the data until you get two totals that match.

Drill 1

a	b	c	d	e	f	g
5	77	114	5,808	1,936	9,300	6,936
46	89	225	3,997	2,825	8,250	3,896
3	78	336	9,408	3,796	10,475	7,140
17	85	725	5,650	8,625	7,125	4,874
28	98	825	3,714	9,436	12,740	2,515
9	69	936	2,825	8,514	12,850	8,360
10	97	704	6,796	4,174	9,674	1,794

Drill 2

a	b	c	d	e	f	g
99	795	1,581	1,881	2,642	4,573	2,185
67	657	1,691	1,991	2,772	4,683	3,274
88	234	1,339	2,202	2,992	5,477	9,396
96	359	1,221	2,432	3,743	6,409	4,585
84	762	1,101	3,303	3,853	6,886	5,872
100	485	1,144	4,650	4,714	7,936	6,903

Drill 3

a	b	c	d	e	f
1,077	3,006	5,208	7,104	1,774	7,417
1,400	3,609	5,502	8,205	2,885	8,528
1,700	3,900	5,205	9,303	3,996	9,639
2,008	4,107	6,309	7,407	4,174	3,936
2,500	4,400	6,600	8,508	5,285	5,828
2,805	1,704	6,900	9,609	6,396	4,717

Drill 4

a	b	c	d	e	f
1.4	14.00	170.40	1,714.70	7,410.95	1,147.74
2.5	17.00	170.43	2,825.80	8,520.55	2,258.88
3.6	25.00	250.90	3,936.90	9,630.65	3,369.93
7.4	28.00	288.50	4,747.17	10,585.78	7,144.74
8.5	36.00	369.63	5,878.25	11,474.85	8,255.85
9.6	39.00	390.69	6,969.39	12,696.95	9,366.63

UNIT 33 LESSONS 145 – 147

Reinforce Document Processing Skills

Learning Goals

1. To reinforce letter/memorandum processing skills.
2. To reinforce table processing skills.
3. To reinforce report processing skills.
4. To reinforce language skills.

Format Guides

1. Paper guide at *0* (for typewriters).
2. LL: 70 for drills and language skills activities; as required by document formats.
3. LS: SS for drills and language skills activities unless otherwise instructed; as required by document formats.
4. PI: 5 spaces, when appropriate.

Lesson 145 *Reinforce Letter/Memo Processing Skills*

145a ▶ 5 Conditioning Practice

each line twice SS (slowly, then faster); DS between 2-line groups; if time permits, rekey selected lines

alphabet 1 Major Quantz will leave the five packages by the box next to the desk.

figures 2 I delivered pizzas to 3910 Lake Road, 876 B Street, and 425 Lana Lane.

double letters 3 Will Emmalou be successful when she attempts to pass the zoology exam?

speed 4 If the firm pays for the social, the eight city officials may also go.

| 1 | 2 | 3 | 4 | 5 | 6 | 7 | 8 | 9 | 10 | 11 | 12 | 13 | 14 |

145b ▶ 20 Build Speed: Letters/Memos

plain full sheets; block format; open punctuation

1. Review special letter parts on page 222.
2. A 5′ writing on the letter to determine *gwam.*
3. Take two 1′ writings on date through subject line of the letter. If you complete the lines before time is called, QS and start over.
4. Take two 1′ writings on complimentary close through enclosures. If you complete the lines before time is called, QS and start over.
5. Take another 5′ writing on the letter. Try to increase your *gwam* by 4-8 words.

gwam 5′

February 10, 19-- REGISTERED Attention Ms. Claudia W. Seymore Fenton 3
Manufacturing Company 3829 Douglas Road Fort Wayne, IN 46835-7553 5
Ladies and Gentlemen Subject: Education Classes 7

(¶ 1) Even the most user-friendly computer hardware/software will gather 10
dust unless employees have been properly trained. When you purchased 13
your system from us, we told you we provide the necessary training. 16
(¶ 2) Our next session of beginner's classes in word processing and 18
spreadsheets will be offered again in March. The word processing class 21
is scheduled for Monday nights. This class starts on March 6 and runs 24
through April 24. The spreadsheet applications class is scheduled for 27
Wednesday nights starting on March 8. April 26 will be the completion 30
date of this class. Both classes meet from 7 p.m. to 8 p.m. 32
(¶ 3) Registration materials are enclosed. Since the classes fill quite 35
rapidly, you must register as soon as possible. 37

Sincerely COMPUTER SPECIALISTS Todd W. Rush Education Specialist xx 39
Enclosures: Registration Materials Course Syllabi 43

gwam 5′ | 1 | 2 | 3 |

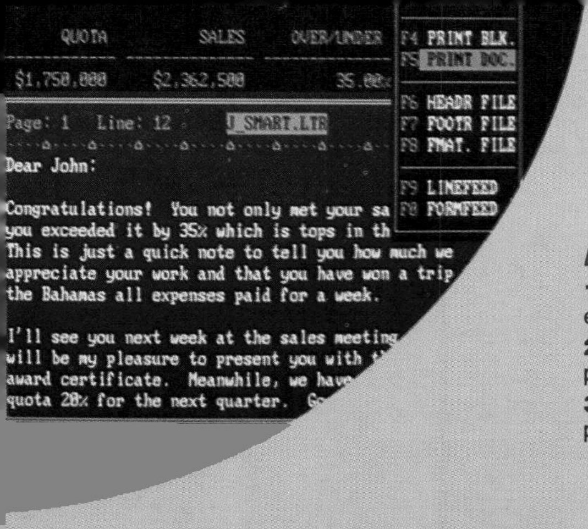

APPENDIX B

Automatic Features/Editing Functions of Electronic Equipment

Learning Goals

1. To learn the basic functions of electronic equipment.

2. To learn the specific commands for your particular software package.

3. To apply these functions and commands to perform the activities.

Practice Procedure

Follow the directions for each activity. Practice the drills until you feel comfortable enough to move to the next activity.

Study the software documentation and note the command for each function.

KNOW WHAT'S HAPPENING . . .
"For the times they are a-changin" went the words of a popular tune some years ago. And my how they've changed! A quick look at the composition of the United States labor force illustrates only one component of change. In 1920, close to 80 percent of the work force consisted of agricultural and industrial workers. The dominant sector of today's labor force, close to 90 percent, consists of information and service workers. Today's information technologies--such as electronic typewriters, personal computers, FAX machines, scanners, intelligent copiers and printers, electronic mail, and telecommunication devices--are having a major impact on workplace roles. Due to the information explosion, many of the new career opportunities in today's marketplace are based on computer technology.

The tools we work with have changed and will continue to change. For example, look what's happened to the typewriter and the world of document preparation. The user of a manual typewriter purchased an eraser to correct errors. The user of an electric may have had the luxury of correct-o-type to fix blunders. The electronic typewriter user may be able to store a few phrases or pages before printing a document. A personal computer, also called a microcomputer, makes document creation, formatting, and editing even easier when word processing software is used.

As the tools we work with continue to change, we ourselves must adapt to remain successful workers and fulfilled individuals. This section has been designed to inform you of some of the features and functions you will encounter when using an electronic typewriter and/or personal computer with word processing software to prepare documents.

KNOW THE "IN BRIEF" SECTION . . .
"In Brief" is designed to give you a generic description of the most commonly used word processing features. Read each one carefully. Since directions for each feature differ from program to program and not all programs contain every feature, study your software user's manual to learn the specific step-by-step instructions for your particular program. The software commands given in "In Brief" are for WordPerfect Versions 4.2 and 5.0.

KNOW YOUR SOFTWARE . . . Software is a program, a set of directions (instructions) that tells your computer to perform a specific task. Word processing software is a package that allows the user to create and format a document, save (store/file) it, retrieve and edit the text, and print the document. Some commonly used word processing features are insert and delete, center, move, copy, indent, columns and decimal alignment, page numbering, boldface, underline, and print. It is important to become familiar with your software package.

KNOW WHAT TO DO . . . (1) Read the "In Brief" feature section. (2) Study the user's manual for your equipment. (3) Study your software documentation for the specific function. (4) Read the directions for the lesson, then key the drills accordingly.

KNOW YOUR EQUIPMENT . . . THE KEYBOARD . . . For a quick review of the components of a personal computer, refer to pages viii and ix. Since many word processing functions require the user to strike a combination of keys, the keyboard arrangement of the three popular machines shown on these pages may help. Use the numbered items listed there to identify each key. If you are using a different computer, consult the instruction booklet that came with the equipment.

140b-144b (continued)

Job 11
LP p. 141

Processing Instructions From Annette O'Toole

Mr. Caswell would like the items on the attached sheet ordered. Prepare Purchase Order **#387-609** *to order these items. You will need to figure and enter the extensions in the total column and grand total of the order.*

March 4, 19--

Order from LaSalle Computer Supplies, 3418 Biscayne Street, Miami, FL 33139-5812

2	No. D83-98	Computer workstation--at $279.50 each
1	No. A23-56	Computer printer stand--at $249.50
1	No. A15-70	File cabinet--at $169.99
2	No. M26-63	Computer workstation chair--at $184.59 each

LaSalle's terms of sale are 3/10, net 30. Have order shipped by United Freight.

Job 12
LP p. 143

Processing Instructions From Annette O'Toole

Attached is a handwritten sales report prepared by Mr. Colfax. Prepare the report in final form.

EPI

MONTHLY SALES REPORT

Month of February

Sales Representative	Territory	Sales For Month	Total Sales For Year
Adams, Becky	South Carolina	$ 18,760	$ 34,810
Brown, Janice	Tennessee	5,195	5,195
Chan, Regina	Tennessee	21,240	39,490
Rodriguez, Mario	Florida	12,560	22,380
Vanberg, Shawn	Georgia	13,500	27,980
Russell, Karin	Alabama	12,345	23,120
Jones, Lisa	North Carolina	15,895	33,125
Hernandez, Felipe	Florida	6,870	6,870
Nelson, Nancy	Virginia	18,755	34,900
Conrad, Greg	Kentucky	21,179	37,500
Vue, Cha	Mississippi	12,790	23,410
Spencer, Briget	North Carolina	16,050	36,185
McCarver, Maureen	South Carolina	7,385	7,385
Ryan, Shari	Alabama	15,380	25,790
Okenek, Jarom	Georgia	14,760	31,850
Lange, Diane	Mississippi	13,780	27,650
Cloud, Lee	Florida	10,980	21,860
Newton, Steve	Florida	15,760	29,485
Thomas, Jan	Georgia	15,675	27,390
	Total Sales	$268,859	$496,375

Activity 1 *Backspace Erase Feature*

1. Read the "In Brief" copy at right.

2. Study software documentation to learn to use the backspace erase feature.

3. Read sentences at right.

4. Key each line twice DS using the backspace erase feature when needed.

BACKSPACE ERASE

An electronic editing tool that allows you to backspace and delete a previously keyed character (or characters).

Every time you strike the backspace erase key, the character to the left of the cursor is automatically erased (deleted).

1 Work is not only a way to make a living: It's the way to make a life!

2 The majority of new jobs will come from small, independent businesses.

3 Planning a career today requires more thought than it ever did before.

Activity 2 *Cursor (Arrow) Keys*

1. Read the "In Brief" copy at right.

2. Study software documentation to learn to use cursor keys.

3. Read sentences at right.

4. Key the sentences DS.

5. Using arrow keys, move the cursor to:

x in **flexibility,** line 1
v in **effectively,** line 3
d in **attitudes,** line 1
p in **compete,** line 3
m in **motivation,** line 2

CURSOR

A blinking light on the screen that identifies the position where text (copy) will be entered or edited. Arrow keys (cursor keys) used to move the cursor around the screen may be located on your computer's numeric keypad or as a separate group of keys between the main keyboard and the keypad.

LEFT/RIGHT CURSOR (ARROW) KEYS

These keys move the cursor one space at a time in a left or a right direction.

UP/DOWN CURSOR (ARROW) KEYS

These keys move the cursor up or down one line at a time.

1 Today, job seekers must possess a flexibility of skills and attitudes.

2 Getting the job you want requires motivation, energy, and preparation.

3 To compete effectively for the most attractive jobs, be well informed.

Activity 3 *Strikeover, Insert, and Delete Editing Features*

1. Read the "In Brief" copy at right.

2. Study software documentation to learn to use strikeover, insert, and delete features.

3. Read sentences at right.

4. Key each sentence DS as shown.

5. Make these changes (use the arrow keys to move the cursor):

Line
1, insert **"** after **career (career")**
1, replace 2d **e** in **seperate** with an **a**
2, delete **b** in **jobb**
2, delete **r** in **carreer (career)**
2, delete space in **it self**
3, insert **c** in **piking (picking)**
3, insert **e** in **carer (career)**
3, insert **l** in **chalenge (challenge)**
4, delete **s** in **keys**
4, replace 2d **s** in **sequense** with **c**
4, insert **c** and **s** in **aces (access)**

STRIKEOVER/REPLACEMENT MODE

Editing feature that allows you to position the cursor and key over (strikeover) characters. Existing text is automatically erased and replaced by new text.

INSERT

Editing feature that allows you to add characters without rekeying the entire document. New text is inserted and existing text is pushed to the right or down to make room for the addition.

DELETE

Editing feature that removes (erases) any character or characters, including blank spaces, identified (highlighted) by the cursor. Existing text to right moves over and text below moves up to close the space.

1 Today the two terms "career and "job" have totally seperate meanings.

2 Consider your jobb as a way to a carreer, not a career in and of it self.

3 No longer is piking a carer to get a job the chalenge workers face.

4 The keys is choosing the best sequense of jobs with aces to a career.

140b-144b (continued)

Job 9

LP p. 139

Processing Instructions From **Annette O'Toole**

Key the attached material as a formal memorandum for **Lynda V. Lopez, Committee Chair.** *Make all the changes marked on the copy as well as any unmarked errors you detect. Be sure to include an enclosure notation. Date the memo* **February 28.**

```
Product Development Evaluation Committee Members

MARCH 15 COMMITTEE MEETING

The next meeting of the Product development Evaluation Commitee
will be held wednesday, march fifteenth, at 2:30 P.M. in the con-
ference room.  Mark Sanderson will be demonstrating the computer
math program, Back to the Basics, which he recently developed.
Because of the time liness of the product, mr. Caswell has re-
quested Susan St. Claier and Dave Master's to present information
at our meeting on production costs and sales.  Jason Hibbard will
present an estimate of the cost/price structure for the software
package.  Mr. Caswell and I agree that we should move as quickly
as possible in order to assure that this program is on the makret
before something appears from another company.  A copy of Mr.
Caswells letter to president Boswell which provides edditional
background information is attached.
```

(Handwritten corrections: "Commitee" → "Committee"; "fifteenth" → "15"; "P.M." → "p.m." (lc); quotation marks around "Back to the Basics,"; "time liness" → "timeliness"; "Claier" → "Clair"; "Master's" → "Masters"; insert "potential" after "sales"; new paragraph before "Mr. Caswell and I agree"; insert "very innovative" before "program"; "makret" → "market"; insert "similar" after "something"; "edditional" → "additional"; commas around "which provides additional background information"; "attached" → "enclosed")

Job 10

LP p. 141

Processing Instructions From **Annette O'Toole**

Prepare an invoice from the order form prepared by Ms. Jan Thomas. Be sure to check the accuracy of extensions and the total column before keying. Use today's date **(February 28).** *Order No.* **892-611A,** *and* **Net 30** *days. Our Order No.* **385.**

EPI ■ EDUCATIONAL PRODUCTS, INC.

▲ 3929 Braddock Road, Fort Meyers, FL 33912-8357 (813) 277-6600

PURCHASE ORDER

Carlton School of Business
488 Willowbrook Drive, SW
Atlanta, GA 30311-7485

Purchase Order No.:

Date:

Terms:

Shipped Via:

Quantity	Description/Stock Number	Price		Per	Total	
20 sets	Creative Business Letters--E561	125	00	set	2,400	00
20 sets	Quick Key WP--B731	75	00	set	1,500	00
5 sets	English Enhancement--E320	219	00	set	1,095	00
2 sets	The Art Gallery--B839	249	00	set	498	00
					5,493	00

By ______________________

Activity 4
Margins, Tabs, and Vertical Spacing

1. Read the "In Brief" copy at right.
2. Study software documentation to learn to set a 60-space line, 5-space paragraph indent tab, and double spacing.
3. Read copy below right.
4. Key the paragraph.

RULER/FORMAT LINE

Line at the top or botom of the screen or accessible within a document used to set the document format consisting of left and right margins, tab stops, text alignment and line-spacing.

MARGINS

The blank space on the left and right sides and at the top and bottom of a page. Left and right margins can be adjusted according to the desired line space; top and bottom margins can also be adjusted.

TABS

Stops set in the ruler/format line that allow you to indent paragraphs and lists and to align columns in tables. When you strike the TAB key, the cursor moves to the desired tab stop. If you key more than one line, the following lines align with the left margin instead of the tab stop.

SPACING

The space between lines of text. Line-spacing may be set for SS (1) or DS (2). A quadruple space is keyed by striking the return an appropriate number of times.

The average person spends 9 percent of the time writing, 16 percent reading, 30 percent speaking, and 45 percent listening. The fact that an individual is given two ears and only one mouth indicates the proper proportion of listening to speaking. Therefore, take heed of the Korean proverb: "Fools chatter; wise men listen."

Activity 5
Word Wrap and Soft and Hard Returns

1. Read the "In Brief" copy at the right.
2. Study software documentation to learn to use the word wrap and soft and hard returns.
3. Read paragraphs at right.
4. Use your program's default settings (or set a 70-space line and a 5-space paragraph indent tab).
5. Key the paragraphs DS using hard returns only between paragraphs.
6. As you key, correct any mistakes using the backspace key.
7. Proofread; make any necessary corrections using the strikeover, insert, and delete functions.
8. With the arrow keys, move the cursor to the beginning of the first ¶. Change to a 50-space line, 5-space paragraph indent tab. Then strike the down arrow repeatedly. What happened?
9. With the arrow keys, move the cursor to the beginning of the first ¶. Change to a 60-space line, 5-space paragraph indent tab. Then strike the down arrow repeatedly. What happened?

WORD WRAP

An automatic feature that determines whether the word being keyed will extend beyond the right margin. If so, the program automatically "wraps the text around" to the beginning of the next line while the user continues keying. A carriage return is necessary only when mandatory, such as at the end of a paragraph or a line of statistical copy.

SOFT RETURN

Automatically entered by the program at the end of a line of copy when text is being "wrapped around" to the next line. When you adjust the margins or insert and/or delete copy, the program automatically changes the position of the soft return.

HARD RETURN

Entered by striking the return key. Hard returns can be removed only by deleting them with backspace erase or the delete feature.

How does your word processing program know where to set the margins when you don't key the numbers? Simple. The program sets them according to the default. A default is a setting entered into a program by the designer. Paper size (8½ × 11 inches), pitch (pica--10), left and right margins, and tab settings are example of preset defaults.

Let's say your program has a default setting of 10 for the left margin and 74 for the right. Should you desire a longer or shorter line of copy, simply change the default setting. Defaults are created to appeal to the majority of users most of the time. Designers try to assume exactly what settings users will want to work with.

140b-144b (continued)

a depleted sales force.
significant decrease in Georgia can be attributed to ~~having~~
terminated employment
two sales representatives ~~quit~~ during the year without
prior
giving notice. This not only created a problem in there
districts, but also in the districts of the representatives
who ed for them
~~that tried to~~ cover ~~two districts~~ while replacements were
being hired and trained.

Comments and Projections

Overall, the past year was a vary successful one. Our goal for this year is to increase total sales by 10 percent, with no state falling below a 7.5 percent gain.

The new products showcased at the January board meeting along with the improvements made to existing product lines should have a significant impact on sales during the next year. The addition of much needed sales representatives in Tennessee Florida and South Carolina will also create a positive impact on the total sales picture. DS

Steps are being taken to establish a new policy for
distribution of sales commissions. This is being done to
r such as those d
prevent future occurences of the problems ~~we~~ experiences in
Georgia. The combination of all these factors should make
Southern
it quite easy for the region to achieve and exceed the 10
projected
percent increase.

Job 8
plain full sheet

Processing Instructions From **Annette O'Toole**

Ms. Lopez would like the attached agenda keyed as soon as possible.

AGENDA

Product Developement Evaluation Committee Meeting
2:30 p.m., March 15

1. Introductory Comments . . . . Lynda Lopez
2. Presentation of "Back to Math Basics" . . . . Mark Sanderson
3. Special Reports
   Production Cost Projections. . . . . Susan St. Claire
   Market Projections. . . . . Dave Masters
   Cost / Price Structure Projections . . . . Jason Hibbard
4. Discussion of Proposal . . . . Committee Members
5. Summary of Discussion: Pros and Cons. . . . . . Griffin Caswell
6. Call for Vote. . . . . Lynda Lopez
7. Adjournment

Activity 6
Review Setting Margins, Tabs, Vertical Spacing, Word Wrap, Insert, Delete, and Strikeover Features

1. Read the ¶s at the right.

2. LL: 60 spaces; LS: DS; ¶ indent tab: 5 spaces.

3. Key ¶s as is; do not correct errors; use a hard return only between ¶s.

4. Make these changes:

Paragraph 1
Line
1, replace **s** in **sertain** with **c**
2, replace 2d **e** in **seperate** with **a**
2, delete space in **up scale**
2, delete space in **down scale**
3, hyphenate **not so rich**
3, change **people** to **individuals**
4, replace **there** with **their**
4, change **area** to **field**
5, insert **entertainment** after **education**
6, change **you** to **yourself**
7, change **imagine** to **picture**

Paragraph 2
Line
8, delete **l** in **successfull**
9, change **they're** to **they are**
10, delete space in **any one**
10, delete space in **under stand**
11, change **&** to **and**
11, replace **T** in 2d **They** with **t**
12, delete space in **care fully**
12, delete **r** and insert **l** in **generraly (generally)**

1 Research has shown that sertain personality traits
2 seperate the up scale from the down scale, the rich from
3 the not so rich. These traits bring people success
4 regardless of there chosen area--business, sports,
5 education, or politics. One of the necessary
6 traits is the ability to envision you succeeding. If you
7 can imagine it, you can achieve it.
8 Another trait of successfull individuals is goal
9 setting. Usually they're not any more intelligent than
10 any one else. However, they set their goals, under stand
11 them, & make sure they are achieved. They don't rush; They
12 plan their actions care fully. Generraly they live by the
13 rule "plan your work, then work your plan."

Activity 7
Underline Text Automatically While Keying

1. Read the "In Brief" copy.

2. Study software documentation to learn to underline existing text and how to underline text automatically while keying.

3. LL: 70 spaces; LS: DS.

4. Read sentences at right.

5. Key sentences using automatic underscore where shown.

6. When finished, proofread your work, making any corrections using insert, delete, and strikeover features.

7. Underline these words in the existing text:

Line:
1, **listening**
2, **information, notes**
3, **listening**
4, **First**

UNDERLINE EXISTING TEXT

Position the cursor (or printwheel) at the beginning of the existing text. Hold down the left shift key and strike the hyphen key. You may have to identify the block of text by entering a specific command *(such as the Alternate and F4 keys)* and then enter the underline command *(such as the F8 key)*.

UNDERLINE TEXT AS YOU KEY (AUTOMATIC)

Turn on automatic (continuous) underlining by striking a keystroke combination *(such as Code and u)*, or strike the assigned function key *(such as F8)*. As you key, the text will be underlined. When you're finished, turn automatic underlining off by striking the same key or combination.

1 The four steps to listening are: sense, interpret, evaluate, respond.
2 Active listening involves processing the information and taking notes.
3 A conversation requires both listening for main ideas and interacting.
4 First on the list of very nonproductive listening habits is fidgeting.
5 If you fidget, you may tug your earlobe, shuffle your feet, or squirm.

Job 7
plain full sheets

Processing Instructions From Annette O'Toole

Mr. Colfax would like the attached report prepared in unbound format. The last two columns of the table you prepared for Document 5 will be needed to complete the table in the report. Correct any unmarked errors.

SOUTHERN REGION SALES REPORT DS
Educational Products, Inc. QS

The Southern Region of EPI (sp) increased overall sales by 5.5 percent ~~last~~ over the previous year, ~~with~~ total sales amount~~ing~~ed too $3,014,730; this increase was 1.5% (sp) higher then forecast for the year.

~~The~~ Sales by States figures for each state in the rgion are outlined below. ~~The~~ Figures are presented for total dollar sales and for percentafge of increase or decrease for the state for the year.

Total dollar sales. Florida replaced Georgia as the state generating the highest total dollar sales with sales of $525,650. Georgia ($406,310) was the only other state with ~~total~~ sales in excess of $400,000. The remaining seven states in the region generated sales between $265,300 ~~to~~ and $338,250. A complete breakdown ~~by~~ for each state in the Southern region is shown below:

State	19-- Sales	% Change
Alabama		
Florida		
Georgia		
Kentucky		
Mississippi		
North Carolina		
South Carolina		
Tennesses		
Virginia		

Use information from the last two Columns of Southern Region Sales Comparison table.

Percentage increase/decrease. ~~As can been seen from the above table,~~ The sales information shows that Virginia had the greatest percentage of total sales increase with 30.3 percent; Florida was second with a 22.4 percent increase. ~~Both states~~ The increase in both States is do to the addition of a sales representative. A knew rep (sp) was added to Floridas sales force in March and to Virginia's in July.

Two states decreased in sales ~~this year~~--Georgia by 18.7 percent and North Carolina by 1.6 percent. The

Activity 8
Bold Text

1. Read the "In Brief" copy.
2. Study software documentation to learn to bold text.
3. Set a 70-space line, DS.
4. Key the sentences using the bold feature where shown.
5. Proofread your work. Make any necessary corrections and print a copy.

BOLD TEXT

The bold feature emphasizes text by printing characters darker than others. This bold effect is created when the printer strikes each designated character twice. Turn on the bold command by striking the assigned key or keystroke combination *(such as the F6 key or the Code and b keys)*. Key the text to be printed in bold, which may appear highlighted on the screen. Turn off the bold command by striking the same key or keystroke combination.

1 **Boom boxes** and various other background noises are **distractions** to us.

2 Your **emotions** and **personal ideas** influence your reaction to a speaker.

3 One huge roadblock we all face is an **overestimation** of our **importance.**

4 A **passive listener** simply nods in **agreement** throughout a **conversation.**

Activity 9 Center
Text Horizontally

1. Read the "In Brief" copy.
2. Study software documentation to learn to center text.
3. Set a 50-space line, SS.
4. Read the drills below.
5. Key each line of each drill using automatic centering, if offered. If not, center each drill manually. Underline and bold the text as shown.

AUTOMATIC CENTERING

To center automatically, position the cursor (or printwheel) at the left margin. Hold down the designated key combination *(such as Code and c);* the cursor moves to the center of the line. As you key, the cursor backs up (but does not print). To print the centered copy, strike the return key. You may have to enter the center command *(such as shift and F6 keys)*. The cursor moves to the center of the line. As you key, the letters back up once for every two characters. Strike the return key (hard return).

Drill 1

STAND UP AND DELIVER

Express Your Opinion Concisely
Be Confident
Beware--Your Body Language is also "Speaking"
Your Tone of Voice Says it All
Pay Attention to Your Listener
Observe Body Language of Others

Drill 2

A KEY TO EFFECTIVE COMMUNICATION:
MATCHING STYLES WITH CONTENT

Small Talk--Chatty, Noncommittal
Control Talk--Take Charge
Search Talk--Analyze Problems; Possible Solutions
Straight Talk--Handle Conflicts Constructively

Drill 3

GAMESMANSHIP PROBLEMS AT WORK

Answer a Question with a Question
Discuss Others Rather than One's Self
Send Incomplete Messages
Provide Superficial Information About an Issue
Use We or They rather than I or You
Withhold Important Information

140b-144b (continued)

Job 5
LP p. 137

Processing Instructions From Annette O'Toole

Process the attached letter for Mr. Colfax's signature. Date the letter **February 28** *and address the letter to*

Ms. Regina R. Chan
EPI Sales Representative
310 Rushmore Drive, NW
Knoxville, TN 37923-7492

Correct any unmarked errors you find in the copy.

Dear Ms. Chan:

Your proposal that EPI sponsor a software institute for business education teachers prior to the tennessee vocational conference is excellent. When teachers preview our software programs, they are much more receptive if they have received instruction during the preview from one of our specialists. This conference would be a perfect place to provide such instruction.

On March 17 I will be meeting with president Boswell to discuss the merits of your proposal. Prior to the meeting, I will need a detailed budget outlining the anticipated expenditures for the institute.

Sincerely,

Troy S. Colfax
Regional Vice President

Job 6
plain full sheet

Processing Instructions From Annette O'Toole

Prepare the attached table in final form for Mr. Colfax.

SOUTHERN REGION

19--/19-- Sales Comparison

State	Previous Year	Current Year	% Change
Alabama	$ 258,960	$ 275,980	+6.6
Florida	429,395	525,650	+22.6
Georgia	499,800	406,310	-18.7
Kentucky	265,290	275,390	+3.8
Mississippi	320,180	338,250	+2.5
North Carolina	340,395	334,970	-1.6
South Carolina	288,345	325,390	+12.8
Tennessee	250,200	265,300	+6.0
Virginia	205,320	267,490	+30.3
Totals	$ 2,857,885	$ 3,014,730	+5.5

Activity 10
Required Space Feature

1. Read the "In Brief" copy at right.
2. Study software documentation to learn to use the required space feature.
3. Set a 60-space line, DS.
4. Read sentences at right.
5. Key sentences using required space feature where needed.
6. Proofread; make any necessary corrections.
7. Print a final copy.

HARD (REQUIRED) SPACE

A feature that guards against breaking a line of printed text between title and surname (Mr. Magoo), initials (B. L. Smith), month and date (December 7, 1941), and parts of a formula (a + b + c), etc. Inserting hard (required) spaces between items of text causes the printer to regard the phrase as one word. When you strike a specific key *(such as the Home key)*, along with the space bar, you enter a "hard space." (A special symbol or code may appear on the screen.) The printer will print the text containing the hard space on one line.

1 A cartoon personality that won the hearts of many was Mr. Magoo.

2 The movies have brought us many stars; for example, Zsa Zsa Gabor.

3 The Declaration of Independence was signed on Thursday, July 4, 1776.

Activity 11
Review Margins, Tabs, Spacing, Required Space, Automatic Center, Underline, and Bold Features

1. Read paragraphs at right.
2. Set a 70-space line, 5-space paragraph indent tab, DS.
3. Center headings; use underline and bold where shown.
4. Key the document.
5. Proofread your work. Make any necessary corrections and print a copy.

PERSONAL STYLE

HOW TO MAKE YOURSELF SPECIAL

The basis for style--one's distinctive manner of expression--comes from within. Style is not something we're born with but rather a combination of abilities that we learn as we mature, just as we learn to speak Russian, repair leaky faucets, or drive a car. Style is a very personal achievement; it's a quality that money cannot buy. As a matter of fact, style has nothing at all to do with money.

WHAT IT TAKES...

Personal style is a mixture of six main elements. (1) Knowing what to add and when to stop is a matter of **balance** and **restraint.** (2) Paying **attention to detail** allows you to think things through to create comfort and satisfaction. (3) **Consideration** means you are alert to other people's needs and sensitivities and respond to them. (4) **Poise, grace,** and **self-confidence** come from knowing one's self without being vain. (5) The ability to **make good choices** helps you make the right decision at the right time. (6) **Individuality** is the distinctive expression of your personal preferences. (7) **Identity** means you have a point of view that marks your place in the game plan of life.

140b-144b (continued)

Job 3
LP p. 135

Processing Instructions From Annette O'Toole

Mr. Griffin Caswell, Director of Product Development, would like the attached material formatted as a two-page letter to **Mr. Henry Boswell, President.** *Date the letter* **February 28** *and use* **New Software Developments** *for the subject line.*

Job 4
plain full sheet

Processing Instructions From Annette O'Toole

Mr. Griffin Caswell, Director of Product Development, would like the same letter reformatted as a simplified memorandum to the **Product Development Staff.** *Date the memorandum* **February 28** *and use* **New Software Developments** *for the subject line.*

The information from the educational survey you had Jay Hancock of Research Associates conduct for us ~~conducted~~ has been most helpful in planning for the future. The responses from 350 elementary school teachers support our belief that teachers are eager for additional computer-aided instructional materials.

Over 40 percent of the respondents indicated that they are currently using some type of instructional materials requiring the computer. A very high percentage (93%) ~~of the respondents~~ felt that future curricular revisions will require the use of computers in their classrooms.

The survey respondents listed math as the subject area ~~as the course~~ in which they would like to see additional software materials developed. Many of the respondents indicated that they would like to have an individualized ~~math~~ program for students with math difficulties.

Currently two computer programs for individualized math instruction are being pilot tested by our department. ~~which~~ These programs appear to meet the elementary teachers' requirements. Mark Sanderson's individualized computer program, "Back to Math Basics," has great sales potential. With a few modifications the software could serve a wide market.

Instructional objectives, periodic self-checks, and posttests are all enhanced by the computer graphics which should be very appealing to elementary students. Jennifer Shields has worked with Mark to develop a more advanced math package which can be used after completing the "Back to the Basics" program.

It is our plan to have a ~~complete~~ comprehensive elementary math ~~individualized~~ program completed within the next two years. ~~I will provide periodic~~ Updates on the progress will be provided periodically ~~of these two individualized math programs~~.

Activity 12
Learn to Use the Hyphenation Feature

1. Read the "In Brief" copy at right.

2. Study software documentation to learn to use the hyphenation feature.

3. Read paragraph at right; identify the required, soft, and/or hard hyphen character features.

4. Set a 70-space line and a 5-space paragraph tab, then key the paragraph DS using your program's hyphenation feature.

5. When finished, proofread your work making any corrections and/or changes.

6. Print a final copy.

HARD (REQUIRED) HYPHEN

Entered when the user strikes the hyphen key. Regardless of where the hyphen appears within the paragraph, the program prints it. Hard hyphens are used in telephone numbers, a numeric range, certain phrases that should not be broken (jack-o-lantern), and compound words (self-confident). A hard hyphen can be deleted by the user.

SOFT (GHOST OR NONREQUIRED) HYPHEN

An electronic feature that allows the user to decide whether a word should be hyphenated to avoid a very ragged right margin. When the hyphenation feature is "on," the cursor stops when a word will not fit on the line. Some programs automatically insert a soft hyphen; others allow the user to make the decision. Should the location of the hyphenated word change during reformatting, the soft hyphen is deleted automatically.

HYPHEN CHARACTER

A feature used for keying dates or minus signs in formulas. The hyphen character may require the user to strike a specific key *(such as the Home key)* before striking the hyphen key. The feature prevents a minus or a dash from being separated from related characters when it occurs at the end of a line.

Most of us never realize the important role imagination plays in our lives. Imagination sets the goal "picture" upon which we act (or fail to act). Imagination is the way we are built--our automatic mechanism works on our "creative imagination." Depending on what a person imagines to be true about herself/himself and her/his environment, that individual will always act and feel and perform accordingly. Therefore, why not imagine yourself successful? If you picture yourself performing in a certain manner, it is almost the same as the actual performance. Mental practice helps to make perfect.

Activity 13
Learn About Pagination (Page Format) Features

1. Read the "In Brief" copy at right and on the next page.

2. Study software documentation to learn about pagination (page format) features.

3. Identify the features available on your software.

4. Create a checklist on "how to perform" each feature; use a step-by-step enumerated format.

5. Set a 60-space line and a 5-space indent tab for the enumerations.

6. Key each checklist, center the headings; indent each step (enumerations).

7. When finished, proofread your work making any corrections using any of the electronic features introduced thus far.

PAGE BREAK

The point (generally a given line count) at which a page ends. When the printer reaches the page break, it automatically advances a new sheet or allows the user to insert paper.

AUTOMATIC (SOFT/NONREQUIRED) PAGE BREAKS

A feature (sometimes called page format) that allows the user to select the number of lines allowed on the page (generally 54). When the program recognizes the given number of lines, it automatically inserts a soft page break. When repagination occurs (a paragraph is added or deleted, for example), all soft page breaks are deleted and new ones inserted automatically.

CONTROLLED (HARD/REQUIRED) PAGE BREAKS

A special command inserted by the user to ensure that a page remains intact during automatic pagination. When the program recognizes the special command, it breaks the page at that point. Usually hard page breaks must be deleted by the user.

HEADER/FOOTER

Text line (or lines) printed consistently in the top margin (header) or bottom margin (footer) of each page of a multiple-page document. A header/footer may include such information as the document title, page number, and date. Rarely does a single document contain both a header and a footer.

(continued, p. A-15)

140b-144b (continued)

Job 2

LP pp. 129-133

Processing Instructions From Annette O'Toole

A copy of the form letter that was sent to sales representatives on **February 1** *and the cards for three new sales representatives are attached. Ms. McLaughlin would like you to key the letter with the changes marked on the copy and send it to the new sales reps.*

Add the following postscript to the letter.

Congratulations on your new position with Educational Products, Inc. I am looking forward to working with you.

Note: The <mail merge feature> was used in preparing the original document. You will use the information on the cards to supply the information for each <variable>. If you use a typewriter, you must rekey the letter each time, supplying the necessary variables.

February ~~1~~ 25, 19--

<Sales Representative>
<Address>
<City>, <State> <Zip>

Dear <Name>:

Subject: New Product Sales Information

~~Nine~~ Sixteen new/revised software programs have been released by our Product Development Division since you received the first quarter price list. Attached is a listing of those products, the purchase order numbers, and the prices. The second quarter price list will be mailed to you prior to April 1.

Our Shipping Department has been instructed to send copies of these software packages along with the promotional materials that have been developed. You should receive them within the next ten days. Any questions you may have about these programs should be directed to our support specialists at (813) 277-6601.

If there are additional materials that will assist you in your sales efforts, please let us know.

Sincerely,

Sarah R. McLaughlin
Director of Marketing

xx

Attachment

EPI ■ EDUCATIONAL PRODUCTS, INC.
▲ 3929 Braddock Road, Fort Meyers, FL 33912-8357

Miss Janice B. Brown
Representative

(813) 277-6600

Home address:
310 Rossville Avenue
Chattanooga, TN 37408-8340

EPI ■ EDUCATIONAL PRODUCTS, INC.
▲ 3929 Braddock Road, Fort Meyers, FL 33912-8357

Mrs. Maureen C. McCarver
Representative

(813) 277-6600

Home address:
849 Rockridge Drive
Columbia, SC 29203-7401

EPI ■ EDUCATIONAL PRODUCTS, INC.
▲ 3929 Braddock Road, Fort Meyers, FL 33912-8357

Mr. Felipe R. Hernandez
Representative

(813) 277-6600

Home address:
2230 Atlantic Road
Miami, FL 33149-1745

WIDOW/ORPHAN

The widow/orphan feature prevents the printing of the last line of a paragraph at the top of a new page (widow) and the first line of a paragraph at the bottom of a page (orphan). The widow/orphan feature "protects" documents from containing these undesirable formatting features.

Before the widow/orphan feature is turned on, the cursor must be at the beginning of the text to be protected--usually at the beginning of the document. The feature may be turned on and off within a document. Use widow/orphan protection for proper page breaks in all documents of two or more pages.

Activity 14
Applying What You've Learned About Pagination

1. Read the copy at right.

2. Set a 60-space line and 5-space paragraph tab.

3. Center the title on line 10, pica; line 12 elite; QS between title and first line of body.

4. Key this document; DS all paragraphs.

5. If available, use the soft hyphen feature as you key.

6. Use the pagination feature allowing 54 lines per page; do not allow widows and orphans.

7. Create a header on line 6 of the second page; place the title **JOB HUNT** at the left margin and the page number flush right.

8. Proofread your work; make any necessary corrections.

9. Print a copy.

SHAKING THE BUSHES--THE JOB HUNT!

Finding a job can be faster and easier--and even more enjoyable--if you chart your course in the right direction.

First and foremost, know what you want to do. You should have some idea about "what you want to be when you grow up." Be active; don't let fate control your course! Take the initiative in your job hunt. Visit many prospects. The more you interview, the more comfortable you become. Another plus: Your enthusiasm about job hunting starts to soar.

Don't be too aggressive. Coming straight out and asking for a job is an approach considered to be too direct by many employers.

Be a Sherlock Holmes. Search for those individuals who are in the position to hire you. Try information interviewing. Talk to the people you will be working for (and with) as well as those to whom you will report directly. By asking questions such as How do you like your job? What do you do here? and What problems do you encounter? you gather information about a potential career.

The lyrics from a recent Broadway play said it well: **"Who am I anyway; am I my resume?"** Absolutely! Make sure your resume relates specifically to your objective. Focus on your skills, knowledge, experiences, and activities. Today's employer is looking for a well-rounded individual who can make a contribution to the company as well as to the community.

Sell yourself. Stress your fine points, such as your ability to communicate (oral and written skills), adaptability, flexibility, ability to learn, and your willingness to be retrained if need be. Smile! It's the enthusiasm in your eyes that clinches the interview.

Follow through. Send a thank-you note to the interviewer. Call to let the person know you're genuinely interested. Remember--persistence pays off.

140a-144a ▶ 5 (daily)

Warm up daily before starting job tasks by keying each line twice (slowly, then faster).

alphabet 1 Jack was extremely hopeful of having the Marquette jazz bands perform.

figures 2 You can call her at 836-4807 before 9 a.m. or at 836-2510 after 9 a.m.

fig/sym 3 Invoice #8604 totalled $371.29 after deducting the 15% sales discount.

speed 4 The girl may dismantle the bicycle and then go to the island to visit.

| 1 | 2 | 3 | 4 | 5 | 6 | 7 | 8 | 9 | 10 | 11 | 12 | 13 | 14 |

140b-144b ▶ 45 (daily)

Work Assignments

Job 1

plain full sheet

Processing Instructions From **Annette O'Toole**

Attached is a copy of the **New Product Price List.** *Rekey the document with the changes marked on the document.*

NEW PRODUCT PRICE LIST

February ~~1~~ 25, 19--

Number	Software	Price
B929	Basic Spreadsheets	$ 139
E246	Computer Geography	~~269~~ 259
E786	Computerized Reading	189
E561	Creative Business Letters	125
B821	Data Controller	~~329~~ 309
E320	English Enhancement	219
B689	Financial Advisor	99
E758	Keyboarding Composition Skills	155
E615	Language Arts Skills	139
B731	Quick Key WP	75
E641	Spelling Mastery	139
B658	Telephone Directory	119
B839	The Art Gallery	249
~~B658~~	~~Telephone Directory~~	~~119~~
B794	Your Time Manager	69
B952	Tax Assistant	129
B586	Graphics Designer	165

Activity 15
Learn to Search a Document for a Character String

1. Read the "In Brief" copy.
2. Study software documentation to learn to use the search feature.
3. Set 60-space line and 10-space paragraph tab.
4. Read paragraph at right, then key it DS as is.
5. Position cursor at beginning of text; search for character string **halo effect.** How many occurrences?
6. Return to beginning of document; search for the string **psychologists.** How many?

SEARCH

A *string* is a group of characters. A group of letters (hugs), numbers (394,823,315), symbols ("@&%!@#+*), or alphanumeric characters (A34C23Z9884TI) are all regarded as a string. A search feature allows you to search forward (and sometimes backward) through the document to locate a character string or a code (tab, hard return, etc.).

When you enter the proper command *(such as striking the F4 key)*, the program prompts (asks) you to enter the word to search for. When you strike the same key (or the return key), the program begins searching the document. Every time the designated string is found, the program highlights it or positions the cursor on it.

Research has shown that most employers make up their minds about job applicants in the first 30 seconds of an interview. These findings are based on what many psychologists refer to as the halo effect. The term halo effect refers to the first impression a person makes. A good first impression is called by psychologists a positive halo effect. A not-so-good first impression is called a negative halo effect. The point is that the first impression lingers--like a halo--causing it to become a lasting impression.

Activity 16
Learn to Use the Search and Replace Feature

1. Read the "In Brief" copy.
2. Study software documentation to learn to use the search and replace feature.
3. Set a 70-space line and a 10-space paragraph tab.
4. Read paragraph at right, then key it DS as is.
5. Move cursor to the beginning of text.
6. Search for every occurrence of **affect** and replace it with **effect.**
7. Move cursor to the beginning of document again.
8. Search for every occurrence of **hula** and replace it with **halo.**

SEARCH AND REPLACE

A feature that searches forward (or backward) through a document until it finds the designated character string or code and then replaces it with a new string that the user designates. Some programs also allow you to delete a string using the replace feature. A *discretionary replace* (sometimes called *selective search* or *search with confirmation*) allows you to replace character strings selectively. A *global replace* will automatically replace every occurrence of the designated character string. By entering the proper command, the program prompts you with special directions such as "Search For:" and "Replace With:". When the command is executed, the program locates each occurrence of the character string and replaces it with the new string.

Regardless of whether the hula affect is negative or positive, it radiates in all directions from the first affect or impression. People with a positive hula affect project a positive self-image, have a firm handshake, maintain eye contact, and smile. Generally, individuals who do not paint a confident and competent image have a cold, clammy handshake, do not maintain eye contact, and, therefore, radiate a negative hula affect.

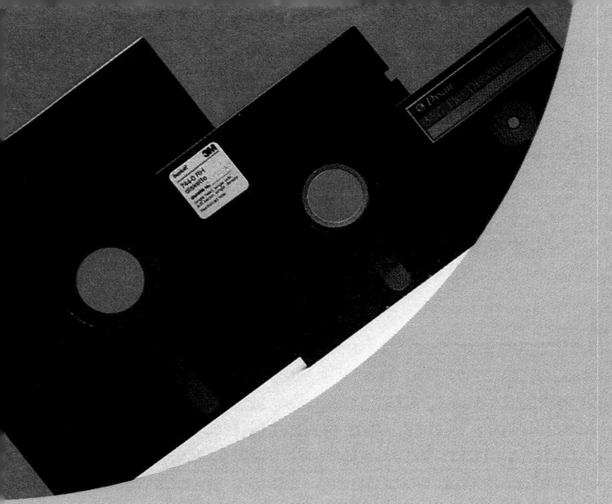

UNIT 32 *LESSONS 140 – 144*

Educational Products, Inc. (An Office Job Simulation)

Learning Goals

1. To become familiar with the keyboarding/formatting tasks in a firm that produces/markets educational software.

2. To learn selected terms frequently used in word processing.

3. To improve your ability to work from different copy sources and to detect and correct unidentified errors.

Documents Processed

1. Tables
2. Letters
3. Memorandums
4. Report/Sales Report
5. Agenda
6. Forms: Invoice and Purchase Order

EDUCATIONAL PRODUCTS, INC. AN OFFICE JOB SIMULATION

Before you begin processing the documents in this unit, read the information at the right carefully.

Make notes of any standard procedures that you think will save you time during the completion of the document production activities.

Daily work plan:

Conditioning practice .... 5′
Work on simulation ....45′

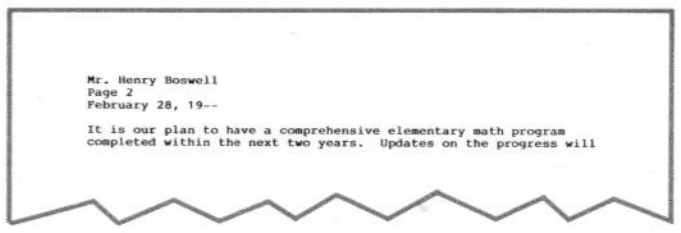

Mr. Henry Boswell
Page 2
February 28, 19--

It is our plan to have a comprehensive elementary math program completed within the next two years. Updates on the progress will

Second-Page Heading

Work Assignment

You have accepted a part-time position in the document processing center of Educational Products, Inc. (EPI) as a document processing trainee. EPI manufactures and sells educational software. The company is located at 3929 Braddock Road, Fort Meyers, FL 33912-8357. Your supervisor is Ms. Annette O'Toole, supervisor of the document processing center. In addition to training personnel, Ms. O'Toole is responsible for scheduling and coordinating the work load of the center's document processing specialists and trainees.

During your training program, you were instructed to format all company letters in block format with mixed punctuation. The originator's business title is to be keyed on the line below the originator's keyed name in the closing lines. The originators of the documents will specify the format they prefer for the memorandums you format.

Processing instructions from the supervisor of the center will be attached to each document you are given to complete. For some documents specific instructions are not given; you will be expected to make appropriate decisions on the basis of your knowledge and experience. Since EPI has based its word processing manual on your textbook, you can also use the text as a reference to assist you in making formatting decisions.

Some documents contain undetected errors that have been overlooked by the individual submitting the document. Correct those errors along with any keying errors you make before submitting your work to Ms. O'Toole.

Special guides for jobs requiring unusual specifications are provided in "Excerpts from EPI's Document Processing Procedures Manual." Review these guides before you begin your work.

Note: Students using electronic equipment should utilize the capabilities of the equipment in creating, editing, and storing documents. For example, Job 2 should be completed using the mail merge function.

Excerpts from EPI's Document Processing Procedures Manual

Leaders. Leaders are a series of periods and spaces (. . .) that are keyed between two items in tabular material to make reading easier. They "lead the reader's eye" from one columnar item to another. They are primarily used when the distance between certain items in two columns is so great that matching columnar items is difficult.

Leaders are made by alternating the period (.) and a space. The lines of leaders should be aligned in vertical rows and should end at the same point at the right.

To align leaders, key all periods on either the odd or the even numbers on the line-of-writing scale guided by their position in the first line of leaders. Begin the first line of leaders on the second space after the first item in the column and end the leaders 2 or 3 spaces to the left of the beginning of the next column.

Agenda. An agenda is one example of a business document that makes use of leaders. Educational Products, Inc. uses the nonjustified format for agendas (all items in Column 2 begin at the same horizontal point). The margins used for the agenda are: top, 1 or 1½″; side 1″; and bottom, 1″. The heading as well as the body of the agenda are double spaced. Study carefully the agenda shown below.

AGENDA

Marketing Meeting

February 12, 19--

1.	Call to Order	Sarah McLaughlin
2.	Minutes of Last Meeting	Greg White
3.	Special Reports	
	Southern Region Sales	Troy Colfax
	Eastern Region Sales	Sally Marshall

Second-page heading for correspondence. The heading for a two-page letter or memorandum begins on line 6. Key the heading SS in block format at the left margin. Include the name of the addressee, the page number, and the date. DS between the heading and the body.

Activity 17
Learn to Copy a Block of Text

1. Read the "In Brief" copy.
2. Study software documentation to learn to copy a text block.
3. Set a 60-space line and 5-space paragraph tab.
4. Read paragraph at right, then key it DS. Center the title using the bold feature.
5. Since the paragraph does not flow very well, it is your asignment to edit it.
6. Instead of trying to rewrite the original paragraph, copy it below its present location.
7. Use all the editing features you have learned until the paragraph is exactly as you want it.
8. Delete the original paragraph.
9. Print a copy.

COPY

Editing feature that allows you to define a block of text (word, phrase, sentence, paragraph, page, or document) in one location of a document and copy (repeat) it in another location of the same document or in a different document. The original block remains intact. First you identify the copy command by striking a specific keystroke combination *(such as the shift and F4 keys)*. Next you identify the block to be copied (word, phrase, etc.). Then you position the cursor in the location where the copied text will appear. To complete the copy function, strike the return key or a special function key as directed in your documentation.

THE RIGHT STUFF

Are you "cut out" to be an entrepreneur? Do you have the "right stuff" to launch a successful business? Some say success depends on education. Others base it on business savvy. Many still call it luck--being in the right place at the right time! What about an individual's personality? Clearly there is no single set of experiences from which today's entrepreneur emerges. What are your goals? Do you have a burning desire to be your own boss? If not, perhaps your goal is to start a business that grows rapidly and helps you amass a fortune. Depending on your goal, personality may be the key in determining your success and happiness.

Activity 18
Learn to Move a Block of Text

1. Read the "In Brief" copy.
2. Study software documentation to learn to move a text block.
3. Set a 70-space line and a 5-space paragraph tab.
4. Read paragraphs at right, then key SS as shown.
5. Using the move feature, make the following changes:

Line
1, move **today** after **loosely**
3, move **simply** after **it;** switch **tear** and **wear**
4, move **people** after **often**
10, move **television** after **viewing**
13 and 14, switch position of lines

6. Use the move feature to move second paragraph to end of the document.
7. Print a copy.

MOVE

Editing feature commonly called "cut and paste" that allows you to remove (cut) a block of text from one location in a document and place (paste) it in a different location within the same document. The original block is removed. First you identify the move command by striking a specific keystroke combination. Next you identify the block to be moved (cut out). Then you position the cursor in the location where the moved text will be retrieved (pasted). Finally, strike the return key or a special function key.

Stress today is a term used very loosely. Even though stress is something we are all aware of, we may find the term very difficult to define. To simply put it, stress is the rate of tear and wear within the body. People often report events as stressful when in reality these events turn out to be only symptoms. Some of the more frequently reported stressful events include the following:

Unfortunately, a common mistake we all make is to respond to stressful situations by avoiding them! A pizza binge, a night of television viewing for eight hours straight, or sleeping the weekend away produces nothing but guilt.

* Disagreements and conflict with friends and family.
* Too heavy a workload with never-ending deadlines.
* Demands being made by everyone around you.
* Social activities that are much more pressure than fun.

139a ▶ 5 Conditioning Practice

each line twice SS (slowly, then faster); DS between 2-line groups; if time permits, rekey selected lines

alphabet 1 Mrs. Waxler enjoyed checking the problems on the quiz she gave Friday.
figures 2 My 1992 salary was $28,741.56; however, after taxes it was $20,683.12.
fig/sym 3 This model (#94A-683) is $1,250; the other model (#94A-783) is $1,495.
speed 4 The proficient man did the work on the bicycle for them on the island.

| 1 | 2 | 3 | 4 | 5 | 6 | 7 | 8 | 9 | 10 | 11 | 12 | 13 | 14 |

139b ▶ 15 Language Skills: Compose at Keyboard

plain full sheets; SM: 1″

1. Applicants are often asked to respond to the questions at the right during an interview. Select four of the questions and compose your response. Number your responses and DS between paragraphs.

2. Edit your copy, marking corrections and changes to improve sentence structure and organization.

1 What would you like to be doing five years from now?
2 Give me three reasons why our firm should hire you.
3 Do your grades accurately reflect your ability? Explain why or why not?
4 Are you considering further education? Explain why or why not.
5 What are your greatest weaknesses.
6 What salary do you feel you should be paid during the first year?
7 What are your major accomplishments in life?
8 What have you learned from previous employment?

139c ▶ 30 Prepare Follow-Up Letters

plain full sheets; modified block format; blocked paragraphs; mixed punctuation; proofread and correct errors

Document 1

Format and key the follow-up letter at the right. Use personal-business letter format. Refer to page 240 for Ms. Murphy's address. Use **May 27, 19--** for the date. Supply missing letter parts.

Document 2

Study the guides for follow-up letters on page 239. Assume that you interviewed for the job you applied for in 136b, Document 2. Compose your follow-up letter; edit and prepare a final copy. Submit your first draft and final copy.

words

opening lines 10

Mr. Juan R. Gutierrez Director of Human Resources Cres- 20
well Manufacturing Co. 8352 West Oxford Avenue 29
Denver, CO 80236-7483 38

Thank you for talking with me about the secretarial 48
opening with Creswell Manufacturing Co. From our 58
discussion, I have a more complete understanding of 68
the requirements for the position. 76

My meeting with Ms. Karlstad was very beneficial. Why 87
those working with her speak so highly of her was quickly 98
apparent. Replacing Ms. Karlstad would be a challenge. I 110
would like the opportunity to face that challenge. 120

If there is further information that would be helpful as 132
you consider my application, please let me know. 142

closing lines 149

Activity 19
Learn to Use the Indent Feature

1. Read the "In Brief" copy.
2. Study software documentation to learn to use the indent feature.
3. Set a 60-space line and 5-space paragraph tab stop.
4. Read the copy at right.
5. Key the copy; DS paragraphs, SS indented text, underline and bold where indicated.
6. Proofread and correct your work; then print a copy.

INDENT

A tab stop set in the ruler/format line to mark the position where every line of text (paragraph or column) will begin from the left margin. When word wrap is on, strike a specific key *(such as F4)* and the indent feature remains in effect until the return key is struck.

THE LIFE OF THE PARTY?

Experts assure us that we're all boring people every now and then. Being judged boring makes most people more upset than being judged incompetent! Since boring people are often rejected because of their conversational style, don't let it happen to you. Be aware of these helpful tips:

1. **Behavior that is tedious.** A boring conversationalist drags a two-minute story into a fifteen-minute event.

2. **Preoccupation with one's self.** Often the most boring individual is the one who wants to talk only about herself/himself.

3. **Out to impress others.** Boring people work too hard to be funny and nice. They're always out to impress others. Often they lack a sense of humor resulting in a conversation that is always "serious."

To avoid being a "yawner" who puts others to sleep at a social gathering, give these tips a try:

1. **Help other people get involved.** Always try to involve other persons in conversation by making clear to each of them that they are as valuable as you.

2. **Ask questions.** To find out what another individual wants to talk about, ask questions. How else can you find a topic that interests her or him?

3. **Gain insight into the other person's feelings.** Ask the other person what he or she thinks about a specific topic. Then talk about that person's ideas and thoughts.

4. **Be natural; always be yourself.** Don't attempt to be witty or clever unless you are witty or clever.

5. **Smile!** A smile is the light in your window that tells people you're a caring individual--someone they'll like a lot.

138c ▶ 7
Simulated Employment Test: Straight-Copy Timed Writing

1. A 5′ writing on all ¶s.
2. Find *gwam* and number of errors.

all letters used	A	1.5 si	5.7 awl	80% hfw

gwam 3′ | 5′

Preparing employment documents is a vital part of securing a job. 4 3
These documents consist of a letter of application, a data sheet, and a 9 6
follow-up letter. Since these documents may be the most important docu- 14 8
ments that you will ever prepare, it is crucial that extra care be taken 19 11
to assure high quality. Within a few seconds a prospective employer 24 14
forms an initial opinion of you based on the letter of application and 28 17
the data sheet. If the opinion is a positive one, the documents will 33 20
be looked at further, and you may be invited for an interview. 37 22

An impressive data sheet is one that leaves the reader with a favor- 42 25
able impression of you and your abilities. The data sheet provides the 47 28
reader with detailed information about you. The reader learns who you 51 31
are, where you live, and how to contact you from the specifics outlined 56 34
by the first section of the data sheet. Other sections inform the reader 61 37
of your education, school activities, and work history. The last part of 66 40
the data sheet is often used to supply the reader with the names of peo- 71 42
ple to contact to acquire further specifics about you and your potential. 76 45

The letter of application accompanies the data sheet. It emphasizes 80 48
how you are qualified and why you should be hired for the job. If the 85 51
data sheet and letter impress the reader, you will be invited for an in- 90 54
terview. During the interview, you will be given the time to convince 95 57
the interviewer that you have the background and are the appropriate per- 99 60
son for the job. A day or two after the interview, a follow-up letter to 104 63
convey your appreciation to the interviewer for spending time with you 109 65
and to specify again your interest in the job is appropriate. 113 68

gwam 3′ | 1 | 2 | 3 | 4 | 5
gwam 5′ | 1 | 2 | 3

Activity 20
Learn to Use the Hanging Indent Feature

1. Read the "In Brief" copy.

2. Study software documentation to learn to use the hanging indent feature.

3. Set a 60-space line and 5- and 10-space tab stops.

4. Read the drill at right.

5. Key the drill; DS paragraphs, SS hanging indented text; bold where indicated.

6. Proofread and correct your work; then print a copy.

HANGING INDENT

When you enter a specific command *(such as striking the F4 key then holding down on the shift key and striking Tab),* this feature positions the first line of a paragraph at the left margin and the remaining lines indented at a specific tab stop from the left margin. Hanging indent remains until the return key is struck.

GETTING YOUR ACT TOGETHER

Are you involved in the drama club, student council, band, or sports? Have you acquired new interests during the past year? Is your head swimming with new projects? If so, you've probably been asking yourself the same question over and over: "How can I make sure I'll have time to fit everything into my busy schedule?"

The answer: A crash course in time management. Time management skills help you to make the most of each day and to meet your goals almost effortlessly. Consider the following tips for time management.

DAILY TO DOs. Take 10 minutes each morning (when you're fresh and alert) to make a daily "to do" list. Put everything on the list, from feeding the fish and paying a bill to meeting friends for dinner and studying for a test.

"A" AND "B" LISTS. Divide your list into two categories: the "A" items, things that are a must for today; and the "B" items, things that you can put off until tomorrow. When you've completed the lists, rank each item according to its importance, such as A1, A2, B1, B2, etc. This ranking helps you eliminate nonessential, time-consuming tasks from your schedule.

HAVE A MEETING--WITH YOURSELF. Do you let interruptions and distractions get in the way of accomplishing your goals? When the phone rings or a friend stops over to visit, do you stop what you're doing? If that behavior continues, you'll never achieve your objectives. Start setting aside an hour or an hour and a half each day for yourself. Turn off the radio and don't allow interruptions to distract you. Choose a time when your creativity is generally at its peak. Soon you'll find that scheduling a meeting with yourself allows you to accomplish many of your goals.

GET ORGANIZED! Stop spreading yourself thin. If you're like most people, you probably keep information in separate places: a calendar, a phone book, a schedule of appointments, and a datebook. Then you can't find the information when you need it. Purchase a pocket-sized reference folder (the handy, go-anywhere kind) and put all of your information in it. That way you're sure to have what you need when you need it.

138b (continued)

Document 3
Unbound Report

Format and key the material given at the right as an unbound report using the internal citation method for referencing. Use **INTEGRATED SOFTWARE** for the title of the report.

Document 4

Prepare a reference page from the information given below.

References

Clark, J. F., and others. Computers and Information Processing. 2d ed. Cincinnati: South-Western Publishing Co., 1990.

VanHuss, S. H., and W. R. Daggett, Jr. Electronic Information Systems. Cincinnati: South-Western Publishing Co., 1990.

words

title 4

Software packages are now available that combine word 18
processing, data base, and spreadsheet applications. This 29
allows the user to perform each of the applicatoins 40
seperately, or to merge information between applications. 53
Software packages that have this capability are called in- 64
tegrated software. These pack ages may include several dif- 76
ferent applications; however, wordprocessing, data base, and 88
spreadsheets are currently the most common applications. 101

Word Processing 107

Word Processing software provides the program to enable 115
a computer to do word processing applications. This allows 129
a user to create edit, and print documents using a computer. 143

The editing capability is extremely valuable. Editing 154
can be done at any time by loading a document back into 166
memory and display it on the scren. Various function keys 179
are used to insert, delete, copy, replace, and move informa- 191
tion. This has a great effect on the time and effort re- 207
quired to edit documents. 212

Spreadsheets 217

Spreadsheet programs allow the use of data for deci- 229
sion making purposes. Various forms of manual spreadsheets 241
have been used for many years. Computers which utilize cur- 253
rent spreadsheet softwar provide users with electronic 264
spreadsheets. Spreadsheets are being used by business firms 283
for financial analysis. Information gained from spread- 295
sheets decreases the uncertainty related to the outcomes of 307
potential decisions (VanHuss, 1990, 254-255). 318

Data Base 322

Data base software is used for collecting and maintaining 334
information (Clark and others, 1990, 215). This application 346
allows the extraction of information in different ways. 357
Those in decision-making positions are provided with more 369
information in a timely as well as cost-effective manner, 381
allowing the various alternatives to be considered more 393
thoroughly. 394

Activity 21
Learn to Set Column Tabs

1. Read the "In Brief" copy.
2. Study software documentation to learn to set column tabs.
3. Format the table SS; DS below the main heading.
4. Proofread and correct your work; then print the table.

COLUMN TABS

1. Identify the longest item in each column and determine the number of spaces to be placed between columns.
2. Use the automatic centering feature: key these items and spaces (Step 1) on the line.
3. Move the cursor to the beginning of the first column; note (write down) the cursor position.
4. Repeat Step 3 for each remaining column.
5. Clear all tabs in the ruler line.
6. Set tabs in the ruler line at the positions noted in Steps 3 and 4.
7. Delete the line keyed in Step 2.
8. Key the table.

SPELLING WORDS FOR WEEK OF 01/02/--

accommodate	committee	industrial	participation
appreciate	correspondence	interest	personnel
appropriate	customer	maintenance	possibility
categories	eligible	monitoring	recommend
commitment	immediately	necessary	services

Activity 22
Learn to Set Right Alignment Tabs

1. Read the "In Brief" copy.
2. Study software documentation to learn to set right alignment tabs.
3. Format Drill 1 DS.
4. Proofread and correct your work; then print the table.
5. Repeat Steps 3 and 4 for Drill 2.

RIGHT ALIGNMENT TAB

A tab position set in the ruler line to align a column of text on the right (called "flush right" or "right justified"). A right alignment tab is set in the last position of the longest line in the column.

Often a right alignment tab is set by striking R, which then may display on the ruler line. Copy that is keyed at that tab will "back up" from the tab, ending where the tab is set.

Follow the usual procedure for determining and setting the left margin and for noting (writing down) the position, EXCEPT place right tabs at the <u>end</u> of the column.

Drill 1

WOMEN'S TEAM CAPTAINS

Basketball	Diana Lindsay
Gymnastics	Lili Wong
Soccer	Adia Lopez
Softball	Nancy Brand
Volleyball	Glenda Ford

Drill 2

MEN'S TEAM CAPTAINS

Baseball	Ken Morrison
Basketball	Cy Briggs
Football	Joe Hererra
Gymnastics	Kevin Kwan
Soccer	Bo Simpson

Activity 23
Learn to Set Decimal Tabs

1. Read the "In Brief" copy.
2. Study software documentation to learn to set decimal tabs.
3. Format the table SS.
4. Proofread and correct the table; then print it.

DECIMAL TAB

A tab position set in the ruler line to align numbers at the decimal point. Follow the usual procedure for determining and setting the left margin and for determining tab positions, EXCEPT place decimal tabs at the decimal position, not at the beginning of the column. A decimal tab often is indicated by striking D, which then may display in the ruler line.

Figures entered at a decimal tab "back up" from the tab until the decimal key (.) is struck; then the figures appear aligned at the decimal point. Whole numbers are treated by the decimal tab feature as though a decimal point follows the last figure.

TEST SCORES/AVERAGE SCORE--UNITS 1-3

Adams, R.	75	89.5	82.75	82.42
Ellis, L.	89.25	94	96.25	93.17
Jenkins, Z.	68.75	75.25	71	71.67
Oblinger, S.	85	89	93.5	89.17
Trabel, D.	71.5	68.25	75	71.58
Worrell, K.	82.75	89	75.5	82.42

138a ▶ 5 Conditioning Practice

each line twice SS (slowly, then faster); DS between 2-line groups; if time permits, rekey selected lines

alphabet 1 Jared Buckly reviewed the next eight steps required for modernization.
figures 2 The librarian purchased 5,790 books during 1991 and 4,863 during 1992.
fig/sym 3 The order for 19 desks (invoice #8A23) came to $7,640 with the 5% tax.
speed 4 The neighbor of the tax auditor of the firm did the work on the docks.

| 1 | 2 | 3 | 4 | 5 | 6 | 7 | 8 | 9 | 10 | 11 | 12 | 13 | 14 |

138b ▶ 38 Simulated Employment Test: Letter, Table, Report

Time Schedule

Applicant Time to Review Documents and Ask Questions .... 6′
Employment Production Test .... 30′
(includes proofreading time--applicant will be notified when five minutes remain)

plain full sheet; correct errors as you key

Document 1
Letter
block format; open punctuation

words

November 15, 19-- | Mr. Joshua D. Cline, President | Chadwick Insurance 14
Company | 3209 Roosevelt Way, NE | Seattle, WA 98105-6385 | Dear Mr. Cline | 28
Subject: Bellevue Branch Office 34

The renovation of the building we leased for the new branch office in 48
Bellevue is scheduled to be completed by December 1. This schedule should 63
give us ample time to have the branch operational by the target date of 78
December 15. 81

Erika Tudor from the Seattle home office has been promoted to branch 94
manager and will be in Bellevue by the first of December. Jason Reeves has 110
agreed to transfer from the Tacoma branch to be Erika's assistant. I am 124
confident they will do an exceptional job. 133

A complete roster of the Bellevue office personnel is enclosed. Two of 147
the agents are transferring from Seattle. The others are new and will have 163
completed our trainee program by December 10. 172

I will keep you informed on the progress of the Bellevue branch; I am sure 187
that it will be an excellent addition to our company. (163) 198

Sincerely | Parker S. Hawthorne | District Supervisor | xx | Enclosure 210/**231**

Document 2
Table
plain full sheet; DS;
CS: 8; center column headings

Bellevue Branch 3
November 15, 19-- 7

Name and Position	Location	Phone	
			21
Erika Tudor, Branch Manager	100b	252-1903	29
Jason Reeves, Assistant	102	252-4871	37
Dyan Silverhill, Secretary	100a	252-3010	46
Courtney Edinburg, Agent	110	252-9618	54
Phillip Guerrero, Agent	104	252-1765	62
Forrest Hewitt, Agent	108	252-6913	69
Chieh Kaneko, Agent	106	252-1655	76

Begin all tables on line 10 or as directed by your teacher. Clear all preset tabs from the ruler line before setting tabs for a table.

Activity 24
Two-Column Table with Right Alignment Tab

1. Format the table at the right DS. Use the centering feature to center the main and secondary headings; use a right alignment tab for the right-hand column.

2. Proofread and correct errors; then print the table.

Riverfront Dinner Show

Week of March 12-16

Dinner Music	Lou Springer
Emcee	Eric Simpson
Dance Demo	Valley School of Dance
Music and Humor	Halcyon Days
Comedy	Fred Hines
Dance Band	Halcyon Days

Activity 25
Three-Column Table with Column and Right Alignment Tabs

1. Format the table at the right SS. Use the centering feature to center the main and secondary headings; use the bold feature for the main heading. Block the column heads as shown.

2. Use the underline feature to key a line a DS below the table; then DS to the source note. (If your equipment will not display or print the line, insert the line with a pen on the printed table.)

MOTION PICTURE ACADEMY AWARDS (OSCARS)

1980 - 1989

Year	Movie Title	Studio
1989	Ordinary Peopel	Paramount
1981	Chariots of Fire	Warner Bros
1982	Gandhi	Columbia
1983	Terms of Endeerment	Paramount
1984	Amadeus	Orion Pictures
1985	Out of Africa	Universal
1986	Platoon	Orion Pictures
1987	The Last Emperor	Columbia
1988	Rain Main	United Artists
1989	Driving Miss Daisy	Warner Bros.

Source: Information Please Almanac, 1990.

Activity 26
Multi-Column Table with Decimal Tab

1. Format the table at the right DS. Use the centering feature to center the main and secondary headings. To determine the left margin (center the table), use the column heading if it is the longest line in the column. Key the column headings before setting decimal table.

2. Use the underline feature to key a line between the table and source note or use a pen to insert the line on the printed table.

3. Proofread and correct the table; then print.

Temperature of Selected Metropolitan Areas

Average Monthly Fahrenheit Degrees

Metro Area	January	April	July	October
Chicago	21.4	48.8	73	53.5
Dallas-Fort Worth	44	65.9	86.3	67.9
Detroit	23.4	47.3	71.9	51.9
Houston	51.4	68.7	83.1	69.7
Los Angeles	56	59.5	69	66.3
New York	31.8	51.9	76.4	57.5
Washington	35.2	56.7	78.9	59.3

Source: Information Please Almanac, 1990.

APPLICATION FOR EMPLOYMENT

AN EQUAL OPPORTUNITY EMPLOYER

PLEASE PRINT WITH BLACK INK OR USE TYPEWRITER

NAME (LAST, FIRST, MIDDLE INITIAL)	SOCIAL SECURITY NUMBER	CURRENT DATE
Murphy, Leslie-Ann	520-38-8151	May 21, 19--

ADDRESS (NUMBER, STREET, CITY, STATE, ZIP CODE)	HOME PHONE NO.
358 Knox Court, Denver, CO 80219-6482	(303) 492-2950

REACH PHONE NO.	U.S. CITIZEN?	DATE YOU CAN START
	YES X NO	June 10, 19--

ARE YOU EMPLOYED NOW?	IF SO, MAY WE INQUIRE OF YOUR PRESENT EMPLOYER?
No	

TYPE OF WORK DESIRED	REFERRED BY	SALARY DESIRED
Secretarial	Ms. Carolyn Baxter	$ Open

IF RELATED TO ANYONE IN OUR EMPLOY, STATE NAME AND POSITION

	YES	NO	IF YES, EXPLAIN
DO YOU HAVE ANY PHYSICAL CONDITION THAT MAY PREVENT YOU FROM PERFORMING CERTAIN KINDS OF WORK?		X	
HAVE YOU EVER BEEN CONVICTED OF A FELONY?		X	

EDUCATION

	EDUCATIONAL INSTITUTION	LOCATION (CITY, STATE)	DATES ATTENDED FROM MO.	FROM YR.	TO MO.	TO YR.	DIPLOMA, DEGREE, OR CREDITS EARNED	CLASS STANDING (CHK QUARTER) 1	2	3	4	MAJOR SUBJECTS STUDIED
COLLEGE												
HIGH SCHOOL	Lincoln High School	Denver, Colorado	8	87	5	91	Diploma	X				Admin. Services
GRADE SCHOOL												
OTHER												

LIST BELOW THE POSITIONS THAT YOU HAVE HELD (LAST POSITION FIRST)

1. NAME AND ADDRESS OF FIRM The Exercise Place 315 Bellaire Way Denver, CO 80233-4302	DESCRIBE POSITION RESPONSIBILITIES Maintained customer data base, responded to customer inquiries, and assisted with customer billing.
NAME OF SUPERVISOR Miss Linda Morrison	
EMPLOYED (MO-YR) FROM: 9/90 TO: 5/91	REASON FOR LEAVING Co-op program during school year.
2. NAME AND ADDRESS OF FIRM Copper Mountain Resort P.O. Box 3001 Copper Mountain, CO 80443-7011	DESCRIBE POSITION RESPONSIBILITIES Processed mail and telephone reservations for resort guests.
NAME OF SUPERVISOR Mr. Jarome Nielson	
EMPLOYED (MO-YR) FROM: 5/90 TO: 8/90	REASON FOR LEAVING Summer employment.
3. NAME AND ADDRESS OF FIRM Lakeside Amusement Park 4601 Sheridan Boulevard Denver, CO 80212-1240	DESCRIBE POSITION RESPONSIBILITIES Ride attendant.
NAME OF SUPERVISOR Mr. Jason Anderson	
EMPLOYED (MO-YR) FROM: 5/89 TO: 8/89	REASON FOR LEAVING Summer employment.

I UNDERSTAND THAT I SHALL NOT BECOME AN EMPLOYEE UNTIL I HAVE SIGNED AN EMPLOYMENT AGREEMENT WITH THE FINAL APPROVAL OF THE EMPLOYER AND THAT SUCH EMPLOYMENT WILL BE SUBJECT TO VERIFICATION OF PREVIOUS EMPLOYMENT, DATA PROVIDED IN THIS APPLICATION, ANY RELATED DOCUMENTS, OR RESUME. I KNOW THAT A REPORT MAY BE MADE THAT WILL INCLUDE INFORMATION CONCERNING ANY FACTOR THE EMPLOYER MIGHT FIND RELEVANT TO THE POSITION FOR WHICH I AM APPLYING, AND THAT I CAN MAKE A WRITTEN REQUEST FOR ADDITIONAL INFORMATION AS TO THE NATURE AND SCOPE OF THE REPORT IF ONE IS MADE.

Leslie-Ann Murphy

SIGNATURE OF APPLICANT

Application for Employment Form

Begin all tables on line 10 or as directed by your teacher. Clear all preset tabs from the ruler line before setting tabs for a table.

Activity 27
Three-Column Table with Right, Column, and Decimal Tab

1. Format the table at the right DS, setting the appropriate tab for each column. Block the column headings as shown. Key the column headings before setting tabs.

2. Proofread; correct errors; print the table.

PRICE QUOTATION FOR MORTON ASSOCIATES INC.

Item No.	Description	Unit Price
PC-4001A	Microprocessor	$2,895
PC-4031A	Input/Output Units	589
PC-4041A	Dual Disk Drive	416
4050N	Color Monitor	325
4054M	B/W Monitor	195
840X	Glare Guard	94.94
PC-4024A	Dot Matrix Printer	325
7210X	Printer Stand	194.95
704X	Power Surge Stripe	69.95

Activity 28
Four-Column Table with Varied Tabs

1. Format the table at the right DS, using the appropriate tab for each column. Note (write down) the positions where columns begin and end; on a separate list note the position for each tab.

2. To center column headings, add the numbers representing the beginning and ending positions of the column; divide by 2. (The result is the center of the column.) Count the spaces in the column heading; divide by 2. Subtract the result from the center position. (Begin the column heading in this position.)

3. Proofread your work, checking for format errors as well as misstrokes. Make necessary corrections; then print the table.

CLIENT CONTACTS MADE BY SHEILA SANDERS

Week Ending February 2, 19--

Client	Date	Hours	Site
Swatzky	January 28	1.5	His Office
Grossmane	January 29	.17	Telephone
Schlosser	January 29	.42	Telephone
Wagner	January 30	2	Their Office
Cook	January 30	2.25	Their Office
Washburn	January 31	1.75	Their Office
Murphy	January 31	1	My Office
O'Connor	February 1	.75	Telephone
Daniel	February 1	1.5	Their Office
Miller	February 2	2.5	Their Office

Activity 29
Four-Column Table with Decimal and Right Alignment Tabs

1. Format the table at the right SS, using the appropriate tab for each column. Center the column headings (See Step 2, Activity 28).

2. Use the underline feature as you key the last number in each amount column. (If necessary, insert the underlines on the printed table with a pen.)

3. Proofread carefully before printing the table.

Regional Sales
(In Millions)

Region	This Year	Last Year	% Change
Central	$3.0	$2.8	7% inc.
Northeast	.6	.5	20% inc.
Northwest	2.1	2.0	5% inc.
Southeast	1.8	1.8	0% none
Southwest	1.6	1.4	14% inc.
Total	$9.1	$8.5	

136b (continued)

Document 2

Review the application letter guidelines on p. 239. Compose at the keyboard a rough-draft letter applying for one of the positions shown at the right. Edit/revise your letter; then process it in final form.

SECRETARY

Immediate opening for school secretary. Full-time position requires good communication skills, telephone etiquette, and keyboarding skill of 45-55 wpm. Knowledge of modern office equipment is a must.

Must be able to work with students, faculty, and school visitors. Send data sheet and letter of application to

Wayne S. Jorgenson
Superintendent
North School District
7523 Mcgregor Street
Detroit, MI 48209-2431

ADMINISTRATIVE ASSISTANT

Assistant to the Marketing Vice President. Large company seeks outgoing individual with good keyboarding and shorthand skills.

Interested applicants must have a minimum keyboarding skill of 50 wpm and a minimum shorthand skill of 80 wpm. Experience preferred, but will consider applicants with no previous experience who possess excellent keyboarding and shorthand skills.

To apply, send letter of application and data sheet to

Director of Human Resources
Steele Manufacturing Company
697 Brookwood Court
Joliet, IL 60435-9203

WORD PROCESSING

Bachman Consulting Services has an opening in the Word Processing Department for a detail-oriented individual with excellent transcription skills.

Machine transcription and word processing training desirable. Must have keyboarding skill of 50 wpm.

Send letter of application and data sheet to

Miss Judith L. Painter
Personnel Director
Bachman Consulting Services
840 Belvidere Street
Boston, MA 02115-7301

KEYBOARDING OPERATOR

Small insurance company has full-time position for a keyboarding operator. Applicant must be able to key 40 wpm, perform basic math operations, and project professional telephone image.

Apply to

Ms. Mary A. Stetson
Office Manager
Crandall Insurance Company
330 University Drive
Pine Bluff, AR 71601-4011

Lesson 137 Application Form/Composing

137a ▶ 5 Conditioning Practice

each line twice SS (slowly, then faster); DS between 2-line groups; if time permits, rekey selected lines

alphabet 1 I would be very amazed if he objects to the back exercising equipment.
figures 2 Table A on page 3 lists 2,068 births in 1991 and 3,754 births in 1992.
fig/sym 3 A 17% discount off the marked price ($26,930.00) amounts to $4,578.10.
speed 4 If all the girls go to the formal social, she may pay for their gowns.

| 1 | 2 | 3 | 4 | 5 | 6 | 7 | 8 | 9 | 10 | 11 | 12 | 13 | 14 |

137b ▶ 45 Prepare Application Forms

LP pp. 125-127

Document 1 LP p. 125

Format and key the application form on p. 243. Correct any errors you make as you key the copy.

Document 2 LP p. 127

Use LP p. 127 as the application for employment form to apply for the position you selected in 136b.

You should review the form and make a few notes before entering your personal data on the form.

Activity 30

Learn About Boilerplate Documents, the Merge Feature, and Stop Codes

1. Read the "In Brief" copy.

2. Study software documentation to learn which specific features are offered by your program.

3. Format the memo (60-space line) at the right below on plain paper. Set a right alignment tab for the colon sequence and a tab for the text in the memo headings. DS between memo headings.

4. Key the document using your program's stop code (or merge code) wherever the @1, @2, @3, etc., symbol appears.

5. Save the document.

6. Print the document three times; insert the following variables in the first printout.

@1 Olivian DeSouza
@2 (yesterday's date)
@3 Ms. DeSouza
@4 crepe hangers
@5 "It won't work"
@6 downers
@7 Ms. DeSouza
@8 Thursday morning

The second document variables:

@1 Maurizio Chuidioni
@2 (today's date)
@3 Mr. Chuidioni
@4 ones with their chins on their shoes
@5 "It's no use trying"
@6 pessimists
@7 Mr. Chuidioni
@8 Wednesday afternoon

The third document variables:

@1 Miyoki Kojima
@2 (tomorrow's date)
@3 Dr. Kojima
@4 ones who think nothing ever goes their way and
@5 "Are you serious?"
@6 negativists
@7 Dr. Kojima
@8 Tuesday afternoon

BOILERPLATE DOCUMENT

A document, such as a form letter or sales contract that is used again and again, in which most of the text remains the same each time. Only names and certain details, such as amounts and dates, are changed here and there within the document.

CONSTANT

The text in a boilerplate document that remains the same for each use of the document.

VARIABLE

The text (names, phrases, dates, etc.) in a boilerplate document that is changed to "personalize" the document.

STOP CODES

A command (or symbol) embedded within a boilerplate document. While printing a document, the printer stops when it recognizes the "stop" command allowing the user to key variable (personalized) information. The user then must strike a designated key to reactivate the printer until the next stop code is recognized.

PRIMARY DOCUMENT

A word processing document made up of the constant and embedded codes.

SECONDARY DOCUMENT

A word processing document consisting only of the variables.

MERGE

Word processing feature that allows the user to combine a primary document and secondary documents to print "personalized" documents.

TO: @1
FROM: Dan Henderson
SUBJECT: Positively! Seminars
DATE: @2

Although they're often reasonably competent people, negativists can unnerve, devitalize, exhaust, and fatigue the best of us. I'm certain, @3, that you've met at least one or two of them. They're the @4 who respond to anyone else's productive suggestion with @5 or "Forget it, we tried that last year" or "Why waste your time; they'll never let you do it."

What is needed to get the best from @6 in the workplace? An upbeat attitude, that's what! Have you checked yours lately? We all have the potential for being dragged down into despair. @7, is your attitude showing?

This question and many others will be answered for you in the Positively! seminars next week. The seminar presenter, Adele Cook, a nationally known speaker/trainer/consultant, will conduct sessions in Conference Room D.

Sessions are scheduled from 1 to 4 on Monday through Thursday and from 9 to 12 on Tuesday through Friday. The people in your area are to attend the @8 session.

This seminar will pick up where Ms. Cook's sessions ended last year. Distribute the attached materials, please.

Attachments

Lesson 135 — Personal Data Sheet/Composing

135a ▶ 5 Conditioning Practice

each line twice SS (slowly, then faster); DS between 2-line groups; if time permits, rekey selected lines

alphabet 1 Vicky Lopez is extremely qualified for a management job with our firm.

figures 2 Crowds of 49,872 and 51,360 saw the games between the Giants and Mets.

fig/sym 3 The invoice (96A103) which is for $2,745 should be paid before June 8.

speed 4 She is apt to yell when they cut down the iris by the giant cornfield.

| 1 | 2 | 3 | 4 | 5 | 6 | 7 | 8 | 9 | 10 | 11 | 12 | 13 | 14 |

135b ▶ 45 Prepare Data Sheets

plain full sheets; SM: 1″; PB: 1″

Document 1

Format and key the data sheet shown on page 240.

Document 2

Compose at the keyboard a rough-draft data sheet for yourself using the guidelines on p. 239 and the model on p. 240. Edit; then key a final copy.

Lesson 136 — Application Letter/Composing

136a ▶ 5 Conditioning Practice

each line twice SS (slowly, then faster); DS between 2-line groups; if time permits, rekey selected lines

alphabet 1 Gavin expects the banker to formalize quite a few details before July.

figures 2 Jay hit .359 with 86 singles, 20 doubles, 7 triples, and 14 home runs.

fig/sym 3 Our 1993-1994 service & supply budget was $16,780, an increase of 25%.

speed 4 The eight girls and the auditor may burn down the shanty by city hall.

| 1 | 2 | 3 | 4 | 5 | 6 | 7 | 8 | 9 | 10 | 11 | 12 | 13 | 14 |

136b ▶ 45 Prepare Application Letters

plain full sheets; modified block format; blocked ¶s; mixed punctuation; proofread and correct errors

Document 1

Format and key the application letter for Ms. Leslie-Ann Murphy. If necessary, refer to the illustration on p. 239. Use personal-business letter format and begin return address on line 10. Refer to data sheet on p. 240 for Ms. Murphy's return address.

words

May 15, 19-- |Mr. Juan R. Gutierrez |Director of Human Resources |Creswell 14
Manufacturing Co. |8352 West Oxford Avenue |Denver, CO 80236-7483 |Dear 28
Mr. Gutierrez: 31

Ms. Carolyn Baxter, my administrative services instructor, informed me of 46
the secretarial position with your company that will be available June 10. 61
She speaks very highly of your organization. After learning more about the 77
position, I am confident that I am qualified and would like to be considered 92
for the assignment. 96

Currently I am completing my senior year at Lincoln High School. All of my 111
elective courses have been in the administrative services area. This includes 127
courses in information processing, shorthand, and business procedures. I 142
have a keyboarding skill of 60 words a minute and a shorthand skill of 80 157
words a minute. The information processing class was taught using com- 171
puters. We were instructed in word processing, spreadsheet, and data base 186
applications. As an office assistant, I have been able to utilize these skills 202
on the job. 204

My work experience and school activities have given me the opportunity to 219
work with people to achieve group goals. Participating in FBLA has given 234
me a better appreciation for the business world. 244

I would appreciate the opportunity to interview with you to discuss the pos- 259
sibility of employment. You may call me weekdays after 3:30 p.m. 272

Sincerely, |Ms. Leslie-Ann Murphy |xx |Enclosure 281

Leslie-Ann Murphy
358 Knox Court
Denver, CO 80219-6482
(303) 492-2950 QS

EDUCATION DS

Senior at Lincoln High School
High School Diploma, pending graduation
Major Emphasis: Administrative Services
Grade Average: 3.50; upper 15% of class DS

SCHOOL ACTIVITIES DS

Future Business Leaders of America Secretary, senior year; member for three years. DS

National Honor Society, junior and senior years. DS

High School Yearbook Treasurer, senior year; member for two years. DS

WORK EXPERIENCE

Office Assistant, The Exercise Place, Denver, Colorado, September 1990 to present. Work 15 hours a week as an office assistant; maintain customer data base, respond to customer inquiries, and assist with customer billing.

Reservations Clerk, Copper Mountain Resort, Copper Mountain, Colorado, summer 1990. Processed mail and telephone reservations for resort guests.

Concessionnaire, Lakeside Amusement Park, Denver, Colorado, summer 1989.

REFERENCES (by permission)

Ms. Carolyn M. Baxter, Administrative Services Instructor, Lincoln High School, 2285 South Federal Boulevard, Denver, CO 80219-4312 (303) 329-3300.

Miss Linda A. Morrison, Owner, The Exercise Place, 3850 Jordan Drive, Denver, CO 80221-9020 (303) 243-2561.

Mr. Jarome C. Nielson, Resort Manager, Copper Mountain Resort, P.O. Box 3001, Copper Mountain, CO 80443-7011 (303) 458-2000.

Data Sheet

CAPITALIZATION GUIDES

Capitalize

1 The first word of every sentence and the first word of every complete direct quotation. Do not capitalize (a) fragments of quotations or (b) a quotation resumed within a sentence.

She said, "Hard work is necessary for success."
He stressed the importance of "a sense of values."
"When all else fails," he said, "follow directions."

2 The first word after a colon if that word begins a complete sentence.

Remember this: Work with good techniques.
We carry these sizes: small, medium, and large.

3 First, last, and all other words in titles of books, articles, periodicals, headings, and plays, except words of four or fewer letters used as articles, conjunctions, or prepositions.

Century 21 Keyboarding — "How to Buy a House"
Saturday Review — "The Sound of Music"

4 An official title when it precedes a name or when used elsewhere if it is a title of distinction.

President Lincoln — She is the Prime Minister.
The doctor is in. — He is the class treasurer.

5 Personal titles and names of people and places.

Miss Franks — Dr. Jose F. Ortez — San Diego

6 All proper nouns and their derivatives.

Canada — Canadian Festival — France — French food

7 Days of the week, months of the year, holidays, periods of history, and historic events.

Sunday — Labor Day — New Year's Day
June — Middle Ages — Civil War

8 Geographic regions, localities, and names.

the North — Upstate New York — Mississippi River

9 Street, avenue, company, etc., when used with a proper noun.

Fifth Avenue — Avenue of the Stars — Armour & Co.

10 Names of organizations, clubs, and buildings.

Girl Scouts — 4-H Club — Carew Tower

11 A noun preceding a figure except for common nouns such as *line*, *page*, and *sentence*, which may be keyed with or without a capital.

Style 143 — Catalog 6 — page 247 — line 10

12 Seasons of the year only when they are personified.

icy fingers of Winter — the soft kiss of Spring

NUMBER EXPRESSION GUIDES

Use words for

1 Numbers from one to ten except when used with numbers above ten, which are keyed as figures. Note: Common business practice is to use figures for all numbers except those which begin a sentence.

Was the order for four or eight books?
Order 8 shorthand books and 15 English books.

2 A number beginning a sentence.

Fifteen persons are here; 12 are at home sick.

3 The shorter of two numbers used together.

ten 50-gallon drums — 350 five-gallon drums

4 Isolated fractions or indefinite amounts in a sentence.

Nearly two thirds of the students are here.
About twenty-five people came to the meeting.

5 Names of small-numbered streets and avenues (ten and under).

1020 Sixth Street — Tenth Avenue

Use figures for

1 Dates and time, except in very formal writing.

May 9, 1982 — 10:15 a.m.
ninth of May — four o'clock

2 A series of fractions.

Key 1/2, 1/4, 5/6, and 7 3/4.

3 Numbers following nouns.

Rule 12 — page 179 — Room 1208 — Chapter 15

4 Measures, weights, and dimensions.

6 ft. 9 in. tall — 5 lbs. 4 oz. — 8 1/2" × 11"

5 Definite numbers used with the percent sign (%); but use *percent* (spelled) with approximations in formal writing.

The rate is 15 1/2%.
About 50 percent of the work is done.

6 House numbers except house number One.

1915-42d Street — One Jefferson Avenue

7 Sums of money except when spelled for extra emphasis. Even sums may be keyed without the decimal.

$10.75 — 25 cents — $300
seven hundred dollars ($700)

PUNCTUATION GUIDES

Use an apostrophe

1 As a symbol for *feet* in billings or tabulations or as a symbol for *minutes.* (The quotation mark may be used as a symbol for *seconds* and *inches.*)

12′ × 16′ 3′ 54″ 8′6″ × 10′8″

2 As a symbol to indicate the omission of letters or figures (as in contractions).

can't wouldn't Spirit of '76

3 To form the plural of most figures, letters, and words used as words rather than for their meaning: Add the *apostrophe and s.* In market quotations, form the plural of figures by the addition of *s* only.

6's A's five's ABC's Century Fund 4s

4 To show possession: Add the *apostrophe and s* to (a) a singular noun and (b) a plural noun which does not end in *s.*

a man's watch women's shoes boy's bicycle

Add the *apostrophe and s* to a proper name of one syllable which ends in *s.*

Bess's Cafeteria Jones's bill

Add the *apostrophe only* after (a) plural nouns ending in *s* and (b) a proper name of more than one syllable which ends in *s* or *z.*

boys' camp Adams' home Melendez' report

Add the *apostrophe* after the last noun in a series to indicate joint or common possession of two or more persons; however, add the possessive to each of the nouns to show separate possession of two or more persons.

Lewis and Clark's expedition
the manager's and the treasurer's reports

Use a colon

1 To introduce an enumeration or a listing.

These are my favorite poets: Shelley, Keats, and Frost.

2 To introduce a question or a long direct quotation.

This is the question: Did you study for the test?

3 Between hours and minutes expressed in figures.

10:15 a.m. 12:00 4:30 p.m.

Use a comma (or commas)

1 After (a) introductory words, phrases, or clauses and (b) words in a series.

If you can, try to visit Chicago, St. Louis, and Dallas.

2 To set off short direct quotations.

She said, "If you try, you can reach your goal."

3 Before and after (a) words which come together and refer to the same person, thing, or idea and (b) words of direct address.

Clarissa, our class president, will give the report.
I was glad to see you, Terrence, at the meeting.

4 To set off nonrestrictive clauses (not necessary to the meaning of the sentence), but not restrictive clauses (necessary to the meaning).

Your report, which deals with the issue, is great.
The girl who just left is my sister.

5 To separate the day from the year and the city from the state.

July 4, 1986 New Haven, Connecticut

6 To separate two or more parallel adjectives (adjectives that could be separated by the word "and" instead of the comma).

a group of young, old, and middle-aged persons

Do not use commas to separate adjectives so closely related that they appear to form a single element with the noun they modify.

a dozen large red roses a small square box

7 To separate (a) unrelated groups of figures which come together and (b) whole numbers into groups of three digits each (however, *policy, year, page, room, telephone,* and most *serial numbers* are shown without commas).

During 1991, 1,750 cars were insured under Policy 806423.
page 1042 Room 1184 (213) 825-2626

Use a dash

1 For emphasis.

The icy road--slippery as a fish--was a hazard.

2 To indicate a change of thought.

We may tour the Orient--but I'm getting ahead of my story.

3 To introduce the name of an author when it follows a direct quotation.

"Hitting the wrong key is like hitting me."--Armour

4 For certain special purposes.

"Well--er--ah," he stammered.
"Jay, don't get too close to the --." It was too late.

Use an exclamation mark

1 After emphatic interjections.

Wow! Hey there! What a day!

2 After sentences that are clearly exclamatory.

"I won't go!" she said with determination.
How good it was to see you in New Orleans last week!

Use a hyphen

1 To join compound numbers from twenty-one to ninety-nine that are keyed as words.

forty-six fifty-eight over seventy-six

2 To join compound adjectives before a noun which they modify as a unit.

well-laid plans six-year period two-thirds majority

3 After each word or figure in a series of words or figures that modify the same noun (suspended hyphenation).

first-, second-, and third-class reservations

4 To spell out a word or name.

s-e-p-a-r-a-t-e G-a-e-l-i-c

5 To form certain compound nouns.

WLW-TV teacher-counselor AFL-CIO

Use parentheses

1 To enclose parenthetical or explanatory matter and added information.

The amendments (Exhibit A) are enclosed.

2 To enclose identifying letters or figures in lists.

Check these factors: (1) period of time, (2) rate of pay, and (3) nature of duties.

3 To enclose figures that follow spelled-out amounts to give added clarity or emphasis.

The total award is five hundred dollars ($500).

Use a question mark

At the end of a sentence that is a direct question; however, use a period after a request in the form of a question.

What day do you plan to leave for Honolulu?
Will you mail this letter for me, please.

Use quotation marks

1 To enclose direct quotations.

He said, "I'll be there at eight o'clock."

2 To enclose titles of articles and other parts of complete publications, short poems, song titles, television programs, and unpublished works like theses and dissertations.

"Sesame Street" "Chicago" by Sandburg
"Laura's Theme" "Murder She Wrote"

3 To enclose special words or phrases, or coined words.

"power up" procedure "Murphy's Law"

Use a semicolon

1 To separate two or more independent clauses in a compound sentence when the conjunction is omitted.

Being critical is easy; being constructive is not so easy.

2 To separate independent clauses when they are joined by a conjunctive adverb (*however, consequently,* etc.).

I can go; however, I must get excused.

3 To separate a series of phrases or clauses (especially if they contain commas) that are introduced by a colon.

These officers were elected: Lu Ming, President; Lisa Stein, vice president; Juan Ramos, secretary.

4 To precede an abbreviation or word that introduces an explanatory statement.

She organized her work; for example, putting work to be done in folders of different colors to indicate degrees of urgency.

Use an underline

1 With titles of complete works such as books, magazines, and newspapers. (Such titles may also be keyed in ALL CAPS without the underline.)

Superwrite The New York Times TV Guide

2 To call attention to special words or phrases (or you may use quotation marks). **Note:** Use a continuous underline unless each word is to be considered separately.

Stop keying when time is called.
Spell these words: steel, occur, separate.

Use a singular verb

1 With a singular subject.

The weather is clear but cold.

2 With an indefinite pronoun used as a subject (each, every, any, either, neither, one, etc.).

Each of you is to bring a pen and paper.
Neither of us is likely to be picked.

3 With singular subjects linked by *or* or *nor.* If, however, one subject is singular and the other is plural, the verb should agree with the closer subject.

Either Jan or Fred is to make the presentation.
Neither the principal nor the teachers are here.

4 With a collective noun (*committee, team, class, jury,* etc.) if the collective noun acts as a unit.

The jury has returned to the courtroom.
The committee has filed its report.

5 With the pronouns *all* and *some* (as well as fractions and percentages) when used as subjects *if* their modifiers are singular. Use a plural verb *if* their modifiers are plural.

All of the books have been classified.
Some of the gas is being pumped into the tank.

6 When *number* is used as the subject and is preceded by *the;* however, use a plural verb if *number* is preceded by *a.*

The number of voters has increased this year.
A number of workers are on vacation.

Use a plural verb

1 With a plural subject.

The blossoms are losing their petals.

2 With a compound subject joined by *and.*

My mother and my father are the same age.

Negative forms of verbs

1 Use the plural verb *do not* (or the contraction *don't*) when the pronoun *I, we, you,* or *they,* as well as a plural noun, is used as the subject.

You don't have a leg to stand on in this case.
The scissors do not cut properly.
I don't believe that answer is correct.

2 Use the singular verb *does not* (or the contraction *doesn't*) when the pronoun *he, she,* or *it,* as well as a singular noun, is used as the subject.

She doesn't want to attend the meeting.
It does not seem possible that winter's here.

Pronoun agreement with antecedents

1 Pronouns (*I, we, you, he, she, it, their,* etc.) agree with their antecedent *in person*--person speaking, first person; person spoken to, second person; person spoken about, third person.

We said we would go when we complete our work.
When you enter, present your invitation.
All who saw the show found that they were moved.

2 Pronouns agree with their antecedents *in gender* (feminine, masculine, and neuter).

Each of the women has her favorite hobby.
Adam will wear his favorite sweater.
The tree lost its leaves early this fall.

3 Pronouns agree with their antecedents *in number* (singular or plural).

A verb must agree with its subject.
Pronouns must agree with their antecedents.
Brian is to give his recital at 2 p.m.
Joan and Carla have lost their homework.

4 When a pronoun's antecedent is a collective noun, the pronoun may be either singular or plural depending on whether the noun acts individually or as a unit.

The committee met to cast their ballots.
The class planned its graduation program.

Commonly confused pronoun sound-alikes

it's (contraction): it is; it has
its (possessive adjective): possessive form of *it*

It's good to see you; it's been a long time.
The puppy wagged its tail in welcome.

their (pronoun): possessive form of *they*
there (adverb/pronoun): at or in that place/used to introduce a clause
they're (contraction): they are

The hikers all wore their parkas.
Will he be there during our presentation?
They're likely to be late because of the snow.

who's (contraction): who is; who has
whose (pronoun): possessive form of *who*

Who's been to the movie? Who's going now?
I chose the one whose skills are best.

Word-division guides

1 Divide words between syllables only; therefore, do not divide one-syllable words. **Note:** When in doubt, consult a dictionary or a word-division manual.

through-out	pref-er-ence	em-ploy-ees
reached	toward	thought

2 Do not divide words of five or fewer letters even if they have two or more syllables.

into also about union radio ideas

3 Do not separate a one-letter syllable at the beginning of a word or a one- or two-letter syllable at the end of a word.

across enough steady highly ended

4 Usually, you may divide a word between double consonants; but, when adding a syllable to a word that ends in double letters, divide after the double letters of the root word.

writ-ten	sum-mer	expres-sion	excel-lence
will-ing	win-ner	process-ing	fulfill-ment

5 When the final consonant is doubled in adding a suffix, divide between the double letters.

run-ning begin-ning fit-ting submit-ted

6 Divide after a one-letter syllable within a word; but when two single-letter syllables occur together, divide between them.

sepa-rate regu-late gradu-ation evalu-ation

7 When the single-letter syllable *a, i,* or *u* is followed by the ending *ly, ble, bly, cle,* or *cal,* divide before the single-letter syllable.

stead-ily	siz-able	vis-ible	mir-acle
cler-ical	but	musi-cal	practi-cal

8 Divide only between the two words that make up a hyphenated word.

self-contained well-developed

9 Do not divide a contraction or a single group of figures.

doesn't $350,000 Policy F238975

10 Try to avoid dividing proper names and dates. If necessary, divide as follows.

Mary J./Pembroke	not	Mary J. Pem-/broke
November 15,/1995	not	November/15, 1995

Letter-placement points

Paper-guide placement

Check the placement of the paper guide for accurate horizontal centering of the letter.

Margins and date placement

Use the following guide:

5-Stroke Words In Letter Body	Side Margins	Dateline
Up to 100	2″	18
101-200	1½″	16*
Over 200	1″	14

*Dateline is moved up 2 line spaces for each additional 25 words.

Letters containing many special features may require changes in these settings. Horizontal placement of date varies according to the letter style.

Address

The address begins on the fourth line (3 blank line spaces) below the date. A personal title, such as Mr., Mrs., Miss, or Ms., should precede the name of an individual. An official title, when used, may be placed on the first or the second line of the address, whichever gives better balance.

Two page-letters

If a letter is too long for one page, at least 2 lines of the body of the letter should be carried to the second page. The second page of a letter, or any additional pages, requires a proper heading. Use the block form shown below, beginning on line 6. Single-space the heading, and double-space below it.

Second-Page Heading

```
Dr. Ronald L. Spitz
Page 2
June 5, 19--
```

Attention line

An attention line, when used, is placed on the first line of the letter address.

Subject line

A subject line, when used, is placed on the second line (a double space) below the salutation. It is usually keyed at the left margin but may be centered in the modified block letter format. A subject line is required in the Simplified Block format; it is placed on the second line below the letter address.

Company name

Occasionally the company name is shown in the closing lines. When this is done, it is shown in ALL-CAPS 2 lines (a double space) below the complimentary close. Modern practice is to omit the company name in the closing lines if a letterhead is used.

Keyed/Printed name/official title

The name of the person who originated the letter and his/her official title are placed a quadruple space (3 blank line spaces) below the complimentary close, or a quadruple space below the company name when it is used. When both the name and official title are used, they may be placed on the same line, or the title may be placed on the next line below the keyed/printed name.

In the Simplified Block format, the name and official title of the originator are placed a quadruple space below the body of the letter.

2-Letter ZIP Code Abbreviations

Alabama AL	Guam GU	Massachusetts MA	New York NY	Tennessee TN
Alaska AK	Hawaii HI	Michigan MI	North Carolina NC	Texas TX
Arizona AZ	Idaho ID	Minnesota MN	North Dakota ND	Utah UT
Arkansas AR	Illinois IL	Mississippi MS	Ohio OH	Vermont VT
California CA	Indiana IN	Missouri MO	Oklahoma OK	Virgin Islands VI
Colorado CO	Iowa IA	Montana MT	Oregon OR	Virginia VA
Connecticut CT	Kansas KS	Nebraska NE	Pennsylvania PA	Washington WA
Delaware DE	Kentucky KY	Nevada NV	Puerto Rico PR	West Virginia WV
District of Columbia DC	Louisiana LA	New Hampshire NH	Rhode Island RI	Wisconsin WI
Florida FL	Maine ME	New Jersey NJ	South Carolina SC	Wyoming WY
Georgia GA	Maryland MD	New Mexico NM	South Dakota SD	

MERKEL-EVANS, Inc.
1321 Commerce Street • Dallas, TX 75202-1648 • Tel. (214) 871-4400

November 10, 19-- QS (space down 4 blank line spaces)

Mrs. Evelyn M. McNeil
4582 Campus Drive
Fort Worth, TX 76119-1835 DS

Dear Mrs. McNeil DS

The new holiday season is just around the corner, and we invite you to beat the rush and visit our exciting Gallery of Gifts. Gift-giving can be a snap this year because of our vast array of gifts "for kids from one to ninety-two."

What's more, many of our gifts are prewrapped for presentation. All can be packaged and shipped right here at the store.

A catalog of our hottest gift items and a schedule of special hours for special charge-card customers are enclosed. Please stop in and let us help you select that special gift, or call us if you wish to shop by phone.

We wish you happy holidays and hope to see you soon. DS

Cordially yours QS

Ms. Carol J. Suess, Manager DS

rj DS
Enclosures

1 Block, open

ASSOCIATION OF OFFICE MANAGERS
518 JUNIPER CIRCLE GOLDEN, CO 80403-6249 (303) 930-7749

September 26, 19-- QS (space down 4 blank line spaces)

Mr. Frank P. Dalton
90 Spring Street
Portland, ME 04101-7430 DS

Dear Mr. Dalton DS

It has come to my attention that several of the publications you ordered in August may not have arrived as yet. According to the enclosed copy of your order, Items 3765A, 4890B, and 5021X have not yet been shipped.

Normally, orders received by the Association of Office Managers are processed within 10 days of receipt. Because of a computer problem, however, it appears that some orders in August may not have been completed.

A copy of Item 3765A is enclosed. Copies of 4890B and 5021X will be sent priority mail within the next few days by Mrs. Carla F. Fernandez, chief of special orders.

We appreciate your interest in our publications and thank you for your patronage. DS

Sincerely yours DS

ASSOCIATION OF OFFICE MANAGERS QS

Brian E. Miller
Director of Publications DS

xx DS
Enclosures
Order
Item 3765A DS

c Mrs. Carla F. Fernandez DS

If you have received these publications previously, please accept these copies with our compliments.

2 Modified block, open

Communication Concepts Inc.
178 S. Prospect Avenue ■ San Bernardino, CA 92410-4567 ■ (714) 586-7934

September 15, 19-- QS

MISS MICHELLE T LAWSON
DEL AMO SECRETARIAL SERVICE
21200 HAWTHORNE AVE
LOS ANGELES CA 90058-2820 DS

SIMPLIFIED BLOCK LETTER FORMAT DS

This letter illustrates the features that distinguish the Simplified Block Letter format from the standard block format. DS

1. The date is placed on line 12 so that the letter address will show through the window of a window envelope when used.

2. The letter address is keyed in the style recommended by the U. S. Postal Service for OCR processing: ALL-CAP letters with no punctuation. Cap-and-lowercase letters with punctuation may be used if that is the format of the addresses stored in an electronic address file. Personal titles may be omitted.

3. A subject line replaces the traditional salutation which some people find objectionable. The subject line may be keyed in ALL-CAP or cap-and-lowercase letters. A double space is left above and below it.

4. The complimentary close, which some people view as a needless appendage, is omitted.

5. The writer's name is placed on the fourth line space below the body of the letter. The writer's title or department name may appear on the line with the writer's name or on the next line below it. The signature block may be keyed in ALL-CAP or cap-and-lowercase letters.

6. A standard-length line is used for all letters. A six-inch line is a common length (60 pica or 10-pitch spaces; 72 elite or 12-pitch spaces). DS

The features listed and illustrated here are designed to bring efficiency to the electronic processing of mail. QS

MRS. MARIA T. LOPEZ, DIRECTOR DS

tms

3 Simplified block

henderson associates
6623 Mitchell Avenue, Tallahassee, FL 32303-4429

INTEROFFICE MEMORANDUM

June 12, 19-- QS

Martin F. Jensen, Chief Financial Officer DS

OFFICE RENOVATION DS

All of the furniture ordered for your office has arrived except for the computer table. It is back ordered, and it should arrive within the next week.

Arrangements have been made for your new carpet to be installed on Saturday, June 26. Since your old furniture will be left in the hallway during the weekend, we will need to take the necessary security precautions. Mike Jackson has agreed to let you store your file cabinets in his office over the weekend. Please let me know by Friday if there are other things you would like stored along with the files, and I will make the necessary arrangements. QS

Karl L. Hayward, Facilities Manager DS

xx

4 Simplified memorandum

Addressing procedure

Envelope address

Set a tab stop (or margin stop if a number of envelopes are to be addressed) 10 spaces left of center for a small envelope or 5 spaces for a large envelope. Start the address here on Line 12 from the top edge of a small envelope and on Line 14 of a large one.

Style

Key the address in *block style,* SS. Use ALL CAPS and omit punctuation. Key the city name, state abbreviation, and ZIP Code on the last address line. The ZIP Code is keyed 2 spaces after the state abbreviation.

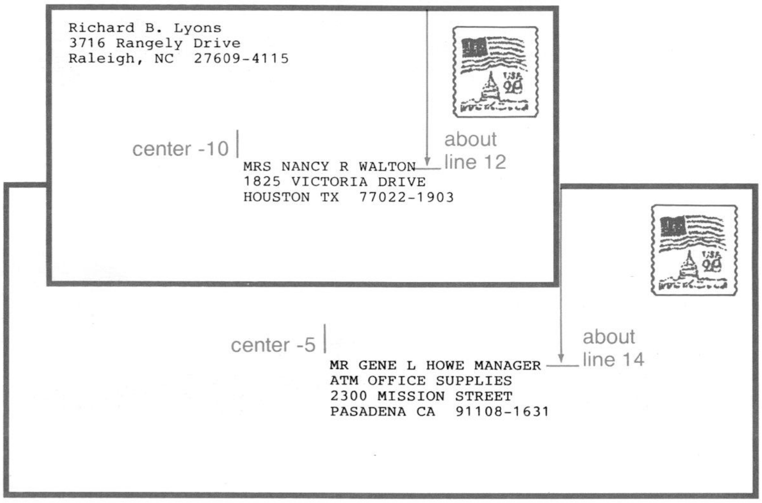

Richard B. Lyons
3716 Rangely Drive
Raleigh, NC 27609-4115
center -10
about line 12
MRS NANCY R WALTON
1825 VICTORIA DRIVE
HOUSTON TX 77022-1903
center -5
about line 14
MR GENE L HOWE MANAGER
ATM OFFICE SUPPLIES
2300 MISSION STREET
PASADENA CA 91108-1631

Addressee notations

Key addressee notations, such as HOLD FOR ARRIVAL, PLEASE FORWARD, or PERSONAL, a double space below the return address and about 3 spaces from the left edge of the envelope. Key these notations in ALL CAPS.

If an *attention line* is used, key it as the first line of the envelope address.

Mailing notations

Key mailing notations, such as SPECIAL DELIVERY and REGISTERED, below the stamp and at least 3 line spaces above the envelope address. Key these notations in ALL CAPS.

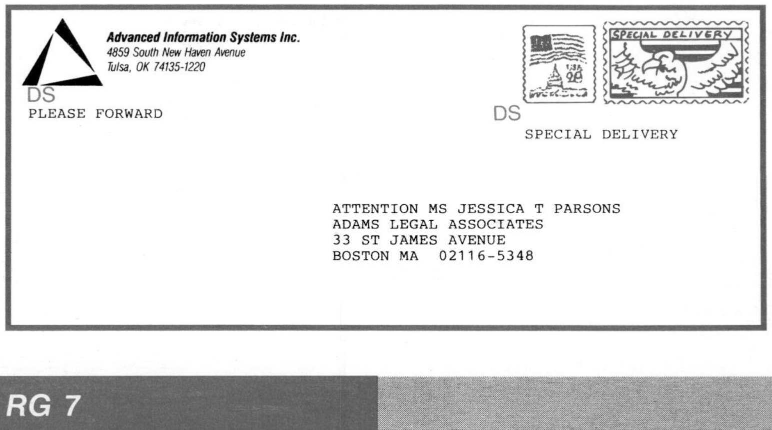

Advanced Information Systems Inc.
4859 South New Haven Avenue
Tulsa, OK 74135-1220
DS
PLEASE FORWARD
SPECIAL DELIVERY
DS
SPECIAL DELIVERY
ATTENTION MS JESSICA T PARSONS
ADAMS LEGAL ASSOCIATES
33 ST JAMES AVENUE
BOSTON MA 02116-5348

Folding and inserting procedure

Small envelopes (No. 6¾, 6¼)

Step 1
With letter face up, fold bottom up to ½ inch from top.

Step 2
Fold right third to left.

Step 3
Fold left third to ½ inch from last crease.

Step 4
Insert last creased edge first.

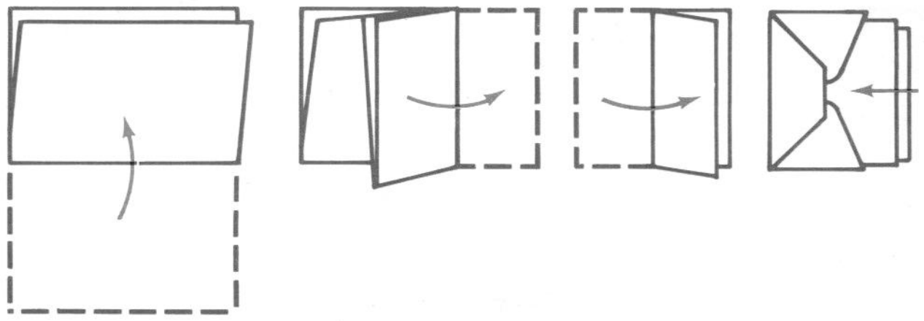

Large envelopes (No. 10, 9, 7¾)

Step 1
With letter face up, fold slightly less than ⅓ of sheet up toward top.

Step 2
Fold down top of sheet to within ½ inch of bottom fold.

Step 3
Insert letter into envelope with last crease toward bottom of envelope.

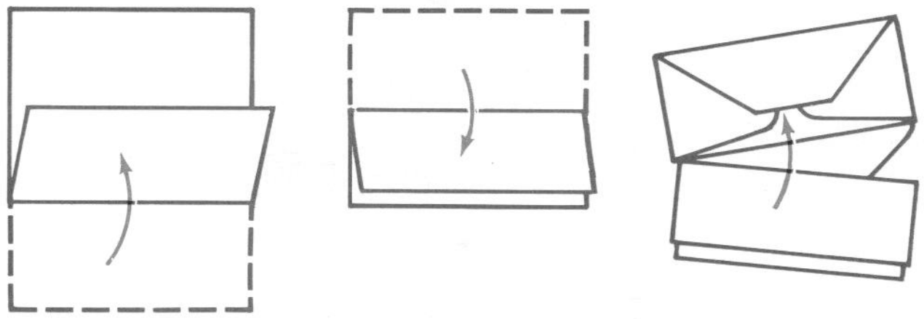

Window envelopes (letter)

Step 1
With sheet face down, top toward you, fold upper third down.

Step 2
Fold lower third up so address is showing.

Step 3
Insert sheet into envelope with last crease at bottom.

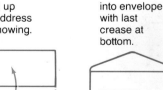

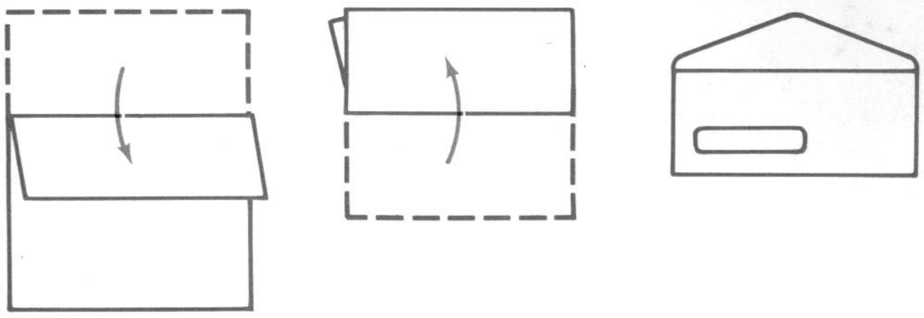

Main head

THE CHANGING OFFICE ← line 10 pica; line 12 elite

QS

A secretary returning to an office job after a 25-year absence would have a difficult time coping with the changes that have taken place during that time. Changing technology would best describe the challenges facing today's office worker. Two "buzzwords" which are currently being used in the office are electronic desktop publishing and electronic mail.

1" 1"

DS

Side head

Electronic Desktop Publishing

DS

Desktop publishing is the process of integrating text and graphics by utilizing computer software to produce professional-looking documents without using professional services. According to Winsor (1987, 29):

DS

Desktop publishing has a bright future. . . . Desktop publishing enables people and businesses to develop their own brochures, newsletters, and other documents at a fraction of the cost and time expended sending the work out to a professional graphics studio.

DS

Since today's firms are more concerned than ever about creating the proper image, it is expected that a greater number of firms will turn to desktop publishing to enhance their images.

DS

Electronic Mail

DS

The second "buzzword" being used extensively in the modern office is electronic mail (E-mail). E-mail is the sending, storing, and delivering of written messages electronically. Reiss and Dolan (1989, 529) identify two categories of electronic mail services:

DS

1. In-house electronic mail. (E-mail which is run on a firm's computer system.)

at least 1"

1 Unbound, page 1

2 line 6

line 8

2. Commercial electronic mail. (E-mail which is supplied by organizations such as General Electric Information Services and MCI Communication.)

Summary

Desktop publishing and electronic mail are but two of the changes which are shaping the future of information processing. Each year new technology enhances the ability of office personnel to produce quality information in less time.

QS

REFERENCES

QS

Reiss, Levi and Edwin G. Dolan. Using Computers: Managing Change. Cincinnati: South-Western Publishing Co., 1989.

DS

Winsor, William M. "Electronic Publishing: The Next Great Office Revolution." The Secretary, June/July 1987.

1" 1"

2 Unbound, page 2

Main head

CAREER PLANNING ← line 10 pica; line 12 elite

QS

Career planning is an important, ongoing process. It is important because the career you choose will affect the quality of your life and will help determine the respect and recognition you receive. Throughout your lifetime you are likely to make three or four career changes.[1]

1½" 1"

DS

Establish a Career Objective

DS

One early, important step in the career planning process is to define your career objective.

The career objective may indicate your area of interest (such as finance or sales), the sort of organization you would like to work for (such as banking or manufacturing), and the level of the position you want.[2]

Complete a Personal Inventory

Another useful step in career planning is to develop a personal profile of your skills, interests, and values.

Skills. An analysis of your skills is likely to reveal that you have many different kinds.

1. Functional skills that determine how well you manage time, communicate, motivate people, write, etc.

2. Adaptive skills that determine how well you will fit into a specific work environment. These skills include personal traits such as flexibility, reliability, efficiency, thoroughness, and enthusiasm for the job.

DS ______________

DS

[1]Susan Bernard, Getting the Right Job, AT&T's College Series (Elizabeth, NJ: AT&T College Market, 1988), p. 6.

DS

[2]William H. Cunningham, Ramon J. Aldag, and Christopher M. Swift, Introduction to Business, 2d ed. (Cincinnati: South-Western Publishing Co., 1989), p. 620.

at least 1"

3 Leftbound, page 1

2 line 6

line 8

3. Technical or work content skills that are required to perform a specific job. These skills may include such things as keyboarding, accounting, computer operation, and language usage skills.[3]

Interests. "Interests refer to the things that you like or dislike."[4] By listing and analyzing them you should be able to identify a desirable work environment. For example, your list is likely to reveal if you like to work with things or people, work alone or with others, lead or follow others, or be indoors or outdoors.

1½" 1"

Values. Values are your priorities in life, and you should identify them early so that you can pursue a career which will improve you chances to acquire them. Some of the more obvious values include the importance you place on family, security, wealth, prestige, creativity, power, independence, and glamour.

DS ______________

DS

[3]Adale Scheele, "Deciding What You Want To Do," Business Week Careers, 1988 ed., p. 7.

DS

[4]Bernard, Getting the Right Job, pp. 1-2.

[5]Cunningham, Introduction to Business, p. 617.

4 Leftbound, page 2

TABLE OF CONTENTS — line 10 pica; line 12 elite

Seminar Presenter 1

DS

Selection 1
Reason 1

Seminar Development 1

Meeting #1 2
Meeting #2 2

Seminar Dates 2

Seminar Content 2

Traits 2
Styles 3

Bibliography 4

1½″ → ← 1″

[5] Leftbound, contents page

3 line 6

BIBLIOGRAPHY ← line 10 pica; line 12 elite

QS

Indent 5

Cunningham, William H., Ramon J. Aldag, and Christopher M. Swift. Introduction to Business. 2d ed. Cincinnati: South-Western Publishing Co., 1989.

Kalinski, Burton S., and Peter F. Meggison. Management of Administrative Office Systems. 2d ed. San Diego: Harcourt Brace Jovanovich, Publishers, 1988.

Simkin, Mark G. Computer Information Systems for Business. Dubuque, Iowa: Wm. C. Brown Publishers, 1987.

Smith, Harold T., William H. Baker, and Marvin P. Evans. The Administrative Manager. 2d ed. Chicago: Science Research Associates, Inc., 1987.

1½″ → ← 1″

[6] Leftbound, bibliography (references)

Main head

FINDLEY HIGH SCHOOL BUSINESS CLUB ACTIVITIES — line 12 pica; line 14 elite

QS

The members of the Findley High School Business Club met last week and decided to conduct the projects listed below. Please consider this document as the club's request for permission to organize and conduct these projects during this school year. The proposed projects will publicize the business education program to students, parents, and other members of the community that Findley High School serves. In addition, they will bring recognition to current business education students.

Fall Semester Projects

The following projects have been suggested for the fall semester. These projects will help to draw students' attention to the business education program early in the school year.

Poster contest. The club will sponsor a poster contest in late September to recruit new members into the Business Club. The posters will be displayed throughout the high school building and the winner will receive a coupon good for two dinners at George's Family Restaurant.

Open house. Club members will participate in the Business Education Department's Fourth Annual Open House. The members will

1. Greet the guests at the main entrance.
2. Escort the guests to the Business Education Department where the program will be held.
3. Demonstrate the computer hardware and software that is used in the business classes.

1″ → ← 1″

at least 1″

[7] Topbound, page 1

EAGLE & SONS
2299 Seward Highway • Anchorage, Alaska • 99503-4100

INTEROFFICE MEMORANDUM

TO: Warren E. Latouch, Director of Administration

FROM: Carla M. Boniface, Chief of Personnel

DATE: May 2, 19--

SUBJECT: Employee Evaluation Program

DS

As the company continues to expand, it is desirable that we establish an effective program for evaluating the performance of all our employees. A sound evaluation program offers many advantages to both the company and our employees, including the following:

1. Assists employees in judging their own value and accomplishments. Ratings should include strong points as well as shortcomings, with suggestions for improvement.

DS

2. Provides managers with information which they may use to determine promotions or lateral reassignments in order to make the most effective use of each employee's abilities.

3. Provides a basis for determining increases in compensation or for bonus payments to reward the most efficient employees.

4. Requires supervisors to analyze the work done by their subordinates and to recognize the contribution they make in the accomplishment of their mutual objectives.

5. Promotes an atmosphere of mutual respect and teamwork among supervisors and employees.

6. Provides an evaluation of the effectiveness of other personnel programs such as recruitment, selection, orientation, and training.

It is essential that clear-cut policies be established for this new evaluation program. To insure success, the objectives of the program must be clearly established, thoroughly understood, and fully accepted by all concerned. A recommended plan of action to accomplish these objectives is attached.

As a matter of priority, I recommend that the establishment of a program to evaluate employee performance be placed on the agenda of the executive committee for consideration at the earliest possible date.

xx

Attachment

1″ → ← 1″

[8] Formal memorandum

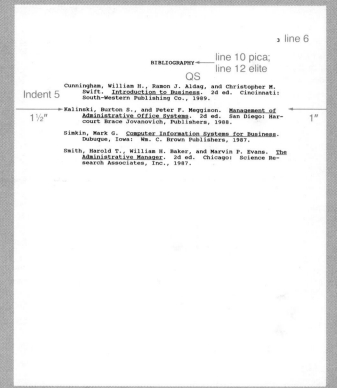

CORRECTION SYMBOLS

■ Proofreader's marks

Sometimes keyed or printed copy may be corrected with proofreader's marks. The keyboard operator must be able to interpret these marks correctly in rekeying the corrected copy or *rough draft* as it may be called. The most commonly used proofreader's marks are shown below.

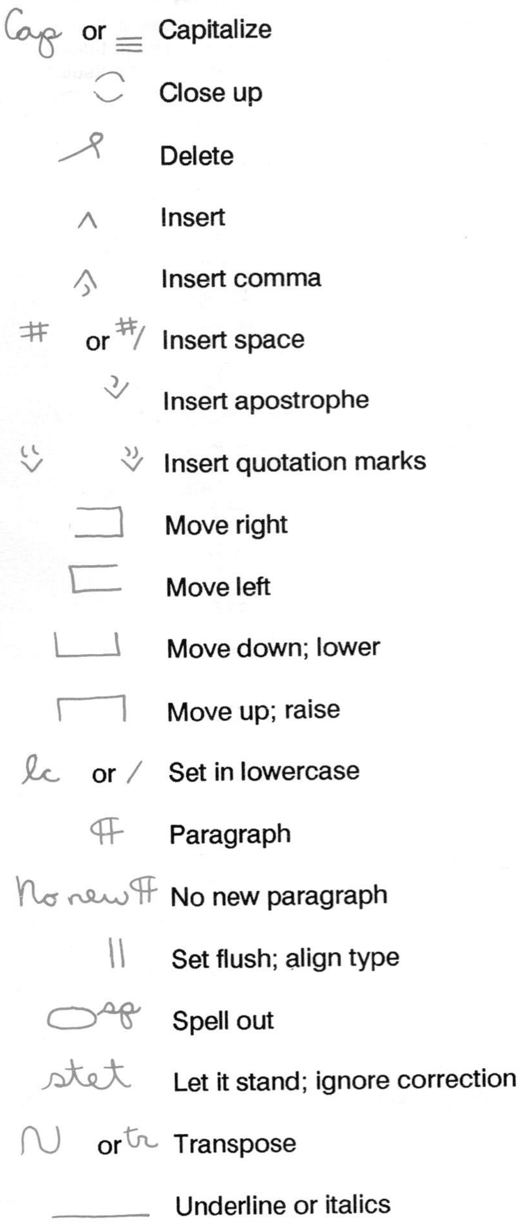
Cap or Capitalize
Close up
Delete
Insert
Insert comma
or #/ Insert space
Insert apostrophe
Insert quotation marks
Move right
Move left
Move down; lower
Move up; raise
lc or / Set in lowercase
Paragraph
No new ¶ No new paragraph
Set flush; align type
sp Spell out
stet Let it stand; ignore correction
or tr Transpose
Underline or italics

CENTERING PROCEDURES

1 Horizontal centering

1 Move margin stops to extreme ends of scale.

2 Clear tab stops; then set a tab stop at center of paper.

3 Tabulate to center of paper.

4 From center, backspace *once* for each 2 letters, spaces, figures, or punctuation marks in the line.

5 Do not backspace for an odd or leftover stroke at the end of the line.

6 Begin to key where backspacing ends.

Formula for finding horizontal center of paper

	Example
Scale reading at left edge of paper	0
+ Scale reading at right edge of paper	102
Total ÷ 2 = Center Point	102 ÷ 2 = 51

2 Horizontal centering for machines with automatic center

1 Insert paper with the left edge at 0.

2 Set margins at the extreme right and left edges of the paper.

3 Strike **Return** to move the carrier to the left margin; then press the **Center** key. (If you are using a microcomputer/word processor, refer to your software user's guide for centering.

4 Key the first line. (Characters will not print as you key the line, but the carrier will move to the left for each character keyed.)

5 Strike **Return** to print the line.

6 Repeat Steps 2-4 to center each line.

3 Vertical centering

Mathematical method

1 Count lines and blank line spaces needed to key problem.

2 Subtract *lines to be used* from *lines available* (66 for full sheet and 33 for half sheet).

3 Divide by 2 to get top and bottom margins. If a fraction results, disregard it.

4 If an even number results, space down that number of times from top of sheet and key the first line. If an odd number results, use the next lower number.

Dropping fractions and using even numbers usually places copy a line or two above exact center--in what is often called *reading position.*

Formula for vertical mathematical placement

$$\frac{\text{Lines available} - \text{lines used}}{2} = \text{top margin}$$

Backspace-from-center method
Basic rule

From vertical center of paper, roll platen (cylinder) back once for each 2 lines, 2 blank line spaces, or line and blank line space. Ignore odd or leftover line.

Steps to follow:

1 To move paper to vertical center, start spacing down from top edge of paper.

a half sheet
down 8 DS (double spaces)
+ 1 SS (Line 17)

b full sheet
down 17 DS (Line 34)

2 From vertical center

a half sheet, SS or DS; follow basic rule, back 1 for 2 lines

b full sheet, SS or DS; follow basic rule, back 1 for 2; then back 2 SS for *reading position.*

Prepare

1 Insert and align paper (typewriter).

2 Clear margin stops by moving them to extreme ends of line-of-writing scale. On electronic equipment, set margins as near as possible to the edges of the paper (so that automatic centering may be used for horizontal placement).

3 Clear all tabulator stops.

4 Move element carrier (carriage) or cursor to center of paper or line-of-writing scale.

5 Decide the number of spaces to be left between columns (for intercolumns)--preferably an even number (4, 6, 8, 10, etc.).

1 Plan vertical placement

Follow either of the vertical centering procedures explained on page RG 10.

Spacing headings. Double-space (count 1 blank line space) between main and secondary headings, when both are used. Double-space between the last table heading (either main or secondary) and the first horizontal line of column items or column headings. Double-space between column headings (when used) and the first line of the column entries. On electronic equipment, use the automatic center feature (see RG 10) to center the *key* line (line made up of the longest item in each column plus the number of spaces between columns). Set a tab stop at the beginning of each column; then discard or delete the *key* line.

Spacing above totals and source notes. Double-space between the total rule and the total figures. Double-space between the last line of the table and the 1½" rule above the source note. Double-space between the 1½" rule and the source note.

2 Plan horizontal placement

On an electronic typewriter, backspace from center of paper (or line-of-writing scale) 1 space for each 2 letters, figures, symbols, and spaces in *longest* item of each column in the table. Then backspace once for each 2 spaces to be left between columns (intercolumns). Set left margin stop where backspacing ends.

If an odd or leftover space occurs at the end of the longest item of a column when backspacing by 2's, carry it forward to the next column. Do not backspace for an odd or leftover character at the end of the last column. (See illustration below.)

Set tab stops. From the left margin, space forward 1 space for each letter, figure, symbol, and space in the longest item in the first column and for each space to be left between Cols. 1 and 2. Set a tab stop at this point for the second column. Follow this procedure for each additional column of the table.

Note: If a column heading is longer than the longest item in the column, it *may* be treated as the longest item in the column in determining placement. The longest columnar entry must then be centered under the heading and the tab stop set accordingly.

3 Center column headings (optional)

Backspace-from-column-center method

From point at which column begins (tab or margin stop), space forward once for each 2 letters, figures, or spaces in the longest item in the column. This leads to the column center point; from it, backspace once for each 2 spaces in column heading. Ignore an odd or leftover space. Key the heading at this point; it will be centered over the column.

Mathematical methods

1 To the number on the cylinder (platen) or line-of-writing scale immediately under the first letter, figure, or symbol of the longest item of the column, add the number shown under the space following the last stroke of the item. Divide this sum by 2; the result will be the center point of the column. From this point on the scale, backspace (1 for 2) to center the column heading.

2 From the number of spaces in the longest item, subtract the number of spaces in the heading. Divide this number by 2; ignore fractions. Space forward this number from the tab or margin stop and key the heading.

MAIN HEADING

Secondary Heading

These	Are	Column	Heads
xxxxxx	*longest*	xxxx	xxxxx
xxxx	*item*	*longest*	xxx
xxxxx	xxxxx	*item*	*longest*
longest	xxxxxx	xxxxx	*item*
item	xxxx	xxx	xxx

longest1234longest1234longest1234longest

4 Horizontal rulings

To make horizontal rulings in tables, depress shift lock and strike the underline key.

Single-space above and double-space below horizontal rulings.

5 Vertical rulings

On a typewriter, operate the automatic line finder. Place a pencil or pen point through the cardholder (or the typebar guide above the ribbon or carrier). Roll the paper up until you have a line of the desired length. Remove the pencil or pen and reset the line finder.

On a computer-generated table, use a ruler and pen or pencil to draw the vertical rulings.

1 Electronic correction

Electronic typewriters, word processors, and computers vary in the way keystroking errors may be corrected. All, however, have a correction key that removes errors from the electronic window/screen and/or paper. Use the User's Manual for your machine to learn the steps for making corrections electronically.

2 Lift-off tape

1 Strike the special backspace/lift-off key to move the printing element (or carrier) to the point of the error.

2 Rekey the error exactly as you made it. In this step, the lift-off tape actually lifts the error off the page. The printing element stays in place.

3 Key the correction.

3 Correction fluid

1 Turn the paper up a few spaces to ease the correction procedure.

2 Shake the bottle; remove the applicator; daub excess fluid on inside of bottle opening.

3 Brush fluid sparingly over the entire error by a light touching action.

4 Return applicator to bottle and tighten cap; blow on the error to speed the drying process.

4 Correction paper

1 Backspace to the beginning of the error.

2 Insert the correction tape or paper strip behind the ribbon and in front of the error, coated side toward the copy.

3 Rekey the error exactly as you made it. In this step, powder from the correction paper is pressed by force into the form of the error, thus masking it.

4 Remove the correction paper; backspace to the point where the correction begins and key the correction.

5 Rubber eraser

1 Turn the paper up a few spaces; then move the element carrier (carriage) to the extreme right or left so that eraser crumbs will not fall into the machine.

2 Move the paper bail out of the way. Pull the original sheet forward (if a carbon copy is being made) and place a card (5″ × 3″ or slightly larger) in front of, not behind, the first carbon sheet to protect the carbon copy from smudges.

3 Flip the original sheet back and make the erasure with a hard eraser. Brush or blow the eraser crumbs off the paper.

4 Move the protective card to a position in front of the second carbon sheet if more than one carbon copy is being made. Erase the error on the first carbon copy with a soft eraser.

5 Remove the card and key the correction.

6 Correcting errors by squeezing/spreading

Letter omitted in a word

1 Remove the word with the omitted letter.

2 Move printing element to second space after preceding word.

3 Pull half-space lever forward (or use electronic incremental backspacer) to move printing element a half space to the left.

4 Hold lever in place as you key the corrected word with the other hand.

5 Release the lever and continue keying.

Error
an omitte letter

an omitted letter
Correction

Letter added in a word

1 Remove the word with the added letter.

2 Move printing element to third space after preceding word.

3 Pull half-space lever forward (or use electronic incremental backspacer) to move printing element a half space to the left.

4 Hold lever in place as you key the corrected word with the other hand.

5 Release the lever and continue keying.

Error
a lettter within

a letter within
Correction

7 Carbon-Pack Assembly

1 Assemble letterhead, carbon sheets (uncarboned side up), and second sheets as illustrated above. *Use one carbon and one second sheet for each copy desired.*

2 Grasp the carbon pack at the sides, turn it so that the *letterhead faces away from you, the carbon side of the carbon paper is toward you, and the top edge of the pack is face down.* Tap the sheets gently on the desk to straighten.

3 Hold the sheets firmly to prevent slipping; insert pack into typewriter. Hold pack with one hand; turn platen with the other.

4 To keep the carbon pack straight when feeding it into the typewriter, place the pack in the fold of a plain sheet of paper (paper trough) or under the flap of an envelope. Remove trough or envelope when the pack is in place.

Photocopier

Offset Printer

Reprographics refers to the making of multiple copies of all kinds of materials. Numerous items should be considered when planning and organizing material for duplication. One important factor is cost. The objective is to select a duplication process that will provide the material at the lowest possible cost per copy. The appearance of the copy in terms of clarity, attractiveness, format, and size must also be considered. Since time available to do the work may affect quality and cost, time is also an important factor.

The four processes used most often in schools, churches, and business offices are photocopier duplication, offset duplication, spirit duplication, and stencil duplication. Each of these processes is described briefly here.

Photocopier Duplication

Photocopiers have virtually replaced spirit and stencil duplication in the business office. The photocopy process, which produces copies directly from an original electronically, is easier, cleaner, quicker, and even less costly when only a few copies are needed, than the other processes described here.

Copiers are often classified by the kind of paper they require and the number of copies they are designed to produce. Plain-paper copiers, which use the regular paper found in the office, are most popular. Coated-paper copiers require the use of more expensive chemically-treated paper.

Copiers also may be classified by volume of copies produced. Low-volume copiers (which will produce about 20 copies per minute) are designed for no more than 20,000 copies per month. Mid-volume copiers (which produce 40-60 copies per minute) are designed to generate 20,000 to 50,000 copies per month. High-volume copiers (which produce up to 120 copies per minute) are designed to produce more than 50,000 copies per month.

Copiers, especially in the mid- and high-volume range, are available with a variety of special features. These include image reduction/enlargement, color duplication, duplex (two-sided) printing, collating/stapling, and automatic feed. All these features improve the usefulness and efficiency of copiers, but also add to their cost.

Offset Printing

Offset printing (which is done from plates made from camera-ready masters) is primarily a commercial printing process used to make thousands of copies of items containing limited numbers of pages. More sophisticated photocopiers have largely replaced offset printers for within-the-office duplication.

Preparing Master Copies for Photocopying and Offset Printing

Because photocopying and offset printing utilize a photographic process, each method begins with the preparation of a master or model copy of each page. The model or master copy can be generated on a standard or an electronic typewriter, on a computer, or on a word processor. The following steps will result in camera-ready copy usable for either photocopying or offset printing.

1. Be sure that the printing element (type, "ball," or daisy wheel) is clean and free of debris (ink, white-out, etc.).

2. Plan margins, spacing, and space to be left for illustrations (if any) before preparing a rough draft of the model.

3. Prepare a rough-draft model on the same size paper to be used for final printing (unless the copy is to be enlarged or reduced).

4. Proofread and correct the rough-draft copy before keying the final copy.

5. Prepare the final (camera-ready) copy on a smooth-finish paper so that the images are clear and sharp.

6. Correct all errors neatly. Use lift-off tape on typewriters so equipped. On other typewriters, use white-out or cover-up paper strips. On equipment with a display, correct errors on screen before printing a hard copy.

7. Give the master copy a final check to be sure it is error-free and free of smudges, wrinkles, tears, or other blemishes that could be picked up by a camera.

(continued, p. RG 14)

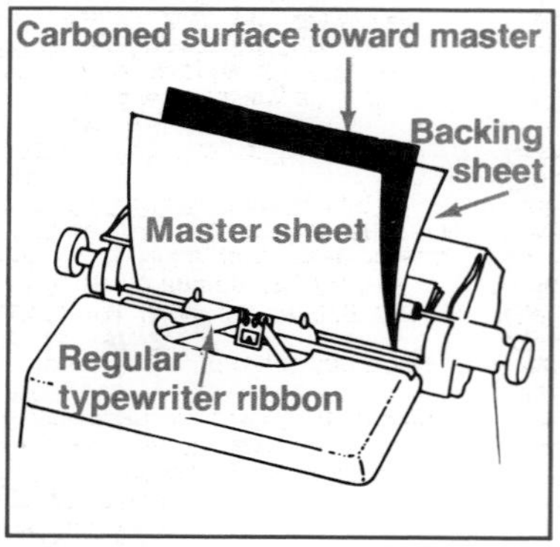

Master Set for
Spirit Duplication

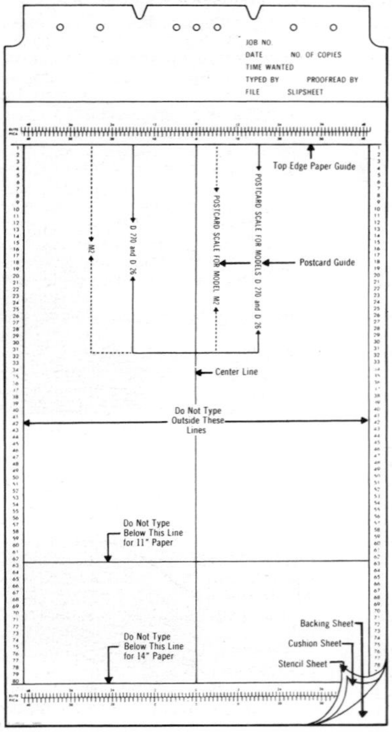

Stencil Set for
Stencil Duplication

Spirit Duplication

The spirit duplicator, sometimes called a "Ditto" (a trade name), is the least expensive way to reproduce up to several hundred copies. The primary print color used is purple, although pale shades of red, blue, green, and black are also available. These copies are not usually as clear and attractive as those produced by other duplicators. This machine is used primarily by churches, schools, and small business firms.

The spirit master set consists of two basic parts: the master sheet and a sheet of special carbon that can be used only once. A backing sheet also may be used to improve the consistency of the print. If a specially prepared master is not available, simply place the carbon paper between the master sheet and the backing sheet, with the glossy side of the carbon toward you. When you key the copy, the carbon copy will be on the *back* of the master sheet. Follow these directions for better masters.

1. Prepare a model copy of the material to be duplicated. Leave at least a one-half inch margin at the top of the master. Proofread the model copy; correct it if necessary.

2. If you do not have a carbon ribbon, you can avoid "fuzzy" type and filled-in characters by preparing the copy with the ribbon indicator in the "stencil" position. This procedure makes it difficult to proofread the copy, however.

3. Insert the open end of the spirit master into the machine first so that you can make corrections easily (see illustration at left). If you make an error, scrape off with a razor blade or knife the incorrect letter or word on the reverse side of the master sheet. Before correcting the error, tear off an unused portion of the carbon and slip it under the part to be corrected. Correct the error and remove the torn portion of carbon as soon as you have done so.

4. On electric and electronic machines, which provide even pressure automatically, key as usual. Use a firm, even stroke to key the master on a nonelectric machine; key capitals a little heavier than usual and punctuation marks a little lighter.

5. Proofread the copy and correct any errors you may have missed before you remove the master from the machine.

6. "Run" the number of copies needed by following the User's Manual that accompanies your spirit duplicator.

Stencil Duplication

Thousands of copies of programs, bulletins, newsletters, and other publications can be reproduced in a short time through the use of the stencil duplication process. A stencil consists of three basic parts: the stencil sheet, the backing sheet, and the cushion sheet. When a key strikes the stencil sheet, it "cuts" an impression in the shape of the type. Note: Only a machine having type bars is capable of "cutting" a stencil adequately. A printing element or wheel may not actually "cut" the stencil sheet. A cushion sheet is placed between the stencil and the backing sheet to absorb the impact of the type bar. A film sheet may be placed over the stencil sheet if darker print is desired. This film also protects the stencil sheet from letter cutout when the type face is extremely sharp. Before "cutting" the stencil, follow these steps.

1. Prepare a model copy of the material to be reproduced. Check it for accuracy of format and keying; correct it if necessary. Be certain that you place the copy on the page so that it will be within the stencil guide marks (see illustration at left).

2. If your machine has a cloth ribbon, clean the printing element thoroughly, paying close attention to the letters where ink tends to accumulate, such as the *o* and the *e*. Adjust the ribbon lever to "stencil" position.

3. Insert the cushion sheet between the stencil sheet and the backing sheet. Place the top edge of the model copy at the corner marks of the stencil to see where to position the first line. The scales at the top and sides of the stencil will help you place the copy correctly.

4. Insert the stencil assembly into the machine. On electric and electronic machines, which provide even pressure automatically, key with the usual force. If you are using a nonelectric typewriter, use a firm, uniform touch. Some keys that are completely closed such as *d* and *p* must be struck more lightly. Capitals and letters such as *m* and *w* must be struck with greater force.

5. If you make an error, it can be corrected easily with stencil correction fluid. If there is a film over the stencil, this must be detached until you resume keying. Use a smooth paper clip to rub the surface of the error on the stencil sheet. Place a pencil between the stencil sheet and the cushion sheet and apply a *light* coat of correction fluid over the error. Let the fluid dry; then make the correction, using a light touch.

INDEX

SPECIAL INDEX

Concentration drills

Guided writing copy

Models illustrated in text

Preapplication manipulative activities

Problems in rough-draft and script

Related communication activities

Skill-transfer timed writings

Straight-copy timed writings

Technique drills

Response patterns:

Appendix A--Numeric Keypad Operation

Appendix B--Automatic Features/Editing Functions of Electronic Equipment